MW00575609

Willmington's
COMPLETE GUIDE TO BIBLE KNOWLEDGE

New Testament Survey

New Testament Survey

Willmington's Complete GUIDE to BIBLE KNOWLEDGE

HAROLD L. WILLMINGTON

Tyndale House Publishers, Inc.
WHEATON, ILLINOIS

This book, the fourth in the series
Willmington's Complete Guide to Bible Knowledge,
is dedicated to Dr. Elmer Towns,
my close friend for more than thirty years.

Library of Congress Cataloging-in-Publication Data
(Revised for vol. 4)

Willmington, H. L.
Willmington's complete guide to Bible knowledge.
Contents: v. 1. Old Testament people — v. 4. New Testament survey.
1. Bible—Handbooks, manuals, etc. I. Title.
B417.W49 1990 220.6'1 90-70187
ISBN 0-8423-8164-3 (v. 4)

Printed in the United States of America

99 98 97 96 95 94 93 92 91
9 8 7 6 5 4 3 2 1

CONTENTS

PART ONE

A **BROAD** OVERVIEW OF THE LIFE OF CHRIST FEATURING FOUR SEPARATE OUTLINE STUDIES ON HIS LIFE AS PRESENTED INDIVIDUALLY BY MATTHEW, MARK, LUKE, AND JOHN

MATTHEW

A SPECIAL REPORT TO THE JEWS:
WHO IS JESUS CHRIST?
HE IS THE KING OF ISRAEL
AND THE LION OF THE TRIBE OF JUDAH.

This report was prepared by Matthew the teacher. In it the sermons of Christ are emphasized. The phrase "the kingdom of heaven" appears 32 times in this book, but nowhere else in the Bible. Matthew's book is the New Testament fulfillment of Psalm 72; Isaiah 9:6-7; 32:1; Jeremiah 23:5; and Zechariah 9:9; 14:9. Matthew presents the first of two New Testament genealogies. (Compare Matt. 1 with Luke 3.)

I. Two of Christ's Longest Discourses Are Found in Matthew. Both were preached on a mountain:
  A. The Sermon on the Mount (ch. 5–7)
  B. The Mount of Olives Discourse (ch. 24–25)
II. Material Found Only in Matthew's Account:
  A. Annunciation to Joseph (1:20-23)
  B. Visit of the Wise Men (2:1-12)
  C. Flight into Egypt (2:13-20)
  D. Healing of two blind men (9:27-31)
  E. Healing of the dumb demoniac (9:32-33)
  F. Parable of the leaven (13:33)
  G. Parable of the hidden treasure (13:44)
  H. Parable of the pearl of great price (13:45-46)
  I. Parable of the sea catch (13:47-50)
  J. Parable of the householder and his treasure (13:52)
  K. Promise of the church (16:13-19)
  L. Miracle of the tribute money (17:24-27)
  M. Parable of the forgiven servant who couldn't forgive (18:23-35)
  N. Parable of the laborers in the vineyard (20:1-16)
  O. Parable of the two sons (21:28-32)
  P. Parable of the wedding guest without a garment (22:1-14)
  Q. Christ's final tears over Jerusalem (23:37-39)
  R. Parable of the ten virgins (25:1-13)
  S. Parable of the eight talents (25:14-30)
  T. Parable of the sheep and the goats (25:31-46)
  U. The resurrection earthquake and temporary blinding of the Roman soldiers (28:1-10)
  V. The bribe of the guards (28:11-15)

There are more Old Testament quotations or allusions found in Matthew than in any other New Testament book. These come from 33 Old Testament books. Matthew is the third longest New Testament book, and 15th longest biblical book, with 28 chapters, 1,071 verses, and 23,684 words.

MATTHEW (Basic Outline)

I. The Preparation of the King
II. The Principles of the King
III. The Power of the King
IV. The Program of the King
V. The Preachers of the King
VI. The Proclamations of the King
VII. The Parables of the King
VIII. The Person of the King
IX. The Preeminence of the King
X. The Plea of the King
XI. The Performance of the King
XII. The Pity of the King
XIII. The Provoking of the King
XIV. The Predictions of the King
XV. The Presentation of the King
XVI. The Purging by the King
XVII. The Pain of the King
XVIII. The Passover of the King
XIX. The Prayers of the King
XX. The Persecution of the King
XXI. The Passion of the King
XXII. The Proof of the King

MATTHEW (Expanded Outline)

I. The Preparation of the King (Matt. 1:1–4:11)
  A. His genealogy (Matt. 1:1-17)
    1. Matthew begins with Abraham and goes forward in time to Joseph.
    2. He gives the royal line of Joseph.
    3. He traces this line through Solomon, David's first son.
    4. His list includes 41 names, four of which are women (Tamar, Rahab, Ruth, Bath-sheba).
  B. His birth announcement (Matt. 1:18-25)
    1. The distress of Joseph (Matt. 1:18)
    2. The decision of Joseph (Matt. 1:19)
    3. The dream of Joseph (Matt. 1:20)
      a. The message in the dream (Matt. 1:20-23)
      b. The marriage following the dream (Matt. 1:24-25)
  C. His worship by the Wise Men (Matt. 2:1-12)

1. The frustration of the Wise Men in Jerusalem (Matt. 2:1-8)
2. The celebration of the Wise Men in Bethlehem (Matt. 2:9-12)

D. His trip to Egypt (Matt. 2:13-20)
1. The reason for this trip (Matt. 2:13-18)
2. The return from the trip (Matt. 2:19-20)

E. His early years in Nazareth (Matt. 2:21-23)

F. His baptism (Matt. 3:13-17)
1. Jesus and John—The agreement (Matt. 3:13-15)
2. Jesus and the Spirit—The anointing (Matt. 3:16)
3. Jesus and the Father—The approval (Matt. 3:17)

G. His temptation (Matt. 4:1-11)
1. Round one
   a. The temptation (Matt. 4:3)
   b. The triumph (Matt. 4:4)
2. Round two
   a. The temptation (Matt. 4:5-6)
   b. The triumph (Matt. 4:7)
3. Round three
   a. The temptation (Matt. 4:8-9)
   b. The triumph (Matt. 4:10)

II. The Principles of the King (Matt. 5–7)—Jesus laid out his moral and spiritual standards during the Sermon on the Mount. "And Jesus went out about all Galilee, teaching in their synagogues and preaching the gospel of the Kingdom" (Matt. 4:23).

A. The believer and the kingdom
1. Positive characteristics—Those things which should be achieved
   a. The role of believers in the world (Matt. 5:3-12)
   b. The relationship of believers to the world (Matt. 5:13-16)
2. Negative characteristics—Those things which should be avoided
   a. Money seeking (Matt. 6:24-25)
   b. Men pleasing (Matt. 6:26)

B. The Old Testament and the kingdom
1. The who of the matter
   a. The divine fulfiller of the Law (Matt. 5:17-18)
   b. The divine fulfilling of the Law (Matt. 7:12)
2. The what of the matter
   a. In relation to murder (Matt. 5:21-26)
      (1) The basic concept (Matt. 5:21)
      (2) The broadened concept (Matt. 5:22)
   b. In relation to adultery (Matt. 5:27-30)
      (1) The basic concept (Matt. 5:27)
      (2) The broadened concept (Matt. 5:28)
   c. In relation to divorce (Matt. 5:31-32)
      (1) The basic concept (Matt. 5:31)
      (2) The broadened concept (Matt. 5:32)
   d. In relation to oath taking (Matt. 5:33-37)
      (1) The basic concept (Matt. 5:33)
      (2) The broadened concept (Matt. 5:34-37)
   e. In relation to retaliation (Matt. 5:38-42)

(1) The basic concept (Matt. 5:38)
(2) The broadened concept (Matt. 5:39-42)
f. In relation to love (Matt. 5:43-48)
(1) The basic concept (Matt. 5:43)
(2) The broadened concept (Matt. 5:44)
C. Worship and the kingdom (Matt. 6:1–7:11)
1. Giving
a. The rules (Matt. 6:1-3)
b. The rewards (Matt. 6:4)
2. Praying (Matt. 6:5-15)
a. Essentials in prayer (Matt. 6:5-7)
b. Example of prayer (Matt. 6:9-13)
c. Encouragements in prayer (Matt. 6:7-11)
3. Fasting (Matt. 6:16-18)
a. As practiced by the hypocrites (Matt. 6:16)
b. As practiced by the humble (Matt. 6:17-18)
4. Earning (Matt. 6:19-23)
a. Earthly treasure is insecure and corruptible (Matt. 6:19).
b. Eternal treasure is secure and incorruptible (Matt. 6:20-21).
5. Serving (Matt. 6:24)
6. Trusting (Matt. 6:25-34)
a. The illustration
(1) The fowls of the air (Matt. 6:26)
(2) The lilies of the field (Matt. 6:28-30)
b. The invitation (Matt. 6:31-34)
7. Judging (Matt. 7:1-5)
8. Witnessing (Matt. 7:6)
D. Entrance to the kingdom (Matt. 7:13-27)
1. The way (Matt. 7:13-14)
a. The gate to hell (Matt. 7:13)
b. The gate to heaven (Matt. 7:14)
2. The warning (Matt. 7:15-23)
a. Concerning false prophets (Matt. 7:15-19)
b. Concerning false professions (Matt. 7:21-23)
3. The wisdom (Matt. 7:24-27)
a. The abundance, as seen by the first builder (Matt. 7:24-25)
b. The absence, as seen by the second builder (Matt. 7:26-27)
III. The Power of the King—His mighty power was shown through his miracles:
A. General healing accounts (Matt. 4:23-25; 8:16-17; 9:35; 12:15; 14:14, 34-36; 15:29-31)
B. Healing of a leper (Matt. 8:1-4)
C. Healing of the centurion's servant (Matt. 8:5-13)
D. Healing of Peter's mother-in-law (Matt. 8:14-15)
E. Stilling of the winds and waves (Matt. 8:23-27)
F. Casting demons from two Gadarene men (Matt. 8:28-34)
G. Healing a paralytic (Matt. 9:1-8)
H. Healing a woman with an issue of blood (Matt. 9:20-22)
I. Raising Jairus's daughter (Matt. 9:18-19, 23-26)
J. Healing two blind men (Matt. 9:27-31)

K. Healing a Galilean demoniac (Matt. 9:32-33)
L. Healing a paralyzed hand (Matt. 12:10-13)
M. Walking on water (Matt. 14:22-33)
N. Healing a Syrophoenician girl with a demon (Matt. 15:21-28)
O. Feeding 4,000 men (Matt. 15:32-39)
P. Providing tax money from a fish (Matt. 17:24-27)
Q. Healing two blind men (Matt. 20:29-34)

IV. The Program of the King (Matt. 13)—The plan and program of heaven's kingdom is overviewed by Jesus in Matthew 13. See VII, The Parables of the King.

V. The Preachers of the King
- A. John the Baptist
  - 1. His ministry
    - a. As predicted by Isaiah and Malachi
      - (1) Isaiah—Compare Isaiah 40:3-5 with Matthew 3:1, 4.
      - (2) Malachi—Compare Malachi 3:1 with Matthew 11:10.
    - b. As proclaimed by John
      - (1) To the Jewish people (Matt. 3:2-3, 5-6)
      - (2) To the Jewish Pharisees (Matt. 3:7-10)
  - 2. His martyrdom
    - a. The doubts of John
      - (1) His request to Jesus (Matt. 11:2-3)
      - (2) His reassurance from Jesus (Matt. 11:4-6)
    - b. The dedication of John (Matt. 11:7-11)—Christ himself spoke of John's faithfulness and zeal.
    - c. The death of John
      - (1) The why of the matter (Matt. 14:3-5)
      - (2) The when of the matter (Matt. 14:6)
      - (3) The who of the matter (Matt. 14:7-9)
      - (4) The how of the matter (Matt. 14:10-11)
- B. The apostles
  - 1. The individuals involved (Matt. 4:18-22; 9:9; 10:2-4)
  - 2. The instruction involved (Matt. 10:1, 5-42)

VI. The Proclamations of the King—In addition to those topics mentioned during his Sermon on the Mount, Jesus touched upon various other subjects.
- A. Repentance (Matt. 4:12-17)
- B. True greatness (Matt. 18:1-5; 20:20-28)
- C. God's love for children (Matt. 18:6-11; 19:13-15)
- D. God's love for the lost (Matt. 18:11-14)
- E. Church discipline (Matt. 18:15-20)
- F. Forgiveness (Matt. 18:21-35)
- G. Divorce (Matt. 19:1-12)
- H. Danger of riches (Matt. 19:16-26)
- I. Rewards (Matt. 19:27-30)
- J. Discipleship (Matt. 8:18-22; 16:24-26)
- K. Vain traditions (Matt. 15:1-20)
- L. The unpardonable sin (Matt. 12:24-37)
- M. His family (Matt. 12:46-50; 13:53-56)
- N. Hypocrisy (Matt. 16:5-12)

O. His authority (Matt. 12:1-8; 21:23-27)
P. The giving of tribute (Matt. 22:15-22)
Q. The resurrection (Matt. 22:23-33)
R. The greatest commandment (Matt. 22:34-40)
S. The Messiah (Matt. 22:41-46)

VII. The Parables of the King
A. The two builders (Matt. 7:24-27)
B. The sower and the soils (Matt. 13:1-9, 18-23)
C. The wheat and the tares (Matt. 13:24-30, 36-43)
D. The mustard seed (Matt. 13:31-32)
E. The leaven (Matt. 13:33)
F. The hidden treasure (Matt. 13:44)
G. The pearl of great price (Matt. 13:45-46)
H. The dragnet (Matt. 13:47-51)
I. The householder (Matt. 13:52)
J. The morning, noon, and evening laborers (Matt. 20:1-16)
K. The two sons (Matt. 21:28-32)
L. The angry vineyard owner (Matt. 21:33-41)
M. The marriage feast (Matt. 22:1-14)
N. The fig tree (Matt. 24:32-35)
O. The faithful and faithless servant (Matt. 24:42-51)
P. The ten virgins (Matt. 25:1-13)
Q. The three servants and their talents (Matt. 25:14-30)
R. The sheep and the goats (Matt. 25:31-46)

VIII. The Person of the King (Matt. 16:13-23)
A. The probing by Christ—"When Jesus came into the coasts of Caesarea Philippi, he asked his disciples, saying, Whom do men say that I the Son of man am?" (Matt. 16:13).
1. The rumors involved (Matt. 16:14-15)
2. The recognition involved—"And Simon Peter answered and said, Thou art the Christ, the Son of the living God" (Matt. 16:16).
3. The revelation involved—"And Jesus answered and said unto him, Blessed art thou, Simon Bar-jona: for flesh and blood hath not revealed it unto thee, but my Father which is in heaven" (Matt. 16:17).

B. The promise of Christ—"And I say also unto thee, That thou art Peter, and upon this rock I will build my church; and the gates of hell shall not prevail against it" (Matt. 16:18).
C. The passion of Christ
1. Caused by sinners—"From that time forth began Jesus to shew unto his disciples, how that he must go unto Jerusalem, and suffer many things of the elders and chief priests and scribes, and be killed, and be raised again the third day" (Matt. 16:21).
2. Caused by Satan (who on this occasion influenced Peter)—"Then Peter took him, and began to rebuke him, saying, Be it far from thee, Lord: this shall not be unto thee. But he turned, and said unto Peter, Get thee behind me, Satan: thou art an offence unto me: for thou savourest not the things that be of God, but those that be of men" (Matt. 16:22-23).

IX. The Preeminence of the King (Matt. 17:1-8)—"And after six days Jesus taketh Peter, James, and John his brother, and bringeth them up into an high mountain apart, And was transfigured before them: and his face did shine as the sun, and his raiment was white as the light" (Matt. 17:1-2).

X. The Plea of the King—"Come unto me, all ye that labour and are heavy laden, and I will give you rest. Take my yoke upon you, and learn of me; for I am meek and lowly in heart: and ye shall find rest unto your souls. For my yoke is easy, and my burden is light" (Matt. 11:28-30).

XI. The Performance of the King—"Behold my servant, whom I have chosen; my beloved, in whom my soul is well pleased: I will put my spirit upon him, and he shall shew judgment to the Gentiles. He shall not strive, nor cry; neither shall any man hear his voice in the streets. A bruised reed shall he not break, and smoking flax shall he not quench, till he send forth judgment unto victory. And in his name shall the Gentiles trust" (Matt. 12:18-21).

XII. The Pity of the King—"But when he saw the multitudes, he was moved with compassion on them, because they fainted, and were scattered abroad, as sheep having no shepherd. Then saith he unto his disciples, The harvest truly is plenteous, but the labourers are few; pray ye therefore the Lord of the harvest, that he will send forth labourers into his harvest" (Matt. 9:36-38).

XIII. The Provoking of the King—The righteous indignation of Christ was aroused on several occasions.

   A. He rebuked his generation (Matt. 11:16-19; 12:38-45; 16:1-4; 17:17).
   B. He rebuked the unbelieving Galilean cities (Matt. 11:20-24).
   C. He rebuked the Pharisees (Matt. 15:1-9; 21:42-45; 23:1-36).

XIV. The Predictions of the King—Matthew records Christ's most detailed prophetical overview of the destruction of Jerusalem and the temple, the coming great tribulation, last-day conditions, etc. This is known as the Mt. Olivet Discourse and is found in chapters 24–25.

XV. The Presentation of the King (Matt. 21:1-11)—"And when they drew nigh unto Jerusalem, and were come to Bethphage, unto the mount of Olives, then sent Jesus two disciples, saying unto them, Go into the village over against you, and straightway ye shall find an ass tied, and a colt with her: loose them, and bring them unto me. And the disciples went, and did as Jesus commanded them, and brought the ass, and the colt, and put on them their clothes, and they set him thereon. And a very great multitude spread their garments in the way; others cut down branches from the trees, and strawed them in the way. And the multitudes that went before, and that followed, cried, saying, Hosanna to the Son of David: Blessed is he that cometh in the name of the Lord; Hosanna in the highest" (Matt. 21:1-2, 6-9).

XVI. The Purging by the King (Matt. 21:12-16)—"And Jesus went into the temple of God, and cast out all them that sold and bought in the temple, and overthrew the tables of the moneychangers, and the seats of them that sold doves" (Matt. 21:12).

XVII. The Pain of the King—"O Jerusalem, Jerusalem, thou that killest the prophets, and stonest them which are sent unto thee, how often would I have gathered thy children together, even as a hen gathereth her chickens under her wings, and ye would not! Behold, your house is left unto you desolate. For I say unto you, Ye shall not see me henceforth, till ye shall say, Blessed is he that cometh in the name of the Lord" (Matt. 23:37-39).

XVIII. The Passover of the King (Matt. 26: 17-30)—"And as they were eating, Jesus took bread, and blessed it, and brake it, and gave it to the disciples, and said, Take, eat; this is my body. And he took the cup, and gave thanks, and gave it to them, saying, Drink ye all of it; for this is my blood of the new testament, which is shed for many for the remission of sins. But I say unto you, I will not drink henceforth of this fruit of the vine, until that day when I drink it new with you in my Father's kingdom" (Matt. 26:26-29).

XIX. The Prayers of the King (Matt. 26:30-46)—"Then cometh Jesus with them unto a place called Gethsemane, and saith unto the disciples, Sit ye here, while I go and pray yonder. And he went a little further, and fell on his face, and prayed, saying, O my Father, if it be possible, let this cup pass from me: nevertheless not as I will, but as thou wilt" (Matt. 26:36, 39).

XX. The Persecution of the King—Throughout his earthly ministry Christ experienced persecution and hostility from sinful humanity.

A. He was accused of being a demon-possessed blasphemer (Matt. 9:3, 34; 12:24; 26:65).
B. He was plotted against (Matt. 12:14).
C. He was denied by a friend (Matt. 26:69-75).
D. He was betrayed by a follower (Matt. 26:47-50).
E. He was illegally tried.
   1. Before Caiaphas and the Jewish leaders (Matt. 26:57, 59-68)
   2. Before Pilate (Matt. 27:11-26)
   3. Before the Roman soldiers (Matt. 27:27)
F. He was spit upon (Matt. 26:67).
G. He was slapped (Matt. 26:67).
H. He was ridiculed (Matt. 26:68; 27:28-30).
I. He was severely beaten (Matt. 27:26).

XXI. The Passion of the King

A. The foretelling of his passion—Christ often predicted his death on the cross.
   1. First occasion (Matt. 16:21-23)—"From that time forth began Jesus to shew unto his disciples, how that he must go unto Jerusalem, and suffer many things of the elders and chief priests and scribes, and be killed, and be raised again the third day" (Matt. 16:21).
   2. Second occasion (Matt. 17:22-23)
   3. Third occasion (Matt. 20:17-19)
   4. Fourth occasion (Matt. 26:6-13)—After being anointed in Bethany by a woman, Jesus said: "For in that she hath poured this ointment on my body, she did it for my burial" (Matt. 26:12).
   5. Fifth occasion (Matt. 26:28)
B. The facts of his passion (Matt. 27:31-50)—"And when they were come unto a place called Golgotha, that is to say, a place of a skull, they gave him vinegar to drink mingled with gall: and when he had tasted thereof, he would not drink. And they crucified him, and parted his garments, casting lots: that it might be fulfilled which was spoken by the prophet, They parted my garments among them, and upon my vesture did they cast lots" (Matt. 27:33-35).

XXII. The Proof of the King (Matt. 28:1-20)—"In the end of the sabbath, as it began to dawn toward the first day of the week, came Mary Magdalene and the other Mary to see the sepulchre. And, behold, there was a great earthquake: for the angel of the Lord descended from heaven, and came and rolled back the stone from the door, and sat upon it" (Matt. 28:1-3).

A. As confirmed by his foes (Matt. 28:4, 11-15)
B. As confirmed by his friends
   1. The women (Matt. 28:5-10)
   2. The Eleven (Matt. 28:16-20)

MARK

A SPECIAL REPORT TO THE ROMANS:
WHO IS JESUS CHRIST?
HE IS THE LOWLY SERVANT.

This report was prepared by Mark the preacher. In it the miracles of Christ are emphasized.

I. Mark's Gospel account is a no-nonsense, action-oriented, bottom-line summary of the life of Jesus.
   A. It is the shortest of the four Gospel accounts.
   B. Mark's book is a fulfillment of Isaiah 42:1-7; 52:13-15; 53.
II. Material found only in Mark's account:
   A. Healing a deaf man with a speech impediment (7:32-37)
   B. Healing a blind man in the temple (8:22-26)
   C. An extended passage on hell (9:42-48)
   D. A passage dealing with tongues and serpents (16:16-18)

There are quotations or allusions in Mark from 25 Old Testament books. Mark is the fifth longest New Testament book, and 22nd longest biblical book, with 16 chapters, 678 verses, and 15,171 words.

MARK (Basic Outline)

I. The Setting Apart of the Servant
II. The Spokesman of the Servant
III. The Sermons and Subjects of the Servant
IV. The Supernaturalness of the Servant
V. The Skeptics of the Servant
VI. The Seekers of the Servant
VII. The Splendor of the Servant
VIII. The Sorrow of the Servant
IX. The Showing of the Servant
X. The Surveillance of the Servant
XI. The Supper of the Servant
XII. The Submission of the Servant
XIII. The Sufferings of the Servant
XIV. The Sacrifice of the Servant
XV. The Sovereignty of the Servant

MARK (Expanded Outline)

I. The Setting Apart of the Servant
  A. His forerunner (Mark 1:2-8)
    1. The prediction concerning John (Mark 1:2-3)
    2. The preaching of John (Mark 1:4-8)
  B. His baptism (Mark 1:9-11)
    1. The servant was anointed by the Spirit (Mark 1:10).
    2. The servant was approved by the Father (Mark 1:11).
  C. His temptation (Mark 1:12-13)—"And immediately the Spirit driveth him into the wilderness. And he was there in the wilderness forty days, tempted of Satan; and was with the wild beasts; and the angels ministered unto him" (Mark 1:12-13).

II. The Spokesman of the Servant
  A. The personal meeting with his apostles
    1. James, John, Peter, and Andrew (Mark 1:16-20)—The former fishermen now became fishers of men.
    2. Matthew (Mark 2:13-14)
  B. The public ministry of his apostles
    1. The official call of the Twelve (Mark 3:13-19)—"And he goeth up into a mountain, and calleth unto him whom he would: and they came unto him" (Mark 3:13).
    2. The official commission to the Twelve (Mark 3:14-15; 6:7-13)—"And he ordained twelve, that they should be with him, and that he might send them forth to preach, and to have power to heal sicknesses, and to cast out devils" (Mark 3:14-15).

III. The Sermons and Subjects of the Servant—"And he said unto them, Let us go into the next towns, that I may preach there also: for therefore came I forth" (Mark 1:38).
  A. The sermons he delivered
    1. The sower and soils (Mark 4:1-34)
    2. A description of defilement (Mark 7:1-23)
    3. The Mt. Olivet Discourse (Mark 13:1-37)
  B. The subjects he discussed
    1. The unpardonable sin (Mark 3:22-30)
    2. True relationships (Mark 3:31-35)
    3. Discipleship (Mark 8:34-38)
    4. Greatness (Mark 9:33-37; 10:42-45)
    5. Sectarianism (Mark 9:38-41)
    6. Hell (Mark 9:42-50)
    7. Divorce (Mark 10:1-12)
    8. Rewards (Mark 10:28-31)
    9. Prayer and faith (Mark 11:20-26)
    10. The Messiah (Mark 12:35-37)

IV. The Supernaturalness of the Servant—"And whithersoever he entered, into villages, or cities, or country, they laid the sick in the streets, and besought him that they might touch if it were but the border of his garment: and as many as touched him were made whole" (Mark 6:56). Mark records no less than 16 miracles performed by Jesus.
  A. Casting out of demons
    1. From a man in Capernaum (Mark 1:21-28)
    2. From a man in Gadara (Mark 5:1-20)

3. From a girl in Tyre (Mark 7:24-30)
4. From a boy near Mt. Hermon (Mark 9:14-29)

B. Healing of diseases
1. Peter's mother-in-law (Mark 1:29-31)
2. A leper (Mark 1:40-45)
3. A palsied man (Mark 2:1-12)
4. A withered hand (Mark 3:1-6)
5. A woman with a bloody issue (Mark 5:25-34)
6. A deaf and mute man (Mark 7:31-37)

C. Feeding the hungry
1. The 5,000 (Mark 6:30-44)
2. The 4,000 (Mark 8:1-10)

D. Controlling the elements
1. Stilling the storm (Mark 4:35-41)
2. Walking on water (Mark 6:45-52)

E. Judging a fruitless fig tree (Mark 11:12-14)

F. Raising a girl from the dead (Mark 5:21-24, 35-43)

V. The Skeptics of the Servant—"And the scribes which came down from Jerusalem said, He hath Beelzebub, and by the prince of the devils casteth he out devils" (Mark 3:22). "And the Pharisees came forth, and began to question with him, seeking of him a sign from heaven, tempting him" (Mark 8:11). "And they send unto him certain of the Pharisees and of the Herodians, to catch him in his words." (Mark 12:13)

A. His confrontation with the skeptics
1. They said he associated with sinners and did not observe all their legalism (Mark 2:18-22).
2. They questioned his authority (Mark 11:27-33).
3. They attempted to trap him.
a. Concerning the subject of paying tribute (Mark 12:13-17)
b. Concerning the subject of the resurrection (Mark 12:18-27)

B. His condemnation of the skeptics
1. He suggested they might have committed the unpardonable sin (Mark 3:22-30).
2. He refused to give them a sign (Mark 8:11-13).
3. He warned against their hypocrisy (Mark 8:14-21).
4. He compared them to some wicked and murderous laborers in a vineyard (Mark 12:1-12).
5. He denounced their self-centeredness and pride (Mark 12:38-40).

VI. The Seekers of the Servant—In contrast to the wicked Jewish leaders who rejected Jesus, there were those who sought him out for various reasons:

A. Some parents with their children (Mark 10:13-16)
1. Rebuked by the apostles (Mark 10:13)
2. Received by the Savior (Mark 10:14-16)

B. The rich young ruler (Mark 10:17-27)
1. The request concerning eternal life (Mark 10:17)
2. The requirements for eternal life (Mark 10:18-21)
3. The rejection of eternal life (Mark 10:22)

C. A sincere scribe (Mark 12:28-34)
1. The request (Mark 12:28)

2. The response
   a. Jesus' reply to the scribe (Mark 12:29-31)
   b. The scribe's reply to Jesus (Mark 12:32-33)
3. The results—"And when Jesus saw that he answered discreetly, he said unto him, Thou art not far from the kingdom of God. And no man after that durst ask him any question" (Mark 12:34).

D. James and John (Mark 10:35-41)
1. The request of the two brothers—"They said unto him, Grant unto us that we may sit, one on thy right hand, and the other on thy left hand, in thy glory" (Mark 10:37).
2. The refusal of the Lord (Mark 10:38-40)
3. The resentment of the ten (Mark 10:41)

E. A widow (Mark 12:41-44)—"And he called unto him his disciples, and saith unto them, Verily I say unto you, That this poor widow hath cast more in, than all they which have cast into the treasury: for all they did cast in of their abundance; but she of her want did cast in all that she had, even all her living" (Mark 12:43-44).

F. A woman in Bethany (Mark 14:3-9)
1. Her gift was precious (Mark 14:3-7)
2. Her gift was prophetical (Mark 14:8-9)

VII. The Splendor of the Servant

A. A declaration of his deity (Mark 8:27-30)—"And Jesus went out, and his disciples, into the towns of Caesarea Philippi: and by the way he asked his disciples, saying unto them, Whom do men say that I am? And they answered, John the Baptist: but some say, Elias; and others, One of the prophets. And he saith unto them, But whom say ye that I am? And Peter answereth and saith unto him, Thou art the Christ" (Mark 8:27-29).

B. A demonstration of his deity (Mark 9:1-13)—"And after six days Jesus taketh with him Peter, and James, and John, and leadeth them up into an high mountain apart by themselves: and he was transfigured before them. And his raiment became shining, exceeding white as snow; so as no fuller on earth can white them" (Mark 9:2-3).

VIII. The Sorrow of the Servant (Mark 6:1-6)

A. Over the disbelief in Nazareth (Mark 6:1-6)—"And he could there do no mighty work, save that he laid his hands upon a few sick folk, and healed them. And he marvelled because of their unbelief. And he went round about the villages, teaching" (Mark 6:5-6).

B. Over the death of John the Baptist (Mark 6:14-29)
1. The why of the matter (Mark 6:17-20)
2. The when of the matter (Mark 6:21)
3. The who of the matter (Mark 6:22-25)
4. The how of the matter (Mark 6:26-30)

IX. The Showing of the Servant (Mark 11:1-11)—"And they brought the colt to Jesus, and cast their garments on him; and he sat upon him. And many spread their garments in the way: and others cut down branches off the trees, and strawed them in the way. And they that went before, and they that followed, cried, saying, Hosanna; Blessed is he that cometh in the name of the Lord: Blessed be the kingdom of our father David, that cometh in the name of the Lord: Hosanna in the highest" (Mark 11:7-10).

X. The Surveillance of the Servant (Mark 11:15-19)

A. What he did—"And they come to Jerusalem: and Jesus went into the temple, and began to cast out them that sold and bought in the temple, and overthrew the tables of the moneychangers, and the seats of them that sold doves" (Mark 11:15).
B. Why he did it—"And he taught, saying unto them, Is it not written, My house shall be called of all nations the house of prayer? but ye have made it a den of thieves" (Mark 11:17).

XI. The Supper of the Servant (Mark 14:12-25)
A. The pitcher (Mark 14:13)
B. The place (Mark 14:14-16)
C. The prophecy (Mark 14:17-21)—"And as they sat and did eat, Jesus said, Verily I say unto you, One of you which eateth with me shall betray me" (Mark 14:18).
D. The picture (Mark 14:22-25)
1. "Jesus took bread, blessed, and brake it"—A picture of his broken body on the cross
2. "And he took the cup"—A picture of his shed blood on the cross

XII. The Submission of the Servant (Mark 14:32-42)—"And he went forward a little, and fell on the ground, and prayed that, if it were possible, the hour might pass from him. And he said, Abba, Father, all things are possible unto thee; take away this cup from me: nevertheless not what I will, but what thou wilt" (Mark 14:35-36).

XIII. The Sufferings of the Servant (Mark 14:1-11)
A. He was plotted against—"After two days was the feast of the passover, and of unleavened bread: and the chief priests and the scribes sought how they might take him by craft, and put him to death. But they said, Not on the feast day, lest there be an uproar of the people" (Mark 14:1-2). "And Judas Iscariot, one of the twelve, went unto the chief priests, to betray him unto them. And when they heard it, they were glad, and promised to give him money. And he sought how he might conveniently betray him" (Mark 14:10-11).
B. He was filled with horror and distress in the Garden.
1. The agony (Mark 14:32-42)
2. The arrest (Mark 14:43-49)
3. The abandonment (Mark 14:50)
C. He was denied by a friend.
1. The revelation of these denials (Mark 14:26-31)—"But Peter said unto him, Although all shall be offended, yet will not I. And Jesus saith unto him, Verily I say unto thee, That this day, even in this night, before the cock crow twice, thou shalt deny me thrice" (Mark 14:29-30).
2. The record of these denials (Mark 14:66-72)—"But he began to curse and to swear, saying, I know not this man of whom ye speak" (Mark 14:71).
D. He was betrayed by a follower (Mark 14:43-46)—"And he that betrayed him had given them a token, saying, Whomsoever I shall kiss, that same is he; take him, and lead him away safely. And as soon as he was come, he goeth straightway to him, and saith, Master, master; and kissed him" (Mark 14:44-45).
E. He was illegally tried.
1. Before the high priest (Mark 14:53-65)
a. Falsely accused (Mark 14:55-59)
b. Condemned to die (Mark 14:60-64)
c. Spit upon, blindfolded, struck, and ridiculed (Mark 14:65)

2. Before Pilate (Mark 15:1-15)
    a. Slandered by the priests (Mark 15:1-5)
    b. Scourged by Pilate (Mark 15:15)
3. Before the Roman soldiers (Mark 15:16-20)
    a. He was mistreated.
    b. He was mocked.

XIV. The Sacrifice of the Servant (Mark 15:20-47)
  A. He was placed on the cross (Mark 15:20-41).
  B. He was placed in the tomb (Mark 15:42-47).

XV. The Sovereignty of the Servant (Mark 16:1-20)
  A. He arose from the grave (Mark 16:1-18).
    1. The announcement (Mark 16:1-8)—"And when the sabbath was past, Mary Magdalene, and Mary the mother of James, and Salome, had bought sweet spices, that they might come and anoint him. And entering into the sepulchre, they saw a young man sitting on the right side, clothed in a long white garment; and they were affrighted. And he saith unto them, Be not affrighted: Ye seek Jesus of Nazareth, which was crucified: he is risen; he is not here: behold the place where they laid him" (Mark 16:1, 5-6).
    2. The appearances (Mark 16:9-18)
        a. To Mary Magdalene (Mark 16:9-11)
        b. To two disciples (Mark 16:12-13)
        c. To the Eleven (Mark 16:14-18)
  B. He ascended into glory (Mark 16:19-20)—"So then after the Lord had spoken unto them, he was received up into heaven, and sat on the right hand of God" (Mark 16:19).

LUKE

A SPECIAL REPORT TO THE GREEKS:
WHO IS JESUS CHRIST?
HE IS THE PERFECT MAN.

This report was prepared by Luke the historian. In it the parables of Christ are emphasized.

Luke is the most lengthy Gospel account and the longest New Testament book. If Paul did not write the book of Hebrews, then Luke authored more of the New Testament than any other writer. Luke's Gospel is the first of a two-volume work addressed to a friend named Theophilus. (Compare Luke 1:3 with Acts 1:1.)

Tradition says Luke was from Antioch in Syria, and remained unmarried. His book offers the second and most complete New Testament genealogy. (See Luke 3.) The Gospel of Luke is a fulfillment of Genesis 3:15; 22:18; Isaiah 7:14-16; 9:6.

I. The Following Things May Be Said About Luke:
   A. He is the only biblical writer who was a physician.
   B. He is the only Gentile biblical writer.
   C. He was probably Paul's most faithful friend and companion.
   D. He was the most educated of the four Gospel writers.

II. Material Found Only in Luke's Account:
   A. The announcement to Zacharias (1:13-25)
   B. The announcement to Mary (1:26-38)
   C. The meeting of Mary and Elisabeth (1:39-45)
   D. The song of Mary (1:46-56)
   E. The birth of John the Baptist (1:57-66)
   F. The praise of Zacharias (1:67-80)
   G. The birth of Christ (2:1-7)
   H. The announcement to the shepherds (2:8-20)
   I. The temple dedication (2:21-38)
   J. The temple visit and early years in Nazareth (2:39-52)
   K. The first sermon at Nazareth (4:14-30)
   L. Resurrection of a widow's son (7:11-18)
   M. Parable of two debtors (7:40-50)
   N. Sending out of the Seventy (10:1-12)
   O. Parable of the Good Samaritan (10:30-37)
   P. Visit with Mary and Martha (10:38-42)
   Q. Parable of the rich fool (12:16-21)
   R. The fruitless fig tree (13:6-9)
   S. Healing of the crippled woman (13:10-17)
   T. Healing of the man with dropsy (14:1-6)
   U. Parable of the banquet dinner (14:7-14)

V. Parable of the three guests (14:15-24)
W. Parable of the lost sheep, silver, and son (15:3-32)
X. Parable of the unjust but clever steward (16:1-13)
Y. Parable of the rich man and Lazarus (16:19-31)
Z. Parable of the duties of faithful servants (17:7-10)
AA. Healing of the ten lepers (17:11-19)
BB. Parable of the widow and judge (18:1-8)
CC. Parable of the Pharisee and the publican (18:9-14)
DD. Conversion of Zacchaeus (19:1-10)
EE. Parable of the ten talents (19:11-27)
FF. Christ before Herod (23:6-12)
GG. Details on the way to the cross (23:27-31)
HH. Dying thief event (23:39-43)
II. His statement on the cross (23:46)—"Father, into thy hands I commend my spirit."
JJ. The Emmaus Road conversation (24:13-32)

There are quotations and allusions in Luke from 31 Old Testament books. Luke is the longest New Testament book, and tenth longest biblical book, with 24 chapters, 1,151 verses, and 25,944 words.

LUKE (Basic Outline)

I. The Explanation
II. The Annunciations
III. The Preparation
IV. The Anticipation
V. The Validation
VI. The Documentation
VII. The Temptation
VIII. The Proclamation
IX. The Eulogization
X. The Deputation
XI. The Demonstrations
XII. The Illustrations
XIII. The Supplications
XIV. The Invitations
XV. The Intoleration
XVI. The Clarification
XVII. The Consecration
XVIII. The Lamentation
XIX. The Presentation
XX. The Purification
XXI. The Observation
XXII. The Confrontations
XXIII. The Condemnation
XXIV. The Symbolization

XXV. The Repudiation
XXVI. The Interrogation
XXVII. The Brutalization
XXVIII. The Authorization
XIX. The Finalization
XXX. The Vindication
XXXI. The Exaltation

LUKE (Expanded Outline)

I. The Explanation—Luke explains to his friend Theophilus his reason for writing an account of the Son of man (Luke 1:1-4).
II. The Annunciations—There were a number of heavenly birth announcements concerning both the Son of man and his forerunner, John the Baptist.
  A. Those announcements preceding his birth
    1. Zacharias and Gabriel (Luke 1:5-25)
      a. Zacharias's devotion to God (Luke 1:6)
      b. Zacharias's duties for God
        (1) The priest and the altar of the Lord (Luke 1:8-10)
        (2) The priest and the angel of the Lord (Luke 1:11-25)
    2. Mary and Gabriel (Luke 1:26-38)
      a. The salvation
        (1) Concerning the birth of Jesus (Luke 1:26-35)
        (2) Concerning the birth of John (Luke 1:36-37)
      b. The submission—"And Mary said, Behold the handmaid of the Lord; be it unto me according to thy word. And the angel departed from her" (Luke 1:38).
    3. Mary and Elisabeth (Luke 1:39-56)
      a. The praise of Elisabeth to Mary (Luke 1:39-45)
      b. The praise of Mary to God (Luke 1:46-56)
    4. Zacharias and the infant John (Luke 1:57-79)
      a. Zacharias, the parent (Luke 1:57-66)
      b. Zacharias, the prophet (Luke 1:67-79)
    5. Mary and Joseph (Luke 2:1-7)
      a. Jesus' birth—The circumstances (Luke 2:1-3)
      b. Jesus' birth—The city (Luke 2:4)
      c. Jesus' birth—The channel (Luke 2:5-7)
  B. Those announcements following his birth
    1. The shepherds and the angels (Luke 2:8-15)
      a. The declaration to the shepherds (Luke 2:8-14)
      b. The decision by the shepherds (Luke 2:15)
    2. The shepherds and the Savior (Luke 2:16-20)
      a. Worshiping (Luke 2:16)
      b. Witnessing (Luke 2:17-20)
    3. Simeon and the Savior (Luke 2:21-35)
      a. The righteousness of Simeon (Luke 2:25)
      b. The revelation to Simeon (Luke 2:26)

c. The recognition by Simeon (Luke 2:27-35)
(1) In regard to the Messiah (Luke 2:27-32)
(2) In regard to the mother (Luke 2:33-35)
4. Anna and the Savior (Luke 2:36-38)
III. The Preparation—The quiet boyhood of Jesus prepared him for his role as the perfect Son of man.
A. As seen in the home of his mother—"And when they had performed all things according to the law of the Lord, they returned into Galilee, to their own city Nazareth. And the child grew, and waxed strong in spirit, filled with wisdom: and the grace of God was upon him. . . . And Jesus increased in wisdom and stature, and in favour with God and man" (Luke 2:39-40, 52).
B. As seen in the house of his Father (Luke 2:41-51)
1. The rebuke by Mary—"And when they saw him, they were amazed: and his mother said unto him, Son, why hast thou thus dealt with us? behold, thy father and I have sought thee sorrowing" (Luke 2:48).
2. The reminder by Jesus—"And he said unto them, How is it that ye sought me? wist ye not that I must be about my Father's business?" (Luke 2:49).
IV. The Anticipation—The preaching of John the Baptist caused great interest in the promised appearance of the Son of man (Luke 3:1-20).
A. John the preacher
1. What John said—"And he came into all the country about Jordan, preaching the baptism of repentance for the remission of sins; as it is written in the book of the words of Esaias the prophet, saying, The voice of one crying in the wilderness, Prepare ye the way of the Lord, make his paths straight. Every valley shall be filled, and every mountain and hill shall be brought low; and the crooked shall be made straight, and the rough ways shall be made smooth; and all flesh shall see the salvation of God" (Luke 3:3-6).
2. To whom it was said
a. The Pharisees (Luke 3:7-9)
b. The crowds (Luke 3:10-11)
c. The publicans (Luke 3:12-13)
d. The soldiers (Luke 3:14)
B. John the prophet (Luke 3:15-20)—"John answered, saying unto them all, I indeed baptize you with water; but one mightier than I cometh, the latchet of whose shoes I am not worthy to unloose: he shall baptize you with the Holy Ghost and with fire" (Luke 3:16).
V. The Validation—At his baptism the Father gives official approval of the Son of man (Luke 3:21-22). "Now when all the people were baptized, it came to pass, that Jesus also being baptized, and praying, the heaven was opened, and the Holy Ghost descended in a bodily shape like a dove upon him, and a voice came from heaven, which said, Thou art my beloved Son; in thee I am well pleased" (Luke 3:21-22).
VI. The Documentation—Luke follows the genealogy of the Son of man backward in time to Adam, tracing his line through Nathan, the second son of King David (Luke 3:23-38).
VII. The Temptation—The Son of man is unsuccessfully tempted on three occasions by Satan (Luke 4:1-13).
A. First occasion (Luke 4:3-4)

1. The temptation (Luke 4:3)
2. The triumph (Luke 4:4)

B. Second occasion (Luke 4:5-8)

1. The temptation (Luke 4:5-7)
2. The triumph (Luke 4:8)

C. Third occasion (Luke 4:9-12)

1. The temptation (Luke 4:9-11)
2. The triumph (Luke 4:12)

VIII. The Proclamation—The Son of man proclaims his message throughout the land (Luke 4:14-15, 42-44). "And he said unto them, I must preach the kingdom of God to other cities also: for therefore am I sent" (Luke 4:43).

A. The sermons he delivered

1. The message at Nazareth on Isaiah 61 (Luke 4:16-30)
2. The Sermon on the Mount (Luke 6:17-49)
3. The Mt. Olivet Discourse (Luke 21:5-38)

B. The subjects he discussed

1. True spiritual relationships (Luke 8:19-21)
2. His future sufferings, death, and resurrection (Luke 9:22, 44-45; 17:25; 18:31-34)
3. Discipleship (Luke 9:23-26, 57-62; 14:25-33)
4. Greatness (Luke 9:46-48; 22:24-27)
5. Sectarianism (Luke 9:49-50)
6. The unbelief and coming judgment upon his generation (Luke 11:29-32)
7. The Holy Spirit (Luke 12:10-12)
8. Covetousness (Luke 12:13-15; 16:14-15)
9. God's care for his own (Luke 12:6-7, 22-34)
10. His watchfulness (Luke 12:35-40)
11. His mission (Luke 12:49-53)
12. Repentance and confession (Luke 12:8-9; 13:1-5)
13. Signs of the times (Luke 12:54-57)
14. False religious profession (Luke 13:22-30)
15. The great white throne judgment (Luke 12:2-5)
16. Divorce (Luke 16:18)
17. Forgiveness (Luke 17:3-4)
18. Faith (Luke 17:5-6)
19. Last day conditions (Luke 17:22-37)
20. Rewards (Luke 18:28-30; 22:28-30)

IX. The Eulogization—The Son of man pays great homage to the imprisoned John the Baptist (Luke 7:19-29).

A. The concern by John

1. His request (Luke 7:19-20)
2. His reassurance (Luke 7:21-23)

B. The commendation of John (Luke 7:24-29)

X. The Deputation—The Son of man chooses and commissions his apostles.

A. The Twelve

1. The call of Andrew, Peter, James, and John (Luke 5:1-11)
2. The call of Levi (Luke 5:27-29)
3. The selection of the Twelve (Luke 6:13-16)

- 4. The sending forth of the Twelve (Luke 9:1-11)
- B. The Seventy (Luke 10:1-24)
    - 1. The job involved (Luke 10:1-16)
        - a. The appointment of the Seventy (Luke 10:1)
        - b. The assignment of the Seventy (Luke 10:2-15)
        - c. The authority (Luke 10:16)
    - 2. The joy involved (Luke 10:17-24)
        - a. As experienced by the Seventy (Luke 10:17-20)
        - b. As experienced by the Savior (Luke 10:21-24)

XI. The Demonstrations—The Son of man exhibits his mighty power by performing 17 miracles, as recorded by Luke.

- A. Casting out of demons
    - 1. The man at Capernaum (Luke 4:31-37)
    - 2. The man at Gadara (Luke 8:26-40)
    - 3. The boy at the base of Mt. Hermon (Luke 9:37-43)
    - 4. A man somewhere in Galilee (Luke 11:14)
- B. Raising the dead
    - 1. The widow's son at Nain (Luke 7:11-18)
    - 2. Jairus's daughter in Galilee (Luke 8:41-42, 49-56)
- C. Feeding the hungry (Luke 9:12-17)
- D. Healing the sick
    - 1. Peter's mother-in-law (Luke 4:38-39)
    - 2. A leper (Luke 5:12-14)
    - 3. Ten lepers (Luke 17:11-19)
    - 4. A paralytic (Luke 5:17-26)
    - 5. A paralyzed hand (Luke 6:6-11)
    - 6. A centurion's servant (Luke 7:1-10)
    - 7. A woman with an issue of blood (Luke 8:43-48)
    - 8. A woman with an 18-year infirmity (Luke 13:10-17)
    - 9. A man with dropsy (Luke 14:1-6)
- E. Calming the sea (Luke 8:22-25)

XII. The Illustrations—The Son of man illustrated both his message and mission through the employment of parables. Here are the 25 parables as recorded by Luke:

- A. The two debtors (Luke 7:40-50)
- B. The sower and the soil (Luke 8:4-15)
- C. The mustard seed (Luke 13:18-19)
- D. The leaven (Luke 13:20-21)
- E. The lighted lamp (Luke 8:16-18; 11:33-36)
- F. The Good Samaritan (Luke 10:25-37)
- G. The generous father (Luke 11:11-13)
- H. The persistent friend (Luke 11:5-8)
- I. Reformation without regeneration (Luke 11:24-26)
- J. The rich fool (Luke 12:16-21)
- K. The faithful and faithless servants (Luke 12:41-48)
- L. The fruitless fig tree (Luke 13:6-9)
- M. The ambitious guest (Luke 14:7-14)
- N. The great supper (Luke 14:16-24)
- O. The lost sheep (Luke 15:1-7)

P. The lost coin (Luke 15:8-10)
Q. The lost son (Luke 15:11-32)
R. The unjust steward (Luke 16:1-13)
S. The rich man and Lazarus (Luke 16:19-31)
T. When our best is but the least (Luke 17:7-10)
U. The persistent widow (Luke 18:1-8)
V. The publican and the Pharisee (Luke 18:9-14)
W. The ten pounds (Luke 19:11-27)
X. The angry vineyard owner (Luke 20:9-18)
Y. The budding fig tree (Luke 21:29-32)

XIII. The Supplications—The Son of man looked upon prayer as an all-important act.
  A. His personal prayers—Jesus prayed:
    1. At his baptism (Luke 3:21)
    2. In the wilderness (Luke 5:16)
    3. Before choosing the Twelve (Luke 6:12)
    4. During his transfiguration (Luke 9:29)
    5. After hearing the report of the returning Seventy (Luke 10:21-22)
    6. Before giving the model prayer (Luke 11:1)
    7. In the Upper Room for Peter—"And the Lord said, Simon, Simon, behold, Satan hath desired to have you, that he may sift you as wheat: But I have prayed for thee, that thy faith fail not: and when thou art converted, strengthen thy brethren" (Luke 22:31-32).
    8. In the Garden—"And he was withdrawn from them about a stone's cast, and kneeled down, and prayed, saying, Father, if thou be willing, remove this cup from me: nevertheless not my will, but thine, be done. And there appeared an angel unto him from heaven, strengthening him. And being in an agony he prayed more earnestly: and his sweat was as it were great drops of blood falling down to the ground" (Luke 22:41-44).
    9. On the cross—"Then said Jesus, Father, forgive them; for they know not what they do" (Luke 23:34). "And when Jesus had cried with a loud voice, he said, Father, into thy hands I commend my spirit" (Luke 23:46).
  B. His pattern prayer—"And he said unto them, When ye pray, say, Our Father which art in heaven, Hallowed be thy name. Thy kingdom come. Thy will be done, as in heaven, so in earth. Give us day by day our daily bread. And forgive us our sins; for we also forgive every one that is indebted to us. And lead us not into temptation; but deliver us from evil" (Luke 11:2-4).
  C. His points on prayer
    1. Who we should pray for (Luke 6:28-29)
    2. When we should pray (Luke 18:1)
    3. Why we should pray (Luke 11:9-10; 21:36; 22:40)

XIV. The Invitations—On two special occasions the Son of man issued a personal invitation.
  A. To a rich young ruler (Luke 18:18-24)
    1. The ruler manifested the right desire (Luke 18:18-22)
    2. The ruler made the wrong decision (Luke 18:23-24)
  B. To a rich tax collector (Luke 19:1-10)
    1. Zacchaeus, the sinner (Luke 19:1-2)
    2. Zacchaeus, the seeker (Luke 19:3-4)
    3. Zacchaeus, the saved (Luke 19:5-10)

XV. The Intoleration—The Son of man witnessed a twofold example of gross intoleration on a specific occasion:
   A. As demonstrated by the Samaritans, directed toward the Savior (Luke 9:51-53)
   B. As demonstrated by the disciples, directed toward the Samaritans (Luke 9:54-56)

XVI. The Clarification—During his visit with Mary and Martha, the Son of man gently corrects Martha for having her priorities in the wrong order (Luke 10:38-42).
   A. The complaint by Martha (Luke 10:38-40)
   B. The correction by Jesus (Luke 10:41-42)

XVII. The Consecration—Some children are brought to the Son of man to be blessed by him (Luke 18:15-17).
   A. The request by the parents—"And they brought unto him also infants, that he would touch them" (Luke 18:15a).
   B. The refusal by the disciples—"But when his disciples saw it, they rebuked them" (Luke 18:15b).
   C. The reaction by the Savior—"But Jesus called them unto him, and said, Suffer little children to come unto me, and forbid them not: for of such is the kingdom of God" (Luke 18:16).

XVIII. The Lamentation—The Son of man weeps over the city of Jerusalem (Luke 19:41-42).

XIX. The Presentation—The Son of man presents himself during the triumphal entry on Palm Sunday (Luke 19:28-40).
   A. The colt involved (Luke 19:28-34)
   B. The celebration involved (Luke 19:35-38)
   C. The complaint involved (Luke 19:39-40)

XX. The Purification—The Son of man cleanses the temple for the second time (Luke 19:45-48).

XXI. The Observation—The Son of man comments concerning those who presented their offerings in the temple (Luke 21:1-4).
   A. The shallow gifts (Luke 21:1)
   B. The sacrificial gift—"And he said, Of a truth I say unto you, that this poor widow hath cast in more than they all: For all these have of their abundance cast in unto the offerings of God: but she of her penury hath cast in all the living that she had" (Luke 21:3-4).

XXII. The Confrontations—The Son of man was often confronted and accused by the wicked Jewish leaders.
   A. They said he was a blasphemer (Luke 5:21).
   B. They accused him of having a demon (Luke 11:15).
   C. They criticized him in various areas:
      1. For associating with sinners (Luke 5:30-32; 7:36-39)
      2. For not observing their ceremonial fastings (Luke 5:33-35)
      3. For not observing their ceremonial washings (Luke 11:37-38)
      4. For allowing his disciples to pluck grain for food on the Sabbath (Luke 6:1-5)
      5. For healing on the Sabbath (Luke 6:6-11)
   D. They challenged his authority (Luke 20:1-8).
   E. They attempted to trap him.
      1. Concerning the paying of tribute (Luke 20:19-22)
      2. Concerning the resurrection of the dead (Luke 20:27-33)

XXIII. The Condemnation—The Son of man utterly condemns the wicked Jewish leaders. "Then in the audience of all the people he said unto his disciples, Beware of the scribes, which desire to walk in long robes, and love greetings in the markets, and the highest seats in the synagogues, and the chief rooms at feasts" (Luke 20:45-46).
  A. They had slandered both Jesus and John the Baptist (Luke 7:30-35).
  B. They were totally corrupt in both their hypocritical attitudes and murderous actions (Luke 11:39-54; 20:47).

XXIV. The Symbolization—The Son of man uses bread and wine in the Upper Room to symbolize his impending death (Luke 22:7-23).
  A. The Passover—"And he sent Peter and John, saying, Go and prepare us the passover, that we may eat" (Luke 22:8).
  B. The place—"And he shall shew you a large upper room furnished: there make ready" (Luke 22:12).
  C. The passion—"And he said unto them, With desire I have desired to eat this passover with you before I suffer" (Luke 22:15).
  D. The prophecies—"For I say unto you, I will not any more eat thereof, until it be fulfilled in the kingdom of God. But, behold, the hand of him that betrayeth me is with me on the table" (Luke 22:16, 21).
  E. The picture
    1. The bread, speaking of his broken body (Luke 22:19)
    2. The wine, speaking of his shed blood (Luke 22:20)

XXV. The Repudiation—The Son of man is betrayed and denied by two followers.
  A. The betrayal by Judas (Luke 22:1-6, 47-48)
    1. Judas plans his wicked work (Luke 22:1-6).
    2. Judas works his wicked plan (Luke 22:47-48).
  B. The denials by Peter (Luke 22:34, 54-62)
    1. The foretelling of these denials (Luke 22:34)
    2. The fulfilling of these denials (Luke 22:54-62)

XXVI. The Interrogation—The Son of man is arrested in Gethsemane and subjected to various unfair trials.
  A. Before the high priest (Luke 22:54, 63-65)—"And the men that held Jesus mocked him, and smote him" (Luke 22:63).
  B. Before the Sanhedrin (Luke 22:66-71)—"Art thou the Christ? tell us. And he said unto them, If I tell you, ye will not believe" (Luke 22:67).
  C. Before Pilate for the first time (Luke 23:1-7)—"Then said Pilate to the chief priests and to the people, I find no fault in this man" (Luke 23:4).
  D. Before Herod (Luke 23:8-12)—"And Herod with his men of war set him at nought, and mocked him, and arrayed him in a gorgeous robe, and sent him again to Pilate" (Luke 23:11).
  E. Before Pilate for the second time (Luke 23:13-25)
    1. The conflict over Jesus (Luke 23:13-23)
      a. The governor's desire to chasten Christ
      b. The Jews' demand to crucify Christ
    2. The condemnation of Jesus (Luke 23:24-25)

XXVII. The Brutalization—The Son of man is put to death at Calvary (Luke 23:26-49).
  A. The trip to the cross (Luke 23:26-31)—"And as they led him away, they laid hold upon one Simon, a Cyrenian, coming out of the country, and on him they laid the cross that he might bear it after Jesus" (Luke 23:26).

1. The weeping of the women (Luke 23:27)
2. The warning of the Savior (Luke 23:28-31)

B. The travail on the cross—"And when they were come to the place, which is called Calvary, there they crucified him, and the malefactors, one on the right hand, and the other on the left" (Luke 23:33).

1. The compassion shown by Jesus for sinners
   a. For those who crucified him—"Then said Jesus, Father, forgive them; for they know not what they do. And they parted his raiment, and cast lots" (Luke 23:34).
   b. For the crucified (Luke 23:39-43)
2. The contempt shown by sinners for Jesus
   a. By the people—"And the people stood beholding. And the rulers also with them derided him, saying, He saved others; let him save himself, if he be Christ, the chosen of God" (Luke 23:35).
   b. By the soldiers—"And the soldiers also mocked him, coming to him, and offering him vinegar" (Luke 23:36).
   c. By the unrepentant thief—"And one of the malefactors which were hanged railed on him, saying, If thou be Christ, save thyself and us." (Luke 23:39)

XXVIII. The Authorization—Joseph of Arimathaea receives permission from Pilate to remove the body of the Son of man and place it in a new tomb (Luke 23:50-53). "And he took it down, and wrapped it in linen, and laid it in a sepulchre that was hewn in stone, wherein never man before was laid" (Luke 23:53).

XIX. The Finalization—The women began anointing the body of the Son of man for final burial (Luke 23:54-56).

XXX. The Vindication—The Son of man is vindicated through his glorious resurrection from the dead (Luke 24:1-48).

A. The announcement to his followers (Luke 24:1-12)

1. The revelation to the women in the tomb (Luke 24:1-8)—"He is not here, but is risen: remember how he spake unto you when he was yet in Galilee" (Luke 24:6).
2. The report by the women concerning the tomb (Luke 24:9-12)—"And returned from the sepulchre, and told all these things unto the eleven, and to all the rest. . . . And their words seemed to them as idle tales, and they believed them not" (Luke 24:9, 11).

B. The appearances to his followers (Luke 24:13-48)

1. To two disciples on the Emmaus Road (Luke 24:13-35)—"And, behold, two of them went that same day to a village called Emmaus, which was from Jerusalem about threescore furlongs. And they talked together of all these things which had happened" (Luke 24:13-14).
   a. The reunion with Jesus (Luke 24:15-16)
   b. The request from Jesus (Luke 24:17)
   c. The reply to Jesus (Luke 24:18-24)
   d. The rebuke of Jesus (Luke 24:25-27)
   e. The recognition of Jesus (Luke 24:28-32)
   f. The report concerning Jesus (Luke 24:33-35)
2. To ten apostles in the Upper Room (Luke 24:36-48)
   a. He reassures them (Luke 24:36-43)—"Behold my hands and my feet, that it is I myself: handle me, and see; for a spirit hath not flesh and bones as ye see me have" (Luke 24:39).

b. He reminds them (Luke 24:44-48)—"And he said unto them, These are the words which I spake unto you, while I was yet with you, that all things must be fulfilled, which were written in the law of Moses, and in the prophets, and in the psalms, concerning me" (Luke 24:44).

XXXI. The Exaltation (Luke 24:49-53)

A. The direction by the Savior—"And, behold, I send the promise of my Father upon you: but tarry ye in the city of Jerusalem, until ye be endued with power from on high" (Luke 24:49).

B. The departure of the Savior—"And it came to pass, while he blessed them, he was parted from them, and carried up into heaven" (Luke 24:51).

JOHN

A SPECIAL REPORT TO THE WORLD:
WHO IS JESUS CHRIST?
HE IS THE SON OF GOD.

This report was prepared by John the theologian. In it the doctrines of Christ are emphasized. In describing the life of Christ, John makes comparisons with the pieces of furniture in the tabernacle of Moses. Note the similarities between the language of Moses and John:

Moses describes the brazen altar (Exod. 27:1-8; 38:1-7). John describes the Lamb of God (John 1:29).

Moses speaks of the brazen laver (Exod. 30:18; 38:8). John speaks of the Water of life (John 4:14).

Moses writes of the table of shewbread (Exod. 25:23-30; 37:10-16). John writes of the Bread of life (John 6:35).

Moses talks of the lampstand (Exod. 25:31-40; 37:17-24). John talks of the Light of the world (John 9:5).

Moses presents the altar of incense (Exod. 30:1-10; 37:25-28). John presents the great prayer of Christ (John 17).

Moses witnesses of the mercy seat (Exod. 25:10-22; 37:1-9). John witnesses of our mercy seat, Christ (1 John 2:2).

John is the only Gospel writer to hint at the rapture (14:2-3). He uses the number seven on numerous occasions.

I. Seven witnesses of Christ
  A. John the Baptist (1:34)
  B. Nathanael (1:49)
  C. Samaritan woman (4:29)
  D. Peter (6:69)
  E. Martha (11:27)
  F. Thomas (20:28)
  G. John the apostle (20:31)
II. Seven precrucifixion miracles
  A. Water into wine (2:1-11)
  B. Healing of the nobleman's son (4:46-54)
  C. Healing of a man at the pool of Bethesda (5:1-47)
  D. Feeding of the 5,000 (6:1-14)
  E. Walking on the water (6:15-21)
  F. Healing of the man born blind (9:1-41)
  G. Raising of Lazarus (11:1-57)
III. Seven "I Am's"
  A. I am the Bread of life (6:35).
  B. I am the Light (8:12).

C. I am the eternal One (8:58).
D. I am the Good Shepherd (10:11).
E. I am the resurrection (11:25).
F. I am the way, the truth, and the life (14:6).
G. I am the true Vine (15:1).

The Gospel of John is the fulfillment of Isaiah 9:6; 40:3-5; 47:4; and Jeremiah 23:6.

IV. Material found only in John's account
A. Earliest dealings with Christ's disciples (1:35-51)
B. Changing water into wine (2:1-12)
C. First temple cleansing (2:13-17)
D. First mention of the death and resurrection (2:18-22)
E. Conversion of Nicodemus (3:1-21)
F. Conversion of the Samaritan woman (4:1-42)
G. Healing of the nobleman's son (4:46-54)
H. Healing of a 38-year-old cripple (5:1-16)
I. The Source of Life sermon (5:17-47)
J. The Bread of Life sermon (6:22-71)
K. The Feast of Tabernacles sermon (7:10-53)
L. The adulterous woman episode (8:1-11)
M. The Temple Treasury sermon (8:12-59)
N. Healing of a man born blind (9:1-41)
O. The Good Shepherd sermon (10:1-42)
P. The raising of Lazarus (11:1-44)
Q. The last high priestly prophecy (11:47-57)
R. The request of some Greeks (12:20-22)
S. The Grain of Wheat sermon (12:23-41, 44-50)
T. The head belief of some fickle priests (12:42-43)
U. Washing of the disciples' feet in the Upper Room (13:1-20)
V. Dipping of sop in the Upper Room (13:21-25)
W. The Thursday night Passover discourse (ch. 14–15)
X. Christ's high priestly prayer (ch. 17)
Y. His dying words to Mary from the cross (19:26-27)
Z. His final words—"It is finished" (19:30).
AA. The breaking of the legs of the two thieves (19:31-37)
BB. Mary Magdalene at the empty tomb (20:1-18)
CC. The meeting with doubting Thomas (20:24-29)
DD. The second draught of fishes (21:1-25)

There are quotations and allusions from 26 Old Testament books in John. John is the fourth longest New Testament book, and 19th longest biblical book, with 21 chapters, 878 verses, and 19,099 words.

JOHN (Basic Outline)

I. The Eternal Son of God (John 1:1-5)
II. The Earthly Son of God (John 1:6–18:11)

A. The forerunner to his ministry (John 1:6-34; 3:22-36)
B. The fruits of his ministry
1. The zeal he displayed
2. The miracles he performed
3. The dialogues he had
4. The sermons he preached
C. The final days of his ministry (John 12:1–18:11)
III. The Executed Son of God (John 18:12–19:42)
IV. The Exalted Son of God (John 20:1–21:25)

JOHN (Expanded Outline)

I. The Eternal Son of God (John 1:1-5)
A. John tells us *who* Christ is (John 1:1-2)
1. He speaks of his eternality—"In the beginning was the Word."
2. He speaks of his equality—"And the Word was with God."
3. He speaks of his deity—"And the Word was God."
B. John tells us *what* Christ did (John 1:3-5).
1. Regarding the creation of this universe—"All things were made by him; and without him was not any thing made that was made" (John 1:3).
2. Regarding the creatures in this universe—"In him was life; and the life was the light of men. And the light shineth in darkness; and the darkness comprehended it not" (John 1:4-5).
II. The Earthly Son of God (John 1:6–18:11)
A. The forerunner to his ministry (John 1:6-34; 3:22-36)
1. The mission of John (John 1:6-9)—"The same came for a witness, to bear witness of the Light, that all men through him might believe" (John 1:7).
2. The Messiah of John (John 1:10-14)—"He was in the world, and the world was made by him, and the world knew him not. He came unto his own, and his own received him not. But as many as received him, to them gave he power to become the sons of God, even to them that believe on his name. . . . And the Word was made flesh, and dwelt among us, (and we beheld his glory, the glory as of the only begotten of the Father,) full of grace and truth" (John 1:10-12, 14).
3. The ministry of John
a. His ministry for Christ
(1) John's testimony to the crowds (John 1:15-18)—"For the law was given by Moses, but grace and truth came by Jesus Christ" (John 1:17).
(2) John's testimony to the religious leaders (John 1:19-28)—"And they asked him, What then? Art thou Elias? And he saith, I am not. Art thou that prophet? And he answered, No. Then said they unto him, Who art thou? that we may give an answer to them that sent us. What sayest thou of thyself? He said, I am the voice of one crying in the wilderness, Make straight the way of the Lord, as said the prophet Esaias. . . . He it is, who coming after me is preferred before me, whose shoe's latchet I am not worthy to unloose" (John 1:21-23, 27).
(3) John's testimony to his own disciples (John 3:22-36)—"Ye yourselves bear me witness, that I said, I am not the Christ, but that I am sent before

him. He that hath the bride is the bridegroom: but the friend of the bridegroom, which standeth and heareth him, rejoiceth greatly because of the bridegroom's voice: this my joy therefore is fulfilled. He must increase, but I must decrease. . . . He that believeth on the Son hath everlasting life: and he that believeth not the Son shall not see life; but the wrath of God abideth on him" (John 3:28-30, 36).

b. His ministry to Christ—John introduces and baptizes the Savior in the Jordan River (John 1:29-34). "The next day John seeth Jesus coming unto him, and saith, Behold the Lamb of God, which taketh away the sin of the world. And I knew him not: but he that sent me to baptize with water, the same said unto me, Upon whom thou shalt see the Spirit descending, and remaining on him, the same is he which baptizeth with the Holy Ghost" (John 1:29, 33).

B. The fruits of his ministry

1. The zeal he displayed (John 2:13-25)

a. The purifying of the temple (John 2:13-17)—"And when he had made a scourge of small cords, he drove them all out of the temple, and the sheep, and the oxen; and poured out the changers' money, and overthrew the tables. . . . And his disciples remembered that it was written, The zeal of thine house hath eaten me up" (John 2:15, 17).

b. The prophecy about the temple (John 2:18-25)—"Jesus answered and said unto them, Destroy this temple, and in three days I will raise it up. Then said the Jews, Forty and six years was this temple in building, and wilt thou rear it up in three days? But he spake of the temple of his body" (John 2:19-21).

2. The miracles he performed

a. First miracle—Turning of water into wine (John 2:1-12)

(1) The occasion (John 2:1-3)
(2) The observation (John 2:4)
(3) The order (John 2:5-7a)
(4) The obedience (John 2:7b-8)
(5) The opinion (John 2:9-10)
(6) The omnipotence (John 2:11)

b. Second miracle—Healing the nobleman's son (John 4:46-54)

(1) Imploration (John 4:49)
(2) Affirmation (John 4:50)
(3) Investigation (John 4:51-52)
(4) Regeneration (John 4:53)

c. Third miracle—Healing of the impotent man (John 5:1-16)

(1) The cripple and the Christ—First meeting
(a) Wallowing on his bed of affliction (John 5:2-7)
(b) Walking with his bed of affliction (John 5:8-9)
(2) The cripple and the critics (John 5:10-13)
(3) The cripple and the Christ—Second meeting
(a) His warning from Jesus (John 5:14)
(b) His witness for Jesus (John 5:15-16)

d. Fourth miracle—Feeding of the 5,000 (John 6:1-14)

e. Fifth miracle—Walking on the water (John 6:15-21)

f. Sixth miracle—Healing of the man born blind (John 9:1-41)
  (1) Inconsideration—The disciples and the blind man (John 9:1-2)
  (2) Evangelization—The Savior and the blind man (their first meeting, John 9:3-7)
  (3) Speculation—The neighbors and the blind man (John 9:8-11)
  (4) Interrogation—The parents and the blind man (John 9:18-23)
  (5) Castigation—The Pharisees and the blind man (John 9:24-29)
    (a) Round one (John 9:16-17)
    (b) Round two (John 9:24-25, 28-33)
    (c) Round three (John 9:34)
  (6) Summarization—The Savior and the blind man (their final meeting, John 9:35-41)

g. Seventh miracle—The raising of Lazarus (John 11:1-57)
  (1) The sickness of Lazarus (John 11:1-3)
  (2) The sermon on Lazarus (John 11:4-16)
  (3) The sorrow over Lazarus (John 11:17-37)
  (4) The summons to Lazarus (John 11:38-44)
  (5) The strategy against Lazarus (John 11:45-57; 12:10)—Hearing of this great miracle at Bethany, the Pharisees meet in Jerusalem and plot to kill both Jesus and, if need be, Lazarus also. "Then gathered the chief priests and the Pharisees a council, and said, What do we? for this man doeth many miracles. . . . Then from that day forth they took counsel together for to put him to death. . . . But the chief priests consulted that they might put Lazarus also to death" (John 11:47, 53; 12:10).

h. Eighth miracle—The supernatural catch of fish (John 21:1-14)

3. The dialogues he had
  a. With Nicodemus (John 3:1-21)
    (1) The character of Nicodemus
      (a) A religious leader (John 3:1)
      (b) A Pharisee (John 3:1)
      (c) A well-known teacher (John 3:10)
    (2) The confession of Nicodemus (John 3:2)
    (3) The concern of Nicodemus (John 3:2-3)
    (4) The confusion of Nicodemus (John 3:4)
    (5) The clarification to Nicodemus—Jesus offered three illustrations to help Nicodemus understand the new birth:
      (a) A physical illustration (John 3:5-6)
      (b) A natural illustration (John 3:8)
      (c) A scriptural illustration (John 3:14)
    (6) The chastisement of Nicodemus (John 3:10, 12)
    (7) The conversion of Nicodemus—Did he accept Christ at this time? Two future events strongly suggest that he did (see John 7:50; 19:39).
  b. With the Samaritan woman (John 4:1-42)—"When therefore the Lord knew how the Pharisees had heard that Jesus made and baptized more disciples than John, (Though Jesus himself baptized not, but his disciples,) he left Judaea, and departed again into Galilee. And he must needs go through Samaria" (John 4:1-4).
    (1) The sinner of Sychar

(a) The contact (John 4:5-9)—"There cometh a woman of Samaria to draw water: Jesus saith unto her, Give me to drink" (John 4:7).
(b) The contrasts—Our Lord contrasts living water to liquid water (John 4:10-15), and real worship to that of ritual worship (John 4:16-26).
(2) The soul winner of Sychar (John 4:27-42)
(a) Her faithfulness (John 4:27-38)
(b) Her fruitfulness (John 4:39-42)
c. With an adulterous woman (John 8:1-11)
(1) The connivers—"And the scribes and Pharisees brought unto him a woman taken in adultery; and when they had set her in the midst, they say unto him, Master, this woman was taken in adultery, in the very act" (John 8:3-4).
(2) The conniving (John 8:5-6a)
(3) The conviction (John 8:6b)
(4) The convicted (John 8:9)
(5) The cleansed (John 8:10-11)
4. The sermons he preached
a. The Source of Life sermons—"For as the Father hath life in himself; so hath he given to the Son to have life in himself" (John 5:26).
(1) The oneness with the Father enjoyed by Christ
(a) His equality with the Father (John 5:18)
(b) His dependence upon the Father (John 5:19)
(c) His responsibilities from the Father (John 5:21-22)
(d) His esteem by the Father (John 5:20, 23)
(e) His submission to the Father (John 5:30)
(f) His authority from the Father (John 5:43)
(2) The twofold resurrection accomplished by Christ
(a) The resurrection of the saved (John 5:24-25, 28-29)
(b) The resurrection of the unsaved (John 5:27, 29)
(3) The fourfold witness concerning Christ
(a) Witnessed to by John the Baptist (John 5:33-35)
(b) Witnessed to by his own works (John 5:36)
(c) Witnessed to by the Father (John 5:37-38)
(d) Witnessed to by the Scriptures (John 5:34, 45-47)
b. The Bread of Life sermons (John 6:22-71)—"And Jesus said unto them, I am the bread of life: he that cometh to me shall never hunger; and he that believeth on me shall never thirst. I am that bread of life" (John 6:35, 48).
(1) Christ and the crowd
(a) He spoke concerning God's salvation (John 6:26, 28-29, 31-33, 35).
(b) He spoke concerning God's sovereignty (John 6:37, 39-40)
(2) Christ and the clergy (John 6:41-58)
(a) They were ignorant concerning his origin (John 6:42).
(b) They were ignorant concerning his offer (John 6:51-52).
(3) Christ and the carnal (John 6:59-66)
(a) Many decided against him (John 6:59-60).
(b) Many departed from him (John 6:66).

(4) Christ and the chosen (John 6:67-71)
(a) Jesus and the 11 apostles (John 6:67-69)
(b) Jesus and the evil apostle (John 6:70-71)

c. The Water of Life sermon (John 7:1-53)—"In the last day, that great day of the feast, Jesus stood and cried, saying, If any man thirst, let him come unto me, and drink. He that believeth on me, as the scripture hath said, out of his belly shall flow rivers of living water. (But this spake he of the Spirit, which they that believe on him should receive: for the Holy Ghost was not yet given; because that Jesus was not yet glorified)" (John 7:37-39).
(1) The disbelief of the brethren of Christ (John 7:1-9)
(a) Their ridicule (John 7:3-5)
(b) His response (John 7:6-7)
(2) The division of the crowds who heard Christ (John 7:10-30, 40-43)
(a) Some thought he was a good man (John 7:12).
(b) Some thought he was a deceiver (John 7:12).
(c) Some thought he was a demoniac (John 7:20).
(d) Some thought he was an ordinary man (John 7:27).
(e) Some thought he was a prophet (John 7:40).
(f) Some thought he was the Messiah (John 7:41).
(3) The disdain of the Pharisees who hated Christ
(a) They attempted to detain him, but were frustrated by their own officials (John 7:32, 44-47)—"Then came the officers to the chief priests and Pharisees; and they said unto them, Why have ye not brought him? The officers answered, Never man spake like this man" (John 7:45-46).
(b) They attempted to denounce him, but were frustrated by one of their own members (John 7:50-51).

d. The Light of Life sermon (John 8:12-59)—"Then spake Jesus again unto them, saying, I am the light of the world: he that followeth me shall not walk in darkness, but shall have the light of life" (John 8:12).
(1) The conflict with some unbelieving Jews
(a) Their questions—They wanted to know who he was (John 8:25); who his Father was (John 8:19); and if he was greater than Abraham (John 8:53).
(b) His answers
1) Concerning himself (John 8:6, 12, 23-24, 28)
2) Concerning his Father (John 8:18-19, 21, 26, 28, 42, 54)
3) Concerning Abraham (John 8:56-58)—"Your father Abraham rejoiced to see my day: and he saw it, and was glad. Then said the Jews unto him, Thou art not yet fifty years old, and hast thou seen Abraham? Jesus said unto them, Verily, verily, I say unto you, Before Abraham was, I am" (John 8:56-58).
(c) Their accusations (John 8:13, 22, 41, 48, 52)
(d) His defense (John 8:14, 16, 18, 49-50)
(e) Their errors (John 8:33, 39)—"They answered him, We be Abraham's seed, and were never in bondage to any man: how sayest thou, Ye shall be made free?" (John 8:33).

(f) His correction (John 8:34, 39-40, 44)—"Jesus answered them, Verily, verily, I say unto you, Whosoever committeth sin is the servant of sin. Ye are of your father the devil, and the lusts of your father ye will do. He was a murderer from the beginning, and abode not in the truth, because there is no truth in him. When he speaketh a lie, he speaketh of his own: for he is a liar, and the father of it" (John 8:34, 44).

(g) Their rejection—"Then took they up stones to cast at him: but Jesus hid himself, and went out of the temple, going through the midst of them, and so passed by" (John 8:59).

(h) His condemnation—"I said therefore unto you, that ye shall die in your sins: for if ye believe not that I am he, ye shall die in your sins" (John 8:24).

(2) The conversion of some believing Jews (John 8:30-32, 36, 51)—"As he spake these words, many believed on him" (John 8:30).

e. The Shepherd of Life sermon (John 10:1-39)

(1) Characteristics of the Shepherd

(a) He does things the right way (John 10:2).

(b) He is recognized by the porter (John 10:3). Note: This may be a reference to the Holy Spirit.

(c) He knows his sheep (John 10:3, 14, 27).

(d) He is known by his sheep (John 10:4, 14, 27).

(e) He leads his sheep (John 10:3).

(f) He is the only true Shepherd (John 10:8-9).

(g) He lays down his life for the sheep (John 10:11, 17-18).

(h) He takes up his life for the sheep (John 10:17-18).

(i) He imparts life to the sheep (John 10:9-10).

(j) He imparts abundant life to the sheep (John 10:10).

(k) He imparts eternal life to the sheep (John 10:28- 29).

(l) He is approved by the Father (John 10:15).

(m) He is loved by the Father (John 10:17).

(n) He is authorized by the Father (John 10:18).

(o) He is one with the Father (John 10:30, 38).

(p) He is the Son of the Father (John 10:36).

(2) Characteristics of the sheep

(a) They will not follow strangers (John 10:5, 8).

(b) They are totally dependent upon the shepherd (John 10:12).

(c) They share the same fold with other sheep (John 10:16).

(3) Characteristics of thieves and robbers (John 10:1, 8, 10)

(a) Their words are evil (John 10:8).

(b) Their works are evil (John 10:1, 10).

(4) Characteristics of the hireling (John 10:12-13)

(a) Unconcerned

(b) Unprotective

(5) Characteristics of the goats (John 10:19-20, 31-39)

(a) They deny the claims of the shepherd (John 10:38).

(b) They slander the shepherd (John 10:20).

(c) They accuse the shepherd (John 10:33, 36).

(d) They attempt to kill the shepherd (John 10:31, 39).

f. The Way, the Truth, and the Life sermon (John 14:1-31)—"Jesus saith unto him, I am the way, the truth, and the life: no man cometh unto the Father, but by me" (John 14:6).

(1) The promise of paradise (John 14:1-11)—"Let not your heart be troubled: ye believe in God, believe also in me. In my Father's house are many mansions: if it were not so, I would have told you. I go to prepare a place for you. And if I go and prepare a place for you, I will come again, and receive you unto myself; that where I am, there ye may be also" (John 14:1-3).

(2) The promise of performance (John 14:12-14)—"Verily, verily, I say unto you, He that believeth on me, the works that I do shall he do also; and greater works than these shall he do; because I go unto my Father. And whatsoever ye shall ask in my name, that will I do, that the Father may be glorified in the Son" (John 14:12-13).

(3) The promise of the paraclete (John 14:15-25)—"And I will pray the Father, and he shall give you another Comforter, that he may abide with you for ever" (John 14:16). The title "Comforter" here is from the Greek word *parakletos*, meaning "One called alongside to help," and is a reference to the Holy Spirit.

(4) The promise of peace (John 14:26-31)—"Peace I leave with you, my peace I give unto you: not as the world giveth, give I unto you. Let not your heart be troubled, neither let it be afraid" (John 14:27).

g. The Abundance of Life sermon (John 15–16)—"I am the vine, ye are the branches: He that abideth in me, and I in him, the same bringeth forth much fruit: for without me ye can do nothing" (John 15:5).

(1) The reasons for this sermon

(a) That we might experience joy (John 15:11)

(b) That we might not stumble (John 16:1)

(c) That we might remember his words (John 16:4)

(d) That we might experience his words (John 16:4)

(2) The relationships in this sermon

(a) Involving the Savior

1) Christ and the Father—"Howbeit when he, the Spirit of truth, is come, he will guide you into all truth: for he shall not speak of himself; but whatsoever he shall hear, that shall he speak: and he will shew you things to come" (John 16:13).

2) Christ and the Holy Spirit (John 15:26; 16:7-11, 13-14)—"But when the Comforter is come, whom I will send unto you from the Father, even the Spirit of truth, which proceedeth from the Father, he shall testify of me" (John 15:26).

3) Christ and the believer (John 15:2-5)—"Abide in me, and I in you. As the branch cannot bear fruit of itself, except it abide in the vine; no more can ye, except ye abide in me" (John 15:4).

(b) Involving the saint

1) The believer and the Father—"For the Father himself loveth you, because ye have loved me, and have believed that I came out from God" (John 16:27).

2) The believer and the Holy Spirit (John 16:7-15)—"Howbeit when he, the Spirit of truth, is come, he will guide you into all truth: for he shall not speak of himself; but whatsoever he shall hear, that shall he speak: and he will shew you things to come" (John 16:13).
3) The believer and other believers (John 15:12-14)—"This is my commandment, That ye love one another, as I have loved you" (John 15:12).
4) The believer and persecution (John 15:18-21; 16:1-3, 21-22)—"Remember the word that I said unto you, The servant is not greater than his lord. If they have persecuted me, they will also persecute you; if they have kept my saying, they will keep yours also" (John 15:20).
5) The believer and fruitbearing (John 15:1-8, 16)—"If ye abide in me, and my words abide in you, ye shall ask what ye will, and it shall be done unto you. . . . Ye have not chosen me, but I have chosen you, and ordained you, that ye should go and bring forth fruit, and that your fruit should remain: that whatsoever ye shall ask of the Father in my name, he may give it you" (John 15:7, 16).

C. The final days of his ministry (John 12:1–18:11)

1. His anointing by Mary (John 12:1-11)

a. The sacrifice of Mary

(1) Her gift was precious (John 12:3).

(2) Her gift was prophetical—"Against the day of my burying hath she kept this" (John 12:7b).

b. The slander of Judas (John 12:4-6)—"Why was not this ointment sold for three hundred pence, and given to the poor? This he said, not that he cared for the poor; but because he was a thief, and had the bag, and bare what was put therein" (John 12:5-6).

2. His triumphal entry (John 12:12-19)

a. The celebration (John 12:12-15)

b. The confusion (John 12:16-18)—"These things understood not his disciples at the first: but when Jesus was glorified, then remembered they that these things were written of him, and that they had done these things unto him" (John 12:16).

c. The complaint—"The Pharisees therefore said among themselves, Perceive ye how ye prevail nothing? behold, the world is gone after him" (John 12:19).

3. His prayer to the Father (John 12:20-28)

a. The request leading to his prayer (John 12:20-26)—"And there were certain Greeks among them that came up to worship at the feast: The same came therefore to Philip, which was of Bethsaida of Galilee, and desired him, saying, Sir, we would see Jesus. Verily, verily, I say unto you, Except a corn of wheat fall into the ground and die, it abideth alone: but if it die, it bringeth forth much fruit" (John 12:20-21, 24).

b. The request mentioned in his prayer (John 12:27-28)—"Now is my soul troubled; and what shall I say? Father, save me from this hour: but for this cause came I unto this hour. Father, glorify thy name. Then came there a voice from heaven, saying, I have both glorified it, and will glorify it again" (John 12:27-28).

4. His dialogue with the people (John 12:29-36)—"And I, if I be lifted up from the earth, will draw all men unto me. This he said, signifying what death he should die" (John 12:32-33).
5. His rejection by the Pharisees (John 12:37-50)—"But though he had done so many miracles before them, yet they believed not on him. . . . Nevertheless among the chief rulers also many believed on him; but because of the Pharisees they did not confess him, lest they should be put out of the synagogue: for they loved the praise of men more than the praise of God" (John 12:37, 42-43).
6. His actions in the Upper Room (John 13:1-38)
   a. Washing (John 13:1-17)—"He riseth from supper, and laid aside his garments; and took a towel, and girded himself. After that he poureth water into a basin, and began to wash the disciples' feet, and to wipe them with the towel wherewith he was girded" (John 13:4-5).
   b. Warning (John 13:18-38)
      (1) Concerning the betrayal by Judas (John 13:18-35)—"When Jesus had thus said, he was troubled in spirit, and testified, and said, Verily, verily, I say unto you, that one of you shall betray me" (John 13:21).
      (2) Concerning the denials by Peter (John 13:36-38)—"Jesus answered him, Wilt thou lay down thy life for my sake? Verily, verily, I say unto thee, The cock shall not crow, till thou hast denied me thrice" (John 13:38).
7. His great high priestly prayer (John 17:1-26)
   a. His prayer for himself (John 17:1-5)—"And now, O Father, glorify thou me with thine own self with the glory which I had with thee before the world was" (John 17:5).
   b. His prayer for his disciples (John 17:6-19)—"And now I am no more in the world, but these are in the world, and I come to thee. Holy Father, keep through thine own name those whom thou hast given me, that they may be one, as we are" (John 17:11).
   c. His prayer for the Church (John 17:20-26)—"Neither pray I for these alone, but for them also which shall believe on me through their word" (John 17:20).
8. His ordeal in Gethsemane (John 18:1-11)

III. The Executed Son of God (John 18:12–19:42)
   A. The denials by Peter (John 18:15-18, 25-27)
   B. The unfair trials of Jesus
      1. Before Annas and Caiaphas (John 18:13-14, 19-24)
      2. Before Pilate (John 18:28-40)
   C. The scourging of Jesus (John 19:1-15)—"Then Pilate therefore took Jesus, and scourged him" (John 19:1).
      1. Jesus is ridiculed by the Roman soldiers—"And the soldiers platted a crown of thorns, and put it on his head, and they put on him a purple robe, and said, Hail, King of the Jews! and they smote him with their hands" (John 19:2-3).
      2. Jesus is reviled by the Jewish leaders—"But they cried out, Away with him, away with him, crucify him. Pilate saith unto them, Shall I crucify your King? The chief priests answered, We have no king but Caesar" (John 19:15).
   D. The crucifixion of Jesus (John 19:16-30)—"And he bearing his cross went forth into a place called the place of a skull, which is called in the Hebrew Golgotha" (John 19:17).

1. The thieves on the cross (John 19:18)
2. The title above the cross (John 19:19-22)—"And Pilate wrote a title, and put it on the cross. And the writing was, JESUS OF NAZARETH THE KING OF THE JEWS" (John 19:19).
3. The tormentors below the cross (John 19:23-24)—"Then the soldiers, when they had crucified Jesus, took his garments, and made four parts, to every soldier a part; and also his coat: now the coat was without seam, woven from the top throughout" (John 19:23).
4. The talk from the cross (John 19:25-30)
   - a. The family words of Jesus—"When Jesus therefore saw his mother, and the disciple standing by, whom he loved, he saith unto his mother, Woman, behold thy son! Then saith he to the disciple, Behold thy mother! And from that hour that disciple took her unto his own home" (John 19:26-27).
   - b. The final words of Jesus—"When Jesus therefore had received the vinegar, he said, It is finished: and he bowed his head, and gave up the ghost" (John 19:30).

E. The piercing of Jesus' side (John 19:31-37)—"But one of the soldiers with a spear pierced his side, and forthwith came there out blood and water" (John 19:34).

F. The burial of Jesus (John 19:38-42)

1. The persons involved—Joseph of Arimathaea and Nicodemus secure the body of Christ from Pilate.
2. The place involved—"Now in the place where he was crucified there was a garden; and in the garden a new sepulchre, wherein was never man yet laid" (John 19:41).

IV. The Exalted Son of God (John 20:1–21:25)

A. The anguish concerning the empty tomb (John 20:1-10)—"The first day of the week cometh Mary Magdalene early, when it was yet dark, unto the sepulchre, and seeth the stone taken away from the sepulchre. . . . Then she runneth, and cometh to Simon Peter, and to the other disciple, whom Jesus loved, and saith unto them, They have taken away the Lord out of the sepulchre, and we know not where they have laid him. For as yet they knew not the scripture, that he must rise again from the dead" (John 20:1-2, 9).

B. The appearances confirming the empty tomb (John 20:11–21:25)

1. The appearance of Jesus before Mary Magdalene (John 20:11-18)
   - a. The sorrowful one (John 20:11)
   - b. The shining ones (John 20:12-13)
   - c. The sovereign one
     - (1) Mary's error (John 20:14-15)—"She, supposing him to be the gardener" (John 20:15).
     - (2) Mary's ecstasy
       - (a) Recognizing (John 20:16)
       - (b) Rejoicing (John 20:17)
       - (c) Reporting (John 20:18)
2. The appearance of Jesus before the ten apostles (John 20:19-23)—"Then the same day at evening, being the first day of the week, when the doors were shut where the disciples were assembled for fear of the Jews, came Jesus and stood in the midst, and saith unto them, Peace be unto you" (John 20:19).

3. The appearance of Jesus before Thomas (John 20:24-31)
   a. The report to Thomas—"The other disciples therefore said unto him, We have seen the Lord" (John 20:25a).
   b. The reluctance of Thomas—"But he said unto them, Except I shall see in his hands the print of the nails, and thrust my hand into his side, I will not believe" (John 20:25b).
   c. The recognition by Thomas (John 20:26-28)—"And after eight days again his disciples were within, and Thomas with them: then came Jesus, the doors being shut, and stood in the midst, and said, Peace be unto you. Then saith he to Thomas, Reach hither thy finger, and behold my hands; and reach hither thy hand, and thrust it into my side: and be not faithless, but believing. And Thomas answered and said unto him, My Lord and my God" (John 20:26-28).
4. The appearance of Jesus before seven apostles (John 21:1-25)
   a. The fishermen on the sea (John 21:1-3)
      (1) The place (John 21:1)
      (2) The personalities—"There were together Simon Peter, and Thomas called Didymus, and Nathanael of Cana in Galilee, and the sons of Zebedee, and two other of his disciples" (John 21:2).
      (3) The particulars—"Simon Peter saith unto them, I go a fishing. They say unto him, We also go with thee. They went forth, and entered into a ship immediately; and that night they caught nothing" (John 21:3).
   b. The fisher of men on the shore (John 21:4-25)
      (1) The call (John 21:5)
      (2) The command (John 21:6a)
      (3) The catch (John 21:6b, 11)
      (4) The commitment (John 21:7)
      (5) The coals of fire (John 21:9)
      (6) The communion (John 21:12-13)
      (7) The confessions (John 21:15-17)
      (8) The cross (John 21:18-19)
      (9) The concern (John 21:20-21)
      (10) The chastisement (John 21:22)
      (11) The confusion (John 21:23)
      (12) The confirmation (John 21:24-25)

PART TWO

A **BROAD** OVERVIEW OF THE LIFE OF CHRIST, FEATURING ONE HARMONY OUTLINE STUDY ON HIS LIFE AS PRESENTED COLLECTIVELY BY MATTHEW, MARK, LUKE, AND JOHN

I. A Chronological Summary

A. The introduction to the earthly life of Christ

1. The four biographers (Matthew, Mark, Luke, John)—Each presents a different aspect of the Savior.
2. The two genealogies (Matt. 1:1-17; Luke 3:23-38)
3. The two prefaces (Luke 1:1-4; John 1:1-5)
4. The three announcements
   a. To Zacharias (Luke 1:5-25)
   b. To Mary (Luke 1:26-38)
   c. To Joseph (Matt. 1:18-25)
5. The three songs of praise
   a. That of Elisabeth (Luke 1:39-45)
   b. That of Mary (Luke 1:46-56)
   c. That of Zacharias (Luke 1:57-79)

B. The manifestation of the earthly life of Christ

1. Christ's birth (Luke 2:1-20)
2. Christ's circumcision (Luke 2:21)
3. Christ's dedication (Luke 2:22-38)
4. Christ's visit by the Wise Men (Matt. 2:1-12)
5. Christ's flight into Egypt (Matt. 2:13-20)
6. Christ's early years in Nazareth (Matt. 2:21, 23; Luke 2:40, 52)
7. Christ's temple visit at age 12 (Luke 2:41-51)
8. Christ's forerunner—The ministry of John the Baptist (Matt. 3:1-12; Mark 1:1-8; Luke 1:80; 3:1-18; John 1:6-34; 3:25-30)
9. Christ's baptism (Matt. 3:13-17; Mark 1:9-11; Luke 3:21-22; John 1:32-33)
10. Christ's temptation (Matt. 4:1-11; Mark 1:12-13; Luke 4:1-13)
11. Christ is presented as the Lamb of God (John 1:29).
12. Christ meets his first five disciples.
    a. John, Andrew, and Peter (John 1:35-42)
    b. Philip and Nathanael (John 1:43-51)
13. Christ performs the first temple cleansing (John 2:13-25).
14. Christ meets with Nicodemus (John 3:1-21).
15. Christ meets with the Samaritan woman (John 4:1-42).
16. Christ's first preaching tour of Galilee (Matt. 4:17; Mark 1:15; Luke 4:14-15)
17. Christ's first return trip to Nazareth (Luke 4:16-30)
18. Christ moves into Capernaum and makes this city his northern headquarters (Matt 4:13-16).
19. Christ extends a call to four fishermen (Matt. 4:18-22; Mark 1:16-20; Luke 5:1-11).
20. Christ's second preaching tour of Galilee (Matt. 4:23-25; Mark 1:35-39; Luke 4:42-44)
21. Christ extends a call to Matthew (Matt. 9:9-13; Mark 2:13-17; Luke 5:27-32).
22. Christ's first meeting with John's disciples (Matt. 9:14-17; Mark 2:18-22; Luke 5:33-39)
23. Christ's first Sabbath controversy with the Pharisees (Matt. 12:1-8; Mark 2:23-28; Luke 6:1-5)
24. Christ officially selects the 12 apostles (Matt. 10:2-4; Mark 3:13-19; Luke 6:12-16).

25. Christ's third preaching tour of Galilee (Matt. 9:35-38)
26. Christ sends out the 12 apostles (Matt. 10:1-42; Mark 6:7-13; Luke 9:1-6)
27. Christ's fourth preaching tour of Galilee (Matt. 11:1)
28. Christ denounces some key cities in Galilee (Matt. 11:20-24).
29. Christ issues a universal invitation (Matt. 11:28-30).
30. Christ is anointed in Simon's house (Luke 7:36-39).
31. Christ's fifth preaching tour of Galilee (Luke 8:1-3)
32. Christ refuses on two occasions to show the Pharisees a sign
    a. First occasion (Matt. 12:39-41)
    b. Second occasion (Matt. 16:1-4; Mark 8:11-12)
33. Christ is misunderstood by his own family (Matt. 13:54-56; Mark 6:1-6; John 7:3-9).
34. Christ explains who his real family is (Matt. 12:46-50; Mark 3:31-35; Luke 8:19-21).
35. Christ's second return trip to Nazareth (Matt. 13:54-58; Mark 6:1-6)
36. Christ's forerunner is murdered by Herod (Matt. 14:1-12; Mark 6:14-29; Luke 9:7-9).
37. Christ refuses the offer of the Galileans to crown him king (Matt. 14:22-23; Mark 6:45-46; John 6:14-15).
38. Christ hears Peter's confession and promises to build his church (Matt. 16:13-21; Mark 8:27-31; Luke 9:18-22).
39. Christ rebukes Peter (Matt. 16:22-23).
40. Christ is transfigured (Matt. 17:1-8; Mark 9:2-8; Luke 9:28-36).
41. Christ rebukes James and John on three occasions.
    a. First occasion (Mark 9:38-41; Luke 9:49-50)
    b. Second occasion (Luke 9:51-56)
    c. Third occasion (Matt. 20:20-28; Mark 10:35-45)
42. Christ answers the apostles' argument concerning who was the greatest among them (Matt. 18:1-5; Mark 9:33-37; Luke 9:46-48).
43. Christ warns about mistreating a little child (Matt. 18:6, 10; Mark 9:42).
44. Christ is approached by three would-be disciples.
    a. First candidate (Luke 9:57-58)
    b. Second candidate (Luke 9:59-60)
    c. Third candidate (Luke 9:61-62)
45. Christ is rebuked by his own unbelieving half brothers (John 7:2-9).
46. Christ forgives a woman taken in the act of adultery (John 8:1-11).
47. Christ sends out the 70 disciples (Luke 10:1-24).
48. Christ visits with Mary and Martha (Luke 10:38-42).
49. Christ commands people to repent (Luke 13:1-5).
50. Christ teaches on the subject of discipleship (Matt. 16:24-27; Mark 8:34-38; Luke 9:23-26; 14:25-33).
51. Christ teaches on the subject of forgiveness Matt. 18:21-22).
52. Christ teaches on the subject of hell (Matt. 18:8-9; Mark 9:43-48; Luke 12:4-5).
53. Christ teaches on the subject of church discipline (Matt. 18:15-20).
54. Christ teaches on the subject of divorce (Matt. 5:31-32; 19:3-12; Mark 10:2-12).
55. Christ teaches on the subject of rewards (Matt. 19:27-30; Mark 10:28-30; Luke 18:28-30)
56. Christ teaches on the subject of faith (Matt. 21:21-22; Mark 11:22-24).

57. Christ attends the feast of tabernacles (John 7:37-39).
58. Christ attends the feast of dedication (John 10:22-23).
59. Christ gives his overall purpose for coming to earth (Matt. 20:28; Mark 10:45; John 10:10).
60. Christ blesses some little children (Matt. 19:13-15; Mark 10:13-16; Luke 18:15-17).
61. Christ is approached by a rich young ruler (Matt. 19:16-26; Mark 10:17-27; Luke 18:18-27).
62. Christ meets Zacchaeus (Luke 19:1-10).

C. The completion of the earthly life of Christ
 1. The eight-day period
  a. Day one: Saturday
   (1) Christ is plotted against by Caiaphas, the high priest (Matt. 26:3-5; Mark 14:1-2; Luke 22:2).
   (2) Christ is anointed by Mary in the home of Simon the leper (Matt. 26:6-13; Mark 14:3-9; John 12:1-8).
  b. Day two: Sunday—Christ makes his triumphal entry into Jerusalem (Matt. 21:1-11, 14-17; Mark 11:1-11; Luke 19:29-44).
  c. Day three: Monday
   (1) Christ pronounces judgment upon a fruitless fig tree (Matt. 21:18-19; Mark 11:12-14).
   (2) Christ performs the second temple cleansing (Matt. 21:12-13; Mark 11:15-17; Luke 19:45-46).
   (3) Christ is sought after by some Gentile Greeks (John 12:20-29).
  d. Day four: Tuesday
   (1) Christ confronts the Pharisees and Sadducees (Matt. 21:23-27; 22:15-46; Mark 11:27-33; 12:13-37; Luke 20:1-8, 20-44).
   (2) Christ condemns the Pharisees and Sadducees (Matt. 23:1-39; Mark 12:38-40; Luke 20:45-47).
   (3) Christ observes the widow and her mite (Mark 12:41-44; Luke 21:1-4).
   (4) Christ weeps over Jerusalem for the final time (Matt. 23:37-39).
   (5) Christ preaches the Mt. Olivet Discourse (Matt. 24; Mark 13; Luke 21:5-36).
   (6) Christ relates the parables of the ten virgins, the talents, and the sheep and goats (Matt. 25:1-46).
  e. Day five: Wednesday—Christ is secretly betrayed by Judas (Matt. 26:14-16; Mark 14:10,11; Luke 22:3-6).
  f. Day six: Thursday
   (1) Christ sends Peter and John from Bethany into Jerusalem (Matt. 26:17-19; Mark 14:12-16; Luke 22:7-13).
   (2) Christ meets with his disciples in the Upper Room (Matt. 26:20-35; Mark 14:17-26; Luke 22:14-38; John 13:1-14, 31).
   (3) Christ preaches his sermon on the Father's house (John 14:1-31).
  g. Day seven: Friday
   (1) Christ preaches his sermon on fruitbearing en route to the Mount of Olives (John 15–16).
   (2) Christ prays his great high priestly prayer at the Mount of Olives (John 17).
   (3) Christ arrives in the Garden of Gethsemane (Matt. 26:36-56; Mark 14:32-52; Luke 22:39-53; John 18:1-12).

(4) Christ suffers his first unfair trial—The appearance before Annas (John 18:12-14, 19-23).
(5) Christ suffers his second unfair trial—The appearance before Caiaphas (Matt. 26:57, 59-68; Mark 14:53-65; John 18:24).
(6) Christ is denied by Simon Peter (Matt. 26:58-75; Mark 14:54, 66-72; Luke 22:54-62; John 18:15-18, 25-27).
(7) Christ suffers his third unfair trial—The appearance before the Sanhedrin (Matt. 27:1; Mark 15:1; Luke 22:66-71).
(8) Christ's betrayer shows remorse and commits suicide (Matt. 27:3-10; Acts 1:18-20).
(9) Christ suffers his fourth unfair trial—The first appearance before Pilate (Matt. 27:2, 11-14; Mark 15:1-5; Luke 23:1-5; John 18:28-38).
(10) Christ suffers his fifth unfair trial—The appearance before Herod Antipas (Luke 23:6-12).
(11) Christ suffers his sixth unfair trial—The final appearance before Pilate (Matt. 27:15-26; Mark 15:6-15; Luke 23:13-25; John 18:29—19:16).
(12) Christ suffers his seventh unfair trial—The appearance before the Roman soldiers (Matt. 27:27-30; Mark 15:16-20; John 19:2-3).
(13) Christ walks the road to Calvary (Matt. 27:31-32; Mark 15:20-21; Luke 23:26-32; John 19:16-17).
(14) Christ is crucified on the cross (Matt. 27:33-50; Mark 15:22-37; Luke 23:32-46; John 19:17-30).
(15) Christ's death introduces some supernatural events (Matt. 27:51-56; Mark 15:38-41; Luke 23:45, 47-49).
(16) Christ's body is removed from the cross and placed in a tomb (Matt. 27:57-61; Mark 15:42-47; Luke 23:50-56; John 19:31-42).

h. Day eight: Saturday—Christ's tomb is officially sealed (Matt. 27:62-66).

2. The 40-Day period

a. Day one: Sunday—Christ is risen from the dead (Matt. 28; Mark 16; Luke 24; John 20–21).
(1) The appearance to Mary Magdalene (Mark 16:9-11; John 20:11-18)
(2) The appearance to some women (Matt. 28:9-15)
(3) The appearance to Simon Peter (Luke 24:34; 1 Cor. 15:5)
(4) The appearance to two disciples en route to Emmaus (Mark 16:12-13; Luke 24:13-35)
(5) The appearance to the apostles in the Upper Room (Mark 16:14; Luke 24:36-48; John 20:19-23)

b. Day two through 40—"To whom also he shewed himself alive after his passion by many infallible proofs, being seen by them forty days, and speaking of the things pertaining to the kingdom of God" (Acts 1:3). During this period of time the resurrected Christ makes five final appearances.
(1) The appearance to Thomas and the apostles (John 20:24-31)
(2) The appearance to seven apostles (John 21)
(3) The appearance to the apostles and 500 disciples (Matt. 28:16-20; Mark 16:15-18; 1 Cor. 15:6)
(4) The appearance to James, the half brother of Christ (1 Cor. 15:7)
(5) The appearance to the 11 on the Mount of Olives (Luke 24:49-50; Acts 1:3-8)—"And while they looked stedfastly toward heaven as he went up,

behold, two men stood by them in white apparel; which also said, Ye men of Galilee, why stand ye gazing up into heaven? This same Jesus, who is taken up from you into heaven shall so come in like manner as ye have seen him go into heaven" (Acts 1:10-11).

II. A Topical Summary
  A. The miracles performed by Christ
    1. Turning water into wine (John 2:1-11)
    2. Healing a nobleman's son (John 4:43-54)
    3. Healing a Capernaum demoniac (Mark 1:21-28; Luke 4:31-37)
    4. Healing Peter's mother-in-law (Matt. 8:14-17; Mark 1:29-34; Luke 4:38-41)
    5. The first great catch of fish (Matt. 4:18-22; Mark 1:16-20; Luke 5:1-11)
    6. Healing a leper (Matt. 8:2-4; Mark. 1:40-45; Luke 5:12-16)
    7. Healing a paralytic (Matt. 9:1-8; Mark 2:1-12; Luke 5:17-26)
    8. Healing a withered hand (Matt. 12:9-14; Mark 3:1-6; Luke 6:6-11)
    9. Healing a centurion's servant (Matt. 8:5-13; Luke 7:1-10)
    10. Raising a widow's son (Luke 7:11-17)
    11. Calming the stormy sea (Matt. 8:18, 23-27; Mark 4:35-41; Luke 8:22-25)
    12. Healing the maniac of Gadara (Matt. 8:28-34; Mark 5:1-20; Luke 8:26-39)
    13. Healing the woman of a bloody flux (Matt. 9:20-22; Mark 5:25-34; Luke 8:43-48)
    14. Raising Jairus's daughter (Matt. 9:18-19, 23-26; Mark 5:22-24, 35-43; Luke 8:41-42, 49-56)
    15. Healing two blind men (Matt. 9:27-31)
    16. Healing a dumb demoniac (Matt. 9:32-34)
    17. Healing a cripple of 38 years (John 5:1-16)
    18. Feeding of the 5,000 (Matt. 14:14-21; Mark 6:31-44; Luke 9:10-17; John 6:1-13)
    19. Walking on water (Matt. 14:24-33; Mark 6:47-52; John 6:16-21)
    20. Healing a demoniac girl (Matt. 15:21-28; Mark 7:24-30)
    21. Healing a deaf man with a speech impediment (Mark 7:31-37)
    22. Feeding of the 4,000 (Matt. 15:32-38; Mark 8:1-9)
    23. Healing a blind man in Bethsaida (Mark 8:22-26)
    24. Healing of a man born blind in Jerusalem (John 9:1-41)
    25. Healing of a demoniac boy (Matt. 17:14-21; Mark 9:14-29; Luke 9:37-43)
    26. Miracle of the tribute money (Matt. 17: 24-27)
    27. Healing of a blind and mute demoniac (Matt. 12:22; Luke 11:14)
    28. Healing of a crippled woman of 18 years (Luke 13:10-17)
    29. Healing of the man with dropsy (Luke 14:1-6)
    30. Healing of ten lepers (Luke 17:11-19)
    31. Raising of Lazarus (John 11:1-46)
    32. Healing of blind Bartimaeus (Matt. 20:29-34; Mark 10:46-52; Luke 18:35-43)
    33. Destroying a fig tree (Matt. 21:17-20, 43; Mark 11:12-14, 20-21)
    34. Restoring a severed ear (Luke 22:49-51)
    35. The second great catch of fish (John 21:1-14)
  B. The parables related by Christ
    1. Two houses in a hurricane (Matt. 7:24-27; Luke 6:48-49)
    2. Forgiving the 50 and the 500 (Luke 7:36-50)
    3. Subduing the strong man (Matt. 12:22-37; Mark 3:22-30)
    4. The sovereign sower (Matt. 13:1-9, 18-23; Mark 4:1-9, 13-20; Luke 8:4-15)
    5. The secret of the seed (Mark 4:26-29)

6. Satan's tares in the Savior's field (Matt. 13:24-30)
7. The mighty mustard seed (Matt. 13:31-32; Mark 4:30-32; Luke 13:18-19)
8. The cook's leaven and the kingdom of heaven (Matt. 13:33)
9. Finding a fortune in a field (Matt. 13:44)
10. The price of a pearl (Matt. 13:45-46)
11. Sorting out a sea catch (Matt. 13:47-50)
12. A trained man and his treasure (Matt. 13:52)
13. Feasting friends of the bridegroom (Matt. 9:14-15; Mark 2:18-20; Luke 5:33-35)
14. A new cloth on an old cloth (Matt. 9:16; Mark 2:21; Luke 5:36)
15. New wine and old bottles (Matt. 9:17; Mark 2:22; Luke 5:37-39)
16. A generation of gripers (Matt. 11:16-19; Luke 7:29-35)
17. The forgiven who wouldn't forgive (Matt. 18:21-35)
18. How to know your neighbor (Luke 10:30-37)
19. The spirits and the swept house (Matt. 12:43-45; Luke 11:24-26)
20. A fool in a fix (Luke 12:13-21)
21. Readiness as opposed to carelessness (Matt. 24:42-51; Luke 12:35-48)
22. The fruitless fig tree (Luke 13:6-9)
23. On being a winner at the banquet dinner (Luke 14:7-14)
24. Two fools and a henpecked husband (Luke 14:15-24)
25. The missing sheep, the misplaced silver, and the miserable son (Luke 15:1-32)
26. The stewing of a steward (Luke 16:1-13)
27. When Hades petitioned paradise (Luke 16:19-31)
28. When our best is but the least (Luke 17:7-10)
29. A widow and a weary judge (Luke 18:1-8)
30. A haughty Pharisee and a humble publican (Luke 18:9-14)
31. A diagnosis of defilement (Matt. 15:10-20; Mark 7:14-23)
32. Hourly workers and daily wages (Matt. 20:1-16)
33. Two sons who reversed their roles (Matt. 21:28-32)
34. The vicious vine keepers (Matt. 21:33-46; Mark 12:1-12; Luke 20:9-19)
35. A wedding guest with no wedding garment (Matt. 22:1-14)
36. The fig tree and the future (Matt. 24:32-35; Mark 13:28-31; Luke 21:29-33)
37. Virgins, vessels, and vigilance (Matt. 25:1-13)
38. A nobleman, ten servants, and ten pounds (Luke 19:11-27)
39. A traveler, three stewards, and eight talents (Matt. 25:14-30)
40. Separating the sheep from the goats (Matt. 25:31-46)

C. The sermons preached by Christ
1. The sermon in Nazareth from the scroll of Isaiah (Luke 4:16-30)
2. The Sermon on the Mount (Matt. 5–7)
3. The Source of Life sermon (John 5:17-47)
4. The Bread of Life sermon (John 6:22-71)
5. The Water of Life sermon (John 7:1-53)
6. The Light of Life sermon (John 8:12-59)
7. The Shepherd of Life sermon (John 10:1-39)
8. The Mt. Olivet Discourse (Matt. 24–25)
9. The Way, the Truth, and the Life sermon (John 14:1-31)
10. The Abundance of Life sermon (John 15–16)

D. The prayers uttered by Christ
1. At his baptism (Luke 3:21)

2. Before his first preaching tour of Galilee (Mark 1:35; Luke 4:42)
3. After healing a leper (Luke 5:16)
4. Before choosing his 12 disciples (Luke 6:12)
5. After the feeding of the 5,000 (Matt. 14:23; Mark 6:46; John 6:15)
6. Before hearing Peter's great confession (Luke 9:18)
7. During his transfiguration (Luke 9:28-29)
8. Upon hearing the report of the returning Seventy (Matt. 11:25-27; Luke 10:21-22)
9. After visiting Mary and Martha (Luke 11:1)
10. After receiving some small children (Matt. 19:13-15; Mark 10:13-16; Luke 18:15-17)
11. Before raising Lazarus (John 11:41-42)
12. When some Greeks desired to see him (John 12:20-28)
13. After leaving the Upper Room (John 17:1-26)
14. In the garden (first prayer) (Matt. 26:39; Mark 14:35-36; Luke 22:41-42)
15. In the garden (second prayer) (Matt. 26:42; Mark 14:39; Luke 22:41-42)
16. In the garden (third prayer) (Matt. 26:44)
17. On the cross (first prayer) (Luke 23:34)
18. On the cross (second prayer) (Matt. 27:46-47; Mark 15:34-35)
19. On the cross (third prayer) (Luke 23:46)

E. The sufferings endured by Christ

1. Rejected by:
    a. His nation (John 1:11)
    b. His hometown (Luke 4:28-29)
    c. His friends (Mark 3:21)
    d. His family (John 7:5)
2. Tempted by Satan (Luke 4:1-2, 13; 22:28)
3. Ridiculed because of:
    a. His hometown (John 1:46; 7:52)
    b. His background (John 8:41; 9:24, 29)
4. Threatened constantly:
    a. By Herod (Matt. 2:16)
    b. By his hometown (Luke 4:29)
    c. By the Jews
        (1) Because he healed on the Sabbath (John 5:16; Luke 6:10-11)
        (2) Because of his claims (John 8:58-59; 10:30-33)
        (3) Because of his sermons (John 8:40; Luke 11:53-54; Mark 12:12; Matt. 26:1-4)
        (4) Because of his miracles (John 11:53; see also John 12:10)
    d. By the devil (Matt. 26:37-38; Mark 14:33-34; Luke 22:44)
5. Homeless (Matt. 8:20)
6. Betrayed by a follower (John 13:21)
7. Denied by a friend (Matt. 26:58, 69-75; Mark 14:54, 66-72; Luke 22:54-62; John 18:15-18, 25-27)
8. Misunderstood by his disciples (Matt. 15:16; 17:6-11; Mark 6:52; John 10:6; 12:16)
9. Forsaken by all (Matt. 26:56)
10. Misquoted (Matt. 26:61)
11. Illegally tried seven times:
    a. First trial, before Annas (John 18:12-14, 19-24)

   b. Second trial, before Caiaphas (Matt. 26:57-68; Mark 14:53-65)
   c. Third trial, before the Sanhedrin (Matt. 27:1-2; Mark 15:1; Luke 22:66–23:1)
   d. Fourth trial, before Pilate (John 18:28-38; Matt. 27:2, 11-14; Mark 15:1-5; Luke 23:1-6)
   e. Fifth trial, before Herod (Luke 23:7-12)
   f. Sixth trial, before Pilate (John 18:39–19:16; Matt. 27:15-26; Mark 15:6-15; Luke 23:13-25)
   g. Seventh trial, before the Roman soldiers (Matt. 27:27-31; Mark 15:16-20)
12. Indicted on false charges (Luke 23:1-2)
13. Mocked by:
   a. The Roman soldiers (Luke 23:36-37; Mark 15:16-20)
   b. The watching crowd (Luke 23:35)
   c. The chief priests (Mark 15:31)
   d. The two thieves (Mark 15:32; Matt. 27:44)
14. Tortured—Our Lord was:
   a. Slapped (John 18:22)
   b. Blindfolded (Luke 22:64)
   c. Spit upon (Matt. 26:67)
   d. Buffeted (Matt. 26:67)
   e. Scourged (Matt. 27:26)
   f. Struck upon the head (Matt. 27:30)
   g. Pierced with thorns (Matt. 27:29)
15. Crucified (Matt. 27; Mark 15; Luke 23; John 19)

F. The Old Testament prophecies fulfilled by Christ
1. That he would be born of a virgin (compare Isa. 7:14 with Matt. 1:22-23)
2. That he would be given the throne of David (compare 2 Sam. 7:11-12; Psa. 132:11; Isa. 9:6-7; 16:5; Jer. 23:5 with Luke 1:31-32)
3. That this throne would be an eternal throne (compare Dan. 2:44; 7:14, 27; Mic. 4:7 with Luke 1:33)
4. That he would be called Emmanuel (compare Isa. 7:14 with Matt. 1:23)
5. That he would have a forerunner (compare Isa. 40:3-5; Mal. 3:1 with Luke 1:76-78; 3:3-6; Matt. 3:1-3)
6. That he would be born in Bethlehem (compare Mic. 5:2 with Luke 2:4-6; Matt. 2:5-6)
7. That he would be worshiped by the Wise Men and presented with gifts (compare Psa. 72:10; Isa. 60:3, 6, 9 with Matt. 2:11)
8. That he would be in Egypt for a season (compare Num. 24:8; Hos. 11:1 with Matt. 2:15)
9. That his birthplace would suffer a massacre of infants (compare Jer. 31:15 with Matt. 2:17-18)
10. That he would be called a Nazarene (compare Isa. 11:1 with Matt. 2:23)
11. That he would be zealous for the Father (compare Psa. 69:9; 119:139 with John 2:13-17)
12. That he would be filled with God's Spirit (compare Isa. 11:2; 61:1-2; Psa. 45:7 with Luke 4:18-19)
13. That he would heal many (compare Isa. 53:4 with Matt. 8:16-17)
14. That he would deal gently with the Gentiles (compare Isa. 9:1-2; 42:1-3 with Matt. 12:17-21; 4:13-16)

15. That he would speak in parables (compare Isa. 6:9-10 with Matt. 13:10-15)
16. That he would be rejected by his own (compare Isa. 53:3; Psa. 69:8 with John 1:11; 7:5)
17. That he would make a triumphal entry into Jerusalem (compare Zech. 9:9 with Matt. 21:4-5)
18. That he would be praised by little children (compare Psa. 8:2 with Matt. 21:16)
19. That he would be the rejected Cornerstone (compare Psa. 118:22-23 with Matt. 21:42)
20. That his miracles would not be believed (compare Isa. 53:1 with John 12:37-38)
21. That his friend would betray him for 30 pieces of silver (compare Psa. 41:9; 55:12-14; Zech. 11:12-13 with Matt. 26:14-16, 21-25)
22. That he would be a man of sorrows (compare Isa. 53:3 with Matt. 26:37-38)
23. That he would be forsaken by his disciples (compare Zech. 13:7 with Matt. 26:31, 56)
24. That he would be scourged and spat upon (compare Isa. 50:6 with Matt. 26:67; 27:26)
25. That his price money would be used to buy a potter's field (compare Zech. 11:12-13; Jer. 18:1-4; 19:1-4 with Matt. 27:9-10)
26. That he would be crucified between two thieves (compare Isa. 53:12 with Matt. 27:38; Mark 15:27-28; Luke 22:37)
27. That he would be given vinegar to drink (compare Psa. 69:21 with Matt. 27:34, 48; John 19:28-30)
28. That he would suffer the piercing of his hands and feet (compare Psa. 22:16; Zech. 12:10 with Mark 15:25; John 19:34, 37; 20:25-27)
29. That his garments would be parted and gambled for (compare Psa. 22:18 with Luke 23:34; John 19:23-24)
30. That he would be surrounded and ridiculed by his enemies (compare Psa. 22:7-8 with Matt. 27:39-44; Mark 15:29-32)
31. That he would thirst (compare Psa. 22:15 with John 19:28)
32. That he would commend his spirit to the Father (compare Psa. 31:5 with Luke 23:46)
33. That his bones would not be broken (compare Psa. 34:20; Exod. 12:46; Num. 9:12 with John 19:33-36)
34. That he would be stared at in death (compare Zech. 12:10 with John 19:37; Matt. 27:36)
35. That he would be buried with the rich (compare Isa. 53:9 with Matt. 27:57-60)
36. That he would be raised from the dead (compare Psa. 16:10 with Matt. 28:2-7)
37. That he would ascend (compare Psa. 24:7-10 with Mark 16:19; Luke 24:51)

G. The predictions made by Christ

1. Concerning the Church
   - a. Its symbol (Matt. 13:45)
   - b. Its foundation—Christ himself (Matt. 16:13-19)
   - c. Its ministry (Matt. 28:19-20; Acts 1:8)
   - d. Its field of service (Matt. 28:19; Acts 1:8)
   - e. Its authority (Matt. 16:19; 18:18; John 20:23)
   - f. Its persecution (Matt. 10:16-23, 34; John 15:18-21; 16:1-3, 33)

g. Its discipline (Matt. 18:15-17)
h. Its removal (John 14:2-3)
2. Concerning himself
a. His transfiguration (Matt. 16:28)
b. His betrayal by Judas
(1) Predicted in Galilee
(a) First occasion (John 6:70-71)
(b) Second occasion (Matt. 17:22)
(2) Predicted in the Upper Room (Matt. 26:21, 25)
c. His denial by Peter
(1) Predicted in the Upper Room (John 13:37-38)
(2) Predicted en route to the Mount of Olives and Gethsemane (Matt. 26:30, 34)
d. His abandonment by the Twelve (Matt. 26:31)
e. His sufferings
(1) Predicted in Caesarea Philippi (Matt. 16:21a)
(2) Predicted on the Mount of Transfiguration (Matt. 17:12b)
f. His death
(1) The fact of his death (John 10:11, 15; Matt. 17:23)
(2) The place of his death (Matt. 20:18)
(3) The method of his death (John 3:14; 12:32; Matt. 20:18-19)
g. His resurrection
(1) The fact of his resurrection (John 10:17-18)
(2) The time element in his resurrection (Matt. 12:40; John 2:19)
h. His appearance in Galilee (Matt. 26:32)
i. His ascension (John 7:33; 16:28)
j. His return
(1) In the air (John 14:3)
(2) On the earth (Matt. 16:27; 24:30; 26:63-64)
3. Concerning the resurrection of Lazarus (John 11:11)
4. Concerning the destruction of Jerusalem and the temple
a. The destruction of Jerusalem (Luke 19:43-44)
b. The destruction of the temple (Mark 13:1-2)
5. Concerning the death of Peter (John 21:18-19)
6. Concerning Pentecost and the ministry of the Holy Spirit
a. The fact of his ministry (John 7:37-39; Luke 24:49)
b. The duration of his ministry (John 14:16)
c. The location of his ministry (John 14:17)
d. The nature of his ministry
(1) Regarding the Savior (John 15:26; 16:14)
(2) Regarding the saved (John 14:26; 16:13)
(3) Regarding the sinner (John 16:8)
7. Concerning the last days (Luke 17:26-30; Matt. 24:32-34)
8. Concerning the nation Israel
a. Its blindness (Matt. 23:37-39)
b. Its rejection (Matt. 21:43)
c. Its regathering (Matt. 24:31)
9. Concerning the great tribulation (Matt. 24:21, 29; Luke 21:22-26)

10. Concerning the coming of Elijah (Matt. 17:11)
11. Concerning the coming Antichrist (John 5:43; Matt. 24:15)
12. Concerning the battle of Armageddon (Luke 17:34-37; Matt. 24:28)
13. Concerning the resurrection of the dead (John 5:28-29)
14. Concerning the future rewards (Matt. 10:41-42; 19:29)
15. Concerning the millennium (Matt. 8:11; 13:43; 19:28; 25:34)
16. Concerning the great white throne judgment (Matt. 25:31-33)
17. Concerning hell (Matt. 13:49-50; 18:8-9; 5:28-29)
18. Concerning heaven (John 14:2-3)

PART THREE

A **BASIC** OVERVIEW OF THE LIFE OF CHRIST, FEATURING NINE OUTLINE STUDIES ON THE MOST IMPORTANT EVENTS IN HIS EARTHLY LIFE

I. The Birth of Christ (Luke 2)

A. Joseph and Mary are brought to Bethlehem because of an enrollment decree which commanded each Hebrew citizen to be counted from that town where he or she was born. Note: This is the third all-important trip made to Bethlehem. Ruth and Naomi made the first journey. (See Ruth 1:22.) Samuel the prophet made the second journey. (See 1 Sam. 16.)

B. Mary gives birth to the Savior—She "wrapped him in swaddling clothes, and laid him in a manger; because there was no room for them in the inn" (Luke 2:7).

1. This was the fourth greatest day in human history.
2. The third greatest day in human history occurred some 34 years later when this Babe grew into glorious manhood, only to be put to death between a pair of thieves on Calvary's cross. "And when they were come to the place, which is called Calvary, there they crucified him, and the malefactors, one on the right hand, and the other on the left" (Luke 23:33).
3. The second greatest day in human history occurred three days later, when an angel told some sorrowing women: "Fear not ye; for I know that ye seek Jesus, which was crucified. He is not here; for he is risen as he said. Come, see the place where the Lord lay" (Matt. 28:5-6).
4. The greatest day in human history is yet to happen. The Apostle John tells us of this: "And the seventh angel sounded; and there were great voices in heaven, saying, The kingdoms of this world are become the kingdoms of our Lord, and of his Christ, and he shall reign forever and ever" (Rev. 11:15).

C. One may instructively contrast Jesus' birth in the flesh (Luke 2:7) with Daniel 2:11. In this Old Testament passage King Nebuchadnezzar had just ordered the death of his wise men because of their inability to relate a dream he had just experienced. These astrologers thereupon protested, exclaiming: "And it is a rare thing that the king requireth, and there is none other that can shew it before the king, except the gods, whose dwelling is not with flesh" (Dan. 2:11). But at the advent of the fourth greatest day in history all this would change.

D. In John 1:14 we read that the Word was made flesh. One of the most glorious truths of the incarnation was its eternality. This simply means that the results of the fourth day will last forever. He still has and always will have a body of flesh and bone. (See Luke 24:39.)

E. In the 1960s an American astronaut wrote a book entitled *Moon Walk*. In it he related how he had left a pleasant, familiar, and safe place called Earth and had landed on an alien, dangerous, and unfamiliar planet known as the Moon. When rightly understood, Luke 2:7 is the divine account of Christ's earth walk, for it begins the story of how God's Son left the beauty and safety of heaven to dwell upon an alien and sin-cursed planet.

F. Observe how the shepherds *came* and how they *left*.

1. They "came with haste" (Luke 2:16).
2. They left and "made known abroad . . . concerning this child" (Luke 2:17).

G. Luke tells us Mary "pondered" all this in her heart (Luke 2:19). Without doubt, this young mother had more to ponder than did any other human in history. Consider:

1. As she held the newly born baby, she knew he was already infinitely older than his mother, and as old as his Father.

2. As she fed the tiny infant, she realized she was nursing the One who had once fed the animals in the Garden of Eden, and her ancestors in the wilderness of Sinai. In essence, she was providing food for the Bread of Life.

H. At this point, let us stop and consider several questions that may be raised concerning those events leading up to the birth of the Savior.

1. Why did Joseph and Mary wait so long before coming to Bethlehem? We know both believed the angel's message about the Babe in Mary's womb, and they doubtless were well aware of the prophecy in Micah 5:2 which stated that Christ was to be born in Bethlehem. Why did they wait until the last moment to come? In fact, one is somewhat led to believe that, had it not been for the decree of Caesar Augustus, they might not have come at all. Answer: No satisfactory answer has been found by this author. It is best to conclude that Joseph (man of God that he was) had good reasons for acting in the manner he did. The reader may desire to explore this further.
2. Why didn't Mary and Joseph stay with their relatives in Bethlehem? The inns of those days were rather notorious, and Joseph must have been desperate, to consider subjecting his pregnant wife to the sin and noise of such a place. But of course they were even denied this. Answer: It would have been too difficult to explain (or to expect them to understand) the nature of the virgin birth. Every gossip in town doubtless knew by this time that Joseph and Mary had only been married six months, and there she was, expecting a baby at any moment. Was it Joseph's? Did it belong to some stranger? Thus, to spare his beloved wife all this, Joseph did not call upon their relatives.
3. Why was Jesus born in a place which apparently housed animals? Answer: Because lambs are usually born in barns. This was God's Lamb.
4. Why did the angels appear to the shepherds first? Answer: What other earthly group would better understand what God had just accomplished than these men who raised lambs and later sold them for sacrificial purposes in the temple? (See John 1:29; 10:11.) Note: They would eventually understand that in the past the sheep had died for the shepherd, but soon now the Shepherd planned to die for the sheep. (See John 10:11.)
5. Why did God use the angels in the first place? Answer:
   a. Because angels are interested in the things of salvation. (See 1 Pet. 1:12; Exod. 25:20; Dan. 12:5-6; Luke 15:10; Eph. 3:10.)
   b. Because they were present at the creation of this world and shouted for joy (Job 38:7). It is only logical, therefore, that God would allow them to be on hand at the presentation of the Savior of this world.

II. The Visit by the Wise Men (Matt. 2)

A. Who were these Wise Men? It is thought that they were perhaps a group of religious astronomers living in the region of Mesopotamia.

B. How did they associate the star with Christ? There are several possibilities. In the 14th century B.C., a prophet from their area named Balaam had spoken of this star. (See Num. 24:17.) They also had the writings of Daniel, who had been prime minister of both Babylon and Persia some six centuries before Christ. Daniel, of course, wrote much about the second coming.

C. Why did they come? These men were doubtless acquainted with the various religions of the East and knew the emptiness of them all. It would seem they followed this star to find peace and purpose for their lives.

D. When did they arrive in Bethlehem? It was perhaps not until some two years after the angels announced his birth to the shepherds. He is referred to as "the young child" (Matt. 2:9, 11, 13-14) and is not a tiny babe at this time. When Herod later attempted to destroy this unknown Babe, he had all children in the Bethlehem area two years and under slain (Matt. 2:16).

E. How many Wise Men came? There is absolutely no evidence that there were three. On the contrary, the group may have numbered from two to several hundred or more. Tradition, however, claims there were but three and their names were Casper, Melchior, and Balthazar.

F. Why did the star, after leading the Wise Men to Jerusalem, apparently disappear for a brief time and then reappear, taking them directly to Bethlehem? It may be that God intended this visit for the sake of the Jewish leaders. However, they had degenerated to such a level that they were unwilling to travel a few miles from Jerusalem to Bethlehem and see if their Messiah had really come. But here was a group of sincere Gentiles who had traveled across a hostile and extended desert to find him.

G. Was the star a regular one? The astronomer Kepler said there was a conjunction of the planets Jupiter and Saturn about this time in history. However, by no stretch of the imagination could a planet or star located thousands of millions of miles from earth function in the precise way this star did as recorded by Matthew: "the star . . . came and stood over where the young child was" (Matt. 2:9). It is not at all unreasonable, however, to suggest that the star was actually a New Testament appearance of that Old Testament shekinah glory cloud which led Israel across the desert.

H. What gifts did they offer him?
   1. They gave him gold, which spoke of his deity.
   2. They gave him frankincense, which spoke of his humanity.
   3. They gave him myrrh, which spoke of his future sufferings.

III. The Baptism of Christ (Matt. 3; Luke 3)

A. This is the clearest illustration of the doctrine of the Trinity in the entire Bible.
   1. The Father speaks from heaven.
   2. The Son stands in the water.
   3. The Holy Spirit descends.

B. This marks the first of three occasions when the Father orally expresses his approval of his Son.
   1. Here at the baptism
   2. On the Mount of Transfiguration (Matt. 17:5)
   3. In Jerusalem (John 12:28)

C. This event gives us the first reference to Christ's prayer life—"Now when all the people were baptized, it came to pass, that Jesus also being baptized, and praying, the heaven was opened" (Luke 3:21).

D. Why was Christ baptized? It may be stated that his baptism totally refutes that false doctrine of baptismal regeneration; that is, the claim that one must be baptized to be saved. The Savior of all did not need to be saved himself. But why, then, was he baptized?
   1. That he might identify with the message of John the Baptist—Actually, there were two aspects of John's message:
      a. "God's kingdom is at hand! The Messiah is here!"

b. "Repent therefore of your sin and be baptized to demonstrate this repentance." Thus, Christ was baptized to identify with the first part of John's message, while the rest fulfilled the second aspect.

2. That John might know Jesus was the true Messiah—"And I knew him not: but he that sent me to baptize with water, the same said unto me, Upon whom thou shalt see the Spirit descending, and remaining on him, the same is he which baptizeth with the Holy Ghost" (John 1:33).
3. To signal the beginning of his work as the Messiah—This was similar to the Old Testament minister who began his ministry at age 30 after a special ordination service.
4. To identify himself with the office of prophet, priest, and king—In the Old Testament all three were anointed. In Leviticus 8 we have described the threefold anointing of a priest. He was first washed with water; then anointed with oil; then finally with blood. Christ submitted to the first two of these (water baptism and the oil of the Spirit) but not the third.
5. That it might be shown that Jesus had the total support and approval of both the first and third persons in the Trinity.

E. This is the first of various baptisms mentioned in the Gospel accounts. The word *baptism* means "to identify with."

1. The baptism of John the Baptist—This was national baptism. (See Mark 1:4.)
2. The baptism of Jesus
   a. With water by John (Matt. 3:15)
   b. With the Holy Spirit by the Father (Matt. 3:16)
3. The baptism of sin upon Christ at Calvary (Luke 12:50; Matt. 20:22)
4. The baptism of the Holy Spirit upon believers at Pentecost (Matt. 3:11b)
5. The baptism of God's wrath upon sinners during the tribulation (Matt. 3:11b-12; 13:30)
6. The baptism of believers (Matt. 28:19)

IV. The Temptation of Christ (Matt. 4; Luke 4)—Here are some questions and answers concerning the temptations of Christ.

A. In what ways can the temptations experienced by the first Adam and the second Adam be compared and contrasted?

1. The comparison—In his first epistle, John separates all temptations into three general categories or groups (1 John 2:16). These are: the lust of the flesh, the lust of the eyes, and the pride of life.
   a. The first Adam was tempted in each area (Gen. 3:6).
      (1) "The tree was good for food" (the lust of the flesh).
      (2) "It was pleasant to the eyes" (the lust of the eyes).
      (3) "A tree desired to make one wise" (the pride of life)
   b. The second Adam was tempted in each area.
      (1) "Command that these stones be made bread" (the lust of the flesh).
      (2) "The devil . . . sheweth him all the kingdoms of the world and the glory of them" (the lust of the eyes).
      (3) "Cast thyself down: for . . . he shall give his angels charge concerning thee" (the pride of life).
2. The contrast
   a. The first Adam was tempted in a beautiful garden, while the second Adam met Satan in a desolate wilderness.

   b. The first Adam experienced total failure, while the second Adam was completely victorious.

B. Did Satan know whom he was tempting? He did indeed. The account in Matthew 4:3 and 4:6 is in the indicative mode in the Greek and should be rendered, "Since you are the Son of God."

C. What benefits did Satan offer Jesus?
   1. First temptation—To fill his stomach (and thus depend upon his own resources)
   2. Second temptation—To jump off the temple (and thus force the hand of the Father)
   3. Third temptation—To grasp the kingdoms of this world (and thus refuse Calvary).

D. What method did Satan use during the second temptation? He attempted to confuse Christ by quoting Scripture out of context. (Compare Matt. 4:6 with Psa. 91:11-12.) In essence, he did the same thing in dealing with the first Adam (Gen. 3:1).

E. Why are Jesus' temptations associated with a period of 40 days? This number is often one of tempting or testing, as found in the Bible. Examples would be:
   1. Moses (Exod. 24:18; 34:28)
   2. Israel (Deut. 8:2-3)
   3. Elijah (1 Kings 19:8)
   4. Goliath (1 Sam. 17:16)

F. Did Satan really have the right to offer Christ "all the kingdoms of the world and the glory of them" (Matt. 4:8-9)?
   1. In a shallow and temporary sense, yes. (See John 14:30; Eph. 2:2; 6:12; 1 John 5:19; Rev. 13:7.)
   2. In the deepest and most eternal sense, no—"Yet have I set my king upon my holy hill of Zion. I will declare the decree: the LORD hath said unto me, Thou art my Son; this day have I begotten thee. Ask of me, and I shall give thee the heathen for thine inheritance, and the uttermost parts of the earth for thy possession. Thou shalt break them with a rod of iron; thou shalt dash them in pieces like a potter's vessel" (Psa. 2:6-9). "And the seventh angel sounded; and there were great voices in heaven, saying, The kingdoms of this world are become the kingdoms of our Lord, and of his Christ; and he shall reign for ever and ever" (Rev. 11:15).

G. How did Christ answer Satan? By the Word of God.
   1. First temptation—"It is written, man shall not live by bread alone, but by every word that proceedeth out of the mouth of God." (Compare Matt. 4:4 with Deut. 8:3.)
   2. Second temptation—"It is written again, Thou shalt not tempt the Lord thy God." (Compare Matt. 4:7 with Deut. 6:16.) This temptation was probably an attempt to prematurely (and wrongly) fulfill Malachi 3:1. "Behold, I will send my messenger, and he shall prepare the way before me; and the Lord, whom ye seek, shall suddenly come to his temple, even the messenger of the covenant, whom ye delight in; behold, he shall come, saith the LORD of hosts." Satan's supreme object in the temptation ordeal was to cause Christ to act by himself, independently of the Father. Just what does it mean to tempt God? Israel is said to have tempted God on ten specific occasions en route to the Promised Land. (See Num. 14:11, 22; Heb. 3:9.) It means simply to presume upon the goodness

of God. It refers to using this goodness in a selfish way. It means to force God's hand on something. Had Christ actually jumped from this temple pinnacle, God would have been forced to step in and save Christ from smashing his physical body on the ground below.

3. Third temptation—"Get thee hence, Satan: for it is written, thou shalt worship the Lord thy God, and him only shalt thou serve." (Compare Matt. 4:10 with Deut. 6:13.) (See also James 4:7.) Dr. Everett F. Harrison writes the following about the third temptation: "In this final episode Satan is unmasked. Gone is any suggestion that he is working for the best interests of the Son of God. No citation from Scripture is offered. Satan reveals the innermost secret of his being. Much as he enjoys the distinction of being the prince of this world, a distinction only sin has enabled him to achieve, he covets something else infinitely more. He would be like the Most High. He would receive to himself what is most characteristically and exclusively the prerogative of God, namely, worship. A true angel abhors the very thought of being worshiped (Rev. 22:8-9), but this fallen angel fiercely, cravenly covets it. That such an offer was extended to Jesus is a testimony to his greatness. The stakes are high. When Satan made Judas his victim, his bait was a mere 30 pieces of silver. Indeed Satan could not well offer a lesser inducement to our Lord, for the nations were the promised inheritance of the Messiah and the uttermost parts of the earth were his anticipated possession (Psa. 2:8). In Psalm 2 this passage follows immediately the divine recognition of the sonship of the Messiah, the focal point of the temptation. 'Ask of me,' says God, but Satan brazenly usurps the place of the Almighty" (*A Short Life of Christ*, p. 90). As it can be seen here, Christ quotes from the book of Deuteronomy each time. It is no accident that higher criticism in Germany began with Deuteronomy in its vicious attack against the Bible.

H. Is this the only time Satan tempted Christ? No; in Luke 4:13 we are told: "And when the devil had ended all the temptation, he departed from him for a season." Note especially the last three words. Satan tempted Christ all through his ministry. At least three specific instances come to mind here where at a later date Satan continued his tempting work against Christ.

1. As expressed by the 5,000 men Christ fed—"When Jesus therefore perceived that they would come and take him by force, to make him a king, he departed again into a mountain himself alone" (John 6:15). "Bypass the cross and grab the crown!"
2. As expressed by Simon Peter—"From that time forth began Jesus to shew unto his disciples, how that he must go unto Jerusalem, and suffer many things of the elders and chief priests and scribes, and be killed, and be raised again the third day. Then Peter took him, and began to rebuke him, saying, Be it far from thee, Lord: this shall not be unto thee. But he turned, and said unto Peter, Get thee behind me, Satan: thou art an offence unto me: for thou savourest not the things that be of God, but those that be of men" (Matt. 16:21-23). "Don't even talk about the cross!"
3. As expressed by the mob at Calvary—"And they that passed by reviled him, wagging their heads, and saying, Thou that destroyest the temple, and buildest it in three days, save thyself. If thou be the Son of God, come down from the cross" (Matt. 27:39-40). "Come down from the cross!"

I. What happened after the wilderness temptation? "Then the devil leaveth him, and behold, angels came and ministered unto him" (Matt. 4:11). Heaven's angels played an important part in the earthly ministry of Christ.
   1. They announced his birth (Luke 1–2; Matt. 1).
   2. They later ministered to him in Gethsemane (Luke 22:43).
   3. They announced his resurrection (Matt. 28:6).

J. Could Christ have sinned during the temptation experience? He could not; God cannot sin. The Bible declares:
   1. He knew no sin (2 Cor. 5:21).
   2. He did no sin (1 Pet. 2:22; Heb. 4:15).
   3. He had no sin (1 John 3:5; John 14:30). (See also Heb. 7:26.)

K. What then was the purpose for the temptations? The purpose was not to see if he would, but to prove that he could not sin. During the settling of the West, a railroad company faced a problem. A bridge spanning a deep chasm gained the reputation of being unsafe. Careful examination by railroad officials showed this to be totally unfounded, but the rumor persisted. Finally, a train was formed made up of only heavy locomotives. For an entire day, as hundreds watched, this train crossed and recrossed the bridge. Why was this done? Did the railroad engineers arrange the experiment to see if the bridge would hold, or did they do it to prove it would hold? The obvious answer here may be applied to the purpose of Christ's temptations. The purpose was to provide the believer with an experienced High Priest. (See Heb. 4:15; 2:18.)

L. Were both God and Satan involved in the temptation of Christ? Is this the case when we are tempted? The answer to both questions is, Yes. The reason for this is seen in the twofold meaning of the word *temptation.*
   1. First meaning—To test in a good sense with the goal of confirming one in matters of righteousness.
   2. Second meaning—To test in a bad sense with the goal of enticing one in matters of evil. Thus:
      a. The first meaning
         (1) As experienced by Jesus—"Then was Jesus led up of the spirit into the wilderness to be tempted of the devil" (Matt. 4:1). "For we have not an high priest which cannot be touched with the feeling of our infirmities; but was in all points tempted like as we are, yet without sin" (Heb. 4:15).
         (2) As experienced by believers—"And it came to pass after these things, that God did tempt Abraham, and said unto him, Abraham: and he said, Behold, here I am" (Gen. 22:1). "My brethren, count it all joy when ye fall into divers temptations; Blessed is the man that endureth temptation: for when he is tried, he shall receive the crown of life, which the Lord hath promised to them that love him" (James 1:2, 12).
      b. The second meaning
         (1) As experienced by Jesus—Satan made a desperate attempt to entice Jesus into evil.
         (2) As experienced by believers—"And Satan stood up against Israel, and provoked David to number Israel" (1 Chron. 21:1). "Let no man say when he is tempted, I am tempted of God: for God cannot be tempted with evil, neither tempteth he any man: but every man is tempted, when he is drawn away of his own lust, and enticed" (James 1:13-14).

V. Christ's Meeting with Nicodemus (John 3)

A. This is the first of but three occasions where the term "born again" is found in the Word of God. (See John 3:3, 7; 1 Pet. 1:23.) However, John often uses the phrase "born of God." (See John 1:13; 1 John 3:9; 5:18.)

B. Several questions may be raised here.

1. Why did Nicodemus come by night? We do not know, and it is unfair to brand him a coward. Perhaps the heavy schedules of both men required this.
2. What did Nicodemus know about Jesus? He knew he was from God because of his supernatural miracles. (Compare John 3:2 with 20:30-31.)
3. What did Jesus mean by his expression, "Except a man be born of water and of the Spirit, he cannot enter into the kingdom of God" (John 3:5)? Here five main views have been offered.
    a. He was referring to baptismal regeneration. This, of course, is totally refuted by other biblical passages. (See Eph. 2:8-9; 1 Cor. 1:17; Rom. 5:1.)
    b. He was referring to that watery sac which accompanies physical birth and thus contrasts physical birth with spiritual birth.
    c. He was saying that the one requirement to live on this earth is to have had a physical birthday; and likewise, the one requirement to someday live in heaven is to have a spiritual birthday. Those who hold this view point to John 3:6 where they feel Jesus clarifies his position.
    d. He was referring to John's baptism of repentance in the Jordan, which baptism the Pharisees had rejected. (Compare Luke 3:3 with 7:30.)
    e. He was referring to the Word of God (the water) and the Spirit of God (Spirit), without which no man can ever be saved. (See John 16:8-11; Rom. 11:6-15.) Advocates of this position point out that water in the Bible is often the recognized symbol for the Word of God. (See Psa. 119:9; John 4:14; Eph. 5:25-26; Titus 3:5.)

C. Although this man was both a ruler and a religious teacher, he needed the new birth. Note Jesus' question in John 3:10, "Art thou a master of Israel, and knoweth not these things?" In the Greek the definite article is used, meaning, "Are you the teacher in Israel?" Nicodemus may have been the most famous teacher of his day.

D. In John 3:12 Jesus connects earthly things with heavenly things, indicating that a right view of the second is based squarely on a right view of the first. This only serves to emphasize the supreme importance of accepting at face value the historical words of Moses concerning creation (Gen. 1–2), as one would do with Christ's words concerning redemption.

E. It may be said that one cannot fully grasp the most famous verse in the Bible, John 3:16, unless he has some understanding of its background, which is found in John 3:14: "And as Moses lifted up the serpent in the wilderness, even so must the Son of man be lifted up."

F. Jesus illustrated his visitor's need by referring to Moses and the brazen serpent. (Compare John 3:14 with Num. 21:9.) On this occasion in the Old Testament account God had sent poisonous serpents to punish rebellious Israel. The people repented and a cure was provided. A serpent of brass was placed atop a wooden pole where all could view it. Anyone bitten needed only to look upon the brass serpent to be healed.

G. To paraphrase, here is what Jesus tells Nicodemus: "Nicodemus, like those Old Testament Israeli individuals, you have been bitten by a serpent—the serpent of sin. It is an incurable and fatal bite. But soon God is going to erect a crosslike pole just outside Jerusalem. And on that cross he will place a Savior."

H. An overview of John 3:16.
  1. It is the most important verse, because it contains the gospel in a nutshell.
  2. It is the greatest verse, because it contains nine of the most profound truths ever recorded.
    a. "For God"—The greatest Person
    b. "So loved the world"—The greatest truth
    c. "That he gave"—The greatest act
    d. "His only begotten Son"—The greatest gift
    e. "That whosoever"—The greatest number
    f. "Believeth in him"—The greatest invitation
    g. "Should not perish"—The greatest promise
    h. "But have"—The greatest certainty
    i. "Everlasting life"—The greatest destiny

VI. Christ's Promise to Build the Church (Matt. 16)

A. Was Jesus building his church upon Peter and planning to make him its first pope? It may be clearly stated that he was not.
  1. Because Christ later gave the same responsibilities to the other apostles which he here gives to Peter. (Compare Matt. 16:19 with John 20:22-23.)
  2. Because the New Testament clearly presents Christ only as the foundation of his church. (See Acts 4:11-12; 1 Cor. 3:11; 1 Pet. 2:4-8.)
  3. Because the New Testament clearly presents Christ and Christ only as the Head of his church. (See Eph. 1:20-23; 5:23; Col. 1:18; 2:18-19.)
  4. Because of the Greek language—There is a play upon words here. Jesus said, "Thou art Peter *[petros,* a little stone], and upon this rock *[petra,* a massive cliff or rock] I will build my church" (Matt. 16:18a)
  5. Because of Peter's personal testimony. (See 1 Pet. 5:1-4.)
  6. Because James, and not Peter, later officiated at the Jerusalem church. (See Acts 15:13, 19.)

B. What then, was Christ doing? The answer is given in Ephesians: "Now therefore ye are no more strangers and foreigners, but fellowcitizens with the saints, and of the household of God; and are built upon the foundation of the apostles and prophets, Jesus Christ himself being the chief corner stone; in whom all the building fitly framed together groweth unto an holy temple in the Lord: in whom ye also are builded together for an habitation of God through the Spirit" (Eph. 2:19-22).

C. What did he mean by "The gates of hell shall not prevail against it" (Matt. 16:18b)? J. Vernon McGee writes: "The *gates of hell* refer to the 'gates of death.' The word used here is the *hades* and *sheol* of the Old Testament which refers to the unseen world and means death: The gates of death shall not prevail against Christ's church" (Matthew, Volume II, p. 23).

D. What were the "keys of the kingdom of heaven" that Jesus gave Peter? A key, of course, unlocks doors and makes available something which was previously closed. Jesus here predicts that Peter would be given the privilege of opening the door of salvation to various peoples. This he later did.
  1. He opened the door of Christian opportunity to Israel at Pentecost (Acts 2:38-42).

2. He did the same thing for the Samaritans (Acts 8:14-17).
3. He performed this ministry to the Gentiles at Cornelius's house at Caesarea (Acts 10).

E. What did Christ mean by the binding and loosing of Matt. 16:19? This authority was given to all the apostles and even other believers. (See Matt. 18:18; John 20:22-23.) W. A. Criswell writes: "In Greek the future perfect tense is used to express the double notion of an action terminated in the past but whose effects are still existing in the present. 'Having been bound and still bound,' and 'having been loosed and still loosed.' The meaning is: if the disciples act in their proper capacity as stewards, they will be acting in accordance with the principles and elective purposes ordained beforehand in heaven" (*Expository Notes on Matthew,* p. 101). In other words, all the actions of the Spirit-filled believer, whether positive or negative in nature, will carry with them the awesome authority of heaven itself.

F. What shocking revelation did Jesus give during this occasion? "From that time forth began Jesus to shew unto his disciples, how that he must go unto Jerusalem, and suffer many things of the elders and chief priests and scribes, and be killed, and be raised again the third day" (Matt. 16:21). This sobering truth would be hammered home repeatedly by the Savior. Examples: "And while they abode in Galilee, Jesus said unto them, The Son of man shall be betrayed into the hands of men: and they shall kill him, and the third day he shall be raised again. And they were exceeding sorry" (Matt. 17:22-23). "Behold, we go up to Jerusalem; and the Son of man shall be betrayed unto the chief priests and unto the scribes, and they shall condemn him to death, and shall deliver him to the Gentiles to mock, and to scourge, and to crucify him: and the third day he shall rise again" (Matt. 20:18-19).

G. How did the devil react to this announcement? "Then Peter took him, and began to rebuke him, saying, Be it far from thee, Lord; this shall not be unto thee. But he turned and said unto Peter, Get thee behind me, Satan. Thou art an offense unto me; for thou savorest not the things that are of God, but those that be of men" (Matt. 16:22-23). Here Satan employs a familiar tactic, using a secondary source through which to spew forth his poison. The first successful attempt occurred in the Garden of Eden. "Now the serpent was more subtil than any beast of the field which the Lord God had made. And he said unto the woman, Yea, hath God said, Ye shall not eat of every tree of the garden?" (Gen. 3:1).

VII. The Transfiguration of Christ (Matt. 17; Mark 9; Luke 9)—Thoughts on the transfiguration

A. The Scriptures suggest that this may have been a night scene, for the three disciples had just awakened from a deep sleep. (See Luke 9:32.)

B. Note that the light was from within, and not from some giant cosmic spotlight suddenly focusing down upon Jesus. His countenance was affected first, then his garments. This was the same glory that shone in both the Old Testament tabernacle (Exod. 40) and the temple (1 Kings 8). It would later be withdrawn because of Israel's sin in the days of Ezekiel (Ezek. 10—11). Later it was revealed to the shepherds (Luke 2:9), to the disciples (Acts 1:9), to Stephen (Acts 7:55), to Saul (Acts 9:3), and to John the apostle (Rev. 1:16). Finally, at Christ's second coming this glory will be revealed to the entire world. "And then shall appear the sign of the Son of man in heaven: and then shall all the tribes of the earth mourn, and they shall see the Son of man coming in the clouds of heaven with power and great glory" (Matt. 24:30). Christ's eternal glory was not surrendered at the time of the incarnation, but was rather covered and contained by his fleshly body. The body of Christ was to the disciples what the veil of the tabernacle was to Old Testament Israel.

1. Both "veils" housed and protected the glory of God from within.
2. Both "veils" were broken at Calvary—"And he took bread, and gave thanks, and broke it, and gave unto them, saying, This is my body which is given for you: this do in remembrance of me" (Luke 22:19). "And, behold, the vail of the temple was rent in twain from the top to the bottom; and the earth did quake, and the rocks rent" (Matt. 27:51). Satan tries (unsuccessfully) to initiate this inward splendor of Christ (2 Cor. 11:14).

C. The word "transfigured" is *metamorpho* in the Greek language. We get our word "metamorphosis" from this. It brings to mind a caterpillar in the cocoon coming forth as a butterfly. The transfiguration of Christ does not set forth his deity, but rather, his humanity. Transformation is the goal of humanity. We shall experience this at the rapture. Adam and Eve may well have been clothed by a light of innocence proceeding from within. But all this was lost through sin.

D. Why the appearance of both Moses and Elijah?

1. Because of what they represented—The main reason for the writing of the Old Testament was to prepare us for Christ. Jesus himself testified of this: "Search the scriptures . . . they . . . testify of me" (John 5:39). "And beginning at Moses and all the prophets, he expounded unto them in all the scriptures, the things concerning himself" (Luke 24:27). While he was on earth, Jesus had a very simple way of summarizing the entire Old Testament: "Think not that I am come to destroy the law, or the prophets: I am not come to destroy, but to fulfill" (Matt. 5:17). Why, then, the appearance of these two men?
    a. Moses was there because he represented the Law.
    b. Elijah was there because he represented the prophets.
2. Because of who they represented—Why were Moses and Elijah, of all Old Testament people, present on this occasion? Perhaps these two men and the disciples suggest all the categories of people who will be in Jesus' coming kingdom. The disciples represent individuals who will be present in physical bodies. Moses represents saved individuals who have died or will die. Elijah represents saved individuals who will not experience death, but will be caught up to heaven alive (1 Thess. 4:17). These three groups will be present when Christ institutes his kingdom on earth. Furthermore the Lord will be in his glory as he was at the transfiguration, and the kingdom will take place on earth, as this obviously did. The disciples were thus enjoying a foretaste of the kingdom the Lord promised (Matt. 16:28) (*Bible Knowledge Commentary,* New Testament Volume, p. 59).
3. Because of their future ministry during the great tribulation—Many believe Moses and Elijah will be the two witnesses referred to in Revelation 11:3-12. (See also Mal. 4:4-5.) If this is true, the transfiguration event would thus serve as a "trial run." In fact, Jesus had suggested this very thing on the way down from the mountain: "And Jesus answered and said unto them, Elias truly shall first come, and restore all things" (Matt. 17:11).

E. Both Moses and Elijah had previously experienced a special revelation from God (see Exod. 33:17-23 and 1 Kings 19:9-13.), and at the same place (Mt. Sinai/Horeb).

The transfiguration answered Moses' twofold request: "To see the glory of God" (see Exod. 33:18.) "To enter the Promised Land" (see Deut. 32:48-52.)

F. Peter here (thoughtlessly) suggests the building of three booths. It may be that at this time the Feast of Tabernacles (booths) was being celebrated in Jerusalem. This was to be a type of the coming millennium as well as a reminder of Israel's redemption from Egypt. (See Lev. 23:34-44.) But before this could happen (the millennium), another feast would take place—the Passover. (See Lev. 23:4-8 and Matt. 26-27.) "For even Christ, our passover, is sacrificed for us" (1 Cor. 5:7).

G. Peter would never forget this great event. He later writes about it. (See 2 Pet. 1:16-18.)

H. Jesus spoke to Moses and Elijah concerning his "decease" (Luke 9:31). The word here is actually "exodus" and is used by Peter at a later date in describing his approaching death. (See 2 Pet. 1:13-14.)

I. Mark concludes the transfiguration event with the following words: "And as they came down from the mountain, he charged them that they should tell no man what things they had seen, till the Son of man were risen from the dead. And they kept that saying with themselves, questioning one with another what the rising from the dead should mean" (Mark 9:9-10).

J. The Jews were familiar with the doctrine of the resurrection (see Job 19:25-26; Isa. 25:8; Hosea 13:14), but the resurrection of the Son of man astonished them, for their theology had no place for a suffering and dying Messiah. This is especially seen in John 12:32-39.

VIII. The Crucifixion of Christ (Matt. 27; Mark 15; Luke 23; John 19)—The following is a brief overview of our Lord's seven statements uttered from the cross.

A. First statement

1. The context—"And the people stood beholding. And the rulers also derided him, saying, He saved others; let him save himself, if he be Christ, the chosen of God" (Luke 23:35).
2. The comment—"Then said Jesus, Father, forgive them, for they know not what they do" (Luke 23:34a).
3. The critique

a. This prayer has bothered some, as it seems to be a blanket pardon for all involved in Jesus' crucifixion. Of course, we know this is not the case. Forgiveness can only come through faith (Eph. 2;8-9). It has been pointed out by some that the word "forgive" here can also mean "to allow," and is actually translated thereby on at least 13 other occasions in the New Testament. If this should be the case here, Christ then would pray, "Father, allow them to crucify me." Thus the prayer would be a plea to stay the wrath of a righteous Father as he viewed his beloved Son being murdered by sinful and wicked people. (See Matt. 3:15; 19:14; Mark 1:34.) However, most Bible students would accept the word "forgive" at face value and interpret his prayer as a request for God not to add this horrible crime of regicide (the killing of one's own king) to the personal accounts of those individuals who killed him. Peter and Paul would amplify on this in later sermons (Acts 3:14-15, 17): "But ye denied the Holy One and the Just, and desired a murderer to be granted unto you; and killed the Prince of life, whom God hath raised from the dead; whereof we are witnesses. And now, brethren, I wot that through ignorance ye did it, as did also your rulers."

(See also 1 Cor. 2:8.) "Which none of the princes of this world knew: for had they known it, they would not have crucified the Lord of glory."

b. The sinlessness of our Savior is again proven here, for he did not pray, "Father, forgive me." He needed no forgiveness for he knew no sin. In summary, the first cross utterance did not mean that humans are excusable, but rather forgivable. (Contrast Rom. 2:1 with 1 Tim. 1:13.)

B. Second statement

1. The context—"And one of the malefactors which were hanged railed on him, saying, If thou be Christ, save thyself and us. But the other answering rebuked him, saying, Dost not thou fear God, seeing thou art in the same condemnation? And we indeed justly; for we receive the due reward of our deeds: but this man hath done nothing amiss. And he said unto Jesus, Lord, remember me when thou comest into thy kingdom" (Luke 23:39-42).
2. The comment—"And Jesus said unto him, Verily I say unto thee, To day shalt thou be with me in paradise" (Luke 23:43).
3. The critique—This statement emphasizes several facts concerning salvation.

a. That salvation is offered to anyone, anywhere. Are deathbed conversions valid? They are indeed, for here is one. But we quickly note:

(1) There is one deathbed conversion in the Bible, so no dying person will despair.

(2) There is only one, so no living person will presume. D. L. Moody once said: "Did ever the new birth take place in so strange a cradle?" Observe the contrast here: In the morning the thief was nailed to a cross. In the evening he was wearing a crown. In the morning he was an enemy of Caesar. In the evening he was a friend of God. In the morning he was spurned by men. In the evening he was fellowshiping with angels. In the morning he died as a criminal on earth. In the evening he lived as a citizen of heaven.

b. That salvation is by grace through faith alone. This conversion refutes:

(1) The doctrine of sacramentalism—He was saved apart from confirmation, sprinkling, Holy Communion, and church membership.

(2) The doctrine of baptismal regeneration

(3) The doctrine of purgatory

(4) The doctrine of universalism—Only one thief was saved.

c. That salvation will be rejected by some in spite of everything God can do. The other thief died, eternally lost. Here we see three men:

(1) One was dying for sin (the Savior).

(2) One was dying from sin (the repentant thief).

(3) One was dying in sin (the lost thief). All classes of humanity were represented at the cross. There were the indifferent ("the people stood beholding," Luke 23:35); the religious ("the rulers derided him," Luke 23:35); the materialistic ("the soldiers parted his raiment and cast lots," Luke 23:34); and the earnest seekers ("Lord, remember me" Luke 23:42). The cross is indeed the judgment of this world. (See John 12:31.)

C. Third statement

1. The context—"Now there stood by the cross of Jesus his mother, and his mother's sister, Mary the wife of Cleophas, and Mary Magdalene" (John 19:25).

2. "When Jesus therefore saw his mother, and the disciple standing by, whom he loved, he saith unto his mother, Woman, behold thy son! Then saith he to the disciple, Behold thy mother! And from that hour that disciple took her unto his own home" (John 19:26-27).
3. The critique
   a. It is probable that Joseph was dead, for had he been alive it would not have been necessary for Jesus to have entrusted Mary to John.
   b. John was apparently the only apostle present at Jesus' crucifixion. The others were probably in hiding somewhere. Judas, of course, had committed suicide by this time.
   c. Our Lord's words to Mary may have reminded her of Simeon's prophecy given at the time of Jesus' dedication as an infant in the temple. "And Simeon blessed them, and said unto Mary his mother, Behold, this child is set for the fall and rising again of many in Israel; and for a sign which shall be spoken against; (yea, a sword shall pierce through thy own soul also,) that the thoughts of many hearts may be revealed" (Luke 2:34-35).

D. Fourth statement
1. The context—"Now from the sixth hour there was darkness over all the land unto the ninth hour" (Matt. 27:45).
2. The comment—"And about the ninth hour Jesus cried with a loud voice, saying, Eli, Eli, lama sabachthani? that is to say, My God, my God, why hast thou forsaken me?" (Matt. 27:46).
3. The critique
   a. This prayer is deeper in its mystery and higher in its meaning than any other single prayer in the Bible. God forsaken by God! Who can understand that? The wisest and most profound Bible student feels utterly inadequate as he approaches it. It can never be mastered by the mortal mind, even though that mind has experienced new birth. Eternity alone will exegete this. Elizabeth Clephane has so well phrased it:

   But none of the ransomed ever knew,
   How deep were the waters crossed;
   Nor how dark was the night, That the Lord passed through,
   Ere he found his sheep that was lost.

   b. There are so many unexplained "whys" raised here.
      (1) Why did the Father turn his back upon the Son?
      (2) Why did not even the Son know the reason?
      (3) Why did innocent blood have to be shed for the forgiveness of sin?
   c. The first and third of these questions are partially answered in Hebrews 9:22; 1 Peter 2:24; 3:18; Isaiah 53. But what of the second question? Did not Christ know? According to Philippians 2:5-8, Christ voluntarily abstained from employing some of his divine attributes while upon this earth. Thus:
      (1) He abstained from using his omnipresence for a period (John 11:15).
      (2) He abstained from using his omnipotence for a period (John 5:19).
      (3) He abstained from using his omniscience for a period (Luke 8:45; Mark 13:32). (See also Luke 2:40.)

E. Fifth statement
   1. The context—"After this, Jesus knowing that all things were now accomplished, that the scriptures might be fulfilled" (John 19:28a).
   2. The comment—"I thirst" (John 19:28b).
   3. The critique—Thus, he who began his ministry by suffering intense hunger (Matt. 4:2), will now end it by experiencing terrible thirst. And yet, the amazing truth remains:
      a. The hungry One was and is the eternal Bread of Life.
      b. The thirsty One was and is the eternal Water of Life.

F. Sixth statement
   1. The context—"Now there was set a vessel full of vinegar: and they filled a spunge with vinegar, and put it upon hyssop, and put it to his mouth" (John 19:29).
   2. The comment—"When Jesus therefore had received the vinegar, he said, It is finished: and he bowed his head, and gave up the ghost" (John 19:30).
   3. The critique
      a. The sixth statement of Jesus is actually one word in the original Greek. It is *tetelestai,* meaning, "It was finished, and as a result it is forever done." This phrase was a farmer's word. When into his herd there was born an animal so beautiful and shapely that it seemed absolutely destitute of faults and defects, the farmer gazed upon the creature with proud, delighted e yes: *"Tetelestai!"* he said. It was also an artist's word. When the painter or the sculptor had put the last finishing touches to the vivid landscape or the marble bust, he would stand back a few feet to admire his masterpiece, and, seeing in it nothing that called for correction or improvement, would murmur fondly, *"Tetelestai! Tetelestai!"*
      b. Our Lord cries out, "It is finished!"—There are three important places where the Scriptures employ this word "finish." It is used in Genesis 2:1, referring to the creation of God's works. It is used here in John 19:30, referring to the salvation of his works. (See also John 4:34; 5:36; 17:4.) It is used in Revelation 10:7 and 16:17, referring to the completion of his works.
      c. With gladness we note that he did not say, "I am finished," for he was just beginning.

Lifted up was He to die,
'It is finished,' was His cry;
Now in heav'n exalted high;
Hallelujah! What a Savior!"

G. Seventh statement
   1. The context—"And the sun was darkened, and the vail of the temple was rent in the midst" (Luke 23:45).
   2. The comment—"And when Jesus had cried with a loud voice, he said, Father, into thy hands I commend my spirit: and having said thus, he gave up the ghost" (Luke 23:46).
   3. The critique
      a. With this statement Jesus ended his Calvary ordeal as he had begun it, by praying to his Father.

b. His death was in and by itself a miracle, for he dismissed his spirit. No mortal can do this through an act of the will without using a gun, knife, poison, etc.

c. All four Gospel accounts record the death of Christ. But one wonders how such a thing could happen? Was not Christ God incarnate? Indeed he was. How, then, could God have actually died on the cross? To explain this, we must return briefly to the book of Genesis. Here we are told of Adam's creation and of his tragic sin. God had warned him that disobedience would result in death, and so it did. In fact, it brought down upon the head of mankind two kinds of death: physical and spiritual. Both kinds of death here can be defined by one word: separation. That is the biblical and theological meaning of the word death. Physical death is separation, the parting of the soul from one's body. Spiritual death is likewise separation, the parting of the unsaved person from God. This is sometimes called the second death" (see Rev. 20:6, 14; 21:8).

d. So then, these two hellish enemies, physical and spiritual death, let loose by Adam, continued to curse and terrorize the human race for over 40 centuries. Then, in the fullness of time, God sent his beloved Son to our world. The Father referred to his Son as the last Adam (among other names) in 1 Corinthians 15:45.

e. Why this title? Because he had come to undo what the first Adam had previously done; that is, he came to rid mankind of those two evil enemies, physical and spiritual death. This he did while on the cross, where he died spiritually, being separated from God; and died physically as he accomplished both tasks. Spiritual death was immediately given the death blow. Paul later assures us that nothing can now separate the believer from the love of God (Rom. 8:35-39). But what about physical death? Paul answers this question in 1 Corinthians 15:51-55: "Behold, I shew you a mystery; we shall not all sleep, but we shall all be changed. In a moment, in the twinkling of an eye, at the last trump: for the trumpet shall sound, and the dead shall be raised incorruptible, and we shall be changed. For this corruptible must put on incorruption, and this mortal must put on immortality. So when this incorruptible shall have put on incorruption, and this mortal shall have put on immortality, then shall be brought to pass the saying that is written, Death is swallowed up in victory. O death, where is thy sting? O grave, where is thy victory?"

IX. The Resurrection of Christ (Matt. 28; Mark 16; Luke 24; John 20–21)—The risen Savior would make ten appearances during those 40 days transpiring between his resurrection and his ascension. Five of these occurred on that first Easter Sunday. The final five took place in the remaining 39 days. Here is an overview of these ten appearances.

A. First appearance—To Mary Magdalene (Mark 16:9-11; John 20:11-18)

1. The revelation—"The first day of the week cometh Mary Magdalene early, when it was yet dark, unto the sepulchre, and seeth the stone taken away from the sepulchre. . . . But Mary stood without at the sepulchre weeping: and as she wept, she stooped down, and looked into the sepulchre, and seeth two angels in white sitting, the one at the head, and the other at the feet, where the body of Jesus had lain. And they say unto her, Woman, why weepest thou? She saith

unto them, Because they have taken away my Lord, and I know not where they have laid him. And when she had thus said, she turned herself back, and saw Jesus standing, and knew not that it was Jesus. Jesus saith unto her, Woman, why weepest thou? whom seekest thou? She, supposing him to be the gardener, saith unto him, Sir, if thou have borne him hence, tell me where thou hast laid him, and I will take him away" (John 20:1, 11-15).

2. The reaction—"Jesus saith unto her, Mary. She turned herself, and saith unto him, Rabboni; which is to say, Master. Jesus saith unto her, Touch me not; for I am not yet ascended to my Father: but go to my brethren, and say unto them, I ascend unto my Father, and your Father; and to my God, and your God. Mary Magdalene came and told the disciples that she had seen the Lord, and that he had spoken these things unto her" (John 20:16-18).
3. The review
   a. This was undoubtedly one of the two most dramatic "recognition meetings" in all the Bible. The first involved Joseph revealing himself to his brothers in Egypt (see Gen. 45:1-3).
   b. It was a Samaritan woman to whom Christ first revealed his messiahship. (See John 4:25-26.) It is now to another woman, Mary Magdalene, that Christ first appears in his resurrection body. Both were formerly women of questionable moral backgrounds. (See Mark 16:9.)
   c. Note his phrase, "Go to my brethren." There is a progressive intimacy between Jesus and his disciples. He calls them servants (John 13:13), friends (John 15:15), and here, brethren.
   d. Note also the phrase, "I ascend unto my Father." Some hold that Christ ascended that very first Easter Sunday to sprinkle his blood as the ultimate sacrifice within the heavenly sanctuary.
   e. Why did Mary not recognize Jesus? Probably for several reasons:
      (1) Her eyes were blinded with tears.
      (2) The early morning light was still too dim.
      (3) She was not expecting to see him.

B. Second appearance—To a group of women (Matt. 28:9-15)
1. The revelation—"And the angel answered and said unto the women, fear not ye: for I know that ye seek Jesus, which was crucified. He is not here: for he is risen, as he said. Come, see the place where the Lord lay. And go quickly, and tell his disciples that he is risen from the dead; and, behold, he goeth before you into Galilee; there shall ye see him: lo, I have told you. And they departed quickly from the sepulchre with fear and great joy; and did run to bring his disciples word" (Matt. 28:5-8).
2. The reaction—"And as they went to tell his disciples, behold, Jesus met them, saying, All hail. And they came and held him by the feet, and worshipped him. Then said Jesus unto them, Be not afraid: go tell my brethren that they go into Galilee, and there shall they see me" (Matt. 28:9-10).
3. The review
   a. This account contains what surely must be the three most thrilling words in all the Bible, "He is risen!"
   b. The angel predicts Jesus' disciples would later meet him by the Sea of Galilee, which they did (John 21).

C. Third appearance—To two disciples en route to Emmaus (Luke 24:13-32; Mark 16:12-13)

1. The revelation—"And it came to pass, that, while they communed together and reasoned, Jesus himself drew near, and went with them. But their eyes were holden that they should not know him. And he said unto them, What manner of communications are these that ye have one to another, as ye walk, and are sad? And the one of them, whose name was Cleopas, answering said unto him, Art thou only a stranger in Jerusalem, and hast not known the things which are come to pass there in these days? And he said unto them, What things? And they said unto him, Concerning Jesus of Nazareth, which was a prophet mighty in deed and word before God and all the people: and how the chief priests and our rulers delivered him to be condemned to death, and have crucified him" (Luke 24:15-20). "Then he said unto them, O fools, and slow of heart to believe all that the prophets have spoken: Ought not Christ to have suffered these things, and to enter into his glory? And beginning at Moses and all the prophets, he expounded unto them, in all the scriptures, the things concerning himself. And they drew nigh unto the village, whither they went; and he made as though he would have gone further. But they constrained him, saying, Abide with us; for it is toward evening, and the day is far spent. And he went in to tarry with them. And it came to pass, as he sat at meat with them, he took bread, and blessed it, and brake, and gave it to them. And their eyes were opened, and they knew him; and he vanished out of their sight" (Luke 24:25-31).
2. The reaction—"And they said one to another, Did not our heart burn within us, while he talked with us by the way, and while he opened to us the scriptures? And they rose up the same hour, and returned to Jerusalem, and found the eleven gathered together, and them that were with them, Saying, The Lord is risen indeed, and hath appeared to Simon. And they told what things were done in the way, and how he was known of them in breaking of bread" (Luke 24:32-35).
3. The review
   a. The two disciples reminded their unrecognized friend that "the day is far spent." Spiritually speaking, however, it was just the opposite. The terrible night of Calvary was far spent. The glorious morning of the resurrection was now at hand. "The night is far spent, the day is at hand: let us therefore cast off the works of darkness, and let us put on the armour of light" (Rom. 13:12).
   b. Following his resurrection our Lord was eventually recognized when he performed the simplest of tasks:
      (1) After pronouncing a name (John 20:16)
      (2) After a simple greeting (Matt. 28:9)
      (3) After the breaking of bread (Luke 24:30-31)

D. Fourth appearance—To Simon Peter (Luke 24:34; 1 Cor. 15:5). What a meeting this must have been! The last time these two saw each other, the one was bitterly cursing and denying the other.

E. Fifth appearance—To the apostles in the Upper Room (Mark 16:14; Luke 24:36-38; John 20:19-23)

1. The revelation—"And as they thus spake, Jesus himself stood in the midst of them, and saith unto them, Peace be unto you. But they were terrified and

affrighted, and supposed that they had seen a spirit. And he said unto them, Why are ye troubled? and why do thoughts arise in your hearts? Behold my hands and my feet, that it is I myself: handle me, and see; for a spirit hath not flesh and bones, as ye see me have" (Luke 24:36-39).

2. The reaction—"And when he had so said, he shewed unto them his hands and his side. Then were the disciples glad, when they saw the Lord" (John 20:20). "And while they yet believed not for joy, and wondered, he said unto them, Have ye here any meat? And they gave him a piece of a broiled fish, and of an honeycomb. And he took it, and did eat before them" (Luke 24:41-43).
3. The review—What kind of body did Jesus have after his resurrection? This is of great importance to the Christian, for he or she will someday have a similar body, as testified to by both Paul and John (see Phil. 3:21; 1 John 3:1-3).
   a. His new body had flesh and bone (Luke 24:39-40).
   b. He ate food in the new body (Luke 24:41-43; John 21:12- 13; Acts 10:41).
   c. His new body still bore the marks of his crucifixion (John 20:25-27; Luke 24:40; Rev. 5:6).
   d. His new body was not subjected to material laws (John 20:19; Luke 24:31, 36).

F. Sixth appearance—To Thomas and the ten apostles (John 20:24-31)

1. The revelation—"But Thomas, one of the twelve, called Didymus, was not with them when Jesus came. The other disciples therefore said unto him, We have seen the Lord. But he said unto them, Except I shall see in his hands the print of the nails, and put my finger into the print of the nails, and thrust my hand into his side, I will not believe. And after eight days again his disciples were within, and Thomas with them: then came Jesus, the doors being shut, and stood in the midst, and said, Peace be unto you. Then saith he to Thomas, Reach hither thy finger, and behold my hands; and reach hither thy hand, and thrust it into my side: and be not faithless, but believing" (John 20:24-27).
2. The reaction—"And Thomas answered and said unto him, My Lord and my God. Jesus saith unto him, Thomas, because thou hast seen me, thou hast believed: blessed are they that have not seen, and yet have believed" (John 20:28-29).
3. The review—In recent times there are those who have boasted of being favored by exotic appearances of Christ himself. One such evangelist claimed to have seen a 900-foot image of Jesus. If this highly unlikely story were true, the evangelist would have been less blessed than the rest of God's people who, unlike Thomas, are praised for believing without seeing.

G. Seventh appearance—To seven apostles by the Sea of Galilee (John 21)

1. The revelation—"But when the morning was now come, Jesus stood on the shore: but the disciples knew not that it was Jesus. Then Jesus saith unto them, Children, have ye any meat? They answered him, No. And he said unto them, Cast the net on the right side of the ship, and ye shall find. They cast therefore, and now they were not able to draw it for the multitude of fishes" (John 21:4-6).
2. The reaction—"Therefore that disciple whom Jesus loved saith unto Peter, It is the Lord. Now when Simon Peter heard that it was the Lord, he girt his fisher's coat unto him, (for he was naked,) and did cast himself into the sea. And the other disciples came in a little ship; (for they were not far from land, but as it were two hundred cubits,) dragging the net with fishes. As soon then as they were come to land, they saw a fire of coals there, and fish

laid thereon, and bread. Jesus saith unto them, Bring of the fish which ye have now caught. Simon Peter went up, and drew the net to land full of great fishes, an hundred and fifty and three: and for all there were so many, yet was not the net broken. Jesus then cometh, and taketh bread, and giveth them, and fish likewise. So when they had dined, Jesus saith to Simon Peter, Simon, son of Jonas, lovest thou me more than these? He saith unto him, Yea, Lord; thou knowest that I love thee. He saith unto him, Feed my lambs. He saith to him again the second time, Simon, son of Jonas, lovest thou me? He saith unto him, Yea, Lord; thou knowest that I love thee. He saith unto him, Feed my sheep. He saith unto him the third time, Simon, son of Jonas, lovest thou me? Peter was grieved because he said unto him the third time, Lovest thou me? And he said unto him, Lord, thou knowest all things; thou knowest that I love thee. Jesus saith unto him, Feed my sheep" (John 21:7-11, 13, 15-17).

a. There may have been a double miracle involved here, for Jesus already had fish and bread available even before the disciples had brought in their catch.
b. Jesus' question, "Lovest thou me more than these?" may have referred to at least one of three things. He could have meant: "Do you love me more than you love these men?" "Do you love me more than fishing?" "Do you love me more than these men love me?"
c. It would seem that Jesus had the third meaning in mind, based on Matthew 26:33. "Peter answered and said unto him, Though all men shall be offended because of thee, yet will I never be offended."
d. Three times he is asked if he really loves the Savior. Three times he answers in the affirmative. In the Greek New Testament there are two different kinds of love. One is *phileo* love, which refers to that warm affection between two human beings. The other kind of love is an *agapao* love, which is a divine love—God's love for sinful people.
e. This love is never found in the heart of any person prior to the ascension of Christ. In fact, Jesus asks Peter on three occasions (John 21:15-19) if he really loves him. The first two times Jesus uses the second kind of love and asks the following question: "Peter, do you *agapao* me?" On both occasions Peter answers by choosing the first word. He says, "Lord, you know I *phileo* you." Finally, our Lord uses the first word also. The reason for all this (as Peter would later find out) is explained in Romans 5:5 by Paul—"the love *agapao* of God is shed abroad in our hearts by the Holy Ghost which is given unto us."
f. Thus, the reason Peter answered the way he did was because the Holy Spirit had not yet come at Pentecost and it was therefore impossible for him to love Christ with this divine *agapao* love. Also to be noted here is Jesus' request that Peter feed his lambs (John 21:15) and his sheep (21:16-17). Again, there is a play on the Greek here, for Christ uses two different words for "feed." He says "be grazing my baby lambs, but discipline my older sheep." Today we have this truth in reverse. We discipline the young and feed the old.
g. Peter had once denied Christ three times in the presence of the Savior's enemies. Jesus now gives him the opportunity to affirm his love on three occasions. God is the God of the second chance.

(1) As seen in the life of Jonah—"And the word of the Lord came unto Jonah the second time, saying, Arise, go unto Nineveh, that great city, and preach unto it the preaching that I bid thee" (Jon. 3:1-2).

(2) As seen in the life of John Mark—This young man had once failed God by abandoning Paul and Barnabas during their first missionary journey (see Acts 13:13; 15:36-39). But Mark, like Jonah and Peter, served the God of the second chance. Years later, just prior to his martyrdom in Rome, the Apostle Paul testifies of this. "Only Luke is with me. Take Mark, and bring him with thee: for he is profitable to me for the ministry" (2 Tim. 4:11).

h. In essence, Christ's words here constituted the final part of a twofold commission given to Peter. Both parts were issued by Jesus on the shores of Galilee. Each occurred following a supernatural catch of fish. One part was spoken at the beginning of Jesus' ministry, before his crucifixion; the other at the end of his ministry, after his resurrection. Here is this twofold commission.

(1) First part—"Catch fish." "When Simon Peter saw it, he fell down at Jesus' knees, saying, Depart from me; for I am a sinful man, O Lord. For he was astonished, and all that were with him, at the draught of the fishes which they had taken: and so was also James, and John, the sons of Zebedee, which were partners with Simon. And Jesus said unto Simon, Fear not; from henceforth thou shalt catch men" (Luke 5:8-10).

(2) Second part—"Feed sheep."

i. Thus, in Luke 5 Jesus stressed soul winning; but here in John 21, he emphasizes sheep tending. To his credit Peter would faithfully carry out both parts of Christ's commission.

(1) He fulfilled the first section at Pentecost through the spoken word when he let down his net and caught fish—some 3,000 of them. (See Acts 2:41.)

(2) He fulfilled the second section at Babylon through the written word where he wrote 1 and 2 Peter that he might feed sheep. "As newborn babes, desire the sincere milk of the word, that ye may grow thereby" (1 Pet. 2:2). Feed the flock of God which is among you, taking the oversight thereof, not by constraint, but willingly, not for filthy lucre, but of a ready mind; neither as being lords over God's heritage, but being ensamples to the flock" (1 Pet. 5:2-3).

H. Eighth appearance—To the apostles and 500 disciples (Matt. 28:16-20; Mark 16:15-18; 1 Cor. 15:6)

1. The revelation—"After that, he was seen of above five hundred brethren at once; of whom the greater part remain unto this present, but some are fallen asleep" (1 Cor. 15:6). "And Jesus came and spake unto them, saying, All power is given unto me in heaven and in earth. Go ye therefore, and teach all nations, baptizing them in the name of the Father, and of the Son, and of the Holy Ghost: teaching them to observe all things whatsoever I have commanded you: and, lo, I am with you alway, even unto the end of the world" (Matt. 28:18-20).

2. The reaction—"And when they saw him, they worshipped him: but some doubted" (Matt. 28:17).

3. The review

a. Here a distinction should be made between an apostle and a disciple.

(1) The meaning of the word *apostle* is literally, "one sent forth." Jesus had previously chosen 12 men and had sent them forth.

(2) The meaning of *disciple* is "a learner," and referred to any and all followers of Christ. Thus it can be seen that while all apostles were learners (Judas excepted), not all disciples were apostles.

b. Who were these 500 disciples? Doubtless they included such individuals as Nicodemus, Joseph of Arimathaea, Barnabas, Silas, Stephen, Philip the Evangelist, Matthias, etc.

I. Ninth appearance—To James, the half brother of Christ (1 Cor. 15:7). Prior to this, James had been an unbeliever (John 7:5); but now he accepts his older half brother as Messiah. James later becomes part of the church in Jerusalem and also author of the book of James.

J. Tenth appearance—To the Eleven on the Mount of Olives (Luke 24:49-50; Acts 1:3-8)

1. The revelation—"And he led them out as far as to Bethany; and he lifted up his hands, and blessed them" (Luke 24:50). "And, being assembled together with them, commanded them that they should not depart from Jerusalem, but wait for the promise of the Father, which, saith he, ye have heard of me" (Acts 1:4).
2. The reaction—"When they therefore were come together, they asked of him, saying, Lord, wilt thou at this time restore again the kingdom to Israel? And he said unto them, It is not for you to know the times or the seasons, which the Father hath put in his own power. But ye shall receive power, after that the Holy Ghost is come upon you: and ye shall be witnesses unto me both in Jerusalem, and in all Judaea, and in Samaria, and unto the uttermost part of the earth. And when he had spoken these things, while they beheld, he was taken up; and a cloud received him out of their sight. And while they looked stedfastly toward heaven as he went up, behold, two men stood by them in white apparel; which also said, Ye men of Galilee, why stand ye gazing up into heaven? this same Jesus, which is taken up from you into heaven, shall so come in like manner as ye have seen him go into heaven" (Acts 1:6-11).
3. The review

a. Especially observe Acts 1:8.

(1) We note that they were to be witnesses—Not potentates, or psychologists, or promoters, but witnesses.

(2) This verse is actually a table of contents and divine outline for the entire book of Acts. Note:

(a) Witnessing in Jerusalem (Acts 1–7)

(b) Witnessing in Judea and Samaria (Acts 8–12)

(c) Witnessing unto the uttermost part of the earth (Acts 13–28)

b. Acts 1:11 says, "This same Jesus . . . shall so come in like manner as ye have seen him go" Thus:

(1) The going was personal, and so shall the return be (1 Thess. 4:16).

(2) The going was visible, and so shall the return be (Phil. 3:21).

(3) The going was from the Mount of Olives, and so shall the return be (Zech. 14:4).

PART FOUR

ACTS THROUGH REVELATION

ACTS

THE BIRTH OF THE BRIDE
A TREMENDOUS TALE
OF GROWING, GLOWING, AND GOING FOR GOD

Preface

The Book of Acts is in reality a letter written by Luke.

The person to whom Luke wrote—"The former treatise have I made, O Theophilus . . ." (1:1a). Luke writes his second letter to Theophilus. His first one (the Gospel of Luke) was written to tell what Christ did while on earth through his physical body (see Luke 1:1-4). His second letter (the Book of Acts) was written to tell what Christ was doing while in heaven through his spiritual body, the church. He begins by reminding Theophilus "of all that Jesus began both to do and teach" (1:1). This, of course, was in stark contrast to the wicked Pharisees, who, according to the Savior, "say, and do not" (Matt. 23:3). Luke speaks of the "many infallible proofs" which surrounded the resurrection ministry. During that time our Lord appeared at least 10 different times to his followers.

The person of whom Luke wrote—"Of all that Jesus began both to do and teach, until the day in which he was taken up, after that he through the Holy Ghost had given commandments unto the apostles whom he had chosen: To whom also he shewed himself alive after his passion by many infallible proofs, being seen of them forty days, and speaking of the things pertaining to the kingdom of God: And, being assembled together with them, commanded them that they should not depart from Jerusalem, but wait for the promise of the Father, which, saith he, ye have heard of me. For John truly baptized with water; but ye shall be baptized with the Holy Ghost not many days hence" (Acts 1:1b-5).

A. Interesting facts about the Book
1. The book of Acts is the true story relating the first 30 years of the early church. In many ways it is the highmark of Christian witness.
2. The action centers around two great "crusades," the Greater Jerusalem Crusade (Acts 1–12) headed up by Peter, and the Global Crusade (Acts 13–28), led by Paul.
3. The associates involved in their campaigns were John the apostle, Stephen, Philip, Barnabas, Silas, Timothy, and Luke. The record tells us of the first:
   a. Deacons—Philip, Stephen, *et al* (6:1-5)
   b. Martyrs—Stephen, James (7:60; 12:2)
   c. Missionaries—Paul, Barnabas, Silas (13:1-3; 15:40)
   d. Evangelists—Philip, Apollos (8:5, 26; 18:24-28)
4. The book of Acts is in reality a fulfillment of John 15:26-27. "But when the Comforter is come, whom I will send unto you from the Father, even the Spirit

of truth, which proceedeth from the Father, he shall testify of me: And ye also shall bear witness, because ye have been with me from the beginning."

5. Believers were first called Christians during this time (11:26).
6. The preaching of the gospel is viciously attacked by the devil when he attempted to:
   a. Ban it—The Jewish religious leaders (4:18; 5:28)
   b. Buy it—Simon the sorcerer (8:9-11, 18-19)
   c. Bury it—Saul of Tarsus (9:1-2)
   d. Bridle it—The legalists (15:1)
   e. Blur it—The demon-possessed girl (16:16-18)
   f. Belittle it—The Stoics and Epicureans (17:18-21, 32)
   g. Blaspheme it—Demetrius the silversmith (19:24-34)
7. Both angels and demons are seen in action. An angel protects an apostle (Peter, 12:7-8) and plagues a king (Herod, 12:23). Demons possess sorcerers (8:9; 13:6-10), damsels (16:16-18), and vagabonds (19:13-16).
8. Both revivals (19:18-20) and riots break out (19:28-34).
9. The book of Acts lists three significant conversions.
   a. The eunuch (8:36-38), a descendant of Ham (Gen. 10:6-20)
   b. Saul (9:1-6), a descendant of Shem (Gen. 10:21-31)
   c. Cornelius (10:44-48), a descendant of Japheth (Gen. 10:2-5). The convert number jumps from 120 (1:15) to 3,120 (2:41), to 8,120 (4:4), to untold multitudes (5:14).
10. Acts provides for us the final two of five of the most famous New Testament sermons.
    a. The Sermon on the Mount (Matt. 5–7)
    b. The sermon on the kingdom of heaven (Matt. 13)
    c. The sermon on the second coming (Matt. 24–25)
    d. The sermon at Pentecost (Acts 2)
    e. The sermon on Mars Hill (Acts 17)
11. In fact, an outstanding feature of the book of Acts is the number of speeches and sermons. No less than 24 messages are found in its 28 chapters.
12. The book opens with Peter preaching in Jerusalem, the Jewish religious capital, and ends with Paul preaching in Rome, the Gentile political capital (2:14; 28:31).
13. Paul preached before *prison keepers* (16:25-34), *philosophers* (17:16-31), *Pharisees* (23:6), and *potentates* (24:24-25; 26:24-28).
14. The ministry of prayer plays an all-important role in Acts.
    a. The prayers of the apostles
       (1) In the Upper Room (1:14, 24)
       (2) Following Pentecost (2:42)
       (3) In the hour of persecution (4:23-30)
       (4) Upon ordaining the deacons (6:6)
    b. The prayers of Peter and John
       (1) In the temple (3:1)
       (2) At Samaria (8:15)
    c. The prayers of Peter
       (1) At Joppa, at the raising of Dorcas (9:40)
       (2) At Joppa, resulting in his vessel vision (10:9)
    d. The prayer of Cornelius at Caesarea (10:4)

- e. The prayer of the Jerusalem church for Peter (12:12)
- f. The prayer of the Antioch church upon ordaining Saul and Barnabas (13:3)
- g. The prayers of Paul and Barnabas for the churches founded during their missionary journey (14:23)
- h. The prayers of Paul and Silas
    - (1) At Philippi, by a riverside (16:13)
    - (2) At Philippi, inside a prison (16:25)
- i. The prayers of Paul
    - (1) In Damascus following his conversion (9:11)
    - (2) In Jerusalem (22:17)
    - (3) In Miletus (20:36)
    - (4) In Tyre (21:5)
    - (5) On the Isle of Melita (28:8)

15. The books of Luke and Acts may be favorably compared.
    - a. Both were written by the same author, Luke.
    - b. Both were written to the same individual, Theophilus.
    - c. Luke is the longest New Testament book.
    - d. Acts is the second longest New Testament book.
    - e. Luke records the birth of the Son of God.
    - f. Acts records the birth of the Church of God.
    - g. Luke tells us what the Father began to do through the body of his Son (the Savior).
    - h. Acts tells us what the Father continued to do through the body of his Spirit (the saints).
16. Acts 2 and Genesis 11 may be instructively compared.
    - a. In Genesis 11 human language was confused by God.
    - b. In Acts 2 human language was clarified by God.
    - c. In Genesis 11 the builders are seen working for human glory.
    - d. In Acts 2 the believers are seen waiting for God's glory.
17. Acts lists two of nine famous biblical teams.
    - a. Moses and Aaron (Exod. 5:1)
    - b. Joshua and Caleb (Num. 14:6-9)
    - c. Elijah and Elisha (1 Kings 19:19-21)
    - d. Zerubbabel and Joshua (Ezra 3:2)
    - e. Haggai and Zechariah (Ezra 5:1)
    - f. Ezra and Nehemiah (Neh. 8:9)
    - g. Peter and John (Luke 22:7; Acts 3:1)
    - h. Paul and Barnabas/Silas (Acts 13:2; 15:40)
    - i. Elijah and possibly Moses (Rev. 11:3-12)

B. Acts—a Book of Firsts and Lasts

1. In essence, the following may be said about the book of Acts.
    - a. It is a bridge book, which leads across the gap between the Gospel accounts and the epistles.
    - b. We read of several "firsts" and "finals" in Acts.
        - (1) First (in the Bible)
            - (a) First example of tongue speaking (2:1-4)
            - (b) First official religious and political persecution of believers (4:3, 18; 5:17-18, 40)

(c) First practice of commonism (2:44-47) Note: This is a far cry from communism. The first says, "What is mine is thine," while the second says, "What is thine is mine."
(d) First example of sin unto death (5:1-11)
(e) First church election of deacons (6:5-6)
(f) First Christian martyr—Stephen (7:59)
(g) First apostolic martyr—James (12:2)
(h) First view of the ascended Savior (7:55-56)
(i) First missionary journey (13:2-4)

(2) Finals (in the Bible)
(a) Final appearance of God's glory cloud (1:9)
(b) Final mention of Mary (1:14)
(c) Final listing of the 12 apostles (1:13)
(d) Final casting of lots (1:26). Other instances include: to choose the scapegoat (Lev. 16:8); to divide the land (Josh. 18:10); to obtain Christ's garment (Matt. 27:35).

2. Three of the greatest evangelistic meetings in the New Testament were conducted in Acts.
   a. The meeting at Pentecost (2:41)
   b. The meeting in Samaria (8:5-8)
   c. The meeting in Ephesus (19:18-20)
3. Acts 10 is the greatest example showing how God arranges those circumstances to bring together a seeking sinner and a soul winner.
4. Acts 12 gives us the most dramatic New Testament account of an angel ministering to a believer.
5. Acts 15 describes the most important church council ever held.
6. Acts 16 records the most important New Testament vision (vv. 9-10).
7. Acts 16 presents the most dramatic conversion of a Gentile in the Bible (vv. 22-34).
8. Acts 20 records for us the most touching farewell address in the New Testament.
9. Acts 24:25 records one of the saddest responses to the gospel message in the Bible. Compare with Luke 18:23.
10. Acts 27 describes possibly the most severe ocean storm since the great flood.
11. There are quotations or allusions in Acts from 25 Old Testament books. Acts is the second longest New Testament book and 14th longest biblical book, with 28 chapters, 1,007 verses, and 24,250 words.
12. Great passages would include:
    a. 1:8
    b. 1:11
    c. 2:17-21
    d. 2:37-38
    e. 2:41-47
    f. 3:6
    g. 4:11-12
    h. 4:33
    i. 5:29
    j. 7:54-55
    k. 9:3-6

l. 10:34-35
m. 15:15-18
n. 16:30-31
o. 17:31
p. 20:35
q. 24:24-25
r. 26:28

THE BOOK OF ACTS

PART ONE: The Holy Land, Greater Jerusalem Crusade—Headed by Peter the fisherman; assisted by John, Stephen, and Philip (Acts 1–12)

I. The Activities of Peter
  A. Peter and the 120 (Acts 1:1-26)
    1. On the Mount of Olives (Acts 1:1-12)
      a. Receiving the assurance from Christ
        (1) The confusion—"When they therefore were come together, they asked of him, saying, Lord, wilt thou at this time restore again the kingdom to Israel?" (Acts 1:6).

---

†1:6 *The disciples' question here was in direct response to Jesus' prophecy in 1:5 that they would soon be baptized with the Holy Spirit. Stanley Toussaint writes: "In the disciples' minds the outpouring of the Holy Spirit and the coming of the promised kingdom were closely associated. And well they should be, because the Old Testament frequently joined the two (cf. Isa. 32:15-20; 44:3-5; Ezek. 39:28-29; Joel 2:28–3:1; Zech. 12:8-10). When Christ told the disciples of the soon-coming Spirit baptism, they immediately concluded that the resurrection of Israel's kingdom was near in time"* (Bible Knowledge Commentary, *New Testament edition, p. 354).*

---

        (2) The commission—"And he said unto them, It is not for you to know the times or the seasons, which the Father has put in his own power. But ye shall receive power, after that the Holy Ghost is come upon you: and ye shall be witnesses unto me both in Jerusalem, and in all Judaea, and in Samaria, and unto the uttermost part of the earth" (Acts 1:7-8).

---

†1:8
A. We note that they were to be witnesses—not potentates, or psychologists, or promoters—but witnesses.
B. This verse is actually a table of contents and divine outline for the entire book of Acts. Note:
  1. Witnessing in Jerusalem (Acts 1–7)
  2. Witnessing in Judea and Samaria (Acts 8–12)
  3. Witnessing unto the uttermost part of the earth (Acts 13–28)

---

b. Witnessing the ascension of Christ

(1) The action involved—"And when he had spoken these things, while they beheld, he was taken up; and a cloud received him out of their sight" (Acts 1:9).

---

†1:9 *When he had spoken these words, our Lord was taken up by God's shekinah glory cloud. This marks the seventh of at least nine appearances of this dazzling and divine cloud. Note that it appeared:*

A. To Israel en route to Palestine (Exod. 13:21; 14:19-20)
B. Over the tabernacle holy of holies (Lev. 16:2)
C. Over the temple holy of holies (2 Chron. 5:13-14)
D. In Ezekiel's time (Ezek. 10)
E. At the birth of Christ (Luke 2:9-11)
F. At his transfiguration (Matt. 17:5)
G. Here at this ascension (Acts 1:9)
H. It will appear next at the Rapture (1 Thess. 4:17)
I. It will appear again during his second coming (Matt. 24:30).

---

(2) The attendants involved—"And while they looked stedfastly toward heaven as he went up, behold, two men stood by them in white apparel" (Acts 1:10).

(3) The announcement involved—"Which also said, Ye men of Galilee, why stand ye gazing up into heaven? this same Jesus, which is taken up from you into heaven, shall so come in like manner as ye have seen him go into heaven" (Acts 1:11).

---

†1:11 *These two individuals may have been heavenly men (like Moses and Elijah; see Matt. 17:3) or angels (see Luke 24:4; John 20:12). At any rate, we are told several things concerning his return:*

A. The going was personal, and so shall the return be (1 Thess. 4:16).
B. The going was visible, and so shall the return be (Phil. 3:21).
C. The going was from the Mount of Olives, and so shall the return be (Zech. 14:4).

---

2. In the Upper Room (Acts 1:13-26)

a. The prayer meeting (Acts 1:13-14)—"These all continued with one accord in prayer and supplication, with the women, and Mary the mother of Jesus, and with his brethren" (Acts 1:14).

---

†1:14

A. The 11 apostles return to Jerusalem where they join an assembly of believers totaling 120 in a large upper room. This was probably the same upper room where the Last Supper was held (Luke 22:12); and where Jesus appeared to them after his resurrection (John 20:19, 26). It may have been the home of John Mark's mother. (See Acts 12:12.) We are not to believe, however, that the number of disciples was limited at that time to 120 (see 1 Cor. 15:6).

B. We are told that "these [120] all continued with one accord in prayer and supplication" (1:14). The words "with one accord" come from a single Greek word, homothumadon, *meaning "like-mindedness." It is used 12 times in the Greek New Testament, and 11 instances are found in the book of Acts. This word was a favorite with both the people of God and people of Satan.*

1. As used by God's people (2:1; 2:46; 4:24; 5:12; 15:25)

2. As used by Satan's people (7:57; 12:20; 18:12; 19:29)

C. We note, then, that the early believers acted with one accord in matters of:

1. Supplication (1:14)

2. Expectation (2:1)

3. Communication (2:46)

4. Consecration (4:24)

5. Separation (5:12)

6. Cooperation (15:25)

D. Among the 120 were "the women, and Mary, the mother of Jesus, and . . . his brethren" (1:14). Note:

1. The women—A reference to those godly women who had followed Jesus from Galilee. These would include (among many others):

a. Joanna, the wife of Herod's steward (Luke 8:3)

b. Mary and Martha (John 11)

c. Mary, the mother of James the Less (Mark 15:40)

d. Mary Magdalene (Mark 16:9)

e. Salome (Mark 15:40)

f. Susanna (Luke 8:3)

2. Mary, the mother of Jesus (Acts 1:14)—This is the final mention of Mary in the Bible.

3. His brethren—These were Jesus' half brothers (Matt. 13:55; Mark 6:3), who had been unbelievers during his earthly ministry (John 7:3-5) but were now believers. Two of these are thought to have written the New Testament epistles of James and Jude, which bear their names.

---

b. The business meeting (Acts 1:15-26)

(1) Concerning the defection of Judas (Acts 1:15-20)—"For he was numbered with us, and had obtained part of this ministry. For it is written in the book of Psalms, Let his habitation be desolate, and let no man dwell therein: and his bishoprick let another take" (Acts 1:17, 20).

---

†1:20

A. During the prayer meeting Simon Peter discusses the defection and death of Judas, which required the election of a new apostle to take his place (1:15-26).

1. Peter quotes two Old Testament passages to show that the apostasy of Judas demands his replacement. Psalm 69:25 predicted his removal, and 109:8 his replacement. Jesus had already related Judas to Psalm 41:9 (John 13:18-19).

2. It should be noted, however, that it was the defection of Judas and not his death that caused the replacement. No effort was made later to replace the martyred apostle James (see Acts 12:2).

B. The account of Judas's violent end in 1:18—"He burst asunder in the midst and all his bowels gushed out," seems to contradict Matthew 27:5, which starkly says he "hanged himself."

Stanley Toussaint observes: "One explanation is that Judas' intestines quickly became swollen and distended after he hanged himself, so he burst open. Another explanation, more probable, is that Judas hanged himself over a cliff and the rope or branch of the tree he was using broke. When he fell to the rocks below, he burst open" (Bible Knowledge Commentary, *New Testament edition, p. 356).*

---

(2) Concerning the election of Matthias (Acts 1:21-26)—"And they prayed, and said, Thou, Lord, which knowest the hearts of all men, shew whether of these two thou hast chosen, and they gave forth their lots; and the lot fell upon Matthias; and he was numbered with the eleven apostles" (Acts 1:24, 26).

---

†1:26

A. There were two requirements concerning the replacement.

1. The man had to have been a follower of Christ throughout his ministry, and not a recent convert (see John 15:27).

2. He had to have been a witness to the resurrection.

B. At this point, two questions have been asked:

1. Was the method of the election appropriate? We are told the disciples "gave forth their lots" (1:26). How was this carried out? Dr. Charles Ryrie writes: "The two names were put on lots, placed in an urn, and then the one which first fell from the urn was taken to be the Lord's choice" (The Acts of the Apostles, p. 16). This method was in perfect harmony with Old Testament practice. The high priest used this method to choose the scapegoat (Lev. 16:8); and, later, to divide the land of Palestine among the tribes (Num. 26:55).

2. Was the election itself correct? There are those who would say it was in error, that God apparently intended for Paul and not Matthias to become the 12th apostle. However, there is no proof whatsoever of this. The title of apostle was not limited to the 12, for Barnabas (Acts 14:14), James (Gal. 1:19; 1 Cor. 15:7), and Apollos (1 Cor. 4:6-9) were all called apostles also. Apparently it will be Matthias who will be included in the fulfillment of such promises as Matthew 19:28 and Revelation 21:14.

B. Peter and the crowd at Pentecost (Acts 2:1-47)

1. The cloven tongues (Acts 2:1-4)—"And there appeared unto them cloven tongues like as of fire, and it sat upon each of them. And they were all filled with the Holy Ghost, and began to speak with other tongues, as the Spirit gave them utterance" (Acts 2:3-4).

---

†2:1-4

A. This is the first of but four instances of tongue speaking in the entire Bible.

1. The apostles in Jerusalem (Acts 2:4)

2. The Gentiles (Cornelius and his household in Caesarea (Acts 10:46)

3. The disciples of John the Baptist in Ephesus (Acts 19:6)

4. The church members in Corinth (1 Cor. 14)

B. Luke begins by saying, "When the day of Pentecost was fully come" (Acts 2:1). Here is a summary of that historical day.

1. *The chronology of Pentecost. Pentecost (a Greek word which simply means 50) was the third of six great Israelite feasts mentioned in Leviticus 23:*
   a. *The Passover, unleavened bread feast (Lev. 23:4-8, a reference to Calvary)*
   b. *The sheaf of firstfruits (Lev. 23:9-14, a reference to the resurrection)*
   c. *The feast of seven weeks (Lev. 23:15-21, a prophetical reference to Pentecost)*
   d. *The feast of trumpets (Lev. 23:23-35, a reference to the Rapture and second coming of Christ)*
   e. *The feast of atonement (Lev. 16; 23:26-32, a reference to the coming tribulation)*
   f. *The feast of tabernacles (Lev. 23:33-43, a reference to the millennium)*
2. *The comparison of Pentecost*
   a. *New Testament Pentecost may be compared with Old Testament Pentecost. Old Testament Pentecost occurred 50 days after Israel left Egypt. Note: the Passover lamb was slain on April 14, 1491* B.C.*, and Israel left Egypt the next night (Exod. 12:1-2, 6, 12, 31). Exactly 50 days later they arrived at Mt. Sinai during the first week of June (Exod. 19:1).*

      New Testament Pentecost *occurred 50 days after Christ rose from the dead. Note: Our Lord was, of course, crucified during the Passover week in April (John 19:14). He then spent 40 days with his disciples after the resurrection (Acts 1:3). Then, some 10 days later (Acts 1:5; 2:1) New Testament Pentecost occurred.*

      Old Testament Pentecost *celebrated a birthday, that of the nation Israel (Exod. 19:5).*
      New Testament Pentecost *celebrated a birthday, that of the church (Acts 2:41-47).*
      Old Testament Pentecost *witnessed the slaying of some 3,000 souls (Exod. 32:28).*
      New Testament Pentecost *witnessed the saving of some 3,000 souls (Acts 2:41).*
      Old Testament Pentecost *was introduced in a mighty way (Exod. 19)—"And it came to pass on the third day in the morning, that there were thunders and lightnings, and a thick cloud upon the mount, and the voice of the trumpet exceedingly loud, so that all the people that was in the camp trembled, and Mount Sinai was altogether on a smoke, because the Lord descended upon it in fire; and the smoke thereof ascended as the smoke of a furnace, and the whole mount quaked greatly" (Exod. 19:16, 18).*

      New Testament Pentecost *was also introduced in a mighty way—"And when the day of Pentecost was fully come, they were all with one accord in one place. And suddenly there came a sound from heaven as of a rushing mighty wind, and it filled all the house where they were sitting. And there appeared unto them cloven tongues like as of fire, and it sat upon each of them. And they were all filled with the Holy Ghost, and began to speak with other tongues, as the Spirit gave them utterance" (Acts 2:1-4).*
   b. *New Testament Pentecost may be compared to Bethlehem. At Bethlehem, God the Father was preparing a body for his Son to work through—"Wherefore, when he cometh into the world, he saith, Sacrifice and offering thou wouldest not, but a body has thou prepared me" (Heb. 10:5). At Pentecost God the Father was preparing a body for his Spirit to work through—"What? Know ye not that your body is the temple of the Holy Ghost which is in you, which ye have of God, and ye are not your own?" (1 Cor. 6:19).*
   c. *New Testament Pentecost may be compared to Old Testament Babel. At Babel we see sinful people working for their own glory (Gen. 11:4). At Pentecost we see saved people waiting for God's glory (Acts 1:14). At Babel, God confounded human language (Gen. 11:9). At Pentecost God clarified human language (Acts 2:8). At Babel, God scattered people throughout the world (Gen. 11:9). At Pentecost God gathered people within the Church (Eph. 1:10).*

2. The congregation (Acts 2:5-11)—"And they were all amazed and marvelled, saying one to another, Behold, are not all these which speak Galilaeans? And how hear we every man in our own tongue, wherein we were born?" (Acts 2:7-8).
3. The confusion—"And they were all amazed, and were in doubt, saying one to another, What meaneth this? Others mocking said, These men are full of new wine" (Acts 2:12-13).

---

†2:13 *Peter quickly denies this. However, a comparison can be made between being filled with wine and being filled with the Holy Spirit. (See Eph. 5:18.) Note:*

A. Both are the result of a crushing process (see John 7:37-39).
B. Both give a new boldness to the one under their control.
C. Both produce a longing for more.

---

4. The clarification—"But Peter, standing up with the eleven, lifted up his voice, and said unto them, Ye men of Judaea, and all ye that dwell at Jerusalem, be this known unto you, and hearken to my words: For these are not drunken, as ye suppose, seeing it is but the third hour of the day" (Acts 2:14-15).
5. The comparison (Acts 2:16-21)
   a. The Old Testament prophet—"But this is that which was spoken by the prophet Joel" (Acts 2:16).
   b. The Old Testament prophecy—"And it shall come to pass in the last days, saith God, I will pour out of my Spirit upon all flesh: and your sons and your daughters shall prophesy, and your young men shall see visions, and your old men shall dream dreams: and on my servants and on my handmaidens I will pour out in those days of my Spirit; and they shall prophesy: And I will shew wonders in heaven above, and signs in the earth beneath; blood, and fire, and vapour of smoke: The sun shall be turned into darkness, and the moon into blood, before that great and notable day of the Lord come: And it shall come to pass, that whosoever shall call on the name of the Lord shall be saved" (Acts 2:17-21).

---

†2:21 *Peter compares what has just happened with Joel's Old Testament prophecy concerning the visitation of God's Spirit upon all flesh (Joel 2:28-32; cf. Acts 2:16-21). It should, however, be noted that the ultimate fulfillment of Joel's prophecy will occur during the tribulation (Acts 2:19-20; cf. Isa. 13:10; Ezek. 32:7; Matt. 24:29; Rev. 6:12).*

---

6. The condemnation (Acts 2:22-28)
   a. The Messiah had been crucified by his foes (Acts 2:22-24)—"Him, being delivered by the determinate counsel and foreknowledge of God, ye have taken, and by wicked hands have crucified and slain" (Acts 2:23).

---

†2:23 *This is but the first of at least eight occasions in which the Jewish leaders are accused of crucifying their own Messiah.*

A. Peter accuses them (2:23, 36; 3:15; 4:10; 5:30; 10:39).
B. Stephen accuses them (7:52).
C. Paul accuses them (13:28).

---

b. The Messiah had been resurrected by his Father—"Whom God hath raised up, having loosed the pains of death: because it was not possible that he should be holden of it" (Acts 2:24).

---

†2:24 *Both Peter and Paul repeatedly stress that all-important doctrine of Christ's resurrection in the book of Acts.*
A. The references of Peter (2:24, 32; 3:15, 26; 4:10; 5:30; 10:40)
B. The references of Paul (13:30, 33-34, 37; 17:31; 26:23)

---

7. The conclusion (Acts 2:29-36)—"Therefore let all the house of Israel know assuredly, that God hath made that same Jesus, whom ye have crucified, both Lord and Christ" (Acts 2:36).
   a. As predicted by the prophet—"Men and brethren, let me freely speak unto you of the patriarch David, that he is both dead and buried, and his sepulchre is with us unto this day. Therefore being a prophet, and knowing that God had sworn with an oath to him, that of the fruit of his loins, according to the flesh, he would raise up Christ to sit on his throne; he seeing this before spake of the resurrection of Christ, that his soul was not left in hell, neither his flesh did see corruption" (Acts 2:29-31).
   b. As performed by the Father—"This Jesus hath God raised up, whereof we all are witnesses. Therefore being by the right hand of God exalted, and having received of the Father the promise of the Holy Ghost, he hath shed forth this, which ye now see and hear" (Acts 2:32-33).
8. The conviction—"Now when they heard this, they were pricked in their heart, and said unto Peter and to the rest of the apostles, Men and brethren, what shall we do?" (Acts 2:37).

---

†2:37 *Here is the first instance of the convicting ministry of the Holy Spirit as promised by Jesus in John 16:8-9. For other instances, see:*
A. The Samaritans (8:12)
B. Saul (9:18; 22:16)
C. Cornelius (10:47-48)
D. Lydia (16:15)
E. The Philippian jailor (16:33)

---

9. The command—"Then Peter said unto them, Repent, and be baptized every one of you in the name of Jesus Christ for the remission of sins, and ye shall receive the gift of the Holy Ghost. For the promise is unto you, and to your children, and to all that are afar off, even as many as the Lord our God shall call" (Acts 2:38-39).

---

†2:39 *What did Peter mean by his command to be baptized "for the remission of sins"?*

A. It must be remembered that the book of Acts is a dispensational, and therefore, transitional book. This was a message to Israel concerning their national crime of murdering their own Messiah.

B. The preposition eis, *here translated "for," can also be rendered "because of," as it is in Luke 14:35; Matthew 3:11; 12:41.*

C. Whatever Peter meant here, it must be understood that nowhere do the Scriptures teach us that salvation is dependent upon water baptism (1 Cor. 1:27; cf. 15:1-4). Here Paul clearly states what the gospel is, and baptism is definitely not included. Thus, those who insist upon baptismal regeneration literally "rob Paul to pay Peter" (see also 2 Pet. 3:15-16).

---

10. The challenge—"And with many other words did he testify and exhort, saying, Save yourselves from this untoward generation" (Acts 2:40).
11. The conversions—"Then they that gladly received his word were baptized: and the same day there were added unto them about three thousand souls" (Acts 2:41).
12. The communion—"And they continued stedfastly in the apostles' doctrine and fellowship, and in breaking of bread, and in prayers. And all that believed were together, and had all things common" (Acts 2:42, 44).

---

†2:44 *This early system of mutual ownership was commonism, but definitely not communism. Observe the difference:*

A. Commonism says, "What is mine is thine."

B. Communism says, "What is thine is mine."

C. It should be noted that: This system was temporary. It had its problems (Acts 5:1; 6:10). It soon failed (2 Thess. 3:7-10).

C. Peter and the lame man (Acts 3:1-26)
   1. The miracle (Acts 3:1-11)
      a. The need for the healing—"And a certain man lame from his mother's womb was carried, whom they laid daily at the gate of the temple which is called Beautiful, to ask alms of them that entered into the temple" (Acts 3:2).
      b. The name in the healing—"Then Peter said, Silver and gold have I none; but such as I have give I thee: In the name of Jesus Christ of Nazareth rise up and walk" (Acts 3:6).

---

†3:6 *In* A.D. *1260, St. Thomas Aquinas visited the Roman Pope Innocent IV, who showed him all the fabulous wealth of the papacy. After the tour, Innocent said, "So you see, good Thomas, unlike the first pope, I cannot say, 'Silver and gold have I none.'" Aquinas nodded in quiet agreement, and then said softly: "And neither can you say, 'In the name of Jesus Christ of Nazareth, rise up and walk.'"*

---

      c. The new convert after the healing—"And he leaping up stood, and walked, and entered with them into the temple, walking, and leaping, and praising God" (Acts 3:8).

†3:8 *This verse is a reminder of Israel's future golden age, as described by Isaiah: "Then shall the lame man leap as an hart, and the tongue of the dumb sing: for in the wilderness shall waters break out, and streams in the desert" (Isa. 35:6).*

---

2. The message (Acts 3:12-26)—Peter now delivers a powerful sermon on the cross.
   a. The promoters of the cross—The Jews. "The God of Abraham, and of Isaac, and of Jacob, the God of our fathers, hath glorified his Son Jesus; whom ye delivered up, and denied him in the presence of Pilate, when he was determined to let him go. But ye denied the Holy One and the Just, and desired a murderer to be granted unto you; and killed the Prince of life, whom God hath raised from the dead; whereof we are witnesses" (Acts 3:13-15).
   b. The prophecies about the cross—The Old Testament scriptures. "But those things, which God before had shewed by the mouth of all his prophets, that Christ should suffer, he hath so fulfilled" (Acts 3:18).
   c. The power of the cross
      (1) It had healed the body of a man—"And his name through faith in his name hath made this man strong, whom ye see and know: yea, the faith which is by him hath given him this perfect soundness in the presence of you all" (Acts 3:16).
      (2) It could heal the souls of all men—"Unto you first God, having raised up his Son Jesus, sent him to bless you, in turning away every one of you from his iniquities" (Acts 3:26).
   d. The program of the cross (Acts 3:15, 18, 21)
      (1) Christ would suffer and die (Acts 3:18).
      (2) God would raise him from the dead (Acts 3:15).
      (3) He would be taken up for awhile—"Whom the heaven must receive until the times of restitution of all things, which God hath spoken by the mouth of all his holy prophets since the world began" (Acts 3:21).
      (4) He will come again—"Repent ye therefore, and be converted, that your sins may be blotted out, when the times of refreshing shall come from the presence of the Lord; and he shall send Jesus Christ, which before was preached unto you" (Acts 3:19-20).
   e. The plea of the cross (Acts 3:19, 26)—"Repent ye therefore, and be converted, that your sins may be blotted out" (Acts 3:19).

D. Peter and the high priest Annas (Acts 4:1-37)—Annas the high priest has Peter and John arrested.
   1. The reason for the arrest—"Being grieved that they taught the people, and preached through Jesus the resurrection from the dead" (Acts 4:2).
   2. The evidence supporting the arrest—"Howbeit many of them which heard the word believed; and the number of the men was about five thousand" (Acts 4:4).

---

†4:4 *The numerical growth as experienced by the early church was nothing less than supernatural.*
A. It began with 120 (1:15).
B. Then 3,000 were added (2:41).

C. And 5,000 men were added (4:4).
D. Multitudes of men and women were added (5:14).
E. A great number of Jewish priests were added (6:7).

---

3. The dialogue in the arrest
   a. The demand—"And when they had set them in the midst, they asked, By what power, or by what name, have ye done this?" (Acts 4:7).

---

†**4:7** *The Sanhedrin was, here (however impure the motives were), acting within its jurisdiction, for the Mosaic Law specified that whenever someone performed a miracle and used it for the basis of teaching, he was to be examined and stoned, if the teaching was false (Deut. 13:1-5).*

---

   b. The declaration—"Be it known unto you all, and to all the people of Israel, that by the name of Jesus Christ of Nazareth, whom ye crucified, whom God raised from the dead, even by him doth this man stand here before you whole. Neither is there salvation in any other: for there is none other name under heaven given among men, whereby we must be saved" (Acts 4:10, 12).

---

†**4:12** *Peter, filled with the Holy Spirit, tells the assembly that the miracle was performed through the name of the Messiah, whom they had crucified. (Note: Peter's defense here was the first direct fulfillment of Jesus' promise in Matt. 10:16-20. See also Peter's later testimony and advice in 1 Pet. 3:15.) He then associates Jesus with the Old Testament prophecy by showing that Christ is the cornerstone spoken of in Psalm 118:22. Jesus had previously applied this passage to himself (Mark 12:10; 1 Pet. 2:4-8).*

---

4. The conference during the arrest (Acts 4:13-18)
   a. The astonishment—"Now when they saw the boldness of Peter and John, and perceived that they were unlearned and ignorant men, they marvelled; and they took knowledge of them, that they had been with Jesus" (Acts 4:13).
   b. The acknowledgment—"And beholding the man which was healed standing with them, they could say nothing against it. But when they had commanded them to go aside out of the council, they conferred among themselves, saying, What shall we do to these men? for that indeed a notable miracle hath been done by them is manifest to all them that dwell in Jerusalem; and we cannot deny it" (Acts 4:14-16).

---

†**4:16** *There is little doubt that they would have denied it if they could have (Matt. 28:11-15). Not only could they not deny the miracle; neither could they deny Peter's message concerning the resurrection of Christ. There is no record that here or at any other time the Sanhedrin ever attempted to deny the historical fact of Christ's resurrection. It may be said in passing that, concerning the healed cripple, there is no argument against the evidence of a transformed life.*

---

c. The agreement—"But that it spread no further among the people, let us straitly threaten them, that they speak henceforth to no man in this name" (Acts 4:17).

5. The warning accompanying the arrest (Acts 4:18-22)
   a. You can't continue—"And they called them, and commanded them not to speak at all nor teach in the name of Jesus" (Acts 4:18).
   b. We must continue—"But Peter and John answered and said unto them, Whether it be right in the sight of God to hearken unto you more than unto God, judge ye. For we cannot but speak the things which we have seen and heard" (Acts 4:19-20).
6. The praise service following the arrest (Acts 4:23-30)—"And being let go, they went to their own company, and reported all that the chief priests and elders had said unto them. And when they heard that, they lifted up their voice to God with one accord, and said, Lord, thou art God, which hast made heaven, and earth, and the sea, and all that in them is: And now, Lord, behold their threatenings: and grant unto thy servants, that with all boldness they may speak thy word" (Acts 4:23-24, 29).
7. The blessings resulting from the arrest (Acts 4:31-37)
   a. The believers were filled by the Spirit of God—"And when they had prayed, the place was shaken where they were assembled together; and they were all filled with the Holy Ghost, and they spake the word of God with boldness" (Acts 4:31).
   b. The brotherhood was supplied by the grace of God—"And the multitude of them that believed were of one heart and of one soul: neither said any of them that ought of the things which he possessed was his own; but they had all things common. Neither was there any among them that lacked: for as many as were possessors of lands or houses sold them, and brought the prices of the things that were sold, and laid them down at the apostles' feet: and distribution was made unto every man according as he had need" (Acts 4:32, 34-35).

E. Peter and Ananias and Sapphira (Acts 5:1-11)
1. The couple's deception—"But a certain man named Ananias, with Sapphira his wife, sold a possession, and kept back part of the price, his wife also being privy to it, and brought a certain part, and laid it at the apostles' feet" (Acts 5:1-2).

---

†**5:2** *The account here is reminiscent of that of Achan in Joshua 7.*
A. Satan used both Achan and Ananias to attack God's people from within the camp.
B. The sin of both involved greed and lying.
C. Each was confronted and condemned by God's chief leader.
1. Joshua dealt with Achan.
2. Peter dealt with Ananias.
D. Both men, along with their wives, were killed for their sin.
E. Both served as an example (Acts 5:11; 1 Cor. 10:6).

---

2. Their discovery—"But Peter said, Ananias, why hath Satan filled thine heart to lie to the Holy Ghost, and to keep back part of the price of the land? Whiles it

remained, was it not thine own? and after it was sold, was it not in thine own power? why hast thou conceived this thing in thine heart? thou hast not lied unto men, but unto God" (Acts 5:3-4).

---

†**5:4** *The two "whys" used here by Peter strongly support the position that Ananias was a saved man. One does not ask an unsaved person why he commits sin.*

---

3. Their deaths—"And Ananias hearing these words fell down, and gave up the ghost: and great fear came on all them that heard these things. . . . Then fell she down straightway at his feet, and yielded up the ghost: and the young men came in, and found her dead, and, carrying her forth, buried her by her husband" (Acts 5:5, 10).

---

†**5:5** *These two thus become the first recorded believers to commit the sin unto death (see 1 Cor. 11:30-32; 1 John 5:16). Peter perhaps had Ananias and his wife in mind when he later wrote: "For the time is come that judgment must begin at the house of God: and if it first begin at us, what shall the end be of them that obey not the gospel of God?" (1 Pet. 4:17).*

F. Peter and the sick (Acts 5:12-16)—"Insomuch that they brought forth the sick into the streets, and laid them on beds and couches, that at the least the shadow of Peter passing by might overshadow some of them. There came also a multitude out of the cities round about unto Jerusalem, bringing sick folks, and them which were vexed with unclean spirits: and they were healed every one" (Acts 5:15-16).

G. Peter and the lawyer Gamaliel (Acts 5:17-42)—For the second time Peter is arrested for preaching Christ.

1. The anger of the Sadducees—"Then the high priest rose up, and all they that were with him, (which is the sect of the Sadducees,) and were filled with indignation, and laid their hands on the apostles, and put them in the common prison" (Acts 5:17-18).
2. The appearance of the Lord—"But the angel of the Lord by night opened the prison doors, and brought them forth, and said, Go, stand and speak in the temple to the people all the words of this life" (Acts 5:19-20).

---

†**5:20**

A. This is the first of three miracles involving individuals being released from prison in Acts.

1. *The apostles are released (5:19-20).*
2. *Peter is released (12:6-10).*
3. *Paul and Silas are released (16:26-27).*

B. It also marks the first of six angelic appearances in Acts.

1. *An angel frees the apostles from prison (5:19).*
2. *An angel directs Philip to the Gaza desert (8:26).*
3. *An angel instructs Cornelius to send for Peter (10:3, 22).*
4. *An angel frees Peter from death row (12:7).*

5. An angel judges Herod Agrippa I (12:23).
6. An angel encourages Paul during an ocean storm (27:23).

---

3. The astonishment of the jailors—"But when the officers came, and found them not in the prison, they returned, and told, saying, The prison truly found we shut with all safety, and the keepers standing without before the doors: but when we had opened, we found no man within. Then came one and told them, saying, Behold, the men whom ye put in prison are standing in the temple, and teaching the people" (Acts 5:22-23, 25).
4. The accusation of the council—"And when they had brought them, they set them before the council: and the high priest asked them, saying, Did not we straitly command you that ye should not teach in this name? and, behold, ye have filled Jerusalem with your doctrine, and intend to bring this man's blood upon us" (Acts 5:27-28).
5. The address of the apostles
   a. The witness involved—"Then Peter and the other apostles answered and said, We ought to obey God rather than men. The God of our fathers raised up Jesus, whom ye slew and hanged on a tree. Him hath God exalted with his right hand to be a Prince and a Saviour, for to give repentance to Israel, and forgiveness of sins. And we are his witnesses of these things; and so is also the Holy Ghost, whom God hath given to them that obey him" (Acts 5:29-32).

---

†5:32 *Note the expression, "We ought to obey God rather than men" (5: 29). Peter believed in law and order (1 Pet. 2:13-14), but on this occasion had to submit to God's higher law.*

---

   b. The wrath involved—"When they heard that, they were cut to the heart, and took counsel to slay them" (Acts 5:33).
6. The advice of Gamaliel—"Then stood there up one in the council, a Pharisee, named Gamaliel, a doctor of the law, had in reputation among all the people, and commanded to put the apostles forth a little space" (Acts 5:34).
   a. His warning—"And said unto them, Ye men of Israel, take heed to yourselves what ye intend to do as touching these men" (Acts 5:35).
      (1) The first illustration—"For before these days rose up Theudas, boasting himself to be somebody; to whom a number of men, about four hundred, joined themselves: who was slain; and all, as many as obeyed him, were scattered, and brought to nought" (Acts 5:36).
      (2) The second illustration—"After this man rose up Judas of Galilee in the days of the taxing, and drew away much people after him: he also perished; and all, even as many as obeyed him, were dispersed" (Acts 5:37).
   b. His wisdom—"And now I say unto you, Refrain from these men, and let them alone: for if this counsel or this work be of men, it will come to nought: but if it be of God, ye cannot overthrow it; lest haply ye be found even to fight against God" (Acts 5:38-39).

---

†5:39 *A Persian wife once gave similar advice to her wicked husband: "And Haman told Zeresh his wife and all his friends every thing that had befallen him. Then said his wise men and Zeresh his wife unto him, 'If Mordecai be of the seed of the Jews, before whom thou hast begun to fall, thou shalt not prevail against him, but shalt surely fall before him'" (Esther 6:13).*

---

7. The attitude of the apostles (Acts 5:40-42)
    a. Their pain—"And to him they agreed: and when they had called the apostles, and beaten them, they commanded that they should not speak in the name of Jesus, and let them go" (Acts 5:40).
    b. Their praise—"And they departed from the presence of the council, rejoicing that they were counted worthy to suffer shame for his name" (Acts 5:41).
    c. Their persistence—"And daily in the temple, and in every house, they ceased not to teach and preach Jesus Christ" (Acts 5:42).

H. Peter and Simon the Sorcerer (Acts 8:9-25)

1. The pride of Simon—"But there was a certain man, called Simon, which beforetime in the same city used sorcery, and bewitched the people of Samaria, giving out that himself was some great one" (Acts 8:9).
2. The popularity of Simon—"To whom they all gave heed, from the least to the greatest, saying, This man is the great power of God. And to him they had regard, because that of long time he had bewitched them with sorceries" (Acts 8:10-11).
3. The pretense of Simon—"But when they believed Philip preaching the things concerning the kingdom of God, and the name of Jesus Christ, they were baptized, both men and women. Then Simon himself believed also: and when he was baptized, he continued with Philip, and wondered, beholding the miracles and signs which were done" (Acts 8:12-13).
4. The perversion of Simon
    a. The bribe—"And when Simon saw that through laying on of the apostles' hands the Holy Ghost was given, he offered them money" (Acts 8:18).
    b. The blasphemy—"Saying, Give me also this power, that on whomsoever I lay hands, he may receive the Holy Ghost" (Acts 8:19).

---

†8:19 *His action has given to the vocabulary of church history the word "Simony," which denotes the buying and selling of ecclesiastical rights and offices. He was not saved. Jesus himself had previously discounted this kind of false faith (John 2:23-25; 6:26, 66).*

---

5. The problem of Simon
    a. Peter tells Simon what he was doing—"But Peter said unto him, Thy money perish with thee, because thou hast thought that the gift of God may be purchased with money. Thou hast neither part nor lot in this matter: for thy heart is not right in the sight of God. Repent therefore of this thy wickedness, and pray God, if perhaps the thought of thine heart may be forgiven thee" (Acts 8:20-22).

---

†8:20 *In the 1880s the American circus showman and promoter P. T. Barnum attempted to entice the great London Baptist preacher Charles H. Spurgeon to "join his act." Spurgeon would be furnished*

with a huge tent, guaranteed a full house, and paid $1,000 per "preaching performance." All Barnum wanted in return was to pocket the ticket take. Upon receiving this brazen offer, Spurgeon answered as follows:
"Dear Mr. Barnum:
I have before me your offer to come to America. You will find my answer in the book of Acts, Chapter 8 and verse 20.
Very sincerely,
C. H. Spurgeon."
Had the materialistic promoter turned to Acts, he would have read: "Thy money perish with thee, because thou hast thought that the gift of God may be purchased with money."

---

b. Peter tells Simon why he was doing it—"For I perceive that thou art in the gall of bitterness, and in the bond of iniquity" (Acts 8:23).

6. The plea of Simon—"Then answered Simon, and said, Pray ye to the Lord for me, that none of these things which ye have spoken come upon me" (Acts 8:24).

I. Peter and Aeneas (Acts 9:32-35)

1. The misery (Acts 9:32-33)—"And there he found a certain man named Aeneas, which had kept his bed eight years, and was sick of the palsy" (Acts 9:33).

2. The miracle

a. In the physical realm—"And Peter said unto him, Aeneas, Jesus Christ maketh thee whole: arise, and make thy bed. And he arose immediately" (Acts 9:34).

b. In the spiritual realm—"And all that dwelt at Lydda and Saron saw him, and turned to the Lord" (Acts 9:35).

J. Peter and Dorcas (Acts 9:36-42)

1. The deeds of Dorcas—"Now there was at Joppa a certain disciple named Tabitha, which by interpretation is called Dorcas: this woman was full of good works and almsdeeds which she did" (Acts 9:36).

2. The death of Dorcas—"And it came to pass in those days, that she was sick, and died: whom when they had washed, they laid her in an upper chamber" (Acts 9:37).

3. The deliverance of Dorcas—"And forasmuch as Lydda was nigh to Joppa, and the disciples had heard that Peter was there, they sent unto him two men, desiring him that he would not delay to come to them" (Acts 9:38).

a. The grief of the widows—"Then Peter arose and went with them. When he was come, they brought him into the upper chamber: and all the widows stood by him weeping, and shewing the coats and garments which Dorcas made, while she was with them" (Acts 9:39).

b. The gladness of the widows—"But Peter put them all forth, and kneeled down, and prayed; and turning him to the body said, Tabitha, arise. And she opened her eyes: and when she saw Peter, she sat up. And he gave her his hand, and lifted her up, and when he had called the saints and widows, presented her alive. And it was known throughout all Joppa; and many believed in the Lord" (Acts 9:40-42).

---

†9:42 *After raising Dorcas, Peter remains for a while in Joppa at the house of a tanner named Simon. Apparently Peter's attitude toward the restrictions of Judaism was already widening (even though* *he would still need the sheet vision from God); for here he was, staying with a skin tanner. This was an unclean trade in the eyes of the Jews, for it involved the handling of dead bodies (9:43).*

K. Peter and Cornelius (Acts 9:43–10:48)
  1. Cornelius, a religious sinner in Caesarea (Acts 10:1-8)
    a. His veneration for God—"There was a certain man in Caesarea called Cornelius, a centurion of the band called the Italian band, a devout man, and one that feared God with all his house, which gave much alms to the people, and prayed to God alway" (Acts 10:1-2).

---

†10:2 *We are immediately told three things about this man:*
  A. He was a centurion—This would make him commander of 100 Roman soldiers. The various centurions in the New Testament are usually pictured in a good light. (See Matt. 8:5-10; 27:54; Acts 22:25-26; 27:1, 3, 42-44.)
  B. He was devout—He desired to know about God. Jesus had once said: "If any man will to do his will, he shall know of the doctrine . . . of God" (John 7:17).
  C. He was nevertheless lost (cf. Nicodemus, John 3).

---

    b. His visitation from God (Acts 10:3-8)
      (1) The messenger involved—"He saw in a vision evidently about the ninth hour of the day an angel of God coming in to him, and saying unto him, Cornelius. And when he looked on him, he was afraid, and said, What is it, Lord? And he said unto him, Thy prayers and thine alms are come up for a memorial before God" (Acts 10:3-4).
      (2) The message involved—"And now send men to Joppa, and call for one Simon, whose surname is Peter: He lodgeth with one Simon a tanner, whose house is by the sea side: he shall tell thee what thou oughtest to do" (Acts 10:5-6).

---

†10:6 *It can be said that there are three factors necessary for the salvation of a sinner:*
  A. The Spirit of God (John 16:8)
  B. The Word of God (Rom. 10:17)
  C. The soul winner of God (Rom. 1:14)

---

  2. Peter, a reluctant soul winner in Joppa (Acts 10:9-23)—"On the morrow, as they went on their journey, and drew nigh unto the city, Peter went up upon the housetop to pray about the sixth hour: And he became very hungry, and would have eaten: but while they made ready, he fell into a trance" (Acts 10:9-10).
    a. The message of the trance—"And saw heaven opened, and a certain vessel descending unto him, as it had been a great sheet knit at the four corners, and let down to the earth: wherein were all manner of fourfooted beasts of the earth, and wild beasts, and creeping things, and fowls of the air. And there came a voice to him, Rise, Peter; kill, and eat. But Peter said, Not so, Lord; for I have never eaten any thing that is common or unclean" (Acts 10:11-14).

†10:14 *Peter's reply here was in the form of a great contradiction. If he is Lord, one cannot say "Not so"; and if one says, "Not so," he cannot be Lord.*

---

b. The meaning of the trance (Acts 10:15-23)—"And the voice spake unto him again the second time, What God hath cleansed, that call not thou common. This was done thrice: and the vessel was received up again into heaven. Now while Peter doubted in himself what this vision which he had seen should mean, behold, the men which were sent from Cornelius had made inquiry for Simon's house, and stood before the gate, while Peter thought on the vision, the Spirit said unto him, Behold, three men seek thee. Arise therefore, and get thee down, and go with them, doubting nothing: for I have sent them" (Acts 10:15-17, 19-20).

---

†10:20 *It is thrilling to note that God prepares both sinner and soul winner, for whenever he is at work, God leads at both ends of the line. The Lord always prepares us for what he is preparing for us (10:17-21). We note that this marks the second time in history that God sent a Jewish missionary from Joppa to reach some Gentiles. (See also Jonah 1:3.)*

---

3. Peter and Cornelius, redeemed saints in Christ (Acts 10:24-48)
   a. The conversation with Cornelius (Acts 10:24-35)
      (1) The reception—"And as Peter was coming in, Cornelius met him, and fell down at his feet, and worshipped him. But Peter took him up, saying, Stand up; I myself also am a man" (Acts 10:25-26).

---

†10:26 *This is the first of at least four occasions in the New Testament in which a man was forbidden to fall down before anyone (human or angel) other than God.*

A. Paul rebukes the people at Lystra for this—"Then the priest of Jupiter, which was before their city, brought oxen and garlands unto the gates, and would have done sacrifice with the people. Which when the apostles, Barnabas and Paul, heard of, they rent their clothes, and ran in among the people, crying out, and saying, Sirs, why do ye these things? We also are men of like passions with you, and preach unto you that ye should turn from these vanities unto the living God, which made heaven, and earth, and the sea, and all things that are therein" (Acts 14:13-15).

B. An angel rebukes John the apostle on Patmos for this.

1. *First occasion—"And I fell at his feet to worship him. And he said unto me, See thou do it not: I am thy fellowservant, and of thy brethren that have the testimony of Jesus: worship God: for the testimony of Jesus is the spirit of prophecy" (Rev. 19:10).*
2. *Second occasion—"And I John saw these things, and heard them. And when I had heard and seen, I fell down to worship before the feet of the angel which shewed me these things. Then saith he unto me, See thou do it not: for I am thy fellowservant, and of thy brethren the prophets, and of them which keep the sayings of this book: worship God" (Rev. 22:8-9).*

---

(2) The perception—"And he said unto them, Ye know how that it is an unlawful thing for a man that is a Jew to keep company, or come unto one of another nation; but God hath shewed me that I should not call any man common or unclean. . . . Then Peter opened his mouth, and

said, Of a truth I perceive that God is no respecter of persons: But in every nation he that feareth him, and worketh righteousness, is accepted with him" (Acts 10:28, 34-35).

b. The clarification to Cornelius (Acts 10:36-43)—Peter's sermon

(1) He talked about the Word of God—"The word which God sent unto the children of Israel, preaching peace by Jesus Christ: (he is Lord of all:) That word, I say, ye know, which was published throughout all Judaea, and began from Galilee, after the baptism which John preached" (Acts 10:36-37).

(2) He talked about the work of God—"How God anointed Jesus of Nazareth with the Holy Ghost and with power: who went about doing good, and healing all that were oppressed of the devil; for God was with him" (Acts 10:38).

(3) He talked about the witnesses of God—"And we are witnesses of all things which he did both in the land of the Jews, and in Jerusalem; whom they slew and hanged on a tree: Him God raised up the third day, and shewed him openly; not to all the people, but unto witnesses chosen before of God, even to us, who did eat and drink with him after he rose from the dead" (Acts 10:39-41).

(4) He talked about the will of God—"And he commanded us to preach unto the people, and to testify that it is he which was ordained of God to be the Judge of quick and dead. To him give all the prophets witness, that through his name whosoever believeth in him shall receive remission of sins" (Acts 10:42-43).

c. The conversion of Cornelius (Acts 10:44-48)

(1) The divine baptizer—"While Peter yet spake these words, the Holy Ghost fell on all them which heard the word. And they of the circumcision which believed were astonished, as many as came with Peter, because that on the Gentiles also was poured out the gift of the Holy Ghost" (Acts 10:44-45).

(2) The human baptizer—"For they heard them speak with tongues, and magnify God. Then answered Peter, Can any man forbid water, that these should not be baptized, which have received the Holy Ghost as well as we? And he commanded them to be baptized in the name of the Lord. Then prayed they him to tarry certain days" (Acts 10:46-48).

L. Peter and the Jewish believers at Jerusalem (Acts 11:1-18)

1. The accusation (Acts 11:1-3)—"And when Peter was come up to Jerusalem, they that were of the circumcision contended with him, Saying, Thou wentest in to men uncircumcised, and didst eat with them" (Acts 11:2-3).

2. The argumentation (Acts 11:4-17)

a. Peter presents his case—"But Peter rehearsed the matter from the beginning, and expounded it by order unto them, saying, And as I began to speak, the Holy Ghost fell on them, as on us at the beginning. Then remembered I the word of the Lord, how that he said, John indeed baptized with water; but ye shall be baptized with the Holy Ghost" (Acts 11:4, 15-16).

b. Peter presents his conclusion—"Forasmuch then as God gave them the like gift as he did unto us, who believed on the Lord Jesus Christ; what was I, that I could withstand God?" (Acts 11:17).

3. The acceptance—"When they heard these things, they held their peace, and glorified God, saying, Then hath God also to the Gentiles granted repentance unto life" (Acts 11:18).

---

†11:18 *Stanley Toussaint writes: "With Peter the saints recognized that the conversion of Gentiles was initiated by God and that they should not stand in His way. This response had two ensuing and significant results. First, it preserved the unity of the body of Christ, the church. Second, it drove a huge wedge between church-age believers and temple worshippers in Jerusalem. Before this the common Jewish people looked on Christians with favor (cf. 2:47; 5:13, 26), but soon thereafter the Jews opposed the church. This antagonism is attested by Israel's response to the execution of James (12:2-3; cf. 12:11). Perhaps this concourse with Gentiles was a starting point of the Jewish opposition"* (Bible Knowledge Commentary, *New Testament edition, p. 382).*

M. Peter and the angel of the Lord (Acts 12:1-24)

1. The angel in a prison (Acts 12:1-18)

a. The martyrdom of James—"Now about that time Herod the king stretched forth his hands to vex certain of the church. And he killed James the brother of John with the sword" (Acts 12:1-2).

---

†12:2 *King Herod Agrippa I, the murderer of John the Baptist and the ruler who questioned Jesus (Matt. 14:1-12; Luke 23:6-12), suddenly and viciously orders the murder of James the apostle, and puts Peter on death row. James thus becomes the first apostle to die a martyr's death. His death is the only recorded one (with the exception of Judas) among the 12. This execution was no doubt a fulfillment of Matthew 20:23; Mark 10:39. It is believed that James' brother, John, was the last of the 12 to die.*

---

b. The freedom of Peter (Acts 12:3-18)

(1) His success in escaping a prison house—"Peter therefore was kept in prison: but prayer was made without ceasing of the church unto God for him. And when Herod would have brought him forth, the same night Peter was sleeping between two soldiers, bound with two chains: and the keepers before the door kept the prison. And, behold, the angel of the Lord came upon him, and a light shined in the prison: and he smote Peter on the side, and raised him up, saying, Arise up quickly. And his chains fell off from his hands. When they were past the first and the second ward, they came unto the iron gate that leadeth unto the city; which opened to them of his own accord: and they went out, and passed on through one street; and forthwith the angel departed from him" (Acts 12:5-7, 10).

---

†12:6 *On the eve of his scheduled execution Peter is sound asleep in prison. He no doubt had full confidence in Jesus' promise that he would live to be an old man (John 21:18).*

---

(2) His struggle in entering a prayer house—"And when he had considered the thing, he came to the house of Mary the mother of John, whose surname was Mark; where many were gathered together praying. And

as Peter knocked at the door of the gate, a damsel came to hearken, named Rhoda. And when she knew Peter's voice, she opened not the gate for gladness, but ran in, and told how Peter stood before the gate. And they said unto her, Thou art mad. But she constantly affirmed that it was even so. Then said they, It is his angel. But Peter continued knocking: and when they had opened the door, and saw him, they were astonished" (Acts 12:12-16).

---

†12:12 *"This verse introduces the reader to John Mark, who figures prominently in Paul's first missionary journey. Evidently his mother, Mary, was a woman of prominence and means. Probably her house was a principal meeting place of the church, so it must have been spacious. Because John Mark's father is not named, Mary may have been a widow. This same Mark is considered to be the writer of the Gospel bearing his name" (cf. Mark 14:51-52; 1 Pet. 5:13)* (Ibid., *p. 385).*

With some amusement we note that it was far easier for Peter to escape the prison house than to enter this house of prayer! It is ironic but true that often the most surprised people of all, when God performs a miracle, are the very ones who prayed the hardest for it.

---

2. The angel in a palace (Acts 12:19-24)
   a. The particulars—"And Herod was highly displeased with them of Tyre and Sidon: but they came with one accord to him, and, having made Blastus the king's chamberlain their friend, desired peace; because their country was nourished by the king's country. And upon a set day Herod, arrayed in royal apparel, sat upon his throne, and made an oration unto them" (Acts 12:20-21).
   b. The pride—"And the people gave a shout, saying, It is the voice of a god, and not of a man" (Acts 12:22).
   c. The punishment—"And immediately the angel of the Lord smote him, because he gave not God the glory: and he was eaten of worms, and gave up the ghost" (Acts 12:23).

---

†12:23 *Herod Agrippa I should have learned from the historical account of Nebuchadnezzar how God hates and humbles the proud—"The king spake, and said, Is not this great Babylon, that I have built for the house of the kingdom by the might of my power, and for the honour of my majesty? While the word was in the king's mouth, there fell a voice from heaven, saying, O king Nebuchadnezzar, to thee it is spoken; the kingdom is departed from thee. And they shall drive thee from men, and thy dwelling shall be with the beasts of the field: they shall make thee to eat grass as oxen, and seven times shall pass over thee, until thou know that the most High ruleth in the kingdom of men, and giveth it to whomsoever he will" (Dan. 4:30-32).*

N. Peter and the Jerusalem Council (Acts 15)—"And certain men which came down from Judaea taught the brethren, and said, Except ye be circumcised after the manner of Moses, ye cannot be saved. . . . And the apostles and elders came together for to consider of this matter" (Acts 15:1, 6).
   1. His comments—"And when there had been much disputing, Peter rose up, and said unto them, Men and brethren, ye know how that a good while ago God made choice among us, that the Gentiles by my mouth should hear the

word of the gospel, and believe. And God, which knoweth the hearts, bare them witness, giving them the Holy Ghost, even as he did unto us; and put no difference between us and them, purifying their hearts by faith" (Acts 15:7-9).

2. His caution—"Now therefore why tempt ye God, to put a yoke upon the neck of the disciples, which neither our fathers nor we were able to bear?" (Acts 15:10).
3. His conclusion—"But we believe that through the grace of the Lord Jesus Christ we shall be saved, even as they" (Acts 15:11).

II. The Activities of Stephen (Acts 6:1–7:60)

A. The complaint of the leaders (Acts 6:2-4)—"And in those days, when the number of the disciples was multiplied, there arose a murmuring of the Grecians against the Hebrews, because their widows were neglected in the daily ministration" (Acts 6:1).

---

†6:1 *The Grecian Jews were those who could not speak Aramaic, the native tongue of Jews living in Israel. They may have been born and raised outside of Israel, speaking both Greek and their native tongue. This Grecian group may have also included Gentile proselytes to Judaism who later became Christians.*

B. The conference of the leaders (Acts 6:2-4)

1. Their dilemma—"Then the twelve called the multitude of the disciples unto them, and said, It is not reason that we should leave the word of God, and serve tables" (Acts 6:2).

---

†6:2 *The word for tables here is* trapezal, *and often denotes banks, for moneylenders sat at tables to conduct their business (Matt. 21:12). Thus the stated need here was to find some qualified superintendents, and not just mere table waiters and cooks.*

---

2. Their decision—"Wherefore, brethren, look ye out among you seven men of honest report, full of the Holy Ghost and wisdom, whom we may appoint over this business" (Acts 6:3).

---

†6:3

A. Five requirements are listed for this new office.

1. They must be men.
2. They had to be saved.
3. They were to be reputable.
4. They were to be spiritual.
5. They were to possess wisdom.

B. We note that there existed no "double standard" between pastors and the deacons and trustees in the early church.

C. Stanley Toussaint suggests: "Selecting seven men may go back to the tradition in Jewish communities where seven respected men managed the public business in an official council" (Bible Knowledge Commentary, *New Testament edition, p. 367).*

---

3. Their dedication—"But we will give ourselves continually to prayer, and to the ministry of the word" (Acts 6:4).

C. The choice of the laborers (Acts 6:5-7)

1. The individuals—"And the saying pleased the whole multitude: and they chose Stephen, a man full of faith and of the Holy Ghost, and Philip, and Prochorus, and Nicanor, and Timon, and Parmenas, and Nicolas a proselyte of Antioch" (Acts 6:5).

---

†6:5 *All seven had Greek names and may have all come from the Grecian group. If so, this was a gracious gesture to the complainers.*

---

2. The installation—"Whom they set before the apostles: and when they had prayed, they laid their hands on them" (Acts 6:6).

---

†6:6 *The laying on of hands was done in the Bible:*

A. As an act of benediction (Matt. 19:13, 15; Gen. 48:14-20)

B. For the purpose of healing (Mark 5:23; 6:5)

C. To impart the Holy Spirit (Acts 8:17, 19; 9:17)

D. For the purpose of ordination (Acts 6:6; 13:3; 1 Tim. 4:14; 2 Tim. 1:6; Num. 8:9-10)

---

3. The increase—"And the word of God increased; and the number of the disciples multiplied in Jerusalem greatly; and a great company of the priests were obedient to the faith" (Acts 6:7).

---

†6:7 *These Jewish leaders, unlike those described in the Gospel of John, displayed the courage of their convictions. Note the sad account of the former group: "Nevertheless among the chief rulers also many believed on him; but because of the Pharisees they did not confess him, lest they should be put out of the synagogue: For they loved the praise of men more than the praise of God" (John 12:42-43).*

D. The champion of the Lord

1. The maturity of Stephen
   - a. He was a man of faith (Acts 6:5).
   - b. He was controlled by the Spirit (Acts 6:5, 10).
   - c. He possessed divine wisdom (Acts 6:10).
2. The miracles of Stephen—"And Stephen, full of faith and power, did great wonders and miracles among the people" (Acts 6:8).
3. The maligning of Stephen (Acts 6:9-14)—Stephen was viciously slandered by a group of religious men.
   - a. Who they were—"Then there arose certain of the synagogue, which is called the synagogue of the Libertines, and Cyrenians, and Alexandrians, and of them of Cilicia and of Asia, disputing with Stephen" (Acts 6:9).

---

†6:9 *The preaching ministry of Stephen had offended the synagogue of the Libertines, a group of former slaves who apparently had their own synagogue in Jerusalem.*

---

b. What they said—"Then they suborned men, which said, We have heard him speak blasphemous words against Moses, and against God. And they stirred up the people, and the elders, and the scribes, and came upon him, and caught him, and brought him to the council, and set up false witnesses, which said, This man ceaseth not to speak blasphemous words against this holy place, and the law: For we have heard him say, that this Jesus of Nazareth shall destroy this place, and shall change the customs which Moses delivered us" (Acts 6:11-14).

c. Why they said it—"And they were not able to resist the wisdom and the spirit by which he spake" (Acts 6:10).

---

†6:10 *This blessed unanswerable wisdom was a fulfillment of Jesus' words in Luke 21:12-15: "But before all these, they shall lay their hands on you, and persecute you, delivering you up to the synagogues, and into prisons, being brought before kings and rulers for my names sake. And it shall turn to you for a testimony. Settle it therefore in your hearts, not to meditate before what ye shall answer: For I will give you a mouth and wisdom, which all your adversaries shall not be able to gainsay nor resist."*

---

4. The meekness of Stephen—"And all that sat in the council, looking stedfastly on him, saw his face as it had been the face of an angel" (Acts 6:15).

---

†6:15 *This heavenly glow was experienced by Moses in a physical sense and described by Peter in a spiritual sense.*

A. As experienced by Moses—"And it came to pass, when Moses came down from mount Sinai with the two tables of testimony in Moses' hand, when he came down from the mount, that Moses wist not that the skin of his face shone while he talked with him" (Exod. 34:29).

B. As described by Peter—"If ye be reproached for the name of Christ, happy are ye; for the spirit of glory and of God resteth upon you: on their part he is evil spoken of, but on your part he is glorified" (1 Pet. 4:14).

---

5. The message of Stephen (Acts 7:1-53)—As has been seen (Acts 7:13-14), the charge against Stephen was that he had predicted the coming destruction of Israel's second (Herodian) temple. In his defense Stephen points out the following:

a. Israel had been blessed by God even before possession of the first (Solomonic) temple.

(1) God had led Abraham into Canaan (Acts 7:2-8).

(2) God had protected his seed while in Egypt (Acts 7:9-17).

---

†7:17 *At least two apparent discrepancies occur in these verses (7:6-16) during Stephen's address:*

A. Concerning the length of the Egyptian bondage (7:6)—Stephen said it was for 400 years, while Paul gave the time at 430 years (Gal. 3:17). The simplest explanation is that Stephen used round numbers. Stanley Toussaint suggests: "Another explanation is that the 400 years was the actual time of bondage whereas the 430 years described the time from the confirming of the covenant in

Genesis 35:9-15 to the Exodus, which occurred in 1446 B.C." (Bible Knowledge Commentary, *New Testament edition, p. 370).*

B. *Concerning the number in Jacob's family who moved to Egypt (7:14)—Stephen stated the number to be 75, but Moses said it was 70 (Gen. 46:27; Exod. 1:5). One of the most widely accepted solutions is to recognize that Moses includes Jacob, Joseph, and Joseph's two sons, Ephraim and Manasseh (a total of 70); but that Stephen omits Jacob and Joseph but includes Joseph's seven grandchildren (mentioned in 1 Chron. 7:14-15, 20-25).*

---

(3) God had brought them out of Egypt (Acts 7:18-36).

(4) God had led them back into Canaan (Acts 7:37-45).

b. Israel had nevertheless turned from God.

(1) During the days of its first temple—"Yea, ye took up the tabernacle of Moloch, and the star of your god Remphan, figures which ye made to worship them: and I will carry you away beyond Babylon" (Acts 7:43).

---

†7:43

A. *Stephen had apparently been teaching that the Jewish temple was no longer necessary for the worship of the true God. Christ, of course, had already said this (John 4:20-24). To prove his assertion, Stephen pointed out the following facts:*

1. *That God had blessed Abraham and their fathers, even though they had not always lived in Palestine*
2. *That during much of its history while in the land, Israel did not worship God in the temple*
3. *That even the possession of its temple did not save Israel from being rebellious and disobedient*

B. *The purpose of his speech, then, seemed to be to show Israel from her own history that the possession of the temple had been neither a necessity for, nor a guarantee of, the true worship of God.*

---

(2) During the days of her second temple—"Ye stiffnecked and uncircumcised in heart and ears, ye do always resist the Holy Ghost: as your fathers did, so do ye. Which of the prophets have not your fathers persecuted? and they have slain them which shewed before of the coming of the Just One; of whom ye have been now the betrayers and murderers: who have received the law by the disposition of angels, and have not kept it" (Acts 7:51-53).

---

†7:53 *Stephen points out that Israel had rejected Christ (7:52) as that nation had once rejected both Joseph (7:9), and Moses (7:23-29). It is vital to thus observe the following concerning these three persons:*

A. *Both Joseph and Moses, while rejected during their first appearance, were later highly accepted during their second appearance.*

B. *Christ, likewise, was rejected as the Lamb, but will be highly accepted during his second appearance as the Lion.*

---

6. The martyrdom of Stephen (Acts 7:54-60)

a. His persecutors (Acts 7:54, 57-58)

(1) The wickedness involved—"Then they cried out with a loud voice, and stopped their ears, and ran upon him with one accord" (Acts 7:57).
(2) The witness involved—"And cast him out of the city, and stoned him: and the witnesses laid down their clothes at a young man's feet, whose name was Saul" (Acts 7:58).

---

†7:58

A. Here it may be observed that there are three murders in Israel's history that especially mark out her rejection of God's will.
1. The murder of John the Baptist, indicating the rejection of the Father
2. The murder of Christ, showing the rejection of the Son
3. The murder of Stephen, demonstrating the rejection of the Holy Spirit
B. This is the first mention of Saul in the Bible.

---

b. His preview of glory
(1) What he saw—"But he, being full of the Holy Ghost, looked up stedfastly into heaven, and saw the glory of God, and Jesus standing on the right hand of God" (Acts 7:55).

---

†7:55 *Stephen begins his sermon by speaking of the God of glory (7:2); and ends it by seeing the glory of God.*

---

(2) What he said—"And said, Behold, I see the heavens opened, and the Son of man standing on the right hand of God" (Acts 7:56).

---

†7:56

A. Stephen becomes the first of three men to see Jesus after his ascension. The other two are Paul (Acts 9:3-6) and John (Rev. 1:10, 12-16). Note: Stephen saw Jesus standing at God's right hand. This is the only reference to the Savior standing (after his ascension) until one reaches the book of Revelation. In all other descriptions he is said to be seated (See Matt. 26:64; Acts 2:34; Col. 3:1; Eph. 1:20; Heb. 1:3, 13; 8:1; 10:12). Perhaps our Lord rises to welcome his saints home.
B. This verse records the final usage of the name, "Son of man." It was by far the most common name used by the Savior in the Gospels to describe himself.

---

c. His prayers (Acts 7:59-60)
(1) For himself—"And they stoned Stephen, calling upon God, and saying, Lord Jesus, receive my spirit" (Acts 7:59).
(2) For his enemies—"And he kneeled down, and cried with a loud voice, Lord, lay not this sin to their charge" (Acts 7:60a).
d. His passing—"And when he had said this, he fell asleep" (Acts 7:60b).

---

†7:60

A. Stephen dies at the hands of wicked men, as once did his Master.
1. He calls upon God to "receive my spirit" (7:59), as once did Jesus (Luke 23:46).

2. *He prays for his enemies, "Lord, lay not this sin to their charge" (7:60), as once did Jesus (Luke 23:34).*

B. *We are told that, "when he had said this, he fell asleep" (7:60). This is God's description of a believer's death (Matt. 27:52; John 11:11; Acts 13:36; 1 Cor. 15:18, 20, 51; 1 Thess. 4:13-15; 2 Pet. 3:4).*

III. The Activities of Philip (Acts 6:5; 8:5-8, 26-40)
   A. The deacon in Jerusalem—Philip was one of seven men chosen by the early church to serve in the office of a deacon (Acts 6:5).
   B. The evangelist in Samaria (Acts 8:5-8)
      1. His message—"Then Philip went down to the city of Samaria, and preached Christ unto them" (Acts 8:5).

---

†8:5 *We are told that the church at Jerusalem would soon send Peter and John to help Philip in Samaria. The Holy Spirit had done a great work in John's heart, for both he and his brother James had once asked Jesus to call down fire from heaven upon the Samaritans (Luke 9:54).*

---

      2. His miracles—"And the people with one accord gave heed unto those things which Philip spake, hearing and seeing the miracles which he did. For unclean spirits, crying with loud voice, came out of many that were possessed with them: and many taken with palsies, and that were lame, were healed. And there was great joy in that city" (Acts 8:6-8).
   C. The soul winner in Gaza (Acts 8:26-40)
      1. His message from an angel—"And the angel of the Lord spake unto Philip, saying, Arise, and go toward the south unto the way that goeth down from Jerusalem unto Gaza, which is desert" (Acts 8:26).
      2. His ministry to a eunuch
         a. The charge of the eunuch—"And he arose and went: and, behold, a man of Ethiopia, an eunuch of great authority under Candace queen of the Ethiopians, who had the charge of all her treasure, and had come to Jerusalem for to worship" (Acts 8:27).
         b. The confusion of the eunuch
            (1) The passage involved—"Was returning, and sitting in his chariot read Esaias the prophet. The place of the scripture which he read was this, He was led as a sheep to the slaughter; and like a lamb dumb before his shearer, so opened he not his mouth: In his humiliation his judgment was taken away: and who shall declare his generation? for his life is taken from the earth" (Acts 8:28, 32-33).
            (2) The problem involved—"Then the Spirit said unto Philip, Go near, and join thyself to this chariot. And Philip ran thither to him, and heard him read the prophet Esaias, and said, Understandest thou what thou readest? And the eunuch answered Philip, and said, I pray thee, of whom speaketh the prophet this? of himself, or of some other man?" (Acts 8:29-30, 34).

---

†8:31 *Philip asked him if he understood what he was reading. The answer of the eunuch reflects the*

---

tragic condition of all lost sinners: "How can I, except some man should guide me?" (8:31; see Luke 24:32; 45; Rom. 10:13-15, 17).

---

c. The clarification to the Eunuch—"Then Philip opened his mouth, and began at the same scripture, and preached unto him Jesus" (Acts 8:35).

d. The conversion of the eunuch—"And as they went on their way, they came unto a certain water: and the eunuch said, See, here is water; what doth hinder me to be baptized? And Philip said, If thou believest with all thine heart, thou mayest. And he answered and said, I believe that Jesus Christ is the Son of God" (Acts 8:36-37).

e. The confession of the eunuch—"And he commanded the chariot to stand still: and they went down both into the water, both Philip and the eunuch; and he baptized him. And when they were come up out of the water, the Spirit of the Lord caught away Philip, that the eunuch saw him no more: and he went on his way rejoicing" (Acts 8:38-39).

D. The family man in Caesarea—"But Philip was found at Azotus: and passing through he preached in all the cities, till he came to Caesarea" (Acts 8:40).

1. The visitors to Philip's home—"And the next day we that were of Paul's company departed, and came unto Caesarea: and we entered into the house of Philip the evangelist, which was one of the seven; and abode with him" (Acts 21:8).
2. The virgins in Philip's home—"And the same man had four daughters, virgins, which did prophesy" (Acts 21:9).

PART TWO: The Whole Earth, Global Crusade—Headed up by Paul, the tentmaker; assisted by Barnabas, Silas, Timothy, Mark, and Luke (Acts 13–28)

I. The Conversion of Paul (Acts 9:1-19; 22:5-16; 26:12)

A. His vendetta against the saints of God (Acts 9:1-2; 22:4; 26:9-12)

1. Luke's official account of this vendetta—"And Saul, yet breathing out threatenings and slaughter against the disciples of the Lord, went unto the high priest, and desired of him letters to Damascus to the synagogues, that if he found any of this way, whether they were men or women, he might bring them bound unto Jerusalem" (Acts 9:1-2).

---

†**9:2** *This is the first of several instances when believers were referred to as those of "this way." See Acts 19:9, 23; 22:4; 24:14, 22. It doubtless came from Jesus' statement in John 14:6: "Jesus saith unto him, I am the way, the truth, and the life: no man cometh unto the Father, but by me."*

---

2. Paul's personal account of the vendetta—"And I persecuted this way unto the death, binding and delivering into prisons both men and women" (Acts 22:4). "I verily thought with myself, that I ought to do many things contrary to the name of Jesus of Nazareth. Which thing I also did in Jerusalem: and many of the saints did I shut up in prison, having received authority from the chief priests; and when they were put to death, I gave my voice against them. And

I punished them oft in every synagogue, and compelled them to blaspheme; and being exceedingly mad against them, I persecuted them even unto strange cities" (Acts 26:9-11).

B. His vision of the Son of God (Acts 9:3-9; 22:6-11; 26:12-18)

1. What he saw—A blinding light brighter than the noonday sun (Acts 9:3; 22:6; 26:13)

---

†9:3 *He also saw Jesus at this time. (See 9:17, 27; 22:14; 26:16; 1 Cor. 9:1; 15:8.) This marks the first of at least seven instances when Paul saw the ascended Savior. Other occasions were:*

A. At Troas (16:9-10)
B. In Corinth (18:9-10)
C. In Jerusalem, during his first visit as a believer (22:17-21)
D. In Jerusalem, during his final visit (23:11)
E. En route to Rome (27:23-24)
F. When he was caught up into the third heaven (2 Cor. 12:1-4)

---

2. What he heard

a. He heard the Savior saying, "I am the One you have been persecuting" (Acts 9:4-5; 22:7-8; 26:9-15).

---

†9:4 *We note here in 9:4 that to persecute Christians is in reality to persecute Christ. Jesus thus identifies with his people. (See also Matt. 25:31-34; 1 Cor. 12:12-27.)*

---

b. He heard the Savior saying, "I am the One you shall be proclaiming" (Acts 9:6; 22:10; 26:16-18).

(1) The what of the matter—"But rise, and stand upon thy feet: for I have appeared unto thee for this purpose, to make thee a minister and a witness both of these things which thou hast seen, and of those things in the which I will appear unto thee" (Acts 26:16).

(2) The who of the matter—"Delivering thee from the people, and from the Gentiles, unto whom now I send thee" (Acts 26:17).

(3) The why of the matter—"To open their eyes, and to turn them from darkness to light, and from the power of Satan unto God, that they may receive forgiveness of sins, and inheritance among them which are sanctified by faith that is in me" (Acts 26:18).

C. His visitation by a servant of God (Acts 9:10-18; 22:13-16)

1. Ananias and God

a. The revelation to Ananias—"And there was a certain disciple at Damascus, named Ananias; and to him said the Lord in a vision, Ananias. And he said, Behold, I am here, Lord. And the Lord said unto him, Arise, and go into the street which is called Straight, and enquire in the house of Judas for one called Saul, of Tarsus: for, behold, he prayeth, and hath seen in a vision a man named Ananias coming in, and putting his hand on him, that he might receive his sight" (Acts 9:10-12).

†9:12 *These three words, "Behold, he prayeth" (9:11), are in themselves a summary of Paul's life. Here he begins his ministry by prayer, and ends it in the same way. (See 2 Tim. 4:16.) Paul literally prayed anywhere and everywhere about anything and everything. He prayed for sinners and saints, for potentates and prison guards, for Jews and Gentiles, for leaders and laymen. (See the following references: Acts 16:25; 20:36; 21:5; 22:17; 28:8; Rom. 1:9; 10:1; Eph. 1:16; Phil. 1:4, 9; Col. 1:3, 9; 1 Thess. 1:2; 2 Tim. 1:3; Philem. 1:4.)*

---

b. The reluctance by Ananias—"Then Ananias answered, Lord, I have heard by many of this man, how much evil he hath done to thy saints at Jerusalem: and here he hath authority from the chief priests to bind all that call on thy name" (Acts 9:13-14).

---

†9:14 *Ananias' concern over "how much evil he hath done to thy saints" was totally justified. Note the extent of Saul's "much evil" in his war against the church (Acts 7:57-58; 8:1-4; 22:4-5, 19-20; 26:9-11; 1 Cor. 15:9; Gal. 1:13, 22-24; Phil. 3:6; 1 Tim. 1:13):*

A. He "kept the raiment" of those that murdered Stephen, and consented to his death (Acts 7:57-58; 8:1-2; 22:20).
B. He made havoc of the church (Acts 8:3). This word describes the act of a wild hog viciously uprooting a vineyard.
C. He entered the homes of Christians and dragged them out to prison (Acts 8:3).
D. He hounded Christians to their death in various cities (Acts 22:5).
E. He beat believers (Acts 22:19).
F. He voted to have them put to death (Acts 26:10).
G. He attempted through torture to force them into cursing Christ (Acts 26:11).
H. He persecuted the church beyond measure and "wasted it" (Gal. 1:13).

---

c. The reassurance of Ananias—"But the Lord said unto him, Go thy way: for he is a chosen vessel unto me, to bear my name before the Gentiles, and kings, and the children of Israel: For I will shew him how great things he must suffer for my name's sake" (Acts 9:15-16).

---

†9:16 *Note two phrases here:*

A. "He is a chosen vessel." He surely was. In addition, God would make Saul:
  1. A vessel of mercy (Rom. 9:23)
  2. An earthen vessel (2 Cor. 4:7)
  3. A vessel of honor (Rom. 9:21)
  4. A sanctified and worthy vessel (2 Tim. 2:21)

B. "How great things he must suffer for my name's sake"—In a nutshell, this statement would aptly summarize Paul's future life of service for Jesus.
  1. He was plotted against on at least five occasions.
    a. In Damascus (Acts 9:23-25)
    b. In Jerusalem during his first visit as a believer (Acts 9:29)
    c. In Greece (Acts 20:3)
    d. In Jerusalem during his final visit as a believer (Acts 23:10, 12-14)
    e. In Caesarea (Acts 25:2-3)

2. He was at first mistrusted by believers (Acts 9:26).
3. He was disliked by some believers (Phil. 1:14-16).
4. His work for God was constantly opposed by his own countrymen. This was experienced:
  a. In Antioch (Acts 13:45, 50)
  b. In Iconium (Acts 14:2)
  c. In Thessalonica (Acts 17:5)
  d. In Berea (Acts 17:13)
  e. In Corinth (Acts 18:6)
5. He was on one occasion stoned and left for dead (Acts 14:19).
6. He suffered from repeated beatings (2 Cor. 11:24-25; Gal. 6:17).
7. He experienced at least three shipwrecks (2 Cor. 11:25; Acts 27).
8. He was subjected to intense satanic pressure (Acts 13:8; 16:16-18; 1 Thess. 2:18; 2 Cor. 12:7).
9. He was ridiculed (Acts 17:18, 32; 26:24).
10. He was falsely accused on numerous occasions (Acts 18:13; 21:21; 24:5-6).
11. He probably suffered from eye trouble (Gal. 4:13-14; 6:11).
12. He suffered the bite of a poisonous serpent (Acts 28:3-4).
13. He was imprisoned.
  a. In Philippi (Acts 16:24)
  b. In Caesarea (Acts 24:27)
  c. In Rome, for the first time (Acts 28:30)
  d. In Rome, for the final time (2 Tim. 4:6-9)
14. He was acquainted with physical hardships (2 Cor. 6:4-5; 11:27).
15. He was in constant danger (2 Cor. 11:26).
16. He bore the awful pressure of concerns over his beloved churches (2 Cor. 11:28).
17. He was slapped (Acts 23:2).
18. He was nearly torn apart by an angry mob (Acts 21:30-32).
19. He experienced terrible internal pressure (2 Cor. 1:8; 7:5).
20. He was forsaken by his friends in the final hours (2 Tim. 4:10, 16).

---

2. Ananias and Saul
  a. His message for Saul—"And Ananias went his way, and entered into the house; and putting his hands on him said, Brother Saul, the Lord, even Jesus, that appeared unto thee in the way as thou camest, hath sent me, that thou mightest receive thy sight, and be filled with the Holy Ghost" (Acts 9:17).
  b. His ministry to Saul
    (1) Pastoring—"And immediately there fell from his eyes as it had been scales: and he received sight forthwith, and arose, and was baptized" (Acts 9:18).

---

†9:18

A. The conversion of Saul, the second of three great salvation stories in the first section of Acts, vividly illustrates God's desire to redeem all who will but believe.
B. Following the universal flood, God placed all future humanity into three basic groupings, each headed up by one of Noah's three sons, Ham, Shem, and Japheth (Gen. 10:1). Note:

1. In 8:37, the Ethiopian eunuch, a descendant of Ham, is saved.
2. In 9:6, Saul of Tarsus, a descendant of Shem, is saved.
3. In 10:44, Cornelius, a descendant of Japheth, is saved.

---

(2) Predicting—"And he said, The God of our fathers hath chosen thee, that thou shouldest know his will, and see that Just One, and shouldest hear the voice of his mouth. For thou shalt be his witness unto all men of what thou hast seen and heard" (Acts 22:14-15).

II. The Early Ministry of Paul (Acts 9:19-30; 11:24-30; 12:25–13:3; 22:21; Gal. 1:16; 2:1-10)
- A. Preaching in the Damascus synagogues (Acts 9:19-21)
  1. The message—"And when he had received meat, he was strengthened. Then was Saul certain days with the disciples which were at Damascus. And straightway he preached Christ in the synagogues, that he is the Son of God" (Acts 9:19-20).
  2. The marvel—"But all that heard him were amazed, and said; Is not this he that destroyed them which called on this name in Jerusalem, and came hither for that intent, that he might bring them bound unto the chief priests?" (Acts 9:21).
- B. Retiring to the Arabian desert for a period of several years (Gal. 1:16-17)—"Neither went I up to Jerusalem to them which were apostles before me; but I went into Arabia, and returned again unto Damascus" (Gal. 1:17).
- C. Returning to Damascus with greater knowledge and preaching power (Acts 9:22; Gal. 1:17)—"But Saul increased the more in strength, and confounded the Jews which dwelt at Damascus, proving that this is very Christ" (Acts 9:22).
- D. Escaping from Damascus (Acts 9:23-25)
  1. Why he escaped—"And after that many days were fulfilled, the Jews took counsel to kill him: But their laying await was known of Saul. And they watched the gates day and night to kill him" (Acts 9:23-24).
  2. How he escaped—"Then the disciples took him by night, and let him down by the wall in a basket" (Acts 9:25).
- E. Visiting Jerusalem for the first time since his conversion (Acts 9:26-29; Gal. 1:18-19).

---

†9:26 *This marks the first of at least five trips Paul made to Jerusalem after his conversion. The others are:*
A. His second (Acts 11:30)
B. His third (Acts 15:1-30; Gal. 2:1-10)
C. His fourth (Acts 18:21-23)
D. His final (Acts 21:17–23:35)

---

1. The duration of this visit—"Then after three years I went up to Jerusalem to see Peter, and abode with him fifteen days. But other of the apostles saw I none, save James the Lord's brother" (Gal. 1:18-19).
2. The difficulties during this visit (Acts 9:26-29)
   a. The fears—"And when Saul was come to Jerusalem, he assayed to join himself to the disciples: but they were all afraid of him, and believed not that he was a disciple" (Acts 9:26).

b. The fellowship—"But Barnabas took him, and brought him to the apostles, and declared unto them how he had seen the Lord in the way, and that he had spoken to him, and how he had preached boldly at Damascus in the name of Jesus" (Acts 9:27).

F. Escaping from Jerusalem and settling in Tarsus (Acts 9:29-30; 22:17-21; Gal. 1:21)

1. The plot to destroy Paul—"And he spake boldly in the name of the Lord Jesus, and disputed against the Grecians: but they went about to slay him" (Acts 9:29).

2. The plan to deliver Paul

a. The revelation—"And it came to pass, that, when I was come again to Jerusalem, even while I prayed in the temple, I was in a trance; and saw him saying unto me, Make haste, and get thee quickly out of Jerusalem: for they will not receive thy testimony concerning me" (Acts 22:17-18).

b. The regret—"And I said, Lord, they know that I imprisoned and beat in every synagogue them that believed on thee: and when the blood of thy martyr Stephen was shed, I also was standing by, and consenting unto his death, and kept the raiment of them that slew him" (Acts 22:19-20).

c. The reassurance—"And he said unto me, Depart: for I will send thee far hence unto the Gentiles" (Acts 22:21).

G. Joining Barnabas in the work at Antioch (Acts 11:22-26)

1. The origin of the Antioch church

a. The conflict involved—"Now they which were scattered abroad upon the persecution that arose about Stephen travelled as far as Phenice, and Cyprus, and Antioch, preaching the word to none but unto the Jews only. And some of them were men of Cyprus and Cyrene, which, when they were come to Antioch, spake unto the Grecians, preaching the Lord Jesus" (Acts 11:19-20).

b. The converts involved—"And the hand of the Lord was with them: and a great number believed, and turned unto the Lord" (Acts 11:21).

2. The overseers in the Antioch church

a. Barnabas

(1) The missionary of God—"Then tidings of these things came unto the ears of the church which was in Jerusalem: and they sent forth Barnabas, that he should go as far as Antioch. Who, when he came, and had seen the grace of God, was glad, and exhorted them all, that with purpose of heart they would cleave unto the Lord" (Acts 11:22-23).

(2) The man of God—"For he was a good man, and full of the Holy Ghost and of faith: and much people was added unto the Lord" (Acts 11:24).

b. Saul—"Then departed Barnabas to Tarsus, for to seek Saul: and when he had found him, he brought him unto Antioch. And it came to pass, that a whole year they assembled themselves with the church, and taught much people. And the disciples were called Christians first in Antioch" (Acts 11:25-26).

---

†**11:26** *This is the first of three occasions on which believers are called Christians in the Bible. The other two references are:*

A. King Agrippa uses the term (Acts 26:28).

B. Simon Peter uses the term (1 Pet. 4:16).

H. Visiting Jerusalem for the second time carrying a love offering for the needy there (Acts 11:27-30; Gal. 2:1)
   1. The messages from the Spirit of God directing the visit (Acts 11:28; Gal. 2:2)
      a. The revelation to Agabus—"And there stood up one of them named Agabus, and signified by the Spirit that there should be great dearth throughout all the world: which came to pass in the days of Claudius Caesar" (Acts 11:28).
      b. The revelation to Paul (Gal. 2:2)
   2. The meeting with the saints of God during the visit (Gal. 2:9)—"And when James, Cephas, and John, who seemed to be pillars, perceived the grace that was given unto me, they gave to me and Barnabas the right hands of fellowship; that we should go unto the heathen, and they unto the circumcision" (Gal. 2:9).

I. Returning to Antioch to preach and teach the word—"And Barnabas and Saul returned from Jerusalem, when they had fulfilled their ministry, and took with them John, whose surname was Mark. Now there were in the church that was at Antioch certain prophets and teachers; as Barnabas, and Simeon that was called Niger, and Lucius of Cyrene, and Manaen, which had been brought up with Herod the tetrarch, and Saul" (Acts 12:25–13:1).

---

†13:1

A. The ministers in Antioch—This church was blessed to have a number of godly prophets and teachers, five of whom are named. Two deserve special consideration:
   1. Simeon, called Niger—He may have been the Simon of Cyrene mentioned in Mark 15:21. "Niger" means black, indicating he may have been from North Africa.
   2. Manaen—The adjective describing Manaen means foster brother. He and wicked King Herod the Great had apparently once been raised together in the royal court.

B. The missionaries from Antioch—Two of these five are sent out to preach the gospel. "As they ministered to the Lord, and fasted, the Holy Ghost said, Separate me Barnabas and Saul for the work whereunto I have called them. And when they had fasted and prayed, and laid their hands on them, they sent them away" (Acts 13:2-3).
   1. Note what these men were doing at the time. They were ministering to *the Lord. It does not say* for, *but* to *the Lord. What is involved here? In essence, to minister* to *God signifies the* worship *of God. Two examples can be cited at this point:*
      a. The example of King David—"For David said, The LORD *God of Israel hath given rest unto his people, that they may dwell in Jerusalem for ever: and also unto the Levites; they shall no more carry the tabernacle, nor any vessels of it for the service thereof. Because their office was to wait on the sons of Aaron for the service of the house of the* LORD, *in the courts, and in the chambers, and in the purifying of all holy things, and the work of the service of the house of God; and to stand every morning to thank and praise the* LORD, *and likewise at even" (1 Chron. 23:25-26, 28, 30).*
      b. The example of heaven's angels—"And the four beasts had each of them six wings about him; and they were full of eyes within: and they rest not day and night, saying, Holy, holy, holy, Lord God Almighty, which was, and is, and is to come" (Rev. 4:8).
   2. After a hand-laying dedication service, the Antioch church sends forth the world's first Christian foreign missionaries. We note here that the church at Antioch was totally

independent of the Jerusalem church and recognized no ecclesiastical hierarchy whatsoever. A beautiful cooperation is seen here between a local church and the Holy Spirit (13:2-4).

III. The First Missionary Journey of Paul (Acts 13:2–14:2)
  A. First stop, Cyprus (Acts 13:4-12)
    1. Preaching at Salamis, the island's eastern city—"And when they were at Salamis, they preached the word of God in the synagogues of the Jews: and they had also John to their minister" (Acts 13:5).
    2. Preaching at Paphos, the island's western city (Acts 13:6-12)
      a. The openness to the Word of God—"And when they had gone through the isle unto Paphos, they found a certain sorcerer, a false prophet, a Jew, whose name was Bar-jesus: which was with the deputy of the country, Sergius Paulus, a prudent man; who called for Barnabas and Saul, and desired to hear the word of God" (Acts 13:6-7).
      b. The opposition to the Word of God
        (1) The blasphemy of Elymas—"But Elymas the sorcerer (for so is his name by interpretation) withstood them, seeking to turn away the deputy from the faith" (Acts 13:8).
        (2) The blindness of Elymas—"Then Saul, (who also is called Paul,) filled with the Holy Ghost, set his eyes on him, and said, O full of all subtilty and all mischief, thou child of the devil, thou enemy of all righteousness, wilt thou not cease to pervert the right ways of the Lord? And now, behold, the hand of the Lord is upon thee, and thou shalt be blind, not seeing the sun for a season. And immediately there fell on him a mist and a darkness; and he went about seeking some to lead him by the hand" (Acts 13:9-11).
      c. The obedience to the Word of God—"Then the deputy, when he saw what was done, believed, being astonished at the doctrine of the Lord" (Acts 13:12).
  B. Second stop, Perga (Acts 13:13)—John Mark leaves the team at this point.

---

†**13:13** *Stanley Toussaint writes: "What caused Mark to desert is open to speculation: (1) Perhaps he was disillusioned with the change in leadership. After all, Barnabas, the original leader, was John Mark's cousin. (2) The new emphasis on Gentiles may have been too much of an adjustment for a Palestinian Jew like Mark. (3) Possibly he was afraid of the dangerous road over the Taurus Mountains to Antioch which Paul was determined to travel. (4) There is some evidence Paul became quite ill in Perga, possibly with malaria, as the city of Perga was subject to malarial infections. Furthermore, Paul preached to the people of Galatia 'because of an illness' (Gal. 4:13). The missionary party may have gone inland to higher ground to avoid the ravages of malaria and Mark in discouragement over this may have returned home. (5) Some think Mark was homesick. His mother may have been a widow (Acts 12:12); perhaps Mark became lonesome for her and home. Whatever the reason, Paul considered it a defection and a fault (cf. 15:38)"* (Bible Knowledge Commentary, *New Testament edition, p. 388).*

  C. Third stop, Antioch in Pisidia (Acts 13:14-50)—Paul spends several weeks here and preaches two sermons in the synagogues in Antioch.

1. His first sermon (Acts 13:14-43)—It was a sermon about a Savior.
   a. The preparation for this Savior
      (1) Historical preparations—He would come from a special nation.
         (a) God chose a nation—Israel (Acts 13:17).
         (b) He led that nation out of Egypt into Canaan (Acts 13:18-19).
         (c) He sent judges to deliver them (Acts 13:20).
         (d) He chose kings to rule over them (Acts 13:21).
      (2) Prophetical preparations—The Psalms had predicted his death and resurrection (Acts 13:33-37). "God hath fulfilled the same unto us their children, in that he hath raised up Jesus again; as it is also written in the second psalm, Thou art my Son, this day have I begotten thee. Wherefore he saith also in another psalm, Thou shalt not suffer thine Holy One to see corruption" (Acts 13:33, 35).
      (3) Homiletical preparation—John the Baptist had preached sermons on him. "When John had first preached before his coming the baptism of repentance to all the people of Israel. And as John fulfilled his course, he said, Whom think ye that I am? I am not he. But, behold, there cometh one after me, whose shoes of his feet I am not worthy to loose" (Acts 13:24-25).
   b. The identity of this Savior
      (1) He came from the seed of David (Acts 13:23).
      (2) His name is Jesus (Acts 13:23).
   c. The rejection of this Savior (Acts 13:27-29)—"And though they found no cause of death in him, yet desired they Pilate that he should be slain. And when they had fulfilled all that was written of him, they took him down from the tree, and laid him in a sepulchre" (Acts 13:28-29).
   d. The resurrection of this Savior—"But God raised him from the dead: and he was seen many days of them which came up with him from Galilee to Jerusalem, who are his witnesses unto the people. And we declare unto you glad tidings, how that the promise which was made unto the fathers" (Acts 13:30-32).
   e. The salvation from this Savior—"Be it known unto you therefore, men and brethren, that through this man is preached unto you the forgiveness of sins: And by him all that believe are justified from all things, from which ye could not be justified by the law of Moses" (Acts 13:38-39).
2. His second sermon Acts 13:44-50—"And the next sabbath day came almost the whole city together to hear the word of God" (Acts 13:44).
   a. Rejected by the Jewish listeners (Acts 13:45-46, 50)
      (1) The incrimination against Paul—"But when the Jews saw the multitudes, they were filled with envy, and spake against those things which were spoken by Paul, contradicting and blaspheming" (Acts 13:45).
      (2) The indictment by Paul—"Then Paul and Barnabas waxed bold, and said, It was necessary that the word of God should first have been spoken to you: but seeing ye put it from you, and judge yourselves unworthy of everlasting life, lo, we turn to the Gentiles" (Acts 13:46).

---

†13:46 *This statement, first uttered in Antioch of Pisidia, would be repeated at Corinth (Acts 18:6), and at Rome (Acts 28:23-28).*

b. Received by the Gentile listeners (Acts 13:47-49)
(1) They heard God's Word—"For so hath the Lord commanded us, saying, I have set thee to be a light of the Gentiles, that thou shouldest be for salvation unto the ends of the earth" (Acts 13:47).
(2) They honored God's Word—"And when the Gentiles heard this, they were glad, and glorified the word of the Lord: and as many as were ordained to eternal life believed" (Acts 13:48).

D. Fourth stop, Iconium (Acts 13:51–14:5)
1. The revival—"And it came to pass in Iconium, that they went both together into the synagogue of the Jews, and so spake, that a great multitude both of the Jews and also of the Greeks believed. Long time therefore abode they speaking boldly in the Lord, which gave testimony unto the word of his grace, and granted signs and wonders to be done by their hands" (Acts 14:1, 3).
2. The riot—"But the unbelieving Jews stirred up the Gentiles, and made their minds evil affected against the brethren. But the multitude of the city was divided: and part held with the Jews, and part with the apostles" (Acts 14:2, 4).

E. Fifth stop, Lystra (Acts 14:6-23)
1. The cripple—"And there sat a certain man at Lystra, impotent in his feet, being a cripple from his mother's womb, who never had walked" (Acts 14:8).

---

†**14:8** *This marks the final of three occasions in Acts on which a cripple was healed. (See 3:1-10; 9:33-35.)*

---

2. The cure—"The same heard Paul speak: who stedfastly beholding him, and perceiving that he had faith to be healed, said with a loud voice, Stand upright on thy feet. And he leaped and walked" (Acts 14:9-10).
3. The commotion—"And when the people saw what Paul had done, they lifted up their voices, saying in the speech of Lycaonia, The gods are come down to us in the likeness of men" (Acts 14:11).
4. The confusion—"And they called Barnabas, Jupiter; and Paul, Mercurius, because he was the chief speaker" (Acts 14:12).
5. The corruption—"Then the priest of Jupiter, which was before their city, brought oxen and garlands unto the gates, and would have done sacrifice with the people" (Acts 14:13).

---

†**14:13** *The Roman poet Ovid (43 B.C.) records the ancient myth concerning a visit of Zeus and Hermes (two Greek gods) to this area once, disguised as mortals. All turned them away except one old couple. Later a flood supposedly came in judgment and drowned all except this couple. Determining not to make the same mistake, the priest of Jupiter in Lystra prepares to worship the team by the sacrifice of animals and flowers.*

---

6. The consternation—"Which when the apostles, Barnabas and Paul, heard of, they rent their clothes, and ran in among the people, crying out" (Acts 14:14).
7. The correction (Acts 14:15-18)—"And saying, Sirs, why do ye these things? We also are men of like passions with you, and preach unto you that ye should

turn from these vanities unto the living God, which made heaven, and earth, and the sea, and all things that are therein" (Acts 14:15).

8. The condemnation (Acts 14:19-20)
   a. The murder—"And there came thither certain Jews from Antioch and Iconium, who persuaded the people, and, having stoned Paul, drew him out of the city, supposing he had been dead" (Acts 14:19).
   b. The miracle—"Howbeit, as the disciples stood round about him, he rose up, and came into the city: and the next day he departed with Barnabas to Derbe" (Acts 14:20).

---

†14:20 *Some believe Paul actually died here and was then resurrected by God, experiencing at this time his heavenly visit spoken of in 2 Corinthians 12:1-9. However, there is a time problem here, for the stoning occurred in* A.D. *47 or 48 and Paul wrote 2 Corinthians some seven years later in* A.D. *55. But in 2 Corinthians he said the event occurred 14 years prior. At any rate, this may have been where he received the scars he bore for Jesus' sake mentioned in Galatians 6:17. Whether he was dead or simply unconscious, a miracle is seen here; and we get the impression that he immediately rose up, and came into the city (14:20).*

---

9. The confirmation (Acts 14:21-23)—"Confirming the souls of the disciples, and exhorting them to continue in the faith, and that we must through much tribulation enter into the kingdom of God. And when they had ordained them elders in every church, and had prayed with fasting, they commended them to the Lord, on whom they believed" (Acts 14:22-23).

---

†14:23 *Dr. Homer Kent writes: "In each church they visited the believers were organized by the choosing of elders. The word 'ordained' (14:23) translates a Greek term that originally meant to elect by a vote of raised hands. The word also developed the more general sense of 'choose' or 'appoint,' as the compound verb in Acts 10:41 indicates. Does 14:23 mean that Paul and Barnabas appointed the elders for each church, or does the more restricted meaning prevail with the sense that the missionaries established elders in the churches by arranging for congregational elections? Although there is no question but that the term is capable of either meaning, the following factors favor the interpretation of an election: (1) The choice of the verb cheirotoneo rather than one of the many general words for 'appoint' suggests that the special characteristics of this word should be understood. (2) The only other New Testament use of this exact verb is clearly with the sense of a congregational selection (2 Cor. 8:19). (3) Congregational selection was the apostolic practice in the choice of the Seven (Acts 6:3)"* Jerusalem to Rome, *pp. 118-119).*

F. Sixth stop, back to Antioch in Syria (Acts 14:24-28)—"And when they were come, and had gathered the church together, they rehearsed all that God had done with them, and how he had opened the door of faith unto the Gentiles" (Acts 14:27).

IV. The Jerusalem Council, attended by Paul (Acts 15:1-35)
   A. The reason for the council (Acts 15:1-2, 5-6)—"And certain men which came down from Judaea taught the brethren, and said, Except ye be circumcised after the manner of Moses, ye cannot be saved. And the apostles and elders came together for to consider of this matter" (Acts 15:1, 6).

B. The reports given in the council
  1. Peter's report (Acts 15:7-11)
    a. His reminder—"And when there had been much disputing, Peter rose up, and said unto them, Men and brethren, ye know how that a good while ago God made choice among us, that the Gentiles by my mouth should hear the word of the gospel, and believe" (Acts 15:7).
    b. His rebuke—"Now therefore why tempt ye God, to put a yoke upon the neck of the disciples, which neither our fathers nor we were able to bear?" (Acts 15:10).
    c. His rationale—"But we believe that through the grace of the Lord Jesus Christ we shall be saved, even as they" (Acts 15:11).
  2. Paul's report—"Then all the multitude kept silence, and gave audience to Barnabas and Paul, declaring what miracles and wonders God had wrought among the Gentiles by them" (Acts 15:12).
  3. James' report (Acts 15:13-21)
    a. The summary—James summarizes the no-circumcision-for-Gentiles position through two arguments.
      (1) A practical argument—God had already saved Gentiles without the rite of circumcision (Acts 15:14). "Simeon hath declared how God at the first did visit the Gentiles, to take out of them a people for his name" (Acts 15:14).
      (2) A prophetical argument—Amos the prophet had already predicted this would happen (Acts 15:15-18). "And to this agree the words of the prophets; as it is written, After this I will return, and will build again the tabernacle of David, which is fallen down; and I will build again the ruins thereof, and I will set it up: that the residue of men might seek after the Lord, and all the Gentiles, upon whom my name is called, saith the Lord, who doeth all these things" (Acts 15:15-17).
    b. The suggestion (Acts 15:19-21)—"Wherefore my sentence is, that we trouble not them, which from among the Gentiles are turned to God" (Acts 15:19).

---

†15:19 *We note that the final decision was announced not by Simon Peter, but by James, the pastor of the Jerusalem church. Nowhere in the history of the early church is Peter seen exercising ecclesiastical authority over the other apostles. This decision (directed by the Holy Spirit, see v. 28) showed great wisdom, in that it avoided undue and unnecessary offending of the unsaved Jew. (See also 1 Cor. 10:32-33.)*

C. The recommendation of the council (Acts 15:22-29)
  1. Concerning the messengers who carried their recommendation (Acts 15:22-27).
    a. Who they were—"Then pleased it the apostles and elders, with the whole church, to send chosen men of their own company to Antioch with Paul and Barnabas; namely, Judas surnamed Barsabas, and Silas, chief men among the brethren" (Acts 15:22).
    b. What they were—"Men that have hazarded their lives for the name of our Lord Jesus Christ" (Acts 15:26).

2. Concerning the message contained in their recommendation (Acts 15:28-35)—"For it seemed good to the Holy Ghost, and to us, to lay upon you no greater burden than these necessary things; that ye abstain from meats offered to idols, and from blood, and from things strangled, and from fornication: from which if ye keep yourselves, ye shall do well. Fare ye well" (Acts 15:28-29).

D. The return following the council—"So when they were dismissed, they came to Antioch: and when they had gathered the multitude together, they delivered the epistle: Paul also and Barnabas continued in Antioch, teaching and preaching the word of the Lord, with many others also" (Acts 15:30, 35).

V. The Disagreement between Paul and Barnabas (Acts 15:36-40)

A. The background of the disagreement (Acts 15:36-38)—"And Barnabas determined to take with them John, whose surname was Mark. But Paul thought not good to take him with them, who departed from them from Pamphylia, and went not with them to the work" (Acts 15:37-38).

B. The blessing from the disagreement—"And the contention was so sharp between them, that they departed asunder one from the other: and so Barnabas took Mark, and sailed unto Cyprus; and Paul chose Silas, and departed, being recommended by the brethren unto the grace of God" (Acts 15:39-40). Thus, there were now twice as many missionaries on the field. Paul probably wrote Galatians at this time from Antioch.

---

†15:40 *Barnabas takes John Mark and leaves for Cyprus. Happily, the New Testament records that Paul was later reconciled to both Barnabas (1 Cor. 9:6) and John Mark (Col. 4:10; Philem. 24; 2 Tim. 4:11). This is the last mention of Barnabas in the book of Acts.*

VI. The Second Missionary Journey of Paul (Acts 15:41–18:22)

A. First stop, Lystra (Acts 16:1-5)

1. The choosing of Timothy (Acts 16:1-2)
2. The circumcising of Timothy (Acts 16:3)

---

†16:3 *He is circumcised by Paul because he was partly Jewish, so he would not give undue offense to the Jews. Later, Paul would refuse to circumcise Titus, a Gentile (Gal. 2:3). This was an application of Paul's stated principle in 1 Corinthians 9:20.*

B. Second stop, Troas (Acts 16:6-10)

1. Forbidden by the Holy Spirit to go north or south (Acts 16:6-7)
2. Bidden by the Holy Spirit to go west (Acts 16:9-10)

a. The visitation—"And a vision appeared to Paul in the night; there stood a man of Macedonia, and prayed him, saying, Come over into Macedonia, and help us" (Acts 16:9).

b. The verification—"And after he had seen the vision, immediately we endeavoured to go into Macedonia, assuredly gathering that the Lord had called us for to preach the gospel unto them" (Acts 16:10).

†16:10

A. We note that the need alone did not by itself constitute the call. It may be also said that they did not attempt to second-guess God. They had just come from the east; they had been forbidden to go south or north; but still they waited. God's perfect will is not always the easiest thing on earth to find; but once found, it becomes the most blessed. (See Matt. 7:7-8; Luke 11:9-10.)

B. The gospel team leaves immediately for Macedonia, now being joined by the beloved Greek physician, Luke. Acts 16:10 is the first of several "we" sections in this book. (See also 20:5-6; 21:18; 27:1.)

C. Third stop, Philippi (Acts 16:11-40)—At Philippi three tremendous conversions took place.

1. The salvation of a business woman (Acts 16:13-15)
   a. Her business—"And a certain woman named Lydia, a seller of purple of the city of Thyatira" (Acts 16:14a).
   b. Her new birth—"Whose heart the Lord opened that she attended unto the things which were spoken of Paul" (Acts 16:14b).
   c. Her baptism—"And when she was baptized, and her household, she besought us, saying, If ye have judged me to be faithful to the Lord, come into my house, and abide there. And she constrained us" (Acts 16:15).

---

†16:15 *There are at least seven New Testament "household salvation" accounts; that is, the conversion of an individual along with his or her entire family. These persons and their households are:*

A. Cornelius (Acts 10:24, 44)
B. Lydia (Acts 16:15)
C. The Philippian jailer (Acts 16:31)
D. Crispus (Acts 18:8)
E. Aristobulus (Rom. 16:10)
F. Narcissus (Rom. 16:11)
G. Stephanas (1 Cor. 1:16)

---

2. The salvation of a demoniac girl (Acts 16:16-18)
   a. The demon in this girl
      (1) The money it produced through her—"And it came to pass, as we went to prayer, a certain damsel possessed with a spirit of divination met us, which brought her masters much gain by soothsaying" (Acts 16:16).
      (2) The message it proclaimed through her—"The same followed Paul and us, and cried, saying, These men are the servants of the most high God, which shew unto us the way of salvation" (Acts 16:17).

---

†16:17 *Note the cleverness of the demon here who attempted to identify with the message of Paul's true gospel in order to continue deceiving the people with the false gospel propagated through this poor girl.*

---

b. The deliverance of this girl—"And this did she many days. But Paul, being grieved, turned and said to the spirit, I command thee in the name of Jesus Christ to come out of her. And he came out the same hour" (Acts 16:18).

3. The salvation of a prison keeper (Acts 16:19-40)
   a. The charges—"And when her masters saw that the hope of their gains was gone, they caught Paul and Silas, and drew them into the marketplace unto the rulers, and brought them to the magistrates, saying, These men, being Jews, do exceedingly trouble our city, and teach customs, which are not lawful for us to receive, neither to observe, being Romans" (Acts 16:19-21).
   b. The cruelty—"And the multitude rose up together against them: and the magistrates rent off their clothes, and commanded to beat them. And when they had laid many stripes upon them, they cast them into prison, charging the jailor to keep them safely" (Acts 16:22-23).
   c. The confinement—"Who, having received such a charge, thrust them into the inner prison, and made their feet fast in the stocks" (Acts 16:24).
   d. The consternation
      (1) The singing of the prisoners—"And at midnight Paul and Silas prayed, and sang praises unto God: and the prisoners heard them" (Acts 16:25).

---

†**16:25** *We thus have the first sacred concert ever held in Europe. They sang, as did Christ on the eve of his passion (Matt. 26:30; Mark 14:26).*

---

      (2) The shaking of the prison—"And suddenly there was a great earthquake, so that the foundations of the prison were shaken: and immediately all the doors were opened, and every one's bands were loosed" (Acts 16:26).
   e. The command—"And the keeper of the prison awaking out of his sleep, and seeing the prison doors open, he drew out his sword, and would have killed himself, supposing that the prisoners had been fled. But Paul cried with a loud voice, saying, Do thyself no harm: for we are all here" (Acts 16:27-28).
   f. The confusion—"And brought them out, and said, Sirs, what must I do to be saved?" (Acts 16:30).
   g. The clarification—"And they said, Believe on the Lord Jesus Christ, and thou shalt be saved, and thy house" (Acts 16:31).
   h. The conversion
      (1) The jailer's belief in Christ—"And they spake unto him the word of the Lord, and to all that were in his house" (Acts 16:32).
      (2) The jailer's baptism in Christ—"And he took them the same hour of the night, and washed their stripes; and was baptized, he and all his, straightway" (Acts 16:33).
   i. The celebration—"And when he had brought them into his house, he set meat before them, and rejoiced, believing in God with all his house" (Acts 16:34).
   j. The conclusion—"And when it was day, the magistrates sent the serjeants, saying, Let those men go. But Paul said unto them, They have beaten us openly uncondemned, being Romans, and have cast us into prison; and now do they thrust us out privily? nay verily; but let them come

themselves and fetch us out. And the serjeants told these words unto the magistrates: and they feared, when they heard that they were Romans. And they came and besought them, and brought them out, and desired them to depart out of the city" (Acts 16:35, 37-39).

D. Fourth stop, Thessalonica (Acts 17:1-9)
  1. The faithfulness of Paul—"And Paul, as his manner was, went in unto them, and three sabbath days reasoned with them out of the scriptures, opening and alleging, that Christ must needs have suffered, and risen again from the dead; and that this Jesus, whom I preach unto you, is Christ" (Acts 17:2-3).
  2. The fruits of Paul—"And some of them believed, and consorted with Paul and Silas; and of the devout Greeks a great multitude, and of the chief women not a few" (Acts 17:4).
  3. The foes of Paul
    a. Their assaults—"But the Jews which believed not, moved with envy, took unto them certain lewd fellows of the baser sort, and gathered a company, and set all the city on an uproar, and assaulted the house of Jason, and sought to bring them out to the people" (Acts 17:5).
    b. Their accusations—"And when they found them not, they drew Jason and certain brethren unto the rulers of the city, crying, These that have turned the world upside down are come hither also; whom Jason hath received: and these all do contrary to the decrees of Caesar, saying that there is another king, one Jesus" (Acts 17:6-7).

E. Fifth stop, Berea (Acts 17:10-14)
  1. The openness to God's Word
    a. The Bereans researched it—"These were more noble than those in Thessalonica, in that they received the word with all readiness of mind, and searched the scriptures daily, whether those things were so" (Acts 17:11).
    b. The Bereans received it—"Therefore many of them believed; also of honourable women which were Greeks, and of men, not a few" (Acts 17:12).
  2. The opposition to God's Word—"But when the Jews of Thessalonica had knowledge that the word of God was preached of Paul at Berea, they came thither also, and stirred up the people" (Acts 17:13). Timothy and Silas remain in Berea.

F. Sixth stop, Athens (Acts 17:15-34)—Here Paul preached his famous sermon on Mars Hill.
  1. The need for this sermon (Acts 17:16-17)—"Now while Paul waited for them at Athens, his spirit was stirred in him, when he saw the city wholly given to idolatry" (Acts 17:16).
  2. The audience of this sermon (Acts 17:18-21)
    a. Who they were—"Then certain philosophers of the Epicureans, and of the Stoicks, encountered him. And some said, What will this babbler say? other some, He seemeth to be a setter forth of strange gods: because he preached unto them Jesus, and the resurrection" (Acts 17:18).

---

†17:18

A. This first group was named after their founder, Epicurus (341-270 B.C.). They believed that while God existed, he had no interest whatsoever in the welfare of men, and the chief end of life was pleasure. The second group was founded by Zeno (300 B.C.) and believed God was the world's soul which indwelt all things. They held life's goal was to rise above all things and show no emotion whatsoever to either pain or pleasure.

B. Both groups took a dim view of Paul's theology, referring to him as a "babbler" (17:18). This word in Greek is spermologos, *used literally of birds making their nests.*

---

b. What they did—"For all the Athenians and strangers which were there spent their time in nothing else, but either to tell, or to hear some new thing" (Acts 17:21).

---

†17:21 *This may be considered a simplified description of godless, worldly, manmade philosophy. Someone has defined this kind of philosophy as that futile and foolish attempt to learn more and more about less and less until finally one knows everything about nothing.*

---

3. The introduction to this sermon (Acts 17:22)—"Then Paul stood in the midst of Mars' hill, and said, Ye men of Athens, I perceive that in all things ye are too superstitious" (Acts 17:22).
4. The text of this sermon (Acts 17:23)—"For as I passed by, and beheld your devotions, I found an altar with this inscription, TO THE UNKNOWN GOD. Whom therefore ye ignorantly worship, him declare I unto you" (Acts 17:23).
5. The points in this sermon (Acts 17:24-31)
   a. Regarding the past—God was the Creator of all (Acts 17:24-26, 28-29).
   b. Regarding the present—God desires to be the Savior of all (Acts 17:27, 30).
      (1) Providing they reach out (Acts 17:27)—"That they should seek the Lord, if haply they might feel after him, and find him, though he be not far from every one of us" (Acts 17:27).
      (2) Providing they repent—"And the times of this ignorance God winked at; but now commandeth all men everywhere to repent" (Acts 17:30).
   c. Regarding the future—God will judge all people (Acts 17:31). "Because he hath appointed a day, in the which he will judge the world in righteousness by that man whom he hath ordained; whereof he hath given assurance unto all men, in that he hath raised him from the dead" (Acts 17:31).

---

†17:31

A. Paul presents four great truths about God.
   1. He is the Creator (17:24-25).
   2. He is the Governor (17:26-29).
   3. He is the Savior (17:30).
   4. He is the Judge (17:31).

B. During the course of his sermon (17:28) Paul quotes from one of their own heathen poets (Arotus). (See also Titus 1:12.) If this fact of the appointed judgment day were well known, Easter Sunday morning would become the most dreaded day of all the year for unsaved people (see Rev. 20:11-15).

C. Stanley Toussaint observes: "At this point Paul introduced a distinctively Christian viewpoint. His reference to the man *clearly looks to Daniel 7:13-14 which speaks of the Son of man. This One,* appointed *by God the Father, will judge the world with* justice *(cf. John 5:22). The authentication of Christ's person and work was his resurrection. Here again the resurrection of Jesus was preached. The idea of resurrection (cf. Acts 17:18, 32) was incompatible with Greek philosophy. The Greeks wanted to get rid of their bodies, not take them on again. A personal judgment was also unpalatable to Greeks. The gospel message struck at the center of the Athenians' needs.*

Paul (vv. 30-31) discussed the topics of sin ('to repent'), righteousness ('justice'), and judgment ('He will judge'), the same areas in which Jesus said the Holy Spirit would convict people (John 16:5-11)" (Ibid., *p. 404).*

---

6. The reaction to this sermon (Acts 17:32-34)
   a. Some mocked (Acts 17:32).
   b. Some delayed (Acts 17:32).
   c. Some believed (Acts 17:34).

G. Seventh stop, Corinth (Acts 18:1-18)
1. Paul's friends in this city (Acts 18:1-5)
   a. The tentmakers (Acts 18:1-3)—He meets a godly couple, Aquila and Priscilla who, like Paul, were tentmakers by trade.

---

†18:3 *This remarkable couple is mentioned six times in the New Testament. There are inscriptions in the catacombs which hint that Priscilla was of a distinguished family of high standing in Rome. Later in Ephesus a church met in their home (1 Cor. 16:19). In later years, they apparently moved back to Rome (Rom. 16:3-5).*

---

   b. The team members (Acts 18:5)—Silas and Timothy now catch up with Paul from Macedonia.
2. Paul's foes in this city (Acts 18:5-6, 12-17)
   a. Their identity (Acts 18:5)—"Paul was pressed in the spirit, and testified to the Jews that Jesus was Christ" (Acts 18:5).
   b. Their insolence (Acts 18:6)—"And when they opposed themselves, and blasphemed, he shook his raiment, and said unto them, Your blood be upon your own heads; I am clean: from henceforth I will go unto the Gentiles" (Acts 18:6).
   c. Their insurrection (Acts 18:12-17)
      (1) The futility of their efforts (Acts 18:12-16)—They unsuccessfully attempt to indict Paul before Gallio, the Roman deputy.
      (2) The irony of their efforts (Acts 18:17)—"Then all the Greeks took Sosthenes, the chief ruler of the synagogue, and beat him before the judgment seat. And Gallio cared for none of those things" (Acts 18:17).
3. Paul's fruits in this city (Acts 18:8, 11)—"And Crispus, the chief ruler of the synagogue, believed on the Lord with all his house; and many of the Corinthians hearing believed, and were baptized. . . . And he continued there a year and six months, teaching the word of God among them" (Acts 18:8, 11).
4. Paul's heavenly Father in this city (Acts 18:9-10)—"Then spake the Lord to Paul in the night by a vision, Be not afraid, but speak, and hold not thy peace: For I am with thee, and no man shall set on thee to hurt thee: for I have much people in this city" (Acts 18:9-10). *Paul wrote 1 and 2 Thessalonians from Corinth.*

†18:10

A. Every minister and missionary serving in God's perfect will can boldly claim this precious promise concerning their particular field of service.

B. A similar promise is later given to the church in the city of Philadelphia: "I know thy works: behold, I have set before thee an open door, and no man can shut it: for thou hast a little strength, and hast kept my word, and hast not denied my name" (Rev. 3:8).

H. Eighth stop, Ephesus (Acts 18:19-21)
1. He is accompanied by his friends Aquila and Priscilla (Acts 18:18).
2. He is asked by his converts to dwell in Ephesus (Acts 18:20-21)—"But bade them farewell, saying, I must by all means keep this feast that cometh in Jerusalem: but I will return again unto you, if God will. And he sailed from Ephesus" (Acts 18:21).

---

†18:21 *Paul's last phrase here should condition all our plans (see 21:14; 1 Cor. 4:19; 16:7; Heb. 6:3; James 4:15).*

I. Final stop, back to Antioch (Acts 18:22)

VII. The Third Missionary Journey of Paul (Acts 18:23–21:14)

A. First stop, Asia Minor (Acts 18:23)—Paul revisits these churches to exhort and instruct them.

B. Second stop, Ephesus (Acts 18:24–19:41)
1. The forerunner of Paul in Ephesus (Acts 18:24-28)—"And a certain Jew named Apollos, born at Alexandria, an eloquent man, and mighty in the scriptures, came to Ephesus" (Acts 18:24).
   a. The teaching of Apollos (Acts 18:25)—"This man was instructed in the way of the Lord; and being fervent in the spirit, he spake and taught diligently the things of the Lord, knowing only the baptism of John" (Acts 18:25).
   b. The teachers of Apollos—"And he began to speak boldly in the synagogue; whom when Aquila and Priscilla had heard, they took him unto them, and expounded unto him the way of God more perfectly" (Acts 18:26).
2. The fruits of Paul in Ephesus (Acts 19:1-41)
   a. The disciples of John (Acts 19:1-7)—Paul finds 12 disciples of John the Baptist who knew only of the ministry of Christ and nothing of Pentecost. He brings them up to date. "When they heard this, they were baptized in the name of the Lord Jesus. And when Paul had laid his hands upon them, the Holy Ghost came on them; and they spake with tongues, and prophesied" (Acts 19:5-6).

---

†19:6

A. This is the final of three instances in Acts in which individuals spoke in tongues (see 2:1-4 and 10:44-47 for the first two).

B. This is also the only instance in the entire Bible where people were rebaptized.

C. Finally, this marks the last of nine occasions on which individuals were baptized in the book of Acts. The first eight were:

1. *The 3,000 at Pentecost (2:41)*
2. *The believers at Samaria (8:12)*
3. *The Ethiopian eunuch in the desert of Gaza (8:38)*
4. *Saul at Damascus (9:18)*
5. *Cornelius at Caesarea (10:48)*
6. *Lydia and her household at Philippi (16:15)*
7. *The jailer and his household at Philippi (16:33)*
8. *Crispus and his household at Corinth (18:8)*

---

b. The duration with Tyrannus (Acts 19:8-10)—"And he went into the synagogue, and spake boldly for the space of three months, disputing and persuading the things concerning the kingdom of God. But when divers were hardened, and believed not, but spake evil of that way before the multitude, he departed from them, and separated the disciples, disputing daily in the school of one Tyrannus. And this continued by the space of two years; so that all they which dwelt in Asia heard the word of the Lord Jesus, both Jews and Greeks" (Acts 19:8-10).

---

†**19:10** *During this time the churches at Colosse, Laodicea, and Hierapolis were founded (Col. 4:13). It is also possible that all seven churches of Revelation 2–3 were started at this time.*

---

c. The distribution of prayer cloths (Acts 19:11-12)—"And God wrought special miracles by the hands of Paul: so that from his body were brought unto the sick handkerchiefs or aprons, and the diseases departed from them, and the evil spirits went out of them" (Acts 19:11-12).

d. The divinations of Sceva (Acts 19:13-17)—"Then certain of the vagabond Jews, exorcists, took upon them to call over them which had evil spirits the name of the Lord Jesus, saying, We adjure you by Jesus whom Paul preacheth. And there were seven sons of one Sceva, a Jew, and chief of the priests, which did so" (Acts 19:13-14).

(1) The hostile answer by the evil spirit—"And the evil spirit answered and said, Jesus I know, and Paul I know; but who are ye?" (Acts 19:15).

(2) The hostile action by the evil spirit—"And the man in whom the evil spirit was leaped on them, and overcame them, and prevailed against them, so that they fled out of that house naked and wounded" (Acts 19:16).

---

†**19:16** *This is the final of at least 11 New Testament instances of demon-possessed individuals. These are:*

A. *Man of Capernaum, healed by Christ in the synagogue on the Sabbath (Mark 1:24; Luke 4:35)*
B. *Maniac of Gadara, possessed by and healed of a legion of demons (Matt. 8:28-32; Mark 5:2-13; Luke 8:33)*
C. *A mute man healed by Christ, causing the multitudes to rejoice (Matt. 9:32-33)*
D. *A girl from Tyre and Sidon, healed at the request of her heartbroken mother (Matt. 15:28; Mark 7:29)*

E. A boy at the base of Mount Hermon, healed at the request of his heartbroken father (Matt. 17:18; Mark 9:25; Luke 9:42)
F. A blind and deaf man whom Christ was accused of healing by the power of Beelzebub (Matt. 12:22; Luke 11:14)
G. Woman with an 18-year infirmity, healed by Christ in a synagogue on the Sabbath (Luke 13:10-13)
H. Mary Magdalene, healed by Christ of seven demons (Mark 16:9; Luke 8:2)
I. Judas Iscariot, possessed by Satan himself (Luke 22:3; John 6:70; 13:27)
J. A slave girl with powers of divination, healed by Paul at Philippi (Acts 16:16-18)
K. Sceva's sons, renegade Jews at Ephesus (Acts 19:15-16)

---

e. The dedication of the converts (Acts 19:18-20)—"And many that believed came, and confessed, and shewed their deeds. Many of them also which used curious arts brought their books together, and burned them before all men: and they counted the price of them, and found it fifty thousand pieces of silver. So mightily grew the word of God and prevailed" (Acts 19:18-20).
f. The decision of Paul (Acts 19:21-22)—At this time Paul determines to visit Rome someday.
g. The defenders of Diana (Acts 19:23-41)
(1) The libel of Demetrius (Acts 19:23-28)—An anti-Paul meeting is conducted by Demetrius, a silversmith who had profited by making silver shrines for the goddess Diana. At the meeting he said: "Moreover ye see and hear, that not alone at Ephesus, but almost throughout all Asia, this Paul hath persuaded and turned away much people, saying that they be no gods, which are made with hands: so that not only this our craft is in danger to be set at nought; but also that the temple of the great goddess Diana should be despised, and her magnificence should be destroyed, whom all Asia and the world worshippeth" (Acts 19:26-27).

---

†19:27 *The temple of Diana (the Greek name was Artemis) was one of the seven wonders of the ancient world. The image within the temple was of a woman carved with many breasts to signify the fertility of nature. The original stone from which the image had been carved was reported to have fallen from heaven, leading some historians to believe it may have been a meteorite.*

---

(2) The lunacy of the crowd (Acts 19:29-34)—"And the whole city was filled with confusion: and . . . rushed with one accord into the theater" (Acts 19:31). "Some therefore cried one thing, and some another: for the assembly was confused; and the more part knew not wherefore they were come together" (Acts 19:32). For the next two hours this mob screamed out: "Great is Diana of the Ephesians!" (Acts 19:34).
(3) The logic of the town clerk (Acts 19:35-41)—This intelligent Greek official calms down the mob through four logical arguments:
(a) The divinity of the statue (Acts 19:35-36)—"And when the town-clerk had appeased the people, he said, Ye men of Ephesus, what man is there that knoweth not how that the city of the Ephesians is a worshipper of the great goddess Diana, and of the image which fell

down from Jupiter? Seeing then that these things cannot be spoken against, ye ought to be quiet, and to do nothing rashly" (Acts 19:35-36).

---

†**19:36** *This argument was somewhat similar to one once made by Joash, father of Gideon, concerning the Canaanite god Baal (Judg. 6:31). In essence, both were saying, "These are well-known gods, so let them defend themselves."*

(b) The honesty of the opponents (Acts 19:37)—"For ye have brought hither these men, which are neither robbers of churches, nor yet blasphemers of your goddess" (Acts 19:37).

(c) The legality of the matter (Acts 19:38-39)—"Wherefore if Demetrius, and the craftsmen which are with him, have a matter against any man, the law is open, and there are deputies: let them implead one another" (Acts 19:38).

(d) The (possible) hostility of the Romans (Acts 19:40)—"For we are in danger to be called in question for this day's uproar, there being no cause whereby we may give an account of this concourse" (Acts 19:40). *Paul wrote 1 and 2 Corinthians from Ephesus.*

C. Third stop, Greece (Acts 20:1-5)—After a stay of three months he leaves to escape a plot of the Jews to kill him. *Paul wrote Romans from Greece.*

D. Fourth stop, Troas (Acts 20:6-12)

1. The midnight address (Acts 20:7)—"And upon the first day of the week, when the disciples came together to break bread, Paul preached unto them, ready to depart on the morrow; and continued his speech until midnight" (Acts 20:7).

---

†**20:7** *Note: Especially significant in this portion of Scripture is the phrase, "Upon the first day of the week" (20:7). The New Scofield Bible observes: "Although Paul was in Troas seven days (v. 6), apparently neither he nor the local church met for the breaking of bread until the first day of the week (v. 7).*

The fact that Paul and others sometimes attended Sabbath services in Jewish synagogues (17:1-3) does not prove that the apostolic Church kept the seventh day as a special day of worship. It only shows that the early missionaries took the Gospel message wherever and whenever they found people gathered together (5:19-20; 13:5; 16:13, 25-33; 17:17, 19, 22; 18:7; 19:9; 25:6, 23). This witness was carried on daily (2:47; 17:17; 19:9) in every possible way (1 Cor. 9:19-22).

The early churches were specifically warned against submitting themselves to the bondage of any legalistic observance of Sabbath days (Col. 2:16, cf. Gal. 4:9-11). On the other hand, in the exercise of their Christian liberty (Rom. 14:5-6), these same churches voluntarily chose the first day of the week as an appropriate time for fellowship and worship (Acts 20:7; 1 Cor. 16:2), the day on which the Lord arose and repeatedly appeared to his disciples (John 20:19-29). It was a new day for a new people belonging to a new creation (2 Cor. 5:17), a day of commemoration and joy (Matt. 28:9, marg.), service (Matt. 28:10), and spiritual rest (Heb. 4:9-10). This observance of the first day of the week is corroborated by the early fathers: in the writings of Barnabas (c. A.D. 100), Ignatius (A.D. 107), Justin Martyr (A.D. 145-150), and Irenaeus (A.D. 155-202). The edict of Laodicea (fourth century A.D.) did not change the day of worship from the seventh to the first day of the week, as is sometimes alleged, but rather put the stamp of official approval upon an observance already long established in the early churches." (The New Scofield Bible, *pp. 1194-1195*).

---

2. The midmorning accident (Acts 20:8-9)—"And there sat in a window a certain young man named Eutychus, being fallen into a deep sleep: and as Paul was long preaching, he sunk down with sleep, and fell down from the third loft, and was taken up dead" (Acts 20:9).
3. The miraculous awakening (Acts 20:10-12)—"And Paul went down, and fell on him, and embracing him said, Trouble not yourselves; for his life is in him. And they brought the young man alive, and were not a little comforted" (Acts 20:10, 12).

---

†20:12 *This marks the final of eight resurrections in the Bible. This number does not include the resurrection of Christ, nor the ones who arose with him. The eight resurrections are:*

A. *The son of a widow at Zarephath, raised by Elijah (1 Kings 17:22)*
B. *The son of the Shunammite woman, raised by Elisha (2 Kings 4:35)*
C. *A man, raised by Elisha (2 Kings 13:21)*
D. *The son of a widow at Nain, raised by Jesus (Luke 7:14-15)*
E. *The daughter of Jairus, raised by Jesus (Luke 8:54-55)*
F. *Lazarus, at Bethany, raised by Jesus (John 11:44)*
G. *Dorcas, at Joppa, raised by Peter (Acts 9:40)*
H. *Eutychus, at Troas, raised by Paul (Acts 20:12)*

E. Fifth stop, Miletus (Acts 20:13-38)—"And from Miletus he sent to Ephesus, and called the elders of the church" (Acts 20:17).
   1. He reviews the past—"Therefore watch, and remember, that by the space of three years I ceased not to warn every one night and day with tears" (Acts 20:31).
      a. His role as a servant of Christ (Acts 20:19)—"Serving the Lord with all humility of mind, and with many tears, and temptations, which befell me by the lying in wait of the Jews" (Acts 20:19).
      b. His role as a teacher of saints (Acts 20:20, 27)—"And how I kept back nothing that was profitable unto you, but have shewed you, and have taught you publickly, and from house to house, for I have not shunned to declare unto you all the counsel of God" (Acts 20:20, 27).
      c. His role as a witness to sinners (Acts 20:21, 26)—"Testifying both to the Jews, and also to the Greeks, repentance toward God, and faith toward our Lord Jesus Christ. Wherefore I take you to record this day, that I am pure from the blood of all men" (Acts 20:21, 26).

---

†20:26 *He had taught "publickly, and from house to house" the grace of God to sinners and saints alike (20:20-21). It is significant that the world's most famous theologian was also a great soul winner.*

---

      d. His role as an example to all (Acts 20:33-35)—"I have coveted no man's silver, or gold, or apparel. Yea, ye yourselves know, that these hands have ministered unto my necessities, and to them that were with me. I have shewed you all things, how that so labouring ye ought to support the weak, and to remember the words of the Lord Jesus, how he said, It is more blessed to give than to receive" (Acts 20:33-35).

---

†**20:35** *Note: This statement is not found in the four Gospel accounts (although perhaps implied in Luke 14:12). His own life, of course, perfectly exemplified it. (See 2 Cor. 8:9; Eph. 5:2; Phil. 2:5-8; also John 21:25.)*

---

2. He views the present.
   a. Summarizing his situation (Acts 20:22-23, 25)—"And now, behold, I go bound in the spirit unto Jerusalem, not knowing the things that shall befall me there: save that the Holy Ghost witnesseth in every city, saying that bonds and afflictions abide me. And now, behold, I know that ye all, among whom I have gone preaching the kingdom of God, shall see my face no more" (Acts 20:22-23, 25).
   b. Summarizing their situation (Acts 20:28, 32)
      (1) What they were to do (Acts 20:28)—"Take heed therefore unto yourselves, and to all the flock, over the which the Holy Ghost hath made you overseers, to feed the church of God, which he hath purchased with his own blood" (Acts 20:28).
      (2) How they were to do it (Acts 20:32)—"And now, brethren, I commend you to God, and to the word of his grace, which is able to build you up, and to give you an inheritance among all them which are sanctified" (Acts 20:32).
3. He previews the future.
   a. What his desire was (Acts 20:24)—"But none of these things move me, neither count I my life dear unto myself, so that I might finish my course with joy, and the ministry, which I have received of the Lord Jesus, to testify the gospel of the grace of God" (Acts 20:24).
   b. What their dangers would be (Acts 20:29-30)—"For I know this, that after my departing shall grievous wolves enter in among you, not sparing the flock. Also of your own selves shall men arise, speaking perverse things, to draw away disciples after them" (Acts 20:29-30).

---

†**20:30** *Paul later writes Timothy, who is in Ephesus, concerning the "grievous wolves" (1 Tim. 1:3-7). His prophecy concerning apostasy from "your own selves" was tragically fulfilled by men like Hymenaeus, Alexander, Philetus, and others. (See 1 Tim. 1:20; 2 Tim. 2:17.)*

F. Sixth stop, Tyre (Acts 21:1-6)
   1. A message from the Spirit (Acts 21:4)—"And finding disciples, we tarried there seven days: who said to Paul through the Spirit, that he should not go up to Jerusalem" (Acts 21:4).

†21:4

A. *It would seem that the apostle missed God's will here. He had already been warned during the beginning of his ministry by the Lord to: "Make haste, and get thee quickly out of Jerusalem: for they will not receive thy testimony concerning me" (22:18).*

B. *Paul's motive for going to Jerusalem at this time seems to have been his great love for his people (Rom. 9:1-5) and his hope that the gifts of the Gentile churches, sent by him to the poor saints at Jerusalem (Rom. 15:25-28), would open the hearts of the law-bound Jewish believers to the Gospel of God's grace. At any rate, it is very significant that his Jerusalem stop (even though brief) is one of the very few at which absolutely no fruit is recorded.*

---

2. A meeting on the sand (Acts 21:5-6)—"And when we had accomplished those days, we departed and went our way; and they all brought us on our way, with wives and children, till we were out of the city: and we kneeled down on the shore, and prayed" (Acts 21:5).

G. Seventh stop, Ptolemais (Acts 21:7)—"And when we had finished our course from Tyre, we came to Ptolemais, and saluted the brethren, and abode with them one day" (Acts 21:7).

H. Eighth stop, Caesarea (Acts 21:8-14)

1. The warrior of God (Acts 21:8)—"And the next day we that were of Paul's company departed, and came unto Caesarea: and we entered into the house of Philip the evangelist, which was one of the seven; and abode with him" (Acts 21:8).
2. The women of God (Acts 21:9)—"And the same man had four daughters, virgins, which did prophesy" (Acts 21:9).

---

†21:9 *He visits the home of Philip the evangelist and his four unmarried daughters, all of whom are prophetesses. These young women are the last mentioned in the Bible who had this gift. Others were:*

A. *Miriam (Exod. 15:20)*
B. *Deborah (Judg. 4:4)*
C. *Isaiah's wife (Isa. 8:3)*
D. *Huldah (2 Kings 22:14)*
E. *Anna (Luke 2:36)*

---

3. The warning from God (Acts 21:10-11)—"And as we tarried there many days, there came down from Judaea a certain prophet, named Agabus. And when he was come unto us, he took Paul's girdle, and bound his own hands and feet, and said, Thus saith the Holy Ghost, So shall the Jews at Jerusalem bind the man that owneth this girdle, and shall deliver him into the hands of the Gentiles" (Acts 21:10-11).
4. The will of God (Acts 21:12-14)—"And when we heard these things, both we, and they of that place, besought him not to go up to Jerusalem. Then Paul answered, What mean ye to weep and to break mine heart? for I am ready not to be bound only, but also to die at Jerusalem for the name of the Lord Jesus. And when he would not be persuaded, we ceased, saying, The will of the Lord be done" (Acts 21:12-14).

VIII. The Final Visit to Jerusalem by Paul (Acts 21:15-30)

A. The rumors against Paul (Acts 21:18-22, 27-30)

1. That he had denounced the Law of Moses (Acts 21:18-21)—James informs Paul that many Jews were saying this about him. "And they are informed of thee, that thou teachest all the Jews which are among the Gentiles to forsake Moses, saying that they ought not to circumcise their children, neither to walk after the customs" (Acts 21:21).
2. That he had desecrated the temple of God (Acts 21:27-30)—He was incorrectly accused of bringing a Gentile named Trophimus into the temple.

B. The reaction by Paul (Acts 21:23-26)—To counteract these false rumors Paul agrees to put himself back under the Law, shaves his head, and takes a seven-day vow.

C. The rescue of Paul (Acts 21:20-32)—In spite of Paul's efforts the rumors persist and he is set upon by a murderous Jewish mob. "And all the city was moved, and the people ran together: and they took Paul, and drew him out of the temple: and forthwith the doors were shut. And as they went about to kill him, tidings came unto the chief captain of the band, that all Jerusalem was in an uproar. Who immediately took soldiers and centurions, and ran down unto them: and when they saw the chief captain and the soldiers, they left beating of Paul" (Acts 21:30-32).

D. The replies by Paul (Acts 21:33–23:10)

1. His replies to the chief captain

a. First dialogue (Acts 21:33-39)

(1) The captain's confusion—"Art not thou that Egyptian, which before these days madest an uproar, and leddest out into the wilderness four thousand men that were murderers?" (Acts 21:38).

(2) The apostle's correction—"But Paul said, I am a man which am a Jew of Tarsus, a city in Cilicia, a citizen of no mean city: and, I beseech thee, suffer me to speak unto the people" (Acts 21:39).

b. Second dialogue (Acts 22:24-30)

(1) The command of the captain (Acts 22:24)—In an attempt to secure more information, the captain orders Paul to be scourged. The apostle then said: "And as they bound him with thongs, Paul said unto the centurion that stood by, Is it lawful for you to scourge a man that is a Roman, and uncondemned?" (Acts 22:25).

(2) The concern of the captain (Acts 22:28-29)—"And the chief captain answered, With a great sum obtained I this freedom. And Paul said, But I was free born. Then straightway they departed from him which should have examined him: and the chief captain also was afraid, after he knew that he was a Roman, and because he had bound him" (Acts 22:28-29).

2. His reply to the Jewish mob (Acts 21:40–22:23)—"And when he had given him licence, Paul stood on the stairs, and beckoned with the hand unto the people. And when there was made a great silence, he spake unto them in the Hebrew tongue" (Acts 21:40).

a. The speech (Acts 22:1-21)

(1) His conversion (Acts 22:1-16)—"And it came to pass, that, as I made my journey, and was come nigh unto Damascus about noon, suddenly there shone from heaven a great light round about me. And I fell unto the ground, and heard a voice saying unto me, Saul, Saul, why persecutest thou me? And I answered, Who art thou, Lord? And he said unto me, I

am Jesus of Nazareth, whom thou persecutest. . . . And I said, What shall I do, Lord? And the Lord said unto me, Arise, and go into Damascus; and there it shall be told thee of all things which are appointed for thee to do" (Acts 22:6-8, 10).

---

†*Paul continues relating his salvation experience and meeting with Ananias, as first recorded in Acts 9:15-17. Here though, before this Jewish mob, Paul includes a comment made by Ananias not found in the original account: "And now why tarriest thou? arise, and be baptized, and wash away thy sins, calling on the name of the Lord" (Acts 22:16).*

Stanley Toussaint writes: "Two questions revolve about this verse. First, when was Paul saved—on the Damascus Road or at Judas' house? Several factors suggest he was saved on the Damascus Road: (1) The gospel was presented to him directly by Christ (Gal. 1:11-12), not later by Ananias. (2) Already (Acts 22:10) Paul said he had submitted in faith to Christ. (3) Paul was filled with the Spirit before *his baptism with water (9:17-18). (4) The Greek aorist participle,* epikalesamenos, *translated* calling on His name *refers either to action, which is simultaneous with, or before that of the main verb. Here Paul's calling on Christ's name (for salvation) preceded His water baptism. The participle may be translated, 'having called on His name.'*

"Second, what then do the words wash your sins away *mean? Do they teach that salvation comes by water baptism? Because Paul was already cleansed spiritually [see comments in preceding paragraph], these words must refer to the symbolism of baptism. Baptism is a picture of God's inner work of washing away sin (cf. 1 Cor. 6:11; 1 Pet. 3:21)"* (Ibid., *p. 418).*

---

(2) His call (Acts 22:17-21)—"And it came to pass, that, when I was come again to Jerusalem, even while I prayed in the temple, I was in a trance; and saw him saying unto me, Make haste, and get thee quickly out of Jerusalem: for they will not receive thy testimony concerning me. And he said unto me, Depart: for I will send thee far hence unto the Gentiles" (Acts 22:17-18, 21).

b. The screams (Acts 22:22-23)—"And they gave him audience unto this word, and then lifted up their voices, and said, Away with such a fellow from the earth: for it is not fit that he should live. And as they cried out, and cast off their clothes, and threw dust into the air" (Acts 22:22-23).

3. His reply to the Sanhedrin (Acts 23:1-10)

a. The reprisal (Acts 23:1-2)—"And Paul, earnestly beholding the council, said, Men and brethren, I have lived in all good conscience before God until this day. And the high priest Ananias commanded them that stood by him to smite him on the mouth" (Acts 23:1-2).

b. The retaliation (Acts 23:3)—"Then said Paul unto him, God shall smite thee, thou whited wall: for sittest thou to judge me after the law, and commandest me to be smitten contrary to the law?" (Acts 23:3).

---

†**23:3** *The phrase "whited wall" suggested a tottering wall whose precarious position had been disguised by a generous coat of whitewash. The meaning was that, although he held a high position, he would someday fall. In fact, he was assassinated some eight years later.*

---

c. The regret (Acts 23:4-5)—"And they that stood by said, Revilest thou God's high priest? Then said Paul, I wist not, brethren, that he was the high priest: for it is written, Thou shalt not speak evil of the ruler of thy people" (Acts 23:4-5).

d. The ruse (Acts 23:6-10)—"But when Paul perceived that the one part were Sadducees, and the other Pharisees, he cried out in the council, Men and brethren, I am a Pharisee, the son of a Pharisee: of the hope and resurrection of the dead I am called in question. And when he had so said, there arose a dissension between the Pharisees and the Sadducees: and the multitude was divided. For the Sadducees say that there is no resurrection, neither angel, nor spirit: but the Pharisees confess both. And there arose a great cry: and the scribes that were of the Pharisees' part arose, and strove, saying, We find no evil in this man: but if a spirit or an angel hath spoken to him, let us not fight against God. And when there arose a great dissension, the chief captain, fearing lest Paul should have been pulled in pieces of them, commanded the soldiers to go down, and to take him by force from among them, and to bring him into the castle" (Acts 23:6-10).

E. The revelation to Paul (Acts 23:11)—"And the night following the Lord stood by him, and said, Be of good cheer, Paul: for as thou hast testified of me in Jerusalem, so must thou bear witness also at Rome" (Acts 23:11).

---

†23:11 *Paul had often hoped to get to Rome (Rom. 1:13). In Ephesus he had made definite plans to go, but at this point he was not sure he would get away from Jerusalem alive (Rom. 15:31-32). But now, for the first time, God had said it.*

F. The revenge against Paul (Acts 23:12-15)—"And when it was day, certain of the Jews banded together, and bound themselves under a curse, saying that they would neither eat nor drink till they had killed Paul. And they were more than forty which had made this conspiracy. And they came to the chief priests and elders, and said, We have bound ourselves under a great curse, that we will eat nothing until we have slain Paul. Now therefore ye with the council signify to the chief captain that he bring him down unto you to-morrow, as though ye would enquire something more perfectly concerning him: and we, or ever he come near, are ready to kill him" (Acts 23:12-15).

G. The relative of Paul (Acts 23:16-22)

1. Overhearing the plot against his uncle—"And when Paul's sister's son heard of their lying in wait, he went and entered into the castle, and told Paul" (Acts 23:16).
2. Overturning the plot against his uncle—"Then Paul called one of the centurions unto him, and said, Bring this young man unto the chief captain: for he hath a certain thing to tell him. Then the chief captain took him by the hand, and went with him aside privately, and asked him, What is that thou hast to tell me? And he said, The Jews have agreed to desire thee that thou wouldest bring down Paul to morrow into the council, as though they would enquire somewhat of him more perfectly" (Acts 23:17, 19-20).

H. The removal of Paul (Acts 23:23-32)

1. The soldiers (Acts 23:23-24)—"And he called unto him two centurions, saying,

Make ready two hundred soldiers to go to Caesarea, and horsemen threescore and ten, and spearmen two hundred, at the third hour of the night; and provide them beasts, that they may set Paul on, and bring him safe unto Felix the governor" (Acts 23:23-24).

2. The salutation (Acts 23:25-32)—The chief captain wrote a letter to Felix explaining the circumstances surrounding Paul's arrest.

IX. The Imprisonment of Paul in Caesarea (Acts 23:33–26:32)

A. Paul before Felix (Acts 23:33–24:27)

1. Felix reviews a lawsuit against Paul—"Who, when they came to Caesarea, and delivered the epistle to the governor, presented Paul also before him. . . . I will hear thee, said he, when thine accusers are also come. And he commanded him to be kept in Herod's judgment hall" (Acts 23:33, 35).

---

†23:35

A. Both officially and personally, Felix was noted for his evil deeds. Tacitus, the Roman historian, writes: "Felix, indulging in every kind of barbarity and lust, exercised the power of a king in the spirit of a slave." Felix was later guilty of having the Jewish high priest Jonathan (Annas's son) assassinated.

B. He is one of three Roman procurators referred to in the New Testament. The others are:

1. Pontius Pilate (Matt. 27:2)

2. Porcius Festus (Acts 24:27)

---

a. The defamation by the prosecution—"And after five days Ananias the high priest descended with the elders, and with a certain orator named Tertullus, who informed the governor against Paul" (Acts 24:1). This articulate Jewish lawyer accused Paul of three things.

(1) That he was a political rebel—"For we have found this man a pestilent fellow, and a mover of sedition . . . throughout the world" (Acts 24:5a).

(2) That he was a religious heretic—"and a ringleader of the sect of the Nazarenes" (Acts 24:5b).

(3) That he desecrated the temple—"Who also hath gone about to profane the temple" (Acts 24:6a).

b. The defense by the prisoner

(1) Paul pleads innocent concerning charges 1 and 3—"Because that thou mayest understand, that there are yet but twelve days since I went up to Jerusalem for to worship. And they neither found me in the temple disputing with any man, neither raising up the people, neither in the synagogues, nor in the city: Neither can they prove the things whereof they now accuse me" (Acts 24:11-13).

(2) Paul pleads guilty concerning charge number 2—"But this I confess unto thee, that after the way which they call heresy, so worship I the God of my fathers, believing all things which are written in the law and in the prophets: and have hope toward God, which they themselves also allow, that there shall be a resurrection of the dead, both of the just and unjust. And herein do I exercise myself, to have always a conscience void of offence toward God, and toward men. Or else let these same here say, if

they have found any evil doing in me, while I stood before the council, except it be for this one voice, that I cried standing among them, touching the resurrection of the dead I am called in question by you this day" (Acts 24:14-16, 20-21).

c. The decision by the politician—"And when Felix heard these things, having more perfect knowledge of that way, he deferred them, and said, When Lysias the chief captain shall come down, I will know the uttermost of your matter. And he commanded a centurion to keep Paul, and to let him have liberty, and that he should forbid none of his acquaintance to minister or come unto him" (Acts 24:22-23).

2. Felix refuses a lecture delivered by Paul—"And after certain days, when Felix came with his wife Drusilla, which was a Jewess, he sent for Paul, and heard him concerning the faith in Christ. And as he reasoned of righteousness, temperance, and judgment to come, Felix trembled, and answered, Go thy way for this time; when I have a convenient season, I will call for thee" (Acts 24:24-25).

---

†24:25

A. *Both Felix and Drusilla are affected by Paul's preaching. This girl, not yet 20, is the youngest daughter of Herod Agrippa I (murderer of James, Acts 12:1-2), and the sister of Agrippa II and Bernice, mentioned in 25:13. She had left a pagan Syrian king to marry Felix. (Drusilla died 21 years later in the eruption of Mt. Vesuvius.)*

B. *Felix thought he could call upon God in a "convenient season," a time, of course, which never comes. (See Prov. 27:1; Luke 12:16-20; James 4:13-14.)*

---

3. Felix requests some lucre (money) from Paul—"He hoped also that money should have been given him of Paul, that he might loose him: wherefore he sent for him the oftener, and communed with him" (Acts 24:26).

B. Paul before Festus (Acts 25:1-12)

1. Festus and the plotters

a. Their ungodly plan—"Now when Festus was come into the province, after three days he ascended from Caesarea to Jerusalem. Then the high priest and the chief of the Jews informed him against Paul, and besought him, and desired favour against him, that he would send for him to Jerusalem, laying wait in the way to kill him" (Acts 25:1-3).

b. Their unsuccessful plan—"But Festus answered, that Paul should be kept at Caesarea, and that he himself would depart shortly thither. Let them therefore, said he, which among you are able, go down with me, and accuse this man, if there be any wickedness in him. And when he had tarried among them more than ten days, he went down unto Caesarea; and the next day sitting on the judgment seat commanded Paul to be brought" (Acts 25:4-6).

2. Festus and the prisoner

a. The accusations—"And when he was come, the Jews which came down from Jerusalem stood round about, and laid many and grievous complaints against Paul, which they could not prove" (Acts 25:7).

b. The answer—"While he answered for himself, Neither against the law of the Jews, neither against the temple, nor yet against Caesar, have I offended any thing at all" (Acts 25:8).
c. The appeasement—"But Festus, willing to do the Jews a pleasure, answered Paul, and said, Wilt thou go up to Jerusalem, and there be judged of these things before me?" (Acts 25:9).
d. The appeal—"Then said Paul, I stand at Caesar's judgment seat, where I ought to be judged: to the Jews have I done no wrong, as thou very well knowest. For if I be an offender, or have committed any thing worthy of death, I refuse not to die: but if there be none of these things whereof these accuse me, no man may deliver me unto them. I appeal unto Caesar" (Acts 25:10-11).

---

†**25:11** *The Caesar to whom Paul appeals is Nero, who began his reign in* A.D. *54. His early years were gentle in nature and gave no hint of the cruelties which would follow.*

---

e. The agreement—"Then Festus, when he had conferred with the council, answered, Hast thou appealed unto Caesar? unto Caesar shalt thou go" (Acts 25:12).

C. Paul before Agrippa (Acts 25:13–26:32)

1. Learning about Paul—"And after certain days King Agrippa and Bernice came unto Caesarea to salute Festus. And when they had been there many days, Festus declared Paul's cause unto the king, saying, There is a certain man left in bonds by Felix: about whom, when I was at Jerusalem, the chief priests and the elders of the Jews informed me, desiring to have judgment against him" (Acts 25:13-15).

---

†**25:13** *Stanley Toussaint writes: "The King Agrippa referred to here was Agrippa II, son of Herod Agrippa I (Acts 12:1) and a great-grandson of Herod the Great (Matt. 2:1). At this time he was a young man of about 30 years of age and the ruler of territories northeast of Palestine with the title of King. Because he was a friend of the Roman imperial family he was awarded the privilege of appointing the Jewish high priest and also had been made the custodian of the temple treasury. His background made him eminently qualified to hear Paul; he was well acquainted with the Jews' religion (cf. Acts 25:26-27). Agrippa II and his sister Bernice came to Caesarea to pay their respects to Festus. Though Bernice had a tendency to support the Jews, she lived a profligate life. She had an incestuous relationship with Agrippa, her brother"* (Ibid., *p. 423).*

---

2. Listening to Paul
   a. The pomp involved—"And on the morrow, when Agrippa was come, and Bernice, with great pomp, and was entered into the place of hearing, with the chief captains, and principal men of the city, at Festus' commandment Paul was brought forth" (Acts 25:23).
   b. The permission involved—"Then Agrippa said unto Paul, Thou art permitted to speak for thyself. Then Paul stretched forth the hand, and answered for himself" (Acts 26:1).

c. The preaching involved
(1) Paul reviews his life as a religious man—"My manner of life from my youth, which was at the first among mine own nation at Jerusalem, know all the Jews; which knew me from the beginning, if they would testify, that after the most straitest sect of our religion I lived a Pharisee. . . . I verily thought with myself, that I ought to do many things contrary to the name of Jesus of Nazareth. Which thing I also did in Jerusalem: and many of the saints did I shut up in prison, having received authority from the chief priests; and when they were put to death, I gave my voice against them. And I punished them oft in every synagogue, and compelled them to blaspheme; and being exceedingly mad against them, I persecuted them even unto strange cities" (Acts 26:4-5, 9-11).
(2) Paul reviews his life as a redeemed man—"Whereupon as I went to Damascus with authority and commission from the chief priests, at midday, O king, I saw in the way a light from heaven, above the brightness of the sun, shining round about me and them which journeyed with me. And when we were all fallen to the earth, I heard a voice speaking unto me, and saying in the Hebrew tongue, Saul, Saul, why persecutest thou me? it is hard for thee to kick against the pricks. And I said, Who art thou, Lord? And he said, I am Jesus whom thou persecutest. But rise, and stand upon thy feet: for I have appeared unto thee for this purpose, to make thee a minister and a witness both of these things which thou hast seen, and of those things in the which I will appear unto thee; delivering thee from the people, and from the Gentiles, unto whom now I send thee, to open their eyes, and to turn them from darkness to light, and from the power of Satan unto God, that they may receive forgiveness of sins, and inheritance among them which are sanctified by faith that is in me. Whereupon, O king Agrippa, I was not disobedient unto the heavenly vision" (Acts 26:12-19).

d. The protest involved—"And as he thus spake for himself, Festus said with a loud voice, Paul, thou art beside thyself; much learning doth make thee mad. But he said, I am not mad, most noble Festus; but speak forth the words of truth and soberness" (Acts 26:24-25).

e. The persuasion involved—"For the king knoweth of these things, before whom also I speak freely: for I am persuaded that none of these things are hidden from him; for this thing was not done in a corner. King Agrippa, believest thou the prophets? I know that thou believest. Then Agrippa said unto Paul, Almost thou persuadest me to be a Christian. And Paul said, I would to God, that not only thou, but also all that hear me this day, were both almost, and altogether such as I am, except these bonds" (Acts 26:26-29).

---

†**26:29** *Note: It cannot be determined from this verse that Agrippa was at the point of accepting Christ. The Greek text reads: "In short, you are trying to persuade me to be a Christian." The king may have meant he could not be convinced in such a brief period of time.*

---

f. The postscript involved—"And when he had thus spoken, the king rose up, and the governor, and Bernice, and they that sat with them: And when they were gone aside, they talked between themselves, saying, This man doeth nothing worthy of death or of bonds. Then said Agrippa unto Festus, This man might have been set at liberty, if he had not appealed unto Caesar" (Acts 26:30-32). *Paul may have written Hebrews at this time in Caesarea.*

X. The Voyage of Paul to Rome (Acts 27:1–28:15)

A. Phase one—From Caesarea to Fair Havens (Acts 27:1-12)

1. Julius's kindness to Paul (Acts 27:1, 3)—"And when it was determined that we should sail into Italy, they delivered Paul and certain other prisoners unto one named Julius, a centurion of Augustus' band. And the next day we touched at Sidon. And Julius courteously entreated Paul, and gave him liberty to go unto his friends to refresh himself" (Acts 27:1, 3).

2. Paul's caution to Julius (Acts 27:9-11)—"Now when much time was spent, and when sailing was now dangerous, because the fast was now already past, Paul admonished them, and said unto them, Sirs, I perceive that this voyage will be with hurt and much damage, not only of the lading and ship, but also of our lives. Nevertheless the centurion believed the master and the owner of the ship, more than those things which were spoken by Paul" (Acts 27:9-11).

---

†27:11 *At this time it is late autumn. Among the ancients the dangerous season for sailing was from September 14 to November 11. After this date all navigation on the open sea was discontinued. In spite of this knowledge, and over the protests of Paul (who had already been through at least three shipwrecks; see 2 Cor. 11:25), the boat officials set sail for Phoenix, planning to winter there.*

B. Phase two—From Fair Havens to Melita (Acts 27:13-44)

1. The fearful storm (Acts 27:14-20)—"But not long after there arose against it a tempestuous wind, called Euroclydon. And when the ship was caught, and could not bear up into the wind, we let her drive. And we being exceedingly tossed with a tempest, the next day they lightened the ship; and the third day we cast out with our own hands the tackling of the ship. And when neither sun nor stars in many days appeared, and no small tempest lay on us, all hope that we should be saved was then taken away" (Acts 27:14-15, 18-20).

---

†27:20 *This is the final, perhaps most furious of four well-known biblical storms. The other three are:*

A. *The storm experienced by Jonah (Jonah 1:4-15)*

B. *The first storm experienced by the disciples (Matt. 8:23-27; Mark 4:35-41; Luke 8:22-25).*

C. *The second storm experienced by the disciples (Matt. 14:22-32; Mark 6:45-52; John 6:15-21)*

---

2. The cheerful saint (Acts 27:21-26, 33-37)—"But after long abstinence Paul stood forth in the midst of them, and said, Sirs, ye should have hearkened unto me, and not have loosed from Crete, and to have gained this harm and loss. And now I exhort you to be of good cheer" (Acts 27:21-22).

a. The prophetical aspect—"For there stood by me this night the angel of God, whose I am, and whom I serve, Saying, Fear not, Paul; thou must be brought before Caesar: and, lo, God hath given thee all them that sail with thee. Wherefore, sirs, be of good cheer: for I believe God, that it shall be even as it was told me" (Acts 27:23-25).

(1) There would be no loss of life (Acts 27:22).

(2) Only the ship would be lost (Acts 27:22).

(3) They would be cast on an island (Acts 27:26).

b. The practical aspect (Acts 27:33-37)—"And while the day was coming on, Paul besought them all to take meat, saying, This day is the fourteenth day that ye have tarried and continued fasting, having taken nothing. Wherefore I pray you to take some meat: for this is for your health: for there shall not an hair fall from the head of any of you. And when he had thus spoken, he took bread, and gave thanks to God in presence of them all: and when he had broken it, he began to eat. Then were they all of good cheer, and they also took some meat. And we were in all in the ship two hundred threescore and sixteen souls" (Acts 27:33-37).

c. The political aspect (Acts 27:39-44)—"And falling into a place where two seas met, they ran the ship aground; and the forepart stuck fast, and remained unmoveable, but the hinder part was broken with the violence of the waves. And the soldiers' counsel was to kill the prisoners, lest any of them should swim out, and escape. But the centurion, willing to save Paul, kept them from their purpose; and commanded that they which could swim should cast themselves first into the sea, and get to land: and the rest, some on boards, and some on broken pieces of the ship. And so it came to pass, that they escaped all safe to land" (Acts 27:41-44).

C. Phase three—At Melita (Acts 28:1-10)

1. Paul and the people (Acts 28:1-6)

a. First viewed as a murderer (Acts 28:2-4)—"And the barbarous people shewed us no little kindness: for they kindled a fire, and received us every one, because of the present rain, and because of the cold. And when Paul had gathered a bundle of sticks, and laid them on the fire, there came a viper out of the heat, and fastened on his hand. And when the barbarians saw the venomous beast hang on his hand, they said among themselves, No doubt this man is a murderer, whom, though he hath escaped the sea, yet vengeance suffereth not to live" (Acts 28:2-4).

b. Finally viewed as a messiah (Acts 28:5, 7)—"And he shook off the beast into the fire, and felt no harm. Howbeit they looked when he should have swollen, or fallen down dead suddenly: but after they had looked a great while, and saw no harm come to him, they changed their minds, and said that he was a god" (Acts 28:5-6).

---

†28:6

A. This event was a direct fulfillment of Jesus' prophecy in Mark 16:18 and Luke 10:19.

B. This is the second time in Acts when Paul was looked upon as a god (see 14:11-15).

---

2. Paul and Publius (Acts 28:7-10)

a. Healing a father (Acts 28:8)—"And it came to pass, that the father of Publius

lay sick of a fever and of a bloody flux: to whom Paul entered in, and prayed, and laid his hands on him, and healed him" (Acts 28:8).
b. Healing his friends (Acts 28:9)
D. Phase four—From Melita to Rome (Acts 28:11-15)

---

†28:15 *Luke informs us that "when the brethren heard of us, they came to meet us." The phrase in 28:15 "to meet us" is the same word found concerning the rapture of all believers in 1 Thessalonians 4:17, where we read, "to meet the Lord in the air." It is a term regularly used of the official welcome tendered by a delegation who went out to meet a visiting official and accompany him into the city.*

E. Phase five—At Rome (Acts 28:16-31)
1. The two meetings—During which the gospel is explained to the Roman Jews (Acts 28:17-29)
a. First meeting (Acts 28:17-22)
(1) The review of the apostle—He gives them the background for his appearing there in chains (Acts 28:17-20).
(2) The reaction of the audience (Acts 28:21-22)—"And they said unto him, We neither received letters out of Judaea concerning thee, neither any of the brethren that came shewed or spake any harm of thee. But we desire to hear of thee what thou thinkest: for as concerning this sect, we know that every where it is spoken against" (Acts 28:21-22).
b. Second meeting (Acts 28:12-19)
(1) The Son of God—"And when they had appointed him a day, there came many to him into his lodging; to whom he expounded and testified the kingdom of God, persuading them concerning Jesus, both out of the law of Moses, and out of the prophets, from morning till evening. And some believed the things which were spoken, and some believed not" (Acts 28:23-24).
(2) The Scripture of God—"And when they agreed not among themselves, they departed, after that Paul had spoken one word, Well spake the Holy Ghost by Esaias the prophet unto our fathers, Saying, Go unto this people, and say, Hearing ye shall hear, and shall not understand; and seeing ye shall see, and not perceive" (Acts 28:25-26).
(3) The salvation of God—"Be it known therefore unto you, that the salvation of God is sent unto the Gentiles, and that they will hear it" (Acts 28:28).
2. The two years—During which the gospel is explained to all (Acts 28:30-31). "And Paul dwelt two whole years in his own hired house, and received all that came in unto him, preaching the kingdom of God, and teaching those things which concern the Lord Jesus Christ, with all confidence, no man forbidding him" (Acts 28:30-31). *Paul wrote the books of Ephesians, Colossians, Philemon, and Philippians from Rome.*

ROMANS

THE FORT KNOX IN BIBLE DOCTRINE
BASIC THEOLOGY IN ITS PUREST FORM

The most profound discussion about the most profound subject in all of Scripture—God's plan and purpose for saving sinners

A. These words can only refer to one book in the Bible, and that is Romans.
B. If one were to attempt to determine the worth of this amazing no-nonsense, bottom-line summary of God's person, plan, and purpose in matters of doctrine, practical living, and prophecy, and by the untold millions of saints and theologians its pages have produced during the last 20 centuries, then every single one it its 9,447 words would be equal to at least a billion dollars each.
C. This marvelous manuscript is in reality the Declaration of Independence, Constitution, and Bill of Rights of the Christian faith.
D. The founder of the Roman church is unknown.
  1. It was definitely not Paul.
  2. It was probably not Peter (see 15:20-21).
E. Both Peter and Paul, however, were later martyred at Rome (2 Pet. 1:14; 2 Tim. 4:6-8).
F. The church was probably founded by converts at Pentecost (Acts 2:10).
G. The membership consisted of both Jews and Gentiles, but mostly Gentiles (1:13; 11:13; 15:16).
H. Paul was anxious to visit this church (1:8-11).
I. God later assured Paul he would indeed go to Rome (Acts 23:11).
J. Paul knew many believers there in Rome, sending his greeting to 26, calling them by name (Rom. 16).
K. He requests prayer from this church (15:30-32).
L. At least four facts are brought out concerning the internal affairs of this church.
  1. The positive things:
    a. They shared their faith (1:8).
    b. They were obedient to the faith (16:19).
  2. The negative things:
    a. Some were guilty of judging others (14:10).
    b. Some were causing divisions (16:17).
M. Romans provides us with the most detailed indictment of God's hatred for sexual perversion in all the Bible (1:18-32).
N. This book is a book about righteousness. It says, God *is* righteous, God *demands* righteousness, and God *provides* righteousness. We are told just what righteousness is, what it isn't, who needs it, why it is needed, where one may and may not find it.

O. Romans provides the greatest contrast between Christ and Adam in the Bible (5:12-21).
P. It gives us the most expanded explanation of God's past, present, and future dealings with Israel in all the Bible (9–11).
Q. It includes the most comforting verse in the Scriptures for Christians in distress (8:28).
R. Romans 8 is considered by many as the most profound and precious chapter in the New Testament.
S. This book spells out in great detail the vocabulary of salvation—terms such as: justification, sanctification, glorification, preservation, and transformation. All of them deal directly with the power of the gospel and the person (Christ) of the gospel.
T. Romans is the only New Testament book with no less than five distinct benedictions. (See 11:33-36; 15:13; 15:30-33; 16:20; 16:24-27.)
U. There are quotations or allusions from 23 Old Testament books in Romans. Romans is the eighth longest New Testament book, and 29th longest biblical book, with 16 chapters, 433 verses, and 9,447 words.
V. Great passages would include:
   1. 1:16-17
   2. 3:10-19
   3. 5:1-11
   4. 6:1-5
   5. 8:33-39
   6. 11:33-36
   7. 12:1-2

THE BOOK OF ROMANS

The Courthouse of Law—God's Wrath (Condemnation and Justification)—Romans 1–5

I. The Court Reporter (Rom. 1:1-17)
   A. The credentials of the reporter—How Paul describes himself
      1. He was a servant (Rom. 1:1).
      2. He was an apostle and a separated saint (Rom. 1:1).

---

†1:1

A. He was a called apostle. Two things were necessary for apostleship:
   1. He had to have seen Jesus (1 Cor. 9:1; 15:8-9).
   2. His call must have come from God (John 6:70; Acts 9:15)—No man should enter the ministry unless God calls him. (See John 15:16; Matt. 9:38; Heb. 5:14; Jer. 23:21; Ezek. 13:4-6, 10.)
B. He was a separated saint—There are three specific separations which took place in Paul's life.
   1. At his birth (Gal. 1:15)
   2. On the Damascus Road (Acts 9:15-16)—His conversion to Christ
   3. At Antioch (Acts 13:1-2)—His call to service. Paul was separated, as were Jeremiah (Jer. 1:5) and John the Baptist (Luke 1:15).

---

3. He was a gospel preacher (Rom. 1:2).
4. He was a missionary to the Gentiles (Rom. 1:5, 13-14).

B. The Christ of the reporter
1. As prophesied in the Old Testament—"Which he had promised afore by his prophets in the holy scriptures" (Rom. 1:2).
2. As proclaimed in the New Testament—"Concerning his Son Jesus Christ our Lord, which was made of the seed of David according to the flesh; and declared to be the Son of God with power, according to the spirit of holiness, by the resurrection from the dead" (Rom. 1:3-4).

---

†1:5 *Paul lists six facts about the glorious gospel in 1:2-5.*

A. It is not new—Paul said the Old Testament prophets spoke of it. In Romans he quotes from the Old Testament no less than 61 times, from 14 books. This totally refutes any claims of cults to have new and exotic truth concerning the gospel. It is rightly observed that "if something is new, it's probably not true, and if it's true, then it is not new."

B. It is about Jesus—The founder and finisher of the gospel is Christ.

C. It was manifested through the incarnation—Paul speaks of the virgin birth and humanity of Christ in 1:3. Christ is the seed of David.

D. It was declared through the resurrection—The Greek word "declared" in 1:4 is horizo *(from which comes our word "horizon"), meaning "to mark out by sure signs." Thus, God's clear boundary between earth and heaven is Christ, the Son of God.*

1. His humanity *is spoken of, as seen by the following:*
   a. He grew (Luke 2:40, 52).
   b. He looked like a man (John 4:9; 20:15).
   c. He became hungry (Matt. 4:2).
   d. He knew thirst (John 19:28).
   e. He grew weary (Mark 4:38; John 4:6).
   f. He wept (John 11:35; Luke 19:41).
   g. He suffered, bled, and died (1 Pet. 2:21; John 19:34; Matt. 27:50).
2. His deity *is spoken of, as seen by the following:*
   a. He is called God (Titus 2:13).
   b. He is eternal (Rev. 1:8, 18).
   c. He is unchanging (Heb. 13:8).
   d. He is all-powerful (Heb. 1:3).
   e. He is all-knowing (Col. 2:3).
   f. He is ever-present (Matt. 18:20). Both natures are spoken of in Isaiah 9:6; Galatians 4:4; and 1 Timothy 3:16. Note: The phrase "by the resurrection from the dead" (1:4) is literally "of the dead ones." Christ's resurrection is always referred to in the plural as it takes in all believers. (See Rom. 6:4; John 5:21; 1 Cor. 15:22.)

E. It bestows both salvation and service—Note Paul's testimony here: "By whom we have received grace and apostleship" (1:5). We note that grace precedes apostleship. A man must be saved before he can serve. Unsaved ministers are described in 2 Corinthians 11:13-15. Jesus must say, "Come unto me," before he says, "Go ye into all the world." John Wesley was a great example of this.

F. It is received by faith (see also Rom. 5:1; Eph. 2:8-9).

C. The concern of the reporter—Paul addresses his thoughts to a specific local church.
   1. The identity of this church—"Among whom are ye also the called of Jesus Christ: To all that be in Rome, beloved of God, called to be saints: Grace to you and peace from God our Father, and the Lord Jesus Christ" (Rom. 1:6-7).

---

†1:7 *We note here that grace precedes peace. There can be no peace apart from grace. (See Isa. 57:21; Jer. 6:14; Luke 7:50; 8:48; Rom. 5:1; 1 Thess. 5:3.) Paul prefaces every single one of his 13 epistles with these words, "Grace and peace." Peter (1 Pet. 1:2; 2 Pet. 1:2) and John (2 John 3) do the same. Grace is "unmerited favor" and is first mentioned in Genesis 6:8. It is perhaps God's second greatest characteristic (after holiness) and may be spelled out and thought of as "God's righteousness at Christ's expense." (See Rom. 5:20; Eph. 2:8-9; 1 Pet. 3:18; 1 Cor. 15:10.)*

---

   2. The intercession for this church
      a. His praise for them—"First, I thank my God through Jesus Christ for you all, that your faith is spoken of throughout the whole world" (Rom. 1:8).

---

†1:8 *Paul commends them for their universally known faith (1:8). We know that the Emperor Claudius had forced the Jews out of Rome because of one Chrestus, which is thought to be a misspelling for "Christ." (See also 1 Thess. 1:6-8.)*

---

      b. His prayers for them—"For God is my witness, whom I serve with my spirit in the gospel of his Son, that without ceasing I make mention of you always in my prayers; making request, if by any means now at length I might have a prosperous journey by the will of God to come unto you" (Rom. 1:9-10).

---

†1:10 *God later answered this prayer, but not in the way that Paul might have supposed (Acts 27–28). In Romans 16 Paul refers to 26 Roman saints by name.*

---

   3. The interest in this church
      a. Paul desired to see them—"For I long to see you, that I may impart unto you some spiritual gift, to the end ye may be established" (Rom. 1:11).
      b. Paul desired to serve them—"Now I would not have you ignorant, brethren, that oftentimes I purposed to come unto you, (but was let hitherto,) that I might have some fruit among you also, even as among other Gentiles" (Rom. 1:13).

---

†1:13 *He desired to come that he might both remit and receive a blessing (1:12). He had planned to come previously, but was hindered concerning his plans, once by Satan (1 Thess. 2:18) and once by God (Acts 16:6-7). Thus, Paul's human plans were no more inspired than those of Christians today (see Rom. 15:22-23). The spiritual gift mentioned in 1:11 was probably doctrine (1 Pet. 2:2).*

---

   4. The indebtedness to this church—"I am debtor both to the Greeks, and to the Barbarians; both to the wise, and to the unwise. So, as much as in me is, I am ready to preach the gospel to you that are at Rome also" (Rom. 1:14-15).

†1:15 *He felt he owed a great gospel debt to every sinner (1:14; see also 2 Kings 7:9). Because of this, Paul could say: "So, as much as in me is [literally, my side is ready], I am ready to preach the gospel to you that are at Rome also" (1:15). Paul preached at Jerusalem (the religious center of the world) and was mobbed (Acts 21:31; 22:22-23). He preached at Athens (the intellectual center) and was mocked (Acts 17:32). He would later preach in Rome (the political center) where he would be martyred (2 Tim. 4:6).*

D. The confidence of the reporter—"For I am not ashamed of the gospel of Christ: for it is the power of God unto salvation to every one that believeth; to the Jew first, and also to the Greek" (Rom. 1:16).

---

†1:16 *The gospel is God's power (1:16). There are two standards by which God's power is measured in the Bible. In the Old Testament it was according to that power by which God brought Israel out of Egypt. (See Exod. 14–15; Psa. 78.) In the New Testament the unit of measurement is the resurrection of Jesus (Eph. 1:20). The Greek word for "power" is* dunamis, *from which two words come: (1) dynamite-destructive power, and (2) dynamo-constructive power. The gospel of Christ is both. (See 2 Cor. 2:16.)*

E. The conclusion of the reporter—"For therein is the righteousness of God revealed from faith to faith: as it is written, The just shall live by faith" (Rom. 1:17).

---

†1:17

A. The gospel produces righteousness (1:17). This word, simply defined, means "right clothing." The Bible teaches that all sinners are naked before God (Gen. 3:10; Heb. 4:13; Rev. 3:17). Some sinners realize this and attempt to make their own suit of spiritual clothes; but God looks upon such clothes as filthy rags (Isa. 64:6). However, the gospel provides new clothes to all repenting sinners. (See 2 Cor. 6:7; Eph. 6:14; Rev. 19:7-8.) This word may be used to summarize the book of Romans in a threefold manner:

1. God is righteous.

2. God demands righteousness.

3. God provides righteousness.

B. The gospel says, "The just shall live by faith" (1:17b). These six words started the Protestant Reformation when Martin Luther experienced them. The phrase originates in Habakkuk 2:4 and is quoted three times in the New Testament.

1. Here in Romans 1:17, where the emphasis is on "the just."

2. In Galatians 3:11, where the emphasis is on "shall live."

3. In Hebrews 10:38, where the emphasis is on "by faith."

C. Bishop Lightfoot has pointed out the following concerning these six words:

1. The whole Law was given to Moses in 613 precepts.

2. David reduces them to 11 in Psalm 15.

3. Isaiah brings it down to six.

4. Micah limits it to three.

5. Isaiah in another passage narrows it to two.

6. But Habakkuk and Paul here summarize God's plan in a single statement. Faith has been defined as "the hand of the heart."

II. The Court Record (Rom. 1:18–4:25)

A. The charge—High treason against the King of the universe (Rom. 1:18-19). "For the wrath of God is revealed from heaven against all ungodliness and unrighteousness of men, who hold the truth in unrighteousness" (Rom. 1:18).

---

†1:18

A. God's fierce wrath is revealed against all ungodliness (sins against his person) and unrighteousness (sins against his will). The first category is vertical while the second is horizontal in nature.

B. This wrath is manifested in a threefold way:

1. In the biblical account itself (John 3:36)

2. In the cross of Calvary (Matt. 27:46; 1 Pet. 3:18)

3. In the natural world (through tornadoes, earthquakes, famines, etc.)

B. The defendants:

1. A heathen—The pagan (Rom. 1:18-32)
2. A hypocrite—The moral person (Rom. 2:1-16)
3. A Hebrew—The religious person (Rom. 2:17–3:8)

C. The detailed indictment

1. First indictment—Ingratitude (Rom. 1:21). "Because that, when they knew God, they glorified him not as God, neither were thankful; but became vain in their imaginations, and their foolish heart was darkened" (Rom. 1:21).

---

†1:21 *The fall of both Lucifer and Adam through pride and self-will was doubtless prompted by their thankless hearts. Thus, the real antidote or cure for pride in the life of the believer is not humility, but thanksgiving. A thankful person is automatically a humble person. (See 1 Thess. 5:18; Phil. 4:6.)*

---

2. Second indictment—Insolence (Rom. 1:22). "Professing themselves to be wise, they became fools" (Rom. 1:22).

---

†1:22 *They thought themselves to be wise. The Greek word for "became fools" here is* moraino, *a verb form of* moros, *from which we get our word "moron." This was the beginning of human philosophy, a term ill-named, for it means "a lover of wisdom." (See Acts 17:18-21; 1 Cor. 1:18-21; 1 Tim. 6:3-5, 20; 2 Tim. 3:7; 4:4.)*

---

3. Third indictment—Idolatry (Rom. 1:23). "And changed the glory of the uncorruptible God into an image made like to corruptible man, and to birds, and fourfooted beasts, and creeping things" (Rom. 1:23).

---

†1:23

A. They preferred idols to the living God and exchanged *(not changed, for no man, angel, or demon can do this) his glory for that of:*

1. Humans—The Greeks worshiped the human body, as does Hollywood today.
2. Birds—The Assyrians bowed down to birds.
3. Beasts—The Egyptians looked to cows and crocodiles.
4. Creeping things—The pagans worshiped snakes.

B. We note the vivid downward trend of humanity described here in 1:23. The Bible teaches devolution, not evolution.

---

4. Fourth Indictment—Immorality (Rom. 1:24-27). "Wherefore God also gave them up to uncleanness through the lusts of their own hearts, to dishonour their own bodies between themselves" (Rom. 1:24).
   a. Lesbianism—"For this cause God gave them up unto vile affections: for even their women did change the natural use into that which is against nature" (Rom. 1:26).
   b. Homosexuality—"And likewise also the men, leaving the natural use of the woman, burned in their lust one toward another; men with men working that which is unseemly, and receiving in themselves that recompence of their error which was meet" (Rom. 1:27).

---

†1:27 *They gave their bodies over to sexual perversions (1:26-27). The sin of homosexuality is usually the final stage in those civilizations that turn from God. It was for this crime that God burned Sodom off the map of the Middle East (Gen. 19) and later ordered the destruction of Jericho, along with other Old Testament cities (1 Kings 14:24). In recent years the number of homosexuals in Western civilization has increased drastically. The so-called Gay Liberation movement is neither gay nor liberating.*

---

5. Fifth indictment—Incorrigibility (Rom. 1:28-32). "And even as they did not like to retain God in their knowledge, God gave them over to a reprobate mind, to do those things which are not convenient" (Rom. 1:28).
   a. They enjoyed their wicked deeds—"Being filled with all unrighteousness, fornication, wickedness, covetousness, maliciousness; full of envy, murder, debate, deceit, malignity; whisperers, backbiters, haters of God, despiteful, proud, boasters, inventors of evil things, disobedient to parents, without understanding, covenant breakers, without natural affection, implacable, unmerciful" (Rom 1:29-31).

---

†1:31 *Note the nature of these wicked deeds, some 22 in number:*

A. Fornication—Sexual sins in general
B. Wickedness—This word, first found in Genesis 6:5 is mentioned over 360 times in the Bible.
C. Covetousness—The final of the Ten Commandments warns against this sin (Exod. 20:17). It was the specific sin that caused Paul to comprehend his fallen nature and need for redemption (Rom. 7:7).
D. Maliciousness—Unusual cruelty
E. Envy—Unlawfully desiring something belonging to another
F. Murder—This is the only sin which cannot be forgiven by its victim.
G. Debate—Contention and strife

H. *Deceit—The placing of a bait or snare*
I. *Malignity—Malice, holding or harboring hatred*
J. *Whisperers—Secret slanderings*
K. *Backbiters—Open slanderings. The name "Satan" literally means, "the one who slanders."*
L. *God-haters—This person begins by despising the* authority *of the Bible and winds up by hating its* Author.
M. *Despiteful—Insolent and insulting*
N. *Proud—Having to do with one's features*
O. *Boasters—Having to do with one's words*
P. *Inventors of evil*
Q. *Disobedient to parents—This is the beginning of lawlessness and anarchy.*
R. *Without understanding—See Ephesians 4:18-19*
S. *Covenant breakers*
T. *Without natural affection*
U. *Implacable—Unable to be satisfied*
V. *Unmerciful*

---

b. They endorsed their wicked deeds—"Who knowing the judgment of God, that they which commit such things are worthy of death, not only do the same, but have pleasure in them that do them" (Rom. 1:32).

---

†1:32 *They knew the seriousness of their crimes, but still continued and even encouraged others to join them (Mark 14:10-11; Rev. 11:10). For these crimes, God gave them over to a reprobate mind (a mind incapable of rational judgment) (Prov. 1:24-31; Rom. 1:24, 26, 28).*

D. The jury
1. The conscience of a person (Rom. 1:19)—"Because that which may be known of God is manifest in them; for God hath shewed it unto them" (Rom. 1:19).

---

†1:19 *Conscience may be thought of as one of four main characteristics which make up the human soul. These are:*
A. *Intellect—That aspect of the soul which tells me whether a given issue is right or wrong.*
B. *Sensibility—That aspect which tells me what I would like to do about the issue.*
C. *Conscience—That aspect which tells me what I should do.*
D. *Will—That aspect which determines what I shall do.*

---

2. The deeds of a person (Rom. 2:6)—"Who will render to every man according to his deeds" (Rom. 2:6).
3. The works of God (Rom. 1:20)—"For the invisible things of him from the creation of the world are clearly seen, being understood by the things that are made, even his eternal power and Godhead; so that they are without excuse" (Rom. 1:20).

---

†1:20 *All people have both the witness of conscience (1:19) and that of nature (1:20). (See Isa. 40:26; Psa. 8:3; 19:1-3; Acts 14:17; 17:29.) In other words, God does not reap wrath where he has not sown* *knowledge. These twin witnesses are thus unmistakable and universal. As a result, all people are exposed both to them and by them.*

---

4. The Law of God (Rom. 2:12)—"For as many as have sinned without law shall also perish without law: and as many as have sinned in the law shall be judged by the law" (Rom. 2:12).

E. The defense
1. The pagan's defense
   a. His plea rendered—"I should be acquitted on the ground of ignorance."
   b. His plea refuted—"You have the witness of conscience" (Rom. 1:19). "You have the witness of nature" (Rom. 1:20).
2. The moral person's defense
   a. His plea rendered—"I should be acquitted on the ground of comparison—that is, that I'm not as bad as the pagan."
   b. His plea refuted—"You do the same basic things, but in a more refined way." "Therefore thou art inexcusable, O man, whosoever thou art that judgest: for wherein thou judgest another, thou condemnest thyself; for thou that judgest doest the same things" (Rom. 2:1).

---

†2:1

A. The plea refuted—"You do the same basic things, but in a more refined way." A classic example of one person judging another for the very thing he himself had committed was when David condemned a rich farmer who stole from a poor one (2 Sam. 11–12).

B. The self-righteous moral person, like the unrighteous pagan, will be judged by the twin witnesses of nature and conscience (Rom. 1:19-20; 2:12-15). The Bible lists various kinds of conscience.
1. *A good conscience (1 Tim. 1:5, 19)*
2. *A weak conscience (1 Cor. 8:12)*
3. *A convicting conscience (John 8:9)*
4. *A defiled conscience (Titus 1:15)*
5. *A seared conscience (1 Tim. 4:2)*

C. It should be noted that a person's conscience does not function legislatively, but only judicially. It is like an umpire that calls the strikes, but does not make the rules. Conscience, then, is a goad, but not a guide. Paul summarizes this section by saying: "For as many as have sinned without law shall also perish without law; and as many as have sinned in the law shall be judged by the law" (Rom. 2:12; see also Luke 12:47-48).

---

c. His plea reviewed
   (1) He was indifferent (Rom. 2:4-5).
      (a) Concerning God's forbearance (God's act of holding back his wrath)
      (b) Concerning God's goodness (God's act of holding forth his grace)
   (2) He was ignorant.
      (a) He knew nothing concerning *who* God would judge—"Who will render to every man according to his deeds: . . . For there is no respect of persons with God" (Rom. 2:6, 11).
      (b) He knew nothing concerning *how* God would judge—"To them who by patient continuance in well doing seek for glory and honour and

immortality, eternal life: But unto them that are contentious, and do not obey the truth, but obey unrighteousness, indignation and wrath. . . . for as many as have sinned without law shall also perish without law: and as many as have sinned in the law shall be judged by the law. . . . For when the Gentiles, which have not the law, do by nature the things contained in the law, these, having not the law, are a law unto themselves" (Rom. 2:7-8, 12, 14).

(c) He knew nothing concerning *when* God would judge —"In the day when God shall judge the secrets of men by Jesus Christ according to my gospel" (Rom. 2: 16).

---

†**2:16** *An overview summary of the moral person's problems is as follows:*

A. Self-righteous people make one of two capital mistakes:
- *1. They misunderstand the height of God's Law.*
- *2. They underestimate the depth of their own moral conduct.*

B. They desire the fruit of Christianity without the root.

C. They underestimate the awesome knowledge of God (2:1). But God knows all the facts.
- *1. God knows the number of the stars (Psa. 147:4).*
- *2. God knows our thoughts and words (Psa. 139:1-2, 4, 23-24).*
- *3. God knows the number of hairs on one's head (Matt. 10:30).*
- *4. God knows the past, present, and future (Acts 15:18).*
- *5. God even knows what might have been (Matt. 11:23).*

D. They despise his goodness and forbearance (2:4). To despise is to belittle, or to look down upon (Gen. 25:34; Heb. 12:2, 5). Thus, the moral person was despising:
- *1. God's forbearance; that is, his act of holding back his wrath.*
- *2. God's goodness; that is, his act of holding forth his grace.*

E. The moral person takes lightly both God's extended hand and his clenched fist.

F. They assume their morality will excuse them from his judgment (2:3). It has been suggested that there are four possible ways one might escape human punishment:
- *1. He might commit an undetected crime or remain an undetected criminal.*
- *2. He might escape beyond the jurisdiction of the Law.*
- *3. He might hire a smart lawyer and "beat the rap."*
- *4. He might escape, after being put in prison.*

G. But with God there is no escape (Heb. 2:3). Our only hope is to settle out of court. Without this settlement, all people will be judged concerning their thoughts *(Rom. 2:16),* words *(Matt. 12:36), and* deeds *(Rev. 20:12). This will happen "for there is no respect of persons with God" (2:11). (See also Deut. 10:17; Acts 10:34; James 2:1, 9; Eph. 6:9; Col. 3:25.)*

---

3. The religious person's defense (Rom. 2:17–3:8)
   a. His plea rendered—"I should be acquitted on the grounds that I know the law of God and teach courses in religion." "Behold, thou art called a Jew, and restest in the law, and makest thy boast of God. . . . And art confident that thou thyself art a guide of the blind, a light of them which are in darkness" (Rom. 2:17, 19).
   b. His plea refuted—You simply do not practice what you preach (Rom. 2:25-29). "Thou therefore which teachest another, teachest thou not thyself?

thou that preachest a man should not steal, dost thou steal? Thou that sayest a man should not commit adultery, dost thou commit adultery? thou that abhorrest idols, dost thou commit sacrilege? . . . For the name of God is blasphemed among the Gentiles through you, as it is written. . . . For he is not a Jew, which is one outwardly; neither is that circumcision, which is outward in the flesh: But he is a Jew, which is one inwardly; and circumcision is that of the heart, in the spirit, and not in the letter; whose praise is not of men, but of God" (Rom. 2:21-22, 24, 28-29).

c. His plea reviewed
   (1) Fact # 1: The Jew had a national advantage, but no spiritual advantage (Rom. 3:1-2).
   (2) Fact # 2: Even though Israel had rejected Christ, God's promises would not fail (Rom. 3:3-4). "For what if some did not believe? shall their unbelief make the faith of God without effect?" (Rom. 3:3).
   (3) Fact # 3: Israel's unrighteousness had simply demonstrated God's righteousness (Rom. 3:5).
   (4) Fact # 4: Israel would be punished for its unrighteousness (Rom. 3:6-8).

---

†3:8 *An overview summary of the religious person's problems is as follows:*

A. His law could not save him (2:17-24). The Jew had defiled this law and his knowledge of God and had become a horrible testimony to the Gentiles (2:24; also Gen. 34:30; Ezek. 36:17, 20). It was performance of God's will, and not the possession of his Law which averted judgment. Israel had simply not kept the Law (Matt. 21:13; 23:4-36; Acts 15:10).

B. His circumcision could not save him (2:25-27). The Jews believed Abraham (the first to be circumcised—see Gen. 17:11) stood at the gate of hell to assure that no circumcised Jew would ever enter there. While circumcision was indeed the seal *of God's promise, inward faith alone was the* source. *(See Deut. 10:12, 16; 30:6.) The rite of circumcision had already been set aside in Acts 15. His birth could not save him (2:28-29). Salvation comes not through place, face, or race, but by grace. (See John 8:39, 44.)*

C. Paul then quickly summarizes the case against Israel (3:1-8)—Even though the Jews had a national advantage over the Gentiles "because that unto them were committed the oracles of God" (Rom. 3:2), they had no spiritual advantage whatsoever. Even though Israel's unrighteousness had simply "commended the righteousness of God" (that is, showed it in a clearer light), God would still judge them along with the uncircumcised Gentiles. The end never *justifies the means.*

F. The verdict (Rom. 3:9-23)—"What then? are we better than they? No, in no wise: for we have before proved both Jews and Gentiles, that they are all under sin; as it is written, There is none righteous, no, not one: There is none that understandeth, there is none that seeketh after God. Now we know that what things soever the law saith, it saith to them who are under the law: that every mouth may be stopped, and all the world may become guilty before God" (Rom. 3:9, 10-11, 19).

1. Man's character is depraved (Rom. 3:12)—"They are all gone out of the way, they are together become unprofitable; there is none that doeth good, no, not one" (Rom. 3:12).

---

†**3:12** *All had become unprofitable. This is a reference to something originally good which goes bad, like sour milk, rotten meat, or moldy bread (Isa. 1:6). Thus, people are unrighteous, unreasonable, unresponsive, and unrepentant.*

---

2. People's conversation is depraved (Rom. 3:13-14)—"Their throat is an open sepulchre; with their tongues they have used deceit; the poison of asps is under their lips: whose mouth is full of cursing and bitterness" (Rom. 3:13-14).
3. People's conduct is depraved (Rom. 3:15-18).
   a. They murder their brothers (Rom. 3:15-17)—"Their feet are swift to shed blood" (Rom. 3:15).
   b. They mock their God (Rom. 3:18)—"There is no fear of God before their eyes" (Rom. 3:18).

G. The sentence (Rom. 6:23)—"For the wages of sin is death" (Rom. 6:23a).

---

†**6:23** *The sentence: Spiritual death, to be forever separated from God to suffer throughout all eternity in the lake of fire (Rom. 6:23; Rev. 20:11-15). The greatest crime of all can only be punished by the greatest penalty of all, if justice is to prevail.*

H. The miracle (Rom. 3:21-31; 6:23)—"But the gift of God is eternal life through Jesus Christ our Lord" (Rom. 6:23b).

1. The nature of this miracle (Rom. 3:24)—"Being justified freely by his grace through the redemption that is in Christ Jesus" (Rom. 3:24).

---

†**3:24** *Up to this point the case of God against the accused has pretty well followed the format of earthly jurisprudence. But suddenly something totally different and unexpected takes place that would surely cause every earthly court reporter to gasp in utter amazement. After the Judge has carefully heard all the evidence and patiently listened to all the pleas, he finds no other choice but to invoke the supreme penalty, lest true justice be denied. But before the terrible sentence can be carried out, this same Judge quietly closes the case book, lays down the heavenly gavel, rises to his feet, takes off his judicial robes, and goes out to die for these three convicted defendants. This and this alone is justification. The corrupt, doomed, and naked sinner may now be cleansed, delivered, and clothed in the very righteousness of Christ himself.*

---

2. The persons in this miracle—The Father and Son (Rom. 3:25). "Whom God hath set forth to be a propitiation through faith in his blood, to declare his righteousness for the remission of sins that are past, through the forbearance of God."
3. The source of this miracle (Rom. 3:24, 28)
   a. Freely by his grace" (Rom. 3:24)
   b. "By faith" (Rom. 3:28)
   c. "Without the deeds of the law" (Rom. 3:28)
4. The scope of this miracle—unlimited in scope (Rom. 3:22, 29)
   a. "Unto all . . . for there is no difference" (Rom. 3:22).
   b. "The God of the Jews . . . of the Gentiles also" (Rom. 3:29)
5. The bestowal of this miracle—limited in bestowal (Rom. 3:22, 26)

a. "Upon them that believe" (Rom. 3:22).
b. "Him which believeth in Jesus" (Rom. 3:26).

6. The witnesses of this miracle (Rom. 3:21)—"But now the righteousness of God without the law is manifested, being witnessed by the law and the prophets."

---

†3:21 *"The law and the prophets"—The Mosaic Law required two witnesses to attest to any fact (Deut. 19:15). This righteousness was often foreshadowed by the Law through the temple priesthood and offerings. This righteousness was often foretold by the prophets through their writings (Isa. 53; Luke 24:25-27; John 5:46; 1 Pet. 1:10-11).*

---

7. The legal accomplishments of this miracle—*Question:* How to reconcile God's justice and his mercy. Note the two problem words in Romans 3:25: "Whom God hath set forth to be a propitiation through faith in his blood, to declare his righteousness for the remission of sins that are past, through the forbearance of God."

---

†3:25 *The word* propitiation *means "satisfaction" and is a reference to the Old Testament temple mercy seat. It was upon this golden seat that the priest sprinkled the blood of a lamb to separate God's wrath from man's sin. (See 1 John 2:2; 4:10; Heb. 10:11-12.) Why did Christ die? Among other reasons, to preserve and vindicate the justice of God.*

---

a. Remission: To let something pass by (that is, the sins of the Old Testament saints)
b. Forbearance: To hold something back (that is, God's wrath upon those sins).

8. *Answer:* "Christ Jesus . . . whom God hath set forth to be a propitiation" (Rom. 3:24-25). "That he might be just, and the justifier of him which believeth in Jesus" (Rom. 3:26).
9. The harmony seen in this miracle—"Do we then make void the law through faith? God forbid: yea, we establish the law" (Rom. 3:31).

I. The two spokesmen for the court—The Judge introduces two well-known faith experts who swear to the fact that they both anticipated and experienced the miracle of justification centuries ago (Rom. 4:1-25).

1. Abraham, Israel's racial father (Rom. 4:1-5, 9-25)
   a. Abraham and his salvation
      (1) The method of his salvation—"For what saith the scripture? Abraham believed God, and it was counted unto him for righteousness" (Rom. 4:3). "Therefore it is of faith, that it might be by grace" (Rom. 4:16a).

---

†4:3 *The Old Testament Scripture quoted here is Genesis 15:6. This word* counted *could also be translated "imputed." To impute is to add something to someone's account. There are three major imputations in the Bible.*

A. First, the imputation of Adam's sin to the human race (Rom. 3:23; 5:12; 1 Cor. 15:22)
B. Second, the imputation of the race's sin upon Christ (Isa. 53:5; Heb. 2:9; 2 Pet. 2:24; 2 Cor. 5:14)

C. Third, the imputation of God's righteousness to all believers (Phil. 3:9) "Through the righteousness of faith" (Rom. 4:13b). "Therefore it is of faith, that it might be by grace" (Rom. 4:16a).

---

(2) The time of his salvation—"How was it then reckoned? when he was in circumcision, or in uncircumcision? Not in circumcision, but in uncircumcision" (Rom. 4:10).

---

†**4:10** *When was Abraham saved? Was he saved before or after circumcision? In Genesis 15:6, Abraham is said to have been justified. At this time he was 85 years old (Gen. 16:16). In Genesis 17:24 we are told of his circumcision, at the age of 99. Thus, he was justified by faith and a child of God nearly 14 years before he was circumcised.*

---

(3) The seal of his salvation—"And he received the sign of circumcision, a seal of the righteousness of the faith which he had yet being uncircumcised: that he might be the father of all them that believe, though they be not circumcised; that righteousness might be imputed unto them also" (Rom. 4:11).

---

†**4:11** *Why was Abraham saved? "That he might be the father of all them that believe" (4:11). This includes both the uncircumcised (believing Gentiles) and the circumcision (believing Jews). Paul here once again points out that circumcision was merely the* seal *of Abraham's faith, while justification was the* source. *Dr. Allen Johnson writes: "A good illustration of this is the old twenty-dollar gold piece. The seal of the United States was imprinted on the coin as a sign that it was U.S. currency, but the value of the coin remained the same even if it was melted down and the seal obliterated. Now the same seal can be impressed on an iron slug, but the presence of the sign doesn't alter the intrinsic worthlessness of the slug"* (The Freedom Letter, *p. 76).*

---

b. Abraham and his seed

(1) His earthly seed (Rom. 4:17-22)—Isaac was his earthly seed. "And being not weak in faith, he considered not his own body now dead, when he was about an hundred years old, neither yet the deadness of Sarah's womb: He staggered not at the promise of God through unbelief; but was strong in faith, giving glory to God; and being fully persuaded that, what he had promised, he was able also to perform" (Rom. 4:19-21).

(2) His spiritual seed (Rom. 4:11-12, 16, 23-25)—Believers are his spiritual seed. "Now it was not written for his sake alone, that it was imputed to him; but for us also, to whom it shall be imputed, if we believe on him that raised up Jesus our Lord from the dead; who was delivered for our offences, and was raised again for our justification" (Rom. 4:23-25).

2. David, Israel's royal father (Rom. 4:6-8)—"Even as David also describeth the blessedness of the man, unto whom God imputeth righteousness without works, saying, Blessed are they whose iniquities are forgiven, and whose

sins are covered. Blessed is the man to whom the Lord will not impute sin" (Rom. 4:6-8).

a. The felonies of David—He was guilty of adultery and murder (see 2 Sam. 11–12).

b. The forgiveness of David—He was forgiven by faith in God's grace. See Psalms 51 and 52.

III. The Court Review (Rom. 5:1-21)

A. A summary of justification (Rom. 5:1-11)

1. The believer has peace with God—"Therefore being justified by faith, we have peace with God through our Lord Jesus Christ" (Rom. 5:1).

2. The believer has access to God (Rom. 5:2).

---

†5:2

A. Access to God (5:2)—The believer can now approach God because of his new standing. In the Bible there is a distinction between our standing and our state.

1. Our standing *refers to our position in heaven and never changes (1 Cor. 15:1; 2 Cor. 5:17).*

2. Our state *refers to our condition on earth and may change (for better or worse) daily (Phil. 2:19; Col. 4:7).*

B. Our new standing now gives us that blessed privilege not experienced by either Jew or Gentile in the Old Testament. We now have access to God's throne itself. In the Old Testament there was very little of this. Consider:

1. A Gentile was barred at the gates of the temple.

2. A Jewish woman was stopped at the woman's court.

3. A non-Levite Hebrew could not enter the inner court.

4. The high priest himself could only enter into the holy of holies once a year. But on Calvary this veil separating us from God's glory was rent in two by Christ. (See Matt. 27:51; Heb. 10:19.)

---

3. The believer receives assurance from God—"And not only so, but we glory in tribulations also: knowing that tribulation worketh patience; and patience, experience; and experience, hope" (Rom. 5:3-4).

---

†5:4

A. Patience (see Heb. 10:36; James 1:3)—This leads to:

B. Experience (see Psa. 94:12; 2 Cor. 1:3-5; Gal. 4:19; Eph. 4:14-15)—This leads to:

C. Hope—There are three requirements of an earthly hope:

1. It must concern the future.

2. It must concern something good in the future.

3. It must concern something possible in the future.

D. This hope fulfills all three requirements (Eph. 1:17-22; 1 Pet. 1:3-4; Titus 2:11). There are two kinds of hope, a verb and a noun.

1. The verb "hope" says, "I hope to have" (earthly hope).

2. The noun "hope" says, "I have a hope" (heavenly hope).

E. This assurance from God once prompted Andrew Murray to write: "First, He brought me here, it is by His will I am in this strait place; in that fact I will rejoice. Next, He will keep me here in His love, and give me grace as His child. Then, He will make the trial a blessing, teaching me the lessons He intends for me to learn, and working in me the grace He meant to bestow. Last, in His good time He can bring me out again—how and when He knows. Thus: I am (1) here by God's appointment, (2) in His keeping, (3) under His training, and (4) for His time."

---

4. The believer is indwelled by God—"And hope maketh not ashamed; because the love of God is shed abroad in our hearts by the Holy Ghost which is given unto us" (Rom. 5:5).

---

†5:5

A. *There are three separate and distinct words for love in the Greek New Testament. In Romans Paul uses all three.*
   1. Storgos—*A natural, gravitational love; an instinctive concern for one's offspring, found in both animals and humans. Only the negative form, astorgos, is used in Scripture (Rom. 1:31).*
   2. Philos—*A beautiful and friendly love. Paul describes this love in Romans 12:10.*
   3. Agapao—*A divine love, found only in God. This love is not dependent upon the beauty of the object being loved. It is found 320 times in the Greek New Testament, but rarely in classical writings. (Homer used it ten times and Euripedes three times.)*

      This love is never found in the heart of any man prior to the ascension of Christ. In fact, Jesus asks Peter on three occasions (John 21:15-19) if he really loves him. The first two times Jesus uses the third kind of love and asks the following question; "Peter, do you agapao *me?" On both occasions Peter answers by choosing the second word. He says, "Lord, you know I* phileo *you."*

      Finally, our Lord uses the second word also. The reason for all this (as Peter would later find out) is explained in Romans 5:5 by Paul: "The love (agapao) *of God is shed abroad in our hearts by the Holy Ghost which is given unto us." Thus, the reason why Peter answered the way he did was because the Holy Spirit had not yet come at Pentecost and it was therefore impossible for him to love Christ with this divine* agapao *love.*

      In John 11 we have a similar case in which we are told that Lazarus loved Jesus with a phileo *love, but that Jesus loved Lazarus with an* agapao *love (11:3, 5).*

B. *There are two beloved New Testament passages in which this* agapeo *love is in view. (See John 3:16; Eph. 5:25.)*

---

5. The believer is preserved in God (Rom. 5:6-11).
   a. Through Christ's past work on Calvary's cross—"For when we were yet without strength, in due time Christ died for the ungodly. For scarcely for a righteous man will one die: yet peradventure for a good man some would even dare to die. But God commendeth his love toward us, in that, while we were yet sinners, Christ died for us" (Rom. 5:6-8).
   b. Through Christ's present work at God's right hand—"Much more then, being now justified by his blood, we shall be saved from wrath through him. For if, when we were enemies, we were reconciled to God by the death of his Son, much more, being reconciled, we shall be saved by his life" (Rom. 5:9-10).

†5:10

A. The Bible records many clear statements about Christ's blood.

1. It was innocent blood (Matt. 27:4, 19, 24)—This was the testimony of Judas, Pilate's wife, and Pilate.

2. It was shed blood (Matt. 26:28).

3. It was precious blood (1 Pet. 1:18-19).

4. It was cleansing blood (1 John 1:9).

5. It was condemning blood (Matt. 27:25).

B. Why did Christ shed his precious blood?

1. To show forth God's love

2. To save us from God's wrath

a. This includes present-day wrath (John 3:36; Rom. 1:18).

b. This includes tribulational wrath (1 Thess. 1:10; 5:9).

c. This includes eternal wrath (Rev. 20:15).

C. This has been called the chapter of the "much mores." (See 5:9-10, 15, 17, 20.) My salvation was purchased by his bleeding and is preserved through his interceding (see Heb. 1:3; 6:18-20; 7:25; 9:24).

B. A summary of condemnation (Rom. 5:12-21)—In these verses Paul contrasts the work of Adam (the father of all) with the work of Christ (the Savior of all).

1. The work of Adam

a. The reality of his act—"Wherefore, as by one man sin entered into the world" (Rom. 5:12).

---

†5:12 *Adam brought sin into the world. At this point it may prove helpful to review both the origin and meaning of sin.*

A. The origin of sin: In the universe, it was introduced by Satan. (See Ezek. 28:11-19; Isa. 14:12-15; Luke 10:18; 1 John 3:8; Rev. 12:3-4.) In the world, it was introduced by Adam. (See Gen. 2:16-17; Rom. 5:12; 1 Cor. 15:22; 1 Tim. 2:14.)

B. The meaning of sin

1. First meaning—"To miss the mark" (Greek is hamartia*). Here sin may be pictured as any attitude or act of a person which does not hit the bull's-eye of God's glory target (Rom. 3:23). The secular use of its verbal form is illustrated in Judges 20:16.*

2. Second meaning—"To overstep the forbidden line" (Greek is parabasis*. See 1 John 3:4; Acts 1:25; James 2:11.) Sin thus covers both our inability to do right and our inclination to do wrong.*

---

b. The scope of his act—"And so death passed upon all men, for that all have sinned" (Rom. 5:12b).

c. The nature of his act—"By one man's disobedience" (Rom. 5:19).

d. The results of his act

(1) Immediate judgment upon himself

(2) Imputed judgment upon his posterity—"Nevertheless death reigned from Adam to Moses, even over them that had not sinned after the similitude of Adam's transgression, who is the figure of him that was to come" (Rom. 5:14).

---

†**5:14** *He brought death into the world.*
A. This includes physical death (Gen. 3:19; 5:5; Psa. 90:10).
B. This includes spiritual death (Matt. 7:23; 25:41; Rev. 2:11; 20:6, 14; 21:8).

---

3) Eternal judgment upon all unsaved—"The judgment was by one to condemnation" (Rom. 5:16). "Judgment came upon all men to condemnation" (Rom. 5:18).

---

†**5:18**
A. There are several theories about Adam's sin and its relationship to me.
1. The Pelagian view—This says that Adam's sin affected only himself, and merely resulted in a bad moral example.
2. Semi-Pelagian view—That Adam's sin merely weakened the will not to sin.
3. Federal (or Augustinian) view—That because of the unity of the human race, Adam's sin was imputed to posterity; corrupt nature begets corrupt nature. This position is taken by Paul, both here in Romans 5 and in 3:23: "For all have sinned [aorist tense, a once-for-all act in history] and come short [imperfect tense, repeatedly coming short] of the glory of God."
B. The Bible thus distinguishes between sin (the root *of my problem, caused by Adam) and sins (the* fruit *of my problem, caused by myself). I am therefore not a sinner because I sin, but I sin because I am a sinner.*

---

e. The relationship of the Law to his act—"Moreover the law entered, that the offence might abound" (Rom. 5:20).
2. The work of Christ
a. The reality of his act—He introduced grace and righteousness into the world.
(1) These blessings were free (Rom. 5:16).
(2) These blessings were abundant (Rom. 5:17).
b. The scope of his act—"The gift . . . hath abounded unto many" (Rom. 5:15b). "The free gift came upon all men" (Rom. 5:18).
c. The nature of his act—"So by the obedience of one shall many be made righteous" (Rom. 5:19b).
d. The results of his act
(1) Justification—"The free gift . . . unto justification" (Rom. 5:16b).
(2) Sanctification—"They which receive . . . grace and . . . righteousness shall reign in life" (Rom. 5:17b).
(3) Glorification—"Even so might grace reign . . . unto eternal life by Christ Jesus our Lord" (Rom. 5:21b).
e. The relationship of sin to his act—"But where sin abounded, grace did much more abound" (Rom. 5:20b).

The Power Plant of Grace—God's Way (Sanctification and Preservation)—Romans 6–8. Paul does discuss the sanctification of a saint. But from this point on, he does not discuss the justification of a sinner. It will prove helpful here to contrast these two words:
1. *Justification* is an act, while *sanctification* (which simply means "to set apart") is a work.

2. Justification is the means, while sanctification is the end.
3. The first removes the guilt and penalty of sin, while the second removes the growth and power of sin.
4. The former works for us, while the latter works in us.
5. The one declares us righteous, while the other makes us righteous.
6. Justification furnishes the track which leads to heaven, while sanctification furnishes the train.

We have already noted that sanctification simply means "to set apart." Thus, in the Bible:

1. Physical objects were said to be sanctified (Exod. 40: 10-11; 19:23).
2. People could sanctify themselves (Exod. 19:22).
3. One person could sanctify another (Exod. 13:2).
4. Evildoers could sanctify themselves to do iniquity (Isa. 66:17).
5. God sanctified Christ (John 10:36).
6. Christ sanctified himself (John 17:19).
7. A believer could sanctify an unbeliever (1 Cor. 7:14).
8. Carnal Christians are said to be sanctified (1 Cor. 1:2; 3:1-2).
9. Believers are commanded to sanctify God (1 Pet. 3:15). Chapters 6–8 go to make up the second "building" in the book of Romans. There are three "floors" to this power plant of grace.

I. The Plan—First Floor of Sanctification (Rom. 6:1-23)—In this chapter Paul lists God's threefold method leading to sanctification.
   A. Know ye (Rom. 6:1-10)—"Know ye not" (Rom. 6:3). Paul wants us to know three things.
      1. That we have been baptized with Christ into his death (Rom. 6:3)

---

†**6:3** *Here Paul states not only that Christ died* for *me, but* as *me. The word "baptism" simply means "identification." This identification with Christ on Calvary is one of many "dry baptisms" in the Bible. Others would include:*

A. The baptism of sin and suffering upon Christ (Matt. 20:22)
B. The baptism of the Holy Spirit upon believers at Pentecost (Acts 1:5)
C. The baptism of believers into the body of Christ (1 Cor. 12:13)
D. The baptism "for the dead" (1 Cor. 15:29). Note: This is thought to refer to that act of living believers identifying themselves with martyred believers by picking up their fallen banners.
E. The baptism "unto Moses" (1 Cor. 10:2)
F. The baptism of judgment during the tribulation (Matt. 3:11-12)

---

      2. That we have been planted together in the likeness of his resurrection—"For if we have been planted together in the likeness of his death, we shall be also in the likeness of his resurrection" (Rom. 6:5).

---

†**6:5** *The believer has now been "transplanted" three times:*

A. To the Garden of Eden where he sinned with Adam
B. To the cross, where he died with Christ
C. To the tomb, where he arose with Christ

---

3. That because of these two facts, the believer is:
   a. Delivered from his sin—"God forbid. How shall we, that are dead to sin, live any longer therein? . . . Knowing this, that our old man is crucified with him, that the body of sin might be destroyed, that henceforth we should not serve sin. For he that is dead is freed from sin" (Rom. 6:2, 6-7).

---

†6:7 *Death cancels all obligations. Sin here is personified as a cruel tyrant who taxes his subjects beyond all endurance. The only way to pay is to die. This, then, renders inactive (but does not remove) the body of sin and makes it powerless (see also Eph. 4:22-24; Col. 3:9-10).*

---

   b. Delivered to his Savior—"Now if we be dead with Christ, we believe that we shall also live with him: knowing that Christ being raised from the dead dieth no more; death hath no more dominion over him. For in that he died, he died unto sin once: but in that he liveth, he liveth unto God" (Rom. 6:8-10).

B. Reckon ye (Rom. 6:11-12)—"Likewise reckon ye also yourselves to be dead indeed unto sin, but alive unto God through Jesus Christ our Lord" (Rom. 6:11).

---

†6:11 *This simply means that by* faith *we are to act upon these facts regardless of any personal* feelings.

C. Yield ye (Rom. 6:13-15)
1. The rationale for this yielding
   a. The *who* of the matter—"Yield yourselves unto God as those that are alive from the dead" (Rom. 6:13).

---

†6:13

A. We are to stop yielding (present tense) our body members as instruments of unrighteousness.
B. We are to once for all (aorist tense) yield our body members as instruments of righteousness.

---

   b. The *what* of the matter (Rom. 6:13, 19)—"I speak after the manner of men because of the infirmity of your flesh: for as ye have yielded your members servants to uncleanness and to iniquity unto iniquity; even so now yield your members servants to righteousness unto holiness" (Rom. 6:19).
   c. The *why* of the matter—"For sin shall not have dominion over you: for ye are not under the law, but under grace. What then? shall we sin, because we are not under the law, but under grace? God forbid. Know ye not, that to whom ye yield yourselves servants to obey, his servants ye are to whom ye obey; whether of sin unto death, or of obedience unto righteousness?" (Rom. 6:14-16).
2. The rewards of this yielding—"But now being made free from sin, and become servants to God, ye have your fruit unto holiness, and the end everlasting life. For the wages of sin is death; but the gift of God is eternal life through Jesus Christ our Lord" (Rom. 6:22-23).

†6:23 *"Being made free from sin" (6:22). This marks the sixth time Paul has stated this fact. (See 6:2, 6-7, 14, 18). There are three Latin theological terms which may help clarify this precious doctrine. These are:*

A. Non posse non pecare—*Not able not to sin. This refers to believers before their salvation.*

B. Posse non pecare—*Able not to sin. This describes them after their salvation. They now have the power to live victorious lives.*

C. Non posse pecare—*Not able to sin. This describes existence after the Rapture.*

II. The Pain—The Second Floor of Frustration (Rom. 7:1-25). Paul now discusses what part the Law plays in God's plan of sanctification.

A. The spiritual man and the Law (Rom. 7:1-6)

1. His relationship to the Law

a. He is as a widow, being freed from her husband (Rom. 7: 1-3).

b. He is as a dead man, being freed from his lust (Rom. 7:5).

---

†7:5 *The Greek speaks of a violent death here: that of Calvary. In a sense it may be said it was necessary for both Christ and the believer to die in order to get together. Ponder the following:*

A. In the Old Testament, Christ was married to unfaithful Israel. (See the book of Hosea.)

B. In the New Testament, sinners are bound by the power of sin and the chains of the Law.

C. Then, Christ died, freeing him of his Old Testament relationship with sinful Israel (during this dispensation of the church). At the same time the believer died, freeing him from the Law and sin.

D. This blessed relationship will be fully consummated at the marriage of the Lamb. (See Rev. 19:7-8.)

---

2. His relationship to the Savior

a. He has been raised by Christ (Rom. 7:4).

b. He will be married to Christ (Rom. 7:4).

c. He is now able to produce fruit through Christ (Rom. 7:4). Thus, the spiritual person is delivered from the Law.

B. The natural person and the Law (Rom. 7:7-13)—Here the Law is used in a twofold manner.

1. The condemnation usage—Sin uses the Law to rekindle the sinfulness of the flesh (Rom. 7:7-11). "The Law . . . said, Thou shalt not covet. But sin, taking occasion by the commandment, wrought in me all manner of concupiscence" (Rom. 7:7-8). "For sin taking occasion by the commandment, deceived me, and by it slew me" (Rom. 7:11).

---

†7:11

A. The Law was used by sin to slay Paul (7:9-11). This may have been a reference to his bar mitzvah (a religious ceremony observed by all 13-year-old Jewish boys) at which time he formally took upon him the solemn responsibilities of the Law. His carefree days of childhood were then over. He was accountable to God for his actions.

B. The Law was used by sin to work in him "all manner of concupiscence [forbidden and evil desires]" (7:8). In other words, the Law both revealed *and, as used by sin,* revived *Paul's sin nature. Sin thus used the Law as its basis of operation in its war against Paul.*

2. The illustration usage—God uses the Law to reveal the sinfulness of the flesh (Rom. 7:12-13). "Wherefore the law is holy, and the commandment holy, and just, and good. Was then that which is good made death unto me? God forbid. But sin, that it might appear sin, working death in me by that which is good; that sin by the commandment might become exceeding sinful" (Rom. 7:12-13).

---

†7:13

A. The Law in itself is not evil, but rather is "holy, and just, and good" (7:12).

1. It is holy because it came from God (7:14).

2. It is just because it rightfully condemns the sinner.

3. It is good because it prepared the sinner for Christ (Gal. 3:24).

B. The Law was ineffective only because of the weakness of the flesh (7:18). Herein is the real problem. The finest and most experienced football coach in America would lose every single game if he had a team composed of crippled and blind players.

Thus, the natural person is doomed by the Law.

C. The carnal person and the Law (Rom. 7:14-25)—"For we know that the law is spiritual: but I am carnal, sold under sin" (Rom. 7:14).

1. Any attempt to keep the Law will lead to carnality. "For I know that in me (that is, in my flesh,) dwelleth no good thing: for to will is present with me; but how to perform that which is good I find not. For the good that I would I do not: but the evil which I would not, that I do" (Rom. 7:18-19).

2. No attempt to keep the Law can lead to spirituality.

a. The agony of Paul's problem (Rom. 7:22-24)—"O wretched man that I am! who shall deliver me from the body of this death?" (Rom. 7:24).

---

†7:24

A. This may have been a spiritual comparison to the Roman act of punishing a murderer by binding to him the corpse of his victim, thus using its very rot and stench to execute the killer. Phillips writes: "Suppose a biologist were to perform an experiment by grafting, at a given stage of development, a butterfly to a spider and do so in such a way that the two creatures were fused into one and thus grew to maturity. What a clash of instincts there would be in a monstrosity like this! One part of the creature's nature would long for the clear vault of heaven, while the other part would crave a web in a dark corner and a diet of blood. What could be done with such a creature? Nothing, except put it to death. There is a sense in which, in the Garden of Eden, Satan performed just such diabolical surgery on the human race" (Exploring Romans, *p. 120).*

B. Paul thus realizes that the believer cannot control, change, cleanse, conquer, command, correct, or crucify the flesh.

---

b. The answer to Paul's problem (Rom. 7:25)—"I thank God through Jesus Christ our Lord. So then with the mind I myself serve the law of God; but with the flesh the law of sin" (Rom. 7:25). *Thus, the carnal person is defeated by the Law.* Paul ends chapter 6 with the statement that eternal life comes only through Jesus Christ (6:23). He ends chapter 7 by concluding that the victorious life can come only through Jesus Christ.

Note: Before leaving chapter 7 it may prove helpful to briefly summarize the purpose and ministry of the Old Testament Law.

The Law consisted of three sections:
1. The Ten Commandments (Exod. 20:3-17; Deut. 5:7-21)
2. The social regulations concerning the people (Exod. 21–23)
3. The religious ordinances concerning the tabernacle (Exod. 24–40).

The Law followed the Abrahamic covenant by some five centuries, and therefore did not in any way abrogate God's previous promises (Gen. 12:1-3; Gal. 3:17-18). It was a way *of* life, but not a way *to* life (see Gal. 2:15-16; 3:21; 2 Cor. 3:7, 9). Why did not Christ come during Abraham's time? Faith was then present (see Gen. 15; Rom. 4). The answer is that the chief meaning of the Law lies in the developing of an expectation of the Redeemer by revealing human sinfulness. It was therefore an addition, because the covenant with Abraham lacked a sufficient emphasis on sin. God used the ministry of two men to fully develop the meaning of faith repentance which leads to salvation. Note these two men:
1. Moses introduced the curse (Gal. 3:13).
2. Abraham introduced the blessing (Gal. 3:9, 14).
3. Moses pointed to the system of death (2 Cor. 3:6; Rom. 7: 9-10).
4. Abraham pointed to the system of life (Rom. 4:17-25; Heb. 11:19).
5. Moses led to the crucifixion (Gal. 2:19-20; 3:13).
6. Abraham led to the resurrection (Heb. 11:19; Rom. 4:17, 19, 23-25). "But they both belong together, for the sinner is to be redeemed, and to this end renewal and new birth are needful. But the new birth has man's conversion as a presupposition, and conversion is twofold: a turning from and a turning to, a *No* to oneself and a YES to God, or, as the New Testament puts it, *repentance* and *faith!* Only here is revealed to us the true meaning of the Old Testament histories:

Throughout centuries God spoke the word 'faith' into the history of salvation—this is the meaning of the Covenant with Abraham. Throughout 2,000 years it was an education in faith. Throughout centuries God spoke the word 'repent' into the history of salvation—this is the meaning of the law of Moses. For some 1,500 years it was an education in repentance" (Erich Sauer, *Dawn of World Redemption*, pp. 122-123).

Then came Jesus "into Galilee, preaching the gospel of the kingdom of God, and saying, The time is fulfilled, and the kingdom of God is at hand: repent ye, and believe the gospel" (Mark 1:14-15). Thus, in one statement, Jesus joins perfectly both the message of Moses and that of Abraham (see also Acts 20:21.) We may therefore conclude that the Law functioned as:
1. A *bridle,* whereby God could control Israel from above.
2. A *hedge,* which separated Israel from the nations of the world.
3. A *mirror,* revealing the true condition of human beings.
4. A *stimulant,* bringing to surface the hidden sin of human beings.
5. A *schoolteacher,* preparing us for, and delivering us to, Christ (Gal. 3:19. 24; Rom. 3:20; 7:7).

III. The Prize—Third Floor of Preservation (Rom. 8:1-39).
Paul has thus far discussed the following: *One:* Why does the sinner need to be saved? Answer: Condemnation. *Two:* How is the sinner saved? Answer: Justification. *Three:* What is to happen after the sinner gets saved? Answer: Sanctification. *Four:* Will the sinner remain saved? This is the question answered in Romans 8, and the

answer is yes, he or she will, indeed, because of preservation.

It has been observed that if the Bible were likened to a beautiful ring set with jewels, the book of Romans would be the most beautiful jewel in the ring, and the eighth chapter the most beautiful facet in the jewel. Romans 8 is in essence an amplification of John 5:24 and Revelation 21:5. "Verily, Verily, I say unto you, he that heareth my word, and believeth on him that sent me, hath everlasting life, and shall not come into condemnation; but is passed from death unto life" (John 5:24).

"And he that sat upon the throne said, Behold, I make all things new. And he said unto me, write: for these words are true and faithful'" (Rev. 21:5). Will the believing sinner remain saved? He will, because of seven new things:

A. The believer has a new position (Rom 8:1-8).
   1. His position in regard to the Son of God: He is now in Christ. "There is therefore now no condemnation to them which are in Christ Jesus, who walk not after the flesh, but after the Spirit" (Rom. 8:1).

---

†8:1 *Note: We observe that Paul does not say there is no fault, or sin, or imperfection, but* no condemnation. *We also observe the time element—it is* now *no condemnation.*

---

   2. His position in regard to the law of God—He now fulfills its demands through Christ.
      a. The failure involved—"Because the carnal mind is enmity against God: for it is not subject to the law of God, neither indeed can be. So then they that are in the flesh cannot please God" (Rom. 8:7-8).
      b. The facts involved—"For the law of the Spirit of life in Christ Jesus hath made me free from the law of sin and death. For what the law could not do, in that it was weak through the flesh, God sending his own Son in the likeness of sinful flesh, and for sin, condemned sin in the flesh" (Rom. 8:2-3).
      c. The fruit involved—"That the righteousness of the law might be fulfilled in us, who walk not after the flesh, but after the Spirit. For they that are after the flesh do mind the things of the flesh; but they that are after the Spirit the things of the Spirit. For to be carnally minded is death; but to be spiritually minded is life and peace" (Rom. 8:4-6).

B. The believer has a new guest (Rom. 8:9-13)—"But ye are not in the flesh, but in the Spirit, if so be that the Spirit of God dwell in you. Now if any man have not the Spirit of Christ, he is none of his. . . . But if the Spirit of him that raised up Jesus from the dead dwell in you, he that raised up Christ from the dead shall also quicken your mortal bodies by his Spirit that dwelleth in you" (Rom. 8:9, 11).

C. The believer has a new adoption (Rom. 8:14-17)—"Ye have received the Spirit of adoption" (Rom. 8:15).

---

†8:15

A. This verse contains the first of but five references to the word adoption in the Bible. All five come from the pen of Paul. These are: Romans 8:15, 23; 9:4; Galatians 4:5; Ephesians 1:5.

B. Here is an overview of biblical adoption:

1. *The theology of adoption: Defined, the word literally means "the placing of a son." Adoption logically follows regeneration. Regeneration gives one his nature as a child of God, whereas adoption gives him his position as a son of God (Rom. 8:15-23; Gal. 4:4-6; Eph. 1:5; 2 Cor. 6:18).*
2. *Contrasted—How spiritual adoption differs from civil adoption:*
   a. *We never adopt our own children, but God never adopts any other than his own.*
   b. *Civil adoption provides comfort for the childless, but God had a beloved Son (Matt. 3:17; 17:5) prior to adopting us.*
   c. *There are usually many pleasing characteristics in a civil-adopted child, but not in God's children prior to their adoption (Rom. 3:10-18).*
   d. *Civil adoption could never give a child the same nature of the Father, but God's adopted are given the very mind of Christ (1 Cor. 2:16).*
   e. *In some cases, civil adoption could be declared null and void, but God's adopted are absolutely secure.*
3. *Compared—How spiritual adoption compares with civil adoption:*
   a. *The Father must begin the action leading to adoption (Isa. 1:18; John 3:16).*
   b. *Both adoptions give an inheritance to one who previously had none (Rom. 8:17; 1 Pet. 1:1-9).*
   c. *Both adoptions provide a new name (Rev. 2:17; John 1:42).*

---

1. We have an intimacy with the Father (Rom. 8:15)—"Whereby we cry, Abba, Father" (Rom. 8:15).
2. We have an inheritance with the Son (Rom. 8:17)—"And if children, then heirs; heirs of God, and joint-heirs with Christ; if so be that we suffer with him, that we may be also glorified together" (Rom. 8:17).
3. We have an illumination by the Spirit (Rom. 8:14, 16).
   a. He walks with us—"For as many as are led by the Spirit of God, they are the sons of God" (Rom. 8:14).
   b. He witnesses to us—"The Spirit itself beareth witness with our spirit, that we are the children of God" (Rom. 8:16).

D. The believer has a new hope (Rom. 8:18-25)—The nature of this hope is the full and final redemption of all things. This includes:
1. The Christian himself (Rom. 8:18, 23)—"For I consider that the sufferings of this present time are not worthy to be compared with the glory that is to be revealed in us" (Rom. 8:18).

   "We ourselves, having the first fruits of the Spirit . . . groan within ourselves, waiting eagerly for our adoption as sons, the redemption of our body" (Rom. 8:23, NASB).

---

†8:23

A. *It will be a body like Christ's body (1 John 3:2).*
B. *It will be a body of flesh and bone (Luke 24:39). Our Lord both spoke (John 20:17) and ate and drank (Luke 24:30, 41-43; John 21:13) in his resurrected body.*
C. *It will be a recognizable body (1 Cor. 13:12). Jesus was recognized by all believers after his resurrection.*
D. *It will be a body in which the Spirit predominates (1 Cor. 15:44, 49).*
E. *It will be a body unlimited by time and space (John 20:19).*

2. The creation itself (Rom. 8:19-22)—"For the anxious longing of the creation waits eagerly for the revealing of the sons of God. For the creation was subjected to futility, not of its own will, but because of him who subjected it, in hope that the creation itself also will be set free from its slavery to corruption into the freedom of the glory of the children of God. For we know that the whole creation groans and suffers the pains of childbirth together until now" (Rom. 8:19-22, NASB).

E. The believer has a new prayer helper (Rom. 8:26-27).

1. The identity of this helper—The Holy Spirit himself.
2. The necessity for this helper—"Likewise the Spirit also helpeth our infirmities: for we know not what we should pray for as we ought" (Rom. 8:26a).

---

†8:26a

A. *In the Greek, the word* infirmities *is in the singular. Paul had but a single infirmity in mind here: our ignorance and inability in prayer. "For we know not what we should pray for as we ought" (8:26).*

B. *The word* helpeth *should not be overlooked at this point. It means "to aid in the completion of a task." The same word is used in Luke 10:40. All this simply means the Holy Spirit expects the believer to do his share of praying also.*

---

3. The intensity of this helper—"The Spirit itself maketh intercession for us with groanings which cannot be uttered" (Rom. 8:26).

---

†8:26b *This is the third "groan" mentioned in chapter 8.*

A. *The groan of nature (8:22)*
B. *The groan of the believer (8:23)*
C. *The groan of the Holy Spirit (8:26)*

---

4. The infallibility of this helper—He cooperates with Christ. "And he that searcheth the hearts knoweth what is the mind of the Spirit, because he maketh intercession for the saints according to the will of God" (Rom. 8:27).

F. The believer has a new confidence (Rom. 8:28)—"And we know that all things work together for good to them that love God, to them who are the called according to his purpose" (Rom. 8:28).

---

†8:28 *Here we should note two things this verse does* not *say:*

A. *It does not say all things in and by themselves are good, but rather that they work together* for *good. A classic Old Testament example of this is Joseph's testimony to his brothers. (See Gen. 45:5-8; 50:20. See also Psa. 76:10.) Jacob (Joseph's father) did not always understand this principle; thus his troubled conclusion in Genesis 42:36.*

B. *It does not say that this is true for all people, but only for God-lovers. But for these, it is an all-inclusive statement. It covers the good and the bad, the bright and the dark, the sweet and the bitter, the easy and the hard, the happy and the sad. It may be depended upon in prosperity and poverty, in health and sickness, in the calm and in the storm, in life and in death.*

G. The believer has a new destiny (Rom. 8:29-39).
   1. The nature of this goal—"For whom he did foreknow, he also did predestinate to be conformed to the image of his Son, that he might be the firstborn among many brethren" (Rom. 8:29).

---

†8:29 *God has one supreme purpose on this earth today, and that is to conform the largest number of people in the least amount of time into the image of his dear Son.*

---

   2. The steps involved in this goal—We have been foreknown, predestinated, called, justified, and glorified already in the mind of God. These five words form a golden chain of God's grace and glory, linking up from eternity past to eternity future.
   3. The guarantee of this goal
      a. Question: "Who shall separate us from the love of Christ?" (Rom. 8:35a).
      b. Answer: No one. This is true in the face of tribulation, distress, persecution, famine, nakedness, peril, sword, death, life, and includes angels, principalities, powers, things present, things to come, height, depth, or any other creature (see Rom. 8:35, 38-39). "What shall we then say to these things? If God be for us, who can be against us? Who shall lay any thing to the charge of God's elect? It is God that justifieth. Nay, in all these things we are more than conquerors through him that loved us" (Rom. 8:31, 33, 37).

---

†8:37 *When the staunch believer John Chrysostom was brought before the Roman Emperor in the fifth century and threatened with banishment for his faith, he replied, "Thou canst not banish me, for this world is my Father's house." "But I will slay thee," said the Emperor. "Nay, thou canst not," said the noble champion of the faith, "for my life is hid with Christ in God." "I will drive thee away from man and thou shalt have no friend left." "Nay, thou canst not, for I have a friend in heaven from whom thou canst not separate me! I defy thee, for there is nothing that thou canst do to hurt me!"*

---

      c. Reason: Because of the threefold work of Christ
         (1) His death guarantees it (Rom. 8:32)—"He that spared not his own Son, but delivered him up for us all, how shall he not with him also freely give us all things?" (Rom. 8:32).
         (2) His resurrection guarantees it—"It is Christ that died, yea, rather, that is risen again" (Rom. 8:34a).
         (3) His intercession guarantees it—"Who is even at the right hand of God, who also maketh intercession for us" (Rom. 8:34b).

The *Synagogue* of Israel—God's *Wisdom* (Explanation and Vindication) Romans 9–11. Paul writes these chapters to answer two questions. *First,* how does God look upon Israel's rejection of their Messiah? *Second,* how does Israel fit into God's plan for the church?

I. The Sovereignty of God and Israel's Selection in the Past (Rom. 9)—"I say the truth in Christ, I lie not, my conscience also bearing me witness in the Holy Ghost, that I have great heaviness and continual sorrow in my heart. For I could wish that myself were accursed from Christ for my brethren, my kinsmen according to the flesh" (Rom. 9:1-3).

†**9:3** *Paul shared the compassion of both Moses (Exod. 32:31-32) and Christ (Matt. 23:37) over Israel's sinful condition. (See also Gal. 1:8-9.)*

A. The nine spiritual advantages of this sovereign selection (Rom. 9:4-5)
  1. They were Israelites (a special nation).
  2. They had been adopted by God.
  3. They had the glory cloud—This is a reference to the shekinah cloud, that visible luminous appearance of God's presence.
    a. It led them across the wilderness (Exod. 13:21-22; Num. 9:17-22).
    b. It protected them at the Red Sea (Exod. 14:19-20, 24).
    c. It filled the tabernacle during Moses' dedication (Exod. 40:34-38).
    d. It filled the temple during Solomon's dedication (1 Kings 8:10-11; 2 Chron. 5:13-14).
    e. It was removed during Ezekiel's time (Ezek. 10).
  4. They had the covenants.
    a. The Abrahamic covenant—Promising a mighty nation (Gen. 12:2-3, 7; 13:14-17; 15:5, 18; 17:8).
    b. The Palestinian covenant—Promising a land (Deut. 30:3).
    c. The Davidic covenant—Promising an eternal kingdom (2 Sam. 7:12-16; 23:5; 2 Chron. 13:5).
    d. The New Covenant—Promising new hearts (Jer. 31:31-34).
  5. They had the Law.
  6. They performed services for God (ministering in both tabernacle and temple).
  7. They had the messianic promise.
  8. They had a regenerate ancestry (Abraham, Moses, David, etc.).
  9. They were the people from which Christ came.

B. The historical example of this sovereign selection (Rom. 9:6-29)
  1. The example of Ishmael and Isaac (Rom. 9:6-9)—"Not as though the word of God hath taken none effect. For they are not all Israel, which are of Israel: Neither, because they are the seed of Abraham, are they all children: but, In Isaac shall thy seed be called" (Rom. 9:6-7). God chose Isaac (Abraham's son through Sarah) over Ishmael (his son through Hagar).
  2. The example of Esau and Jacob (Rom. 9:10-13)—"(For the children being not yet born, neither having done any good or evil, that the purpose of God according to election might stand, not of works, but of him that calleth;) It was said unto her, The elder shall serve the younger. As it is written, Jacob have I loved, but Esau have I hated" (Rom. 9:11-13).

     God chose Jacob (second-born twin of Isaac) over Esau (firstborn twin). Some have been troubled over Paul's statement here in verse 13: "As it is written, Jacob have I loved, but Esau have I hated." It should be noted that the statement obviously does *not* refer to the two boys, but to the nations they founded, namely, Israel and Edom. This Old Testament prophet Obadiah clearly tells us *why* God hated Edom. In each case here (9:6-13), God rejected men who had been firstborn into patriarchal families. In each case the parent wished to see the rejected one inherit the problem. Abraham pleaded for Ishmael (Gen. 17:18) and Isaac attempted to pass the blessing on to Esau (Gen 27:1, 4, 30, 33).

3. The example of Pharaoh (Rom. 9:14-24)
   a. The facts
      (1) God determined to pardon sinful Israel with undeserved grace. "For he saith to Moses, I will have mercy on whom I will have mercy, and I will have compassion on whom I will have compassion. So then it is not of him that willeth, nor of him that runneth, but of God that sheweth mercy" (Rom. 9:15-16).
      (2) God determined to punish sinful Pharaoh with deserved judgment—"For the scripture saith unto Pharaoh, Even for this same purpose have I raised thee up, that I might shew my power in thee, and that my name might be declared throughout all the earth" (Rom. 9:17).

---

†9:17

A. Some would claim that he was unfair in hardening Pharaoh's heart. It should be noted that on at least seven occasions in the book of Exodus we are told that God hardened the heart of Pharaoh (4:21; 7:3; 9:12; 10:1, 20, 27; 11:10). How are we to understand this? A partial (and only partial) answer may be found in the following observation: The manner in which a given object will react when confronted by an outside influence is wholly dependent upon the nature of that object. For example, imagine a winter scene and a frozen river. On either side is a bank of yellow clay. Suddenly the sun comes from behind the clouds and shines brightly down upon the river and the banks. What happens next? The reaction is this: The ice will melt but the clay will harden. Thus we see in nature the same outside, heavenly influence softening one object but hardening the other.

B. Furthermore, it should be pointed out that on four occasions we are informed that Pharaoh hardened his own heart (Exod. 7:22; 8:15, 19; 9:35). The word "hardeneth" in 9:18 (kabed) *is translated "heavy" in Exodus 17:12; 18:18; Psalm 38:4; and Isaiah 1:4. Thus, God left his heart heavy with iniquities.*

---

   b. The fairness—Paul answers two questions here.
      (1) Is God righteous? Yes (Rom. 9:14, 21-24)—"What shall we say then? Is there unrighteousness with God? God forbid. . . . Hath not the potter power over the clay, of the same lump to make one vessel unto honour, and another unto dishonour?" (Rom. 9:14, 21).

---

†9:21 *Paul spends little time on this objection, simply pointing out that the potter has power over the clay he works with in choosing the kind of vessel he makes. It should be noted here (9:21) that Paul does not say God* made *the clay as it was, but that he* worked *with it. (See Jer. 18:1-6; Isa. 45:9; 64:6-8.) Two kinds of vessels are described here: "The vessels of wrath fitted to destruction" (9:22). This is in the middle voice, meaning "to fit oneself." "The vessels of mercy, which he had afore prepared unto glory" (9:23). The conclusion of the matter is that* hell *(destruction) is the deserved destination of the sinful person, while* heaven *(glory) is the undeserved destination of the saved person.*

---

      (2) Are we responsible? *Yes* (Rom. 9:19-20). "Thou wilt say then unto me, Why doth he yet find fault? For who hath resisted his will? Nay but,

O man, who art thou that repliest against God? Shall the thing formed say to him that formed it, Why hast thou made me thus?" (Rom. 9:19-20).

4. The example from Hosea (Rom. 9:25-26)—"As he saith also in Osee, I will call them my people, which were not my people; and her beloved, which was not beloved" (Rom. 9:25).
5. The example from Isaiah (Rom. 9:27-29)—"Esaias also crieth concerning Israel, Though the number of the children of Israel be as the sand of the sea, a remnant shall be saved. . . . And as Esaias said before, Except the Lord of Sabaoth had left us a seed, we had been as Sodoma, and been made like unto Gomorrha" (Rom. 9:27, 29).

---

†9:29

A. In Hosea's example, God's sovereignty is seen in reference to the saved Gentiles (1 Pet. 2:9-10).
B. In Isaiah's example, God's sovereignty is seen in reference to the saved Israelite remnant.

C. The two conclusions concerning this sovereign selection (Rom. 9:30-33)
1. Through faith the Gentiles had attained righteousness without even seeking it (Rom. 9:30).
2. Through the Law Israel had not attained righteousness even after seeking it (Rom. 9:31-33).

---

†9:33 *They looked for a bold lion; but God sent them a bleeding lamb. They wanted a throne; they were offered a cross.*

II. The Righteousness of God and Israel's Rejection at the Present (Romans 10)
Introduction: Romans 9 and 10 should always be read together. Chapter 9 shows why some Jews are saved; and chapter 10 explains why most are lost.
A. The prayer for God's righteousness (Rom. 9:1-3; 10:1-2)—At the beginning of chapters 9 and 10 Paul reveals his great soul agony over Israel's lost condition. "Brethren, my heart's desire and prayer to God for Israel is, that they might be saved. For I bear them record that they have a zeal of God, but not according to knowledge" (Rom. 10:1-2).
B. The source of God's righteousness (Rom. 10:4-5)—"For Christ is the end of the law for righteousness to every one that believeth. For Moses describeth the righteousness which is of the law, that the man which doeth those things shall live by them" (Rom. 10:4-5).

---

†10:4 *We might reword this verse to say that Christ is the end of the Old Testament Law to the believer after the Cross, as George Washington was the end of the British law to the American after the Revolutionary War. (See 2 Cor. 3:6-11; Heb. 7:11-19; Gal. 3:24; Eph. 2:15; Col. 2:14.)*

C. The availability of God's righteousness (Rom. 10:6-8)—"But what saith it? The word is nigh thee, even in thy mouth, and in thy heart: that is, the word of faith, which we preach" (Rom. 10:8). This is true because of two historical facts.

1. The incarnation of Christ (Rom. 10:6)—"But the righteousness which is of faith speaketh on this wise, Say not in thine heart, Who shall ascend into heaven? (that is, to bring Christ down from above)" (Rom. 10:6).
2. The resurrection of Christ (Rom. 10:7)—"Or, Who shall descend into the deep? (that is, to bring up Christ again from the dead)" (Rom. 10:7).

D. The method of God's righteousness (Rom. 10:9-10)—"That if thou shalt confess with thy mouth the Lord Jesus, and shalt believe in thine heart that God hath raised him from the dead, thou shalt be saved" (Rom. 10:9).

---

†10:9-10 *Some have made oral confession a condition of salvation on the basis of 10:10: "For with the heart man believeth unto righteousness; and with the mouth confession is made unto salvation." The Bible, of course, does not impose this limitation. Paul evidently was stressing the same truth found in James 2:20; that is, a genuine possession of Christ in one's heart will surely lead to a confession of Christ with one's mouth. The fruit will prove the root. (See Matt. 10:32; Luke 12:8; John 12:42-43; Matt. 12:34.) The method, then, of righteousness, is faith in Christ.*

E. The scope of God's righteousness (Rom. 10:11-13)—"For whosoever shall call upon the name of the Lord shall be saved" (Rom. 10:13).

---

†10:13 *Paul had earlier shown that all were lost. He now says that all can be saved. Compare the "whosoever" mentioned here with that in Revelation 20:15.*

F. The presentation of God's righteousness (Rom. 10:14-15)—"How then shall they call on him in whom they have not believed? and how shall they believe in him of whom they have not heard? and how shall they hear without a preacher? And how shall they preach, except they be sent? as it is written, How beautiful are the feet of them that preach the gospel of peace, and bring glad tidings of good things!" (Rom. 10:14-15). There are three reasons why God sends preachers.

1. A sinner must call upon the Lord to be saved.
2. He must believe in order to call.
3. He must hear in order to believe.

G. The rejection of God's righteousness (Rom. 10:16-21)

1. Isaiah had prophesied this rejection—"But they have not all obeyed the gospel. For Esaias saith, Lord, who hath believed our report? . . . But Esaias is very bold, and saith, I was found of them that sought me not; I was made manifest unto them that asked not after me. But to Israel he saith, All day long I have stretched forth my hands unto a disobedient and gainsaying people" (Rom. 10:16, 20-21).
2. Moses had prophesied this rejection—"But I say, Did not Israel know? First Moses saith, I will provoke you to jealousy by them that are no people, and by a foolish nation I will anger you" (Rom. 10:19).

III. The Wisdom of God and Israel's Restoration in the Future (Rom. 11)—Paul here just discussed the rejection of Israel in chapter 10. He will now show that this rejection was neither *total* nor *final* (vv. 26-36).

A. This restoration is assured because Israel's rejection was not total (Rom. 11:1-25).

1. The factions of Israel (Rom. 11:1-10)
   a. The minority group—"I say then, Hath God cast away his people? God forbid. For I also am an Israelite, of the seed of Abraham, of the tribe of Benjamin. God hath not cast away his people which he foreknew. Wot ye not what the scripture saith of Elias? how he maketh intercession to God against Israel, saying, Lord, they have killed thy prophets, and digged down thine altars; and I am left alone, and they seek my life. But what saith the answer of God unto him? I have reserved to myself seven thousand men, who have not bowed the knee to the image of Baal. Even so then at this present time also there is a remnant according to the election of grace" (Rom. 11:1-5). This group is represented by Paul (Rom. 11:1) and Elijah (Rom. 11:2-4).

---

†**11:4** *Elijah felt he was the only believer during his day, and he actually made "intercession to God against Israel" (11:2). But God (who will* never *answer this kind of prayer, regardless of who prays it) quickly informed him that: "I have reserved to myself seven thousand men, who have not bowed the knee to the image of Baal" (Rom. 11:4; see also 1 Kings 19:10, 14, 18).*

---

   b. The majority group (Rom. 11:6-10)—"What then? Israel hath not obtained that which he seeketh for; but the election hath obtained it, and the rest were blinded" (Rom. 11: 7).

---

†**11:7** *Both Isaiah and David predicted this. Present-day Israel is thus plagued with a threefold blindness:*
A. The blindness caused by the fall of Adam (Eph. 4:18)
B. The blindness caused by Satan (2 Cor. 4:4)
C. The blindness caused by God (Rom. 11:8)

---

      (1) Isaiah: Compare Romans 11:8 with Isaiah 29:10—"(According as it is written, God hath given them the spirit of slumber, eyes that they should not see, and ears that they should not hear;) unto this day" (Rom. 11:8).
      (2) David: Compare Romans 11:9-10 with Psalm 69:22-23—"And David saith, Let their table be made a snare, and a trap, and a stumblingblock, and a recompence unto them: Let their eyes be darkened, that they may not see, and bow down their back alway" (Rom. 11:9-10).

2. The fullness of the Gentiles (Rom. 11:11-25)—"For I would not, brethren, that ye should be ignorant of this mystery, lest ye should be wise in your own conceits; that blindness in part is happened to Israel, until the fullness of the Gentiles be come in" (Rom. 11:25).
   a. The definition of this period (as contrasted to the times of the Gentiles)—"And they shall fall by the edge of the sword, and shall be led away captive into all nations: and Jerusalem shall be trodden down of the Gentiles, until the times of the Gentiles be fulfilled" (Luke 21:24).
      (1) The *fullness* refers to that time span involved in the completing of the

body of Christ consisting of both saved Jews and Gentiles) from Pentecost to the Rapture (see Acts 15:14; 1 Cor. 12:12-13; Eph. 4:11, 13).

(2) The *times* refers to that time span from the Babylonian Captivity until the end of the tribulation. (See Deut. 28:28-68; 2 Chron. 36:21; Dan. 9:24-27.)

b. The details of this period

(1) The *facts*—Paul offers a parable from nature

(a) An olive tree—Symbolizing the faith of Abraham (Rom. 11:16, 18). "For if the firstfruit be holy, the lump is also holy: and if the root be holy, so are the branches" (Rom. 11:16).

(b) Some natural branches broken off—Symbolizing unbelieving Israel (Rom. 11:17), a past event

(c) Some wild branches grafted on—Symbolizing believing Gentiles (Rom. 11:17, 19), a present event

(d) Some natural branches grafted back on—Symbolizing believing Israel (Rom. 11:23-24), a future event

(2) The *fiction*—This parable does not teach that the church has replaced Israel. This parable does not teach that a believer can lose his salvation. He is simply saying that since God did not spare the nation Israel when they were apostate, he will likewise not spare an apostate church. Christendom is going in the same direction today as Israel once did, and God will reject and judge them for it. (See 1 Tim. 4:1-3; 2 Pet. 2:1-22; Rev. 3:14-22; 17:3-18.)

(3) The *future*

(a) Israel's unbelief once led to the riches of the Gentiles (Rom. 11:12).

(b) Israel's belief will lead to the redemption of the globe—"For if the casting away of them be the reconciling of the world, what shall the receiving of them be, but life from the dead?" (Rom. 11:15).

B. This restoration is assured because Israel's rejection was not permanent (Rom. 11:26-36).

1. The Israel of God (Rom. 11:26-32)

a. To be restored through their promised Christ (Rom. 11:26)—"And so all Israel shall be saved: as it is written, There shall come out of Sion the Deliverer, and shall turn away ungodliness from Jacob" (Rom. 11:26).

---

†**11:26** *Note: In the previous verse (11:25), Paul describes this future restoration as a* mystery.

A. A mystery in the Bible is a previously hidden truth, not revealed in the Old Testament, but declared and, at times, explained in the New Testament.

B. There are 12 such mysteries. Without amplification, these are:

1. The mystery of the kingdom of heaven (Matt. 13:3-50; Mark 4:1-25; Luke 8:4-15)

2. The mystery of the Rapture (1 Cor. 15:51-52; 1 Thess. 4:16)

3. The mystery of the church as the body of Christ (Eph. 3: 1-11; 6:19; Col. 4:3; Rom. 16:25)

4. The mystery of the church as the bride of Christ (Eph. 5: 28-32)

5. The mystery of the indwelling Christ (Gal. 2:20; Col. 1:26-27)

6. The mystery of the incarnate Christ (Col. 2:2, 9; 1 Cor. 2:7)

7. The mystery of godliness (1 Tim. 3:16)

8. The mystery of iniquity (2 Thess. 2:3-12; Matt. 13:33)

9. The mystery of Israel's present blindness (Rom. 11:25)

10. The mystery of the seven stars (Rev. 1:20)

11. The mystery of Babylon the harlot (Rev. 17:5, 7)

12. The mystery of God (Rev. 10:7; 11:15-19)

C. In Romans 11:25 the mystery *is that "blindness in part is happened to Israel until the fullness of the Gentiles be come in."*

---

b. To be restored through their promised covenant (Rom. 11:27)—"For this is my covenant unto them, when I shall take away their sins. . . . For the gifts and calling of God are without repentance" (Rom. 11:27, 29).

2. The God of Israel (Rom. 11:33-36)—"O the depth of the riches both of the wisdom and knowledge of God! how unsearchable are his judgments, and his ways past finding out! For who hath known the mind of the Lord? or who hath been his counsellor? Or who hath first given to him, and it shall be recompensed unto him again? For of him, and through him, and to him, are all things: to whom be glory for ever. Amen" (Rom. 11:33-36).

The Temple of God—God's Will (Transformation and Exhortation)—Romans 12–16

I. Personal Responsibilities for All the Redeemed (Rom. 12:1–15:13)

A. The believer and self (Rom. 12:1-2)

1. What he is to offer: Body dedication—"I beseech you therefore, brethren, by the mercies of God, that ye present your bodies a living sacrifice, holy, acceptable unto God, which is your reasonable service" (Rom. 12:1).

---

†12:1

A. Note: Paul does not issue a curt command, but rather a pleading request. Loving service simply cannot be commanded. This is the language of grace and the method of the apostle. (See also 1 Cor. 4:16; Eph. 4:1; 1 Tim. 2:1; contrast this with Luke 12:20.)

B. What is the believer invited to do? He is to present his body "a living sacrifice, holy, acceptable unto God." Note:

1. It is to be his body. *God is not primarily interested in our time, talents, or treasury. The only gift which satisfies the Redeemer Creator is the body of his redeemed creature. (See 1 Cor. 3:16; 6:19-20; 2 Cor. 8:5.)*

2. It is to be his living *body. Sometimes it is easier to die for the Lord than it is to live for him.*

3. It is to be a separated *(holy) living body.*

C. Why is the believer invited to do this?

1. Because he has already experienced God's mercy. All other faiths make sacrifice the root of mercy, but Christianity makes it the flower. (Contrast this with 1 Kings 18:26-29; 2 Kings 3:26-27.)

2. Because it is not only the proper and requested course of action, but also the practical and reasonable route.

a. To the sinner, *God says, "Come now, and let us reason together, saith the Lord: Though your sins be as scarlet, they shall be as white as snow; though they be red like crimson, they shall be as wool" (Isa. 1:18). The proper and practical thing for the sinner to do is to give God his* heart.

b. To the saint, God says, "Present your bodies . . . unto God, which is your reasonable service." The proper and practical thing for the saint to do is give God his body.

---

2. What he is to avoid: Worldly conformation—"And be not conformed to this world" (Rom. 12:2a).

3. What he is to achieve: Godly transformation—"But be ye transformed by the renewing of your mind, that ye may prove what is that good, and acceptable, and perfect, will of God" (Rom. 12:2b).

---

†12:2 *The word "transformed" is* metamorpheo *in the Greek, from whence we get our word* metamorphosis, *that biological change whereby a caterpillar becomes a butterfly. The same word is used in the transfiguration of Jesus in Matthew 17:2. (See also 2 Cor. 3:18.) This transformation refers to that act of a believer arranging his outward* position *so that it agrees with his inward* condition. *(See 1 Pet. 1:14; 1 John 2:15.) The renewing of the mind here in 12:2 is probably a reference to constant Bible study and prayer (Eph. 4:23; Col. 3:10). This daily renewing is the only safeguard against failure (1 Cor. 9:24-27).*

B. The believer and service (Rom. 12:3-21)—"For I say, through the grace given unto me, to every man that is among you, not to think of himself more highly than he ought to think; but to think soberly, according as God hath dealt to every man the measure of faith" (Rom. 12:3).

1. The tools for Christian service—Seven gifts of the spirit (Rom. 12:4-8). "For as we have many members in one body, and all members have not the same office: So we, being many, are one body in Christ, and every one members one of another" (Rom. 12:4-5).

   "Having then gifts differing according to the grace that is given to us" (Rom. 12:6).

   a. Foretelling and forthtelling (Rom. 12:6)
   b. Serving (Rom. 12:7a)
   c. Teaching (Rom. 12:8b)
   d. Exhorting (Rom. 12:8)
   e. Giving (Rom. 12:8)
   f. Ruling (Rom. 12:8b)
   g. Mercy showing (Rom. 12:8c)

2. The techniques of service—A list of 24 commands from the Spirit (Rom. 12:9-21). "Let love be without dissimulation. Abhor that which is evil; cleave to that which is good" (Rom. 12:9).

---

†12:9 *"To dwell above, with saints in love, that will indeed be glory; to dwell below with saints we know, well, that's a different story!"*

---

a. How to deal with one's friends (Rom. 12:10, 13-15)—"Be kindly affectioned one to another with brotherly love; in honour preferring one another. . . . Distributing to the necessity of saints; given to hospitality. Bless them which persecute you: bless, and curse not. Rejoice with them that do rejoice, and weep with them that weep" (Rom. 12:10, 13-15).

---

†12:15 *We are to "rejoice with them that do rejoice, and weep with them that weep." Jesus did this (John 2; 11). (The theological reason for this is discussed in 1 Cor. 12:26.)*

---

b. How to deal with one's foes (Rom. 12:17-21)—"Dearly beloved, avenge not yourselves, but rather give place unto wrath: for it is written, Vengeance is mine; I will repay, saith the Lord. Therefore if thine enemy hunger, feed him; if he thirst, give him drink: for in so doing thou shalt heap coals of fire on his head" (Rom. 12:19-20).

---

†12:20 *We are to "destroy" our enemies. The way we are to do this is to make them our friends (12:18-21). Two classic Old Testament examples of this are found in David's treatment of King Saul (1 Sam. 24, 26) and Joseph's attitude toward his brothers (Gen. 45).*

C. The believer and society (Rom. 13:1-14)

1. The *what* of the matter

a. His duties toward the rulers of the state (Rom. 13:1-7)—"Let every soul be subject unto the higher powers. For there is no power but of God: the powers that be are ordained of God. Render therefore to all their dues: tribute to whom tribute is due; custom to whom custom; fear to whom fear; honour to whom honour" (Rom. 13:1, 7).

---

†13:1-7

A. *He is to be in subjection to the higher powers, for "the powers that be are ordained of God" (13:1). The Bible teaches that a child of God is not to love the* systems *of this world, or be conformed to its* patterns, *but nevertheless is to obey its* laws. *The Scriptures present both a separation from and a submission to the state on the part of the Christian (Titus 3:1; 1 Pet. 2:13). The Jews of the Roman Empire were notoriously bad citizens. They refused to obey and used Deuteronomy 17:14-15 as their proof text. However, Paul taught subjection to the state in spite of the shameful and shabby treatment he had often received at its hands (Acts 16:22-24, 37-38; see Prov. 8:15-16; Dan. 2:21; 4:17; John 19:10-11). Thus, human government is a divine institution given by God after the flood (Gen. 9) to assure order and prevent anarchy (see Judg. 17:6).*

B. *He is to know that "whosoever therefore resisteth the power, resisteth the ordinance of God" (13:2). It should be noted that Paul is here establishing general principles to guide the Christian living in a society governed by laws. He does not deal with what action the believer is to take when these laws are immoral or unscriptural. This question is answered in another passage (Acts 5:29).*

C. *He is to render tribute (federal and local taxes), and custom (sales taxes to the coffers of the state), and fear and honor to the keepers of that state (13:7). A man once stopped D. L. Moody in Chicago and asked him where he was going. The great evangelist replied, "To cast my vote in the forthcoming elections." Somewhat shocked, the man admonished him, "But, brother Moody, don't you realize you are a citizen of heaven and that this world is not your final home?" Moody smiled and said, "That's true, but in the meanwhile I pay my taxes in Cook County!"*

---

b. His duties toward the rest of the state (Rom. 13:8-10)—"Owe no man any thing, but to love one another: for he that loveth another hath fulfilled the law. Love worketh no ill to his neighbour: therefore love is the fulfilling of the law" (Rom. 13:8, 10).

†**13:8-10** *This passage does not prohibit a Christian from buying a home or car on the installment plan. Taken in context, it simply says we are to pay our debts to society. Paul has already said, however, that all believers owe the Gospel to the unsaved with whom they come into contact (Rom. 1:14).*

---

2. The *why* of the matter—"And that, knowing the time, that now it is high time to awake out of sleep: for now is our salvation nearer than when we believed. The night is far spent, the day is at hand: let us therefore cast off the works of darkness, and let us put on the armour of light" (Rom. 13:11-12).

---

†**13:12** *Paul speaks of the night as almost over, while Jesus says it is yet to come (John 9:4). Both are right. To the saint, the day breaks; but to the sinner, the night comes. This present world is the only hell the Christian will ever know, and it is the only heaven the unsaved will experience. This long night of sin has extended for thousands of years, beginning with Adam's rebellion. But the Morning Star has already appeared (Luke 2). Soon the Sun of Righteousness will arise with healing in his wings. Every single New Testament epistle writer believed this. (See 1 Cor. 15:51; 1 Thess. 4:16; James 5:8; 1 Pet. 4:7; 1 John 2:18, 28; Jude 18.) Especially to be noted is Paul's phrase, "the day is at hand" in verse 12. This is the first of at least ten important "days" in the Bible, all future. These are:*

A. The day of the Rapture (Rom. 13:12; Eph. 4:30; Phil. 1:6, 10; 2:16; Heb. 10:37; 2 Pet. 1:19)—This may be regarded as a literal 24-hour day.

B. The judgment seat of Christ day (1 Cor. 3:13; 5:5; 2 Tim. 1:18; 4:8; 1 John 4:17)—This may be regarded as a literal 24-hour day and will include only Christians.

C. The Day of the Lord (Joel 1:15; 2:1-2, 11, 31; Acts 2:20; 2 Thess. 2:3; Rev. 6:17)—This "day" covers the entire tribulation, a period of seven years.

D. The day of Christ's second coming (Matt. 24:36; 26:29; 1 Thess. 5:2-4; 2 Thess. 1:10)—This may be regarded as a literal 24-hour day.

E. The day of Armageddon (Rev. 16:14)—This may be regarded as a literal 24-hour day.

F. The "resurrection of the just" day (John 6:39-40, 44, 54; 11:24)—This may be regarded as a literal 24-hour day and includes all Old Testament saints and tribulational believers.

G. The "fallen angel" judgment day (Jude 6)—This may be regarded as a literal 24-hour day.

H. The day of Christ (1 Cor. 1:8; 2 Cor. 1:14; 2 Tim. 1:12)—This "day" covers the entire millennium, a period of 1,000 years.

I. The great white throne judgment day (Matt. 7:22; 11:22; John 12:48; Acts 17:31; Rom. 2:5, 16; 2 Pet. 2:9)—This may be regarded as a literal 24-hour day.

J. The "new creation" day (2 Pet. 3:7-13)—This may be regarded as a literal 24-hour day. Paul then exhorts the believer to "put on the armor of light" (13:12; see Eph. 6:10-17 for the specific pieces of this armor).

---

3. The *who* of the matter—"But put ye on the Lord Jesus Christ, and make not provision for the flesh, to fulfil the lusts thereof" (Rom. 13:14).

D. The believer and weaker saints (Rom. 14:1-23)

1. No believer is to be judged by another down here.
   a. We are not to criticize his legalism (Rom. 14:1-9)—"For none of us liveth to himself, and no man dieth to himself. For whether we live, we live unto the Lord; and whether we die, we die unto the Lord: whether we live therefore, or die, we are the Lord's" (Rom. 14:7-8).

(1) Don't judge in matters of diet (Rom. 14:2-3)—"Let not him that eateth despise him that eateth not; and let not him which eateth not judge him that eateth: for God hath received him" (Rom. 14:3).

(2) Don't judge in matters of days (Rom. 14:5-6)—"He that regardeth the day, regardeth it unto the Lord; and he that regardeth not the day, to the Lord he doth not regard it. He that eateth, eateth to the Lord, for he giveth God thanks; and he that eateth not, to the Lord he eateth not, and giveth God thanks" (Rom. 14:6).

b. We are not to corrupt our liberty (Rom. 14:13-23)—"I know, and am persuaded by the Lord Jesus, that there is nothing unclean of itself: but to him that esteemeth any thing to be unclean, to him it is unclean. But if thy brother be grieved with thy meat, now walkest thou not charitably. Destroy not him with thy meat, for whom Christ died. Let not then your good be evil spoken of: For the kingdom of God is not meat and drink; but righteousness, and peace, and joy in the Holy Ghost. . . . Let us therefore follow after the things which make for peace, and things wherewith one may edify another. . . . It is good neither to eat flesh, nor to drink wine, nor any thing whereby thy brother stumbleth, or is offended, or is made weak" (Rom. 14:14-17, 19, 21).

2. All believers will be judged up there (Rom. 14:10-12)—"But why dost thou judge thy brother? or why dost thou set at nought thy brother? for we shall all stand before the judgment seat of Christ. For it is written, As I live, saith the Lord, every knee shall bow to me, and every tongue shall confess to God. So then every one of us shall give account of himself to God" (Rom. 14:10-12).

---

†**14:12** *There are some 14 special categories of judgment in the Bible. In the book of Romans Paul refers to at least four of these.*

A. The Garden of Eden judgment of Adam (Rom. 5:12)
B. The Calvary judgment of Christ (Rom. 4:25)
C. The judgment seat of Christ (Rom. 14:10)
D. The tribulational judgment of Satan (Rom. 16:20)

E. The believer and the Savior (Rom. 15:1-13)—The earthly ministry of Christ is presented here as a pattern for Christians. (See also 1 Pet. 2:21-25.)

1. It was a sacrificial ministry—"We then that are strong ought to bear the infirmities of the weak, and not to please ourselves. Let every one of us please his neighbour for his good to edification" (Rom. 15:1-2).

   "For even Christ pleased not himself" (Rom. 15:3a).

2. It was a suffering ministry—"But, as it is written, the reproaches of them that reproached thee fell on me" (Rom. 15:3b).

3. It was a sharing ministry (Rom. 15:1, 7)—"Wherefore receive ye one another, as Christ also received us to the glory of God" (Rom. 15:7).

4. It was a settling ministry—"For whatsoever things were written aforetime were written for our learning, that we through patience and comfort of the scriptures might have hope. Now the God of patience and consolation grant you to be likeminded one toward another according to Christ Jesus: That ye may with

one mind and one mouth glorify God, even the Father of our Lord Jesus Christ. . . . Now the God of hope fill you with all joy and peace in believing, that ye may abound in hope, through the power of the Holy Ghost" (Rom. 15:4-6, 13).

5. It was a sure ministry (Rom. 15:8-12).
   a. To the Jews—"Now I say that Jesus Christ was a minister of the circumcision for the truth of God, to confirm the promises made unto the fathers" (Rom. 15:8).
   b. To the Gentiles (Rom. 15:8-12)—"And that the Gentiles might glorify God for his mercy; as it is written, For this cause I will confess to thee among the Gentiles, and sing unto thy name" (Rom. 15:9).

II. Personal Remarks to the Roman Redeemed (Rom. 15:14–16:67)
   A. Paul reviews his past (Rom. 15:14-21).
      1. He mentions his specialized ministry—"That I should be the minister of Jesus Christ to the Gentiles, ministering the gospel of God, that the offering up of the Gentiles might be acceptable, being sanctified by the Holy Ghost" (Rom. 15:16).
      2. He mentions his miracles—"Through mighty signs and wonders, by the power of the Spirit of God" (Rom. 15:19a).

---

†15:19a *The book of Acts records many of Paul's miracles:*
A. Striking a sorcerer with blindness in Paphos of Cyprus (13:11-12)
B. Various miracles in Iconium (14:3-4)
C. Healing a cripple in Lystra (14:8-18)
D. Curing a demoniac girl in Philippi (16:16-18)
E. Healing many of diseases and demons at Ephesus (19:11-12)
F. Raising Eutychus at Troas (20:9-10)
G. Restoring Publius's father of a fever and healing others on the Isle of Melita (28:8-9)

---

      3. He mentions his mission field—"So that from Jerusalem, and round about unto Illyricum [modern Yugoslavia], I have fully preached the gospel of Christ" (Rom. 15:19b).
      4. He mentions his *modus operandi*—"Yea, so have I strived to preach the gospel, not where Christ was named, lest I should build upon another man's foundation" (Rom. 15:20).
   B. Paul previews his future.
      1. He determines to visit them at a later time, as he goes to Spain (Rom 15:22-24, 28-29).

---

†15:29 *The Pillars of Hercules, the westernmost reaches of mainland Europe, and the civilized world in his day, beckoned to Paul. Did he later get to Spain? Just before his death he would write, "I have finished my course" (2 Tim. 4:7). Since Spain was on his itinerary we assume he did indeed get there.*

---

      2. He desires their prayers at the present time, as he goes to Jerusalem (Rom. 15:25-27, 30-32). "But now I go unto Jerusalem to minister unto the saints" (Rom. 15:25).

a. The request for their prayers—"Now I beseech you, brethren, for the Lord Jesus Christ's sake, and for the love of the Spirit, that ye strive together with me in your prayers to God for me" (Rom. 15:30).
b. The reason for their prayers—"That I may be delivered from them that do not believe in Judaea; and that my service which I have for Jerusalem may be accepted of the saints" (Rom. 15:31).

3. He delivers greetings to his many Roman friends.
a. Special greetings to three (Rom. 16:13)—"I commend unto you Phebe our sister, which is a servant of the church which is at Cenchrea: That ye receive her in the Lord, as becometh saints, and that ye assist her in whatsoever business she hath need of you: for she hath been a succourer of many, and of myself also. Greet Priscilla and Aquila my helpers in Christ Jesus" (Rom. 16:1-3).
b. General greetings to 25 (Rom. 16:4-16)—"Salute one another with an holy kiss. The churches of Christ salute you" (Rom. 16:16).

---

†16:3 *Paul briefly leaves the mountain peaks of doctrine to come down to the pavements of Rome. He began his epistle by saying that "without ceasing I make mention of you always in my prayers" (1:9). At the end of his letter he mentions no less than 28 of them by name.*

---

4. He denounces troublemakers (Rom. 16:17-18)—"Now I beseech you, brethren, mark them which cause divisions and offences contrary to the doctrine which ye have learned; and avoid them" (Rom. 16:17).

---

†16:17

A. The New Testament gives three reasons for dismissing a member from the fellowship of a local church.
1. For troublemaking (Rom. 16:17; 2 Thess. 3:6; Prov. 6:19). Note: When Paul finally reached Rome, he found those troublemakers hard at work. (See Phil. 1:14-18; 3:18.)
2. For immorality (1 Cor. 5)
3. For heresy (Titus 3:10)

B. The procedure for dismissing such a person is described in 1 Corinthians 5:4 and Matthew 18:15-17. (See also 2 Thess. 3:14-15.)

---

5. He declares the doom of Satan (Rom. 16:20)—"And the God of peace shall bruise Satan under your feet shortly. The grace of our Lord Jesus Christ be with you. Amen" (Rom. 16:20).

---

†16:20

This prophecy of the bruising of Satan will be fulfilled in a twofold manner:
A. When he is cast into the bottomless pit for a thousand years during the millennium (Rev. 20:1-3)
B. When he is cast into the lake of fire forever after the millennium (Rev. 20:10)

---

6. He delivers his final benediction (Rom. 16:24-27)—"The grace of our Lord Jesus Christ be with you all. Amen. Now to him that is of power to stablish you according

> to my gospel, and the preaching of Jesus Christ, according to the revelation of the mystery, which was kept secret since the world began, but now is made manifest, and by the scriptures of the prophets, according to the commandment of the everlasting God, made known to all nations for the obedience of faith: to God only wise, be glory through Jesus Christ for ever" (Rom. 16:24-27).

---

†16:24 *Paul both begins and concludes this as he does with all others by commending his readers to the* grace of God. *Note:*

A. The introduction to his epistles:

1. *Romans 1:7b—"Grace to you and peace from God our Father, and the Lord Jesus Christ."*
2. *1 Corinthians 1:3—"Grace be unto you, and peace, from God our Father, and from the Lord Jesus Christ."*
3. *2 Corinthians 1:2—"Grace be to you, and peace from God our Father, and from the Lord Jesus Christ."*
4. *Galatians 1:3—"Grace be to you and peace from God the Father, and from our Lord Jesus Christ."*
5. *Ephesians 1:2—"Grace be to you, and peace, from God our Father, and from the Lord Jesus Christ."*
6. *Philippians 1:2—"Grace be unto you, and peace, from God our Father, and from the Lord Jesus Christ."*
7. *Colossians 1:2b—"Grace be unto you, and peace, from God our Father, and the Lord Jesus Christ."*
8. *1 Thessalonians 1:1b—"Grace be unto you, and peace from God our Father, and the Lord Jesus Christ."*
9. *2 Thessalonians 1:2—"Grace unto you, and peace, from God our Father and the Lord Jesus Christ."*
10. *1 Timothy 1:2b—"Grace, mercy, and peace, from God our Father and Jesus Christ our Lord."*
11. *2 Timothy 1:2b—"Grace, mercy, and peace, from God the Father and Christ Jesus our Lord."*
12. *Titus 1:4b—"Grace, mercy, and peace, from God the Father and the Lord Jesus Christ our Saviour."*
13. *Philemon 3—"Grace to you, and peace, from God our Father and the Lord Jesus Christ."*

B. The conclusion to his epistles:

1. *Romans 16:24—"The grace of our Lord Jesus Christ be with you all."*
2. *1 Corinthians 16:23—"The grace of our Lord Jesus Christ be with you."*
3. *2 Corinthians 13:14—"The grace of the Lord Jesus Christ, and the love of God, and the communion of the Holy Ghost be with you all."*
4. *Galatians 6:18—"Brethren, the grace of our Lord Jesus Christ be with your spirit. Amen."*
5. *Ephesians 6:24 (NIV)—"Grace to all who love our Lord Jesus Christ with an undying love."*
6. *Philippians 4:23 (NIV)—"The grace of the Lord Jesus Christ be with your spirit."*
7. *Colossians 4:18—"Grace be with you."*
8. *1 Thessalonians 5:28—"The grace of our Lord Jesus Christ be with you."*
9. *2 Thessalonians 3:18—"The grace of our Lord Jesus Christ be with you all."*
10. *1 Timothy 6:21b—"Grace be with thee."*
11. *2 Timothy 4:22—"The Lord Jesus Christ be with thy spirit. Grace be with you."*
12. *Titus 3:15b—"Grace be with you all."*
13. *Philemon 25—"The grace of our Lord Jesus Christ be with your spirit."*

---

1 CORINTHIANS

GOD'S MEDICAL JOURNAL— A DESCRIPTION OF AND PRESCRIPTION FOR VARIOUS LOCAL CHURCH DISEASES

A. This is what 1 Corinthians is all about: The church at Corinth had been infected by a number of both satanic and fleshly viruses.

B. There is almost no modern-day church problem that is not covered in 1 Corinthians. The church was filled with theological and personal problems.

1. They had perverted the doctrine of baptism (chapter 1).
2. They were bragging about what little human wisdom they had (chapter 1).
3. They were carnal to the core (3:1).
4. They had deceived themselves (3:18).
5. They had defiled their bodies (3:17).
6. They were puffed up (4:18).
7. They were tolerating horrible immorality (5:1).
8. They were suing each other in heathen courts 6:1).
9. They were confused about marriage (7:1).
10. They had abused the doctrine of Christian liberty (8:9).
11. They were not dressing properly in the house of God (11:6).
12. They had made a mockery of the Lord's Supper (11:30).
13. They had corrupted the gifts of the Spirit, especially tongues (chapter 14).
14. They were confused on the subject of the resurrection (chapter 15).
15. They had let down on their offerings.

It has been said that if sins were horses, this church could have filled many stables.

C. The greatest human missionary of all times was the Apostle Paul. This ex-Pharisee, who had once hated and hounded Christians, made three great missionary trips, during which he established dozens of local New Testament churches. Thus the former vicious "wolf of the flock" became one of God's finest "sheepdogs."

D. The fact is that the New Testament is made up basically of some letters Paul wrote to some of these churches he started, and to their pastors. This list would contain:

1. The epistle to Rome (Romans)
2. The epistle to Ephesus (Ephesians)
3. The epistle to Colosse (Colossians)
4. The epistle to Philippi (Philippians)
5. The Epistle to Galatia (Galatians)
6. The two epistles to Thessalonica (1 and 2 Thessalonians)
7. The two epistles to a pastor named Timothy (1 and 2 Timothy)
8. The epistle to a pastor named Titus (Titus)
9. The two epistles to Corinth (1 and 2 Corinthians)

E. Here, then, we have an amazing fact: Out of the 27 New Testament books, no less than 12 were written by Paul to his beloved mission churches.

F. Paul would have had little time, it would seem, for those modern "Christian movements" that bypass, downplay, and outright ignore the ministry and importance of local churches.

G. Of all his church letters, Romans is no doubt the most important, but 1 Corinthians is probably second in importance. This is so because of its great section on the resurrection of Christ and the believer (1 Cor. 15), and, if for no other reason, because of its sheer bulk, for 1 Corinthians is by far the longest epistle written by Paul.

H. In a nutshell, through Paul's efforts, the church was now in Corinth, but somehow Corinth had gotten into the church. This is probably the second most carnal New Testament church. The church at Laodicea was undoubtedly the worst. (See Rev. 3:14-22.)

I. This then is Paul's description of their problem. He therefore offers the proper prescription for their problems.
   1. The reminder—"What? Know ye not that your body is the temple of the Holy Ghost which is in you, which ye have of God, and ye are not your own?" (6:19).
   2. The solution—"Now I beseech you, brethren, by the name of our Lord Jesus Christ, that ye all speak the same thing, and that there be no divisions among you; but that ye be perfectly joined together in the same mind and in the same judgment" (1:10).

      "Whether therefore ye eat, or drink, or whatsoever ye do, do all to the glory of God" (10:31).

      "Therefore, my beloved brethren, be ye steadfast, unmoveable, always abounding in the work of the Lord, forasmuch as ye know that your labour is not in vain in the Lord" (15:58).

J. Background to the founding of the church at Corinth
   1. It was founded by Paul during his second missionary journey.
   2. Acts 18 relates the "ground breaking" ceremonies.
      a. He leaves on his second trip with Silas (Acts 15:40).
      b. At Lystra they pick up Timothy (Acts 16:1).
      c. At Troas Paul receives his Macedonian vision (Acts 16:9).
      d. At Philippi a woman named Lydia, a demon-possessed girl, and a Roman jailer are all three saved (Acts 16:14-34).
      e. From Philippi Paul moves to Thessalonica (Acts 17:1)
      f. From there to Berea (Acts 17:10)
      g. From Berea to Athens (Acts 17:15)
      h. From Athens, finally to Corinth (Acts 18:1)
   3. In Corinth Paul soon meets Aquila and Priscilla. Crispus, the chief ruler of the synagogue, is saved (Acts 18:8).
   4. God comforts Paul in a vision (Acts 18:9-10).
   5. Paul stays at least 18 months in Corinth before departing (Acts 18:11).
   6. The Corinthian church was then pastored by a man called Apollos.

K. Background of Paul's first letter to the church at Corinth
   1. During the summer of A.D. 53, Paul starts on his third missionary journey, apparently alone (Acts 18:23).
   2. He arrives at Ephesus and spends three years there (Acts 20:31).
   3. While at Ephesus he is visited by a delegation from Corinth with news concerning the tragic situation in their local church.
   4. With a heavy heart, Paul sits down and writes 1 Corinthians.

L. The most exciting single word in the Bible is found here in 1 Corinthians: MARANATHA! (16:22).
M. The book also includes perhaps the greatest verse on temptation in an apostolic church (10:13).
N. In essence, 1 Corinthians provides the most amount of information on the following subjects.
   1. Characteristics of the natural, carnal, and spiritual person (2:14–3:4)
   2. The judgment seat of Christ (3:9-15)
   3. Rules concerning the married and single life (7)
   4. Christian liberty (8–10)
   5. Communion (11:17-34)
   6. Rules for personal conduct in God's house (11:1-6)
   7. Spiritual gifts in general (12)
   8. The gift of tongues in particular (14)
   9. The importance of love (13)
   10. The doctrine of the resurrection (15)
O. There are quotations or allusions in 1 Corinthians from 18 Old Testament books; 1 Corinthians is the seventh longest New Testament book, and 28th longest biblical book, with 16 chapters, 437 verses, and 9,489 words.
P. Great passages would include:
   1. 1:18-31
   2. 6:19-20
   3. 9:24-27
   4. 10:13
   5. 12:12-26
   6. 13:1-13
   7. 15:21-28
   8. 15:51-58

THE BOOK OF 1 CORINTHIANS

PART ONE: The eight corruptions committed by the Corinthian church (1 Cor. 1–6)

Introduction:
"Paul, called to be an apostle of Jesus Christ through the will of God, and Sosthenes our brother, unto the church of God which is at Corinth, to them that are sanctified in Christ Jesus, called to be saints, with all that in every place call upon the name of Jesus Christ our Lord, both theirs and ours: Grace be unto you, and peace, from God our Father, and from the Lord Jesus Christ. I thank my God always on your behalf, for the grace of God which is given you by Jesus Christ; that in every thing ye are enriched by him, in all utterance, and in all knowledge; even as the testimony of Christ was confirmed in you: so that ye come behind in no gift; waiting for the coming of our Lord Jesus Christ: who shall also confirm you unto the end, that ye may be blameless in the day of our Lord Jesus Christ. God is faithful, by whom ye were called unto the fellowship of his Son Jesus Christ our Lord" (1 Cor. 1:1-9).

†**1:9** *The following is an overview of these first 9 verses:*

A. *Paul and Sosthenes send their regards. This Sosthenes may have been the same one referred to in Acts 18:17. He was the chief ruler of the synagogue in Ephesus who instigated a riot against Paul. It backfired, however, and he himself was beaten by some angry Greeks. This apparently led to his salvation.*

B. *Paul says (1:2): "With all that in every place call upon the name of Jesus." Thus, this epistle was written for* all *believers, as were his others (see 1 Thess. 5:27; Col. 4:16).*

C. *"The Lord Jesus Christ" (1:3)—This great name is mentioned six times in the first ten verses of the epistle, doubtless because the church had not honored this grand title. Here is the reason why* any *local church has difficulties.*

D. *"Ye are enriched . . . in all utterance and . . . knowledge" (1:5). The Corinthian believers* knew *the truth and* could speak *the truth. They simply were not* practicing *the truth.*

E. *"Ye come behind in no gift" (1:7)—The Bible lists some 18 gifts. The church at Corinth apparently had all of them.*

F. *Verse 8 is one of the greatest "security of the believer" statements in the entire Bible. Note the wording:*

 1. *Confirm—This means to establish and make absolutely secure. The same verb is used in Romans 15:8, where Paul states that God confirmed in Christ the promises made in the Old Testament.*
 2. *Blameless—A legal term meaning "not called into court, uncharged, unaccused." It does not mean sinless, but* chargeless. *(See also Col. 1:22, 1 Tim. 3:10.)*
 3. *To the end . . . in the day—A reference to the Rapture. Conclusion: Paul is writing to one of the most backslidden, carnal, confused, and selfish churches on record. He thus could only predict their eventual salvation because of God's eternal security, in spite of their pitiful condition.*

G. *"God is faithful" (1:9)—A brief summary of his faithfulness would include:*

 1. *He is faithful in defending his people—"I have found David my servant; with my holy oil have I anointed him . . . my faithfulness . . . shall be with him. The enemy shall not exact upon him; nor the son of wickedness afflict him" (Psa. 89:20, 24, 22).*
 2. *He is faithful in times of temptation—"There hath no temptation taken you, but such as is common to man; but God is faithful, who will not suffer you to be tempted above that ye are able; but will with the temptation also make a way of escape, that ye may be able to bear it" (1 Cor. 10:13).*
 3. *He is faithful in keeping the Christian saved—"But the Lord is faithful, who shall stablish you, and keep you from evil" (2 Thess. 3:3). "I pray God your whole spirit and soul and body be preserved blameless unto the coming of our Lord Jesus Christ. Faithful is he that calleth you, who also will do it" (1 Thess. 5:23-24).*
 4. *He is faithful in chastening his children—"I know, O Lord, that thy judgments are right, and that thou in faithfulness hast afflicted me" (Psa. 119:75). "For whom the Lord loveth he chasteneth and scourgeth every son whom he receiveth" (Heb. 12: 6).*
 5. *He is faithful in forgiving confessed sin—"If we confess our sins, he is faithful and just to forgive us our sins and to cleanse us from all unrighteousness" (1 John 1:9).*
 6. *He is faithful in hearing our prayers—"Hear my prayer O Lord, give ear to my supplications; in thy faithfulness answer me" (Psa. 143:1). Thus, their calling was through God, and since he is faithful, their salvation was sure. We note with sadness that Paul says nothing about their* present *condition (as in letters to other churches), but only mentions their* past *and* future.

H. *"The fellowship of his Son Jesus Christ" (1:9)—Christians the world over love to talk and write and sing about this fellowship, and well they should; but it should be kept in mind that sometimes this fellowship involves suffering also. As Paul writes: "That I may know him, and the power of his resurrection, and the fellowship of his sufferings, being made conformable unto his death" (Phil. 3:10).*

Too often it would seem we want the first without the second. But there can be no power of the resurrection without the fellowship of his sufferings.

I. First Corruption—They were following human leaders (1 Cor. 1:10-17)—"Now I beseech you, brethren, by the name of our Lord Jesus Christ, that ye all speak the same thing, and that there be no divisions among you; but that ye be perfectly joined together in the same mind and in the same judgment. For it hath been declared unto me of you, my brethren, by them which are of the house of Chloe, that there are contentions among you" (1 Cor. 1:10-11).

---

†1:11

A. *"No divisions among you" (1:10). Greek scholar W. E. Vine lists four distinct steps which may lead downward from harmony to a tragic breakup of Christian unity. These are:*
   1. Stasis—*A strong disagreement, a dissension. (See Acts 15:2; 23:7, 10.)*
   2. Dichostasia: *A standing apart. (See Gal. 5:20; Rom. 16:17.)*
   3. Schisma—*A severe rent, a tear. (See 1 Cor. 11:18; John 7:43; 9:16; 10:19.)*
   4. Hairesis—*A mature and established separation. (See Acts 5:17; 24:5, 14; 26:5; 2 Pet. 2:1; Titus 3:10.) Here the third word is used by Paul,* schisma, *thus suggesting the Corinthian church was in danger of complete breakup.*

B. *"But that ye be perfectly joined together" (1:10). The phrase "perfectly joined together" in this verse comes from one Greek word. That word is* katartizo. *This word is used in three other important New Testament passages:*
   1. *"Through faith we understand that the worlds were framed by the Word of God." (Heb. 11:3). Here the word* katartizo *is translated "framed."*
   2. *"Wherefore when he cometh into the world he saith, sacrifice and offering thou wouldst not, but a body hast thou prepared me" (Heb. 10:5). Here the word is translated "prepared."*
   3. *"And going on from thence, he saw . . . James . . . and John his brother in a ship with Zebedee their father, mending their nets" (Matt. 4:21). In this final passage the word is translated "mending." The point of all the above is simply this: God is desirous that church believers be joined together: As perfectly as the sun, moon, and stars fit together (Heb. 11:3). As perfectly as God formed the body for Jesus to use (Heb. 10:5). As perfectly as a mended net is. Souls are not saved in a church plagued with problems, simply because the net is broken and they get away.*

C. *Paul begins by naming his source of information—"For it hath been declared unto me . . . of Chloe." (See 1:11.) All too often unsigned critical letters are received by Christian leaders, finding fault with either the pastor or some other member in the church. How many times has vicious gossip from the mouths of nameless (and spineless) church members led to the destruction of their own church!*

A. The leaders involved—"Now this I say, that every one of you saith, I am of Paul; and I of Apollos; and I of Cephas; and I of Christ" (1 Cor. 1:12).

B. The lunacy involved—"Is Christ divided? was Paul crucified for you? or were ye baptized in the name of Paul? I thank God that I baptized none of you, but Crispus and Gaius; lest any should say that I had baptized in mine own name. . . . For Christ sent me not to baptize, but to preach the gospel: not with wisdom of words, lest the cross of Christ should be made of none effect" (1 Cor. 1:13-15, 17).

---

†1:17

A. *In verses 12 through 17 Paul writes to straighten out their first basic problem, that of baptism. How many churches have, since that time, been split right down the middle over the subject of baptism. Here the argument, however, was not over the mode or even the purpose, but concerning the different men who had baptized some of these Corinthian believers.*
   1. *Paul had baptized some of them, of course (but very few in reality), when he established the church.*
   2. *Apollos later pastored the church and also baptized some.*
   3. *Peter (Cephas) had apparently baptized a few, although we know nothing as to when or where this might have taken place. Some believe it could have happened at Pentecost.*
   4. *Christ is also mentioned in this list. As with Peter, we have no knowledge whatsoever as to where, when, and indeed if he ever did this.*

B. *At any rate, here is a local New Testament church hopelessly divided into four groups, with each group claiming superiority over the other three because of the man who had baptized them.*
   1. *The Paulite group—The "claim to fame" of the first group was this: "We are of Paul and therefore better than you. Anyone knows Paul is a great* doctrinal *preacher, and that's the only kind to have."*
   2. *The Apollosite group—The second group would probably retort, "We are of Apollos, and anyone with any sense at all will agree that Apollos is an* eloquent *preacher and can preach circles around Paul any day."*
   3. *The Cephasite group—The third group might then answer, "We are of Cephas, and you can brag about doctrine and eloquence all you want to, but there's just nobody as down-to-earth and* practical *as Peter."*
   4. *The Christite group—The fourth group could thereupon be pictured as looking down at the other three and piously saying, "We are of Christ, and therefore look to* no human preacher *to lead us and feed us."*

C. *"Was Paul crucified for you?" (1:13). We note Paul hits his own fan club first. It is easy to rebuke a group if they are wrong, especially if that group is against you anyway, but it is another thing to criticize sharply those who sing your praises the loudest. Paul was truly "sold out" for Jesus.*

D. *"For Christ sent me not to baptize, but to preach the gospel" (1:17). This is probably the strongest verse in the Bible refuting the doctrine of baptismal regeneration (the unscriptural teaching which says one must be baptized to be saved). We would note here that Paul did not say that Christ had forbidden him to baptize, for the apostle often did baptize his converts (see Acts 16:15, 33; 18:8; 19:5). What he is saying here is simply this: Water baptism is not a part of the gospel of Christ. Later in this same epistle, Paul defines the gospel: "Moreover, brethren, I declare unto you the gospel . . . how that Christ died for our sins according to the scriptures; and that he was buried, and that he rose again the third day according to the scriptures" (1 Cor. 15:1, 3-4).*

   This, then, by itself, is the gospel.

II. Second Corruption—They were favoring earthly wisdom (1 Cor. 1:18–2:13). In verses 1:18-31 Paul contrasts false worldly wisdom (which the Corinthians so highly prized but did not themselves have—see 1:26) with true godly wisdom which centers in the cross of Christ.

A. The reaction to God's wisdom
   1. "It is the program of a fool!" (the conclusion of the unsaved)—"For the preaching of the cross is to them that perish foolishness" (1 Cor. 1:18a).
   2. "It is the power of God!" (the conclusion of the saved)—"But unto us which are saved it is the power of God" (1 Cor. 1:18b).

---

†1:18b

A. *Note: In the original it states that the unbelievers are* perishing *and the believers are* being saved. *Both salvation and damnation are put in the* present tense. *(See John 3:18, 26 in regard to the unsaved.) Concerning the saved, the New Testament describes their salvation in three tenses:*
   1. *Past tense—Romans 8:24 (justification)*
   2. *Present tense—1 Corinthians 1:18 (sanctification)*
   3. *Future tense—Romans 5:9 (glorification)*

B. *Dr. Harry Ironside was once asked by a stranger if he was saved. The famous pastor replied, "Yes, I have been, I am being, and I shall be!"*

B. The revelation concerning God's wisdom—"For it is written, I will destroy the wisdom of the wise, and will bring to nothing the understanding of the prudent. Where is the wise? where is the scribe? where is the disputer of this world? hath not God made foolish the wisdom of this world? For after that in the wisdom of God the world by wisdom knew not God, it pleased God by the foolishness of preaching to save them that believe. . . . Because the foolishness of God is wiser than men; and the weakness of God is stronger than men. For ye see your calling, brethren, how that not many wise men after the flesh, not many mighty, not many noble, are called" (1 Cor. 1:19-21, 25-26)

---

†1:26

A. *Concerning 1:19—In both 1:19 and 3:19 Paul quotes from two Old Testament passages comparing God's wisdom with human wisdom:*
   1. *"For it is written, I will destroy the wisdom of the wise" (1:19). (See Isa. 29:14.)*
   2. *"For it is written, He taketh the wise in their own craftiness" (3:19). (See Job 5:13.) For three classic New Testament examples of just this very thing, see Matthew 21:23-27 (concerning the baptism of John); Matthew 22:15-22 concerning the tribute to Caesar); and John 8:1-11 (concerning an adulterous woman). In his eternal wisdom, God chose instead the method of the cross to save people.*

B. *Concerning 1:26—Paul tactfully reminds the church that it was a good thing God did not choose the intellect and prestige of the world. "For ye see your calling, brethren, how that not many wise men after the flesh, not many mighty, not many noble, are called" (1:26). The great John Wesley was often helped during his ministry by a noble lady of high English society named Lady Huntington. This gracious woman who gave so much of her time, talent, and treasure to Christ would often testify as follows: "I am only going to heaven through the letter M. How thankful I am that Paul did not say that not* any *noble are called, but rather not* many *noble are called. Therefore, I am only going to heaven through the letter M!"*

C. The results of God's wisdom
1. To the Jews, who demanded signs, it was a stumbling block (1 Cor. 1:22-23).
2. To the Greeks, who demanded earthly wisdom, it was senseless (1 Cor. 1:22-23).

---

†1:23 *Note: Israel had rejected God's plan in spite of the fact that he had provided them with certain signs. (See John 3:2; 20:30; Acts 2:19, 43; 5:12.)*

---

3. To all believers, who demanded nothing, it is salvation—"But unto them which are called, both Jews and Greeks, Christ the power of God, and the wisdom of God. . . . But of him are ye in Christ Jesus, who of God is made unto us wisdom, and righteousness, and sanctification, and redemption" (1 Cor. 1:24, 30).

D. The reasons for God's wisdom—"But God hath chosen the foolish things of the world to confound the wise; and God hath chosen the weak things of the world to confound the things which are mighty; and base things of the world, and things which are despised, hath God chosen, yea, and things which are not, to bring to nought things that are: that no flesh should glory in his presence" (1 Cor. 1:27-29).

---

†1:29 *Thus, in manifesting his own glory, God delighted in choosing:*
A. The foolish things of this world
1. A bleeding lamb in Exodus 12
2. A smitten rock in Exodus 17
3. A brass snake in Numbers 21
B. The weak things of this world.
1. A rod to defeat the Egyptians in Exodus 4
2. A sling to defeat a mighty giant in 1 Samuel 17
3. A bone to defeat the Philistines in Judges 15
C. The base things of this world.
1. A harlot's son who became a mighty judge in Judges 11
2. A heathen girl who became David's great-grandmother in Ruth 4
3. An immoral woman who became a great soul winner in John 4

E. The review of God's wisdom (1 Cor. 2:1-13)—In these verses Paul reviews his past visit to their city during which time he established the churches at Corinth. He reminds them:
1. That the message of the cross is not of this world (1 Cor. 2:1-6)—"And I, brethren, when I came to you, came not with excellency of speech or of wisdom, declaring unto you the testimony of God. For I determined not to know any thing among you, save Jesus Christ, and him crucified. And I was with you in weakness, and in fear, and in much trembling. And my speech and my preaching was not with enticing words of man's wisdom, but in demonstration of the Spirit and of power" (1 Cor. 2:1-4).

---

†2:4 *Prior to his visit in Corinth, Paul had spoken to the Greek philosophers on Mars Hill in Athens (Acts 17:16-34). Here he delivered a powerful and eloquent message, using philosophy, poetry, and*

---

history along with great scriptural truths. The sermon, however, produced little fruit. Some (but not all) have therefore concluded that the apostle here in 1 Corinthians 2:1-4 is recording his determination to depend henceforth only and always upon the Holy Spirit and not to rely at all upon eloquence, philosophy, etc. Others have felt that his condition as described in 2:3 was purely physical, perhaps due to nervous exhaustion. (See also 2 Cor. 7:5.)

---

2. That the message of the cross had been ordained before the world—"But we speak the wisdom of God in a mystery, even the hidden wisdom, which God ordained before the world unto our glory: which none of the princes of this world knew: for had they known it, they would not have crucified the Lord of glory" (1 Cor. 2:7-8).
3. That the message of the cross is reserved for the heirs of this world (1 Cor. 2:9-13).
   a. This inheritance is concealed to unbelievers—"But as it is written, Eye hath not seen, nor ear heard, neither have entered into the heart of man, the things which God hath prepared for them that love him" (1 Cor. 2:9).
   b. This inheritance is revealed to believers—"But God hath revealed them unto us by his Spirit: for the Spirit searcheth all things, yea, the deep things of God" (1 Cor. 2:10).

III. Third Corruption—They were floundering in the flesh (1 Cor. 2:14–3:7). In these remarkable verses Paul divides all people into three spiritual categories. These are:
   A. The corpse (the natural person) (2:14)—Controlled by Satan. "But the natural man receiveth not the things of the Spirit of God: for they are foolishness unto him: neither can he know them, because they are spiritually discerned" (1 Cor. 2:14).

---

†2:14 *Characteristics of the natural person:*
A. He may not be totally depraved (as evil as he could possibly be), but he is totally helpless to comprehend God's Word (see Acts 8:31).
B. He thus concludes that the Scriptures are senseless (see Acts 17:18, 32; 26:24).
C. He is dead and must be resurrected, for he cannot be revived (see Rom. 5:12; Eph. 2:1).

   B. The crybaby (the carnal person) (3:1-4)—Controlled by the flesh. "And I, brethren, could not speak unto you as unto spiritual, but as unto carnal, even as unto babes in Christ. I have fed you with milk, and not with meat: for hitherto ye were not able to bear it, neither yet now are ye able. For ye are yet carnal: for whereas there is among you envying, and strife, and divisions, are ye not carnal, and walk as men? For while one saith, I am of Paul; and another, I am of Apollos; are ye not carnal? Who then is Paul, and who is Apollos, but ministers by whom ye believed, even as the Lord gave to every man? I have planted, Apollos watered; but God gave the increase" (1 Cor. 3:1-6).

---

†3:6 *Characteristics of the carnal person:*
A. He is helpless, as a newborn infant. The word "babes" used here is nepios *in the original, and carries with it weakness without power of speech, immaturity and inexperience. This condition*

is also pictured in Ephesians 4:14. "That we henceforth be no more children, tossed to and fro, and carried about with every wind of doctrine" (see also Gal. 4:3; 2 Pet. 1:9).

B. He is unable to receive anything but milk (3:2). This condition always suggests either infancy or infirmity. Milk is proper for awhile (1 Pet. 2:2), but "strong meat belongeth to them that are of full age, even those who by reason of use have their senses exercised to discern both good and evil" (Heb. 5:14; see also Heb. 5:11-13).

C. He walks and talks like an unsaved person. "Are ye not carnal and walk as men?" (3:3b). All believers should consider this pointed question: "If you were arrested and charged with being a 'Christian,' would there be enough evidence to convict you?" It would seem the Corinthians, to a large extent, would get off scot-free.

D. He compares spiritual leaders instead of spiritual truths. (See 2:13 as opposed to 3:4.) Paul answers this by saying: "I have planted, Apollos watered; but God gave the increase" (3:6). Only God can do this (see also 1 Kings 18:30-38).

C. The conqueror (the spiritual person) (2:15)—Controlled by the Spirit. "But he that is spiritual judgeth all things, yet he himself is judged of no man" (1 Cor. 2:15).

---

†2:15 *Characteristics of the spiritual person:*

A. He (or she) is not *sanctimonious.*

B. This person is not *superior (in matters of brains, strength, background, money, etc.).*

C. She is not *sensational.*

D. He is not *sugary sweet.*

E. This person is not *straightlaced.*

F. He is not *segregated from society.*

G. She is not *superficial.*

H. He is not *spineless.*

I. He or she is spiritual. To be spiritual is to be in harmony with God, as are his laws (Rom. 7:14). Thus, a spiritual person is simply one controlled and motivated by the Holy Spirit. (See 1 Cor. 15:46; Gal. 5:16, 25.) Because of this, he or she can correctly judge "all things" (2:15). (See also 2 Tim. 2:15 as opposed to 2 Pet. 3:14-17.) Paul states that "we have the mind of Christ" (2:16). All believers enjoy this positionally (2 Cor. 5:17), but the spiritual person has it experientially (Phil. 2:5).

IV. Fourth Corruption—They were forgetting future judgment (1 Cor. 3:8-23). "Every man's work shall be made manifest: for the day shall declare it" (1 Cor. 3:13a).

A. The meaning of this judgment—This is the same judgment mentioned by Paul in two other passages. "For we shall all stand before the judgment seat of Christ" (Rom. 14:10b). "For we must all appear before the judgment seat of Christ" (2 Cor. 5:10a).

---

†2 Corinthians 5:10a *The Greek word* bema *(translated "judgment seat" in the King James Version) was a familiar term to the people of Paul's day. Dr. Lehman Strauss writes: "In the large Olympic arenas, there was an elevated seat on which the judge of the contest sat. After the contests were over, the successful competitors would assemble before the* bema *to receive their rewards or crowns. The* bema *was not a judicial bench where someone was condemned; it was a reward seat.*

Likewise, the Judgment Seat of Christ is not a judicial bench . . . the Christian life is a race, and the divine umpire is watching every contestant. After the church has run her course, he will gather every member before the bema *for the purpose of examining each one and giving the proper reward to each"* (God's Plan for the Future, *p. 111).*

B. The individuals in this judgment—Only believers will be included. "For we are labourers together with God: ye are God's husbandry, ye are God's building" (1 Cor. 3:9).

C. The purpose of this judgment—It is to determine the quality of my service for Christ from the moment of my salvation until my death or Rapture.

A. Negative considerations

1. *The purpose of the* bema *judgment is* not *to determine whether a particular individual enters heaven or not, for every person's eternal destiny is already determined before he leaves this life.*
2. *The purpose of the* bema *judgment is not to punish believers for sins committed either before or after their salvation. The Scriptures are very clear that no child of God will have to answer for his sins after this life. "He hath not dealt with us after our sins, nor rewarded us according to our iniquities. For as the heaven is high above the earth, so great is his mercy toward them that fear him. As far as the east is from the west, so far hath he removed our transgressions from us" (Psa. 103:10-12). "But thou hast in love to my soul delivered it from the pit of corruption: for thou hast cast all my sins behind thy back" (Isa. 38:17b). "I have blotted out . . . thy transgressions and . . . thy sins" (Isa. 44:22a). "Thou wilt cast all their sins into the depths of the sea" (Micah 7:19b). "For I will be merciful . . . and their sins and their iniquities will I remember no more" (Heb. 8:12). "The blood of Jesus Christ his Son cleanseth us from all sin" (1 John 1:7b).*

B. Positive considerations—What, then, is the purpose of the bema *judgment? In 1 Corinthians 4:2, Paul says that all Christians should conduct themselves as faithful stewards of God: "Moreover it is required in stewards, that a man be found faithful." The Apostle Peter later writes in a similar way: "Minister . . . as good stewards of the manifold grace of God" (1 Pet. 4:10). In the New Testament world, a steward was the manager of a large household or estate. He was appointed by the owner and was entrusted to keep the estate running smoothly. He had the power to hire and fire and to spend and save, being answerable to the owner alone. His only concern was that periodic meeting with his master, at which time he was required to account for the condition of the estate up to that point. With this background in mind, it may be said that someday at the* bema *judgment all stewards will stand before their Lord and Master and be required to give an account of the way they have used their privileges and responsibilities from the moment of their conversion. In conclusion, it can be seen that:*

1. *In the past, God dealt with us as sinners (Eph. 2:1-3; 1 Cor. 6:9-11; Rom. 5:6-8).*
2. *In the present, God deals with us as sons (Rom. 8:14; Heb. 12:5-11; 1 John 3:1-2).*
3. *In the future, God will deal with us (at the* bema*) as stewards.*

D. The materials to be tested in this judgment—"According to the grace of God which is given unto me, as a wise masterbuilder, I have laid the foundation, and another buildeth thereon. But let every man take heed how he buildeth thereupon. For other foundation can no man lay than that is laid, which is Jesus Christ. Now if any man build upon this foundation gold, silver, precious stones, wood, hay, stubble" (1 Cor. 3:10-12).

E. The method of testing at this judgment—"Every man's work shall be made manifest: for the day shall declare it, because it shall be revealed by fire; and the fire shall try every man's work of what sort it is" (1 Cor. 3:13).

F. The results of this judgment—"If any man's work abide which he hath built thereupon, he shall receive a reward. If any man's work shall be burned, he shall suffer loss: but he himself shall be saved; yet so as by fire" (1 Cor. 3:14-15).

---

†3:15

A. A twofold consideration concerning the bema *judgment:*

1. Negative considerations—It should be noted immediately that this passage does not *teach the false doctrine known as purgatory, for it is the believer's* works *and not the believer* himself *that will be subjected to the fires.*

2. Positive considerations—From these verses it is apparent that God classifies the works of believers into one of the following six areas: gold, silver, precious stones, wood, hay, stubble. There has been much speculation about the kinds of work down here that will constitute gold or silver up there. But it seems more appropriate to note that the six objects can be readily placed into two categories:

a. Those indestructible and worthy objects which will survive and thrive in the fires. These are gold, silver, and precious stones.

b. Those destructible and worthless objects which will be totally consumed in the fires. These are the wood, hay, and stubble.

B. A twofold conclusion concerning the bema *judgment:*

1. Those who receive rewards

a. The basis for these rewards—Though it is difficult to know just what goes to make up a "golden work" or a "stubble work," we are nevertheless informed of certain general areas in which God is particularly interested.

(1) How we treat other believers (Heb. 6:10; Matt. 10:41-42)

(2) How we exercise our authority over others (Heb. 13:17; James 3:1)

(3) How we employ our God-given abilities (2 Tim. 1:6; 1 Cor. 12:4, 11; 1 Pet. 4:10). To these verses can be added the overall teaching of Jesus' parables of the ten pounds (Luke 19:11-26) and the eight talents (Matt. 25:14-29).

(4) How we use our money (1 Tim. 6:17-19; 2 Cor. 9:6-7; 1 Cor. 16:2)

(5) How we spend our time (Eph. 5:16; Col. 4:5; 1 Pet. 1:17)

(6) How much we suffer for Jesus (Matt. 5:11-12; Mark 10:29-30; Rom. 8:18; 2 Cor. 4:17; 1 Pet. 4:12-13)

(7) How we run that particular race which God has chosen for us (1 Cor. 9:24; Phil. 3:13-14; Heb. 12:1; Phil. 2:16)

(8) How effectively we control the old nature (1 Cor. 9:25-27)

(9) How many souls we witness to and win for Christ (Prov. 11:30; 1 Thess. 2:19-20; Dan. 12:3)

(10) How we react to temptation (James 1:2-3; Rev. 2:10)

(11) How much Christ's second coming means to us (2 Tim. 4:8)

(12) How faithful we are to the Word of God and the God of the Word (1 Pet. 5:2-4; 2 Tim. 4:1-2; Acts 20:26-28)

b. The nature of these rewards

(1) The incorruptible crown—Given to those who master the old nature (1 Cor. 9:25-27)

(2) The crown of rejoicing—Given to soul winners (Prov. 11:30; 1 Thess. 2:19-20; Dan. 12:3)

(3) The crown of life—Given to those who successfully endure temptation (James 1:2-3; Rev. 2:10)

(4) The crown of righteousness—Given to those who especially love the doctrine of the Rapture (2 Tim. 4:8)

(5) The crown of glory—Given to faithful preachers and teachers (1 Pet. 5:2-4; 2 Tim. 4:1-2; Acts 20:26-28). It has been suggested that these "crowns" will actually be talents and abilities with which to glorify Christ. Thus, the greater the reward, the greater the ability.

2. Those who suffer loss

a. "If any man's work shall be burned, he shall suffer loss" (1 Cor. 3:15). This word for "suffer" is zemioo *in the Greek New Testament, and is used again by Paul in Philippians chapter 3, where he describes those things which were the greatest source of pride to him prior to salvation. He tells us, "For I went through the Jewish initiation ceremony when I was eight days old, having been born into a pure-blooded Jewish home that was a branch of the old original Benjamin family. So I was a real Jew if there ever was one! What's more, I was a member of the Pharisees who demand the strictest obedience to every Jewish law and custom. And sincere? Yes, so much so that I greatly persecuted the church; and I tried to obey every Jewish rule and regulation right down to the very last point" (Phil. 3:5-6, TLB).*

b. But after his conversion, Paul writes, "For whom I have suffered the loss of all things . . . that I may win Christ" (Phil. 3:8). The point of all these teachings is simply this: at the bema *judgment the carnal Christian will suffer the loss of many past achievements, even as Paul did, but with one important exception: Paul was richly compensated, since he suffered his loss to win Christ, while the carnal believer will receive nothing to replace his burned-up wood, hay, and stubble. Before leaving this section, the question may be asked, "Is it possible for someone who has earned certain rewards down here to lose them somehow through carnality?" Some believe this to be tragically possible on the basis of the following verses: "Look to yourselves, that we lose not those things which we have wrought, but that we receive a full reward" (2 John 8). "Behold, I come quickly; hold that fast which thou hast, that no man take thy crown" (Rev. 3:11). "Let no man beguile you of your reward" (Col. 2:18).*

c. The passage in 3:14-17 actually lists three kinds of builders:

(1) The wise builder (3:14)

(2) The worldly builder (3:15)

(3) The wicked builder (3:17)—The wicked builder, of course, will not *stand before the* bema, *but will be at the great white judgment throne (Rev. 20:11-15). The word "destroy" in 3:17 is* phtheiro *in the original and is often associated in the Greek New Testament with false doctrine and corrupt teachers. (See 1 Cor. 15:33; Eph. 4:22; 2 Pet. 2:12; Jude 10; Rev. 19:2.)*

d. It should also be observed that we shall account for not only what we did *but what we* could *have done if we would have (Rev. 3:1-3; Luke 12:48; 1 Cor. 4:1), and what we* would *have done if we could have (Matt. 26:41; 1 Kings 8:18).*

G. The admonition in light of this judgment—"Know ye not that ye are the temple of God, and that the Spirit of God dwelleth in you? If any man defile the temple of God, him shall God destroy; for the temple of God is holy, which temple ye are. . . . Therefore let no man glory in men. For all things are yours. . . . And ye are Christ's; and Christ is God's" (1 Cor. 3:16-17, 21, 23).

V. Fifth Corruption—They were flattering themselves.

A. Their twofold problem

1. They were overestimating their own abilities—"For who maketh thee to differ from another? and what hast thou that thou didst not receive? now if thou didst receive it, why dost thou glory, as if thou hadst not received it? Now ye are full, now ye are rich, ye have reigned as kings without us: and I would to God ye did reign, that we also might reign with you" (1 Cor. 4:7-8).

---

†4:8 *David Lowery writes: "The posture of humility should be taken by all Christians. Paul set forth the pattern of Christ's life to the Philippians (Phil. 2:5-11). It was marked first by humiliation and then crowned by exaltation. The Corinthians had apparently dispensed with the first half. They wanted their exaltation immediately—no more sickness, no more suffering, no more pain. This is no more possible today than it was when Paul wrote to these self-deluded Corinthians, but nonetheless, many follow in their train. The Corinthians thought they had* all *they wanted (1 Cor. 4:8a), but they should have been hungering and thirsting for the practical righteousness they so desperately needed (Matt. 5:6). They thought of themselves as kings in need of nothing, when in fact, they were as needy as the foolish king in the children's tale of the emperor's new clothes, who blithely paraded nakedly before his subjects (cf. Rev. 3:17-18)"* (Bible Knowledge Commentary, *p. 513).*

---

2. They were underestimating the abilities of others—"And these things, brethren, I have in a figure transferred to myself and to Apollos for your sakes; that ye might learn in us not to think of men above that which is written, that no one of you be puffed up for one against another" (1 Cor. 4:6).

B. Paul's threefold solution

1. He offers a prophetical reminder—The judgment seat of Christ, at which time the Lord would deal with them (1 Cor. 4:1-6). "Let a man so account of us, as of the ministers of Christ, and stewards of the mysteries of God. Moreover it is required in stewards, that a man be found faithful. . . . Therefore judge nothing before the time, until the Lord come, who both will bring to light the hidden things of darkness, and will make manifest the counsels of the hearts: and then shall every man have praise of God" (1 Cor. 4:1-2, 5).
2. He announces a planned visit—At which time he would deal with them (1 Cor. 4:18-21). "Now some are puffed up, as though I would not come to you. But I will come to you shortly, if the Lord will, and will know, not the speech of them which are puffed up, but the power. For the kingdom of God is not in word, but in power. What will ye? shall I come unto you with a rod, or in love, and in the spirit of meekness?" (1 Cor. 4:18-21).
3. He points to a personal example—his own sufferings for Christ (1 Cor. 4:8-17).

a. The facts of his sufferings—"For I think that God hath set forth us the apostles last, as it were appointed to death: for we are made a spectacle unto the world, and to angels, and to men. . . . Even unto this present hour we both hunger, and thirst, and are naked, and are buffeted, and have no certain dwellingplace; and labour, working with our own hands: being reviled, we bless; being persecuted, we suffer it: being defamed, we intreat: we are made as the filth of the world, and are the offscouring of all things unto this day" (1 Cor. 4:9, 11-13).

---

†**4:13** *It has been observed that the trouble with Christians in our country today is that no one is trying to kill them.*

---

b. The (hoped for) fruits from his sufferings—"I write not these things to shame you, but as my beloved sons I warn you. For though ye have ten thousand instructors in Christ, yet have ye not many fathers: for in Christ Jesus I have begotten you through the gospel. Wherefore I beseech you, be ye followers of me. For this cause have I sent unto you Timotheus, who is my beloved son, and faithful in the Lord, who shall bring you into remembrance of my ways which be in Christ, as I teach every where in every church" (1 Cor. 4:14-17).

---

†**4:17** *We note Paul admonishes them to "be ye followers of me." He repeats this request on at least three other occasions (see 1 Cor. 11:1; 2 Thess. 3:9; Phil. 3:17). In light of this it is unscriptural for a pastor or Christian leader (however sincere) to admonish his people, saying: "Don't look at my life, don't do as I do or say. Don't even look at men as your examples, look only to Christ!" See the words of Jesus on this in Matthew 5:13-16. Also to be noted are Paul's words, "I have begotten you" (4:15), which may be compared with those found in Galatians 4:19 and 1 Thessalonians 2:11.*

VI. Sixth Corruption—They were failing to discipline (1 Cor. 5:1-13).

A. The need for discipline—"It is reported commonly that there is fornication among you, and such fornication as is not so much as named among the Gentiles, that one should have his father's wife" (1 Cor. 5:1).

---

†**5:1** *The Greek word for fornication is* porneia *(root word of English pornography). Paul uses this word 17 times in all his writings. Eleven of these are found in 1 Corinthians. Here the sin involved a man living with his stepmother in a sexual way. We note:*

A. He was a church member. This is implied:

1. Because his sinning partner is not rebuked—Paul is here only concerned with that sin committed by a member. The woman was apparently not a member.

2. Because Paul orders him to be dismissed from the fellowship of the church

B. He was guilty as charged—"It is reported commonly" (5:1).

C. He was unrepentant.

B. The breakdown in discipline—"And ye are puffed up, and have not rather mourned, that he that hath done this deed might be taken away from among you" (1 Cor. 5:2).

---

†5:2

A. They were puffed up, not because of the sin itself, but because of their tolerance and pride. At times tolerance can be downright treason.

B. Paul rebukes them for not mourning over this tragedy. How much better had the vain Corinthians heeded the advice of the following verses: "Be afflicted and mourn and weep: let your laughter be turned to mourning and your joy to heaviness" (James 4:9). "The sacrifices of God are a broken spirit: a broken and a contrite heart, O God, thou wilt not despise" (Psa. 51:17).

C. But regardless of their brazen attitude, this church corruption had broken the tender heart of Paul, who would later write: "For out of much affliction and anguish of heart I wrote unto you with many tears" (2 Cor. 2:4).

C. The authority to discipline—"In the name of our Lord Jesus Christ, when ye are gathered together, and my spirit, with the power of our Lord Jesus Christ" (1 Cor. 5:4).

---

†5:4 *Although the individual Christian is warned not to sit in judgment upon another Christian (1 Cor. 4:5), the assembled church does indeed have this right and responsibility. (See also Matt. 18:20.)*

D. The seriousness of discipline—"To deliver such an one unto Satan for the destruction of the flesh, that the spirit may be saved in the day of the Lord Jesus" (1 Cor. 5:5).

---

†5:5

A. What does it mean to do this? The Greek word for destruction *here is* olethros, *a reference to the act of spoiling or marring something. Apparently Paul was saying this: "If this fellow is having so much fun in his sin, then remove him entirely from your fellowship and let Satan kick him around a little. Let him taste what it's like to face a hostile world without the prayers and ministry of a local church!"*

B. Thus, when a local Bible-believing church removes a person like this, it literally fulfills the divine command of Job 2:6: "The Lord said unto Satan, Behold, he is in thine hand; but save his life."

C. Paul was forced to take this drastic action against two other individuals at a later date. "Holding faith, and a good conscience: which some having put away concerning faith have made shipwreck: Of whom is Hymenaeus and Alexander: whom I have delivered unto Satan, that they may learn not to blaspheme" (1 Tim. 1:19-20).

E. The reason for discipline—"Your glorying is not good. Know ye not that a little leaven leaveneth the whole lump? Purge out therefore the old leaven, that ye may be a new lump, as ye are unleavened. For even Christ our passover is sacrificed for us" (1 Cor. 5:6-7).

---

†5:7 *At least three reasons can be listed for this church discipline:*

A. To help the man find his way back to God. It worked, too, for the fellow did indeed repent (see 2 Cor. 2:6-8).

B. To keep the sin from spreading throughout the church—"Know ye not that a little leaven leaveneth the whole lump?" (5:6b). Leaven is a type of evil in the Bible (see Matt. 16:6; Gal. 5:9).

C. To maintain the standards of Christ to a watching world. (See Acts 5:1-13.) One reason why the church has so little influence in the world today is because the world has so much influence in the church.

F. The extent of discipline (1 Cor. 5:9-13)—Here Paul says church discipline is to be limited to church members. "For what have I to do to judge them also that are without? do not ye judge them that are within? But them that are without God judgeth. Therefore put away from among yourselves that wicked person" (1 Cor. 5:12-13).

---

†5:13

A. Negative—The church is not to judge the outside world; that is, to nag and rebuke unbelievers for their smoking, card playing, etc., but rather to lead them to Christ.

B. Positive—The New Testament lists at least three types of individuals to be dismissed from the fellowship of a local church.

1. A constant troublemaker (Prov. 6:19; 2 Thess. 3:6, 11, 14)

2. An immoral person (as seen here in 1 Cor. 5)

3. A heretic (one who denies the virgin birth, etc.; Titus 3:10; Rom. 16:17-18)

G. The procedure in discipline. (See Matt. 18:15-20.)

---

† *A. First step: "Go and tell him his fault between thee and him alone" (Matt. 18:15a). At this initial stage the spirit of Galatians 6:1 should prevail: "Brethren, if a man be overtaken in a fault, ye which are spiritual, restore such a one in the spirit of meekness; considering thyself, lest thou also be tempted" (Gal. 6:1).*

B. Second step: "If he will not hear thee, then take with thee one or two more, that in the mouth of two or three witnesses every word may be established" (Matt. 18:16).

C. Third step: "If he shall neglect [literally, disregard] to hear them, tell it unto the church" (18:17a).

D. Fourth step: "If he neglect to hear the church, let him be unto thee as an heathen man and a publican" (Matt. 18:17). "Yet count him not as an enemy, but admonish him as a brother" (2 Thess. 3:15).

H. The results of discipline—In this case, it worked. (See 2 Cor. 2:6-8.)

VII. Seventh Corruption—They were fragmenting the body of Christ (1 Cor. 6:1-11). The Corinthians had been unjustly taking fellow believers to court in legal matters.

A. This action was improper (1 Cor. 6:1-7).

1. Because of whom they were judging—Namely, fellow believers. "Dare any of you, having a matter against another, go to law before the unjust, and not before the saints?" (1 Cor. 6:1).

---

†6:1 *Paul is not condemning the court system here as an institution, for he himself had used it (see Acts 25:10-11). What he is saying is that feuding believers should use every means at their disposal to settle their legal difficulties and not drag each other before pagan courts.*

---

2. Because of whom they someday would judge—Namely, this world, and fallen angels. "Do ye not know that the saints shall judge the world? and if the world shall be judged by you, are ye unworthy to judge the smallest matters? Know ye not that we shall judge angels? how much more things that pertain to this life?" (1 Cor. 6:2-3).

---

†6:3 *See Daniel 7:18, 22; Matthew 19:28; 2 Peter 2:4; Revelation 20:4.*

B. This action was illegal (1 Cor. 6:8)—"Nay, ye do wrong, and defraud, and that your brethren" (1 Cor. 6:8).

---

†6:8 *In other words, they not only refused to settle their petty problems out of court, but now planned to cheat one another in court.*

C. This action was inconsistent (1 Cor. 6:9-11)—They had apparently conveniently forgotten their own terrible past prior to their salvation. "Know ye not that the unrighteous shall not inherit the kingdom of God? Be not deceived: neither fornicators, nor idolaters, nor adulterers, nor effeminate, nor abusers of themselves with mankind, nor thieves, nor covetous, nor drunkards, nor revilers, nor extortioners, shall inherit the kingdom of God. And such were some of you: but ye are washed, but ye are sanctified, but ye are justified in the name of the Lord Jesus, and by the Spirit of our God" (1 Cor. 6:9-11).

VIII. Eighth Corruption—They were falling into sexual immorality (1 Cor. 6:12-20). Paul condemns this terrible sin, pointing out:

A. That our bodies are members of the Savior—"Know ye not that your bodies are the members of Christ? shall I then take the members of Christ, and make them the members of an harlot? God forbid. What? know ye not that he which is joined to an harlot is one body? for two, saith he, shall be one flesh" (1 Cor. 6:15-16).

---

†6:16 *The believer is thus forbidden to unscripturally involve himself in the systems of this present evil world. The child of God is to flee from unlawful involvements in sex (1 Cor. 6:18; 2 Tim. 2:22), silver (1 Tim. 6:10-11), and society (idolatry; see 1 Cor. 10:14).*

B. That our bodies are temples of the Spirit—"Flee fornication. Every sin that a man doeth is without the body; but he that committeth fornication sinneth against his own body. What? know ye not that your body is the temple of the Holy Ghost which is in you, which ye have of God, and ye are not your own? For ye are bought with a price: therefore glorify God in your body, and in your spirit, which are God's" (1 Cor. 6:18-20).

PART TWO: The six questions submitted by the Corinthian Church (1 Cor. 7–16):

I. Question Number One: What about marriage? (1 Cor. 7)

A. The two problems connected with this chapter

1. Did Paul consider marriage to be unproductive?

a. The fiction—Paul thought lightly of marriage, as indicated by the following verses: "But I would have you without carefulness. He that is unmarried careth for the things that belong to the Lord, how he may please the Lord: But he that is married careth for the things that are of the world, how he may please his wife" (1 Cor. 7:32-33).
b. The facts—This error Paul himself amply refutes.
(1) Refuted by his other writings. (See Eph. 5:22-33; 1 Tim. 3:2; 4:1-5; 5:14; Titus 1:6; 2:4-5; Heb, 13:4.)
(2) Refuted by his comments in this same chapter—"But as God hath distributed to every man, as the Lord hath called every one, so let him walk. And so ordain I in all churches. Brethren, let every man, wherein he is called, therein abide with God. I suppose therefore that this is good for the present distress, I say, that it is good for a man so to be" (1 Cor. 7:17, 24, 26). The "present distress" phrase in verse 26 is thought to be a reference to a particular kind of persecution the Corinthian believers were suffering at that time in history.

2. Did Paul consider his writings to be uninspired?
a. The fiction—Paul admitted his thoughts on marriage to be uninspired, as indicated by the following verses: "But I speak this by permission, and not of commandment. . . . But to the rest speak I, not the Lord: If any brother hath a wife that believeth not, and she be pleased to dwell with him, let him not put her away. . . . Now concerning virgins I have no commandment of the Lord: yet I give my judgment, as one that hath obtained mercy of the Lord to be faithful. . . . But she is happier if she so abide, after my judgment: and I think also that I have the Spirit of God" (1 Cor. 7:6, 12, 25, 40).
b. The facts
(1) The word *permission* is literally "a joint opinion" and may refer to the inspired considered opinion of both Paul and Sosthenes. At any rate, Paul was simply saying that this opinion was not a command but rather a divine suggestion. (For a comparable passage, see Rom. 12:1.)
(2) Verse 12 can be explained by comparing it with verse 10. In verse 10, Paul quotes a command uttered by the Lord Jesus himself while he was upon the earth (see Matt. 19:6). But here is a group situation (one partner saved, one unsaved) to whom Jesus issued no command while on earth, but now does so in heaven through Paul's inspired pen.
(3) The same answer given for verse 12 also applies here in verse 25.
(4) The word *think* here could be translated "persuaded" (1 Cor. 7:40). (See Matt. 22:42; 1 Cor. 8:2 where the same Greek word is used. See also Paul's statements in 1 Tim. 3:16; 1 Cor. 2:4.)

B. The five persons considered in this chapter
1. Singles (1 Cor. 7:1)—"Now concerning the things whereof ye wrote unto me: It is good for a man not to touch a woman" (1 Cor. 7:1).
2. Christian couples (1 Cor. 7:2-7, 10-11)

---

†7:5 *Both partners are to render "due benevolence" to each other (7:3). This phrase is translated "good will" in Ephesians 6:7. Neither partner is to "defraud" the other (7:5). The context shows this* *to be in regard to sexual rights. Paul reminds both that neither has "power" over his own body. This is to say that separate ownership of oneself does not exist in the marriage state. No partner may rightfully quote the words of Matthew 20:15 to the other partner: "Is it not lawful for me to do what I will with mine own?" Thus, to defraud (deny) sexual rights one to the other is to invite being tempted by Satan. (See also 2 Cor. 2:11; 1 Pet. 5:8.)*

---

a. Rules for the husband
   (1) He is to render his duty to his wife (1 Cor. 7:3).
   (2) He is to render his body to his wife (1 Cor. 7:4).
   (3) He must not divorce her (1 Cor. 7:11).
b. Rules for the wife
   (1) She is to remain with her husband if at all possible (1 Cor. 7:10).
   (2) She is to remain his wife even if separation becomes necessary (1 Cor. 7:11).
   (3) She is to attempt reconciliation after the separation (1 Cor. 7:11).
   (4) She is to render her duty to her husband (1 Cor. 7:3).
   (5) She is to render her body to her husband (1 Cor. 7:4).
c. Rules for both—"Defraud ye not one the other, except it be with consent for a time, that ye may give yourselves to fasting and prayer; and come together again, that Satan tempt you not for your incontinency" (1 Cor. 7:5).

3. Unmarried, widowers, and widows
   a. The unmarried
      (1) If possible, feel free to remain unmarried—"For I would that all men were even as I myself. But every man hath his proper gift of God, one after this manner, and another after that. I say therefore to the unmarried and widows, It is good for them if they abide even as I" (1 Cor. 7:7-8).
      (2) If impossible, feel free to become married—"But if they cannot contain, let them marry: for it is better to marry than to burn" (1 Cor. 7:9). "If a virgin marry, she hath not sinned" (1 Cor. 7:28).
   b. The widowers and widows—"Art thou bound unto a wife? seek not to be loosed. Art thou loosed from a wife? seek not a wife" (1 Cor. 7:27). "But and if thou marry, thou hast not sinned" (1 Cor. 7:28). "The wife is bound by the law as long as her husband liveth; but if her husband be dead, she is at liberty to be married to whom she will; only in the Lord" (1 Cor. 7:39).
4. Mixed couples—"But to the rest speak I, not the Lord: If any brother hath a wife that believeth not, and she be pleased to dwell with him, let him not put her away. And the woman which hath an husband that believeth not, and if he be pleased to dwell with her, let her not leave him. For the unbelieving husband is sanctified by the wife, and the unbelieving wife is sanctified by the husband: else were your children unclean; but now are they holy. But if the unbelieving depart, let him depart. A brother or a sister is not under bondage in such cases: but God hath called us to peace. For what knowest thou, O wife, whether thou shalt save thy husband? or how knowest thou, O man, whether thou shalt save thy wife?" (1 Cor. 7:12-16). The saved partner is to remain with the unsaved spouse if at all possible. Two reasons are given for this.
   a. Because of the sanctity of marriage itself (1 Cor. 7:14)
   b. Because of the sanctification of the lost partner (1 Cor. 7:14)—The Holy

Spirit can more easily work in the heart of an unsaved spouse if the other partner is a believer.

5. The father (or guardian) of a young virgin (1 Cor. 7:36-38)
   a. He may feel it best for her marriage to be performed.
   b. He may feel it best for her marriage to be prevented or postponed.

II. Question Number Two: What about Christian liberty? (1 Cor. 8–10). Can a Christian do any lawful thing he or she desires to do? Paul answers this in these chapters by employing three examples:

A. A current example—The Corinthian believers (1 Cor. 8)

1. The confusion—Should a Christian eat meat that had previously been sacrificed to pagan idols?

---

†*There were many pagan temples at Corinth upon which tons of animal meat was sacrificed daily. Some of this meat was consumed by the priests while the remainder was placed on sale in the various city meat markets. It probably sold cheaper, due to its previous usage. Some believers, spotting a bargain, were apparently buying this meat for their table. Other Christians were shocked at this. Here, then, was the question: Should saved people eat meat which had previously been sacrificed to idols?*

---

2. The clarification—"But meat commendeth us not to God: for neither, if we eat, are we the better; neither, if we eat not, are we the worse" (1 Cor. 8:8).
3. The conclusion—"Howbeit there is not in every man that knowledge: for some with conscience of the idol unto this hour eat it as a thing offered unto an idol; and their conscience being weak is defiled. Wherefore, if meat make my brother to offend, I will eat no flesh while the world standeth, lest I make my brother to offend" (1 Cor. 8:7, 13).
4. The challenge
   a. Avoid becoming a stumbling stone—"But take heed lest by any means this liberty of yours become a stumbling block to them that are weak. . . . And through thy knowledge shall the weak brother perish, for whom Christ died? But when ye sin so against the brethren, and wound their weak conscience, ye sin against Christ" (1 Cor. 8:9, 11-12).

---

†8:12

A. The Scriptures declare that a Christian is responsible to at least five classes of people.

1. The world in general (Matt. 5:16; 1 Tim. 3:7)
2. His or her immediate family (Eph. 5–6)
3. All believers in general (Eph. 4:32)
4. Weaker believers in particular (Rom. 14:1; 15:1)—He is thus to be careful:
   a. Lest he cause a weaker brother to defile his conscience (1 Cor. 8:7, 10)
   b. Lest he cause a weaker brother to sin against Christ (8:12)
5. The local church (1 Tim. 3:10; 1 Cor. 10:32)

B. How, though, can one decide upon that which is right or wrong? The Bible declares an action may be wrong on two counts.

1. Because of an inherent *sin factor. There are certain things that are always wrong because they go against the very grain of God's holiness. Such things would be murder, lying, adultery, stealing, idolatry, etc.*

2. *Because of an* acquired *sin factor. There are certain things that, in and by themselves, are harmless, but through time and custom have acquired the taint of being evil. An example of this would be the wearing of cosmetics, which was once considered sinful, but now (if modestly applied) is generally accepted among Christian women.*

The first factor is character *sin, and the second can be referred to as* reputation *sin. The child of God is to avoid both.*

---

b. Attempt becoming a stepping stone—"Now as touching things offered unto idols, we know that we all have knowledge. Knowledge puffeth up, but charity edifieth" (1 Cor. 8:1).

---

†8:1

A. The Greek word for "edifieth" is oikodomeo *and speaks of that action which builds a house (see John 2:20; Matt. 7:24). The New Testament teaches that:*

1. The believer is to build himself up (see Jude 20).

2. He is to build up other Christians (see 1 Thess. 5:11; Rom. 14:19).

3. He is to help build up the entire church (see 1 Cor. 14:12).

B. The word "puffeth up" is found but seven times in the Greek New Testament, six of which are used here in 1 Corinthians. (See 4:6, 18-19; 5:2; 8:1; 13:4.) In every case it is associated with worldly knowledge. Note the following three quotes: "And if any man think that he knoweth anything, he knoweth nothing yet as he ought to know" (1 Cor. 8:2). "Knowledge is that act of passing from a state of unconscious ignorance to a state of conscious ignorance" (L. S. Chafer). "I do not know what I may appear to the world; but to myself I seem to have been like a boy playing on the seashore and diverting myself, now and then finding a smoother pebble or a prettier shell than ordinary, while the great ocean of truth lay all undiscovered before me" (Sir Isaac Newton).

B. A personal example—The Apostle Paul (1 Cor. 9)—Here Paul points out that no one had more right to exercise Christian liberty than he did.

1. The basis of his rights—"Am I not an apostle? am I not free? have I not seen Jesus Christ our Lord? are not ye my work in the Lord?" (1 Cor. 9:1).

2. The extent of his rights

a. To enjoy food—"Have we not power to eat and to drink?" (1 Cor. 9:4).

b. To enjoy family life—"Have we not power to lead about a sister, a wife, as well as other apostles, and as the brethren of the Lord, and Cephas?" (1 Cor. 9:5).

c. To enjoy financial support—"For it is written in the law of Moses, Thou shalt not muzzle the mouth of the ox that treadeth out the corn. Doth God take care for oxen? . . . Even so hath the Lord ordained that they which preach the gospel should live of the gospel" (1 Cor. 9:9, 14).

(1) A soldier is paid, and he was Christ's warrior—"Who goeth a warfare any time at his own charges?" (1 Cor. 9:7).

(2) A husbandman enjoys the fruit from his field, and he had planted many vineyards—"Who planteth a vineyard, and eateth not of the fruit thereof?" (1 Cor. 9:7).

(3) A shepherd drinks of the milk of his flock and he had nurtured many lambs—"Or who feedeth a flock, and eateth not of the milk of the flock?" (1 Cor. 9:7).

(4) A priest lives off the temple gifts, as did God's minister to the Gentiles—"Do ye not know that they which minister about holy things live of the things of the temple? and they which wait at the altar are partakers with the altar?" (1 Cor. 9:13).

3. The employment of his rights
   a. The *what* of the matter—"Nevertheless we have not used this power; but suffer all things" (1 Cor. 9:12b). "I preach the gospel . . . of Christ without charge" (1 Cor. 9:18).
   b. The *who* of the matter
      (1) Concerning the Jew—"And unto the Jews I become as a Jew" (1 Cor. 9:20a). This he did, however, without being *legalistic*.
      (2) Concerning the Gentiles—"To them that are without law, as without law" (1 Cor. 9:21). This he did, however, without being *lawless*.
      (3) Concerning the weak—"To the weak became I as weak" (1 Cor. 9:22). This he did, however, without being *limp*.
   c. The *why* of the matter—Paul explains the reasons for using his Christian rights sparingly. "We . . . suffer all things, lest we should hinder the gospel of Christ" (1 Cor. 9:12b). "For though I be free from all men, yet have I made myself servant unto all, that I might gain the more" (1 Cor. 9:19). "I am made all things to all men, that I might by all means save some" (1 Cor. 9:22b).

---

†9:22b *His life was a living testimony of these statements. Thus:*

A. In ministering to the Jews (9:20)—He circumcised Timothy in Lystra because the Jews in that area knew the young man's father was a Greek. He later preached in Hebrew before a mob of Jews in Jerusalem (see Acts 16 and 22).

B. In ministering to the Gentiles (9:21)—He stood to preach, a practice of the Gentiles, while delivering a message in Antioch. He quoted from Greek literature when addressing some Greeks on Mars Hill (see Acts 13 and 17).

C. In ministering to the weak believers (9:22)—He refrained from eating meat, and commanded that weak Christians everywhere be received into full fellowship (see 1 Cor. 8:13; Rom. 14:1; 15:1).

---

   d. The *how* of the matter—"I therefore so run, not as uncertainly; so fight I, not as one that beateth the air: but I keep under my body, and bring it into subjection: lest that by any means, when I have preached to others, I myself should be a castaway" (1 Cor. 9:26-27).

---

†9:27 *Here the word "castaway" is* adokimos *in the Greek, meaning "disapproved." The same word is found in 2 Timothy 2:15.*

---

   e. The *when* of the matter—Here Paul refers to the judgment seat of Christ. "Know ye not that they which run in a race run all, but one receiveth the prize? So run, that ye may obtain. And every man that striveth for the mastery is temperate in all things. Now they do it to obtain a corruptible crown; but we an incorruptible" (1 Cor. 9:24-25).

C. An Old Testament example—The nation Israel (1 Cor. 10). Paul here records what happened to Old Testament Israel when that nation abused its liberty and blessings from God.

1. The narration (10:1-10).
   a. The review of this freedom (1 Cor. 10:1-4)—"Moreover, brethren, I would not that ye should be ignorant, how that all our fathers were under the cloud, and all passed through the sea; and were all baptized unto Moses in the cloud and in the sea; and did all eat the same spiritual meat; and did all drink the same spiritual drink: for they drank of that spiritual Rock that followed them: and that Rock was Christ" (1 Cor. 10:1-4).
   b. The rebellion against this freedom (1 Cor. 10:5-10)
      (1) They were guilty of idolatry (1 Cor. 10:7)—"Neither be ye idolaters, as were some of them; as it is written, The people sat down to eat and drink, and rose up to play" (1 Cor. 10:7).
      (2) They were guilty of immorality (1 Cor. 10:8)—"Neither let us commit fornication, as some of them committed, and fell in one day three and twenty thousand" (1 Cor. 10:8).
      (3) They were guilty of insubordination (1 Cor. 10:9-10)—"Neither let us tempt Christ, as some of them also tempted, and were destroyed of serpents. Neither murmur ye, as some of them also murmured, and were destroyed of the destroyer" (1 Cor. 10:9-10).
   c. The removal of this freedom (1 Cor. 10:5)—"But with many of them God was not well pleased: for they were overthrown in the wilderness" (1 Cor. 10:5).
      (1) Their idolatry was punished by the sword—"Then Moses stood in the gate of the camp, and said, Who is on the LORD's side? let him come unto me. And all the sons of Levi gathered themselves together unto him. And he said unto them, Thus saith the LORD God of Israel, Put every man his sword by his side, and go in and out from gate to gate throughout the camp, and slay every man his brother, and every man his companion, and every man his neighbour. And the children of Levi did according to the word of Moses: and there fell of the people that day about three thousand men" (Exod. 32:26-28).
      (2) Their immorality was punished by a scourge—"And those that died in the plague were twenty and four thousand" (Num. 25:9).

---

†**Numbers 25:9** *Note: A contradiction has been imagined here, for Moses tells us 24,000 were killed in this plague (Num. 25:9), while Paul says 23,000 died (1 Cor. 10:8). However, the apostle limits his number to those who "fell in one day," while Moses gives the total death figure for the entire period.*

---

      (3) Their insubordination was punished by serpents—"And the people spake against God, and against Moses, Wherefore have ye brought us up out of Egypt to die in the wilderness? for there is no bread, neither is there any water; and our soul loatheth this light bread. And the LORD sent fiery serpents among the people, and they bit the people; and much people of Israel died" (Num. 21:5-6).

2. The application (1 Cor. 10:11-13)—"Now all these things happened unto them for ensamples: and they are written for our admonition, upon whom the ends of the world are come" (1 Cor. 10:11).
   a. This was recorded to remind us concerning our fallibility—"Wherefore let him that thinketh he standeth take heed lest he fall" (1 Cor. 10:12).

---

†10:12 *Especially important here are Paul's two words, "Take heed." In the Bible God commands us to take heed concerning:*
A. Our speech (Psa. 39:1)
B. Overconfidence (1 Cor. 10:12)
C. Being deceived by others (Matt. 24:4)
D. Our ministry to others (Acts 20:28; 1 Tim. 4:16; Col. 4:17)

---

   b. This was recorded to reassure us concerning God's dependability—"There hath no temptation taken you but such as is common to man: but God is faithful, who will not suffer you to be tempted above that ye are able; but will with the temptation also make a way to escape, that ye may be able to bear it" (1 Cor. 10:13).

---

†10:13 *It will prove helpful at this point to review the biblical doctrine of temptation.*
A. The definition of temptation
1. To entice to do evil—Satan tempted Christ and tempts Christians this way. (See Matt. 4:1; Heb. 2:18; 4:15; James 1: 13.)
2. To test or prove with the intent of making one stronger—God "tempts" his children this way. (See Gen. 22:1.)
3. To presume upon the goodness of God—Israel tempted God in this manner, as believers can today. (See Psa. 78:18; Acts 5:9; Matt. 4:7.)
B. The source of temptation
1. The world (see Matt. 13:22; John 16:33; Titus 2:12; 2 Pet. 1:4; Gal. 1:4; 2 Tim. 4:10; 1 John 2:15).
2. The flesh (see Matt. 26:41; Rom. 7:18; Gal. 5:19-21).
3. The devil (see 1 Chron. 21:1; Eph. 4:27; 6:11; 1 Tim. 3:6-7; James 4:7.)
C. The purpose of temptation—As we have already seen, God allows temptation to strengthen his children. It is therefore not *a sin to be tempted. (See James 1:2, 12; 1 Pet. 1:6-7.)*
D. The victory over temptation. (See 1 Pet. 4:19; 2 Pet. 2:9.)

---

3. The summation (1 Cor. 10:14-33)—Paul summarizes this entire section on Christian liberty by the following statements.
   a. What our actions should be
      (1) Beware, lest our conduct among unbelievers be compromised (1 Cor. 10:14-22)—"Ye cannot drink the cup of the Lord, and the cup of devils: ye cannot be partakers of the Lord's table, and of the table of devils" (1 Cor. 10:21).
      (2) Beware, lest our conscience among believers be compromised (1 Cor. 10:25-29)—"But if any man say unto you, This is offered in sacrifice unto idols, eat not for his sake that shewed it, and for conscience sake: for the earth is the Lord's, and the fullness thereof: Conscience, I say, not thine

own, but of the other: for why is my liberty judged of another man's conscience?" (1 Cor. 10:28-29).

b. What our attitude should be—"All things are lawful for me, but all things are not expedient: all things are lawful for me, but all things edify not. Let no man seek his own, but every man another's wealth. Whether therefore ye eat, or drink, or whatsoever ye do, do all to the glory of God. Give none offence, neither to the Jews, nor to the Gentiles, nor to the church of God" (1 Cor. 10:23-24, 31-32).

III. Question Number Three: What about church conduct (1 Cor. 11)? "Be ye followers of me, even as I also am of Christ. Now I praise you, brethren, that ye remember me in all things, and keep the ordinances, as I delivered them to you" (1 Cor. 11:1-2).

A. Rules concerning clothing (1 Cor. 11:1-16)

1. The man's appearance

a. His head was to be uncovered—"Every man praying or prophesying, having his head covered, dishonoureth his head" (1 Cor. 11:4).

(1) Demonstrating his relationship to his Savior—"But I would have you know, that the head of every man is Christ; and the head of the woman is the man; and the head of Christ is God" (1 Cor. 11:3). For a man indeed ought not to cover his head, forasmuch as he is the image and glory of God: but the woman is the glory of the man" (1 Cor. 11:7).

---

†11:7 *Thus, no male in a Christian service should wear a hat, as did the Roman priests and Jewish Rabbis, who wore a head covering called a tallis. The custom began due to a misinterpretation of Moses and his veil. (Compare Exod. 34:33 with 2 Cor. 3:13.)*

---

(2) Demonstrating his relationship to his wife—"And the head of the woman is the man" (1 Cor. 11:3b). "But the woman is the glory of the man" (1 Cor. 11:7b). "For the man is not of the woman; but the woman of the man. Neither was the man created for the woman; but the woman for the man" (1 Cor. 11:8-9).

b. His hair was to be cut—"Doth not even nature itself teach you, that, if a man have long hair, it is a shame unto him?" (1 Cor. 11:14). This demonstrated his relationship to society. Back then one of the marks of a homosexual was his long hair.

2. The woman's appearance

a. Her head was to be covered (1 Cor. 11:5, 10).

(1) Demonstrating her submission to her husband (1 Cor. 11:5)

(2) Demonstrating her spirituality to the angels—"For this cause ought the woman to have power on her head because of the angels" (1 Cor. 11:10).

---

†11:10 *Some believe this passage suggests church members may share their pews with angels. (See Psa. 138:1; Eph. 3:10; 1 Tim. 5:21; Heb. 1:14; 1 Pet. 1:10, 12.)*

---

b. Her hair was not to be cut—"For if the woman be not covered, let her also be shorn: but if it be a shame for a woman to be shorn or shaven, let her be covered. But if a woman have long hair, it is a glory to her: for her hair is given her for a covering" (1 Cor. 11:6, 15). This demonstrated her standards to the world. In those days only female slaves and harlots wore short hair.

B. Rules concerning communion (1 Cor. 11:17-34)

1. The person of communion—The Lord Jesus Christ. The table of the Lord is to magnify the Lord of the table. "For I have received of the Lord that which also I delivered unto you, That the Lord Jesus the same night in which he was betrayed took bread" (1 Cor. 11:23). "After the same manner also he took the cup, when he had supped" (1 Cor. 11:25a).

---

†11:25 *Paul did not receive his information concerning the historical details of the Last Supper from any of the apostles who attended, but from Christ himself. This was also true concerning the details surrounding the preaching, death, and resurrection of the Savior. (See 1 Cor. 15:3; Acts 20:35; Gal. 1:11, 22.)*

---

2. The perversion of communion
   a. The Corinthian error—"For first of all, when ye come together in the church, I hear that there be divisions among you; and I partly believe it. . . . When ye come together therefore into one place, this is not to eat the Lord's supper. For in eating every one taketh before other his own supper: and one is hungry, and another is drunken" (1 Cor. 11:18, 20-21).

---

†11:21 *At their communion service the fickle and self-centered Corinthians had so involved themselves in the supper that they had totally ignored both other saints and the Savior. As a result some (the well-to-do) would stuff themselves with food and drink while others (the poor) would go away hungry. Many things happened on that momentous night in the Upper Room, but here in 11:23, Paul singles out Jesus' betrayal by Judas, which may have been a hint describing what the Corinthians were actually doing also. It should be noted that Paul does not teach here (11:22) against having fellowship banquets in a church basement.*

---

   b. The current errors
      (1) That the bread and cup are sacraments—This is refuted by 1 Corinthians 11:24. "This do in remembrance of me."
      (2) That the bread and cup are changed to flesh and blood—This is refuted by 1 Corinthians 11:28 where they remain the same.
3. The purposes of communion
   a. It serves as a backward look to the *Cross*—"For as often as ye eat this bread, and drink this cup, ye do show the Lord's death" (1 Cor. 11:26).
   b. It serves as an inward look to the *conscience*—"But let a man examine himself, and so let him eat of that bread, and drink of that cup" (1 Cor. 11:28).
   c. It serves as a forward look to the *crown*—"Till he comes" (1 Cor. 11:26).
4. The partakers of communion
   a. Generally speaking—All believers, but only believers
   b. Specifically speaking—Two groups are forbidden to partake.
      (1) The unsaved sinner—He may qualify by obeying John 3:16.

(2) The unclean saint—He may qualify by obeying 1 John 1:9.

5. The penalty of communion—"For he that eateth and drinketh unworthily, eateth and drinketh damnation to himself, not discerning the Lord's body. For this cause many are weak and sickly among you, and many sleep" (1 Cor. 11:29-30).

---

†**11:30** *Here several words deserve our consideration.*

A. Unworthily—The word here is an adverb and not an adjective. Paul does not say, "If anyone who is not worthy partakes," but rather, "If anyone partakes in an unworthy manner."

B. Damnation—In the Greek this is the word krima, *and should here be translated "judgment." (See Rom. 11:33; 1 Pet. 4:17; and Rev. 20:4, where the same word appears.) This judgment may be manifested in a twofold manner:*

1. Through physical sickness (11:30)

2. Through physical death—"And many sleep" (11:30). The Greek word for sleep here is koimao *and refers to physical death. (See John 11:11-12; Acts 7:60; 1 Cor. 15:6, 18, 20, 51.)*

---

6. The profit of communion
   a. It can be used for the judging of ourselves—"For if we would judge ourselves, we should not be judged. But when we are judged, we are chastened of the Lord, that we should not be condemned with the world" (1 Cor. 11:31-32).
   b. It can be used for the giving of ourselves—"Wherefore, my brethren, when ye come together to eat, tarry one for another" (1 Cor. 11:33).

IV. Question Number Four: What about spiritual gifts (1 Cor. 12–14)? "Now concerning spiritual gifts, brethren, I would not have you ignorant" (1 Cor. 12:1).

A. Definition of a spiritual gift—It is a supernatural ability given by Christ through the Holy Spirit to the believer at salvation. (See 1 Cor. 12:7; Eph. 4:7-13.)

---

†*Dr. Charles Ryrie has written the following: "Many think of a spiritual gift as an office in the church which only a privileged few can ever occupy. Or else they consider gifts so out of reach of the ordinary believer that the best he can hope for is that someday he might happen to discover some little gift and be allowed to exercise it in some small way. Both of these conceptions are wrong. A spiritual gift is primarily an ability given to the individual. This means that the gift is not a place of service, for the gift is the ability, not where that ability is exercised. The gift of pastor, for instance, is usually associated with the office or position a person may occupy in the pastorate. But the gift is the ability to give shepherdlike care to people, regardless of where this is done. Of course, the man who occupies the office of a pastor should have and exercise the gift of pastor, but so should a dean of men in a Christian school. Indeed (though this may seem shocking at first), why shouldn't a Christian woman be given the gift of pastor to use among the children in her neighborhood or in her Sunday school class or as dean of women? Now I did not say that women should become pastors of churches to do the preaching and take the leadership of the people. I think that the office or position of the pastorate is reserved for men only; but this does not mean that the gift or the ability cannot be given to women"* (Balancing the Christian Life, *pp. 95-96).*

B. Number of spiritual gifts—In this chapter Paul lists 13 of these gifts. They are:

1. Gift of wisdom (1 Cor. 12:8)

†*There are four kinds of wisdom mentioned in the Bible:*
A. Natural wisdom (Acts 5:38)
B. Worldly wisdom (1 Cor. 1:14-31)
C. Sanctifying wisdom (James 1:5)
D. Stewardship wisdom—This is the wisdom Paul speaks of here in 1 Corinthians 12:8. It can be defined as the ability to apply spiritual principles to contemporary problems.

---

2. Gift of knowledge (1 Cor. 12:8)

---

†*There are (at least) three theories concerning this gift:*
A. The supernatural ability to systematically organize the great theological truths in the Word of God for purposes of study, teaching, and preaching.
B. The supernatural ability to receive a divine revelation of truth.
C. The supernatural ability to function as one of the eight authors of the New Testament.

---

3. The gift of faith (1 Cor. 12:9)

---

†*The Bible describes three kinds of basic faith:*
A. Saving faith—Given to all repenting sinners (Acts 16:31; Rom. 4:5; 5:1; 10:17)
B. Sanctifying faith—Available to all believers (Gal. 2:20; 3:11; 5:22; Eph. 6:16; Rom. 1:17; Heb. 10:38)
C. Stewardship faith—Given to some believers (Rom. 12:3; 1 Cor. 12:9). This is the gift *kind of faith and is a supernatural ability to believe and expect great things from God.*

---

4. The gift of healing (1 Cor. 12:9, 28)

---

†*A supernatural ability to cure human ills, whether of physical, mental, or demonic origin—There is evidence that the sign gifts were phased out during the latter part of the first century at the completion of the scriptural canon. Paul decidedly possessed the gift of healing (Acts 14:10; 16:18; 19:12; 20:10; 28:8-9), but for some reason did not employ it during the final months of his ministry. (See Phil. 2:26-27; 1 Tim. 5:23; 2 Tim. 4:20.)*

Here it should be emphasized that the removal of the sign gifts does not *mean God cannot and will not supernaturally heal a believer today. It does mean, however, that the* gift *of healing through an* individual *has ceased. God's present-day plan for healing is found in James 5:14-16.*

---

5. The gift of miracles (1 Cor. 12:10, 28)

---

†*A supernatural ability to perform those events outside and beyond the realm of nature; the ability to set aside for a time the regular laws of nature—In the Bible there are five periods which witnessed a great outpouring of miracles.*
A. During the time of Moses and Joshua
B. During the time of Elijah and Elisha
C. During the time of Daniel

D. During the time of Christ
E. During the time of Peter and Paul

6. The gift of prophecy (1 Cor. 12:10, 28)

†*There were two aspects to this gift.*
A. To foretell the future—The supernatural ability to receive and transmit a revelation from God, especially that which concerns itself with future events. (See Matt. 13:14; 2 Pet. 1:20-21; Rev. 1:3; Acts 11:27-28; 21:10-11.)
B. To forthtell the present.

7. The gift of discernment (1 Cor. 12:10)

†*The supernatural ability to distinguish between demonic, human, and divine works. (See 1 John 4:1.) Both Peter (Acts 8:23) and Paul (Acts 13:10; 16:16-18) possessed this gift.*

8. The gift of tongues (1 Cor. 12:10, 28)

†*See notes under H.2. on 1 Corinthians 14.*

9. The gift of interpretation of tongues (1 Cor. 12:10)

†*The supernatural ability to clarify and interpret those messages spoken in tongues*

10. The gift of apostleship (1 Cor. 12:28)

†*A reference to certain men called by Christ himself (John 15:16) and endowed with special authority to function as the official "charter members" of the early church.*
A. The requirements—According to both Peter (Acts 1:22) and Paul (1 Cor. 9:1) one must have seen the resurrected Christ to qualify.
B. The number:
1. The original Twelve (Luke 6:13)
2. Matthias (Acts 1:26)
3. Paul (Rom. 1:1)
4. Barnabas (Acts 14:14; Gal. 2:9)
5. James (1 Cor. 15:7; Gal. 1:19)

11. The gift of teaching (1 Cor. 12:28)

†*The supernatural ability to inform, interpret, and inspire concerning the details of the Word of God.*

A. Apollos had this gift (Acts 18:24-25).
B. Aquila and Priscilla possessed it (Acts 18:26)

---

12. The gift of helps (1 Cor. 12:28)

---

†*The supernatural ability to render practical help in both physical and spiritual matters.*
A. Dorcas had this gift (Acts 9:36-39).
B. Phebe had this gift (Rom. 16:1-2).

---

13. The gift of administration (1 Cor. 12:28)
14. In other passages Paul adds at least five more gifts to the list given here. (See Rom. 12:6-8; Eph. 4:7-8.)

---

†*The supernatural ability to organize, administer, and promote either people or projects. (See Titus 1:4-5; see also the book of Nehemiah.)*

C. Extent of the spiritual gifts
   1. Each believer possesses at least one spiritual gift (1 Cor. 12:7, 11)—"But the manifestation of the Spirit is given to every man to profit withal" (1 Cor. 12:7).
   2. No believer possesses all the spiritual gifts (1 Cor. 12:29-30)—"Are all apostles? are all prophets? are all teachers? are all workers of miracles? Have all the gifts of healing? do all speak with tongues? do all interpret?" (1 Cor. 12:29-30).

D. Abuse of the spiritual gifts
   1. Action abuses
      a. Attempting to employ that gift not given to us (1 Cor. 14:34)—"Let your women keep silence in the churches: for it is not permitted unto them to speak; but they are commanded to be under obedience, as also saith the law" (1 Cor. 14:34).
      b. Refusing to employ that gift given to us (1 Cor. 14:1, 12, 23)
      c. Not employing our gift in love—"Though I speak with the tongues of men and of angels, and have not charity, I am become as sounding brass, or a tinkling cymbal" (1 Cor. 13:1).
   2. Attitude abuses
      a. The sin of envy—"If the foot shall say, Because I am not the hand, I am not of the body; is it therefore not of the body? And if the ear shall say, Because I am not the eye, I am not of the body; is it therefore not of the body?" (1 Cor. 12:15-16).
      b. The sin of pride—""And the eye cannot say unto the hand, I have no need of thee: nor again the head to the feet, I have no need of you" (1 Cor. 12:21).

E. Purpose of spiritual gifts
   1. To edify the saints—"He that speaketh in an unknown tongue edifieth himself; but he that prophesieth edifieth the church" (1 Cor. 14:4).
   2. To glorify the Savior—"For he that speaketh in an unknown tongue speaketh not unto men, but unto God: for no man understandeth him; howbeit in the spirit he speaketh mysteries" (1 Cor. 14:2).

F. Analogy of the spiritual gifts—In 12:12-27, Paul links the body of Christ and its many spiritually gifted members to that of the human body with its many physical members. "If the foot shall say, Because I am not the hand, I am not of the body; is it therefore not of the body? And if the ear shall say, Because I am not the eye, I am not of the body; is it therefore not of the body?" (1 Cor. 12:15-16).

1. Each member in both bodies performs a vital task, appointed by God himself—"But now hath God set the members every one of them in the body, as it hath pleased him. . . . That there should be no schism in the body; but that the members should have the same care one for another" (1 Cor. 12:18, 25).
2. No member is to be independent of the other members.
   a. The foot and the ear are not to show envy toward the hand and the eye (1 Cor. 12:15-17).
   b. The eye and the head are not to show pride toward the hand and the feet (1 Cor. 12:21).
3. Every member is to rejoice and suffer with the other members—"And whether one member suffer, all the members suffer with it; or one member be honoured, all the members rejoice with it" (1 Cor. 12:26).

G. Indispensable ingredient in the spiritual gifts—This element is *love* (1 Cor. 13).

---

† *A. The spiritual gifts may be thought of as God's divine bricks to be used in the construction of his holy and earthly temple. In the analogy, charity (love) serves as the "celestial cement" which holds the bricks together. Paul ends the previous chapter with the words: "But covet earnestly the best gifts: and yet show I unto you a more excellent way" (12:31). Thus, chapter 13 is this more excellent way.*

B. It should furthermore be noted that God used Paul, the mighty theologian, to write the greatest poem on love in the history of the world. Each Christmas season the National Safety Council issues the following admonition: "If you drink, don't drive, and if you drive, don't drink, because alcohol and gasoline don't mix." Some have erroneously concluded the same about theology and love. But God has commanded that they are not to be separated (see Rev. 2:1-4). Theology without love leads to dead orthodoxy. Love without theology leads to outright heresy.

---

1. The importance of love (1 Cor. 13:1-3)—"Though I speak with the tongues of men and of angels, and have not charity, I am become as sounding brass, or a tinkling cymbal. And though I have the gift of prophecy, and understand all mysteries, and all knowledge; and though I have all faith, so that I could remove mountains, and have not charity, I am nothing. And though I bestow all my goods to feed the poor, and though I give my body to be burned, and have not charity, it profiteth me nothing" (1 Cor. 13:1-3).
   a. The gift of tongues is useless without it (1 Cor. 13:1).
   b. The gift of prophecy is useless without it (1 Cor. 13:2).
   c. The gift of knowledge is useless without it (1 Cor. 13:2).
   d. The gift of faith is useless without it (1 Cor. 13:2).
   e. The gift of giving is useless without it (1 Cor. 13:3).
2. The impeccability of love (1 Cor. 13:4-7)
   a. In relationship to saints (1 Cor. 13:4a)—It is patient, kind, and not jealous.

b. In relationship to self (1 Cor. 13:4b-5a)—It does not brag, is not arrogant, never acts unbecomingly, nor seeks its own.
c. In relationship to sin (1 Cor. 13:5b-6)—It is not provoked, nor does it hold grudges. It refuses to rejoice in unrighteousness, but finds its joy in truth.
d. In relationship to circumstances (1 Cor. 13:7)—"Beareth all things, believeth all things, hopeth all things, endureth all things" (1 Cor. 13:7).

3. The indestructibility of love (1 Cor. 13:8-13)—"And now abideth faith, hope, charity, these three, but the greatest of these is charity" (1 Cor. 13:13).

---

†13:13 *Note: Paul does not say here that love is more durable than faith and hope, but simply is greater. In some divine manner we will continue using these three virtues even in heaven. Love is greater because:*
A. It is the root of faith and hope.
B. It is for others, while faith and hope are largely personal.
C. It is the very essence of God himself.

---

a. Unlike the other gifts, love is permanent—"Charity never faileth: but whether there be prophecies, they shall fail; whether there be tongues, they shall cease; whether there be knowledge, it shall vanish away" (1 Cor. 13:8).
b. Unlike the other gifts, love is complete—"For we know in part, and we prophesy in part. But when that which is perfect is come, then that which is in part shall be done away. When I was a child, I spake as a child, I understood as a child, I thought as a child: but when I became a man, I put away childish things. For now we see through a glass, darkly; but then face to face: now I know in part; but then shall I know even as also I am known" (1 Cor. 13:9-12).

H. Comparison of the spiritual gifts (1 Cor. 14)—In this chapter Paul contrasts and compares two particular gifts, that of tongues, and the gift of prophecy.

1. The gift of prophecy
a. Meaning of the gift—This gift was twofold:
(1) Forthtelling or proclaiming
(2) Foretelling or predicting—"Let the prophets speak two or three, and let the other judge. If any thing be revealed to another that sitteth by, let the first hold his peace" (1 Cor. 14:29-30).
b. Importance of the gift—It is more important than the gift of tongues (1 Cor. 14:4-6, 19, 39). "Greater is he that prophesieth than he that speaketh with tongues. Now, brethren, if I come unto you speaking with tongues, what shall I profit you, except I shall speak to you either by revelation, or by knowledge, or by prophesying, or by doctrine? . . . Yet in the church I had rather speak five words with my understanding, that by my voice I might teach others also, than ten thousand words in an unknown tongue" (1 Cor. 14:5-6, 19).
c. Purpose of the gift (1 Cor. 14:3-4, 19, 22)
(1) Foretelling aspect—To reveal new divine truths
(2) Forthtelling aspect—To build up, to stir up, and to cheer up. "But he that prophesieth speaketh unto men to edification, and exhortation, and comfort" (1 Cor. 14:3).

d. Regulations of the gift
(1) Only three prophets allowed for each service (1 Cor. 14:29)
(2) Only one of them to speak at any given time (1 Cor. 14:4)
(3) Forthtelling was to take a back seat to foretelling (1 Cor. 14:30).

2. The gift of tongues
a. Meaning of the gift—Three explanations have been given:
(1) The supernatural ability to speak previously unlearned human languages

---

†*This view says that all accounts of New Testament tongue-speaking refer to the same event, that is, the supernatural ability to suddenly speak in previously unlearned human languages. The following are arguments for this view.*

A. *Because of the usage of the same vocabulary—Dr. John Walvoord writes: "The use of identical terms in reference to speaking with tongues in Acts and First Corinthians leaves no foundation for distinction. In all passages, the same vocabulary is used:* laleo *and* glossa, *in various grammatical constructions. On the basis of the Greek and the statement of the text, no distinction is found"* (The Holy Spirit, *p. 183). It is also pointed out that the word* glossa *is found 50 times in the Greek New Testament. Of these, 16 times it refers to the physical organ (see James 3:5); once it refers to flames of fires (Acts 2:3); 33 times it refers to human language.*
B. *Because the word rendered "interpret" in 1 Corinthians 14:13 is* diermeneuo, *and literally means "to translate." Out of the 21 occasions where this word is found in the New Testament, 18 definitely refer to translation. (See Acts 9:36.)*
C. *Because of the description of the events at Pentecost (Acts 2:6-11). Also, Peter says (Acts 11:15) that the tongue-speaking he witnessed at Caesarea was identical to that at Pentecost.*
D. *Because ecstatic gibberish could not be a sign to unbelievers (1 Cor. 14:22)*
E. *Because Jesus warned against tongue-babbling—The Greek words* batta *and* logeo *in Matthew 6:7 refer to the act of babbling, or speaking without thinking*
F. *Because Paul offers no redefinition or clarification of Acts 2 when he writes 1 Corinthians 14*
G. *Because Paul quotes Isaiah 28:11-12 in 1 Corinthians 14:21, which reference is definitely connected to human language. A brief background of Isaiah 28 is needed here. In 721 B.C. the northern kingdom was destroyed. Isaiah warns the southern kingdom (Judah) that the same thing will happen to them unless they repent. He is ridiculed by a group of drunken priests and prophets who disbelieve the warning. Isaiah responds by saying that since they would not listen when God spoke to them in* Hebrew, *they* would *when he spoke to them (through enemy soldiers) in the* Assyrian *language. (See also Moses' words in Deut. 28:15-68, especially v. 49.) (Concerning Titus' invasion in A.D. 70, see Jeremiah 5:15.) Thus, to be addressed in other tongues was a symbol of judgment to the Hebrew mind.*
H. *Because of the advent of higher criticism in the eighteenth and nineteenth centuries—In other words, the critics of the Bible rejected the miracle of speaking unlearned human languages and advocated the ecstatic utterance view, thus identifying biblical tongues with other ancient mystery religions.*

---

(2) The supernatural ability to speak in a heavenly nonhuman language

---

†*This position holds that the language spoken is decidedly nonearthly; rather, it is heavenly in its structure. Arguments supporting this view are:*

A. The tongue-speaking disciples at Pentecost are accused of drunkenness (Acts 2:13), a charge which would not be made if the language was of an earthly nature.

B. Paul says tongues would cease (1 Cor. 13:8), a ridiculous statement if the gift is simply speaking unlearned human language.

C. Because of Paul's words in 1 Corinthians 14:2, "For he that speaketh in an unknown tongue speaketh not unto men, but unto God: for no man understandeth him."

D. Paul had the gift of tongues (1 Cor. 14:18), yet he could not understand the human speech of Lycaonia in Acts 14:11.

E. Because of the distinction made between mind and spirit in 1 Corinthians 14:14-15. Here it is claimed (by some) that God uses the mind *to reveal certain revelation in human language and employs the human spirit to reveal other information in nonhuman language.*

F. Because of the phrase "other tongues" in Acts 2:4. This is a translation of the Greek word heteros, *which means, "another of a different kind." (See also Gal. 1:6-7).*

G. Because of the suggestion in 1 Corinthians 13:1: "Though I speak with the tongues of men and of angels." Note: Here it may be asked what kind of language angels speak. While talking to people on earth they have been known to speak both Hebrew (Gen. 19) and Greek (Luke 1). Even during their heavenly ministry they spoke languages which were understandable. (See Isa. 6; Rev. 4–5.)

---

(3) A combination of the first two—Purpose of the gift

A. Negative

1. It was not for church edification (1 Cor. 14:4, 19).

2. It was not for personal edification. Here an objection may be raised, for does not Paul say, "He that speaketh in an unknown tongue edifieth himself"? He does indeed (1 Cor. 14:4). However, a problem is seen here. If tongues are for personal edification, and if the church house was filled with tongue-speaking (as the context definitely indicates—14:23), then how do we explain that, apart from the church at Laodicea (Rev. 3:14-18), this group at Corinth was the most carnal and confused church in the entire Bible? No gift was to be used for personal edification in a selfish way. Here Paul may actually be rebuking *them for their unscriptural use of this gift.*

3. It was not to demonstrate Spirit baptism. (This erroneous concept is totally refuted in 1 Cor. 12:13; Rom. 6:3-4; Col. 2:9-12; Eph. 4:5; Gal. 3:27-28.)

B. Positive

1. To validate the authority of the apostles and early Christians

2. To demonstrate God's judgment upon unbelieving Israel

3. To serve as a sign to seeking (but lost) individual Jews—"Brethren, be not children in understanding: howbeit in malice be ye children, but in understanding be men. In the law it is written, With men of other tongues and other lips will I speak unto this people; and yet for all that will they not hear me, saith the Lord. *Wherefore tongues are for a sign, not to them that believe, but to them that believe not: but prophesying* serveth *not for them that believe not, but for them which believe" (1 Cor. 14:20-22, emphasis mine).*

a. Here Paul quotes from Isaiah 28:11-12. In that chapter, Isaiah warned sinful Israel as follows:

(1) God could not get their attention when he spoke to them in Hebrew.

(2) God would get their attention when he spoke to them in a foreign tongue.
b. By this Isaiah referred to the language used by the Babylonian soldiers in their impending invasion and destruction of the city of Jerusalem.
c. Thus, for Israel to be addressed by God in a foreign (non-Hebrew) language was in essence to be judged by God. Both Moses (Deut. 28:49) and Jeremiah (Jer. 5:15) had also warned of this.

4. To impart new truths prior to the completion of the canon. When Paul wrote 1 Corinthians there were but four New Testament books in existence (James, 1 and 2 Thessalonians and Galatians). There was no written record available concerning such important issues as:
a. The doctrine of the church (later discussed in Ephesians and Colossians)
b. The doctrine of justification, sanctification, and glorification (later written about in Romans)
c. The doctrine of apostasy (Jude)
d. Christian forgiveness (Philemon)
e. The priesthood of Christ (Hebrews)
f. The life of Christ (the four Gospels)
g. Practical Christian service (1 and 2 Peter)
h. Christian love (as found in 1, 2, and 3 John)
i. Advice to pastors and deacons (as discussed in 1 and 2 Timothy and Titus)—In view of all this, no believer could quote or claim the blessed truth in 2 Timothy 3:16-17, simply because it had not yet been written.

---

b. Regulations of the gift
(1) No more than three tongue speakers are to speak in any given service (1 Cor. 14:27).
(2) No more than one may speak at the same time (1 Cor. 14:27).
(3) An interpreter must translate for all utterances (1 Cor. 14:28)—Paul now lists three analogies to demonstrate the absolute importance of the tongues translator.
(a) First analogy: From the world of music (1 Cor. 14:7)—"Yet even lifeless things, either flute or harp, in producing a sound, if they do not produce a distinction in the tones, how will it be known what is played on the flute or on the harp?" (1 Cor. 14:7, NASB)
(b) Second analogy: From military warfare (1 Cor. 14:8)—"For if the trumpet give an uncertain sound, who shall prepare himself to the battle?" (1 Cor. 14:8).
(c) Third analogy: From daily conversation (1 Cor. 14:9-11)—"So likewise ye, except ye utter by the tongue words easy to be understood, how shall it be known what is spoken? for ye shall speak into the air" (1 Cor. 14:9).
(4) All tongue speaking must be done in an orderly manner—"For God is not the author of confusion, but of peace, as in all churches of the saints. Let all things be done decently and in order" (1 Cor. 14:33, 40).
(5) No woman is permitted to speak in tongues—"Let your women keep silence in the churches: for it is not permitted unto them to speak; but they are commanded to be under obedience, as also saith the law" (1 Cor. 14:34).

†14:34 *In 1 Corinthians 11:3-10 Paul allowed a woman to speak in her natural and native tongue; but here he forbids her to use foreign tongues.*

V. Question Number Five: What about the resurrection (1 Cor. 15)?

† *Without doubt this chapter (along with Rom. 8) simply must be considered as one of the two greatest in the entire Word of God. Here we have the oldest written account of Christ's resurrection.*

A. The prominence of the resurrection (1 Cor. 15:1-4)
   1. It is the focal point in reference to salvation. "Moreover, brethren, I declare unto you the gospel which I preached unto you, which also ye have received, and wherein ye stand; by which also ye are saved, if ye keep in memory what I preached unto you, unless ye have believed in vain" (1 Cor. 15:1-2).
   2. It is the focal point in reference to the scriptures—"For I delivered unto you first of all that which I also received, how that Christ died for our sins according to the scriptures; and that he was buried, and that he rose again the third day according to the scriptures" (1 Cor. 15:3-4).

†15:4

A. The time element in Christ's resurrection—"The third day" (15:4). There are two main theories concerning this phrase.
   1. He was crucified on Friday. The well-known custom of the Jews was to count a part of a day as a whole day. Thus, he would be in the tomb a portion of Friday (from 3:00 P.M. to 6:00 P.M.), all day Saturday, and a part of Sunday.
   2. He was crucified on Wednesday. If Matthew 12:40 is to be taken at face value, then Wednesday is the only day which would allow the necessary three full days and nights.

B. The reason for the resurrection of Christ: "For our sins" (15:3). Christ was not a martyr dying for his faith, but a Savior dying for our sins. He did not say, "I am finished," but, "It is finished." All three persons in the Trinity were involved in his death and resurrection.
   1. The Father (John 3:16; Acts 2:24)
   2. The Son (John 10:11, 18).
   3. The Holy Spirit (Heb. 9:14; Rom. 1:4)

C. The results of the resurrection of Christ—"By which also ye are saved" (15:2).

B. The proof of the resurrection (1 Cor. 15:5-22)
   1. First proof—The manifestations of Christ (1 Cor. 15:5-8). There were actually 10 postresurrection appearances of Christ. Paul lists but six (counting himself) in this passage.
      a. To Peter (1 Cor. 15:5)
      b. To the apostles, with Thomas being absent (1 Cor. 15:5)
      c. To 500 disciples (1 Cor. 15:6)
      d. To James, the half-brother of Christ (1 Cor. 15:7)
      e. To the apostles, with Thomas being present (1 Cor. 15:7)
      f. To Paul (1 Cor. 15:8)
   2. Second proof—The salvation of Paul (1 Cor. 15:9-11). "For I am the least

of the apostles, that am not meet to be called an apostle, because I persecuted the church of God. But by the grace of God I am what I am: and his grace which was bestowed upon me was not in vain; but I laboured more abundantly than they all: yet not I, but the grace of God which was with me" (1 Cor. 15:9-10).

C. The priority of the resurrection (1 Cor. 15:12-19)—"Now if Christ be preached that he rose from the dead, how say some among you that there is no resurrection of the dead?" (1 Cor. 15:12). Obviously some were saying this very thing. Paul then lists many horrible conclusions one must be forced to hold if this statement is true.
 1. Concerning Christ—The Easter story is a lie. "But if there be no resurrection of the dead, then is Christ not risen" (1 Cor. 15:13).
 2. Concerning the gospel preachers—They continue to lie. "Yea, and we are found false witnesses of God; because we have testified of God that he raised up Christ: whom he raised not up, if so be that the dead rise not" (1 Cor. 15:15).
 3. Concerning believers—They swallow the lie.
  a. We are still in our sins—"And if Christ be not raised, your faith is vain; ye are yet in your sins" (1 Cor. 15:17).
  b. Our departed loved ones will never be raised—"Then they also which are fallen asleep in Christ are perished" (1 Cor. 15:18).
  c. We will never be raised (1 Cor. 15:13, 15).
  d. We have no hope in this life—"If in this life only we have hope in Christ, we are of all men most miserable" (1 Cor. 15:19).
  e. The sensual way is the only way (1 Cor. 15:32)—"If the dead rise not . . . let us eat and drink; for tomorrow we die" (1 Cor. 15:32).

D. The program of the resurrection (1 Cor. 15:20-28)—"But now is Christ risen from the dead, and become the firstfruits of them that slept. For since by man came death, by man came also the resurrection of the dead. For as in Adam all die, even so in Christ shall all be made alive" (1 Cor. 15:20-22).

---

†**15:22** *In these verses Paul refers to the third of seven Jewish feasts mentioned in Leviticus 23. It was called the Feast of the First Fruits. Note:*
A. On the first day, selected delegates marked out the spot in the grain field from which the sheaf would be cut.
B. On the second day the sheaf was cut and brought into the temple.
C. On the third day it was presented to the Lord as a pledge sample.

---

 1. The villain—"The last enemy that shall be destroyed is death" (1 Cor. 15:26).
 2. The victors—"But every man in his own order: Christ the firstfruits; afterward they that are Christ's at his coming" (1 Cor. 15:23).

---

†**15:23** *The Greek word for "order" here is* tagma, *a military term referring to troops in order of rank, as in a parade. Thus we see:*
A. The resurrection of Christ (Mark 16:2-8; Matt. 28:5-8; Luke 24:1-8)—His resurrection leads the parade, for it was the very first of its kind. The miracle Christ performed upon Lazarus (John 11),

for example, was not true resurrection, but simply the restoration of a dead mortal body to that of a living mortal body. Lazarus died *again at a later date. But ultimate resurrection carries with it immortality.*

B. *The Rapture resurrection—"Afterward they that are Christ's at his coming" (15:23b). These "troops" follow behind the head of the parade. (See 1 Cor. 15:53; 1 Thess. 4:16.)*

C. *The premillennial resurrection of Old Testament and tribulation saints—"Then cometh the end" (15:24a; see John 5:24; Dan. 12:2; Rev. 20:5-6).*

---

a. "Christ the first fruits"—His own resurrection (1 Cor.15:23)

b. "Afterward they that are Christ's at his coming"—The Rapture resurrection (1 Cor. 15:23b)

c. "Then cometh the end"—Premillennial resurrection of Old Testament and tribulational saints (1 Cor. 15:24b)

3. The victory—"Then cometh the end, when he shall have delivered up the kingdom to God, even the Father; when he shall have put down all rule and all authority and power. For he must reign, till he hath put all enemies under his feet" (1 Cor. 15:24-25).

4. The vindication—"And when all things shall be subdued unto him, then shall the Son also himself be subject unto him that put all things under him, that God may be all in all" (1 Cor. 15:28).

E. The prompting of the resurrection (1 Cor. 15:29-34)

1. The resurrection factor should motivate me to pick up the fallen banner of departed believers. "Else what shall they do which are baptized for the dead, if the dead rise not at all? why are they then baptized for the dead?" (1 Cor. 15:29).

---

†15:29 *This verse has been somewhat of a problem.*

A. *Negative: Whatever its meaning, it does* not *support the totally unscriptural practice of the Mormon church of living people being baptized by proxy for dead people. To die lost is to forever remain lost. (See Luke 16:19-31; Heb. 2:3; Rev. 22:11.)*

B. *Positive: Inasmuch as baptism refers to identification, Paul may be saying here that, if there is no resurrection of the dead, then what is the purpose of living believers picking up the standard left by departed believers?*

---

2. The resurrection factor should motivate me to serve as a martyr if God's will so directs (1 Cor. 15:30-32)

3. The resurrection factor should motivate me toward holy living—"Be not deceived: evil communications corrupt good manners. Awake to righteousness, and sin not; for some have not the knowledge of God: I speak this to your shame" (1 Cor. 15:33-34).

F. The pattern of the resurrection (1 Cor. 15:35-38)—"But some man will say, How are the dead raised up? and with what body do they come?" (1 Cor. 15:35). Paul illustrates the resurrection by a grain of wheat.

1. To be resurrected the grain is planted in the ground.

2. At the resurrection the new stalk retains the likeness of the grains.

† *A. Paul does not describe the method used by God in raising the dead, but instead gives a glorious example, a grain of wheat (15:37).*

B. Several thrilling conclusions can be drawn from this illustration.

1. The old body, like a grain of wheat, has no power to change itself. Only God can grow wheat and raise the dead.

2. The old body, like a grain of wheat, must die to be changed. "Verily, verily I say unto you, except a corn of wheat fall into the ground and die, it abideth alone; but if it die, it bringeth forth much fruit" (John 12:24). Thus death does not suppress the grain, but simply releases it.

3. The new body, like a grain of wheat, does not lose its identity. Both still retain a certain likeness of the former state (1 Cor. 13:12).

G. The perfection of the resurrection (1 Cor. 15:39-50)—"It is sown in dishonour; it is raised in glory: it is sown in weakness; it is raised in power: It is sown a natural body; it is raised a spiritual body. There is a natural body, and there is a spiritual body. And so it is written, The first man Adam was made a living soul; the last Adam was made a quickening spirit. . . . The first man is of the earth, earthy: the second man is the Lord from heaven. . . . And as we have borne the image of the earthy, we shall also bear the image of the heavenly" (1 Cor. 15:43-45, 47, 49).

1. Paul contrasts the new body to the old body.

a. The old body—It is sown a perishable body, sinful by nature, dominated by the flesh, and bounded by time and gravity. It is likened to the sinful body of the first Adam.

b. The new body—It is raised an imperishable body, sinless by nature, dominated by the spirit, and unbounded by time and gravity. It is likened to the sinless body of the last Adam.

---

† *A. In verse 44 Paul writes, "There is a natural body and there is a spiritual body." What is the difference? Consider a book with a sheet of plain white paper stuck inside it. In this illustration the book is human body and the paper sheet is the spirit. Down here the book "bosses" the spirit. It has the final say. This is the natural body, governed by the physical laws of gravity and time.*

B. But now take the white sheet out of the book and wrap it around the book like a cover. Now the sheet (spirit) is on top. It has the final say. This is the spiritual body, which is unaffected by the physical laws of gravity or time, but enjoys the blessings of eternity.

---

2. Paul contrasts the new body with brute bodies (1 Cor. 15:39)—It is as different as human flesh is from animal flesh.

3. Paul contrasts the new body with heavenly bodies (1 Cor. 15:40-41)—It is as different as the sun is from the moon.

H. The promise of the resurrection (1 Cor. 15:51-54)

1. Concerning the bodies belonging to living believers—They will be changed without dying. "Behold, I shew you a mystery; We shall not all sleep, but we shall all be changed" (1 Cor. 15:51). "In a moment, in the twinkling of an eye, at the last trump" (1 Cor. 15:52a). "And this mortal must put on immortality" (1 Cor. 15:53b).

†15:53b

A. *"I shew you a mystery." What mystery? Let us suppose you began reading the Bible in Genesis chapter 1, and read through 1 Corinthians chapter 14. If you stopped your reading here, you would already have learned about many important facts, such as creation, sin, the flood, Bethlehem, Calvary, the resurrection, and the existence of heaven and hell. But you would be forced to conclude that a Christian could go to heaven only after physically dying. You would, of course, note the two exceptions of Enoch (Gen. 5:24) and Elijah (2 Kings 2:11); but apart from these it would be clear that believers have to travel the path of the grave to reach the goal of glory. But now the secret is out, and here it is: Millions of Christians will someday reach heaven without dying. "Behold I shew you a mystery; we shall not all sleep, but we shall all be changed" (1 Cor. 15:51). This, then, is the mystery of the Rapture.*

B. *"We shall all be changed." Observe the word* all. *The Bible does not support a partial Rapture theory.*

C. *"In the twinkling of an eye." This occurs as quickly as a gleam of light shines in the eye, about one fifth of a second.*

---

2. Concerning the bodies belonging to departed believers—They will be raised without corruption. "For the trumpet shall sound, and the dead shall be raised incorruptible" (1 Cor. 15:52b). "For this corruptible must put on incorruptible" (1 Cor. 15:53a).

I. The purpose of the resurrection (1 Cor. 15:54-57)—"So when this corruptible shall have put on incorruption, and this mortal shall have put on immortality, then shall be brought to pass the saying that is written, Death is swallowed up in victory. O death, where is thy sting? O grave, where is thy victory? The sting of death is sin; and the strength of sin is the law. But thanks be to God, which giveth us the victory through our Lord Jesus Christ" (1 Cor. 15:54-57).

---

†15:57

A. *The purpose of the resurrection should be clearly understood by Christians. It is a tragic fact that our world is indeed a materialistic one. Materialism has been defined as the art of knowing the* price *of everything, but the* value *of nothing. On occasion, however, in an attempt to avoid this philosophy, believers go to the other extreme and conclude that God is interested* only *in nonphysical matters. This sad error is sometimes seen in our churches in the separate deacon and trustee boards. Often this attitude imposes a higher moral standard upon deacons than on trustees, for, after all, aren't the "spiritual" matters more important than the "physical" areas? The truth of the matter is that God is* very much *interested in physical things, especially in the bodies of Christians. (See 1 Cor. 6:19-20; 2 Cor. 6:16; Eph. 5:28-29; Rom. 12:1-2.)*

B. *What, then, is the purpose of the resurrection? Among other things, it is to destroy man's final enemy. Paul has already written: "The last enemy that shall be destroyed is death" (15:26). Mankind has five natural enemies:*
   1. *The world (Gal. 1:4; 1 John 2:15; James 4:4).*
   2. *The flesh (Rom. 7:18; 8:8; Gal. 5:17; 1 John 2:16).*
   3. *The devil (Matt. 13:39; Eph. 6:11).*
   4. *Spiritual death (John 5:24; 8:51; Rev. 2:11).*
   5. *Physical death (Psa. 55:4; Heb. 2:15).*

C. Here death is pictured as a venomous serpent and its poisonous fang is sin. But someday God will destroy both the rattler and its fang. Note also the twin phrases:
1. "O death, where is thy sting?" This may refer to living believers who will escape physical death at Christ's coming.
2. "O grave, where is thy victory?" This may refer to departed believers, whose bodies the graves will be forced to give up.

J. The practical value of the resurrection (1 Cor. 15:58)—"Therefore, my beloved brethren, be ye stedfast, unmoveable, always abounding in the work of the Lord, forasmuch as ye know that your labour is not in vain in the Lord" (1 Cor. 15:58).

VI. Question Number Six: What about the collection (1 Cor. 16)? "Now concerning the collection for the saints, as I have given order to the churches of Galatia, even so do ye" (1 Cor. 16:1).

---

†16:1 *The location of the offering: the churches of Galatia. The mention of "the churches of Galatia" is to be noted. The New Testament never speaks of the church in or of a country or province. The official "state church" institution in various countries today is totally foreign to the Bible.*

A. The offering taken (1 Cor. 16:1-4)
1. The source of the offering—"Let every one of you" (1 Cor. 16:2).

---

†16:2b *The local church is to be supported by its members. We note also that it was to be done by everyone.*

---

2. The time of the offering—"Upon the first day of the week" (1 Cor. 16:2a).

---

†16:2a *This, of course, means on Sunday. (See Mark 16:2, 9: Luke 24:1; John 20:1, 19; Acts 20:7.)*

---

3. The amount of the offering—"As God hath prospered him" (1 Cor. 16:2c).

---

†16:2c *Although no actual proportion is laid down, it is unthinkable that a believer would give less to God than that amount he tips a waitress in a restaurant.*

---

4. The purpose of the offering—"For the saints" (1 Cor. 16:1)
5. The custodian of the offering—"Whomsoever ye shall approve" (1 Cor. 16:3)

---

†16:3 *In all financial affairs of an assembly, the responsibility should be in the hand of more than one brother, to avoid the slightest suspicion of improper handling.*

B. The offering taker (1 Cor. 16:5-24)
1. His circumstances

a. To visit Corinth later (1 Cor. 16: 5-7)
b. To stay at Ephesus until June (1 Cor. 16:8)

2. His commitment—"For a great door and effectual is opened unto me, and there are many adversaries" (1 Cor. 16:9).
3. His coworkers—Paul sends greetings from and expresses his appreciation for the following individuals.
   a. Timothy (1 Cor. 16:10-11)
   b. Apollos (1 Cor. 16:12)
   c. Stephanas, Fortunatus, and Achaicus (1 Cor. 16:15-18)
   d. Aquila and Priscilla (1 Cor. 16:19)
4. His challenge—"Watch ye, stand fast in the faith, quit you like men, be strong. Let all your things be done with charity" (1 Cor. 16:13-14).
5. His closing words (1 Cor. 16:21-24)—"If any man love not the Lord Jesus Christ, let him be Anathema Maranatha" (1 Cor. 16:22).

---

†16:22

A. The word anathema *means "fitted for destruction." (See Rom. 9:3; Gal. 1:8-9.)*
B. The word maranatha *means "the Lord comes." (See Phil. 4:5; James 5:7-8; Rev. 1:7; 3:11.)*

---

2 CORINTHIANS

A MUST READING FOR THE MINISTRY: THE MOST INTIMATE ACCOUNT EVER WRITTEN OF THE DUTIES AND DEMANDS, JOYS AND SORROWS, TRIALS AND TRIUMPHS, PAIN AND PRIVILEGES INVOLVED IN THE WORK OF GOD.

A. This book, 2 Corinthians, may be compared with 1 Corinthians. In 1 Corinthians we see the congregation in the pews; but here in 2 Corinthians can be viewed the preacher in his pulpit.
B. Paul had organized the Corinthian church during his second missionary trip (Acts 18:1-18).
C. During his third missionary trip he visits the church (2 Cor. 12:14; 13:1).
D. He sends Titus to Corinth to organize a special love offering for the poverty-stricken saints in Jerusalem (1 Cor. 16:1; 2 Cor. 8:6, 10). Titus does this and returns to Paul.
E. He writes a letter (now lost) to the Corinthian church (1 Cor. 5:9). We must keep in mind that God did not choose to inspire *all* of the many letters written by Paul and early church leaders, but *only* those which are found in the New Testament.
F. After a while, Paul writes another letter. This letter is the 1 Corinthians of the New Testament. There were two basic reasons why he wrote this epistle.
    1. To rebuke the church—Paul had heard about some tragic church factions from the household of Chloe, living there in Corinth (1 Cor. 1:11).
    2. To instruct the church—Paul was visited while in Ephesus by a three-man delegation from Corinth, who handed him a list of questions the church had for him (1 Cor. 7:1; 8:1; 12:1; 16:17).
G. He then sends Timothy to Corinth with this New Testament epistle (1 Cor. 4:17; 16:10-11).
H. Timothy returns to Paul in Ephesus—This young preacher was apparently unable to straighten things out in Corinth (2 Cor. 1:1).
I. Paul desires to visit the church himself at this time, but is unable to (2 Cor. 1:15-17).
J. He soon hears that his work there is being undermined by some legalistic Judaizers who had just arrived from Jerusalem (2 Cor. 3:1; 10:12-18; 11:22-23).
K. He now sends Titus back to Corinth with orders to straighten things out and meet him in Troas (2 Cor. 2:12-13; 7:6-7).
L. Paul comes to Troas, but does not find Titus. After a restless period, he departs to Macedonia (2 Cor. 2:12-13).
M. Here he meets Titus, who gives him a favorable report concerning the work at Corinth.
N. With great relief, Paul writes 2 Corinthians (2 Cor. 7:5-15).
O. Paul is finally able to visit Corinth at a later date for a period of three months. Here he writes the epistle of Romans (Acts 20:3; Rom. 15:22-29; Rom. 16:1, 23).
P. One of the reasons Paul had written 1 Corinthians was to instruct the church to remove an unrepentant member (1 Cor. 5:1-8).

Q. He then wrote 2 Corinthians, instructing the church to receive back that one who had since become repentant (2 Cor. 2:6-11).

R. Paul lists no less than 15 characteristics of the gospel ministry. One of the most important reasons why God allows a Christian to suffer is explained in this book (1:1-6). In no other epistle does Paul refer to his own sufferings as in this letter (4:8-10; 6:4-10; 11:24-33).

S. He also provides the most concise reason why God uses us to do his work (4:7).

T. The most extended discussion of the grace of giving is found in 2 Corinthians (see 8–9).

U. Paul was the first of two human beings allowed to visit paradise and return again. John the apostle was the other. In fact the phrase, "the third heaven," is found but once in the Bible (2 Cor. 12:2).

V. The book of 2 Corinthians also serves as an expose on the person and work of Satan. (See 2:10-11; 4:4; 11:3, 13-15; 12:7.)

W. At least four names for Christians are given in this book which are not found anywhere else in the Bible. These are:
  1. Living epistles (3:2-3)
  2. A sweet savor of Christ (2:15)
  3. Treasure-carrying earthen vessels (4:7)
  4. Ambassadors for Christ (5:20)

X. The book of 2 Corinthians is the only epistle in which Paul takes the time to defend his apostleship against the lies of his enemies. (See 10–11.)

Y. There are quotations or allusions in 2 Corinthians from 14 Old Testament books. The book of 2 Corinthians is the tenth longest New Testament book, and 33rd longest biblical book, with 13 chapters, 257 verses, and 6,092 words.

Z. Great passages would include:
  1. 1:2-5
  2. 4:1-18
  3. 5:1-10
  4. 5:17-21
  5. 6:14-18
  6. 7:10
  7. 8:9
  8. 9:6
  9. 9:15
  10. 12:9-10

THE BOOK OF 2 CORINTHIANS

"Paul, an apostle of Jesus Christ by the will of God, and Timothy our brother, unto the church of God which is at Corinth, with all the saints which are in all Achaia: Grace be to you and peace from God our Father, and from the Lord Jesus Christ" (2 Cor. 1:1-2).

I. Consolation (2 Cor. 1:3-7)

  A. The person of consolation and comfort—"Blessed be God, even the Father of our Lord Jesus Christ, the Father of mercies, and the God of all comfort" (2 Cor. 1:3).

†1:3

A. These two words, "comfort" and "consolation" (both from the same Greek word), are found ten times in the first seven verses. Paul begins this epistle (1:3) and ends it (13:11) with the word comfort. Each member of the blessed Trinity is a Comforter.

1. The Father (2 Cor. 1:3; Isa. 49:13)

2. The Son (John 14:1; Isa. 61:2; 2 Thess. 2:16)

3. The Holy Spirit (John 14:16, 26; 15:26; 16:7)

B. The word for "comfort" comes from two Greek words, para *(alongside) and* kaleo *(to call). Thus, to comfort a person is to answer his call and walk alongside him to cheer him, guide him, and, on occasion, to defend him. The Greek word was often used in a court of justice to denote a legal counsel for the defense, one who would plead another's cause. (See 1 John 2:1.) Furthermore, it may be stated that God is the* only *source of real comfort. The prophetical prayer of Jesus on the cross as given in the Psalms (69:20) perfectly describes all human beings: "Reproach hath broken my heart; and I am full of heaviness: and I looked for some to take pity, but there was none; and for comforters, but I found none."*

C. There are two types of people which need no comfort: the unborn and the dead (see Isa. 40:1-2). C. H. Spurgeon said that the preacher who prepared his sermons for heartbroken people would never lack for an audience.

B. The purpose of consolation and comfort—"Who comforteth us in all our tribulation, that we may be able to comfort them which are in any trouble, by the comfort wherewith we ourselves are comforted of God. For as the sufferings of Christ abound in us, so our consolation also aboundeth by Christ" (2 Cor. 1:4-5).

---

†1:5 *There is a vast difference between* sympathy *and* empathy. *The first can only say, "I'm sorry for what you're going through"; but the second may state, "I know exactly what you're going through." Thus, because our Lord Jesus suffered all things, he is able to offer all comfort. (See Heb. 2:14-18; 4:14-16.) The Savior not only comforts us, but suffers with us (Acts 9:4). The spiritual rule therefore is this: The more one suffers for Christ, the more comfort he receives from Christ, and the more ability he has to comfort other suffering people. Thus, he who has suffered much speaks many languages.*

C. The pattern of consolation and comfort—"And whether we be afflicted, it is for your consolation and salvation, which is effectual in the enduring of the same sufferings which we also suffer: or whether we be comforted, it is for your consolation and salvation" (2 Cor. 1:6).

II. Explanation (2 Cor. 1:8–2:13)

A. Concerning Paul's travel to Asia (1 Cor. 1:8-14)

1. His trials—"For we would not, brethren, have you ignorant of our trouble which came to us in Asia, that we were pressed out of measure, above strength, insomuch that we despaired even of life" (2 Cor. 1:8).

2. His testimony—"But we had the sentence of death in ourselves, that we should not trust in ourselves, but in God which raiseth the dead: who delivered us from so great a death, and doth deliver: in whom we trust that he will yet deliver us" (2 Cor. 1:9-10).

†**1:10** *Paul's faith here was like that of Isaac and Abraham in the Old Testament. (See Gen. 22:1-18; Heb. 11:17-19.) Note his testimony concerning God's threefold deliverance.*
A. "Who delivered us." This speaks of justification.
B. "Who doth deliver." This speaks of sanctification.
C. "Who will yet deliver." This speaks of glorification.

B. Concerning Paul's trip to Macedonia (2 Cor. 1:8-24; 2:1, 12-13)
1. His anticipated trip (2 Cor. 1:15-16)—He intended to visit the Corinthian church on the way back to Judea.
2. His abandoned trip (2 Cor. 1:23, 2:1)—He realized the carnal church would not be receptive to his ministry at that time.
3. His actual trip (2 Cor. 2:12-13)

C. Concerning Paul's tears in Ephesus (2 Cor. 2:2-11)—"For out of much affliction and anguish of heart I wrote unto you with many tears; not that ye should be grieved, but that ye might know the love which I have more abundantly unto you" (2 Cor. 2:4).
1. In the past, the Corinthian church had refused to rebuke an unrepentant believer (see 1 Cor. 5).
2. At the present, the Corinthian church had refused to restore the repentant believer.
a. Paul tells the church what they were to do—"Sufficient to such a man is this punishment, which was inflicted of many. So that contrariwise ye ought rather to forgive him, and comfort him, lest perhaps such a one should be swallowed up with overmuch sorrow. Wherefore I beseech you that ye would confirm your love toward him" (2 Cor. 2:6-8).
b. Paul tells the church why they were to do it—"Lest Satan should get an advantage of us: for we are not ignorant of his devices" (2 Cor. 2:11).

---

†**2:11** *There were at least five things that Paul did not want his readers to be ignorant concerning:*
A. The fact of Israel's past rejection (1 Cor. 10:1)
B. The fact of Israel's future restoration (Rom. 11:25)
C. The fact and nature of spiritual gifts (1 Cor. 12:1)
D. The fact and nature of the Rapture (1 Thess. 4:13)
E. The fact and nature of Satan's deception (2 Cor. 2:11)

III. Characterization (2 Cor. 2:14–6:18)—Paul here lists 15 desired characteristics of the gospel ministry.
A. It is a triumphal one (2 Cor. 2:14-16)—"Now thanks be unto God, which always causeth us to triumph in Christ, and maketh manifest the savour of his knowledge by us in every place" (2 Cor. 2:14).

---

†**2:14** *God has thus assured us of victory—total victory:*
A. Regardless of when the problems arise (always)
B. Regardless of where the problems arise (every place). To illustrate this promise, Paul likens the ministry to a victorious Roman parade during which the successful general (in this case, Jesus)

would lead both conquerors *(the saved) and* captives *(the unsaved) to their respective destinies. From the marching parade there would ascend a sweet fragrance, caused by the burning of incense. Thus: "To the one [captives] we are the savour of death unto death; and to the other [conquerors] the savour of life unto life "(2:16). In the Old Testament, Joseph's presence was death for the baker (Gen. 40:16-19, 22), but life for the butler (Gen. 40:9, 13, 21). Likewise, in the New Testament, Jesus' presence meant death for the unrepentant thief (Luke 23:39), but life for the repentant thief (Luke 23:40-43).*

B. It is a sincere one (2 Cor. 2:17)—"For we are not as many, which corrupt the word of God: but as of sincerity, but as of God, in the sight of God speak we in Christ" (2 Cor. 2:17).

---

† **2:17** *The word "corrupt" means to peddle, or to huckster the Word of God. All false prophets are guilty of this horrible sin. (See Acts 8:18-23; 2 Pet. 3:14-16.)*

C. It is a divinely approved one (2 Cor. 3:1-3)—"Do we begin again to commend ourselves? or need we, as some others, epistles of commendation to you, or letters of commendation from you?" (2 Cor. 3:1). Unlike his enemies the Judaizers, Paul needed no letters of recommendation from finite and carnal people.

1. His authority came from the saints—"Ye are our epistle written in our hearts, known and read of all men" (2 Cor. 3:2).
2. His authority came from the Spirit—"Forasmuch as ye are manifestly declared to be the epistle of Christ ministered by us, written not with ink, but with the Spirit of the living God; not in tables of stone, but in fleshy tables of the heart" (2 Cor. 3:3).

---

†**3:3** *The legalistic Judaizing teachers who plagued Paul's work carried formal and impressive letters of introduction from Jerusalem. Prior to his conversion, the apostle had done this also (Acts 9:2). But now all that had changed. Paul's letters were:*

A. Personal—"Ye are our epistle."
B. Permanent—"Written in our hearts"
C. Public—"Known and read of all men."

D. It is a dependent one (2 Cor. 3:4-5)—"Not that we are sufficient of ourselves to think any thing as of ourselves; but our sufficiency is of God" (2 Cor. 3:5).

E. It is a superior one (2 Cor. 3:6-18)—The apostle now contrasts the gospel of grace with the Law of Moses.

1. Its priests are superior—"Who also hath made us able ministers of the new testament; not of the letter, but of the spirit: for the letter killeth, but the spirit giveth life" (2 Cor. 3:6).
2. Its program is superior (2 Cor. 3:7-13)—The glory of grace will never fade away, as did the glory of the Law. (See Exod. 34:29-35.) "And not as Moses, which put a vail over his face, that the children of Israel could not stedfastly look to the end of that which is abolished" (2 Cor. 3:13).

† **3:13** *Here Paul refers back to Exodus 34:29-35, when Moses came down from Mount Sinai after receiving the Ten Commandments. On that occasion his face had so radiated God's glory that he wore a veil, so he wouldn't frighten the waiting Israelites below. But in 2 Corinthians 3:13 Paul explains that the real reason for the veil was to prevent Israel from viewing the glory which soon faded away. But God's new program is superior to that of Moses, for its glory, as given by Christ, will never fade away. (See also Matt. 26:28; Heb. 8:8, 13.)*

---

3. Its person is superior—"Now the Lord is that Spirit: and where the Spirit of the Lord is, there is liberty" (2 Cor. 3:17).
4. Its purpose is superior (2 Cor. 3:14-18).
    a. Concerning the Israel of God—To remove the veil, that is, to take away the unbelief from their hearts. "But even unto this day, when Moses is read, the vail is upon their heart. Nevertheless when it shall turn to the Lord, the vail shall be taken away" (2 Cor. 3:15-16).
    b. Concerning the child of God—To renew the vision; that is, to transform believers into the image of Christ. "But we all, with open face beholding as in a glass the glory of the Lord, are changed into the same image from glory to glory, even as by the Spirit of the Lord" (2 Cor. 3:18).

---

†**3:18** *Thus, the supreme goal of the believer on this earth is to become as much like Jesus as possible. This, of course, is God's ultimate goal throughout all eternity, but he wants to start this process now. Dr. H. A. Ironside writes in his book on 2 Corinthians: "You remember Hawthorne's story of 'The Great Stone Face.' He tells of a lad who lived in the village below the mountain, and there upon the mountain was that image of the great stone face, looking down so solemnly, so seriously, upon the people. There was a legend that some day someone was coming to that village who would look just like the great stone face, and he would do some wonderful things for the village and would be the means of great blessing. The story gripped this lad, and he used to slip away and hour after hour would stand looking at that great stone face and thinking of the story about the one that was coming. Years passed, and that one did not come, and still the young man did what the boy had done, and went to sit and contemplate the majesty, the beauty of that great stone face. By and by youth passed away and middle age came on, and still he could not get rid of that legend; and then old age came, and one day as he walked through the village someone looked at him and exclaimed, 'He has come, the one who is like the great stone face!' He became like that which he contemplated. If you want to be Christlike, look at Jesus. If you want to grow in grace, contemplate Jesus. You find Him revealed in the Word, so read your Bible and meditate upon it."*

F. It is an open one (2 Cor. 4:1-4)—"But have renounced the hidden things of dishonesty, not walking in craftiness, nor handling the word of God deceitfully; but by manifestation of the truth commending ourselves to every man's conscience in the sight of God" (2 Cor. 4:2).

---

†**4:2** *This openness is vital, for sinners are already blinded by Satan and should not suffer additional harm by the lives of deceitful Christians. The strongest argument against the Bible is the life of a carnal Christian, while the strongest argument for the Bible is the life of a godly Christian.*

G. It is a satanically opposed one (2 Cor. 4:3-4)—"In whom the god of this world hath blinded the minds of them which believe not, lest the light of the glorious gospel of Christ, who is the image of God, should shine unto them" (2 Cor. 4:4).

H. It is a Christ-honoring one (2 Cor. 4:5-7).

1. It stresses who Christ is (2 Cor. 4:5)—"For we preach not ourselves, but Christ Jesus the Lord; and ourselves your servants for Jesus' sake" (2 Cor. 4:5).
2. It stresses what Christ has done (2 Cor. 4:6)—"For God, who commanded the light to shine out of darkness, hath shined in our hearts, to give the light of the knowledge of the glory of God in the face of Jesus Christ" (2 Cor. 4:6).
3. It stresses why Christ uses us (2 Cor. 4:7)—"But we have this treasure in earthen vessels, that the excellency of the power may be of God, and not of us" (2 Cor. 4:7).

---

†**4:7** *One of the world's largest and most famous diamonds (108.3 carats), presented to Queen Victoria in 1850 [which can be viewed inside a thick bullet-proof glass case in the Tower of London], rests upon a simple and inexpensive black cloth. This background thus serves by way of contrast to bring out to the fullest all the dazzling glory of that magnificent national treasure. In similar fashion God has entrusted in earthen vessels (bodies of believers) heaven's most prized treasure, the Lord Jesus Christ, "that the excellency of the power may be of God."*

I. It is a suffering one (2 Cor. 4:8-18).

1. The nature of this suffering (2 Cor. 4:8-16)
   a. Troubled on every side (2 Cor. 4:8)
   b. Perplexed (2 Cor. 4:8)
   c. Persecuted (2 Cor. 4:9)
   d. Cast down (2 Cor. 4:9)
   e. Perishing outer man (2 Cor. 4:16)
2. The victory through this suffering
   a. Troubled, yet not crushed
   b. Perplexed, but not in despair
   c. Persecuted, but not forsaken
   d. Struck down, but not destroyed
   e. Perishing outer person, but renewed inner person
3. The results from this suffering
   a. Immediate blessings
      (1) We experience the power of God—"Always bearing about in the body the dying of the Lord Jesus, that the life also of Jesus might be made manifest in our body" (2 Cor. 4:10).
      (2) We exhibit the glory of God—"For all things are for your sakes, that the abundant grace might through the thanksgiving of many redound to the glory of God" (2 Cor. 4:15).
   b. Future blessings
      (1) The assurance of our bodily resurrection—"Knowing that he which raised up the Lord Jesus shall raise up us also by Jesus, and shall present us with you" (2 Cor. 4:14).

(2) The assurance of our bountiful reward—"For our light affliction, which is but for a moment, worketh for us a far more exceeding and eternal weight of glory; while we look not at the things which are seen, but at the things which are not seen: for the things which are seen are temporal; but the things which are not seen are eternal" (2 Cor. 4:17-18).

J. It is a confident one (2 Cor. 5:1-9)—"Therefore we are always confident" (2 Cor. 5:6). "We are confident, I say" (2 Cor. 5:8).
  1. The basis of our confidence—"Now he that hath wrought us for the selfsame thing is God, who also hath given unto us the earnest of the Spirit" (2 Cor. 5:5).
  2. The vehicle of our confidence—"For we walk by faith, not by sight" (2 Cor. 5:7).
  3. The goal of our confidence
    a. To please our heavenly Father down here—"We are confident, I say, and willing rather to be absent from the body, and to be present with the Lord. Wherefore we labour, that, whether present or absent, we may be accepted of him" (2 Cor. 5:8-9).
    b. To receive our heavenly frame up there—"For we know that if our earthly house of this tabernacle were dissolved, we have a building of God, an house not made with hands, eternal in the heavens" (2 Cor. 5:1).

K. It is a compelling one (2 Cor. 5:10-17)—There were five factors which caused Paul to work night and day in the gospel ministry.
  1. The judgment of saints—"For we must all appear before the judgment seat of Christ; that every one may receive the things done in his body, according to that he hath done, whether it be good or bad" (2 Cor. 5:10).
  2. The need of sinners—"For the love of Christ constraineth us; because we thus judge, that if one died for all, then were all dead" (2 Cor. 5:14).
  3. The terror of the Lord—"Knowing therefore the terror of the Lord, we persuade men" (2 Cor. 5:11a).

---

†**5:11** *Here Paul refers to that reverential fear and respect which should characterize every believer. Paul's fear was that he might displease his glorious Master.*

---

  4. The love of Christ—"For the love of Christ constraineth us" (2 Cor. 5:14). "And that he died for all, that they which live should not henceforth live unto themselves, but unto him which died for them, and rose again" (2 Cor. 5:15).

---

†**5:15** *This glorious gospel therefore assures us that:*
A. We might live through *Christ (1 John 4:9).*
B. We might live with *Christ (1 Thess. 5:10).*
C. We might live for *Christ (2 Cor. 5:15).*

---

  5. The power of the gospel—"Therefore if any man be in Christ, he is a new creature: old things are passed away; behold, all things are become new. . . . For he hath made him to be sin for us, who knew no sin; that we might be made the righteousness of God in him" (2 Cor. 5:17, 21).

L. It is a representative one (2 Cor. 5:18-20).
1. Paul speaks of Christ's work (his atonement)—"And all things are of God, who hath reconciled us to himself by Jesus Christ, and hath given to us the ministry of reconciliation; to wit, that God was in Christ, reconciling the world unto himself, not imputing their trespasses unto them; and hath committed unto us the word of reconciliation" (2 Cor. 5:18-19).
2. Paul speaks of Christ's workers (his ambassadors)—"Now then we are ambassadors for Christ, as though God did beseech you by us: we pray you in Christ's stead, be ye reconciled to God" (2 Cor. 5:20).

---

†**5:20** *There are three facts concerning an ambassador:*
A. An ambassador must be a citizen of the state he represents (Phil. 3:20; Col. 3:1-2).
B. He is chosen (John 15:16).
C. He is called home before war is declared (1 Thess. 1:10; 5:1-10).

M. It is (to be) a blameless one (2 Cor. 6:1-7).
1. Being offensive in nothing—"Giving no offence in any thing, that the ministry be not blamed" (2 Cor. 6:3).
2. Being approved in all things—"But in all things approving ourselves as the ministers of God, in much patience" (2 Cor. 6:4a).
a. During the hardships imposed by circumstances—"In afflictions, in necessities, in distresses" (2 Cor. 6:4b).
b. During the hardships imposed by sinners—"In stripes, in imprisonments, in tumults" (2 Cor. 6:5a).
c. During the hardships imposed by self-discipline—"In labors, in watchings, in fastings" (2 Cor. 6:5b).

N. It is a paradoxical one (2 Cor. 6:8-10).

---

†*A paradox is an apparent (but not real) contradiction. There are a number of paradoxes in the Bible concerning both the saint and the Savior.*
A. Concerning the saint
1. Of finding one's life, yet eventually losing it (John 12:25)
2. Of losing one's life, yet eventually finding it (Matt. 10:39)
3. Of being unknown, yet being well known (2 Cor. 6:9a)
4. Of dying, yet possessing life (2 Cor. 6:9b)
5. Of being sorrowful, yet always rejoicing (2 Cor. 6:10)
6. Of dying, yet able to give life (John 12:24)
7. Of being poor, yet making many rich (2 Cor. 6:10)
8. Of having nothing, yet possessing all things (2 Cor. 6:10)
9. Of hearing words that cannot be expressed (2 Cor. 12:4)
10. Of being strong when one is weak (2 Cor. 12:10)
11. Of knowing the love of Christ which surpasses knowledge (Eph. 3:19)
12. Of seeing the unseen (2 Cor. 4:18)
B. Concerning the Savior—It may be concluded that the very life and ministry of our blessed Savior was itself a divine paradox.
1. He hungered, yet fed multitudes (Matt. 4:2; John 6).

2. He thirsted, yet is the water of life (John 19:28; 4:14).
3. He wearied, yet is our rest (John 4:6; Matt. 11:29-30).
4. He paid tribute, yet is the King of kings (Matt. 17:27; Rev. 19:16).
5. He prayed, yet hears our prayers (Mark 14:32, 35, 39; John 14:12, 14).
6. He wept, yet dries our tears (John 11:35; Rev. 21:4).
7. He was sold for 30 pieces of silver, yet redeems the world (Matt. 26:15; 1 Pet. 1:18-19).
8. He was led as a sheep to the slaughter, and yet is the Good Shepherd (Isa. 53:7; John 10:11).
9. He was put to death, yet raises the dead (John 19:30).

---

1. "As deceivers, and yet true" (2 Cor. 6:8)
2. "As unknown, and yet well known" (2 Cor. 6:9)
3. "As dying, and, behold, we live" (2 Cor. 6:9).
4. "As chastened, and not killed" (2 Cor. 6:9)
5. "As sorrowful, yet always rejoicing" (2 Cor. 6:10)
6. "As poor, yet making many rich" (2 Cor. 6:10)
7. "As having nothing, and yet possessing all things" (2 Cor. 6:10)

O. It is to be a separated one (2 Cor. 6:11-18).
1. The nature of this separation—"Be ye not unequally yoked together with unbelievers" (2 Cor. 6:14a).

---

†**6:14a** *This separation would no doubt cover such human ties as:*
A. Marriage
B. Certain business partnerships
C. Unsound ecclesiastical organizations

---

2. The logic of this separation
a. What partnership has righteousness with lawlessness (2 Cor. 6:14)?
b. What fellowship has light with darkness (2 Cor. 6:14)?
c. What harmony has Christ with Belial (2 Cor. 6:15)?
d. What has a believer in common with an unbeliever (2 Cor. 6:15)?
e. What agreement has the temple of God with idols (2 Cor. 6:16)?
3. The reason for this separation—"For ye are the temple of the living God" (2 Cor. 6:16b).
4. The blessings of this separation (2 Cor. 6:16-18)—"As God hath said, I will dwell in them, and walk in them: and I will be their God, and they shall be my people" (2 Cor. 6:16c).

IV. Gratification (2 Cor. 7:1-16)—Paul is profoundly thankful to God for two things:
A. Upon seeing Titus—He was practically beside himself when Titus did not appear either in Troas or Macedonia as originally planned. (See 2 Cor. 2:12-13.) "For, when we were come into Macedonia, our flesh had no rest, but we were troubled on every side; without were fightings, within were fears. Nevertheless God, that comforteth those that are cast down, comforted us by the coming of Titus" (2 Cor. 7:5-6).
B. Upon hearing Titus (2 Cor. 7:7-16)—Titus, who had been sent by Paul to Corinth, now brings back a twofold report.
1. The church had favorably received Paul's message—He had previously sent

them a letter (probably 1 Corinthians) of rebuke, attempting to straighten out the mess in their congregation. It had worked, according to Titus, and led to their repentance. "For godly sorrow worketh repentance to salvation not to be repented of: but the sorrow of the world worketh death" (2 Cor. 7:10).

2. The church had favorably received Paul's messenger—"Therefore we were comforted in your comfort: yea, and exceedingly the more joyed we for the joy of Titus, because his spirit was refreshed by you all. . . . And his inward affection is more abundant toward you, whilst he remembereth the obedience of you all, how with fear and trembling ye received him" (2 Cor. 7:13, 15).

V. Solicitation (2 Cor. 8:1–9:15)—"I have shewed you all things, how that so labouring ye ought to support the weak, and to remember the words of the Lord Jesus, how he said, It is more blessed to give than to receive" (Acts 20:35).

A. The examples of giving

1. The Macedonians (2 Cor. 8:1-5)

a. They surrendered their bodies to the Lord—"But first gave their own selves to the Lord" (2 Cor. 8:5).

b. They submitted their wills to the apostle—"And unto us by the will of God" (2 Cor. 8:5).

c. They sacrificially shared their wealth with the saints—"How that in a great trial of affliction the abundance of their joy and their deep poverty abounded unto the riches of their liberality" (2 Cor. 8:2).

2. The Savior—"For ye know the grace of our Lord Jesus Christ, that, though he was rich, yet for your sakes he became poor, that ye through his poverty might be rich" (2 Cor. 8:9).

---

†8:9 *Thus, our Lord became what he was not (poor), that we might become what we were not (rich). The sinless Son of God became the Son of man that sinful sons of men might become the sons of God.*

---

3. The Father—"Thanks be unto God for his unspeakable gift" (2 Cor. 9:15).

B. The characteristics of giving

1. It is initiated by God himself (2 Cor. 8:1; 9:8)—"And God is able to make all grace abound toward you; that ye, always having all sufficiency in all things, may abound to every good work" (2 Cor. 9:8).

2. It is to be done purposefully—"Every man according as he purposeth in his heart, so let him give; not grudgingly, or of necessity: for God loveth a cheerful giver" (2 Cor. 9:7).

3. It is to be voluntary (2 Cor. 8:3-4, 8, 12; 9:7)—"They [the Macedonians] were willing" (2 Cor. 8:3). "For if there be first a willing mind, it is accepted" (2 Cor. 8:12). "Not grudgingly, or of necessity" (2 Cor. 9:7).

4. It is to be liberal (2 Cor. 8:2; 9:6)—"But this I say, He which soweth sparingly shall reap also sparingly; and he which soweth bountifully shall reap also bountifully" (2 Cor. 9:6).

5. It is to be preceded by a giving of self to the Lord (2 Cor. 8:5).

6. It is to come from our joy in Christ (2 Cor. 8:2; 9:7).

7. It is to be based on what we have—"According to that a man hath, and not according to that he hath not" (2 Cor. 8:12).

8. It is related to one of the spiritual gifts—"Therefore, as ye abound in every thing, in faith, and utterance, and knowledge, and in all diligence, and in your love to us, see that ye abound in this grace also" (2 Cor. 8:7).
9. It is therefore to be regarded as a ministry—"For as touching the ministering to the saints" (2 Cor. 9:1).

C. The results of giving
1. It serves as an example for others—"Your zeal hath provoked very many" (2 Cor. 9:2).
2. It shows our love for God (2 Cor. 8:8, 24)—"To prove the sincerity of your love" (2 Cor. 8:8). "Wherefore show ye to them, and before the churches, the proof of your love" (2 Cor. 8:24).
3. It guarantees our own spiritual growth—"Now he [God] . . . increase the fruits of your righteousness" (2 Cor. 9:10). "As it is written, He hath dispersed abroad; he hath given to the poor: his righteousness remaineth for ever" (2 Cor. 9:9).
4. It assures us our own need will be provided for—"Being enriched in every thing to all bountifulness, which causeth through us thanksgiving to God" (2 Cor. 9:11).
5. It results in God giving us more that we might in turn give back more—"And God is able to make all grace abound toward you; that ye, always having all sufficiency in all things, may abound to every good work" (2 Cor. 9:8).
6. It provides for the needs of deserving saints—"For the administration of this service not only supplieth the want of the saints, but is abundant also by many thanksgivings unto God" (2 Cor. 9:12).
7. It results in God receiving glory from those needy saints who have been ministered to (2 Cor. 9:12-13). "By many thanksgivings unto God" (2 Cor. 9:12). "By . . . this ministration they glorify God" (2 Cor. 9:13a).
8. It enriches the giver as he is prayed for by the saints he has helped—"And by their prayer for you, which long after you for the exceeding grace of God in you" (2 Cor. 9:14).

VI. Vindication (2 Cor. 10–13)—Paul writes these chapters to defend his name and ministry. Both were being undermined by some envious Judaizers who had probably come to Corinth from Jerusalem to stir up trouble. In his defense he lists a fivefold superiority of his divinely given ministry as contrasted to the false Judaizers.

A. His methods were superior.
1. He did not use a fleshly system—"For though we walk in the flesh, we do not war after the flesh: (For the weapons of our warfare are not carnal, but mighty through God to the pulling down of strong holds;) Casting down imaginations, and every high thing that exalteth itself against the knowledge of God, and bringing into captivity every thought to the obedience of Christ" (2 Cor. 10:3-5).

---

†10:4 *In defeating Satan one cannot fight fire with fire. He must use blood (see Rev. 12:11).*

---

2. He did not use a false standard—"For we dare not make ourselves of the number, or compare ourselves with some that commend themselves: but they

measuring themselves by themselves, and comparing themselves among themselves, are not wise. But he that glorieth, let him glory in the Lord. For not he that commendeth himself is approved, but whom the Lord commendeth" (2 Cor. 10:12, 17-18).

---

†10:18

A. All too often both saved and unsaved people are guilty of this false measurement system.

1. The unsaved person can usually find some poor miserable wretch who is worse than he is, thus relieving his own uneasy conscience and causing him to conclude that his "superior morality" is sufficient, apart from Christ's righteousness.

2. Sometimes Christian leaders fall victim to this snare also by comparing their own ministry to that of another believer's work. This can lead to envy (if his work is bigger than mine) or pride (if the opposite is true).

B. But Paul carefully avoided this trap. Note his words: "But he that glorieth, let him glory in the Lord. For not he that commendeth himself is approved, but whom the Lord commendeth" (10:17-18).

C. In this Paul was supported by both Old and New Testament teachings.

1. 1 Samuel 16:6-7—"And it came to pass, when they were come, that he looked on Eliab, and said, Surely the LORD's anointed is before him. But the Lord said unto Samuel, Look not on his countenance, or on the height of his stature; because I have refused him: for the Lord seeth not as man seeth; for man looketh on the outward appearance, but the LORD looketh on the heart."

2. John 7:24—"Judge not according to the appearance, but judge righteous judgment."

B. His mission field was superior—"To preach the gospel in the regions beyond" (2 Cor. 10:16).

C. His motives were superior—Especially was this true concerning the church. Paul was the concerned shepherd, while his enemies were cruel hirelings.

1. His jealousy over the church—"For I am jealous over you with godly jealousy: for I have espoused you to one husband, that I may present you as a chaste virgin to Christ" (2 Cor. 11:2).

---

†11:2 *At this point let us distinguish between jealousy and envy.*

A. Jealousy: "The desire to possess one's own things." Contrary to popular opinion, this is a good and natural trait, if kept in proper bounds.

B. Envy: "The desire to possess the things of another." This is always wrong.

---

2. His fear for the church—"But I fear, lest by any means, as the serpent beguiled Eve through his subtilty, so your minds should be corrupted from the simplicity that is in Christ" (2 Cor. 11:3).

3. His unselfish service to the church—Even though he was an apostle, Paul functioned as a servant among them. "For I suppose I was not a whit behind the very chiefest apostles" (2 Cor. 11:5).

a. He gave much to them—"I robbed other churches, taking wages of them, to do you service" (2 Cor. 11:8).

- b. He took nothing from them—"And when I was present with you, and wanted, I was chargeable to no man: for that which was lacking to me the brethren which came from Macedonia supplied: and in all things I have kept myself from being burdensome unto you, and so will I keep myself" (2 Cor. 11:9).

4. His warning to the church—He warns the church about their enemies.
   - a. Who they were—"For such are false apostles, deceitful workers, transforming themselves into the apostles of Christ" (2 Cor. 11:13).
   - b. Where they came from—"And no marvel; for Satan himself is transformed into an angel of light. Therefore it is no great thing if his ministers also be transformed as the ministers of righteousness; whose end shall be according to their works" (2 Cor. 11:14-15).
   - c. What they did—"For you bear with anyone if he enslaves you, if he devours you, if he takes advantage of you, if he exalts himself, if he hits you in the face" (2 Cor. 11:20, NASB).
5. His sufferings for the church (2 Cor. 11:23-33)
   - a. Backbreaking labor (2 Cor. 11:23, 27)
   - b. Beatings
     - (1) Beaten with 39 lashes on five occasions (2 Cor. 11:24)
     - (2) Beaten with rods on three occasions (2 Cor. 11:25)
   - c. Stonings (2 Cor. 11:25)
   - d. Three shipwrecks (2 Cor. 11:25)—During one of these he was afloat on the sea (2 Cor. 11:25).
   - e. Wearisome travels (2 Cor. 11:26)
   - f. Constant dangers (2 Cor. 11:26)
     - (1) From swollen rivers
     - (2) From robbers
     - (3) From his own countrymen
     - (4) From Gentiles
     - (5) From false brethren
   - g. Narrow escapes (2 Cor. 11:32-33)—"In Damascus the governor under Aretas the king kept the city of the Damascenes with a garrison, desirous to apprehend me: and through a window in a basket was I let down by the wall, and escaped his hands" (2 Cor. 11:32-33).
   - h. Physical deprivations
     - (1) Lack of food and water (2 Cor. 11:27)
     - (2) Lack of warm clothing (2 Cor. 11:27)
     - (3) Lack of proper rest (2 Cor. 11:27)
   - i. The daily pressure of caring for his local churches (2 Cor. 11:28)

D. His miracles were superior.

1. Paul's supernatural sight—"It is not expedient for me doubtless to glory. I will come to visions and revelations of the Lord. I knew a man in Christ above fourteen years ago, (whether in the body, I cannot tell; or whether out of the body, I cannot tell: God knoweth;) such an one caught up to the third heaven. And I knew such a man, (whether in the body, or out of the body, I cannot tell: God knoweth;) How that he was caught up into paradise, and heard unspeakable words, which it is not lawful for a man to utter" (2 Cor. 12:1-4).

†12:4 *Note: We cannot even speculate upon what Paul actually witnessed on this occasion. At a later date John the apostle apparently viewed a similar sight. (See Rev. 10:4.)*

Some believe Paul actually died during his stoning at Lystra (Acts 14:19) and that during this time he experienced the vision here in 2 Corinthians 12, prior to being raised again from the dead by God.

---

2. Paul's supernatural strength—"And lest I should be exalted above measure through the abundance of the revelations, there was given to me a thorn in the flesh, the messenger of Satan to buffet me, lest I should be exalted above measure. For this thing I besought the Lord thrice, that it might depart from me. And he said unto me, My grace is sufficient for thee: for my strength is made perfect in weakness. Most gladly therefore will I rather glory in my infirmities, that the power of Christ may rest upon me. Therefore I take pleasure in infirmities, in reproaches, in necessities, in persecutions, in distresses for Christ's sake: for when I am weak, then am I strong" (2 Cor. 12:7-10).

---

†12:10

A. Note: This passage marks the fifth reference to Satan by Paul in 2 Corinthians. From these verses we learn:

1. His title: The god of this world (4:4)

2. His tactics:

a. To take advantage of believers (2:11)

b. To inflict suffering upon believers (12:7)—See especially Job 1–2.

c. To blind unbelievers (4:4)

3. His treachery—Disguising himself as an angel of light (11:14)

4. His trustees—False ministers (11:15)

B. What was the nature of this thorn in the flesh? There are various views. The main theory is that he suffered from chronic ophthalmia, a disease of the eyes—not extremely painful, but at times repulsive. It came upon Paul 14 years prior to his writing this epistle, which was about the time of his entrance into Galatia. This was occasioned by some sort of physical infirmity. (See also Gal. 4:13-15; 6:11.)

C. It should also be remembered that he was blinded for a while at his conversion (Acts 9:9). Satan thus may have exploited a natural infirmity.

---

3. Paul's supernatural signs—"Truly the signs of an apostle were wrought among you in all patience, in signs, and wonders, and mighty deeds" (2 Cor. 12:12).

E. His future meeting would be superior—His enemies had met with the Corinthians, but only to confuse and corrupt. His planned meeting would be different.

1. The spirit he would bring with him when he came—"Behold, the third time I am ready to come to you; and I will not be burdensome to you: for I seek not yours, but you: for the children ought not to lay up for the parents, but the parents for the children" (2 Cor. 12:14).

2. The spirit he would expect from them when he came—"For I fear, lest, when I come, I shall not find you such as I would, and that I shall be found unto you such as ye would not: lest there be debates, envyings, wraths, strifes,

backbitings, whisperings, swellings, tumults" (2 Cor. 12:20). "Examine yourselves, whether ye be in the faith; prove your own selves. Know ye not your own selves, how that Jesus Christ is in you, except ye be reprobates? . . . Finally, brethren, farewell. Be perfect, be of good comfort, be of one mind, live in peace; and the God of love and peace shall be with you. Greet one another with an holy kiss. All the saints salute you. The grace of the Lord Jesus Christ, and the love of God, and the communion of the Holy Ghost, be with you all. Amen" (2 Cor. 13:5, 11-14).

GALATIANS

THE IMPERATIVE:
WARNING:
DO NOT MIX, UNDER ANY CIRCUMSTANCES, THE INGREDIENTS:
THE LAW OF GOD AND THE GRACE OF GOD.

A. The book of Galatians is the Magna Charta of the early church. It is Scripture's strongest declaration and defense of the doctrine of justification by faith.
B. One of the problems in dating the book concerns its destination. Was the letter written to the churches in northern Galatia (where Paul visited during his second and third missionary trips) or to the churches in southern Galatia (where he preached during his first trip)?
C. The Galatians themselves were an emotional and intense Celtic people. Caesar said: "They are fickle in their resolves, fond of change, and not to be trusted." This is demonstrated during Paul's first visit to them. In the morning they attempted to worship him, and in the afternoon to murder him (Acts 14). They were a branch of Gauls, originally from north of the Baltic Sea, who had split off from a main migration westward to France and had settled in Asia Minor during the third century B.C.
D. This is probably Paul's first epistle. The book of 2 Timothy would be his last. Paul's work in Galatia had been highly successful. Great multitudes of people, mostly Gentiles, had accepted Christ. But after he left, the Judaizers from Jerusalem (a group of legalistic gospel-perverting Jews) had come to Galatia, teaching that Gentiles must put themselves back under the bondage of the law to be saved. The Galatians had thus received their message with the same zeal that they had accepted Paul's. There was then a general epidemic of circumcision among them.
E. The Judaizers had not only attacked the message of Paul, but also his apostleship.
F. Galatians may have been the only book written personally by the apostle without the aid of a stenographer (see 6:11).
G. It is, next to 2 Corinthians, the most autobiographical of Paul's letters and the only epistle by Paul addressed to a group of local churches.
H. The key word is *liberty*, used 11 times in the letter. This is more than all his other epistles combined.
I. It has been said that Judaism was the cradle of Christianity and very nearly its grave. But God raised up Paul as the Moses of the Christian church to deliver believers from bondage. Galatians finishes what Paul will begin in 2 Corinthians (concerning his apostleship), and begins what Paul will finish in Romans (concerning justification by faith).
J. There is a striking parallel between Galatians and Romans. At least 19 passages may be favorably compared. Galatians is a rough sketch of which Romans is the finished picture.
K. J. Vernon McGee aptly summarizes Galatians: "It is a stern, severe and solemn message (Gal. 1:6-9; 3:1-5). It does not correct conduct, as the Corinthian letters do,

but it is corrective—the Galatian believers were in grave peril. Because the foundations were being attacked, everything was threatened. The epistle contains no word of commendation, praise, or thanksgiving. There is no request for prayer, and there is no mention of their standing in Christ. No one with him is mentioned by name (1:2). Compare this with the other epistles of Paul. The heart of Paul the apostle is laid bare, there is deep emotion and strong feeling. This is his fighting epistle—he has on his war paint. He has no toleration for legalism. Someone has said that Romans comes from the head of Paul while Galatians comes from the heart of Paul. 'Galatians takes up controversially what Romans puts systematically.' It is the declaration of emancipation from legalism of any type. This was Martin Luther's favorite Epistle, and it was on the masthead of the Reformation. It has been called the Magna Charta of the early church, the manifesto of Christian liberty, the impregnable citadel, and a veritable Gibraltar against any attack on the heart of the Gospel. 'Immortal victory is set upon its brow.'

"It is the strongest declaration and defense of the doctrine of justification by faith in or out of the scripture. It is God's polemic on behalf of the most vital truth of the Christian faith against any attack. Not only is a sinner saved by grace through faith, but the saved sinner lives by grace. Grace is a way to life and a way of life" (*Through the Bible*, p. 108).

L. Paul reveals more about his early Christian life activities in this book than in any other of his writings (1:13–2:14). Among these events is the account when he confronted Peter concerning Simon's sinful legalism.

M. Galatians is the first chronological New Testament book to quote Habakkuk 2:4: "The just shall live by faith" (Gal. 3:11). The other two instances are Romans 1:17 and Hebrews 10:38. Chapters 3 and 4 provide the most extensive explanation on the function of the Law of God in all Scripture. The book also contains the greatest contrast between the fruit of the flesh and that of the spirit in the Bible. (See 5:19-23.)

N. There are quotations and allusions in Galatians from ten Old Testament books. Galatians is the 11th longest New Testament book, and 40th longest biblical book, with six chapters, 149 verses, and 3,098 words.

O. Great passages would include:
   1. 2:20
   2. 3:26-29
   3. 4:4-5
   4. 5:22-26
   5. 6:14

THE BOOK OF GALATIANS

"Paul, an apostle, (not of men, neither by man, but by Jesus Christ, and God the Father, who raised him from the dead;) and all the brethren which are with me, unto the churches of Galatia" (Gal. 1:1-2).

I. Justification by Faith—The Foundation (Gal. 1:3-5)

A. The source of our justification—"Grace be to you and peace from God the Father, and from our Lord Jesus Christ" (Gal. 1:3).

B. The sacrifice for our justification—"Who gave himself for our sins, that he might deliver us from this present evil world, according to the will of God and our Father: To whom be glory for ever and ever. Amen" (Gal. 1:4-5).

II. Justification by Faith—The Aberration (Gal. 1:6-9)

A. The concern of Paul—"I marvel that ye are so soon removed from him that called you into the grace of Christ unto another gospel: which is not another; but there be some that trouble you, and would pervert the gospel of Christ" (Gal. 1:6-7).

B. The curse from Paul—"But though we, or an angel from heaven, preach any other gospel unto you than that which we have preached unto you, let him be accursed" (Gal. 1:8).

---

†1:8

A. This "gospel" was really not an allos *(Greek word meaning "another of the same kind"), but a* heteros *(Greek word meaning "another of a different kind").*

B. This "gospel" was not to be received, even though it came from an angel or from Paul himself.

C. This "gospel," if received and believed, would result in divine judgment and damnation upon its recipients. The word "accurse" here is anathema *in the Greek. (See also Acts 23:14; 1 Cor. 12:3; Rom. 9:3; 2 Thess. 1:9.)*

III. Justification by Faith—The Revelation (Gal. 1:10–2:10)

A. The uniqueness of this revelation (Gal. 1:11-12, 17-19)

1. It was not of man, that is, human flesh did not compile it for Paul—"But I certify you, brethren, that the gospel which was preached of me is not after man" (Gal. 1:11).
2. It was not from man, that is, human flesh did not communicate it to Paul—"For I neither received it of man, neither was I taught it, but by the revelation of Jesus Christ" (Gal. 1:12).

---

†1:12 *The Savior also revealed to Paul those facts concerning:*

A. The Last Supper (1 Cor. 11:23)

B. The death and resurrection of Christ (1 Cor. 15:3-4)

B. The need for this revelation (Gal. 1:13-14)—"For ye have heard of my conversation in time past in the Jews' religion, how that beyond measure I persecuted the church of God, and wasted it: and profited in the Jews' religion above many my equals in mine own nation, being more exceedingly zealous of the traditions of my fathers" (Gal. 1:13-14).

---

†1:14 *Here Paul gives his testimony and tells of the horrible life he lived prior to his conversion. The apostle loved to relate this testimony. (See Acts 22:1-16; 26:1-20; 1 Tim. 1:12-16.)*

C. The trips following this revelation

1. Traveling to Arabia and Damascus (Gal. 1:17)
2. Traveling to Jerusalem

a. The *when* of the matter—"Then after three years I went up to Jerusalem . . . and abode . . . fifteen days" (Gal. 1:18).
b. The *who* of the matter—"To see Peter" (Gal. 1:18). "But other of the apostles saw I none, save James the Lord's brother" (Gal. 1:19).

D. The purpose of this revelation (Gal. 2:1-2, 9)—"But when it pleased God, who separated me from my mother's womb, and called me by his grace, to reveal his Son in me, that I might preach him among the heathen; immediately I conferred not with flesh and blood" (Gal. 1:15-16).

---

†1:16 *Two other unborn babies also experienced this early call.*
A. Jeremiah the prophet (Jer. 1:4-10)
B. John the Baptist (Luke 1:15-17)

E. The recognition of this revelation (Gal. 2:1-2, 9)
1. The *when* of the matter—"Then fourteen years after I went up again to Jerusalem with Barnabas, and took Titus with me also" (Gal. 2:1).

---

†2:1 *He visits Jerusalem again along with Barnabas and Titus (Gal. 2:1-10; Acts 11:29-30). It has now been 14 years since his conversion. At this point in the record the Judaizers begin putting pressure upon Paul to mix their devilish legalism with God's pure grace, but they would run into a brick wall in this. James, Peter, and John encourage Paul to keep preaching God's grace to the Gentiles.*

---

2. The *what* of the matter—"And I went up by revelation, and communicated unto them that gospel which I preach among the Gentiles, but privately to them which were of reputation, lest by any means I should run, or had run, in vain. . . . But contrariwise, when they saw that the gospel of the uncircumcision was committed unto me, as the gospel of the circumcision was unto Peter. . . and when James, Cephas, and John, who seemed to be pillars, perceived the grace that was given unto me, they gave to me and Barnabas the right hands of fellowship; that we should go unto the heathen, and they unto the circumcision" (Gal. 2:2, 7, 9).

F. The enemies of this revelation (Gal. 2:3-5)—"But neither Titus, who was with me, being a Greek, was compelled to be circumcised: and that because of false brethren unawares brought in, who came in privily to spy out our liberty which we have in Christ Jesus, that they might bring us into bondage: to whom we gave place by subjection, no, not for an hour; that the truth of the gospel might continue with you" (Gal. 2:3-5).

IV. Justification by Faith: The Confrontation (Gal. 2:11-14)
A. The rebuke involved—"But when Peter was come to Antioch, I withstood him to the face, because he was to be blamed" (Gal. 2:11).

---

†2:14
A. It is difficult to know just when this confrontation took place. Some would feel it happened at a later date, following the Jerusalem Council. At any rate, Peter had allowed the ever-present

Judaizers to pressure him into withdrawing from all Gentile believers upon the arrival of some influential Jews from Jerusalem. Paul soundly rebukes Peter for this. By doing what he did, Peter was denying five major doctrines.

1. The unity of the church (2:14)
2. Justification by faith alone (2:15-16)
3. Freedom from the Law (2:17-18)
4. The all-sufficiency of the indwelling Christ (2:19-20)
5. The grace of God (2:21)

B. Peter's immediate reaction to this rebuke is not recorded. He very obviously did repent and bore Paul no ill will for it (see 2 Pet. 3:15).

B. The reason involved—"For before that certain came from James, he did eat with the Gentiles: but when they were come, he withdrew and separated himself, fearing them which were of the circumcision. And the other Jews dissembled likewise with him; insomuch that Barnabas also was carried away with their dissimulation" (Gal. 2:12-13).

C. The rationale involved—"But when I saw that they walked not uprightly according to the truth of the gospel, I said unto Peter before them all, If thou, being a Jew, livest after the manner of Gentiles, and not as do the Jews, why compellest thou the Gentiles to live as do the Jews?" (Gal. 2:14).

V. Justification by Faith: The Clarification (Gal. 2:15-19)—"Knowing that a man is not justified by the works of the law, but by the faith of Jesus Christ, even we have believed in Jesus Christ, that we might be justified by the faith of Christ, and not by the works of the law: for by the works of the law shall no flesh be justified" (Gal. 2:16).

VI. Justification by Faith: The Transformation (Gal. 2:20-21)—"I am crucified with Christ: nevertheless I live; yet not I, but Christ liveth in me: and the life which I now live in the flesh I live by the faith of the Son of God, who loved me, and gave himself for me" (Gal. 2:20).

VII. Justification by Faith: The Argumentation (Gal. 3:1–4:20)—In chapters 3 and 4 Paul offers a series of arguments that prove the sufficiency of justification by faith alone.

A. The argument from their own experience (Gal. 3:1-2; 4:12-20).

1. He reminds them how they first received the message of justification (Gal. 3:1-5)—"You foolish Galatians, who has bewitched you, before whose eyes Jesus Christ was publicly portrayed as crucified? This is the only thing I want to find out from you: Did you receive the Spirit by the works of the Law, or by hearing with faith? Are you so foolish? Having begun by the Spirit, are you now being perfected by the flesh? Did you suffer so many things in vain—if indeed it was in vain? Does He then who provides you with the Spirit and works miracles among you, do it by the works of the Law, or by the hearing with faith?" (Gal. 3:1-5, NASB).

---

†**3:5** *Warren Wiersbe writes: "The illustration of human birth is appropriate here. Two human parents are required for a child to be conceived and born, and two spiritual parents are required for a child to be born into God's family: the Spirit of God and the Word of God (James 3:1-8; 1 Pet. 1:22-25). When a normal child is born, he has all that he needs for life; nothing need be added.*

When the child of God is born into God's family, he has all that he needs spiritually; nothing need be added! All that is necessary is that the child have food, exercise, and cleansing that he might grow into maturity. It would be strange if the parents had to take the child to the doctor at one month to receive ears, at two months to receive toes, and so on" (Be Free, *p. 57).*

---

2. He reminds them how they first received the messenger of justification (Gal. 4:12-20)—"But you know that it was because of a bodily illness that I preached the gospel to you the first time; and that which was a trial to you in my bodily condition you did not despise or loathe, but you received me as an angel of God as Christ Jesus Himself. Where then is that sense of blessing you had? For I bear you witness, that if possible, you would have plucked out your eyes and given them to me. Have I therefore become your enemy by telling you the truth? " (Gal. 4:13-16, NASB).

B. The argument from the life of Abraham (Gal. 3:6-9)—"Even as Abraham believed God, and it was accounted to him for righteousness. Know ye therefore that they which are of faith, the same are the children of Abraham" (Gal. 3:6-7).

C. The argument from the Law (Gal. 3:10–4:11)

1. The Law and sinners (Gal. 3:10-12)—"For as many as are of the works of the law are under the curse: for it is written, Cursed is every one that continueth not in all things which are written in the book of the law to do them. But that no man is justified by the law in the sight of God, it is evident: for, The just shall live by faith" (Gal. 3:10-11).

---

†3:11

A. God not only pardons sinners by faith, but then preserves them by faith: "The just shall live by faith" (3:11). This all-important statement is taken from the Old Testament book of Habakkuk (2:4) and is used three times in the New Testament. (See Rom. 1:17 and Heb. 10:38.)

B. The New Testament author of the book of James had already written: "For whosoever shall keep the whole law, and yet offend in one point, he is guilty of all" (James 2:10). Thus the Old Testament Law may be likened to a long chain. To break this chain, a person need only snap a single link, and the entire chain is broken.

---

2. The Law and the promise (Gal. 3:15-26)
   a. The law cannot change the promise (Gal. 3:15-18)—"Brethren, I speak after the manner of men; though it be but a man's covenant, yet if it be confirmed, no man disannulleth, or addeth thereto" (Gal. 3:15).
   b. The Law is inferior to the promise (Gal. 3:19-20)—His argument here is that God used a mediator (angels) in giving the law, but gave the promise of faith personally to Abraham.
   c. The Law is not contrary to the promise (Gal. 3:21-26)—"Is the law then against the promises of God? God forbid: for if there had been a law given which could have given life, verily righteousness should have been by the law" (Gal. 3:21).
3. The Law and Israel
   a. It was given to Israel 430 years after the promise (Gal. 3:17).

†3:17 *Warren Wiersbe writes: "The 430 years of verse 16 has puzzled Bible students for many years. From Abraham's call (Gen. 12) to Jacob's arrival in Egypt (Gen. 46) is 215 years. This may be computed as follows:*

A. Abraham was 75 years old when God called him and 100 years when Isaac was born (Gen. 12:4; 21:5). This gives us 25 years.
B. Isaac was 60 when Jacob was born (Gen. 25:26).
C. Jacob was 130 years old when he arrived in Egypt (Gen. 47:9). Thus, 25 + 60 + 130 = 215 years.
D. But Moses tells us that Israel sojourned in Egypt 430 years (Exod. 12:40); so the total number of the law is 645 years, not 430.
E. The length of stay in Egypt is recorded also in Genesis 15:13 and Acts 7:6, where the round number of 400 years is used. Several solutions have been offered to this puzzle, but perhaps the most satisfying is this: Paul is counting from the time Jacob went into Egypt, when God appeared to him and reaffirmed *the Covenant (Gen. 46:1-4). The 430 years is the time from God's confirmation of His promise to Jacob until the giving of the law at Sinai"* (Be Free, *pp. 77-78.)*

---

b. It was an insertion, given because of sin (Gal. 3:19).
c. It was ordained by angels (Gal. 3:19).

---

†3:19 *Note the following verses which attest to this fact of angelic activity on Mount Sinai at the giving of the Law. "The Lord came from Sinai . . . and he came with ten thousands of saints. From his right hand went a fiery law for them" (Deut. 33:2). "The chariots of God are twenty thousand, even thousands of angels; the Lord is among them, as in Sinai, in the holy place" (Psa. 68:17). "Who [sinful Israel] have received the law by the disposition of angels, and have not kept it?" (Acts 7:53). "For the word spoken by angels [the law] was stedfast" (Heb. 2:2).*

---

d. It thus acted as a divine custodian (Gal. 3:23-24)—"But before faith came, we were kept under the law, shut up unto the faith which should afterwards be revealed. Wherefore the law was our schoolmaster to bring us unto Christ, that we might be justified by faith" (Gal. 3:23-24).

---

†3:24 *It thus acted as Israel's "schoolmaster" (child-discipliner, from the Greek word* paidagogos). *"Wherefore the law was our schoolmaster to bring us unto Christ" (3:24). J. Vernon McGee writes: "The key word here is schoolmaster and has nothing to do with a school teacher in a present-day context. The term designated a slave or servant in a Roman home who had charge of any child born in the home. He fed, dressed, bathed, blew the nose of and paddled, the son born in the home. When the little fellow reached school age, he took him by the hand and led him to school. This is where he got the name of* paidagogos *(child leader). The law took mankind by the hand, led him to the cross of Christ and said, 'Little man, you need a Saviour.' The law turns us over to Christ. We are under Christ now and not under the law"* (Through the Bible, *p. 110).*

---

4. The Law and Christ
   a. He has redeemed us from its curse (Gal. 3:13)—"Christ hath redeemed us from the curse of the law, being made a curse for us: for it is written, Cursed is every one that hangeth on a tree" (Gal. 3:13).

---

†3:13 *McGee observes: "This was a very strange law since the method of capital punishment under the law was by stoning. But if the crime was aggravated and atrocious, the body of the criminal was taken after death and hung up to display the seriousness of the crime"* Through the Bible, *p. 110).*

---

b. He did this at God's appointed time through a human body (Gal. 4:4-5)—"But when the fulness of time was come, God sent forth his Son, made of a woman, made under the law, to redeem them that were under the law, that we might receive the adoption of sons" (Gal. 4:4-5).

---

†4:5 *Paul here, of course, does not mean that the Law makes us children of God, while Christ makes us sons of God. But he does contrast the differences between a child and a son under the Roman legal system of the day.*

A. Childhood *refers to my condition in God's family, while* adoption *speaks of my position.*
B. *Through* regeneration *one enters into the family; but by* adoption *he enjoys the family.*
C. *The circumstances leading to* childhood *are private, while those dealing with* adoption *are public.*
D. *A* child *is under guardians, while an* adopted adult *has full liberty.*

---

c. He thus guaranteed our full adoption as sons of God (Gal. 4:1-7)—"And because ye are sons, God hath sent forth the Spirit of his Son into your hearts, crying, Abba, Father. Wherefore thou art no more a servant, but a son; and if a son, then an heir of God through Christ" (Gal. 4:6-7).

---

†4:7 *Paul contrasts the differences between a son and a servant (4:7).*

A. *A* servant *retains his old nature, while a* son *enjoys that of his father.*
B. *A* servant *has a master, while a* son *has a father.*
C. *A* servant *obeys out of law and fear, but a* son *out of liberty and love.*
D. *A* servant *is promised no inheritance, while a* son *can legally expect to inherit all things.*

---

5. The Law and believers (Gal. 3:25-29)—"But after that faith is come, we are no longer under a schoolmaster. For ye are all the children of God by faith in Christ Jesus. For as many of you as have been baptized into Christ have put on Christ. There is neither Jew nor Greek, there is neither bond nor free, there is neither male nor female: for ye are all one in Christ Jesus. And if ye be Christ's, then are ye Abraham's seed, and heirs according to the promise" (Gal. 3:25-29).

---

†3:29 *There were three great divisions in the Roman world:*

A. *Racial and religious—Jew and Greek*
B. *Social and class—bond and free*
C. *Man's world and woman's world—But in Christ there is no* spiritual *distinction whatsoever.*

---

6. The Law and the Galatians (Gal. 4:8-20)
   a. Paul rebukes them for their faithlessness—"Howbeit then, when ye knew

not God, ye did service unto them which by nature are no gods. But now, after that ye have known God, or rather are known of God, how turn ye again to the weak and beggarly elements, whereunto ye desire again to be in bondage? Ye observe days, and months, and times, and years" (Gal. 4:8-10).

---

†4:10 *After being released from spiritual slavery, why did they now desire to put back on their chains of bondage again (4:9-10)? They were doing exactly this by observing* days *(Jewish holy days such as weekly sabbaths and special feast days),* months *(celebrations of new moons which began each month of the Jewish lunar calendar),* times *(seasons of week-long festivals such as the feast of tabernacles, unleavened bread, etc.), and* years *(Sabbatical and Jubilee years).*

---

b. Paul reminds them of his faithfulness—"I am afraid of you, lest I have bestowed upon you labour in vain. Brethren, I beseech you, be as I am; for I am as ye are: ye have not injured me at all. Ye know how through infirmity of the flesh I preached the gospel unto you at the first. And my temptation which was in my flesh ye despised not, nor rejected; but received me as an angel of God, even as Christ Jesus. Where is then the blessedness ye spake of? for I bear you record, that, if it had been possible, ye would have plucked out your own eyes, and have given them to me. Am I therefore become your enemy, because I tell you the truth? . . . My little children, of whom I travail in birth again until Christ be formed in you" (Gal. 4:11-16, 19).

---

†4:19

A. *Where was that happy spirit once enjoyed between the apostle and the Galatians (4:11-15)? He reminds them of their past affection for him, which had made them willing (if it were possible) to pluck out their eyes for him. Some connect this statement in 4:15 with that in 2 Corinthians 12:7 concerning Paul's thorn in the flesh.*

B. *Why had they thus turned from him, viewing him, their real spiritual mother, as their enemy, and attached themselves to false legalizing teachers (4:16-20)? In perhaps no other single verse does the apostle display more of his agony and aspiration for all his converts than he does here in 4:19: "My little children, of whom I travail in birth again until Christ be formed in you."*

VIII. Justification by Faith: The Allegorization (Gal. 4:21-31)—In these verses Paul uses Hagar and Sarah, two Old Testament women, to allegorize the Law of Moses and the grace of God.

A. Hagar (an allegory of the Law)

1. She was a bondwoman.
2. Her marriage to Abraham was fleshly directed.
3. Her son, Ishmael, was naturally born.
4. This son persecuted Abraham's second son, Isaac.
5. Her child was not considered as Abraham's rightful heir.
6. Hagar represented the Mount Sinai Covenant as she bore a slave child (Israel would also be slaves for awhile).
7. She corresponded to earthly Jerusalem (in Paul's day) due to her slavery (Jerusalem was occupied by the Romans at that time).

B. Sarah (an allegory of grace)
1. She was a freewoman.
2. Her marriage to Abraham was spirit-directed.
3. Her son Isaac was supernaturally born.
4. This son was persecuted by Ishmael.
5. Her child was considered as Abraham's rightful heir.
6. Sarah represented the New Covenant, as she bore a free son.
7. She corresponded to heavenly Jerusalem.

IX. Justification by Faith: The Application (Gal. 5:1-15)
A. Assuring us of the freedom of the Son (Gal. 5:1-15)
1. Keeping us from the legalism of the Jews (Gal. 5:1-12) —"Stand fast therefore in the liberty wherewith Christ hath made us free, and be not entangled again with the yoke of bondage. Behold, I Paul say unto you, that if ye be circumcised, Christ shall profit you nothing. For I testify again to every man that is circumcised, that he is a debtor to do the whole law. Christ is become of no effect unto you, whosoever of you are justified by the law; ye are fallen from grace" (Gal. 5:1-4).

---

†5:4 *What does it mean to refuse this glorious liberty in Christ?*

A. It means to trade the blessed yoke of Christ for the burdensome yoke of the Law (5:1). Note the contrast between these two yokes.

1. The yoke of Christ—"Come unto me, all ye that labour and are heavy laden, and I will give you rest. Take my yoke upon you, and learn of me; for I am meek and lowly in heart: and ye shall find rest unto your souls. For my yoke is easy, and my burden is light" (Matt. 11:28-30).

2. The yoke of the Law—"Now therefore why tempt ye God, to put a yoke upon the neck of the disciples, which neither our fathers nor we were able to bear?" (Acts 15:10).

B. It means to become debtor to the entire Mosaic Law (3:3; see also Deut. 27:26). Warren Wiersbe writes: "Imagine a motorist driving down a city street and either deliberately or unconsciously driving through a red light. He is pulled over by a policeman who asks to see his driver's license. Immediately the driver begins to defend himself. 'Officer, I know I ran that red light—but I have never robbed anybody. I've never committed adultery. I've never cheated on my income tax!' The policeman smiles as he writes out the ticket, because he knows that no amount of obedience can make up for one act of disobedience. It is one law, the same law that protects the obedient man and punishes the offender. To boast about keeping part of the law while at the same time breaking another part is to confess that I am worthy of punishment" (Be Free, *pp. 118-119).*

C. It means to fall from grace (5:4). This, of course, does not mean they had lost their salvation, for in the book of Galatians Paul refers to his readers as:

1. Brethren (nine times; see 1:2, 11; 3:15; 4:12, 31; 5:11, 13; 6:1, 18)

2. Children of God (3:26)

3. Sons of God (4:6)

4. Heirs of the promise (3:29)—The Greek word here translated "fallen" is ekpipto, *and is found in Acts 27:17, 26, 29, 32, where it refers to a ship not under control. This is the meaning here in Galatians. To put oneself back under the Law means to deny the sweet and sure control of God's grace. Paul has already stated that it is tragically possible to frustrate (literally, to nullify, to make of none effect) the grace of God. (See Gal. 2:21.)*

2. Keeping us from the license of the Libertines (Gal. 5:13)

---

†5:13 *Paul now warns against the opposite of legalism, which is lawlessness.*

A. In Romans 7 (as here in Gal. 5) Paul connects the commandments of God with the corruption of the flesh. This he does by pointing out the following: The law in itself is good (Rom. 7:7). The trouble came when sin used the Law to make him feel guilty by arousing all kinds of evil and forbidden desires within him (7:8). He concludes by saying: "For I was alive without the law once: but when the commandment came, sin revived, and I died. And the commandment, which was ordained to life, I found to be unto death" (Rom. 7:9-10).

B. Here now in Galatians 5 he lists some 17 works of the flesh, resulting from an illegal use of the Law. These are:

1. *Adultery (sexual sins between married people)*
2. *Fornication (sexual sins between unmarried people)*
3. *Uncleanness (impurity)*
4. *Lasciviousness (sensuality)*
5. *Idolatry (worship of idols)*
6. *Witchcraft (Greek is* pharmakeia, *which can refer to sorcery and/or drugs)*
7. *Hatred (enmity)*
8. *Variances (Greek is* eris, *referring to the god of strife)*
9. *Emulations (rivalry, jealousy)*
10. *Wrath (temper, outburst of anger)*
11. *Strife (factions, cliques)*
12. *Seditions (divisions, dissensions)*
13. *Heresies (sects)*
14. *Envyings (coveting)*
15. *Murders (unlawful killing)*
16. *Drunkenness (rendered helpless by strong drink)*
17. *Revelings (carousings, orgies)*

---

3. Keeping us in the love of the Lord—"For all the law is fulfilled in one word, even in this; Thou shalt love thy neighbour as thyself" (Gal. 5:14).

B. Assuring us the fruit of the Spirit (Gal. 5:15-23)

1. As demonstrated by our fruitbearing (Gal. 5:16-26)
   a. Negative: The fruit of the flesh—"My little children, of whom I travail in birth again until Christ be formed in you, I desire to be present with you now, and to change my voice; for I stand in doubt of you. Tell me, ye that desire to be under the law, do ye not hear the law?" (Gal. 4:19-21).
   b. Positive: The fruit of the Spirit—"But the fruit of the Spirit is love, joy, peace, longsuffering, gentleness, goodness, faith, meekness, temperance: against such there is no law" (Gal. 5:22-23).

---

†5:23

A. Warren Wiersbe writes: "The contrast between works *and* fruit *is important. A machine in a factory* works, *and turns out a product, but it could never manufacture fruit. Fruit must grow out of life, and in the case of the believer, it is the life of the Spirit. When you think of 'works' you think of effort, labor, strain, and toil; when you think of 'fruit' you think of beauty, quietness, the unfolding of life. The flesh produces 'dead works' (Heb. 9:14), but the Spirit produces living fruit . . . the New Testament speaks of several kinds of fruit: people won to Christ (Rom. 1:13), holy living (Rom. 6:22), gifts brought to God (Rom. 15:16-18), good works (Col.. 1:10), and praise (Heb. 13:15). The fruit of the Spirit listed in our passage has to do with character"* (Be Free, *pp. 133-134).*

B. Note now the various aspects of this Spirit-produced fruit.
1. Love (divine concern for others)
2. Joy (inward peace and sufficiency)
3. Peace (a confidence and quietness of the soul)
4. Longsuffering (patience, endurance without quitting)
5. Gentleness (kindness)
6. Goodness (love in action)
7. Faith (dependability)
8. Meekness (subdued strength)
9. Temperance (self-control)

---

2. As demonstrated by our burden-bearing (Gal. 6:1-6)—"Brethren, if a man be overtaken in a fault, ye which are spiritual, restore such an one in the spirit of meekness; considering thyself, lest thou also be tempted. Bear ye one another's burdens, and so fulfil the law of Christ" (Gal. 6:1-2).
3. As demonstrated by our seed-bearing (Gal. 6:7-10)—"Be not deceived; God is not mocked: for whatsoever a man soweth, that shall he also reap. For he that soweth to his flesh shall of the flesh reap corruption; but he that soweth to the Spirit shall of the Spirit reap life everlasting. And let us not be weary in well doing: for in due season we shall reap, if we faint not" (Gal. 6:7-9).
4. As demonstrated by our brand-bearing (Gal. 6:14-17)—"But God forbid that I should glory, save in the cross of our Lord Jesus Christ, by whom the world is crucified unto me, and I unto the world. From henceforth let no man trouble me: for I bear in my body the marks of the Lord Jesus" (Gal. 6:14, 17).

---

†6:17 *J. Sidlow Baxter writes: "This Galatian epistle was written to groups of believers scattered through a rural area, in which most of the people were agricultural workers of one sort or another. In keeping with the mentality and circumstances of the Galatians, Paul uses language and metaphors which are specially appropriate to them. There were four kinds of 'bearing' with which the Galatians were familiar above all else. These were: fruit-bearing, burden-bearing, seed-bearing, and brand-bearing (for as many of the agricultural labourers were slaves, they were branded to indicate whose property they were). See now how Paul makes use of these things in expounding the true liberty of the Spirit:*
A. Fruit-bearing: 'The fruit of the Spirit is love, joy, peace, longsuffering,' etc. (5:22-23).
B. Burden-bearing: 'Bear ye one another's burdens and so fulfill the law of Christ' (6:2).
C. Seed-bearing: 'Whatsoever a man soweth,' etc. (6:7). 'Let us not be weary in well doing, for . . . we shall reap' (6:9).
D. Brand-bearing: 'I bear in my body the marks [or brands] of the Lord Jesus' (6:17). There were five classes of person who were branded, i.e, slaves *(as a mark of ownership),* soldiers *(as a*

mark of allegiance), devotees *(as a mark of consecration),* criminals *(as a mark of exposure), and the* abhorred *(as a mark of reproach). The marks of the Lord Jesus in the body of Paul were all these five in one!"* (Explore the Book, *Vol. 6, pp. 153-154, 158).*

(See 2 Cor. 11:23-28 for a history of some of these marks.)

EPHESIANS

SIX STRIKING SYMBOLS OF THE CHRISTIAN CHURCH

A. The church is likened to:
   1. A body (Eph. 1)
   2. A temple (Eph. 2)
   3. A mystery (Eph. 3)
   4. A new man (Eph. 4)
   5. A bride (Eph. 5)
   6. A soldier (Eph. 6)

B. This is what Ephesians is all about. Ephesians and Colossians have some similarities.
   1. Both were written by the same author—Paul.
   2. Both were written during the same period of time.
   3. Both are prison epistles.
   4. Ephesians emphasizes the body of Christ, which is the church.
   5. Colossians emphasizes the head of that body, which is Christ himself.

C. Note J. Vernon McGee's introduction to this book of Ephesians: "A quartet of men left Rome in the year A.D. 62, bound for the province of Asia, which was located in what is currently designated as Asia Minor. These men had on their persons four of the most sublime compositions of the Christian faith. These precious documents would be invaluable if they were in existence today. Rome did not comprehend the significance of the writings of an unknown prisoner. If she had, these men would have been apprehended and the documents seized. When they bade farewell to the Apostle Paul, each was given an epistle to bear to his particular constituency. These four letters are designated 'The Prison Epistles of Paul' since he wrote them while imprisoned in Rome, awaiting a hearing before Nero, the Caesar at that time, to whom Paul, as a Roman citizen, had appealed his case."

   This quartet of men and their respective places of abode can be identified as:
   1. Epaphroditus from Philippi (Phil. 4:18) had the epistle to the Philippians.
   2. Tychicus from Ephesus (Eph. 6:21) had the epistle to the Ephesians.
   3. Epaphras from Colosse (Col. 4:12) had the epistle to the Colossians.
   4. Onesimus, a slave from Colosse (Philem. 10) had the epistle to Philemon (who was his master). "These epistles present a composite picture of Christ, the church, the Christian life, and the interrelationship and functioning of all. These different facets present the Christian life on the highest plane. Ephesians presents the church 'which is his body'(Eph. 1:22-23)—this is the invisible church, of which Christ is the Head. Colossians presents Christ, 'the head of the body, the church' (Col. 1:18). The emphasis is upon Christ, rather than on the church. Philippians presents Christian living with Christ as the dynamic—'I can do all things through Christ which strengtheneth me' (Phil. 4:13). Philemon presents Christian living in action in a pagan society: 'If thou count

me therefore a partner, receive him as myself. If he hath wronged thee, or oweth thee ought, put that on mine account" (Philem. 17-18). The gospel walked in shoe leather in the first century—it worked" *(Exploring Through Ephesians*, p. 3).

D. Ephesus is the only New Testament church to receive a letter from more than one Bible writer. John the apostle also had a message for them (Rev. 2:1-7).
E. This church had more famous preachers than did any other church. This would include men such as Paul, Apollos, John, and Timothy.
F. Ephesians is the Joshua book of the New Testament.
G. It has been called "Paul's third heaven epistle." It has been referred to as the Alps of the New Testament, the Mount Whitney of the High Sierras of all Scripture.
H. In no other epistle is our preconversion position in the world and postconversion in Christ so vividly described as in this book.
   1. Our preconversion position (2:1-3, 11-13)
   2. Our postconversion position (1:3-14; 2:4-10, 14-22)
I. Ephesians provides the most beautiful New Testament passages describing Christ's relationship to and love for his church. (See 5:22-33.)
J. The Ephesian church was founded by Paul during his second missionary trip.
K. After spending 18 months in Corinth (Acts 18:11), he visited Ephesus with Aquila and Priscilla (Acts 18:18).
L. Paul stayed there for only a short time, but promised to return (Acts 18:19-21).
M. Aquila and Priscilla remained in Ephesus where God led them to instruct a powerful Bible preacher named Apollos in the details of the Word of God (Acts 18:24-26).
N. Paul returned during his third missionary trip and stayed three years (Acts 19:8-10; 20:31).
O. He is later visited by the Ephesian elders during a layover at Miletus, en route to Jerusalem (Acts 20:16-38).
P. It is thought that this epistle may be the one referred to by Paul in Colossians 4:16.
Q. It gives the most detailed description and presentation of the believer as a soldier of Jesus (6:11-17).
R. Two of Paul's greatest prayers for the church are found in this book (1:15-18; 3:14-21).
S. It includes the last of three New Testament passages speaking of spiritual gifts (4:11). Compare with Romans 12:3-8; 1 Corinthians 12:1-31.
T. According to John's letter (Rev. 2:1-7), this church:
   1. Worked hard and possessed patience
   2. Had high church standards
   3. Hated the deeds of the licentious Nicolaitanes
   4. Had left their first love
   5. Needed to repent and return to Christ
U. Ephesians is the 12th longest New Testament book, and 41st longest biblical book, with six chapters, 155 verses, and 3,039 words. There are quotations or allusions from 13 Old Testament books in Ephesians.
V. Great passages would include:
   1. 1:17-23
   2. 2:1-10
   3. 2:19-22

4. 3:17-21
5. 4:1-6
6. 5:16-33
7. 6:10-17

THE BOOK OF EPHESIANS

I. The Church Is Likened to a Body (Eph. 1)—"Which is his body, the fulness of him that filleth all in all" (Eph. 1:23).
   A. The creation of this body (Eph. 1:1-14)
      1. It was wrought and planned by the Father (Eph. 1:1-6) —"Grace be to you, and peace, from God our Father, and from the Lord Jesus Christ. Blessed be the God and Father of our Lord Jesus Christ, who hath blessed us with all spiritual blessings in heavenly places in Christ" (Eph. 1:2-3).

---

†1:3

A. Paul writes to those "at Ephesus, and to the faithful in Christ Jesus." Dr. J. Vernon McGee has written: "The little preposition in (en), *when it precedes Christ, is the most important word of this epistle. Theologians have amassed an array of imposing theological words to define our salvation— such as redemption, atonement, justification, reconciliation, propitiation, and the vicarious substitutionary sacrifice of Christ. All of these are fine, and each presents one aspect of the many facets of our salvation. None, however, seems entirely adequate. What does it mean to be saved? This is a question which is answered in utmost simplicity by the Bible term, 'in Christ.' To be saved means to be in Christ. A sinner who has trusted Christ for his salvation has as much right in heaven as has Christ—or he has no right there at all, for he is in Christ!"* (Exploring Through Ephesians, *p. 11).*

B. Paul writes: "Blessed be the God and Father of our Lord Jesus Christ" (see v. 3). The word "blessed" is eulogetos, *and means "to speak well of, to praise, to celebrate." This adjective is used only of God. (See Mark 14:61; Luke 1:68; Rom. 1:25; 9:5; 2 Cor. 1:3; 11:31; Eph. 1:3; 1 Pet. 1:3.) When the word "blessed" is used of a person, the Greek term is* makarios, *and means "to pronounce happy." (See Matt. 5:3-11.) Thus, God desires for his children to bless him by saying nice things about him. Furthermore, God hears and records these things in his book of remembrance. (See Mal. 3:16.) We note also that Paul carefully distinguishes the difference between Christ's relationship to the Father and our relationship to the Father. See also John 20:17 where Jesus does the same thing. (See also John 1:14, 18; 3:16, 18; 1 John 4:9; Rev. 1:5.)*

---

a. He elected us.
   (1) The time involved—"Before the foundation of the world" (Eph. 1:4).
   (2) The purpose involved—"That we should be holy and without blame before him" (Eph. 1:4).

b. He predestinated us.
   (1) The method—Through Jesus Christ
   (2) The basis—"According to the good pleasure of his will" (Eph. 1:5).

(3) The reason—"To the praise of the glory of his grace, wherein he hath made us accepted in the beloved" (Eph. 1:6).

2. It was bought and purchased by the Son (Eph. 1:7-12).
   a. Redeemed by his blood—"In whom we have redemption through his blood, the forgiveness of sins, according to the riches of his grace" (Eph. 1:7).
   b. Gathered in his name—"That in the dispensation of the fulness of times he might gather together in one all things in Christ, both which are in heaven, and which are on earth; even in him" (Eph. 1:10).

---

†1:10

A. *Special note: The word translated* dispensation *here,* oikonomia, *is employed three times by the Greek text of Ephesians. The apostle writes concerning:*
   1. *The dispensation of the fullness of time (1:10)*
   2. *The dispensation of the grace of God (3:2)*
   3. *The dispensation (translated by the word "fellowship" in the King James Version) of the mystery (3:9)*

B. *It may prove helpful at this point to briefly define the concept of dispensationalism as developed by Paul.*

C. *The Greek word* oikonomia *is found some 19 times in the New Testament. It is translated by the following English words:*
   1. Steward *(Luke 12:42; 16:11; 1 Cor. 4:1-2; Titus 1:7; 1 Pet. 4:10)*
   2. Stewardship *(Luke 16:2-4)*
   3. Dispensation *(1 Cor. 9:17; Eph. 1:10; 3:2; Col. 1:25)*
   4. Fellowship *(Eph. 3:9)*
   5. Edifying *(1 Tim. 1:4)*

D. *Note the following definitions of a dispensation: "It is a period of time during which man is tested in respect of obedience to some specific revelation of the will of God" (from the* Scofield Bible*). Thus the central idea in the word dispensation is that of managing or administrating the affairs of a household. "As far as the use of the word in Scripture is concerned, a dispensation may be defined as a stewardship, administration, oversight or management of others' property. As we have seen, this involves responsibility, accountability, and faithfulness on the part of the steward . . . A dispensation is primarily a stewardship arrangement and not a period of time (though obviously the arrangement will exist during a period of time . . . a dispensation is basically the arrangement involved, not the time involved; and a proper definition will take this into account. A concise definition of a dispensation is this: 'A dispensation is a distinguishable economy in the outworking of God's purpose'"* (Dispensationalism Today, *pp. 25, 29, 31.)*

E. *To summarize: Dispensationalism views the world as a household run by God. In this household world, God is dispensing or administering its affairs according to his own will and in various stages of revelation in the process of time. These various stages mark off the distinguishably different economies in the outworking of his total purpose, and these economies are the dispensations.*

---

   c. Predestinated for his glory—"In whom also we have obtained an inheritance, being predestinated according to the purpose of him who worketh all things after the counsel of his own will: That we should be to the praise of his glory, who first trusted in Christ" (Eph. 1:11-12).

3. It was taught and preserved by the Spirit (Eph. 1:13-14).
   a. The *what* of the matter—"In whom ye also trusted, after that ye heard the word of truth, the gospel of your salvation: in whom also after that ye believed, ye were sealed with that holy Spirit of promise" (Eph. 1:13).

---

†1:13 *He seals us. This indicates the following:*
A. Ownership (1 Cor. 6:19-20; 2 Tim. 2:19)
B. Security (Eph. 4:30)
C. Completed transaction (Jer. 32:9-10; John 17:4; 19:30)

---

   b. The *why* of the matter—"Which is the earnest of our inheritance until the redemption of the purchased possession, unto the praise of his glory" (Eph. 1:14).

---

†1:14 *He becomes our earnest. An earnest is something of value (like money) given as a down payment for a purchased possession. This all happens at the time of salvation. Note: He is called "that holy Spirit of promise" (1:13) because Jesus himself has promised he would come. (See John 14:16-17; 16:7, 13; Acts 1:4-5.) Verse 14 is the third and final doxology in these first few verses. (See verses 6, 12, 14.)*

B. The consecration of this body (Eph. 1:15-23)
1. Paul prays that the church may know the God of glory—"That the God of our Lord Jesus Christ, the Father of glory, may give unto you the spirit of wisdom and revelation in the knowledge of him" (Eph. 1:17).
2. Paul prays that the church may know the glory of God.
   a. As it is seen in his saints—"The eyes of your understanding being enlightened; that ye may know what is the hope of his calling, and what the riches of the glory of his inheritance in the saints, and what is the exceeding greatness of his power to us-ward who believe, according to the working of his mighty power" (Eph. 1:18-19).
   b. As it is seen in his Son—"Which he wrought in Christ, when he raised him from the dead, and set him at his own right hand in the heavenly places, far above all principality, and power, and might, and dominion, and every name that is named, not only in this world, but also in that which is to come" (Eph. 1:20-21).
   c. As it is seen in his church—"And hath put all things under his feet, and gave him to be the head over all things to the church, which is his body, the fulness of him that filleth all in all" (Eph. 1:22-23).

---

†1:23 *Thus, the believer is fighting* from *a victory and not* for *a victory. The divine "cards" have already been stacked; we have already won. (See also Matt. 28:18; Psa. 8:6; 110:1; 1 Cor. 15:25-26.)*

II. The Church Is Likened to a Temple—"In whom all the building fitly framed together groweth unto an holy temple in the Lord" (Eph. 2:21).

A. What we once were (Eph. 2:1-3, 11-12)
   1. Dead in sin (Eph. 2:1)
   2. Influenced by Satan—"Wherein in time past ye walked according to the course of this world, according to the prince of the power of the air, the spirit that now worketh in the children of disobedience" (Eph. 2:2).
   3. Controlled by lust (Eph. 2:3)
   4. Separated from Christ (Eph. 2:12)
   5. Excluded from the promises (Eph. 2:12)
   6. Hopeless in the world (Eph. 2:12)

B. What God did (Eph. 2:4-6, 18)
   1. He loved us—"But God, who is rich in mercy, for his great love wherewith he loved us" (Eph. 2:4).
   2. He liberated us—"Even when we were dead in sins, hath quickened us together with Christ, (by grace ye are saved;) and hath raised us up together, and made us sit together in heavenly places in Christ Jesus" (Eph. 2:5-6).

C. Why God did it (Eph. 2:7)—"That in the ages to come he might shew the exceeding riches of his grace in his kindness toward us through Christ Jesus" (Eph. 2:7).

D. How God did it (Eph. 2:8-9, 13)
   1. By the grace of God—"For by grace are ye saved through faith; and that not of yourselves: it is the gift of God: not of works, lest any man should boast" (Eph. 2:8-9).
   2. By the blood of Christ—"But now in Christ Jesus ye who sometimes were far off are made nigh by the blood of Christ" (Eph. 2:13).

E. What we now are (Eph. 2:10, 14-22)
   1. We are products of God's workmanship (Eph. 2:10)—"For we are his workmanship, created in Christ Jesus unto good works, which God hath before ordained that we should walk in them" (Eph. 2:10).

---

†**2:10** *We are the workmanship of God. The Greek word for workmanship (2:10) is* poema, *from whence our English word "poem" comes. God has two treasured poems in this universe:*
A. The poem of creation (see Rom. 1:20; Rev. 4:11)
B. The poem of salvation (see Eph. 2:10; Rev. 5:9) Thus, we are saved to be sure. This salvation is apart from *works (2:8-9) but* unto *works (2:10).*

---

   2. We are partners with Israel in God's Son (Eph. 2:14-18) —"For He Himself is our peace, who made both groups into one, and broke down the barrier of the dividing wall, by abolishing in His flesh the enmity, which is the Law of Commandments contained in ordinances, that in Himself He might make the two into one new man, thus establishing peace" (Eph. 2:14-15, NASB).

---

†**2:16** *We are (as Gentiles) united with Israel in Christ, that he might reconcile both unto God in one body (2:16). Chrysostom once wrote: "He does not mean that He has elevated us to that high dignity of theirs, but He has raised both of us and them to one still higher. I will give you an illustration. Let us imagine that there are two statues, one of silver and other of lead, and then that both shall be melted down, and the two shall come out gold. So thus He has made the two one."*

---

3. We are parts of God's temple (Eph. 2:19-22)—"And are built upon the foundation of the apostles and prophets, Jesus Christ himself being the chief corner stone; in whom all the building fitly framed together groweth unto an holy temple in the Lord: in whom ye also are builded together for an habitation of God through the Spirit" (Eph. 2:20-22).

III. The Church Is Likened to a Mystery (Eph. 3)—"For this cause I Paul, the prisoner of Jesus Christ for you Gentiles, If ye have heard of the dispensation of the grace of God which is given me to you-ward: how that by revelation he made known unto me the mystery; (as I wrote afore in few words, whereby, when ye read, ye may understand my knowledge in the mystery of Christ)" (Eph. 3:1-4).

A. The time element of this mystery

1. Not known in the Old Testament—"Which in other ages was not made known unto the sons of men" (Eph. 3:5) .
2. Made known in the New Testament—"As it is now revealed unto his holy apostles and prophets by the Spirit" (Eph. 3:5b).

B. The nature of this mystery—"That the Gentiles should be fellowheirs, and of the same body and partakers of his promise in Christ by the gospel" (Eph. 3:6).

---

†3:6 *In the Old Testament, Gentile salvation was known, but not without becoming Jews by proselytization (see Isa. 11:10; 42:6; 60:3; Zech. 2:11; Mal. 1:11). (Compare these Old Testament verses with Eph. 3:5-6; Rom. 16:25; Col. 1:26.)*

C. The recipient of this mystery (Eph. 3:1-4, 7-9)

1. Paul, the man—"How that by revelation he made known unto me the mystery; (as I wrote afore in few words" (Eph. 3:3).
2. Paul, the meek—"Unto me, who am less than the least of all saints, is this grace given, that I should preach among the Gentiles the unsearchable riches of Christ" (Eph. 3:8).
3. Paul, the messenger—"And to make all men see what is the fellowship of the mystery, which from the beginning of the world hath been hid in God, who created all things by Jesus Christ" (Eph. 3:9).

D. The basis of this mystery—"According to the eternal purpose which he purposed in Christ Jesus our Lord" (Eph. 3:11).

E. The reasons for this mystery (Eph. 3:10)

1. That God's wisdom might be experienced by the church—"In order that the manifold wisdom of God might now be made known through the church" (Eph. 3:10, NASB).
2. That God's wisdom might be illustrated to the angels—"To the rulers and authorities in the heavenly places" (Eph. 3:10, NASB).

---

†3:10 *Thus this world becomes a university wherein both demons and angels might study the grace of God. (See also Eph. 1:21; 6:12; Col. 1:16; 2:15; 1 Pet. 1:12.)*

F. The results of this mystery

1. Believers have access to the throne of God—"In whom we have boldness and access with confidence by the faith of him" (Eph. 3:12).
2. Believers are strengthened by the Spirit of God—"For this cause I bow my knees unto the Father of our Lord Jesus Christ, that he would grant you, according to the riches of his glory, to be strengthened with might by his Spirit in the inner man" (Eph. 3:14, 16).
3. Believers can know the love of God—"That Christ may dwell in your hearts by faith; that ye, being rooted and grounded in love, may be able to comprehend with all saints what is the breadth, and length, and depth, and height; and to know the love of Christ, which passeth knowledge, that ye might be filled with all the fulness of God" (Eph. 3:17-19).

---

†**3:19** *There are two great prayers in this epistle.*

A. In 1:15-23, Paul prays for the eyes of the believers: "That . . . the eyes of your understanding being enlightened" (1:18). Here he wanted them to know the tremendous power of God.
B. In 3:14-21 Paul prays for the hearts of the believers: "That Christ may dwell in your hearts" (3:17). Here he wanted them to know the tender love of Christ.

---

4. Believers can request the power of God—"Now unto him that is able to do exceeding abundantly above all that we ask or think, according to the power that worketh in us" (Eph. 3:20).
5. Believers can display the glory of God—"Unto him be glory in the church by Christ Jesus throughout all ages, world without end. Amen" (Eph. 3:21).

IV. The Church Is Likened to a New Man (Eph. 4:13-24)—"Till we all come in the unity of the faith, and of the knowledge of the Son of God, unto a perfect man, unto the measure of the stature of the fulness of Christ: and that ye put on the new man, which after God is created in righteousness and true holiness" (Eph. 4:13, 24).
A. The position of the new man
1. The unity of his new position—Seven great stabilizers (Eph. 4:4-6)
a. One body

---

†*One body (Christ's body—the church). (See 1 Cor. 12:12, 27; Eph. 5:30.)*

---

b. One spirit

---

†*One Spirit (the Holy Spirit). (See 1 Cor. 12:4.)*

---

c. One hope

---

†*One hope—The Scriptures declare this hope to be:*
A. Good (2 Thess. 2:16)
B. Better (Heb. 7:19)
C. Blessed (Titus 2:13)

D. Glorious (Col. 1:27)
E. Lively (1 Pet. 1:3)
F. Firm (Heb. 3:6; 6:11)
G. Eternal (Titus 3:7)

---

d. One Lord

---

†*One Lord (the Savior) (1 Cor. 12:5)*

---

e. One faith

---

†*One faith (Jude 3; 2 Cor. 13:5; 1 Cor. 16:13; Gal. 1:23; Phil. 1:27; ; 1 Tim. 1:2; 4:1; 5:8; 2 Tim. 4;7: Titus 1:4)*

---

f. One baptism

---

†*One baptism (into Christ's body) (Rom. 6:3-4; 1 Cor. 12:13; Col. 2:9-12; Gal. 3:27-28; 1 Pet. 3:21)*

---

g. One God and Father
2. The unifier of his new position—One great Savior (Eph. 4:7-16)
a. His gifts to believers—"But to each one of us grace has been given as Christ apportioned it. This is why it says: 'When he ascended on high, he led captives in his train and gave gifts to men.' (What does 'he ascended' mean except that he also descended to the lower, earthly regions? He who descended is the very one who ascended higher than all the heavens, in order to fill the whole universe.) It was he who gave some to be apostles, some to be prophets, some to be evangelists, and some to be pastors and teachers" (Eph. 4:7-11, NIV).

---

†**4:11** *Dr. Homer Kent writes the following concerning these verses: "Paul first issues a statement that God has bestowed gifts to believers to enable them to accomplish the goal of walking in unity (4:7). The previous paragraph has emphasized the fact of unity by pointing to the oneness of believers in various respects. Now Paul shows that each believer is an individual participant and recipient of the divine graces which he needs. Each person's grace is in proportion to what Christ in His sovereign wisdom has freely given. Not all receive the same gifts, or the same number of gifts, or the same amount of any one gift. Christ dispenses as He deems best. The scriptural proof (4:8-10) cited for the above assertion is drawn from Psalm 68:18. 'When he ascended up on high, he led captivity captive, and gave gifts unto men.' The historical circumstances of the psalm are uncertain. It depicts a victorious and triumphant return, probably of David to Mount Zion. If the psalm was intended to be Messianic (as this usage in Ephesians certainly suggests), then David is regarded as typical of his greater Son whose passion victory was followed by the ascension. The chief points in the quotation which were significant to the author were the victorious ascent and the dispensing of gifts to men. Certain other features, however, are also of special interest. 'He led captivity captive' is*

translated 'he captured prisoners' (Jerusalem Bible), 'he took many captives with him' (TEV), and 'he led a host of captives' (RSV). Messianically interpreted, this usually referred to Christ's conquering of His enemies: Satan, sin, death, the curse. Others (a minority, but including many of the ancient Fathers) explain these 'captives' as friends, either the redeemed on earth, or Old Testament saints in hades (Heb., sheol). *In support of this last interpretation, arguments such as the following are given:*

A. That which is led captive is taken to heaven. This is not true of Satan, sin, death, or the curse.

B. The past tense (aorist) 'led captive' does not fit the regeneration of subsequent believers as well as some prior action.

C. The interpretation that this refers to the descent of Christ to the realm of the dead at His death accords well with 1 Peter 3:19-20.

D. It fits Matthew 27:50-53, where the visible release of some Old Testament saints from hades may imply the spiritual release of all such.

E. This harmonizes with the apparent change in location of paradise, which in the New Testament era is stated as being above, and equated with heaven (2 Cor. 12:2-4)" (Ephesians, the Glory of the Church, *pp. 68-69).*

---

b. His goal for believers (Eph. 4:12-16)

(1) That we be equipped—"For the perfecting of the saints, for the work of the ministry, for the edifying of the body of Christ" (Eph. 4:12).

(2) That we be unified—"Till we all come in the unity of the faith, and of the knowledge of the Son of God, unto a perfect man, unto the measure of the stature of the fulness of Christ. . . . From whom the whole body fitly joined together and compacted by that which every joint supplieth, according to the effectual working in the measure of every part, maketh increase of the body unto the edifying of itself in love" (Eph. 4:13, 16).

(3) That we be settled—"That we henceforth be no more children, tossed to and fro, and carried about with every wind of doctrine, by the sleight of men, and cunning craftiness, whereby they lie in wait to deceive" (Eph. 4:14).

B. The disposition of the new man

1. His walk

a. Adopt the spiritual walk—"I therefore, the prisoner of the Lord, beseech you that ye walk worthy of the vocation wherewith ye are called, with all lowliness and meekness, with longsuffering, forebearing one another in love; endeavouring to keep the unity of the Spirit in the bond of peace" (Eph. 4:1-3).

---

†4:3

A. In lowliness (Phil 2:3; Matt. 11:29)

B. In meekness (2 Cor. 10:1)

C. In longsuffering (Gal. 5:22)

D. In forebearing (Col. 3:13)

E. In unity (John 17:21; 1 Cor. 12:13)

---

b. Avoid the sensual walk—"This I say therefore, and testify in the Lord, that ye henceforth walk not as other Gentiles walk, in the vanity of their mind, having the understanding darkened, being alienated from the life of God through the ignorance that is in them, because of the blindness of their heart: who being past feeling have given themselves over unto lasciviousness, to work all uncleanness with greediness" (Eph. 4:17-19).

2. His words—"But speaking the truth in love, may grow up into him in all things, which is the head, even Christ. . . . Wherefore putting away lying, speak every man truth with his neighbour: for we are members one of another. . . . Let no corrupt communication proceed out of your mouth, but that which is good to the use of edifying, that it may minister grace unto the hearers. . . . Let all bitterness, and wrath, and anger, and clamour, and evil speaking, be put away from you, with all malice" (Eph. 4:15, 25, 29, 31).

---

†4:31 *Chrysostom wrote the following concerning 4:25: "Let not the eye lie to the foot, nor the foot to the eye. If there be a deep pit and its mouth covered with reeds shall present to the eye the appearance of solid ground, will not the eye use the foot to ascertain whether it is hollow underneath, or whether it is firm and resists? Will the foot tell a lie and not the truth as it is? And what, again, if the eye were to spy a serpent or a wild beast, will it lie to the foot?"*

---

3. His works
   a. Put off the old man—"That ye put off concerning the former conversation the old man, which is corrupt according to the deceitful lusts" (Eph. 4:22).
      (1) Don't lose your temper—"Be ye angry, and sin not: let not the sun go down upon your wrath" (Eph. 4:26).

---

†4:26 *D. L. Moody once remarked that he wouldn't give a dime for a Christian without a temper, but he also wouldn't give a nickel for a believer who couldn't control that temper. There is, of course, righteous anger (see Mark 3:5). However, Satan loves to use uncontrolled anger.*

---

      (2) Don't give place to the devil—"Neither give place to the devil" (Eph. 4:27).
      (3) Don't steal—"Let him that stole steal no more: but rather let him labour, working with his hands the thing which is good, that he may have to give to him that needeth" (Eph. 4:28).

---

†4:28 *Dr. Homer Kent observes: "Paul's actual expression is 'the one stealing.' It is a present participle and can hardly be relegated to the one who 'stole' before he was converted. Rather, it seems to depict the continuing practice of pilfering that still characterized some of these Christians. We must recognize that many of the early Christians came from the ranks of slaves, where pilfering was a way of life. Conversion does not remove all such habits instantaneously, especially in matters where no great conscience has developed.*

"Furthermore, let us recognize that stealing in the broad sense is not unknown among present-day Christians. Deans of students in any Christian school can elaborate on this problem at some length. Income tax returns, insurance claims, and examinations in school are only a few examples of situations where Christians are many times less than honest. The scriptural injunction is not merely

that stealing cease, nor even that restitution be made. The Christian principle is laid down that each man should toil honestly at that which is good, not merely to meet his own needs and thus avoid temptation to thievery, but to be able to amass a surplus to help others in need. This is in stark contrast to the prevalent attitude which assumes that one is entitled to the supply of needs, whether or not he wishes to work. By working diligently, the individual removes some of the temptation to steal, and by assisting others in need, he helps remove the temptation from them also" (Ephesians, the Glory of the Church, *p. 83).*

---

(4) Don't grieve the Holy Spirit—"And grieve not the holy Spirit of God, whereby ye are sealed unto the day of redemption" (Eph. 4:30).

b. Put on the new man—"And be renewed in the spirit of your mind: and that ye put on the new man, which after God is created in righteousness and true holiness. Wherefore putting away lying, speak every man truth with his neighbour: for we are members one of another. . . . Let no corrupt communication proceed out of your mouth, but that which is good to the use of edifying, that it may minister grace unto the hearers. . . . Let all bitterness, and wrath, and anger, and clamour, and evil speaking, be put away from you, with all malice: and be ye kind one to another, tender-hearted, forgiving one another, even as God for Christ's sake hath forgiven you" (Eph. 4:23-25, 29, 31-32).

V. The Church Is Likened to a Bride (Eph. 5)—"For the husband is the head of the wife, even as Christ is the head of the church: and he is the saviour of the body" (Eph. 5:23).

A. The bride: Her duties as the church (Eph. 5:1-23)

1. To be separated (Eph. 5:1-13)

a. To the Lord (Eph. 5:1-2, 8-10)—"Be ye therefore followers of God, as dear children; and walk in love, as Christ also hath loved us, and hath given himself for us an offering and a sacrifice to God for a sweetsmelling savour. . . . For ye were sometimes darkness, but now are ye light in the Lord: walk as children of light: (for the fruit of the Spirit is in all goodness and righteousness and truth;) proving what is acceptable unto the Lord" (Eph. 5:1-2, 8-10).

b. From the world (Eph. 5:3-7, 11-13)—"But fornication, and all uncleanness, or covetousness, let it not be once named among you, as becometh saints; neither filthiness, nor foolish talking, nor jesting, which are not convenient: but rather giving of thanks" (Eph. 5:3-4).

2. To be circumspect (Eph. 5:14-16)—"See then that ye walk circumspectly, not as fools, but as wise, redeeming the time, because the days are evil" (Eph. 5:15-16).

3. To be Spirit-filled (Eph. 5:17-18)—"Wherefore be ye not unwise, but understanding what the will of the Lord is. And be not drunk with wine, wherein is excess; but be filled with the Spirit" (Eph. 5:17-18).

---

†**5:18** *Note: This verse does not encourage "moderate drinking," as some have supposed. The word translated "excess" is* asotia *in the Greek and refers to a riotous and unruly way of life.*

---

4. To be singing (Eph. 5:19)—"Speaking to yourselves in psalms and hymns and spiritual songs, singing and making melody in your heart to the Lord" (Eph. 5:19).

5. To be singleminded (Eph. 5:20)—"Giving thanks always for all things unto God and the Father in the name of our Lord Jesus Christ" (Eph. 5:20).
6. To be submissive (Eph. 5:21-22)—"Submitting yourselves one to another in the fear of God. Wives, submit yourselves unto your own husbands, as unto the Lord" (Eph. 5:21-22).

B. The bridegroom: His devotion to the church (Eph. 5:23-33)

1. This devotion, as illustrated by marriage—"For the husband is the head of the wife, even as Christ is the head of the church: and he is the saviour of the body. Therefore as the church is subject unto Christ, so let the wives be to their own husbands in every thing. . . . So ought men to love their wives as their own bodies. He that loveth his wife loveth himself. For no man ever yet hated his own flesh; but nourisheth and cherisheth it, even as the Lord the church: for we are members of his body, of his flesh, and of his bones. For this cause shall a man leave his father and mother, and shall be joined unto his wife, and they two shall be one flesh. This is a great mystery: but I speak concerning Christ and the church. Nevertheless let every one of you in particular so love his wife even as himself; and the wife see that she reverence her husband" (Eph. 5:23-24, 28-33).
2. This devotion as demonstrated on the cross—"Husbands, love your wives, even as Christ also loved the church, and gave himself for it" (Eph. 5:25).
3. This devotion, as consummated by the Rapture—"That he might sanctify and cleanse it with the washing of water by the word, that he might present it to himself a glorious church, not having spot, or wrinkle, or any such thing; but that it should be holy and without blemish" (Eph. 5:26-27).
   a. A bride without spot—No worldly imperfections
   b. A bride without blemish—No fleshly imperfections

VI. The Church Is Likened to a Soldier (Eph. 6)—"Put on the whole armour of God, that ye may be able to stand against the wiles of the devil" (Eph. 6:11).

A. Boot camp training (Eph. 6:1-9)

1. Example of children and parents (Eph. 6:1-4)—"Children, obey your parents in the Lord: for this is right. Honour thy father and mother; which is the first commandment with promise; That it may be well with thee, and thou mayest live long on the earth. And, ye fathers, provoke not your children to wrath: but bring them up in the nurture and admonition of the Lord" (Eph. 6:1-4).
   a. As a soldier, the child is to honor and obey his parents.

---

†*Both Samson and Absalom are sad warnings to those who would disobey this command. (See Judg. 14:1-3; 2 Sam. 15:1-12; 18:15.)*

---

   b. As a commander, the parent is to discipline and instruct his or her children.

---

†*The parent is to instruct and admonish children in the Lord. (See Prov. 13:24; 19:18; 22:15; 23:13-14; 29:15, 17; Deut. 6:6-7.)*

---

2. Example of servants and master (Eph. 6:5-9)—"Servants, be obedient to them that are your masters according to the flesh, with fear and trembling, in

singleness of your heart, as unto Christ; not with eyeservice, as menpleasers; but as the servants of Christ, doing the will of God from the heart; with good will doing service, as to the Lord, and not to men: knowing that whatsoever good thing any man doeth, the same shall he receive of the Lord, whether he be bond or free. And, ye masters, do the same things unto them, forbearing threatening: knowing that your Master also is in heaven; neither is there respect of persons with him" (Eph. 6:5-9).

a. The servant is to serve his master as he would serve Christ.

b. The master is to treat his servant as he would treat Christ.

B. Front line fighting (Eph. 6:10-24)

1. Our enemy—The devil

a. His cohorts (Eph. 6:12)—"For we wrestle not against flesh and blood, but against principalities, against powers, against the rulers of the darkness of this world, against spiritual wickedness in high places" (Eph. 6:12).

---

†6:12

A. Principalities—A possible reference to Satan's "generals" who have the oversight of entire nations (see Dan. 10).

B. Powers—May refer to his "troops" who possess human beings (see Mark 5: Matt. 17).

C. World rulers—Those demons in charge of Satan's worldly business.

D. Spiritual wickedness—Those demons in charge of worldly religion.

---

b. His cunning (Eph. 6:11)—"The wiles [schemes] of the devil."

---

†6:11 *Greek scholar Kenneth Wuest writes: "Wiles is* methodeia *in the Greek, referring to 'cunning arts, deceit, craft, trickery.' It means to follow up, or investigate by method and settled plan, to follow craftily, frame devices, deceive"* (Ephesians and Colossians, *p. 141). (See also 1 Tim. 3:7; 2 Cor. 2:11.)*

---

c. His cruel tactics (Eph. 6:16)—"The fiery darts [flaming missiles] of the wicked" (Eph. 6:16).

---

†6:16 *This is a reference to arrows tipped with tow, pitch, or such material, then set on fire before they are discharged. (See also 1 Pet. 1:7; 4:12.)*

---

2. Our endeavors—The game plan

a. We are to obey (Eph. 6:10)—"Finally, my brethren, be strong in the Lord, and in the power of his might" (Eph. 6:10).

b. We are to stand (Eph. 6:11, 14).

---

†6:14 *We are to* stand. *No less than four times does Paul exhort us to do this (vv. 11, 13-14). The believer is never told to attack the devil, but to withstand and resist him. (See 1 Pet. 5:8-9.) Thus, when tempted to do wrong, we should flee as did Joseph (Gen. 39:12); but when attacked by Satan* *for doing right, we should stand firm as did Daniel's three friends (Dan. 3). It has been observed that as pilgrims we walk, as witnesses we talk, as contenders we run, but as fighters we stand.*

---

c. We are to pray (Eph. 6:18)—"Praying always with all prayer and supplication in the Spirit"

---

†**6:18** *We are to* pray. *(See Matt. 17:21; Jude 20; 1 Tim. 2:8; 1 Thess. 5:17.)*

---

d. We are to watch (Eph. 6:18).

---

†*We are to* watch. *(See 1 Cor. 16:13; 2 Cor. 6:5; 11:27; Matt. 24:43; Luke 12:37-40; Acts 20:31; 1 Thess. 5:6; 1 Pet. 4:7; 2 Tim. 4:5; Rev. 3:2; 16:15.) We may thus conclude that both watching and praying are the divine twin secrets for overcoming:*
A. The world (see Mark 13:33)
B. The flesh (see Mark 14:38)
C. The devil (see Eph. 6:18)

---

e. We are to persevere (Eph. 6:18).
3. Our equipment—The armor of God. "Put on the whole armour of God, that ye may be able to stand against the wiles of the devil" (Eph. 6:11).
   a. The girdle of truth (Eph. 6:14)
   b. The breastplate of righteousness (Eph. 6:14)
   c. The sandals of the gospel (Eph. 6:15)
   d. The shield of faith (Eph. 6:16)
   e. The helmet of salvation (Eph. 6:17)
   f. The sword of the Spirit (Eph. 6:17)

---

†*Let us carefully note each piece of armor mentioned here. Paul very obviously takes those pieces of armor worn by the Roman soldier and makes spiritual application to each one.*
*A. The girdle of truth—*Expositors' Commentary *says: "First in the list of these articles of equipment mentioned is the girdle. Appropriately so; for the soldier might be furnished with every other part of his equipment, and yet, wanting his girdle, would be neither fully clothed nor securely armed. His belt was no mere adornment of the soldier, but an essential part of his equipment. Passing round the loins and by the end of the breastplate (in later times supporting the sword), it was of special use in keeping other parts in place, and in securing the proper soldierly attitude and freedom of movement." Truth, as mentioned here, probably refers to truthfulness as found in a Christian. Thus a believer whose life is tainted with deceit and falsehood forfeits the very thing which holds other pieces of his armor together.*
B. The breastplate of righteousness—This speaks of right acts as practiced by the believer. The breastplate was to protect the heart of the soldier. Thus, unrighteous acts committed by a Christian rob him of this vital protection and expose his spiritual heart to Satan. (See Heb. 10:22; 13:9; James 1:26; 4:8; 1 John 3:19-22.)
C. The sandals of the gospel—The Roman soldier wore sandals which were bound by thongs over the instep and around the ankle, and the soles were thickly studded with nails. This gave him a

firm footing in time of attack. This may refer to the assurance and confidence which comes from knowing the great doctrinal truths associated with the gospel. (See 1 Pet. 3:15; Eph. 4:14.)

D. The shield of faith—K. Wuest writes: "The word shield *used here designated the shield of the heavy infantry, a large, oblong one, four by two and one-half feet, sometimes curved on the inner side." Hebrews 11 is a commentary on this piece of armor.*

E. The helmet of salvation—The helmet, of course, protected the head and brain. This piece (like the sandals) may refer to the intake of Bible doctrine, lest one's eyes be blinded, his ears deafened, and his mind confused with the attacks from the world, the flesh, and the devil.

F. The sword of the Spirit—Here is the only offensive *weapon listed among the various pieces of armor. The rest are* defensive *in nature. The sword of the Spirit is identified as the Word of God. (See Heb. 4:12.) This, then, is the armor the Christian is commanded to wear. Kenneth Wuest writes concerning the command in 6:13, "Wherefore take unto you the whole armour of God": "'Take unto you' is* analambano, *meaning, 'to take up in order to use.' The verb is aorist imperative, which construction issues a command given with military snap and curtness, a command to be obeyed at once and once for all. Thus, the Christian is to take up and put on all the armor of God as a once-for-all act and keep that armor on during the entire course of his life, not relaxing the discipline necessary for the constant use of such protection. The historian Gibbon relates how the relaxation of discipline and disuse of exercise rendered soldiers less willing and less able to support the fatigue of service. They complained of the weight of armor, and obtained permission to lay aside much of it"* (Ephesians and Colossians, *p. 142).*

---

4. Our examples—Paul and Tychicus (Eph. 6:19-24)
   a. Paul, the chained ambassador (Eph. 6:19-20)—"And for me, that utterance may be given unto me, that I may open my mouth boldly, to make known the mystery of the gospel, for which I am an ambassador in bonds: that therein I may speak boldly, as I ought to speak" (Eph. 6:19-20).
   b. Tychicus, the coming ambassador (Eph. 6:21-22)—"But that ye also may know my affairs, and how I do, Tychicus, a beloved brother and faithful minister in the Lord, shall make known to you all things: whom I have sent unto you for the same purpose, that ye might know our affairs, and that he might comfort your hearts" (Eph. 6:21-22).

---

†6:22 *Dr. Homer Kent writes: "In closing this letter, Paul explains that he will be sending it by his messenger Tychicus, who was also the bearer of the epistles to Philemon and to the Colossians (Col. 4:7). It is most probable that all three letters were carried on the same trip. Tychicus was one of Paul's most trusted colleagues. He was from the province of Asia (Acts 20:4), and could have been from Ephesus, the capital. He had traveled with Paul on the third missionary journey and presumably accompanied him to Jerusalem with the collection. Now he was at Rome with the apostle, and would have the responsible task of delivering these important letters to their destinations, as well as conducting the runaway slave Onesimus safely to his master in Colosse. Years later he would be sent by Paul to Ephesus once again (2 Tim. 4:12). To call him a 'beloved brother' was to emphasize Paul's personal attachment to him. To describe him as a 'faithful minister' points to his trustworthy performance of spiritual responsibilities. 'In the Lord' belongs to both expressions and denotes the spiritual realm in which Paul and Tychicus find the basis for their association"* (Ephesians, the Glory of the Church, *p. 125).*

PHILIPPIANS

CAN IT BE? IS IT POSSIBLE TO OFFER UP PRAISE IN A PRISON AND TO WRITE OF JOY FROM A JAILHOUSE?

A. It is indeed, as demonstrated by the wonderful book of Philippians. The words of joy and rejoicing are found no less than 18 times in Philippians, more than any other biblical book for its size. The secret and source of this joy is Christ, which name in various forms appears some 70 times in this epistle.

B. The church at Philippi was founded as a result of a supernatural vision experienced by Paul while at Troas during his second missionary trip (see Acts 16:8-10).

C. It was apparently Paul's favorite church. During his brief stay there he and Silas saw God work marvelously in the lives of at least three individuals.
   1. An Asian businesswoman named Lydia whom God saved from Judaism (Acts 16:13-15)
   2. A Greek soothsayer whom God saved from demonism (Acts 16:16-18)
   3. A Roman jailer whom God saved from emperorism (the worship of Caesar, Acts 16:27-32)

D. Thus this church, conceived in a vision, would reach its apex in a prison. Strange and wonderful indeed are the ways of God.

E. For its size, Philippians speaks more about Christian unity than any other biblical book. (See 2:1-4; 3:15-17; 4:1-3.)

F. It also describes the second (of two) kinds of peace in the Bible.
   1. The peace *with* God, experienced by all believers (Rom. 5:1)
   2. The peace *of* God, experienced by Spirit-filled believers (Phil. 4:7)

G. This book contains the greatest passage on the humility and exaltation of Christ in the entire Word of God (see 2:5-11).

H. The city of Philippi was founded by Philip of Macedon (father of Alexander the Great) in 357 B.C., and named after him. It was some 700 miles from Rome and enjoyed full Roman citizenship privileges.

I. In A.D. 57, at the end of his third missionary trip (some five years after his first visit), Paul seems to have paid two brief visits to Philippi (see 2 Cor. 1:16; Acts 19:21; 20:1-3).

J. The year A.D. 62 finds the apostle a prisoner in Rome. Acts 28:30-31 indicates that he was confined to his own hired house, being chained to various Roman soldiers every six hours. Although he could not preach in public, he was allowed to write (Eph. 6:20; Phil. 1:7, 14, 16; Col. 4:18; Philem. 1, 10, 13).

K. It was therefore at this time, some ten years after his original visit to Philippi, that Paul wrote the epistle of Philippians to his favorite church.

L. This church, upon learning of his imprisonment in Rome, had sent a love offering by way of Epaphroditus. They had already sent him two other love gifts years back for his missionary endeavors in Thessalonica (Phil. 4:15-16).

M. While in Rome, Epaphroditus had become very ill and nearly died. But God spared his life. Paul thus writes Philippians both to thank them for their gift and also to report the good news of Epaphroditus's recovery.
N. Philippians is the 17th longest New Testament book, and 49th longest biblical book, with four chapters, 104 verses, and 2,002 words. There are quotations or allusions from nine Old Testament books in Philippians.
O. Great passages would include:
   1. 1:21-22
   2. 2:1-11
   3. 3:7-14
   4. 3:20-21
   5. 4:4-8
   6. 4:11-13

THE BOOK OF PHILIPPIANS

I. Christ Is Life's Purpose (Phil. 1)—"For to me to live is Christ, and to die is gain" (Phil. 1:21). The knowledge of this wonderful truth allowed Paul to accomplish three things.
   A. He could rest in God's security—"Being confident of this very thing, that he which hath begun a good work in you will perform it until the day of Jesus Christ" (Phil. 1:6).
      1. Paul's greetings to the saints (Phil. 1:1-2)—"Paul and Timotheus, the servants of Jesus Christ, to all the saints in Christ Jesus which are at Philippi, with the bishops and deacons: Grace be unto you, and peace, from God our Father, and from the Lord Jesus Christ" (Phil. 1:1-2).

---

†**1:2** *Dr. John Walvoord writes: "The mention of bishops and deacons indicates the advanced state of organization of the Church at Philippi now composed of mature and gifted believers from whom recognized leaders had come. As A. R. Fausset notes, 'This is the earliest epistle where bishops and deacons are mentioned, and the only one where they are separately addressed.' Of course, as early as Acts 6, men were appointed in the church to serve in a way similar to deacons. Although not called deacons, the prominence of this appointment of men to special service in Acts seems to recognize its significance. Elders were appointed in every church as early as Acts 14:23, and are mentioned in Acts 11:30; 20:27-28; 1 Thess. 5:12-13)"* (Philippians, Triumph in Christ, *p. 24).*

Greek scholar Kenneth Wuest writes in a similar manner: "The word bishop *is the translation of a Greek word used in secular pursuits of an overseer in any capacity, for instance, the official in charge of the repairing of a temple or an officer in an army. The word itself means 'to look upon.' Paul uses it as another name for an elder, the latter being the title of the office so far as statutes in the church are concerned, the former being the title that indicated the responsibility and activity of the office, that of overseeing the spiritual welfare of the local church. He brings the two names together as designating one individual in Acts 20:17, 28. The word* deacon *is the English spelling of a Greek word that was used as a general term to designate a servant. It covered both slaves and hired servants. It represented a servant, not in his relation to his master, but in his activity. The same word is translated 'minister' in 1 Corinthians 3:5; 2 Corinthians 3:6; Ephesians 3:7. Here it refers to a distinct class of officers in the apostolic church. The origin of the office is given us in Acts 6"* (Word Studies in Philippians, *p. 28).*

As a final note here, consider the comments of J. Dwight Pentecost: "The word 'deacon' comes from a compound Greek word that means 'to stir up the dust.' It presents the picture of one who is moving so rapidly through the dusty lanes of the villages of Palestine to discharge his duty that his feet kick up dust as he goes. There was so much for the deacons to do they could not loiter nor tarry. They went about their ministry with such diligence that they were stirring up the dust; thus those who were set apart to this ministry were called 'those who stir up the dust' or deacons" (The Joy of Living, *p. 114).*

---

2. Paul's thanksgiving for the saints (Phil. 1:3-8)—"I thank my God upon every remembrance of you, always in every prayer of mine for you all making request with joy, even as it is meet for me to think this of you all, because I have you in my heart; inasmuch as both in my bonds, and in the defence and confirmation of the gospel, ye all are partakers of my grace" (Phil. 1:3-4, 7).
3. Paul's prayer concerning the saints (Phil. 1:9-11)—"And this I pray, that your love may abound yet more and more in knowledge and in all judgment; that ye may approve things that are excellent; that ye may be sincere and without offence till the day of Christ; Being filled with the fruits of righteousness, which are by Jesus Christ, unto the glory and praise of God" (Phil. 1:9-11).

---

†1:11

A. *The word "approve" here means to place one's OK upon something after a period of testing. It was used by the Greeks to describe doctors who had passed their examinations. They were then certified physicians.*

B. *The "joy of Christ" phrase is no doubt a reference to the Rapture (1 Thess. 4:14-18; 1 Cor. 15:51-53; Heb. 9:24-28; Rev. 4:1).*

---

4. Paul's explanation to the saints (Phil. 1:12)—"But I would ye should understand, brethren, that the things which happened unto me have fallen out rather unto the furtherance of the gospel" (Phil. 1:12).

B. He could rejoice in great suffering (Phil. 1:13-20).

1. The cause of his fetters (Phil. 1:13)—"So that my imprisonment in the cause of Christ."
2. The circumference of his faith (Phil. 1:13)—"Has become well known throughout the whole praetorian guard and to everyone else" (Phil. 1:13, NASB). "All the saints salute you, chiefly they that are of Caesar's household" (Phil. 4:22).

---

†4:22 *John Walvoord writes: "Paul was guarded by imperial soldiers who were the cream of the Roman army, and the time of this writing was while he was in Rome, the center of the Roman government. Whether in Rome or elsewhere, however, according to the custom, the apostle was probably chained to a Roman soldier twenty-four hours a day, with a new guard every six hours. No doubt this was a most trying experience which subjected Paul to all the evil characteristics and whims of his guard even when he talked to his friends, when he prayed or when he attempted to write. Always there was this Roman guard. The circumstances, however, also afforded him the* *priceless opportunity of witness, and each guard heard Paul's story. The claims of the grace of God and the transformation it afforded in his life subjected him to the scrutiny of each guard to see whether his testimony was genuine. The slightest deviation, impatience, or irritation would disqualify his testimony to the guard, and any lack of consistency in life would soon be communicated to others. The apostle's sincerity and his glowing account of God's grace manifested to him apparently were effective as guard after guard came to know Jesus Christ in an effective way.*

"Only God knows what went on in the rented room in which Paul was permitted to live. There the guards heard the conversation of Paul with his intimate friends and were able to ask questions about the strange words which they heard from their prisoner. In the lonely hours of the dark night, illuminated only by the moon, many a guard probably heard the testimony of Paul—his early career as a Pharisee, his antagonism and persecution of Christians, his remarkable conversion, and the causes of his imprisonment. No doubt all this was the subject of much conversation in the praetorian guard, and raised sympathy among the soldiers as they understood his unjust imprisonment. His chains had become an effective line of communication to the elite soldiers of the Roman Empire who, if converted, could carry the gospel to the ends of the earth as they were moved from place to place. It reminds us that every circumstance of life is a platform on which the transforming grace of God can be manifested in the life of the Lord's own" (Philippians: Triumph in Christ, *pp. 37-38).*

---

3. The courage of his friends—"And many of the brethren in the Lord, waxing confident by my bonds, are much more bold to speak the word without fear" (Phil. 1:14).

---

†1:14 *Paul's imprisonment had apparently jolted some of his timid believer friends into a bolder approach in presenting the gospel. One possibility for this may have been the conversion of several elite Roman soldiers. Thus their testimony would doubtless have given new courage to those regular church members in Rome.*

---

4. The carnality of his foes
   a. Their rebellion—"Some indeed preach Christ even of envy and strife; and some also of good will: The one preach Christ of contention, not sincerely, supposing to add affliction to my bonds: but the other of love, knowing that I am set for the defence of the gospel" (Phil. 1:15-17).

---

†1:17 *The psalmist once wrote: "Surely the wrath of man shall praise thee" (Psa. 76:10). In other words, in spite of the impure and insincere motives of his enemies in proclaiming the gospel, Paul nevertheless rejoiced. The greatest problem of the world, then, as it is today, is not when the gospel is imperfectly preached, but when it is not preached at all.*

---

   b. His reaction—"What then? notwithstanding, every way, whether in pretence, or in truth, Christ is preached and I therein do rejoice, yea, and will rejoice" (Phil. 1:18).
5. The confidence in his future (Phil. 1:19)—"For I know that this shall turn out for my deliverance through your prayers and the provision of the Spirit of Jesus Christ" (Phil. 1:19, NASB).

†**1:19** *The King James Version speaks of the "supply of the Spirit of Jesus Christ." Warren Wiersbe writes: "The word* supply *gives us our English word* chorus. *Whenever a Greek city was going to put on a special festival, someone had to pay for the singers and dancers. The donation called had to be a lavish one, and so this word came to mean 'to provide generously and lavishly.' Paul was not depending upon his own dwindling resources; he was depending on the generous resources of God, ministered by the Holy Spirit"* (Be Joyful, *p. 36).*

C. He could remain in glad service (Phil. 1:21-30)—"For to me to live is Christ, and to die is gain" (Phil. 1:21).

1. God's will for the apostle—"According to my earnest expectation and my hope, that in nothing I shall be ashamed, but that with all boldness, as always, so now also Christ shall be magnified in my body, whether it be by life, or by death" (Phil. 1:20).

---

†**1:20** *Through Paul's body the Savior would be magnified. How can this be done? It has been observed that through the telescope a distant object can be brought near, and through the microscope a small object can be made big. Thus, by rightly applying these instruments in a spiritual way, the believer can, through his body, cause Christ to become both big and near in the eyes of watching saints and sinners alike.*

---

a. His desire was to depart and be with the Savior—"For I am in a strait betwixt two, having a desire to depart, and to be with Christ; which is far better" (Phil. 1:23).

---

†**1:23** *Note: Paul speaks of death as a departure (see also 2 Tim. 4:6). This word* depart *was used by:*
A. Soldiers, when they took down their tent and moved on.
B. Politicians, when they set a prisoner free.
C. Farmers, when they unyoked their oxen.

---

b. His decision was to remain and minister to the saints —"Nevertheless to abide in the flesh is more needful for you" (Phil. 1:24).

2. God's will for the Philippians (Phil. 1:27-30)—"Only let your conversation be as it becometh the gospel of Christ: that whether I come and see you, or else be absent, I may hear of your affairs, that ye stand fast in one spirit, with one mind striving together for the faith of the gospel. . . . For unto you it is given in the behalf of Christ, not only to believe on him, but also to suffer for his sake" (Phil. 1:27, 29).

II. Christ Is Life's Pattern (Phil. 2)—"Let this mind be in you, which was also in Christ Jesus" (Phil. 2:5). The pattern here to be copied by the saints incorporates the two beautiful Christian virtues of unity and humility.

A. The exhortation to these virtues (Phil. 2:1-4)

1. They are available (Phil. 2:1)—"Since therefore there is encouragement in Christ, since there is consolation of love, since there is fellowship of the Spirit [and] affection and compassion" (my personal translation).
2. They are attainable (Phil. 2:2-4)—"Fulfil ye my joy, that ye be likeminded,

having the same love, being of one accord, of one mind. Let nothing be done through strife or vainglory; but in lowliness of mind let each esteem other better than themselves. Look not every man on his own things, but every man also on the things of others" (Phil. 2:2-4).

---

†**2:4** *Plato defined "lowliness" as follows: "That state of mind which submits to the divine order of the universe, and does not impiously exalt itself." The word is used in a secular document of the Nile River at its low stage. How many tragic church splits would be avoided if only this principle was observed.*

B. The examples of these virtues (Phil. 2:5-30)
   1. The example of Christ—"Let this mind be in you, which was also in Christ Jesus: who, being in the form of God, thought it not robbery to be equal with God: but made himself of no reputation, and took upon him the form of a servant, and was made in the likeness of men: and being found in fashion as a man, he humbled himself, and became obedient unto death, even the death of the cross" (Phil. 2:5-8).

---

†**2:8** *Surely these verses rank among the greatest in all Scripture. What exactly did Christ do?*

A. *He left heaven's glory (John 17:5; 2 Cor. 8:9).*

B. *He made himself of no reputation. The Greek word here in 2:7 is* kenoo *and means "to empty." Just what did Christ empty himself of?*
   1. *Negative—He did* not *lay aside in any sense of the word his deity. He was, is, and ever shall be the total Son of God. (See John 1:1; 17:5; 2 Cor. 4:4; Col. 1:15; 2:9; Heb. 1:3.)*
   2. *Positive—He did, for awhile, hide his heavenly fame in an earthly frame. Even though he retained every single attribute of deity while on earth, He did, nevertheless, surrender to the Holy Spirit the independent exercise of those divine characteristics. (See Psa. 22:6; Isa. 53:3; Mark 9:12; Rom. 15:3.) Two phrases need to be examined at this point:*
      a. *"The form of God"—This does not mean that Christ had a physical shape prior to the incarnation. It refers to that inner, essential, and abiding nature of a person or thing.*
      b. *"Robbery to be equal with God"—That is, he did not hold or consider the outer manifestation of his deity in heaven as a treasure to be grasped and retained at all costs. Christ in his incarnation did not concern himself with retaining all this.*

C. *He was made in the likeness of human beings (John 1:14; Rom. 1:3; 8:3; Gal. 4:4; Heb. 2:14, 17). This simple but absolutely staggering fact cannot be even remotely grasped by human minds. The infinite holy Creator suddenly becomes in the likeness of his finite and sinful creatures (yet without sin). Who can comprehend such sacrifice? It is as if a mighty and magnificent earthly king would determine to lay aside for awhile his fantastic storehouse of wealth and, leaving behind an adoring and amazed court, take upon himself the body of a lowly ant. "The Son of man" was, by the way, our Lord's favorite name for himself while on earth.*

D. *He took upon himself the form of a servant. He did not come as a mighty human Caesar or some world-renowned human philosopher. Even this would have been a condescension of colossal proportions. He came, rather, as a lowly servant.*

E. *He humbled himself. That is, he submitted to authority (see 1 Pet. 2:21-24). He agreed to talk our language, to wear our clothes, to eat our food, to breathe our air, and to endure our vile and vicious treatment. Contrast his statement in the Garden with that of Lucifer's statement (Matt. 26:39, 42; Isa. 14:13-14).*

F. He became obedient unto death (Matt. 26:39; John 10:18; Heb. 5:8; 12:2).

G. He died on a cursed cross. He did not just die, but suffered the worst kind of death both physically and judicially (Gal. 3:13; Isa. 53; Psa. 22).

---

a. He gave up (for awhile) the glory of heaven.
b. He emptied himself (he refused to use his divine attributes in an independent way).
c. He was incarnated in the flesh.
d. He took the form of a servant.
e. He humbled himself.
f. He became obedient unto death.
g. He died on a cursed tree.

2. The example of the Father (Phil. 2:9-11)—"Wherefore God also hath highly exalted him, and given him a name which is above every name: that at the name of Jesus every knee should bow, of things in heaven, and things in earth, and things under the earth; and that every tongue should confess that Jesus Christ is Lord, to the glory of God the Father" (Phil. 2:9-11).

---

†2:11

A. He has been highly exalted by the Father himself (Isa. 52:13; John 17:1; Acts 2:33; Heb. 2:9).

B. He has been given a name (position and place of authority) above all other names (Eph. 1:20; Heb. 1:4).

C. He will be universally acknowledged as Lord of all.

1. The methods of this acknowledgment—By the bowing of the knee and the confession of the tongue.

2. The creatures of this acknowledgment

a. "Those in heaven"—The world of angels

b. "Those on earth"—The world of saints and sinners

c. "Those under the earth"—The world of demons. (See Rev. 5:13; 7:9-12; 14:6-7; Isa. 45:23; Rom. 10:9-10.) Note: To confess him in this life as Lord means salvation, but to wait until the next life will result in damnation. Thus, the supreme question is not when *a human being will do this, but rather* where.

---

3. The example of Paul (Phil. 2:12-18)

a. What the apostle had done—"Holding fast the Word of life, so that in the day of Christ I may have cause to glory because I did not run in vain nor toil in vain. But even if I am being poured out as a drink offering upon the sacrifice and service of your faith, I rejoice and share my joy with you all" (Phil. 2:16-17. NASB).

b. What the Philippians were to do (Phil. 2:12-15, 18)

(1) They were to work out their salvation—"Wherefore, my beloved, as ye have always obeyed, not as in my presence only, but now much more in my absence, work out your own salvation with fear and trembling. For it is God which worketh in you both to will and to do of his good pleasure. Do all things without murmurings and disputings" (Phil. 2:12-14).

†2:14

A. We note he did not *say, "Work for your own salvation." The idea here is to complete something. The Greeks used this phrase in bringing a math problem to its logical conclusion and also to work a gold mine in a field.*

B. It is thus not by imitation, but by incarnation (Gal. 2:20). The Christian life is not to be a series of ups and downs, but rather of ins and outs. God works in; *we are to work* out.

---

(2) They were to hold out their illumination—"That ye may be blameless and harmless, the sons of God, without rebuke, in the midst of a crooked and perverse nation, among whom ye shine as lights in the world" (Phil. 2:15).

---

†2:16 *Dr. J. Dwight Pentecost writes: "The apostle uses an interesting word when he says 'holding forth.' It has the idea of two travelers going through the night, one with a light and one without a light. The one extends his light on the other who is following, that light might fall on his footsteps . . . God has set you as a light. The word Paul translates 'light' is the word for* luminary. *It is the word for a light-giving heavenly body, a star if you please. This world is waiting for the sunrise of the Son of righteousness, but until he slips over the horizon to bring his light to this world again, there is a star to cast its light that men might not fall. You are a star to hold forth the word of life; therefore, do all things without murmuring and complaining"* (The Joy of Living, *pp. 101-102).*

---

4. The example of Timothy (Phil. 2:19-24)—"But I trust in the Lord Jesus to send Timotheus shortly unto you, that I also may be of good comfort, when I know your state" (Phil. 2:19).
   a. To the church he had served as a shepherd—"For I have no man likeminded, who will naturally care for your state" (Phil. 2:20).

---

†2:20 *Timothy had a long and intimate contact with this church. (See Acts 16:3; 17:14-15; 19:22; 20:3-4; Phil. 2:19-23.)*

---

   b. To the apostle, he had served as a son—"But ye know the proof of him, that, as a son with the father, he hath served with me in the gospel" (Phil. 2:22).
5. The example of Epaphroditus (Phil. 2:25-30)
   a. His service—"Yet I supposed it necessary to send to you Epaphroditus, my brother, and companion in labour, and fellow-soldier, but your messenger, and he that ministered to my wants" (Phil. 2:25).

---

†2:25

A. This man was a Gentile believer from Philippi. His name means "charming." He had been sent by the Philippian church to minister to Paul and bring him their offering.

B. Note the three titles here:

1. *"My brother"—Indicating they were bound by a common love*
2. *"My companion in labour"—Indicating they were bound by a common work*
3. *"My fellowsoldier"—Indicating they were bound by a common danger*

b. His sickness—"For indeed he was sick nigh unto death: but God had mercy on him; and not on him only, but on me also, lest I should have sorrow upon sorrow" (Phil. 2:27).
c. His sacrifice—"Because for the work of Christ he was nigh unto death, not regarding his life, to supply your lack of service toward me" (Phil. 2:30).

---

†2:30 *Warren Wiersbe aptly summarizes the life of this remarkable man. Wiersbe writes: "Epaphroditus was a balanced Christian! Balance is important in the Christian life. Some people emphasize 'fellowship' so much that they forget the* furtherance *of the Gospel. Others are so involved in defending the 'faith' of the Gospel that they neglect building* fellowship *with other believers. Epaphroditus did not fall into either of these traps. He was like Nehemiah, the man who rebuilt the walls of Jerusalem with his sword in one hand and his trowel in the other (Neh. 4:17). You cannot build with a sword nor battle with a trowel! It takes both to get the Lord's work accomplished. Dr. H. A. Ironside used to tell about a group of believers who thought only of 'fellowship.' They had little concern for reaching the lost or for defending the faith against its enemies. In front of their meeting place they hung a sign: 'JESUS ONLY.' But the wind blew away some of the letters, and the sign read 'US ONLY.' It was a perfect description of a group of people who were not balanced Christians"* (Be Joyful, *p. 76).*

III. Christ Is Life's Prize (Phil. 3)—"Brethren, I count not myself to have apprehended: but this one thing I do, forgetting those things which are behind, and reaching forth unto those things which are before" (Phil. 3:13).
  A. The corrupters of this prize (Phil. 3:1-3, 18-19)
    1. Who they were—The Judaizers. "Beware of the dogs, beware of the evil workers, beware of the false circumcision" (Phil. 3:2, NASB).
    2. What they were—"For many walk, of whom I have told you often, and now tell you even weeping, that they are the enemies of the cross of Christ" (Phil. 3:18).
    3. Where they were headed—"Whose end is destruction, whose God is their belly, and whose glory is in their shame, who mind earthly things" (Phil. 3:19).
  B. The cost of this prize—Becoming a Christian had cost Paul the many natural advantages of his background. "Though I might also have confidence in the flesh. If any other man thinketh that he hath whereof he might trust in the flesh, I more: circumcised the eighth day, of the stock of Israel, of the tribe of Benjamin, an Hebrew of the Hebrews; as touching the law, a Pharisee; concerning zeal, persecuting the church; touching the righteousness which is in the law, blameless" (Phil. 3:4-6).

---

†3:6 *Robert Lightner writes: "Circumcision was named first probably because it was a big issue with the Judaizers. Paul's specific time,* the eighth day, *stressed that he was not a proselyte or an Ishmaelite but a pure-blooded Jew. Proselytes were circumcised later in life and Ishmaelites after age 13 (cf. Gen. 17:25-26). Paul was of* the people of Israel, *which describes his heritage. His parents were both true Jews, unlike some of the Judaizers. He could trace his family lineage all the way back to Abraham. He was a true member of the covenant people (cf. 2 Cor. 11:22). He was also a Benjamite, from which tribe came Israel's first king (1 Sam. 9:1-2). This tribe had a special place of honor and was viewed with great esteem. Even after the kingdom was disrupted the tribe of*

Benjamin remained loyal to the house of David. Hebrew was Paul's native tongue. Unlike some of the Israelites, he did not adopt Greek customs. He knew thoroughly both the language and customs of the people of God. He was a Hebrew son of Hebrew parents. In regard to the Law, Paul was a Pharisee, *a member of the strictest sect among his people. In addition to the Law of Moses, the Pharisees added their own regulations which in time were interpreted as equal to the Law. What greater* zeal *for the Jewish religion could anyone boast of than that he persecuted* the church? *Paul did this relentlessly before his conversion to Christ (Acts 9:1-2). No Judaizer could match such zeal. "In 'legalistic righteousness' Paul also excelled. In fact in his own eyes he was faultless* (amemptos; *the same word is used in Phil. 2:15 where it is rendered 'blameless')"* (Bible Knowledge Commentary, *New Testament Volume, p. 660).*

C. The crown of this prize (Phil. 3:7-17, 20-21)
   1. He gained a new knowledge—"But what things were gain to me, those I counted loss for Christ. Yea doubtless, and I count all things but loss for the excellency of the knowledge of Christ Jesus my Lord: for whom I have suffered the loss of all things, and do count them but dung, that I may win Christ" (Phil. 3:7-8).

---

†**3:8** *Martyred missionary Jim Elliot once wrote: "He is no fool who gives up what he cannot keep to gain what he cannot lose" (See also Jer. 9:23; 1 Cor. 2:2.)*

---

   2. He gained a new righteousness—"And be found in him, not having mine own righteousness, which is of the law, but that which is through the faith of Christ, the righteousness which is of God by faith" (Phil. 3:9).
   3. He gained a new power—"That I may know him, and the power of his resurrection, and the fellowship of his sufferings, being made conformable unto his death" (Phil. 3:10).

---

†**3:10** *Far too many Christians are excited about the implications of the first half of this famous verse but show little interest in the last part. But it must be kept in mind that there is no power of the resurrection without the fellowship of the suffering. These go hand-in-hand. To know Christ in this manner has been the goal of all godly believers throughout history. See the following testimonies:*

A. Moses—Exodus 33:13
B. David—Psalm 42:1-2; 63:1-2
C. Philip—John 1:45 (see also Rom. 6:3-5; 8:17)

---

   4. He gained a new goal (Phil. 3:11-17)—"Brethren, I count not myself to have apprehended: but this one thing I do, forgetting those things which are behind, and reaching forth unto those things which are before, I press toward the mark for the prize of the high calling of God in Christ Jesus" (Phil. 3:13-14).

---

†**3:14**

A. John Walvoord writes: "He begins by saying, 'Not as though I had already attained, either were already perfect' (v. 12). The perfection he would have at the future resurrection was not yet attained, as he still had a sin nature, a sinful body, and was only too aware of the need for further spiritual progress. In stating that he was not already perfect, the apostle Paul used a Greek word, teleioo, *meaning 'to reach a goal or fulfill a purpose.' The Greek word is the root of the English word* teleology *which refers to the design or purpose of the universe. The same word is found in Luke 13:32; John 17:23; 1 Corinthians 2:6; 2 Corinthians 12:9; Ephesians 4:12, and many other passages"* (Philippians, Triumph in Christ, *pp. 90-91).*

B. Note especially Paul's statement in 3:13: "This one thing I do." For other biblical examples, see:
   1. Jesus and the rich young ruler (Mark 10:21)
   2. Martha and Jesus (Luke 10:42)
   3. An ex-blind man (John 9:25)
   4. The psalmist (Psa. 27:4). (See also James 1:8.)

C. Warren Wiersbe writes: "Consecration is the secret of power. If a river is allowed to overflow its banks, the area around it becomes a swamp. But if that river is dammed and controlled, it becomes a source of power" (Be Joyful, *p. 97).*

D. Concerning Paul's phrase, "reaching forth unto those things which are before," see 1 Corinthians 9:24, 26; 2 Timothy 4:7, 8; Hebrews 6:1; 12:1.

---

5. He gained a new role—"Brethren, be followers together of me, and mark them which walk so as ye have us for an ensample" (Phil. 3:17).
6. He gained a new hope—"For our conversation is in heaven; from whence also we look for the Saviour, the Lord Jesus Christ: who shall change our vile body, that it may be fashioned like unto his glorious body, according to the working whereby he is able even to subdue all things unto himself" (Phil. 3:20-21).

---

†3:21 *Paul was a citizen of Rome, but what he is saying here is "Our citizenship is in heaven." Or "We are a colony of heaven." What does that mean? It means that the believer, since he is a citizen of heaven, is to take his orders from up there. He is to obey the laws from heaven. Thus, just as Philippi was a colony of Rome on foreign soil, the church is a colony of heaven on earthly, foreign soil.*

IV. Christ Is Life's Power (Phil. 4)—"I can do all things through Christ which strengtheneth me" (Phil. 4:13).

A. This power can unify (Phil. 4:1-3)—"I beseech Euodias, and beseech Syntyche, that they be of the same mind in the Lord. And I intreat thee also, true yokefellow, help those women which laboured with me in the gospel, with Clement also, and with other my fellowlabourers, whose names are in the book of life" (Phil. 4:2-3).

B. The power can fortify—"Be careful for nothing; but in every thing by prayer and supplication with thanksgiving let your requests be made known unto God. And the peace of God, which passeth all understanding, shall keep your hearts and minds through Christ Jesus" (Phil. 4:6-7).

---

†4:7

A. Note the two golden rules concerning experiencing the peace of God here:
   1. "Be careful about nothing." The word careful *here means "to be pulled in different directions." Paul is not talking about concern here, but about panic. (See Psa. 55:22; 1 Pet. 5:7.)*

2. *Be prayerful about everything. Furthermore, our prayers should be both definite and devotional. It has been noted that there are but two areas over which the Christian is not to worry:*
   a. *Those things which he himself can change. Here* perspiration *is the answer.*
   b. *Those things which he himself cannot change. Here* supplication *is the answer.*

B. *The word* keep *here was often used to describe someone or something which was carefully guarded by the elite Roman soldiers of Caesar's palace. All Christians enjoy the peace* with God *mentioned in Romans 5:1, but only those who have successfully substituted care for prayer can enjoy the peace* of God *which truly passes understanding. Thus we see that this peace guards:*
   1. *Our hearts, protecting us from wrong feelings.*
   2. *Our minds, protecting us from wrong thinking.*

C. *We should observe here that the familiar sign "Prayer changes things" is* not *always true. But prayer does change* us, *by protecting against those matters which were driving us to despair. (See Isa. 26:3; Psa. 119:165; 2 Cor. 10:5.) This, then, is God's marvelous method for keeping peace.*

C. This power can purify—"Finally, brethren, whatsoever things are true, whatsoever things are honest, whatsoever things are just, whatsoever things are pure, whatsoever things are lovely, whatsoever things are of good report; if there be any virtue, and if there be any praise, think on these things" (Phil. 4:8).

D. This power can exemplify—"Those things, which ye have both learned, and received, and heard, and seen in me, do: and the God of peace shall be with you" (Phil. 4:9).

E. This power can satisfy (Phil. 4:10-13)—"Not that I speak in respect of want: for I have learned, in whatsoever state I am, therewith to be content. I know both how to be abased, and I know how to abound: every where and in all things I am instructed both to be full and to be hungry, both to abound and to suffer need" (Phil. 4:11-12).

---

†**4:12** *Paul had learned in all of his circumstances "therewith to be content." It should be added, however, that contentment is* not *complacency; it is containment. The abiding Christ within Paul's body assured him of this satisfaction. Note the two kinds of Christians:*

A. *The thermometer believer—His satisfaction is totally dependent upon outside circumstances. He simply registers the prevailing spiritual temperature.*

B. *The thermostat believer. His satisfaction is totally independent of the outside circumstances. He is not only affected by it, but actually controls that area surrounding him.*

F. This power can ratify—"Now ye Philippians know also, that in the beginning of the gospel, when I departed from Macedonia, no church communicated with me as concerning giving and receiving, but ye only. For even in Thessalonica ye sent once and again unto my necessity" (Phil. 4:15-16).

G. This power can sanctify—"But I have all, and abound: I am full, having received of Epaphroditus the things which were sent from you, an odour of a sweet smell, a sacrifice acceptable, wellpleasing to God" (Phil. 4:18).

H. This power can multiply—"But my God shall supply all your need according to his riches in glory by Christ Jesus" (Phil. 4:19).

I. This power can glorify—"Now unto God and our Father be glory for ever and ever. Amen" (Phil. 4:20).

COLOSSIANS

THE PREEMINENCE OF THE PREEMINENT ONE
THE GLORIES OF THE GLORIOUS ONE.

A. The book of Colossians is the most Christocentric book in the Bible. The greatest passage on the preexistent, omnipotent, exalted and eternal Son of God is found in Colossians. (See 1:15-19.)

B. Colossians in a sense concludes that which Ephesians introduces. In Ephesians Paul dwells upon the body of the church, while in Colossians he writes of the head of that body. Because of this, both books are somewhat similar. For example, 78 out of the 95 verses in Colossians are nearly identical to those in Ephesians.

C. It has been said that Colossians is to Ephesians what Galatians is to Romans.

D. This book provides one of two New Testament commands for the church epistles to be exchanged and read before the various local assemblies (compare Col. 4:16 with 1 Thess. 5:27).

E. Colossians is one of the epistles Paul wrote during his first Roman imprisonment. The others are Ephesians, Philippians, and Philemon.

F. The church at Colosse was probably started during Paul's third missionary journey. Although he personally never visited the city (see Col. 2:1), he did spend two years teaching the Word of God in Ephesus at the house of Tyrannus (see Acts 19:9-10). Colosse was only 90 miles east of Ephesus. It is therefore suggested that one of his students during this time was a man from Colosse named Epaphras. After graduating from the two-year T.B.I. (Tyrannus Bible Institute), Ephaphras may have gone back to evangelize the entire Lycus Valley. This valley, some ten miles long, contained three important cities: Laodicea, Hierapolis, and Colosse. Laodicea was only 12 miles from Colosse.

G. It is therefore possible that Paul's zealous young student started both the church in Colosse and the one in Laodicea. (See also Col. 4:16 and Rev. 3:14-22.)

H. The Colossian church was composed mainly of Gentile membership (see Col. 2:13).

I. Paul intended to visit it upon his release from prison (Philem. 22).

J. The church in Colosse may have met in the home of Philemon, for he lived at Colosse with one of his slaves, Onesimus (Col. 4:9 and the book of Philemon). Some time after its beginning, the church at Colosse was infected by a deadly virus known as Judaistic Gnosticism. This represented the worst of both the Jewish and Greek world of thought. The "J-G virus" consisted of the following:
   1. Salvation could be obtained only through knowledge. This meant only those with superior intellects could hope to achieve salvation. Faith (belief without materialistic proof) was silly and useless.
   2. Matter itself was evil. The J-G virus taught that the world was created by a series of angelic emanations. In other words, God (the original source) created an angel who in turn created another angel, who created yet a third, etc. Finally, the last of these angels created the world as we know it today.
   3. While this philosophy admitted to the *transcendence* of God (that he is above

everything), it denied his *immanence* (that he is also in everything). This view immediately ruled out the incarnation of Christ, special divine creation, prayer, faith, miracles, the second coming, and the accuracy of the Bible.

4. The goal of human life was either morbid *asceticism* (avoiding all joys of life, and abusing the body for the spirit's sake) or that of unrestrained *licentiousness* (if it feels good, do it). The first was known as Stoicism, and the second view Epicureanism. Scofield once observed: "Pure Christianity lives between two dangers ever present: the danger that it will evaporate into a philosophy . . . and the danger that it will freeze into a form."
5. In conclusion, it may be said that the J-G virus error included dietary and Sabbath observations, circumcision rites, worship of angels, and the practice of asceticism. (See Col. 2:11, 16; 2:18; 2:21-23.)

K. Epaphras was apparently unable to deal properly with this vicious strain and thus makes the dangerous and wearisome thousand-mile trip from Colosse to Rome to seek Paul's advice.

L. When he left Colosse, Archippus assumed the pastorate (Col. 4:17). Archippus may have been the son of Philemon (Philem. 2).

M. Upon reaching Rome and informing Paul, Epaphras was evidently also imprisoned (Philem. 23). This was doubtless because of bold preaching.

N. Paul writes the Colossian epistle to deal with the disease and sends it back by one of his trusted top lieutenants named Tychicus (Col. 4:7; cf. Acts 20:4; Eph. 6:21; 2 Tim. 4:12; Titus 3:12).

O. Colossians may be contrasted to other Pauline epistles. Thus:

1. In Romans we are *justified* in Christ.
2. In 1 Corinthians we are *enriched* in Christ.
3. In 2 Corinthians we are *comforted* in Christ.
4. In Galatians we are *free* in Christ.
5. In Ephesians we are *quickened* in Christ.
6. In Philippians we are *happy* in Christ.
7. In Colossians we are *complete* in Christ.

P. This book thus presents the glorious culmination of it all. We are complete in Christ. This completeness is fourfold:

1. Building *downward*—"Grounded and settled and . . . not moved away from the hope of the gospel" (1:23). This is the *deeper* life.
2. Building *upward*—"Built up in him, and stablished in the faith" (2:7). This is the *higher* life.
3. Building *inward*—"For ye are dead, and your life is hid with Christ in God" (3:3). This is the *inner* life.
4. Building *outward*—"Walk with wisdom toward them that are without, redeeming the time" (4:5). This is the *outer* life.

Q. Colossians is the 18th longest New Testament book, and 50th longest biblical book, with four chapters, 95 verses, and 1,998 words. There are quotations or allusions from seven Old Testament books in Colossians.

R. Great passages would include:

1. 1:10-20
2. 2:14-15
3. 3:12-17
4. 3:18-23

THE BOOK OF COLOSSIANS

"Paul, an apostle of Jesus Christ by the will of God, and Timotheus our brother, to the saints and faithful brethren in Christ which are at Colosse: Grace be unto you, and peace, from God our Father and the Lord Jesus Christ" (Col. 1:1-2).

I. The Deity and Preeminence of the Savior (Col. 1)
  A. The thanksgiving for this divine preeminence
    1. It was the source of Paul's praying (Col. 1:3-14)
      a. He thanks the Father for the witness of the Colossians —"We give thanks to God and the Father of our Lord Jesus Christ, praying always for you, since we heard of your faith in Christ Jesus, and of the love which ye have to all the saints. . . . Giving thanks unto the Father, which hath made us meet to be partakers of the inheritance of the saints in light: who hath delivered us from the power of darkness, and hath translated us into the kingdom of his dear Son: in whom we have redemption through his blood, even the forgiveness of sins" (Col. 1:3-4, 12-14).
      b. He prays to the Father for the walk of the Colossians —"For this cause we also, since the day we heard it, do not cease to pray for you, and to desire that ye might be filled with the knowledge of his will in all wisdom and spiritual understanding; that ye might walk worthy of the Lord unto all pleasing, being fruitful in every good work, and increasing in the knowledge of God; strengthened with all might, according to his glorious power, unto all patience and longsuffering with joyfulness" (Col. 1:9-11).
    2. It was the source of Paul's preaching—"Whereof I am made a minister, according to the dispensation of God which is given to me for you, to fulfil the word of God; even the mystery which hath been hid from ages and from generations, but now is made manifest to his saints: to whom God would make known what is the riches of the glory of this mystery among the Gentiles; which is Christ in you, the hope of glory" (Col. 1:25-27).

---

†1:27 *Paul speaks of "this mystery among the Gentiles." A biblical mystery is simply a sacred secret previously kept from people in the Old Testament. There are 11 such mysteries. Paul writes of eight of these; Matthew describes one; and John the apostle lists two. Out of the eight Pauline mysteries, no less than three are found here in Colossians. These are:*
  A. The mystery that the body of Christ (the church) is to be composed of both saved Jews and Gentiles (Col. 4:3; see also Rom. 16:25; Eph. 3:1-12; 6:19).
  B. The mystery of the indwelling Christ (Col. 1:27; see also Gal. 2:20).
  C. The mystery of the incarnation of Christ (Col. 2:2, 9; see also 1 Cor. 2:7).

---

    3. It was the source of Paul's persecution—"But part of my work is to suffer for you; and I am glad, for I am helping to finish up the remainder of Christ's sufferings for his body, the church" (Col. 1:24, TLB).

---

†1:24 *Norman Geisler writes: "By this he did not mean that Christ's suffering on the cross was insufficient (cf. Rom. 3:21-26; Heb. 10:10-14). He was speaking not of salvation but of service.*

Christ's suffering alone procures salvation (1 Pet. 1:11; 5:1; Heb. 2:9). But it is a believer's privilege to suffer for Christ (2 Tim. 3:11; 1 Pet. 3:13-14; 5:9; Heb. 10:32). The word 'affliction' (thlipsis)*—never used in the New Testament of Christ's death—means 'distress,' 'pressure,' or 'trouble' (which Paul had plenty of; 2 Cor. 11:23-29). Ordinarily it refers to trials in life, not the pains of death. Christ does indeed continue to suffer when Christians suffer for Him. He asked Saul (later called Paul) on the Damascus Road, "Why do you persecute Me?" (Acts 9:4). Since the church is Christ's body, He is affected when it is affected. For the sake of Christ's body Paul willingly suffered (Phil. 1:29)."* (Bible Knowledge Commentary, *New Testament Volume, p. 675).*

B. The theology of this divine preeminence
   1. Christ's relationship to the Father—"Who is the image of the invisible God, the firstborn of every creature. . . . For it pleased the Father that in him should all fulness dwell" (Col. 1:15, 19).

---

†1:19

A. *The word "image" here is used to express likeness, and refers to the visible manifestation of something invisible. Christ is not* similar *to God—he is God.*

B. *The word "firstborn" is* prototokos, *a reference to the highest priority of position. It does not speak of time, but of title. Christ is thus ascribed as Lord of all creation. (See Psa. 89:27.) Norman Geisler observes:* "First, *Christ* is the image of the invisible God. *Besides the obvious meaning of likeness (cf. 2 Cor. 4:4), 'image' implies representation and manifestation. Like the head of a sovereign imprinted on a coin, so Christ is 'the exact representation of [the Father's] being' (Heb. 1:3). As Jesus said, 'Anyone who has seen Me has seen the Father' (John 14:9). Anyone who saw Christ, the visible manifestation of the invisible God, has thereby 'seen' God indirectly. For 'no one has ever seen God, but God the only Son . . . has made Him known' (John 1:18). Paul wrote of the 'invisible' God (1 Tim. 1:17), but Christ is the perfect visible representation and manifestation of that God.* Second, *Christ's supremacy is shown in His relationship to Creation. He is the* Firstborn over all Creation. *Though it is grammatically possible to translate this as 'Firstborn in Creation,' the context makes this impossible for five reasons: (1) The whole point of the passage (and the book) is to show Christ's superiority* over all things. *(2) Other statements about Christ in this passage (such as Creator of all [1:16], upholder of Creation [v. 17], etc.) clearly indicate His priority and superiority over Creation. (3) The 'Firstborn' cannot be part of Creation if He created 'all things.' One cannot create himself. (Jehovah's Witnesses wrongly add the word 'other' six times in this passage in their* New World Translation. *Thus they suggest that Christ created all other things after He was created! But the word 'other' is not in the Greek). (4) The 'Firstborn' received worship of all the angels (Heb. 1:6), but creatures should not be worshiped (Exod. 20:4-5). (5) The Greek word for 'Firstborn' is* prototokos. *If Christ were the 'first-created,' the Greek word would have been* protoktisis" (Bible Knowledge Commentary, *New Testament Volume, 672-673).*

---

   2. Christ's relationship to the Church—"And he is the head of the body, the church: who is the beginning, the firstborn from the dead; that in all things he might have the preeminence" (Col. 1:18).

†1:18

A. How can it be said that Christ was the firstborn from the dead when he himself had, before his own resurrection, brought back three individuals from the grave? These were:

1. The son of a widow at Nain (Luke 7:11-15)

2. Jairus's daughter (Luke 8:41-42, 49-56)

3. Lazarus (John 11:43)

B. The answer is both simple and thrilling. Jesus is the firstborn from the dead because:

1. His resurrected body was a new body, not subjected to the laws of sin, time, or gravity.

2. His resurrected body was a permanent body, never to die again, as the three that were raised had to do.

---

3. Christ's relationship to the universe
   a. He was its Creator—"For by him were all things created, that are in heaven, and that are in earth, visible and invisible, whether they be thrones, or dominions, or principalities, or powers: all things were created by him, and for him" (Col. 1:16).
   b. He is its sustainer—"And he is before all things, and by him all things consist" (Col. 1:17).
   c. He shall be its reconciler—"And, having made peace through the blood of his cross, by him to reconcile all things unto himself; by him, I say, whether they be things in earth, or things in heaven. And you, that were sometime alienated and enemies in your mind by wicked works, yet now hath he reconciled in the body of his flesh through death, to present you holy and unblameable and unreproveable in his sight" (Col. 1:20-22).

---

†1:22 *In relationship to the universe, Christ was its past Creator (1:16). He is its present Sustainer (1:17). He shall be its future reconciler (1:20-22). Note:*

A. The nature of this reconciliation—Simply stated, it refers to the bringing about into a right relationship with the Father all those things within this sinful universe. This does not mean, of course, that all people (or any fallen angel) will be eventually saved. It does mean, however, that the glorious truth of Romans 8:28 will someday be totally realized.

B. The time of this reconciliation—It began at the cross, but will be concluded with the sound of the seventh trumpet (see Rev. 11:15).

II. The Danger and Perversion of the Serpent (Col. 2)
   A. The nature of these perversions
      1. Enticing words (persuasive argument)—Verse 4

---

†2:4 *This perversion would doubtless correspond favorably to the liberalism of the 20th century, which has promised so much but produced so little.*

---

2. Philosophy (Col. 2:8)

---

†2:8a *False philosophy is like a blind man looking in a dark room for a black cat that isn't there. It can* *also be described as that science of learning more and more about less and less until finally you know everything about nothing.*

---

3. Vain deceit (empty deception)—(Col. 2:8)
4. Human tradition (Col. 2:8)

---

†2:8c *All traditions, of course, are not bad; but many are. Jesus soundly and severely denounced the wicked traditions of the godless Pharisees. (See Matt. 15:1-9.)*

---

5. Worldly doctrines—"Since you died with Christ to the basic principles of this world, why as though you still belonged to it, do you submit to its rules: Do not handle! Do not taste! Do not touch! These are all destined to perish with use, because they are based on human commands and teachings" (Col. 2:20-22, NIV).
6. Legalism—"Let no man therefore judge you in meat, or in drink, or in respect of an holyday, or of the new moon, or of the sabbath days" (Col. 2:16). "These are a shadow of the things that were to come; the reality, however, is found in Christ" (Col. 2:17, NIV).

---

†2:17 *A believer who puts himself back under legalism would be like a son admiring the photo of his father, but ignoring the father's actual presence.*

---

7. Self-abasement (Col. 2:18, 23)
8. Worship of angels (Col. 2:18)
9. Receiving visions (Col. 2:18)
10. Self-made religion (Col. 2:23)

B. The answer to these perversions
   1. Know who Jesus is—"In whom are hid all the treasures of wisdom and knowledge. . . . For in him dwelleth all the fulness of the Godhead bodily" (Col. 2:3, 9).
   2. Know what he has done for you—"For I would that ye knew what great conflict I have for you, and for them at Laodicea, and for as many as have not seen my face in the flesh; that their hearts might be comforted, being knit together in love, and unto all riches of the full assurance of understanding, to the acknowledgement of the mystery of God, and of the Father, and of Christ" (Col. 2:1-2).
      a. The quickening—"And you, being dead in your sins and the uncircumcision of your flesh, hath he quickened together with him, having forgiven you all trespasses" (Col. 2:13).
      b. The blotting—"Blotting out the handwriting of ordinances that was against us, which was contrary to us, and took it out of the way, nailing it to his cross" (Col. 2:14).

---

†2:14

A. To expound upon the theological blessings of this verse, consider a statement found in Genesis 2:19: "Adam called every living creature . . . the name thereof" (Gen. 2:19b). Adam must have had a tremendous vocabulary. Ernest Mayr, America's leading taxonomist, lists the species existing today—3,500 mammals, 8,600 birds, and 5,500 reptiles and amphibians. In spite of all this, there were seven simple words unknown and unexperienced by Adam prior to his fall. These words were:

1. *Death (Gen. 2:17)*
2. *Nakedness (3:7)*
3. *Cursed (3:14)*
4. *Sorrow (3:17)*
5. *Thorns (3:18)*
6. *Sweat (3:19)*
7. *Sword (3:24)*

B. *After the fall, Adam soon added these bitter and bloody words to his vocabulary. The echo of these wicked words haunted Adam and mankind for over 40 centuries. Then came the second Adam (a name for Jesus).*

C. *The New Testament tells us how he met and dealt with each word.*

1. *Death (John 11:25)*
2. *Nakedness (John 19:23)*
3. *Cursed (Gal. 3:13)*
4. *Sorrow (John 12:27)*
5. *Thorns (John 19:5)*
6. *Sweat (Luke 22:44)*
7. *Sword (John 19:34)*

D. *As a result of this, Paul literally shouts out the truth here in Colossians 2:14 that these terrible works of condemnation have forever been blotted out.*

---

c. The spoiling—"And having spoiled principalities and powers, he made a shew of them openly, triumphing over them in it" (Col. 2:15).

d. The nourishing—"The Head, from whom the entire body, being supplied and held together by the joints and ligaments, grows with a growth which is from God" (Col. 2:19, NASB).

3. Know who you are—"And ye are complete in him, which is the head of all principality and power: buried with him in baptism, wherein also ye are risen with him through the faith of the operation of God, who hath raised him from the dead" (Col. 2:10, 12).

4. Know what you are to do for him—"As ye have therefore received Christ Jesus the Lord, so walk ye in him: rooted and built up in him, and stablished in the faith, as ye have been taught, abounding therein with thanksgiving" (Col. 2:6-7).

III. The Duty and Performance of the Saints (Col. 3–4)

A. In relation to the Son of God (Col. 3:1-4)—"If ye then be risen with Christ, seek those things which are above, where Christ sitteth on the right hand of God. Set your affection on things above, not on things on the earth. For ye are dead, and your life is hid with Christ in God. When Christ, who is our life, shall appear, then shall ye also appear with him in glory" (Col. 3:1-4).

---

†3:4 *Note two phrases in these verses:*

A. *"Christ sitteth on the right hand of God" (v. 1b). This is but one of at least 13 references which*

speak of Christ being seated at God's right hand. The other instances are, as described by:
1. *Jesus himself (Luke 22:69)*
2. *Peter (Acts 2:33; 5:31; 1 Pet. 3:22)*
3. *Stephen (Acts 7:35)*
4. *Paul (Rom. 8:34; Eph. 1:20)*
5. *Author of Hebrews (1:3, 13; 8:1; 10:12; 12:2)*

B. *"Set your affection on things above, not on things on the earth" (Col. 3:2).*
1. Objection—*"But isn't it possible for a Christian to be so heavenly minded that he is no earthly good?"*
2. Observation—*For every one believer so heavenly minded he's no earthly good there are doubtless ten believers so earthly minded that they are no heavenly good. A child of God functions both as a temporary pilgrim (down here) and a permanent citizen (up there). His pilgrimage thus should be governed by his citizenship.*

B. In relation to the Word of God (Col. 3:16)—"Let the word of Christ dwell in you richly in all wisdom; teaching and admonishing one another in psalms and hymns and spiritual songs, singing with grace in your hearts to the Lord" (Col. 3:16).

---

†3:16 *Colossians 3:16 is as vital to the sanctification of a saint as John 3:16 is to the justification of a sinner.*

C. In relation to the work of God (Col. 3:17)—"And whatsoever ye do in word or deed, do all in the name of the Lord Jesus, giving thanks to God and the Father by him" (Col. 3:17).
1. What to put off (Col. 3:5-9)—"Mortify therefore your members which are upon the earth; fornication, uncleanness, inordinate affection, evil concupiscence, and covetousness, which is idolatry: for which things' sake the wrath of God cometh on the children of disobedience: in the which ye also walked some time, when ye lived in them. But now ye also put off all these; anger, wrath, malice, blasphemy, filthy communication out of your mouth. Lie not one to another, seeing that ye have put off the old man with his deeds" (Col. 3:5-9).
2. What to put on (Col. 3:10-12, 14)—"And have put on the new man, which is renewed in knowledge after the image of him that created him. . . . Put on therefore, as the elect of God, holy and beloved, bowels of mercies, kindness, humbleness of mind, meekness, longsuffering. . . . And above all these things put on charity, which is the bond of perfectness" (Col. 3:10, 12, 14).

D. In relation to our talks with God (Col. 4:2-4)
1. Paul's command to pray—"Continue in prayer, and watch in the same with thanksgiving" (Col. 4:2).
2. Paul's request for prayer—"Withal praying also for us, that God would open unto us a door of utterance, to speak the mystery of Christ, for which I am also in bonds: that I may make it manifest, as I ought to speak. . . . The salutation by the hand of me Paul. Remember my bonds. Grace be with you. Amen" (Col. 4:3-4, 18).

E. In relation to our testimony for God
1. Before the unsaved (Col. 4:5-6)—"Walk in wisdom toward them that are

without, redeeming the time. Let your speech be alway with grace, seasoned with salt, that ye may know how ye ought to answer every man" (Col. 4:5-6).

2. In the home (Col. 3:18-21)
   a. Concerning wives—"Wives, submit yourselves unto your own husbands, as it is fit in the Lord" (Col. 3:18).
   b. Concerning husbands—"Husbands, love your wives, and be not bitter against them" (Col. 3:19).
   c. Concerning children—"Children, obey your parents in all things: for this is well pleasing unto the Lord" (Col. 3:20).
   d. Concerning fathers—"Fathers, provoke not your children to anger, lest they be discouraged" (Col. 3:21).
3. On the job (Col. 3:22-25)
   a. Advice to servants—"Servants, obey in all things your masters according to the flesh; not with eyeservice, as menpleasers; but in singleness of heart, fearing God: and whatsoever ye do, do it heartily, as to the Lord, and not unto men; knowing that of the Lord ye shall receive the reward of the inheritance: for ye serve the Lord Christ" (Col. 3:22-24).
   b. Advice to masters—"Masters, give unto your servants that which is just and equal; knowing that ye also have a Master in heaven" (Col. 4:1).
4. In the church (Col. 3:13)—"Forbearing one another, and forgiving one another, if any man have a quarrel against any: even as Christ forgave you, so also do ye" (Col. 3:13).

F. In relation to the ministers of God (Col. 4:7-18)—Paul ends this epistle by sending greetings from eight men and by making a request.
   1. His greetings to the Colossians

A. *Tychicus—The carrier of the Colossian epistle*
B. *Onesimus—The once runaway slave of Philemon*
C. *Aristarchus—A fellow prisoner with Paul at this time*
D. *John Mark—The author of Mark's Gospel*
E. *Justus—Nothing known about him except that he was a coworker with Paul*
F. *Epaphras—The imprisoned Colosse pastor*
G. *Luke—Paul's beloved Greek physician and the author of Luke's Gospel and the book of Acts*
H. *Demas—A coworker who would eventually forsake Paul (2 Tim. 4:10)*
I. *Archippus—The Colossian believer who assumed Epaphras's place as pastor during Paul's imprisonment*

---

   2. His request of the Colossians—"And when this epistle is read among you, cause that it be read also in the church of the Laodiceans; and that ye likewise read the epistle from Laodicea" (Col. 4:16).

1 THESSALONIANS

REPEATED RAPTURE REMINDERS

A. No other biblical book, regardless of its size, gives as much space to the Rapture as does 1 Thessalonians. This glorious event is referred to in each of its five chapters. (See 1:10; 2:19; 3:13; 4:13-18; 5:1-11, 23.) The passage in 4:13-18 is the most detailed single account of the Rapture in the Bible.

B. The church at Thessalonica was founded by Paul during his second missionary journey. (See Acts 17:1-10.) Of the many churches established by the apostle, only a few (six to be exact) would receive a New Testament epistle from Paul. Of the six, only the church at Corinth and the one in Thessalonica were blessed with two inspired letters.

C. Paul was hindered by Satan when he later attempted to visit this city (1 Thess. 2:18).

D. Paul spent at least three weeks in Thessalonica in the home of Jason (possibly a kinsman, see Rom. 16:21) organizing the church, working all the while as a tentmaker, that he might not be a burden to the believers. (See 1 Thess. 2:9; 2 Thess. 3:7-12.)

E. His visit there is short-lived, for the gospel is opposed by some unbelieving Jews. Thus, under cover of night, Paul, Timothy, and Silas leave for Berea.

F. He soon is driven from Berea by the same vicious Jews and heads for Athens. Timothy and Silas remain in Berea.

G. While in Athens he sends word to Timothy requesting that his young helper go back and strengthen the work at Thessalonica, which command Timothy obeys (1 Thess. 3:1-2).

H. From Athens, Paul goes to Corinth. Here at a later date both Silas and Timothy catch up with him. Timothy brings a good report concerning the work in Thessalonica. Paul is overjoyed and writes both 1 and 2 Thessalonians from Corinth at this time.

I. His first letter was written to encourage, establish, instruct, and inspire. The church was apparently composed of a great many Gentiles (Acts 17:4).

J. Henrietta Mears writes: "Paul's success in Thessalonica has not been the usual experience of missionaries among the heathen. Carey in India, Judson in Burma, Morrison in China, and Moffat in Africa waited each seven years for his first convert. But here, the Holy Spirit allowed Paul to reap a sudden harvest" *(What the Bible Is All About*, p. 532).

K. The church was noted for its soul-winning zeal (1 Thess. 1:8).

L. The members were not, however, good Bible students (Acts 17:11).

M. There were difficulties in the congregation.
   1. Some were lazy (2 Thess. 3:10).
   2. Some were busybodies (2 Thess. 3:11).
   3. Some were disobedient (2 Thess. 3:14-15).

N. The book of 1 Thessalonians is the 19th longest New Testament book and 51st longest biblical book, with five chapters, 89 verses, and 1857 words. There are quotations or allusions from eight Old Testament books in 1 Thessalonians.

O. Great passages would include:
   1. 3:12-13
   2. 4:3-4
   3. 4:13-18
   4. 5:16-24

THE BOOK OF 1 THESSALONIANS

"Paul, and Silvanus, and Timotheus, unto the church of the Thessalonians which is in God the Father and in the Lord Jesus Christ: Grace be unto you, and peace, from God our Father, and the Lord Jesus Christ. We give thanks to God always for you all, making mention of you in our prayers. . . . I charge you by the Lord that this epistle be read unto all the holy brethren" (1 Thess. 1:1-2; 5:27).

I. The Reputation of the Church (1 Thess. 1)
   A. It was an energetic church—"Remembering without ceasing your work of faith, and labour of love, and patience of hope in our Lord Jesus Christ, in the sight of God and our Father" (1 Thess. 1:3).

---

†1:3 *The New Scofield Bible observes: "Even though Paul had ministered in Thessalonica for less than a month, many great doctrines of the Christian faith are alluded to in this Epistle: the Trinity (cf. 1:1 with 1:5-6); the Holy Spirit (1:5-6; 4:8; 5:19); Christ's second advent (1:10; 2:19; 3:13; 4:14-17; 5:23); the Day of the Lord (5:1-3); assurance (1:5); conversion (1:9); election (1:4); resurrection (4:14-18); sanctification (4:3; 5:23); and Christian behavior (2:12; 4:1)"* (New Scofield Reference Bible, *p. 1290).*

   B. It was an elect church (1 Thess. 1:4)—"Knowing, brethren beloved, your election of God" (1 Thess. 1:4).

---

†1:4

A. Election is both individual and corporate. It covers both Christian and congregation. The latter is in view here. C. H. Spurgeon was once asked how he reconciled God's election with man's choice. He answered, "I never have to reconcile friends!"

B. Both of these great theological truths are presented in the Bible. They are not contradictory, but complementary. The entire Trinity is directly involved in this election.
   1. In regard to the Father: we were saved before the foundation of the world (Eph. 1:4; 2 Tim. 1:9).
   2. In regard to the Son: we were saved at the cross (Gal. 2:20).
   3. In regard to the Holy Spirit: we were saved at the moment of our decision to accept Christ (1 Cor. 12:13; Titus 3:5).

C. Thomas Constable writes: "That God has chosen to bless some individuals with eternal life is clearly taught in many places in both the Old and New Testaments (Deut. 4:37; 7:6-7; Isa. 44:1-2; Rom. 9; Eph. 1:4-6, 11; Col. 3:12; 2 Thess. 2:13). Equally clear is the fact that God holds each individual personally responsible for his decision to trust or not to trust in Jesus Christ (cf. John 3; Rom. 5). The difficulty in putting divine election and human responsibility together is understanding how both can be true. That *both are true is taught in the Bible.* How *both can be true is apparently incomprehensible to finite human minds; no one has ever been able to explain this antinomy satisfactorily. This task transcends human mental powers, much as seeing angels transcends human visual powers and hearing very high-pitched sounds transcends human auditory powers. The Thessalonians' response to the gospel message proved that God had chosen them for salvation"* (Bible Knowledge Commentary, *New Testament Volume, p. 691).*

C. It was an exemplary church (1 Thess. 1:5-7).
   1. Paul's example to the church—"For our gospel came not unto you in word only, but also in power, and in the Holy Ghost, and in much assurance; as ye know what manner of men we were among you for your sake. And ye became followers of us, and of the Lord, having received the word in much affliction, with joy of the Holy Ghost" (1 Thess. 1:5-6).

---

†1:6 *Paul speaks of preaching the gospel not only in word but in power also.*
A. God's Word *is effective even though preached by a carnal believer (Isa. 55:11; Phil. 1:15-18). It is tragically possible for the divine message to be anointed while the human messenger is not.*
B. *God's* will *is that both his spokesmen and scriptures be in perfect harmony.*

---

   2. Their example to the world—"So that ye were ensamples to all that believe in Macedonia and Achaia" (1 Thess. 1:7).

D. It was an evangelistic church (1 Thess. 1:8)—"For from you sounded out the word of the Lord not only in Macedonia and Achaia, but also in every place your faith to Godward is spread abroad; so that we need not to speak any thing" (1 Thess. 1:8).

---

†1:8 *Charles Ryrie comments: "The word translated 'sounded out' is very picturesque. The Greek letters, simply changed into English characters, spell our word echo. Thus the picture is of the message of the gospel so stirring the strings of the Thessalonians' hearts that it reverberated in strong and clear tones to all Greece and everywhere"* (First and Second Thessalonians, *p. 27). Thus, while waiting for the trumpet of Christ to sound, these Thessalonians were sounding out the trumpet* for *Christ (see 1 Thess. 4:16; see also Rom. 1:8).*

E. It was an expectant church (1 Thess. 1:9-10)—In these verses Paul summarizes the three spiritual stages of saved church members.
   1. In the past—"How ye turned to God from idols" (1 Thess. 1:9).
   2. In the present—"To serve the living and true God" (1 Thess. 1:9).
   3. In the future—"And to wait for his Son from heaven, whom he raised from the dead, even Jesus, which delivered us from the wrath to come" (1 Thess. 1:10).

---

†1:10
A. *All this may be tied in beautifully with Paul's statement concerning them in 1:3 where he writes of their "work of faith, and labour of love, and patience of hope." Thus we see:*
   1. *In the past—Turning, and looking to the Father. This was their work of faith (see John 6:28-29; Acts 20:21).*

2. *In the present—Serving, and looking on the fields. This was their labor of love (see John 4:35; 1 Cor. 15:58; Heb. 6:10).*
3. *In the future—Waiting, and looking for the Son. This was their patience of hope (see 2 Tim. 4:8).*

B. *Dr. John Walvoord writes: "Paul told how God had worked in the Thessalonians. It had resulted in their turning to God from idols to serve the living and true God. This is a very accurate expression and one we should understand. It does not say that they turned* from *idols* to *God. Rather, they turned* to *God* from *idols to serve the living and true God. It was not reformation first and faith in Christ second, but it was faith in Christ first with the result that idols were forsaken. The tense of the word* turned, *as it is found in the Greek New Testament, is in the aorist, which means that they turned once for all. It was a single, definite act"* (The Thessalonian Epistle, *p. 17).*

II. The Review of the Church (1 Thess. 2–3)—In these chapters the apostle reviews those circumstances involved in the founding of their church. "For yourselves, brethren, know our entrance in unto you, that it was not in vain" (1 Thess. 2:1).

A. The activities of the shepherd in Thessalonica (what Paul says about himself)

1. He was a suffering traveler (1 Thess. 2:1-2)—"But even after that we had suffered before, and were shamefully entreated, as ye know, at Philippi, we were bold in our God to speak unto you the gospel of God with much contention" (1 Thess. 2:2). "For verily, when we were with you, we told you before that we should suffer tribulation; even as it came to pass, and ye know" (1 Thess. 3:4).

---

†2:2 *The Greek word translated "contention" is* agonia, *from whence comes our English word* agony.

---

2. He was a faithful steward—"But even after that we had suffered before, and were shamefully entreated, as ye know, at Philippi, we were bold in our God to speak unto you the gospel of God with much contention. For our exhortation was not of deceit, nor of uncleanness, nor in guile: but as we were allowed of God to be put in trust with the gospel, even so we speak; not as pleasing men, but God, which trieth our hearts. For neither at any time used we flattering words, as ye know, nor a cloke of covetousness; God is witness: nor of men sought we glory, neither of you, nor yet of others, when we might have been burdensome, as the apostles of Christ" (1 Thess. 2:2-6).

---

†2:6 *Here the apostle states that his message, motive, and method were all approved by God.*

---

3. He was a gentle mother (1 Thess. 2:7-8)—"But we were gentle among you, even as a nurse cherisheth her children" (1 Thess. 2:7).

---

†2:7 *Dr. Charles Ryrie comments: "The word cherish means 'to warm' and is used of the way a mother bird covers her young (Deut. 22:6); its only other occurrence in the New Testament is our Lord's relationship to his church (Eph. 5:29)"* (First and Second Thessalonians, *p. 37). How a* *mother feeds her child is almost as important as* what *she feeds it. This is also brought out in Ephesians 4:15: "But speaking the truth [the what] in love [the how]."*

---

4. He was a tireless laborer (1 Thess. 2:9)—"For ye remember, brethren, our labour and travail: for labouring night and day, because we would not be chargeable unto any of you, we preached unto you the gospel of God" (1 Thess. 2:9).

---

†2:9 *Richard Wolff writes: "Paul had learned to cut out and stitch the coarse goats' hair cloth used for making tents, shoes, and mats. It was customary for a Rabbi to learn a trade"* (General Epistles of First and Second Thessalonians, *p. 19).*

---

5. He was a consistent example (1 Thess. 2:10)—"Ye are witnesses, and God also, how holily and justly and unblameably we behaved ourselves among you that believe" (1 Thess. 2:10).

---

†2:10 *Note his three key words here:*

A. *Holily—His testimony godward (spiritual)*
B. *Justly—His testimony manward (social)*
C. *Unblameably—His testimony selfward (personal) Thus, the upward, outward, and inward in Paul's life possessed that vital spiritual maturity a good leader simply must have.*

---

6. He was a concerned father (1 Thess. 2:11-12)—"As ye know how we exhorted and comforted and charged every one of you, as a father doth his children, that ye would walk worthy of God, who hath called you unto his kingdom and glory" (1 Thess. 2:11-12).

---

†2:12 *The apostle often pictures himself as a parent. (See 1 Cor. 4:14; 2 Cor. 6:13; Gal. 4:18-19; Phil. 1:10.)*

---

7. He was as a homesick brother (1 Thess. 2:17)—"But we, brethren, being taken from you for a short time in presence, not in heart, endeavoured the more abundantly to see your face with great desire" (1 Thess. 2:17).
8. He was an expectant soul winner (1 Thess. 2:19-20)—"For what is our hope, or joy, or crown of rejoicing? Are not even ye in the presence of our Lord Jesus Christ at his coming? For ye are our glory and joy" (1 Thess. 2:19-20).

---

†2:20

A. *The Word of God mentions at least five possible rewards. These are:*
   1. *The incorruptible crown—Given to those who master the old nature (1 Cor. 9:25-27).*
   2. *The crown of life—Given to those who successfully endure temptation (James 1:2-3; Rev. 2:10).*
   3. *The crown of righteousness—Given to those who especially love the doctrine of the Rapture (2 Tim. 4:8).*

4. The crown of glory—Given to those faithful preachers and teachers (1 Pet. 5:2-4).
5. The crown of rejoicing—Given to soul winners (Prov. 11:30; 1 Thess. 2:19-20).

B. Note Paul's statement in 2:19, "at his coming." The Greek word here is parousia, *and is a technical term for the arrival or visit of a king. The word appears in many key New Testament prophecy passages. (See Matt. 24:3, 27, 37, 39; 2 Thess. 2:8; 1 Cor. 15:22-23; 1 Thess. 4:13-18; James 5:7-8; 1 John 2:28; 2 Pet. 1:16; 3:4.)*

---

9. He was as a missionary superintendent (1 Thess. 3:1-5) —"Wherefore when we could no longer forbear, we thought it good to be left at Athens alone; and sent Timotheus, our brother, and minister of God, and our fellowlabourer in the gospel of Christ, to establish you, and to comfort you concerning your faith: that no man should be moved by these afflictions: for yourselves know that we are appointed thereunto. For verily, when we were with you, we told you before that we should suffer tribulation; even as it came to pass, and ye know" (1 Thess. 3:1-4).

---

†3:2

A. Paul had previously been driven from Thessalonica and Berea by the unbelieving Jews. From Berea he went to Athens. While there he sent Timothy (who had remained in Berea) back to Thessalonica as a short-term missionary to strengthen the young church. In this passage he asks the Thessalonians not to pity him because of his manifold sufferings. The apostle declares that his trials had neither shaken nor surprised him, for, "we are appointed thereunto" (3:3; see also John 16:2; 1 Cor. 4:9; 2 Tim. 3:12; Acts 9:16).

B. William MacDonald has written: "Paul reminds them that even when he was in Thessalonica, he used to tell them that Christians are appointed to afflictions. His predictions came true in their own lives; how well they knew it! Trials form a necessary discipline in our lives:
1. They prove the reality of our faith, and weed out those who are mere professors (1 Pet. 1:7).
2. They enable us to comfort and encourage others who are going through trials (2 Cor. 1:4).
3. They develop certain graces, such as patience, in our character (Rom. 5:3).
4. They make us more zealous in spreading the gospel (Acts 4:29; 5:27-29; 8:3-4).
5. They help to remove the dross from our lives (Job 23:10)" (Letters to the Thessalonians, *p. 44).*

---

10. He was a prayer warrior (1 Thess. 2:13; 3:7-13).
   a. The persistence of his prayers—"For this cause also thank we God without ceasing" (1 Thess. 2:13). "Night and day praying exceedingly" (1 Thess. 3:10).
   b. The purpose of his prayers—"Night and day praying exceedingly that we might see your face, and might perfect that which is lacking in your faith? Now God himself and our Father, and our Lord Jesus Christ, direct our way unto you. And the Lord make you to increase and abound in love one toward another, and toward all men, even as we do toward you: to the end he may stablish your hearts unblameable in holiness before God, even our Father, at the coming of our Lord Jesus Christ with all his saints" (1 Thess. 3:10-13).

B. The activities of the sheep in Thessalonica (what Paul says about his converts)—"For ye, brethren, became followers of the churches of God which in Judaea are in

Christ Jesus: for ye also have suffered like things of your own countrymen, even as they have of the Jews" (1 Thess. 2:14). "But now when Timotheus came from you unto us, and brought us good tidings of your faith and charity, and that ye have good remembrance of us always, desiring greatly to see us, as we also to see you" (1 Thess. 3:6).

C. The activities of the serpent in Thessalonica (what Paul says about his enemies)
   1. The Judaizers—"Who both killed the Lord Jesus, and their own prophets, and have persecuted us; and they please not God, and are contrary to all men: forbidding us to speak to the Gentiles that they might be saved, to fill up their sins alway: for the wrath is come upon them to the uttermost" (1 Thess. 2:15-16).

---

†2:16

A. Paul's worst enemies in Thessalonica (as in other places) had been the vicious Judaizers. How Satan had used them.
   1. They had already "killed the Lord Jesus, and their own prophets" (2:15). See also Acts 2:23; 3:15; 5:30; 7:52.
   2. They had "persecuted us" (2:15).
   3. They "please not God, and are contrary to all men" (2:15).
   4. They had forbidden Paul to "speak to the Gentiles that they might be saved" (2:16). See also Acts 13:50; 14:5, 19; 17:5; 18:12; 22:22.

B. Paul has been accused of being anti-Semitic, but this is totally unfounded. The apostle himself, of course, was an Israelite and proud of his background. (See Phil. 3:4-5.) Furthermore, his great heart practically bled for the conversion of his beloved nation. (See Rom. 9:1-3; 10:1.)

---

   2. The devil—"Wherefore we would have come unto you, even I Paul, once and again; but Satan hindered us" (1 Thess. 2:18).

III. The Removal of the Church (1 Thess. 4)
   A. The challenges of this removal
      1. We are to know God's will (what he wants us to do)—"Furthermore then we beseech you, brethren, and exhort you by the Lord Jesus, that as ye have received of us how ye ought to walk and to please God, so ye would abound more and more" (1 Thess. 4:1). "For this is the will of God, even your sanctification" (1 Thess. 4:3).

---

†4:3 *God has but one will for sinners, and that is that they become saved. (See 1 Tim. 2:4; 2 Pet. 3:9.) In like manner he has only one will for saints and that is that they be sanctified. Here Paul, of course, refers to a daily growing in grace and maturing in the faith. The first step in sanctification is consecration. (See Rom. 12:1-2.)*

---

      2. We are to know God's way (how he wants us to do it).
         a. Concerning self—Purity (1 Thess. 4:3-5). "That ye should abstain from fornication" (1 Thess. 4:3). "That every one of you should know how to possess his vessel in sanctification and honour" (1 Thess. 4:4).

b. Concerning saints—Charity (1 Thess. 4:6-10)

(1) The revelation of the matter—"That no man go beyond and defraud his brother in any matter: because that the Lord is the avenger of all such, as we also have forewarned you and testified. . . . But as touching brotherly love ye need not that I write unto you: for ye yourselves are taught of God to love one another" (1 Thess. 4:6, 9).

(2) The reasons for the matter—"For God hath not called us unto uncleanness, but unto holiness. He therefore that despiseth, despiseth not man, but God, who hath also given unto us his holy Spirit" (1 Thess. 4:7-8).

c. Concerning sinners—Honesty (1 Thess. 4:11-12). "And to make it your ambition to lead a quiet life and attend to your own business and work with your hands just as we commanded you; so that you may behave properly toward outsiders and not be in any need" (1 Thess. 4:11-12, NASB).

B. The chronology of this removal (1 Thess. 4:13-18)

---

†*In this great passage Paul answers a question that had bothered the Thessalonians. When he was among them (Acts 17) they had doubtless learned many precious truths about the glorious return of Christ to earth someday and the establishing of his kingdom. In fact, to some, this all seemed to be just around the corner. But since the apostle's departure, a number of believers had died. They obviously then would not be here on earth at the time of Christ's return. Did this mean they would miss everything? This then is the background to the great Rapture passage before us here in chapter 4.*

---

1. A realization—"But I would not have you to be ignorant, brethren, concerning them which are asleep, that ye sorrow not, even as others which have no hope" (1 Thess. 4:13).

---

†**4:13** *This is but one of five key areas in which Paul would not have believers to be ignorant. The other four are:*

A. The events in the Old Testament (1 Cor. 10:1)
B. The restoration of Israel (Rom. 11:25)
C. The manifestation of spiritual gifts (1 Cor. 12:1)
D. The devices of Satan (2 Cor. 2:11)

---

2. A repose—"For if we believe that Jesus died and rose again, even so them also which sleep in Jesus will God bring with him" (1 Thess. 4:14).

---

†**4:14**

A. The death of a believer is looked upon as a peaceful sleep. (See Matt. 27:52; John 11:11; Acts 7:60; 13:36; 1 Cor. 15:6, 18, 20, 51; 2 Pet. 3:4.) However, it should be quickly stated that this verse in no way teaches soul sleep. That unscriptural doctrine is refuted by Matthew 17:3 and Revelation 6:9-11.

B. The sleep here thus refers to the body of the believer, and not the believer himself. Paul makes this very clear in another passage: "We are confident, I say, and willing rather to be absent from the body, and to be present with the Lord" (2 Cor. 5:8).

---

3. A revelation—"For this we say unto you by the word of the Lord, that we which are alive and remain unto the coming of the Lord shall not prevent them which are asleep" (1 Thess. 4:15).

---

†4:15 *Note Paul's use of the pronoun "we." The apostle apparently hoped to be there when Christ came. He would later know otherwise. (See 2 Tim. 4:6.)*

---

4. A return—"For the Lord himself shall descend from heaven with a shout, with the voice of the archangel, and with the trump of God" (1 Thess. 4:16).

---

†4:16a

A. *"For the Lord himself"—This glorious and personal return will be a fulfillment of the prophecy made at the time of Christ's ascension. "And while they looked stedfastly toward heaven as he went up, behold, two men stood by them in white apparel; which also said, Ye men of Galilee, why stand ye gazing up into heaven? this same Jesus which is taken up from you into heaven, shall so come in like manner as ye have seen him go into heaven" (Acts 1:10-11).*

B. *"The voice of the archangel"—It is often supposed that Michael will be this archangel on the basis of Daniel 12:1-2. However, it is not unreasonable to suggest that Gabriel will be the angel involved at this time because of the vital part he played in those events surrounding the first coming of Christ. (See Luke 1:19, 26; Matt. 1:20; 2:13.)*

---

5. A resurrection—"And the dead in Christ shall rise first" (1 Thess. 4:16b).

---

†4:14b *This makes the second of three resurrections mentioned by Paul in 1 Corinthians 15:23-24:*

A. *The resurrection of Christ ("Christ the first fruits")*
B. *The Rapture resurrection ("they that are Christ's at his coming")*
C. *The resurrection of Old Testament and tribulational saints ("then cometh the end"). See also Revelation 20:4, 6.*

---

6. A Rapture—"Then we which are alive and remain shall be caught up together." (1 Thess. 4:17).
7. A reunion—"With them in the clouds, to meet the Lord in the air: and so shall we ever be with the Lord" (1 Thess. 4:17).
8. A reassurance—"Wherefore comfort one another with these words" (1 Thess. 4:18).

IV. The Responsibility of the Church (1 Thess. 5)

A. The God of purpose (what he wills for us to do) (1 Thess. 5:1-22)

1. Be watchful (1 Thess. 5:1-8)

a. The action involved—"For yourselves know perfectly that the day of the Lord so cometh as a thief in the night" (1 Thess. 5:2).

---

†5:2

A. *"The day of the Lord"—Here is the first reference in the New Testament to this period. It is found often in the Old Testament (e.g., Isa. 13:9-11; Joel 2:28-32; Zeph. 1:14-18; 3:14-15), or a title used to describe the coming great tribulation.*

B. *"As a thief in the night"—Christ's second coming is often compared in this manner (Luke 12:39; 1 Thess. 5:4; 2 Pet. 3:10; Rev. 3:3; 16:15). These verses stress two great truths:*
   1. *Regarding the suddenness of his return.*
   2. *Regarding our watchfulness for his return.*

---

b. The reaction involved
   (1) The children of light—"But ye, brethren, are not in darkness, that that day should overtake you as a thief. Ye are all the children of light, and the children of the day: we are not of the night, nor of darkness. Therefore let us not sleep, as do others; but let us watch and be sober. . . . But let us, who are of the day, be sober, putting on the breastplate of faith and love; and for an helmet, the hope of salvation" (1 Thess. 5:4-6, 8).

---

†5:8 *This is in contrast to the unsaved, who are described as the children of darkness. Someday the Sun of righteousness shall arise with healing in his wings (Mal. 4:2). It is therefore only logical that the children of light should await that glorious day.*

---

   (2) The children of darkness—"For when they shall say, Peace and safety; then sudden destruction cometh upon them, as travail upon a woman with child; and they shall not escape. For they that sleep sleep in the night; and they that be drunken are drunken in the night" (1 Thess. 5:3, 7).

2. Be helpful (1 Thess. 5:9-11, 14).
   a. The *why* of the matter—"For God hath not appointed us to wrath, but to obtain salvation by our Lord Jesus Christ, who died for us, that, whether we wake or sleep, we should live together with him" (1 Thess. 5:9-10).

---

†5:10

A. *Concerning verse 9: This is a reference to both external wrath (John 3:36; Col. 3:6) and tribulational wrath (Rev. 6:17; 15:1; 11:18). Paul begins and ends his epistle to the Thessalonian church with this precious promise. (Compare 1:9 with 5:9.)*

B. *Concerning verse 10—William MacDonald writes: "This verse emphasizes the tremendous price our Lord paid to deliver us from wrath and insure our salvation. He died for us that whether awake or asleep we should live together with Him. There will be two classes of believers at His coming:*
   1. *Those who have died.*
   2. *Those who are living. The former are spoken of as being asleep, the latter as being awake. Whether we are among the living or the dead at the time of His return, we shall live with Him. Christians who die lose nothing. The Lord said the same thing, in effect, to Martha, 'I am the resurrection, and the life: he that believeth on me, though he die [i.e., a Christian who has died], yet shall he live [he will be raised at the Rapture]; and whosoever liveth and believeth on me [a believer alive at the time of the Rapture] shall never die (John 11:25-26)"* (Letter to the Thessalonians, *p. 68).*

---

b. The *who* of the matter—"Wherefore comfort yourselves together, and edify one another, even as also ye do. . . . Now we exhort you, brethren, warn them that are unruly, comfort the feebleminded, support the weak, be patient toward all men" (1 Thess. 5:11, 14).

---

†5:14

A. *Warn the unruly. The Greek word here is* ataktos, *which referred to soldiers who deserted their ranks.*

B. *Comfort the feebleminded. A better word here would be fainthearted.*

C. *Support the weak, the immature. (See Rom. 14.)*

---

3. Be merciful (1 Thess 5:15)—"See that none render evil for evil unto any man; but ever follow that which is good, both among yourselves, and to all men" (1 Thess. 5:15).
4. Be respectful (1 Thess. 5:12-13)—"And we beseech you, brethren, to know them which labour among you, and are over you in the Lord, and admonish you; and to esteem them very highly in love for their work's sake. And be at peace among yourselves" (1 Thess. 5:12-13).
5. Be joyful (1 Thess 5:16)—"Rejoice evermore" (1 Thess. 5:16).

---

†5:16 *This verse in the Greek is the shortest in the New Testament (and not John 11:35). It is often, however, one of the hardest to keep.*

---

6. Be prayerful (1 Thess. 5:17)—"Pray without ceasing" (1 Thess. 5:17).

---

†5:17 *Charles Ryrie writes: "The Christian's joy puts him in the proper mood to pray without ceasing. Paul has already used the words* without ceasing *twice of his own remembrance of the Thessalonians (1:3; 2:13) and now he enjoins it on the believers. Outside the New Testament the word is used of a hacking cough and aptly illustrates what Paul has in mind here about prayer. Just as a person with a hacking cough is not always audibly coughing, though the tendency to cough is always there, so the Christian who prays without ceasing is not always praying audibly and yet prayer is always the attitude of his heart and life"* (First and Second Thessalonians, *p. 80).*

---

7. Be thankful (1 Thess. 5:18).

---

†5:18 *(See also Eph. 5:20; Col. 3:17.) The importance of this command cannot be overstated. The cure for pride in our lives is not to practice humility, lest we become proud of our piousness, but to be thankful. In Romans 1, Paul described the terrible final stages of Gentile world apostasy. The picture he paints is one of the most chilling in all the Bible. What horrible crime could possibly cause all this? Note his answer: "Because, when they knew God, they glorified him not as God, neither were thankful" (Rom. 1:21). Someone has offered the following little rule: Be careful for nothing, be prayerful in everything, and be thankful for anything.*

"In every thing give thanks: for this is the will of God in Christ Jesus concerning you" (1 Thess. 5:18).

8. Be careful (1 Thess. 5:19-22).
    a. Concerning the Spirit of God—"Quench not the Spirit" (1 Thess. 5:19).

---

†**5:19** *The Holy Spirit is like a fire. (See Matt. 3:11; Luke 3:16; Acts 2:3; Heb. 11:34.) To quench the Spirit is one of two sins a believer can commit against this blessed third person of the Trinity who lives in our hearts. The other is to grieve him. (See Eph. 4:30.) To* quench *him is not to do what he wants us to do, while to* grieve *him is to do what he does not want us to do.*

---

b. Concerning the gifts of God—"Despise not prophesyings" (1 Thess. 5:20).
c. Concerning the Word of God—"Prove all things; hold fast that which is good" (1 Thess. 5:21).
d. Concerning my walk for God—"Abstain from all appearance of evil" (1 Thess. 5:22).

B. The God of peace (what he will do for us) (1 Thess. 5: 23-28)—"And the very God of peace sanctify you wholly; and I pray God your whole spirit and soul and body be preserved blameless unto the coming of our Lord Jesus Christ. Faithful is he that calleth you, who also will do it" (1 Thess. 5:23-24).

---

†**5:24**

A. *Verse 23 has been a main support for the doctrine of trichotomy, which teaches that we are a threefold being: spirit, soul, and body. Whatever else may be involved in this verse, Paul is praying that God would sanctify the* total *believer. God is not involved in "saving souls," but in sanctifying individuals. Jesus strongly brings this out. (See Matt. 22:36-40.)*
B. *Note the final words in 5:23, ". . .unto the coming of our Lord Jesus Christ." Paul ends this chapter as he has done the previous four, with a reference to the second appearing of Christ. In the first chapter (1:10) he connects it with* salvation*; in the second (2:19-20), with* service*; in the third (3:13), with* stability*; in the fourth (4:18), with* sorrow*; and here with* sanctification.
C. *This epistle, Paul commanded, was to "be read unto all the holy brethren" (5:27; see also Col. 4:16; 1 Tim. 4:13; Rev. 1:3).*

---

2 THESSALONIANS

THE SIN OF MAN AND THE MAN OF SIN

A. In 2 Thessalonians Paul writes of both.
   1. General facts concerning the sin of man (1:8-9; 3:6-15)
   2. Specific facts concerning the man of sin (2:1-12)

B. The New Testament's two most extended passages dealing with the coming Antichrist are 2 Thessalonians 2:1-12 and Revelation 13:1-8.

C. This book is the shortest of Paul's epistles to local churches.

D. The book of 1 Corinthians was his longest to a local assembly.

E. Paul wrote 1 Thessalonians to tell his converts they had not missed the Rapture. He now writes this epistle assuring them they were not enduring the great tribulation.

F. Merrill Tenney summarizes both 1 and 2 Thessalonians: "Practically every major doctrine in the catalogue of faith is represented in these two small epistles. Although they were not written as doctrinal treatises, nor primarily to present the author's general theological views, they contain a well-rounded body of theological teaching. Paul and those who received his epistles believed in one living God (1 Thess. 1:9), the Father (2 Thess. 1:2), who has loved men and has chosen them to enjoy His salvation (2 Thess. 2:16; 1 Thess. 2:4). He has sent deliverance from wrath through Jesus Christ, His Son (1 Thess. 1:10), and has revealed this deliverance through the message of the gospel (1 Thess. 1:5; 2:9; 2 Thess. 2:14). This message has been confirmed and has been made real by the power of the Holy Spirit (1 Thess. 1:5; 4:8). The gospel concerns the Lord Jesus Christ, who was killed by the Jews (1 Thess. 2:15). He rose from the dead (1 Thess. 1:10; 4:14, 5:10). He is now in heaven (1 Thess. 1:10), but He will come again (1 Thess. 2:19; 4:15, 5:23; 2 Thess. 2:1). To Him is ascribed deity, for He is called Lord (1 Thess. 1:6), God's Son (1 Thess. 1:10), and the Lord Jesus Christ (1 Thess. 1:1; 3; 5:28; 2 Thess. 1:1). Believers (1) receiving the word of God (1 Thess. 1:6), (2) turn from idols, serve God and wait for the return of Christ (1 Thess. 1:9-10). Their normal growth is in sanctification (1 Thess. 4:3, 7; 2 Thess. 2:13). In personal life they are to be clean (1 Thess. 4:4-6), industrious (1 Thess. 4:11-12), prayerful (1 Thess. 5:17), and cheerful (1 Thess. 5:16). Theoretically and practically the Thessalonian letters embody all the essentials of Christian truth" *(New Testament Survey,* p. 283).

G. The book of 2 Thessalonians is the 22nd longest New Testament book, and 60th longest biblical book, with three chapters, 47 verses, and 1,042 words. There are quotations or allusions from nine Old Testament books in this epistle.

H. Great passages would include:
   1. 1:11-12
   2. 2:13-17
   3. 3:3-5

THE BOOK OF 2 THESSALONIANS

"Paul, and Silvanus, and Timotheus, unto the church of the Thessalonians in God our Father and the Lord Jesus Christ: Grace unto you, and peace, from God our Father and the Lord Jesus Christ" (2 Thess. 1:1-2).

I. Explanation—The Way of the Lord (A Pastoral Encouragement, 2 Thess. 1). In this chapter Paul explains (in part) just why God often allows believers to suffer persecution.
  A. God and the persecuted
    1. The saints and the benefits of persecution (we receive the good)
      a. The benefit of sanctification
        (1) Our faith in God is enlarged (2 Thess. 1:3).
        (2) Our love for believers is enlarged (2 Thess. 1:3).

---

†1:3a *Dr. Charles Ryrie states that this verb "groweth exceedingly" is a very strong compound one, found only here in the New Testament, and indicates organic growth, as a healthy plant.*

---

        (3) Our example to all is enlarged (2 Thess. 1:4).
      b. The benefit of preparation—"All this is evidence that God's judgment is right, and as a result you will be counted worthy of the kingdom of God, for which you are suffering" (2 Thess. 1:5, NIV).
    2. The Savior and the benefits of persecution (he receives the glory)—"When he shall come to be glorified in his saints, and to be admired in all them that believe (because our testimony among you was believed) in that day. . . . That the name of our Lord Jesus Christ may be glorified in you, and ye in him, according to the grace of our God and the Lord Jesus Christ" (2 Thess. 1:10, 12).

---

†1:12 *Dr. John Walvoord writes: "This is an expression often used but perhaps not always analyzed or understood as it should be. The Scriptures state: 'The heavens declare the glory of God; and the firmament sheweth his handiwork. Day unto day uttereth speech, and night unto night sheweth knowledge' (Psa. 19:1-2). What does it mean when it is said that the heavens declare the glory of God? The heavens declare that God is perfect. The heavens manifest his wisdom, his power, and his intelligent end. The heavens are manifesting the glory of God in the sense that they reveal what God is and what he can do. But the heavens are not designed to reveal the love of God, the grace of God, nor the righteousness of God. We are designed to show 'the exceeding riches of his grace in his kindness toward us through Christ' (Eph. 2:7)"* (The Thessalonian Epistles, *p. 112).*

  B. God and the persecutors (2 Thess. 1:7-9)
    1. The judge—"And to you who are troubled rest with us, when the Lord Jesus shall be revealed from heaven with his mighty angels" (2 Thess. 1:7).
    2. The judged—"In flaming fire taking vengeance on them that know not God, and that obey not the gospel of our Lord Jesus Christ" (2 Thess. 1:8).

†1:8

A. What a contrast is seen here in regard to angels concerning Christ's first coming and his second coming:

1. First coming—Angels are prohibited from delivering the Savior from the Calvary judgment (Matt. 26:52-53).

2. Second coming—Angels are permitted to deliver sinners to the final judgment.

B. Note also the two categories of sinners here:

1. "Them that know not God"—These are probably those who may never have heard the spoken gospel, but did have both the witness of conscience and nature, and are therefore without excuse. (See especially Rom. 1:18-20; 2:12-16.)

2. "Them . . . that obey not the gospel of our Lord Jesus Christ." Here is doubtless a reference to those who actually heard but then refused the gospel invitation.

---

3. The judgment—"Who shall be punished with everlasting destruction from the presence of the Lord, and from the glory of his power" (2 Thess. 1:9).

---

†1:9 *William McDonald writes: "They shall suffer punishment. A god who doesn't punish sin is no god at all. The idea that a God of love must not punish sin overlooks the fact that God is also holy and must do what is morally right. The nature of the punishment is here defined as eternal destruction. The word translated eternal* (aionios) *is used 70 times in the New Testament. Three times it may mean ages of limited duration (Rom. 16:25; Titus 1:2). The other times it means eternal or endless. It is used in Romans 16:26 to describe the unending existence of God.*

"Destruction never means annihilation. It means loss of well-being, or ruin as far as the purpose of existence is concerned. The wineskins which the Lord Jesus described in Luke 5:37 were destroyed (same word as used here). They did not cease to exist, but they were ruined as far as further usefulness was concerned.

"The punishment of the wicked also includes banishment from the presence of the Lord and from the glory of His might. To perish without Him is to be without Him forever" (Letters to the Thessalonians, *pp. 87-88).*

A final thought may prove helpful before leaving this chapter. In 1 Thessalonians Paul had dealt with the Rapture *of Christ. (See 1 Thess. 4:13-18.) But here in the opening chapter of 2 Thessalonians, he describes the* revelation *of Christ. These two great events are not one and the same and should not be confused. William McDonald offers the following helpful distinction:*

A. The Rapture

1. Christ comes in the air (1 Thess. 4:17).

2. He comes for his saints (1 Thess. 4:16-17).

3. The Rapture is a mystery, i.e., a truth unknown in Old Testament times (1 Cor. 15:51).

4. Christ's coming for his saints is never said to be preceded by signs in the heavens.

5. The Rapture is identified with the day of Christ (1 Cor. 1:8; 2 Cor. 1:14; Phil. 1:6, 10).

6. The Rapture is presented as a time of blessing (1 Thess. 4:18).

7. The Rapture takes place in a moment, in the twinkling of an eye (1 Cor. 15:52). This strongly implies that it will not be witnessed by the world.

8. The Rapture seems to involve the church primarily (John 14: 1-4; 1 Cor. 15:51-58; 1 Thess. 4:13-18).

9. Christ comes as the bright and morning star (Rev. 22:16).

B. The Revelation

1. He comes to the earth (Zech. 14:4).

2. He comes with his saints (1 Thess. 3:13; Jude 14).

3. The revelation is not a mystery; it is the subject of many Old Testament prophecies (Psa. 72; Isa. 11; Zech. 14).

4. Christ's coming with his saints will be heralded by celestial portents (Matt. 24:29-30).

5. The revelation is identified with the day of the Lord (2 Thess. 2:1-12, ASV*).*

6. The main emphasis of the revelation is on judgment (2 Thess. 2:8-12).

7. The revelation will be visible worldwide (Matt. 24:27; Rev. 1:7).

8. The revelation involves Israel primarily, then also the Gentile nations.

9. Christ comes as the sun of righteousness with healing in his wings (Mal. 4:2) (Letters to the Thessalonians, *p. 85).*

II. Tribulation—The Wrath of the Lord (A Prophetical Enlightenment—2 Thess. 2)

A. Facts concerning the day of the Lord (2 Thess. 2:1-12)—The day of the Lord as used here ("day of Christ" in the King James Version)

---

†*We begin this section by noting that the expression "day of Christ" should be translated "day of the Lord." A vast difference separates these two biblical days. The* day of the Lord *refers to the coming seven-year tribulation. (See especially Joel 1:15; 2:1-2; Rev. 6:12-17.) The* day of Christ *points to the future millennium. (See 1 Cor. 1:8; 5:5; Phil. 1:6 ,10; 2:16.) These believers had somehow been tricked by Satan into believing this dreadful day of the Lord had come.*

---

1. The day of the Lord and the church (2 Thess. 2:1-3)

a. The confusion—"Now we request you, brethren, with regard to the coming of our Lord Jesus Christ, and our gathering together to Him, that you may not be quickly shaken from your composure or be disturbed either by a spirit or a message or a letter as if from us, to the effect that the day of the Lord has come" (2 Thess. 2:1-2, NASB).

---

†2:2

A. "Neither by spirit"—That is, don't believe any false prophet who might receive this "through the spirit."

B. "Nor by word"—That is, don't listen to any false teacher who might teach this.

C. "Nor by letter as from us"—That is, don't accept any letter supposedly coming from me which would teach this, for such a letter is false.

---

b. The clarification—"Let no man deceive you by any means: for that day shall not come, except there come a falling away first, and that man of sin be revealed, the son of perdition" (2 Thess. 2:3).

---

†2:3

A. Note the expression, "a falling away first." Some have translated this, "a catching away first," believing it to be a reference to the Rapture. This is a theological possibility, but the Greek word is apostasia, *from whence our English word apostasy comes. It thus would seem more likely to mean the worldwide religious apostasy which Paul would later write (in past) about. (See 1 Tim. 4:1-3; 2 Tim. 3:1-5; 4:3-4.)*

B. *Merrill F. Unger writes: "Before the day of the Lord bursts upon a Christ-rejecting world, there must first come the apostasy, or falling away. This is not simple departure from the faith often characterizing the church age (1 Tim. 4:1-5; 2 Tim. 3:1-8; Rev. 3:14-22), but the wholesale rebellion and thoroughgoing lapse into error and demonism of the period just preceding Christ's advent in glory (Luke 18:8; Rev. 9:20-21)"* (Unger's Bible Handbook, *p. 711).*

C. *What then is the relationship between the church and the day of the Lord? It is simply this: the tribulation cannot begin until the church is removed from the earth.*

---

2. The day of the Lord and the Antichrist (2 Thess. 2:3-5, 8-9)
   a. His titles
      (1) The man of sin (2 Thess. 2:3)
      (2) The son of perdition (2 Thess. 2:3)

---

†**2:3** *Some believe that Judas Iscariot will be the Antichrist, pointing out that the title, "son of perdition," is found but two times in the New Testament. Jesus himself had used it first in reference to Judas (see John 17:12), and now Paul calls the Antichrist by the same name. Such evidence is, of course, far from conclusive.*

---

(3) The mystery of iniquity (2 Thess. 2:7)

---

†**2:7** *The mystery of iniquity in one sense is the evil opposite of the mystery of godliness.*

A. *The mystery of godliness refers to that historical event whereby all the fulness of God both indwelled and empowered Jesus Christ. (See 2 Cor. 5:19; Col. 2:9; 1 Tim. 3:16.)*

B. *The mystery of iniquity refers to that prophetical event whereby all the fullness of Satan will both indwell and empower the Antichrist.*

---

(4) The wicked one (2 Thess. 2:8)

b. His travesty—"Who opposeth and exalteth himself above all that is called God, or that is worshipped; so that he as God sitteth in the temple of God, shewing himself that he is God" (2 Thess. 2:4).

c. His trickery—"Even him, whose coming is after the working of Satan with all power and signs and lying wonders" (2 Thess. 2:9).

d. His termination—"And then shall that Wicked be revealed, whom the Lord shall consume with the spirit of his mouth, and shall destroy with the brightness of his coming" (2 Thess. 2:8).

3. The day of the Lord and the restrainer (2 Thess. 2:6-7)—"And you know what restrains him now, so that in his time he may be revealed. For the mystery of lawlessness is already at work; only he who now restrains will do so until he is taken out of the way" (2 Thess. 2:6-7, NASB).

---

†**2:7** *Who or what is this powerful restrainer? There are several theories:*

A. It is human government. However, this is unlikely, for Satan already exercises strong influence upon the kingdoms of mankind. (See Matt. 4:8.)

B. It is angels. This too is remote. (See Jude 9.)

C. It is the Holy Spirit. This is by far the most logical conclusion. Dr. Charles Ryrie writes: "The pretribulation argument is simply this. The restrainer is God, and the instrument of restraint is the God-indwelt church (cf. Eph. 4:6 for God indwelling; Gal. 2:20 for Christ indwelling; 1 Cor. 6:19 for the Spirit indwelling). It should be remembered that Christ said of the divinely indwelt and empowered church that 'the gates of hell shall not prevail against it' (Matt. 16:18), so we can say that this indwelt, empowered church is an adequate restraining instrument against the forces of darkness. The church will not go through any of the tribulation because the restrainer will be removed before the Man of Sin is revealed, which revelation (with the signing of the covenant with the Jews, Dan. 9:27) begins the tribulation period. Since the restrainer is ultimately God, and since God indwells all Christians, either He must be withdrawn from the hearts of believers while they are left on earth to go through the tribulation, or else when He is withdrawn all believers are taken with Him. Since it is impossible for a believer to be 'disindwelt' the only alternative is that believers too will be taken out of the way before the appearance of the Man of Sin, which signals the start of the tribulation" (First and Second Thessalonians, *p. 112).*

---

4. The day of the Lord and the unsaved (2 Thess. 2:10-12)—"And with all deceivableness of unrighteousness in them that perish; because they received not the love of the truth, that they might be saved. And for this cause God shall send them strong delusion, that they should believe a lie: that they all might be damned who believed not the truth, but had pleasure in unrighteousness" (2 Thess. 2:10-12).

---

†**2:12** *Note it is God who sends these strong delusions. God's divine sovereignty is seen even in the activities of unsaved people and apostate angels. (See Exod. 4:21; Gen. 50:20; Josh. 11:20; 1 Sam. 16:14; 1 Kings 22:19-23; Judg. 9:23.) Dr. John Walvoord writes: "Some understand from verse 11 that if a person in this present age of grace hears the gospel and does not receive Christ as Savior, then when Christ comes and takes His church home to glory these will find it impossible to be saved after the church is translated. It is unlikely that a person who rejects Christ in this day of grace will turn to Him in that awful period of tribulation. But the usual principle of Scripture is that while there is life there is hope. It is possible, though very improbable, that a person who has heard the gospel in this present age of grace will come to Christ after the Rapture. The Scriptures definitely teach that God will send strong delusion to those who do not believe after the church is gone. God will judge their hearts, and if they deliberately turn away from the truth He will permit them to believe a lie. They will honor the man of sin as their god and as their king, instead of acknowledging the Lord Jesus Christ. The result will be 'That they all might be damned who believed not the truth, but had pleasure in unrighteousness'"* (The Thessalonian Epistles, *p. 129).*

B. Facts concerning the destined of the Lord (2 Thess. 2:13-17)—After dealing with the eternal damnation of the lost, Paul now deals with the eternal salvation of the saved.

1. The source and time of our salvation—"But we are bound to give thanks alway to God for you, brethren beloved of the Lord, because God hath from the

beginning chosen you to salvation through sanctification of the Spirit and belief of the truth" (2 Thess. 2:13).

2. The method and means of our salvation—"Through sanctification by the Spirit and faith in the truth" (2 Thess. 2:13, NASB).

---

†2:13b *It has been said that had it not been for the Father and Son, there would have been no salvation feast; and were it not for the Spirit, there would be no guests.*

---

3. The goal of our salvation—"And it was for this He called you through our gospel that you may gain the glory of our Lord Jesus Christ" (2 Thess. 2:14, NASB).

---

†2:14 *That is, that believers might one day share the splendor and honor that Jesus now enjoys, seated at the right hand of the Father. The intrinsic glory of Christ, however, will never be shared with any human being. (See Isa. 42:8; John 17:1, 5.)*

---

4. The responsibilities of our salvation—"Therefore, brethren, stand fast, and hold the traditions which ye have been taught, whether by word, or our epistle" (2 Thess. 2:15).

---

†2:15 *Paul obviously felt this admonition was sorely needed, based upon the original evaluation of the church in Thessalonica, as given in Acts: "And the brethren immediately sent away Paul and Silas by night unto Berea: who coming* thither *went into the synagogue of the Jews. These were more noble than those in Thessalonica, in that they received the word with all readiness of mind, and searched the scriptures daily, whether those things were so" (Acts 17:10-11).*

---

5. The reassurance of our salvation—"Now our Lord Jesus Christ himself, and God, even our Father, which hath loved us, and hath given us everlasting consolation and good hope through grace, comfort your hearts, and stablish you in every good word and work" (2 Thess. 2:16-17).

III. Consecration—The Will of the Lord (A Practical Exhortation, 2 Thess. 3)

A. Paul's request (2 Thess. 3:1-2)—"Finally, brethren, pray for us, that the word of the Lord may have free course, and be glorified, even as it is with you: and that we may be delivered from unreasonable and wicked men: for all men have not faith" (2 Thess. 3:1-2).

B. Paul's reassurance (2 Thess. 3:3-5)—"But the Lord is faithful, who shall stablish you, and keep you from evil. And we have confidence in the Lord touching you, that ye both do and will do the things which we command you" (2 Thess. 3:3-4).

C. Paul's reprimand (2 Thess. 3:6-18)

1. The recipients of this reprimand

a. The disorderly (2 Thess. 3:6, 11)—"Now we command you, brethren, in the name of our Lord Jesus Christ, that ye withdraw yourselves from every brother that walketh disorderly, and not after the tradition which he received of us" (2 Thess. 3:6).

b. The busybodies (2 Thess. 3:11)
c. The loafers (2 Thess. 3:7-10)
(1) Paul's work record—"For yourselves know how ye ought to follow us: for we behaved not ourselves disorderly among you; neither did we eat any man's bread for nought; but wrought with labour and travail night and day, that we might not be chargeable to any of you: not because we have not power, but to make ourselves an ensample unto you to follow us" (2 Thess. 3:7-9).
(2) Paul's work rule—"For even when we were with you, this we commanded you, that if any would not work, neither should he eat" (2 Thess. 3:10).
d. The disobedient—"And if any man obey not our word by this epistle, note that man, and have no company with him, that he may be ashamed" (2 Thess. 3:14).

2. The recommendations in this reprimand
a. First step—Identify them. "And if any man obey not our word by this epistle, note that man" (2 Thess. 3:14).
b. Second step—Admonish them. "Now them that are such we command and exhort by our Lord Jesus Christ, that with quietness they work, and eat their own bread" (2 Thess. 3:12). "Admonish him as a brother" (2 Thess. 3:15).
c. Third step—Excommunicate them. "Now we command you, brethren, in the name of our Lord Jesus Christ, that ye withdraw yourselves from every brother that walketh disorderly, and not after the tradition which he received of us" (2 Thess. 3:6). "Have no company with him, that he may be ashamed" (2 Thess. 3:14b).
d. Fourth step—Love them as a brother or sister through it all. "Yet count him not as an enemy, but . . . as a brother" (2 Thess. 3:15).

1 TIMOTHY

FROM AN OLD MAN OF GOD TO A YOUNG MAN OF GOD

A. The book of 1 Timothy is the first of three New Testament letters written especially to pastors. The other two are 2 Timothy and Titus. Paul probably wrote both this epistle and Titus between his first and second imprisonments.
B. The New Testament has much to say concerning Timothy.
C. His name appears some 24 times.
D. He was from Lystra and probably was saved during Paul's first missionary trip (Acts 14:19-20; 16:1-2).
E. His mother (Eunice) and grandmother (Lois) were godly Jewish women, but his father was a pagan Greek (Acts 16:1; 2 Tim. 1:5).
F. He is invited by Paul to "join the team" during the apostle's second trip (Acts 16:3). This team would consist of Silas, Paul, and Luke.
G. Timothy may have been chosen to take John Mark's place. (See Acts 13:5.)
H. He is circumcised by Paul that he might have freedom to preach the gospel in the various Jewish synagogues (Acts 16:3; see also 1 Cor. 9:20).
I. Timothy is formally ordained by Paul and the presbytery (1 Tim. 4:14; 2 Tim. 1:6).
J. He also accompanies Paul during the third missionary trip (Acts 19:22; 20:4; 2 Cor. 1:1, 19).
K. He becomes Paul's close companion during the apostle's first imprisonment. (See Phil. 1:1; Col. 1:1; Philem. 1:1.)
L. Like Paul, Timothy also suffers imprisonment. (See Heb. 13:23.)
M. He performs a ministry in at least five New Testament churches:
    1. Thessalonica (1 Thess. 3:2, 6)
    2. Corinth (1 Cor. 4:17; 16:10; 2 Cor. 1:19)
    3. Philippi (Phil. 2:19-23)
    4. Berea (Acts 17:14)
    5. Ephesus (1 Tim. 1:2)
N. Timothy may have been a somewhat reserved individual and one who did not always enjoy robust health (1 Tim. 4:12, 14-16).
O. He was, nevertheless, a man of God (see 1 Tim. 6:11).
P. This epistle provides the most extended list explaining the needed qualifications for pastors and deacons in the New Testament. (See 3:1-13.)
Q. It also includes the first of three passages in Paul's writings where he predicts last day conditions. (Compare 1 Tim. 4:1-4 with 2 Tim. 3:1-9; 4:1-4.)
R. The reason for man's headship over the woman is also given in this epistle. (See 2:9-15.)
S. The book of 1 Timothy is the 16th longest New Testament book and 47th longest biblical book, with six chapters, 113 verses, and 2,269 words. There are quotations or allusions from 11 Old Testament books in 1 Timothy.

T. Great passages would include:
1. 2:1-6
2. 3:14-16
3. 4:11-16
4. 6:13-16

THE BOOK OF 1 TIMOTHY

Introduction: This epistle is, in essence, a personal letter to the family of God. "These things write I unto thee, hoping to come unto thee shortly: but if I tarry long, that thou mayest know how thou oughtest to behave thyself in the house of God, which is the church of the living God, the pillar and ground of the truth" (1 Tim. 3:14-15).

I. Paul and the Family of God
A. He was an apostle—"Paul, an apostle of Jesus Christ by the commandment of God our Saviour, and Lord Jesus Christ, which is our hope" (1 Tim. 1:1).
B. He was a father—"Unto Timothy, my own son in the faith: Grace, mercy, and peace, from God our Father and Jesus Christ our Lord" (1 Tim. 1:2).
C. He was a former blasphemer—"Who was before a blasphemer, and a persecutor, and injurious: but I obtained mercy, because I did it ignorantly in unbelief" (1 Tim. 1:13).
D. He became a sinner saved by grace—"And the grace of our Lord was exceeding abundant with faith and love which is in Christ Jesus" (1 Tim. 1:14).

---

†1:14 *Note: Paul lists the three motivating forces in his life:*
A. Love—His love for *Christ constrained him to labor (2 Cor. 5:14).*
B. Faith—His faith in *Christ empowered him to labor (Eph. 1:19).*
C. Grace—His grace from *Christ enabled him to labor (Heb. 12:28). Thus, we are saved* by *grace (Eph. 2:8-9), that we might serve* through *grace (Rom. 12:3-6).*

E. He thus served as God's trophy—"And yet for this reason I found mercy, in order that in me as the foremost Jesus Christ might demonstrate His perfect patience, as an example for those who would believe in Him for eternal life" (1 Tim. 1:16, NASB).

---

†1:16 *Perhaps no other conversion has proven more profitable in soul-winning than has Paul's. He himself mentioned it often (see Gal. 1–2; Phil. 3; Acts 22, 26).*

F. He was a suffering servant—"For therefore we both labour and suffer reproach, because we trust in the living God, who is the Saviour of all men, specially of those that believe" (1 Tim. 4:10).
G. He was, most of all, a preacher.
1. His message—The gospel. "According to the glorious gospel of the blessed God, which was committed to my trust" (1 Tim. 1:11).

2. His mission field—The Gentiles. "Whereunto I am ordained a preacher, and an apostle, (I speak the truth in Christ, and lie not;) a teacher of the Gentiles in faith and verity" (1 Tim. 2:7).
3. His master—The Savior. "And I thank Christ Jesus our Lord, who hath enabled me, for that he counted me faithful, putting me into the ministry" (1 Tim. 1:12).

II. Timothy and the Family of God

A. Timothy's personal responsibilities

1. Stay in Ephesus—"As I besought thee to abide still at Ephesus, when I went into Macedonia, that thou mightest charge some that they teach no other doctrine" (1 Tim. 1:3).
2. Maintain a good conscience—"Keeping faith and a good conscience . . ." (1 Tim. 1:19, NASB).
3. Examine yourself—"Take heed unto thyself" (1 Tim. 4:16).
4. Examine your doctrine—"And unto the doctrine; continue in them: for in doing this thou shalt both save thyself, and them that hear thee" (1 Tim. 4:16).

---

†4:16 *Here Paul is not referring to the eternal salvation of the believer's soul, but rather the earthly salvation of the believer's service. Thus, self-examination and discipline will save one from being placed by God on the shelf of disservice through sin (1 Cor. 9:27).*

---

5. Discipline yourself—"Discipline yourself for the purpose of godliness" (1 Tim. 4:7b, NASB).
6. Be an example—"Let no man look down on your youthfulness, but rather in speech, conduct, love, faith and purity, show yourself an example of those who believe" (1 Tim. 4:12, NASB).
7. Develop your gift—"Neglect not the gift that is in thee, which was given thee by prophecy, with the laying on of the hands of the presbytery. Meditate upon these things; give thyself wholly to them; that thy profiting may appear to all" (1 Tim. 4:14-15).

---

†4:15 *Totally develop your spiritual gift. What we don't use, we lose (see Heb. 2:1-3). The word "profiting" in 4:15 means "to cut forward, to blaze the way, to make a pioneer advance." A growing pastor means a growing church. A man cannot lead others where he has not been himself.*

---

8. Take care of your body—"Drink no longer water, but use a little wine for thy stomach's sake and thine often infirmities" (1 Tim. 5:23).

---

†5:23

A. *This verse* cannot *be used to support the practice of moderate drinking among believers. The wine here was to be taken for medicinal purposes.*

B. *This verse* can *be used to support the position that the spiritual gift of healing through individuals may have been phased out even before the completion of the New Testament. Consider:*

1. *Paul could not heal Timothy.*

2. Paul could not heal Trophimus (2 Tim. 4:20).
3. Paul could not heal himself (2 Cor. 12:7-10).

---

9. Avoid the love of money—"For the love of money is the root of all evil: which while some coveted after, they have erred from the faith, and pierced themselves through with many sorrows" (1 Tim. 6:10).
10. Pursue the good—"But thou, O man of God, flee these things; and follow after righteousness, godliness, faith, love, patience, meekness" (1 Tim. 6:11).
11. Be a soldier—"Fight the good fight of faith, lay hold on eternal life, whereunto thou art also called, and hast professed a good profession before many witnesses. I give thee charge in the sight of God, who quickeneth all things, and before Christ Jesus, who before Pontius Pilate witnessed a good confession; that thou keep this commandment without spot, unrebukeable, until the appearing of our Lord Jesus Christ" (1 Tim. 6:12-14).
12. Be impartial—"I charge thee before God, and the Lord Jesus Christ, and the elect angels, that thou observe these things without preferring one before another, doing nothing by partiality" (1 Tim. 5:21).

B. Timothy's public responsibilities
1. Concerning the pulpit in the church
a. What to honor—The Scriptures of God. "If thou put the brethren in remembrance of these things, thou shalt be a good minister of Jesus Christ, nourished up in the words of faith and of good doctrine, whereunto thou hast attained. These things command and teach. Till I come, give attendance to reading, to exhortation, to doctrine" (1 Tim. 4:6, 11, 13).

---

†**4:13** *The minister of God is to proclaim the Word of God as follows:*
A. He is to provide the information *involved; that is, "What does the text say?" "Give attendance to reading."*
B. He is to provide the interpretation *involved; that is, "What does the text mean?" "Give attendance . . . to doctrine."*
C. He is to provide the application *involved; that is, "How can this text be applied?" "Give attendance to . . . exhortation."*

---

b. What to avoid—Human speculations. "Neither give heed to fables and endless genealogies, which minister questions, rather than godly edifying which is in faith: so do" (1 Tim. 1:4). "O Timothy, keep that which is committed to thy trust, avoiding profane and vain babblings, and oppositions of science falsely so called" (1 Tim. 6:20).

2. Concerning prayers in the church
a. Pray for all—"I exhort therefore, that, first of all, supplications, prayers, intercessions, and giving of thanks, be made for all men; for kings, and for all that are in authority; that we may lead a quiet and peaceable life in all godliness and honesty. For this is good and acceptable in the sight of God our Saviour; who will have all men to be saved, and to come unto the knowledge of the truth" (1 Tim. 2:1-4).

†2:4 *Pray for all (2:1). This is to be done because, if the church will not pray, then who else will? We note that kings are at the top of Paul's list. At this time wicked Nero was on the Roman throne.*

A. Supplications—Asking for one's own needs
B. Prayers—Worship and adoration
C. Intercessions—Asking for another's needs
D. Thanksgiving—Appreciation for past grace and faith for future grace (see Phil. 4:6)

---

b. Pray for all things—"For every creature of God is good, and nothing to be refused, if it be received with thanksgiving: for it is sanctified by the word of God and prayer" (1 Tim. 4:4-5).

3. Concerning women in the church
   a. Their responsibilities—"In like manner also, that women adorn themselves in modest apparel, with shamefacedness and sobriety; not with broided hair, or gold, or pearls, or costly array" (1 Tim. 2:9).
   b. Their restrictions—"But I suffer not a woman to teach, nor to usurp authority over the man, but to be in silence" (1 Tim. 2:12). Two factors are involved in the giving of this rule.
      (1) The fact of the original creation—"For Adam was first formed, then Eve" (1 Tim. 2:13).
      (2) The fact of the original corruption—"And Adam was not deceived, but the woman being deceived was in the transgression" (1 Tim. 2:14).

---

†2:14

A. Do not allow congregational doctrine to be taught by a woman (2:12). Greek scholar Kenneth Wuest points out that here Paul uses the present infinitive tense instead of the aorist tense. Thus the command here should read, "I do not permit a woman to be a teacher." This, of course, does not prohibit her from teaching a ladies' Bible class, Sunday school, etc. But the doctrinal teachers in the family of God are to be men (Acts 13:1; 1 Cor. 12:28-29; Eph. 4:11). Paul now quickly gives Timothy two reasons for this.
   1. Because of the original creation—"For Adam was first formed, then Eve" (2:13; see also Eph. 5:22; 1 Cor. 11:1-16).
   *2. Because of the original corruption—"And Adam was not deceived [*apatao*, to merely deceive], but the woman being deceived [*exapatao*, to totally deceive], was in the transgression" (2:14; see also 1 Cor. 11:8-9).*
   3. The Word of God presents a divinely appointed threefold headship:
      a. The headship of Christ over his body (Col. 1:18)
      b. The headship of the pastor over his flock (Acts 20:28)
      c. The headship of the man over his wife (1 Cor. 11:1-16; 1 Tim. 2:12)

B. The Greek word translated "quietness" in 2:11 and "silent" in 2:12 does not mean total silence, or no talking. It rather means, "settled down," "undisturbed, not unruly," as translated in Acts 22:2 and 2 Thessalonians 3:12. The Greek word meaning "to say nothing" is sigao. *(See Luke 18:39; 1 Cor. 14:34.)*

---

c. Their redemption—"Notwithstanding she shall be saved in childbearing, if they continue in faith and charity and holiness with sobriety" (1 Tim. 2:15).

---

†**2:15** *First Timothy 2:15 has been the object of much speculation: "Notwithstanding she shall be saved in childbearing, if they continue in faith and charity and holiness and with sobriety." There are (at least) three basic interpretations offered to explain this verse.*

A. *That the salvation here refers to spiritual salvation. It is pointed out that the definite article precedes the word "childbearing" and should read "the childbearing," thus referring to the seed of the woman in Genesis 3:15-16. Therefore, according to this view, Paul is saying that, while it was a woman which paved the way for the corruption in Eden, it was also a woman who paved the way for the incarnation at Bethlehem.*

B. *That the "salvation" here is from doctrinal error and warns against women teaching deceptions.*

C. *That they will be kept from the corruption of society by being at home raising children.*

---

4. Concerning widows in the church

---

†*Duane Liftin writes: "Next Paul offered instruction on how Timothy must deal with the widows in the congregation. Throughout the Old and New Testaments, widows, along with aliens and orphans, are viewed as special objects of God's mercy. As such they are to be taken under the wing of the congregation (cf. Deut. 10:18; 14:29; 24:17-21; Acts 6:1-7; James 1:27). As early as Acts 6 the church had established a charitable outreach to widows. Now about 30 years later the ministry to widows, of whom there were no doubt many, showed signs of being a major burden to the congregation. Paul was therefore eager in this passage to identify those who did not truly need help in order to leave enough for those who did"* (Bible Knowledge Commentary, *New Testament edition, p. 742).*

---

a. Widows over 60 with no living children (1 Tim. 5:3, 5, 9) —They are to be honored and provided for.

b. Widows with a family (1 Tim. 5:4, 16)—They are to be provided for by their families.

c. Young widows (1 Tim. 5:6, 11-15)

(1) The rule—Let them remarry and raise children.

(2) The reason—This will keep them from immorality and idle talk.

5. Concerning senior saints in the church (1 Tim. 5:1-2)—"Rebuke not an elder, but intreat him as a father; and the younger men as brethren; the elder women as mothers; the younger as sisters, with all purity" (1 Tim. 5:1-2).

6. Concerning elders in the church

a. To be carefully chosen—"Lay hands suddenly on no man" (1 Tim. 5:22).

---

†**5:22**

A. *The exhortation—"Lay hands suddenly on no man."*

B. *The explanation—A. Duane Liftin observes: "All people are heading toward judgment, carrying with them either their* sins *or their* good *works. For some, their* sins *or* good *works go before them and* are *obvious to all observers. For others their sins or good works* trail behind, *hidden from view, becoming known only after the individual has passed. Thus Paul emphasized the difficulties inherent in choosing qualified candidates for the ordination. Hasty, superficial assessments, whether positive or negative, are sometimes inaccurate, leading to the enlistment of unqualified men or the overlooking of those whose fine qualities are less obvious. With time, however, a man's true colors will emerge to an astute observer. Thus the perceptive observations of verses 24-25 are designed to underline the warning of verse 22: do not rush to ordain someone"* (Bible Knowledge Commentary, *New Testament edition, p. 745).*

---

b. To be honored—"Let the elders that rule well be counted worthy of double honour, especially they who labour in the word and doctrine. For the scripture saith, Thou shalt not muzzle the ox that treadeth out the corn. And, The labourer is worthy of his reward" (1 Tim. 5:17-18).

c. To be assumed innocent until proven guilty—"Against an elder receive not an accusation, but before two or three witnesses" (1 Tim. 5:19).

7. Concerning the rich in the church (1 Tim. 6:6-10, 17-19)

a. Their faith—It is to be placed in God, and not in gold. "Charge them that are rich in this world, that they be not highminded, nor trust in uncertain riches, but in the living God, who giveth us richly all things to enjoy" (1 Tim. 6:17).

b. Their fortune—It is to be shared with others. "That they do good, that they be rich in good works, ready to distribute, willing to communicate" (1 Tim. 6:18).

8. Concerning servants (1 Tim. 6:1-2)

a. Those working for unsaved masters—"Let as many servants as are under the yoke count their own masters worthy of all honour, that the name of God and his doctrine be not blasphemed" (1 Tim. 6:1).

b. Those working for saved masters—"And they that have believing masters, let them not despise them, because they are brethren; but rather do them service, because they are faithful and beloved, partakers of the benefit. These things teach and exhort" (1 Tim. 6:2).

III. Church Officers and the Family of God (1 Tim. 3:1-13)

A. Qualifications for the office of bishop (1 Tim. 3:1-7) —"This is a true saying, If a man desire the office of a bishop, he desireth a good work" (1 Tim. 3:1).

---

†**3:1** Bishops *(3:1-7; see also Titus 1:5-9)—"If any man desire the office of a bishop, he desireth a good work" (3:1). The Greek word for "bishop" is* episkopos *and refers to an overseer. Here, of course, Paul had in mind the office of the pastor. Another name found in the New Testament which may refer to this same position is "elder"* (presbuteros *in the Greek). These two terms, bishop and elder, are often used interchangeably (Acts 20:17-28; Titus 1:5-7). The former term (bishop) speaks of his office responsibility, while the latter term (elder) refers to his spiritual maturity.*

---

1. He must be a male (1 Tim. 3:1).
2. He must be without reproach (1 Tim. 3:2).
3. He must be the husband of one wife (1 Tim. 3:2).

---

†*Few New Testament statements have been the object of so much speculation as this little phrase in 3:2, "The husband of one wife." There are two main interpretations.*

A. *"The prohibition of polygamy" view—According to this theory, Paul is simply saying no church member who had several wives in his home could qualify as a bishop. However, this view has serious problems.*
   1. *Paul had already forbidden this years ago (1 Cor. 7:2 and Rom. 7:1-3).*
   2. *The Roman government had outlawed polygamy at this time. There is no evidence that the early church ever had this problem.*
   3. *This term literally says a "one-woman man" and is found again in 5:9 (though here reversed) where it speaks of a widow as a "one-man woman."*

B. *"The prohibition of divorce" view—According to this theory, a divorced and remarried man is prohibited from occupying the office of the pastorate, regardless of the circumstances which may have surrounded the divorce. It must be kept in mind that Paul in this chapter is not discussing the* salvation *of a sinner, but the qualifications of an officer.*

---

4. He must be temperate (1 Tim. 3:2).
5. He must be prudent (1 Tim. 3:2).
6. He must be respectable (1 Tim. 3:2).
7. He must be given to hospitality (1 Tim. 3:2).
8. He must be able to teach (1 Tim. 3:2).
9. He must not be given to wine (1 Tim. 3:3).
10. He must not be pugnacious (1 Tim. 3:3).
11. He must be gentle (1 Tim. 3:3).
12. He must not be contentious (1 Tim. 3:3).
13. He must be free from the love of money (1 Tim. 3:3).
14. He must rule his own house well (1 Tim. 3:4)—"For if a man know not how to rule his own house, how shall he take care of the church of God?" (1 Tim. 3:5). "But if any provide not for his own, and specially for those of his own house, he hath denied the faith, and is worse than an infidel" (1 Tim. 5:8).
15. He must not be a novice or new convert—"Not a novice, lest being lifted up with pride he fall into the condemnation of the devil" (1 Tim. 3:6).
16. He must have a good reputation in the unsaved community (1 Tim. 3:7).

B. Qualifications for the office of a deacon (1 Tim. 3:8-13). "This is a true saying, If a man desire the office of a bishop, he desireth a good work. A bishop then must be blameless, the husband of one wife, vigilant, sober, of good behaviour, given to hospitality, apt to teach; not given to wine, no striker, not greedy of filthy lucre; but patient, not a brawler, not covetous" (1 Tim. 3:1-3)

---

†**3:8** Deacons *(3:8-13)—The exact nature and duties of this office are nowhere set forth in any systematic way in the New Testament. It seems almost certain that the office was created to solve the organizational problem of the early church, due in part to its rapid growth (Acts 6:1-8). The Greek word for "deacon" is* diakonos. *(See also Rom. 12:7, here translated "ministry," and Phil. 1:1.)*

---

1. He must be a man of dignity (1 Tim. 3:8).
2. He must not be double-tongued (1 Tim. 3:8).
3. He must not be given to wine (1 Tim. 3:8).
4. He must be no lover of money (1 Tim. 3:8).
5. He must possess a pure conscience (1 Tim. 3:9).

6. He must not be a novice (1 Tim. 3:10).
7. If married, he must be the husband of a godly wife (1 Tim. 3:11). "Even so must their wives be grave, not slanderers, sober, faithful in all things" (1 Tim. 3:11).
8. He must be the husband of one wife (1 Tim. 3:12).
9. He must rule his own house well (1 Tim. 3:12).

IV. False Teachers and the Family of God

A. Their theology

1. The source of their teaching—"Now the Spirit speaketh expressly, that in the latter times some shall depart from the faith, giving heed to seducing spirits, and doctrines of devils" (1 Tim. 4:1).
2. The substance of their teaching—"Forbidding to marry, and commanding to abstain from meats, which God hath created to be received with thanksgiving of them which believe and know the truth" (1 Tim. 4:3).

B. Their tactics

1. Arguing—"For every creature of God is good, and nothing to be refused, if it be received with thanksgiving. . . . If thou put the brethren in remembrance of these things, thou shalt be a good minister of Jesus Christ, nourished up in the words of faith and of good doctrine, whereunto thou hast attained. But refuse profane and old wives' fables, and exercise thyself rather unto godliness" (1 Tim. 4:4, 6-7).
2. Stirring up constant friction—"He is conceited and understands nothing; but he has a morbid interest in controversial questions and disputes about words, out of which arise envy, strife, abusive language, evil suspicions, and constant friction" (1 Tim. 6:4-5, NASB).

C. Their transgressions

1. They use the Law in the wrong way (1 Tim. 1:7-10)—"Desiring to be teachers of the law; understanding neither what they say, nor whereof they affirm. But we know that the law is good, if a man use it lawfully" (1 Tim. 1:7-8).
2. They allow their own conscience to be seared (1 Tim. 4:2)—"Speaking lies in hypocrisy; having their conscience seared with a hot iron" (1 Tim. 4:2).
3. They use the church for personal gain (1 Tim. 6:5).
4. They oppose the true faith with false theories of science. "O Timothy, keep that which is committed to thy trust, avoiding profane and vain babblings, and oppositions of science falsely so called" (1 Tim. 6:20).

V. The Savior and the Family of God—Paul offers a brief summary of Christ's work here in this epistle.

A. His incarnation—"God was manifest in the flesh" (1 Tim. 3:16b)

B. His purpose—"This is a faithful saying, and worthy of all acceptation, that Christ Jesus came into the world to save sinners; of whom I am chief" (1 Tim. 1:15). "Who is the Saviour of all men" (1 Tim. 4:10).

C. His deity—"Now unto the King eternal, immortal, invisible, the only wise God, be honour and glory for ever and ever. Amen" (1 Tim. 1:17). "Who only hath immortality, dwelling in the light which no man can approach unto; whom no man hath seen, nor can see: to whom be honour and power everlasting. Amen" (1 Tim. 6:16).

D. His successful ministry—"And without controversy great is the mystery of godliness: God was manifest in the flesh, justified in the Spirit, seen of angels, preached unto the Gentiles, believed on in the world, received up into glory" (1 Tim. 3:16).

†3:16

A. *"God was manifest in the flesh" (3:16; see also John 1:14; Dan. 2:11; Gal. 4:4; Isa. 7:14; 9:6).*

Note: 1 Timothy 3:16 is one of the truly great verses in all the Bible, and may be viewed as an amplification of John 3:16. M. F. Unger writes: "It refers to the basic body of divine revelation made known in Scripture and may well have constituted an early Christian hymn."

B. *"Preached unto the Gentiles" (nations). This probably finds its ultimate fulfillment in the words of the Great Commission in Matthew 28:18-20. Note the little phrase, "seen of angels" in 3:16. The earthly ministry of Christ was viewed by both elect and evil angels. (See Luke 2:13; Matt. 4:11; Luke 22:43—elect angels; and Mark 1:23-26; 5:2-13—evil angels.)*

C. *"Believed on in the world." In spite of Israel's official rejection of him, our Lord left in his wake a powerful "minority group" of dedicated missionaries, numbering perhaps in the thousands (see 1 Cor. 15:6).*

E. His suffering and death—"I give thee charge in the sight of God, who quickeneth all things, and before Christ Jesus, who before Pontius Pilate witnessed a good confession" (1 Tim. 6:13). "Who gave himself a ransom for all, to be testified in due time" (1 Tim. 2:6).

F. His resurrection—"Justified in the Spirit" (1 Tim. 3:16, a reference to the resurrection; see also Rom. 1:4)

G. His ascension—"Received up into glory" (1 Tim. 3:16)

H. His mediatorship—"For there is one God, and one mediator between God and men, the man Christ Jesus" (1 Tim. 2:5).

I. His return—"That thou keep this commandment without spot, unrebukeable, until the appearing of our Lord Jesus Christ" (1 Tim. 6:14).

J. His millennial reign—"Which in his times he shall shew, who is the blessed and only Potentate, the King of kings, and Lord of lords" (1 Tim. 6:15).

---

†6:15 *There are two significant titles for Jesus in this verse:*

A. *Potentate—This is the Greek word,* dunastes, *which means "the mighty ones of great authority." This title is used but once in describing Jesus.*

B. *King of kings and Lord of lords—This title is used but three times. The other two references are Revelation 17:14 and 19:16.*

---

2 TIMOTHY

THE FINAL WORDS OF GOD'S FINEST WITNESS

A. The book of 2 Timothy records these words, as written by Paul.
B. After being released from his first Roman imprisonment (Acts 28), Paul is once again arrested.
C. This arrest may have taken place suddenly in Troas, thus explaining why Paul left there without taking his cloak, parchments, or Old Testament scrolls (2 Tim. 4:13).
D. On July 19, A.D. 64, Rome was burned (probably by Nero) and the Christians were blamed. Christianity then became an illegal religion, and to evangelize was a crime punishable by death.
E. Paul was probably arrested again sometime after July of A.D. 64, and condemned to death.
F. During his second and final imprisonment he wrote 2 Timothy.
G. His second imprisonment was far different from the first.
   1. He was then a political prisoner awaiting trial. He is now a condemned criminal, awaiting death.
   2. Then he lived in his own hired house. Now he huddles in a cold, damp, dark dungeon.
   3. During his first imprisonment he was visited by many. Now he is forsaken by all.
H. This is the most personal letter; in Romans we see Paul the theologian; in 1 Corinthians, Paul the counselor; in 2 Corinthians, Paul the preacher; in Galatians, Paul the defender; in 1 Timothy and Titus, Paul the statesman; but here in 2 Timothy, Paul the man.
I. The letter is rich in personal allusions. Paul mentions 23 men, women, friends, and foes.
J. This epistle is his spiritual swan song, his dying shout of triumph.
K. Paul writes more about last day conditions in this epistle than in any other. (See 3:1-13; 4:1-4.)
L. He also lists (by name) more enemies of the gospel in this epistle. There are Hymenaeus and Philetus (2:17), Jannes and Jambres (3:8), and Alexander the coppersmith (4:14).
M. Dr. J. Vernon McGee writes: "In Second Timothy Paul speaks of the ultimate outcome of gospel preaching. The final fruition will not be the total conversion of mankind, nor will it usher in the Millennium. On the contrary, there will come about an apostasy which will well-nigh blot out 'the faith' from the earth. This is in complete harmony with the startling word of Christ, 'When the Son of man cometh, shall he find faith on the earth?' This is not in keeping, of course, with a social gospel which expects to transform the world by tinkering with the social system. These vain optimists have no patience with the doleful words of 2 Timothy. Nevertheless, the cold and hard facts of history and the events of the present have demonstrated the accuracy of Paul" (*Second Timothy*, p. 196).

N. At least six analogies depicting the Christian life are given here in this book. The believer is likened to a soldier (2:3), athlete (2:5), farmer (2:6), student (2:15), vessel (2:21), and servant (2:24).

O. Finally, Paul's overall evaluation and summary of his own ministry is seen in his closing words. (See 4:6-8.)

P. The book of 2 Timothy is the 20th longest New Testament book, and 53rd longest biblical book, with four chapters, 83 verses, and 1,703 words. There are quotations or allusions from seven Old Testament books in 2 Timothy.

Q. Great passages would include:
1. 1:6-10
2. 1:11-14
3. 2:1-3
4. 2:11-13
5. 2:15
6. 3:16-17
7. 4:1-5
8. 4:7-8

THE BOOK OF 2 TIMOTHY

I. Paul the Preacher (2 Tim. 1)—"Whereunto I am appointed a preacher, and an apostle, and a teacher of the Gentiles" (2 Tim. 1:11).
  A. The preacher and his student (Timothy)
    1. His concern for Timothy
      a. He prayed for him (2 Tim. 1:3).
      b. He knew his tears (2 Tim. 1:4).
    2. His confidence in Timothy
      a. Stir up your gift—"Wherefore I put thee in remembrance that thou stir up the gift of God, which is in thee by the putting on of my hands. For God hath not given us the spirit of fear; but of power, and of love, and of a sound mind" (2 Tim. 1:6-7).

---

†1:6 *The Greek word here translated "stir" literally means to rekindle. This is its only reference in the New Testament. Timothy was evidently not making full use of his pastoral gift.*

---

      b. Don't be ashamed:
        (1) Of Christ's message—"Be not thou therefore ashamed of the testimony of our Lord" (2 Tim. 1:8).
        (2) Of Christ's messenger—"Nor of me his prisoner: but be thou partaker of the afflictions of the gospel according to the power of God" (2 Tim. 1:8).
      c. Hold fast to sound doctrine—"Hold fast the form of sound words, which thou hast heard of me, in faith and love which is in Christ Jesus" (2 Tim. 1:13).
      d. Remain true to your ministry—"That good thing which was committed unto thee keep by the Holy Ghost which dwelleth in us" (2 Tim. 1:14).

B. The preacher and himself
   1. He reviews his past performance—Ministering as:
      a. An apostle (2 Tim. 1:1)
      b. A father (2 Tim. 1:2)
      c. A servant (2 Tim. 1:3)
      d. A prisoner (2 Tim. 1:8)
      e. A preacher (2 Tim. 1:11)
      f. A teacher (2 Tim. 1:11)
      g. A sufferer (2 Tim. 1:12)
   2. He retains his permanent hope—"For the which cause I also suffer these things: nevertheless I am not ashamed: for I know whom I have believed, and am persuaded that he is able to keep that which I have committed unto him against that day" (2 Tim. 1:12).

---

†1:12 *There are two views concerning the use of the word "committed" in this verse.*
A. Paul was here referring to his salvation, which he had deposited with Christ.
B. Paul was here referring to his service, which Christ had deposited with Paul. It may be the apostle had both in mind.

---

   3. He regrets certain actions of some false friends—"This thou knowest, that all they which are in Asia be turned away from me; of whom are Phygellus and Hermogenes" (2 Tim. 1: 15).
   4. He rejoices concerning the actions of a true friend—"The Lord give mercy unto the house of Onesiphorus; for he oft refreshed me, and was not ashamed of my chain: but, when he was in Rome, he sought me out very diligently, and found me. The Lord grant unto him that he may find mercy of the Lord in that day: and in how many things he ministered unto me at Ephesus, thou knowest very well" (2 Tim. 1:16-18).

C. The preacher and his Savior—"Who hath saved us, and called us with an holy calling, not according to our works, but according to his own purpose and grace, which was given us in Christ Jesus before the world began, but is now made manifest by the appearing of our Saviour Jesus Christ, who hath abolished death, and hath brought life and immortality to light through the gospel" (2 Tim. 1:9-10).

II. Paul the Pattern (2 Tim. 2)—"And the things that thou hast heard of me among many witnesses, the same commit thou to faithful men, who shall be able to teach others also" (2 Tim. 2:2). In this chapter Paul likens the work of the ministry to various things.

---

†2:2 *The child of God is assigned a threefold duty concerning the Word of God:*
A. We are to receive it—From others.
B. We are to regard it—Within ourselves.
C. We are to remit it—To others. To state it in another way: we are to read *it, to* heed *it, and to* deed *it.*

A. A soldier—"Thou therefore endure hardness, as a good soldier of Jesus Christ. No man that warreth entangleth himself with the affairs of this life; that he may please him who hath chosen him to be a soldier" (2 Tim. 2:3-4).

B. An athlete—"And also if any one competes as an athlete, he does not win the prize unless he competes according to the rules" (2 Tim. 2:5, NASB).

---

†2:5 *Paul often describes the Christian life in athletic terms.*
A. A wrestler (Eph. 6:12)
B. A fighter (1 Cor. 9:26)
C. A runner (1 Cor. 9:24; Heb. 12:1)

C. A farmer—"The husbandman that laboureth must be first partaker of the fruits" (2 Tim. 2:6).

D. A sufferer (2 Tim. 2:9-13)
1. The report concerning Paul's sufferings—"Wherein I suffer trouble, as an evil doer, even unto bonds; but the word of God is not bound" (2 Tim. 2:9).
2. The reason for Paul's sufferings—"Therefore I endure all things for the elect's sakes, that they may also obtain the salvation which is in Christ Jesus with eternal glory" (2 Tim. 2:10).
3. The rewards of Paul's sufferings—"It is a faithful saying: For if we be dead with him, we shall also live with him: if we suffer, we shall also reign with him: if we deny him, he also will deny us: if we believe not, yet he abideth faithful: he cannot deny himself" (2 Tim. 2:11-13).

---

†2:13 *The word "deny" is mentioned three times in these verses.*
A. "If we deny him," that is, do not allow him first place in our lives
B. "He also will deny us," that is, we will suffer the loss of our rewards at the judgment seat of Christ (see 1 Cor. 3:11-15).
C. "He cannot deny himself," that is, his promise of eternal salvation to the elect is secure regardless of their failures (see 2:10, 19).

E. An instructor (2 Tim. 2:14)—"Of these things put them in remembrance, charging them before the Lord that they strive not about words to no profit, but to the subverting of the hearers" (2 Tim. 2:14).

---

†2:14 *There was apparently a strong (and sinful) tendency in the early church to argue over certain words and concepts found within various false philosophical systems. Note Paul's repeated warnings on this in the pastoral epistles: "Neither give heed to fables and endless genealogies" (1 Tim. 1:4). "Avoiding profane and vain babblings" (1 Tim. 6:20). "But refuse profane and old wives' fables" (1 Tim. 4:7). "Questions and strifes of words, whereof cometh envy" (1 Tim. 6:4). "But shun profane and vain babblings" (2 Tim. 2:16). "But foolish and unlearned questions avoid" (2 Tim. 2:23). "But avoid foolish questions, and genealogies" (Titus 3:9).*

F. A student (2 Tim. 2:15-19, 23)
1. He advises Timothy to study God's Word—"Study to shew thyself approved

unto God, a workman that needeth not to be ashamed, rightly dividing the word of truth" (2 Tim. 2:15).

---

†2:15 *The Greek word translated "rightly dividing" is found only here in the New Testament and literally means, "to cut straight." In light of Paul's former trade he may here have been comparing the art of tentmaking with that of Bible teaching. Careless and crooked cutting of the canvas would weaken the completed tent, thus the importance of each stroke of the knife. Paul's intended lesson here is obvious.*

---

2. He advises Timothy to shun profane words—"But shun profane and vain babblings: for they will increase unto more ungodliness. And their word will eat as doth a canker: of whom is Hymenaeus and Philetus; who concerning the truth have erred, saying that the resurrection is past already; and overthrow the faith of some. Nevertheless the foundation of God standeth sure, having this seal, The Lord knoweth them that are his. And, Let every one that nameth the name of Christ depart from iniquity. . . . But foolish and unlearned questions avoid, knowing that they do gender strifes" (2 Tim. 2:16-19, 23).

G. A vessel
1. The various vessels—"But in a great house there are not only vessels of gold and of silver, but also of wood and of earth; and some to honour, and some to dishonour" (2 Tim. 2:20).
2. The victorious vessel—"If a man therefore purge himself from these, he shall be a vessel unto honour, sanctified, and meet for the master's use, and prepared unto every good work. Flee also youthful lusts: but follow righteousness, faith, charity, peace, with them that call on the Lord out of a pure heart" (2 Tim. 2:21-22).

H. A servant (2 Tim. 2:24-26)—"And the servant of the Lord must not strive; but be gentle unto all men, apt to teach, patient" (2 Tim. 2:24).

III. Paul the Prophet (2 Tim. 3)—"This know also, that in the last days perilous times shall come. . . . But evil men and seducers shall wax worse and worse, deceiving, and being deceived" (2 Tim. 3:1, 13).

---

†3:1 *The word "perilous" here is translated "exceeding fierce" in Matthew 8:28, describing the maniac of Gadara. Thus, in the last days Satan will attempt to turn this world into his own personal graveyard.*

A. The symptoms of this "final days disease" (2 Tim. 3:1-9)
1. Information concerning this disease—"But evil men and seducers shall wax worse and worse, deceiving, and being deceived" (2 Tim. 3:13).
   a. They will be self-lovers (2 Tim. 3:2).
   b. They will be lovers of money (2 Tim. 3:2).
   c. They will be boastful (2 Tim. 3:2).
   d. They will be arrogant (2 Tim. 3:2).
   e. They will be revilers (2 Tim. 3:2).

f. They will be disobedient to parents (2 Tim. 3:2).
g. They will be ungrateful (2 Tim. 3:2).
h. They will be unholy (2 Tim. 3:2).
i. They will be unloving (2 Tim. 3:3).

---

†*Especially to be noted is the little phrase in verse 3, "without natural affection." This phrase is a translation of the Greek word* stergein, *which refers to a special kind of human love. Greek scholar Kenneth Wuest writes: "It is a love that is a natural movement of the soul, something almost like gravitation or some other force of blind nature. It is the love of parents for children and children for parents, of husband for wife and wife for husband, or close relations one for another. It is found in the animal world in the love which the animal has for its offspring. It is a love of obligatoriness, the term being used here not in its moral sense, but in the natural sense. It is a necessity under the circumstances. This kind of love is the binding factor by which any natural or social unit is held together"* (By Paths in the Greek New Testament, *p. 110).*

The point of all the above is that Paul predicts that one of the elements prevalent during the final days will be the absence (in some human circles) of even that stergein *gravitational-type love possessed by the animal kingdom for their young. It would seem in light of this that no more vivid example of Paul's sad prediction can be seen than in the modern abortion movement.*

---

j. They will be irreconcilable (2 Tim. 3:3).
k. They will be malicious gossipers (2 Tim. 3:3).
l. They will be without self-control (2 Tim. 3:3).
m. They will be brutal (2 Tim. 3:3).
n. They will be haters of good (2 Tim. 3:3).
o. They will be treacherous (2 Tim. 3:4).
p. They will be reckless (2 Tim. 3:4).
q. They will be conceited (2 Tim. 3:4).
r. They will be lovers of pleasures rather than lovers of God (2 Tim. 3:4).
s. They will be holding a form of godliness, although denying its power (2 Tim. 3:5).

2. Illustrations of this disease—"For of this sort are they which creep into houses, and lead captive silly women laden with sins, led away with divers lusts, ever learning, and never able to come to the knowledge of the truth. Now as Jannes and Jambres withstood Moses, so do these also resist the truth: men of corrupt minds, reprobate concerning the faith" (2 Tim. 3:6-8).

B. The solution for this "final days disease" (2 Tim. 3:10-17)

1. Continue in the work of God (2 Tim. 3:10-12)—"But thou hast fully known my doctrine, manner of life, purpose, faith, longsuffering, charity, patience, persecutions, afflictions, which came unto me at Antioch, at Iconium, at Lystra; what persecutions I endured: but out of them all the Lord delivered me. Yea, and all that will live godly in Christ Jesus shall suffer persecution" (2 Tim. 3:10-12).
2. Continue in the Word of God (2 Tim. 3:14-17).
   a. What it had done for Timothy the young man—"But continue thou in the things which thou hast learned and hast been assured of, knowing of whom thou hast learned them; and that from a child thou hast known the holy

scriptures, which are able to make thee wise unto salvation through faith which is in Christ Jesus" (2 Tim. 3:14-15).

b. What it would do for Timothy the leader—"All scripture is given by inspiration of God, and is profitable for doctrine, for reproof, for correction, for instruction in righteousness: that the man of God may be perfect, throughly furnished unto all good works" (2 Tim. 3:16-17).

---

†3:17 *In this remarkable passage Paul asserts that the Bible is profitable for:*

A. Doctrine—The Bible may be used as the perfect textbook to present the systematic teachings of the great truths relating to God himself.

B. Reproof—The Bible is to be used to convict us of the wrong in our lives.

C. Correction—The Bible will then show us the right way.

D. Instruction in righteousness—The Bible provides all the necessary details which will allow a Christian to become fully equipped for every good work.

IV. Paul the Pilgrim (2 Tim. 4)—"The time of my departure is at hand" (2 Tim. 4:6).

A. His final charge (2 Tim. 4:1-2, 5)

1. Preach the Word of God—"I charge thee therefore before God, and the Lord Jesus Christ, who shall judge the quick and the dead at his appearing and his kingdom; preach the word; be instant in season, out of season; reprove, rebuke, exhort with all longsuffering and doctrine" (2 Tim. 4:1-2).

2. Reach your world for God—"But watch thou in all things, endure afflictions, do the work of an evangelist, make full proof of thy ministry" (2 Tim. 4:5).

B. His final warning (2 Tim. 4:3-4)—"For the time will come when they will not endure sound doctrine; but after their own lusts shall they heap to themselves teachers, having itching ears; and they shall turn away their ears from the truth, and shall be turned unto fables" (2 Tim. 4:3-4).

C. His final testimony (2 Tim. 4:6-7)—"For I am now ready to be offered, and the time of my departure is at hand. I have fought a good fight, I have finished my course, I have kept the faith" (2 Tim. 4:6-7).

---

†4:7 *The word translated "offered" is a liturgical word and signifies the pouring out of a religious drink offering (Num. 15:1-10). Paul had already regarded his ministry in winning the lost to Christ as an offering to God (Rom. 15:16; Phil. 2:17), and now his approaching death would complete the sacrifice.*

The word "departure" means "to take down a tent, to break camp, to pull in the anchor." His testimony in verse 7 should be contrasted with God's statement to wicked Belshazzar in Daniel 5:26.

D. His final commission (2 Tim. 4:10, 12)

1. Titus is sent to Dalmatia (2 Tim. 4:10).

2. Tychicus is sent to Ephesus (2 Tim. 4:12).

E. His final farewell—"Salute Prisca and Aquila, and the household of Onesiphorus" (2 Tim. 4:19).

F. His final request (2 Tim. 4:9, 11, 13, 21)

1. The persons he desires to see (2 Tim. 4:9, 11)
   a. Timothy—"Do thy diligence to come shortly unto me" (2 Tim. 4:9)
   b. John Mark—"Only Luke is with me. Take Mark, and bring him with thee: for he is profitable to me for the ministry" (2 Tim. 4:11).

---

†**4:11** *Timothy was to come immediately. He was to bring John Mark with him. Years prior to this Mark had, of course, accompanied Paul and Barnabas on their first missionary trip, but had left the team and gone home. Due to this sign of immaturity, Paul had refused to include him in a second proposed trip. This action then prompted a break between Paul and Barnabas. (See Acts 13:3; 15:36-40.) But since that time Mark had so grown in God's grace that Paul desired to see him before his departure.*

---

2. The objects he desires to have (2 Tim. 4:13)
   a. His cloak
   b. His books
   c. His Old Testament scrolls

---

† *A. Timothy was to bring Paul's cloak he had left at Troas (4:13). The great 16th-century Bible translator William Tyndale would later make a similar request while confined to a damp prison cell: "I entreat your lordship, and that by the Lord Jesus, that if I must remain here for the winter, you would beg the Commissary to be so kind as to send me, from the things of mine which he has, a warmer cap, I feel the cold painfully in my head. Also a warmer cloak to patch my leggings. My overcoat is worn out, my shorts even are worn out. He has a woolen shirt of mine, if he will send it. But most of all I entreat and implore your kindness to do your best with the Commissary to be so good as to send my Hebrew Bible, grammar, and vocabulary, that I may spend my time in that pursuit."*

B. He was to bring the parchments—Paul's copies of the Old Testament. This statement is staggering in its implications. Here is a man who conducted the first three missionary trips ever attempted for Christ, who had personally seen the Savior on at least four occasions, who had written approximately half of the New Testament, and who had organized the first 50 or so Christian churches on this earth. Now in his hour of death he requests the Scriptures, for he evidently felt he could still learn from the precious pages. The child of God is in absolutely no danger whatsoever of learning too much about God's Word.

G. His final sorrow
1. Abused by his foes—"Alexander the coppersmith did me much evil: the Lord reward him according to his works: of whom be thou ware also; for he hath greatly withstood our words" (2 Tim. 4:14-15).
2. Abandoned by his friends—"For Demas hath forsaken me, having loved this present world, and is departed unto Thessalonica; Crescens to Galatia, Titus unto Dalmatia" (2 Tim. 4:10). "At my first defense no one supported me, but all deserted me; may it not be counted against them" (2 Tim. 4:16, NASB).

†4:16 *Paul thus was the third and final New Testament person to pray for those who had ill-treated him. Note the statements of the first two:*

A. The words of Jesus in Luke 23:34: "Then said Jesus, Father, forgive them; for they know not what they do. And they parted his raiment, and cast lots."

B. The words of Stephen in Acts 7:59-60: "And they stoned Stephen, calling upon God, and saying, Lord Jesus, receive my spirit. And he kneeled down, and cried with a loud voice, Lord, lay not this sin to their charge. And when he had said this, he fell asleep."

H. His final notes of praise
   1. What God has done for him—"Notwithstanding the Lord stood with me, and strengthened me" (2 Tim. 4:17).
   2. What God would do for him
      a. He would deliver him—"And the Lord shall deliver me from every evil work, and will preserve me unto his heavenly kingdom: to whom be glory for ever and ever. Amen" (2 Tim. 4:18).
      b. He would reward him—"Henceforth there is laid up for me a crown of righteousness, which the Lord, the righteous judge, shall give me at that day: and not to me only, but unto all them also that love his appearing" (2 Tim. 4:8).

TITUS

PAUL'S MESSAGE TO GOD'S MAN IN CRETE

A. The man was Titus and the message was to stay there.
B. Titus, like Timothy, was one of Paul's "preacher boys."
C. Paul had assigned Titus to strengthen a previously established church work on the Isle of Crete. This island, southeast of Greece, was about 150 miles long and 35 miles wide, thus making it the largest of the Mediterranean islands. It was an island of 100 cities, consisting of mountains, but also very fertile valleys. The highest mountain, Mount Ida, was the traditional birthplace of the Greek god Zeus. The Cretans were relatives of the Philistines. They had a notorious reputation of being "always liars, evil beasts, lazy gluttons" (Titus 1:12, NASB). This testimony came from one of their own poets and prophets. The origin of the church there is unknown, but may have been started by the same returning Cretans who were present at Pentecost (see Acts 2:11).
D. The epistle to Titus was written about the same time as 1 Timothy, during that period between Paul's first and second Roman imprisonments.
E. The three pastoral epistles may be favorably compared.
    1. In 1 and 2 Timothy Paul stresses doctrine.
    2. In Titus he emphasizes duty.
    3. The child of God is to protect the gospel in 1 Timothy.
    4. He is to proclaim it in 2 Timothy.
    5. He is to practice it in Titus.
F. A summary of the person and ministry of Titus would include:
    1. He was a Gentile (Greek, see Gal. 2:3).
    2. He was probably a convert of Paul (Titus 1:4).
    3. Some believe he may have been the brother of Luke.
    4. Titus first appears in the sacred account when he accompanied Paul and Barnabas to Jerusalem (Gal. 2:1).
    5. He is later sent by Paul to Corinth to straighten out certain disorders in the church there and to initiate an offering for the poor saints at Jerusalem (2 Cor. 8:6, 10-11).
    6. He then meets Paul in Macedonia and is sent back to Corinth carrying the epistle of 2 Corinthians to pave the way for Paul's coming and to complete their offering (2 Cor. 2:3, 12-13; 7:5-6, 13-14; 8:16-17, 23; 12:14, 18).
    7. He seems to have accompanied Paul during the third missionary trip.
    8. He is last mentioned in 2 Timothy 4:10, at which time Paul sends him from southern Greece to Dalmatia (Yugoslavia).
    9. Titus may have been the only Gentile to receive a New Testament letter.
G. This epistle marks the last of but two instances where the great theological word "regeneration" is used in the New Testament.
    1. It is found in Matthew 19:28 where it refers to mother nature.
    2. It is found in Titus 3:5 where it refers to redeemed sinners.

H. This little epistle contains two of Scripture's greatest passages on the work of Christ and the destiny of believers. (See 2:11-14; 3:4-7.)
I. Titus is the 23rd longest New Testament book, and 61st longest biblical book, with three chapters, 46 verses, and 921 words. There are quotations or allusions from six Old Testament books in Titus.
J. Great passages would include:
   1. 2:11-14
   2. 3:4-7

THE BOOK OF TITUS

I. Titus and the Apostle (Titus 1:1-4)
   A. Paul was God's servant
      1. Serving as an apostle—"Paul, a servant of God, and an apostle of Jesus Christ, according to the faith of God's elect, and the acknowledging of the truth which is after godliness; in hope of eternal life, which God, that cannot lie, promised before the world began" (Titus 1:1-2).

---

†*The God of the Bible is described not only as one who* cannot *lie, but also as the God who* need not *lie. The person lying usually does so to get himself out of an unpleasant situation, to avoid punishment, to impress someone, or to obtain something. But the holy, eternal, all-knowing, all-powerful, and all-sufficient God is never confronted by any of these circumstances.*

---

      2. Serving as a preacher—"But hath in due times manifested his word through preaching, which is committed unto me according to the commandment of God our Saviour" (Titus 1:3).
   B. Titus was Paul's son—"To Titus, mine own son after the common faith: Grace, mercy, and peace, from God the Father and the Lord Jesus Christ our Saviour" (Titus 1:4).
II. Titus and the Elders (Titus 1:5-16)—"For this cause left I thee in Crete, that thou shouldest set in order the things that are wanting, and ordain elders in every city, as I had appointed thee" (Titus 1:5).

---

†**1:5** *Duane Liftin writes: "As with Timothy in Ephesus (1 Tim. 1:3), Paul had left Titus behind to provide leadership to the fledgling church in Crete. Now the apostle reiterated his previous instructions, both for Titus' sake and for the congregation's sake. The organization of the Cretan church was unfinished due to the brevity of Paul's visit. Thus Titus was to straighten out (lit., "set in order") the situation by appointing elders in every town. Titus was now acting as an apostolic agent (cf. Acts 14:23) in Paul's absence. His authority in the Cretan church was an extension of Paul's own. Such authority ended with the close of the Apostolic Age"* (Bible Knowledge Commentary, *New Testament Volume, p. 762).*

   A. The nature of their qualifications
      1. They must be above reproach (Titus 1:6).

2. They must be the husband of one wife (Titus 1:6).
3. They must have children who believe (Titus 1:6).
4. They must not be accused of rebellion (Titus 1:6).
5. They must not be self-willed (Titus 1:7).

---

†*One of the main contrasts between Satan and Christ had to do with the will. Note:*
A. The self-will of Satan (Isa. 14:12-14; Ezek. 28:11-17)
B. The submissive will of Christ (Matt. 26:36-46)

---

6. They must not be quick-tempered (Titus 1:7).
7. They must not be addicted to wine (Titus 1:7).
8. They must not be pugnacious (Titus 1:7).
9. They must not be lovers of money (Titus 1:7).
10. They must be hospitable (Titus 1:8).
11. They must love what is good (Titus 1:8).
12. They must be sensible (Titus 1:8).
13. They must be just (Titus 1:8).
14. They must be devout (Titus 1:8).
15. They must be self-controlled (Titus 1:8).
16. They must be students of the Word (Titus 1:9).

B. The necessity for their qualifications
1. To reprove erring believers—"Holding fast the faithful word as he hath been taught, that he may be able by sound doctrine both to exhort and to convince the gainsayers" (Titus 1:9). "This witness is true. Wherefore rebuke them sharply, that they may be sound in the faith" (Titus 1:13).
2. To renounce apostate unbelievers
   a. Their identity—"For there are many unruly and vain talkers and deceivers, specially they of the circumcision. . . . One of themselves, even a prophet of their own, said, The Cretians are alway liars, evil beasts, slow bellies" (Titus 1:10, 12).
   b. Their iniquity—"Whose mouths must be stopped, who subvert whole houses, teaching things which they ought not, for filthy lucre's sake. Unto the pure all things are pure: but unto them that are defiled and unbelieving is nothing pure; but even their mind and conscience is defiled. They profess that they know God; but in works they deny him, being abominable, and disobedient, and unto every good work reprobate" (Titus 1:11, 15-16).

---

†1:16

A. "Unto the pure, all things are pure." Paul is here, of course, talking about Mosaic dietary laws, and not morals in general (see Matt. 15:11; Rom. 14:14; Acts 10:15).

B. "They profess that they know God." The most dangerous (and often most devilish) groups on earth are those who profess but who do not possess the things of God. Paul would warn Timothy of this same group in his final epistle: "Having a form of godliness, but denying the power thereof" (2 Tim. 3:5). Our Lord had previously soundly condemned such individuals during his earthly ministry (see Matt. 7:21-23; 23:1-39).

III. Titus and the Church (Titus 2:1–3:11)
 A. Its head, the Savior
  1. The what of his work
   a. His incarnation—"For the grace of God that bringeth salvation hath appeared to all men. . . . But after that the kindness and love of God our Saviour toward man appeared" (Titus 2:11; 3:4).
   b. His death—"Not by works of righteousness which we have done, but according to his mercy he saved us, by the washing of regeneration, and renewing of the Holy Ghost; which he shed on us abundantly through Jesus Christ our Saviour" (Titus 3:5-6).
   c. His second coming—"This witness is true. Wherefore rebuke them sharply, that they may be sound in the faith" (Titus 1:13).
  2. The why of his work—"Teaching us that, denying ungodliness and worldly lusts, we should live soberly, righteously, and godly, in this present world. . . . Who gave himself for us, that he might redeem us from all iniquity, and purify unto himself a peculiar people, zealous of good works. . . . That being justified by his grace, we should be made heirs according to the hope of eternal life" (Titus 2:12, 14; 3:7).

---

†**3:7** *We may observe three aspects in verse 12:*
A. The selfward aspect—We are to live soberly.
B. The manward aspect—We are to live righteously.
C. The Godward aspect—We are to live godly.

 B. Its heirs, the saved
  1. Responsibilities of the sheep
   a. The older men—"That the aged men be sober, grave, temperate, sound in faith, in charity, in patience" (Titus 2:2).
   b. The older women—"The aged women likewise, that they be in behaviour as becometh holiness, not false accusers, not given to much wine, teachers of good things" (Titus 2:3).
   c. The younger women—"That they may teach the young women to be sober, to love their husbands, to love their children, to be discreet, chaste, keepers at home, good, obedient to their own husbands, that the word of God be not blasphemed" (Titus 2:4-5).
   d. The younger men—"Young men likewise exhort to be sober minded" (Titus 2:6).
   e. Servants—"Exhort servants to be obedient unto their own masters, and to please them well in all things; not answering again; not purloining, but shewing all good fidelity; that they may adorn the doctrine of God our Saviour in all things" (Titus 2:9-10).
  2. Responsibilities of the undershepherd
   a. To serve as a preacher—"But speak thou the things which become sound doctrine. . . . These things speak, and exhort, and rebuke with all authority. Let no man despise thee" (Titus 2:1, 15). "Put them in mind to be subject to principalities and powers, to obey magistrates, to be ready to every good

work, to speak evil of no man, to be no brawlers, but gentle, shewing all meekness unto all men. For we ourselves also were sometimes foolish, disobedient, deceived, serving divers lusts and pleasures, living in malice and envy, hateful, and hating one another. . . . This is a faithful saying, and these things I will that thou affirm constantly, that they which have believed in God might be careful to maintain good works. These things are good and profitable unto men. But avoid foolish questions, and genealogies, and contentions, and strivings about the law; for they are unprofitable and vain" (Titus 3:1-3, 8-9).

b. To serve as a pattern—"In all things shewing thyself a pattern of good works: in doctrine shewing uncorruptness, gravity, sincerity, sound speech, that cannot be condemned; that he that is of the contrary part may be ashamed, having no evil thing to say of you" (Titus 2:7-8).

c. To serve as a purifier—"A man that is an heretick after the first and second admonition reject; knowing that he that is such is subverted, and sinneth, being condemned of himself" (Titus 3:10-11).

IV. Titus and the Future (Titus 3:12-15)

A. He is instructed to meet Paul in Nicopolis (Titus 3:12).

---

†**3:12** *He would be relieved for awhile by Tychicus. Tychicus had already been sent by Paul on various missions to the churches at Ephesus (Eph. 6:21) and Colosse (Col. 4:7). He would later be sent to Ephesus again (see 2 Tim. 4:12). He was then to meet Paul in southern Greece (Nicopolis).*

B. He is instructed to help Zenas and Apollos (Titus 3:13).

PHILEMON

THIS IS A LETTER
FROM A PRISONER TO A MASTER
ABOUT A SLAVE.

A. The book is Philemon (the master); the slave was Onesimus; and the prisoner was Paul.
B. This book, the shortest of all Paul's epistles, is one of the four letters written during his first Roman imprisonment. The other letters are Philippians, Colossians, and Ephesians.
C. It is one of four personal letters to individuals penned by Paul. The others are 1 and 2 Timothy and Titus.
D. Dr. J. Vernon McGee writes: "The Epistles present a different style in revelation. God had used law, history, poetry, prophecy, and the Gospels heretofore, but in the Epistles He adopted a more personal and direct method. In this intimate way, He looks back to the cross and talks about the church. Someone has said that the Epistles are the love letters of Christ to us. Dr. Deissman divided them into two classifications: epistles and letters. The epistles are general, while the letters are more personal and individual. Under this division, the Epistle of Philemon would be classified as a letter, for it is individual and intimate. There is reason to believe that Paul did not expect its contents to be divulged (at other times he knew that he was writing Scripture). This does not detract from the inspiration and value of Philemon, but rather enhances its value and message" (*Through the Bible,* p. 211).
E. The historical background of Philemon is as follows:
   1. Onesimus, a slave owned by Philemon (wealthy Colossian believer and long time friend of Paul) had robbed his master and run away to Rome.
   2. In some wonderful way, Onesimus's path crosses that of Paul, resulting in his glorious conversion to Christ.
   3. Upon hearing his testimony, Paul determines to send him back to Philemon.
   4. To prepare the way (for what could be a very tense meeting), Paul pens this beautiful letter to Philemon. It is a masterpiece of Christian tact and ethics.
F. The letter provides us with one of the finest illustrations of that great theological truth of imputation (the act of reckoning something to another's account) as can be found anywhere in the Bible.
G. This epistle demonstrates that our letter writing can be a ministry for God if we allow it to be so. Some who find it difficult to speak for God may well write for him.
H. It is Paul's only letter where he hints at his age (Philem. 9).
I. Philemon is the 25th longest New Testament book, and 64th longest biblical book, with one chapter, 25 verses, and 445 words.
J. Its great passage is verses 3-6.

THE BOOK OF PHILEMON

I. The Appreciation for Praise of Philemon (Philem. 1-7)
A. Philemon was a friend.
1. To Paul in Rome—"And to our beloved Apphia, and Archippus our fellow soldier, and to the church in thy house" (Philem. 2).

---

†**v. 1** *Although Paul had never been to Colosse, he had in the past met Philemon. We may suppose this wealthy Colossian believer had prayed for and financially invested in the apostle's ministry.*

---

2. To Christians in Colosse—"Hearing of thy love and faith, which thou hast toward the Lord Jesus, and toward all saints" (Philem. 5).

---

†**v. 5** *No greater tribute can be paid to a believer than this. Paul speaks of Philemon's love for Jesus (because of who he is), and his faith in Jesus (because of what he is).*

"For I have come to have much joy and comfort in your love, because the hearts of the saints have been refreshed through you, brother" (Philem. 7, NASB).

---

†**v. 7** *Philemon's house was probably a free "Holiday Inn" to any and all believers journeying in that area. His life had also touched those saints in the Colosse church.*

B. Philemon was a family man—"And to our beloved Apphia, and Archippus our fellow soldier, and to the church in thy house" (Philem. 2).

---

†**v. 2**

A. *It is believed that Apphia was Philemon's wife and Archippus his son. In his Colossian letter (Col. 4:17) Paul seems to say that Archippus had assumed the role of the pastor there in Colosse when Epaphras (founder of the church) had departed for Rome to visit the imprisoned apostle. At any rate, Philemon seemed to have his family well in hand. He could loudly echo the final words of Joshua: "Choose you this day whom ye will serve . . . but as for me and my house, we will serve the Lord" (Josh. 24:15).*

B. *Note the phrase, "the church in thy house." Edwin C. Deibler writes: "The practice of churches meeting in private homes for worship was common up to A.D. 200. Not until the third century did churches meet in separate buildings. Home churches were also mentioned by Paul in Romans 16:5 and Colossians 4:15"* (Bible Knowledge Commentary, *New Testament volume, p. 771).*

II. The Appeal and Plea for Onesimus (Philem. 8-17)—"I beseech thee for my son Onesimus, whom I have begotten in my bonds" (Philem. 10).

---

†**v. 10** *Onesimus is one of three individuals whom Paul looked upon as his spiritual sons. The other two are:*

A. Timothy (1 Tim. 1:2; 2 Tim. 1:2)
B. Titus (Titus 1:4)

A. The background of this appeal—Onesimus, Philemon's runaway slave, had been led to Christ in Rome by Paul and was now being sent back to Philemon with a request that he be received as a Christian brother.
B. The basis of this appeal
  1. Forgive him for your sake—"Which in time past was to thee unprofitable, but now profitable to thee and to me. . . . For perhaps he therefore departed for a season, that thou shouldest receive him for ever" (Philem. 11, 15).

---

†v. 15 *This former dishonest slave had already learned so much in Rome and had proven to be such a help to the apostle. But his spiritual responsibility would demand that he now return and submit himself to Philemon. If he refused to do this, God's blessing upon him would be limited.*

---

  2. Forgive him for his sake—"No longer as a slave, but more than a slave, a beloved brother . . . in the Lord" (Philem. 16, NASB).

---

†v. 16 *The name Onesimus means "profitable." However, until his conversion, any resemblance between the name and his actions was purely accidental. But now Christ had made all things new. Therefore, if for no other reason (and indeed there were other good reasons), Philemon should restore Onesimus so that he might prove by his actions the meaning of his name.*

---

  3. Forgive him for my sake—"Yet for love's sake I rather beseech thee, being such an one as Paul the aged, and now also a prisoner of Jesus Christ. . . . If thou count me therefore a partner, receive him as myself. If he wronged thee, or oweth thee ought, put that on mine account" (Philem. 9, 17-18)

---

†v. 18 *Paul refers to himself in two ways unique to this epistle:*
A. "Paul, a prisoner of Jesus Christ" (Philem. 1, 9).
B. "Paul, the aged" (Philem. 9)

III. The Assurance and Pledge of Paul (Philem. 19-25)—"I Paul have written it with mine own hand, I will repay it: albeit I do not say to thee how thou owest unto me even thine own self besides" (Philem. 19).

---

†v. 19
A. Paul has already reminded Philemon concerning his sufferings for Christ in that Roman prison (v. 9). This was in contrast, of course, to the "good life" Philemon was probably enjoying there in Colosse. The intended conclusion thus might be: "If I, Paul, am willing to endure this persecution for Christ, cannot you forgive a fellow saint for Christ?"

B. The apostle then gently reminds Philemon that his very conversion experience could be traced back to Paul's ministry.

A. His confidence in Philemon—"Having confidence in thy obedience I wrote unto thee, knowing that thou wilt also do more than I say" (Philem. 21).
B. His request to Philemon—"But withal prepare me also a lodging: for I trust that through your prayers I shall be given unto you" (Philem. 22).

HEBREWS

WHATEVER HAPPENED TO JESUS?
IS HE STILL ALIVE?
WHERE IS HE AND WHAT IS HE DOING?

A. He is indeed alive and well. At this very moment he sits at God's right hand to serve as our great High Priest. This, in essence, is what the book of Hebrews is all about. Let us imagine a conversation between a Hindu and a Christian. The Hindu listens intently as the Christian briefly summarizes the earthly ministry of Jesus Christ. At the conclusion of the message, four basic questions might quickly come to his mind.
Question: Why did Jesus have to be born?
Answer: "No man hath seen God at any time; the only begotten Son, which is in the bosom of the Father, he hath declared him" (John 1:18).
Question: Why did Jesus have to die?
Answer: "Who gave himself for our sins, that he might deliver us from this present evil world, according to the will of God and our Father" (Gal. 1:4).
Question: Why did Jesus have to be resurrected?
Answer: "And if Christ be not risen, then is our preaching vain, and your faith is also vain" (1 Cor. 15:14).
Question: Why did Jesus have to ascend?
Answer: The book of Hebrews

B. The book of Hebrews presents the only full discussion in the New Testament of Christ as the believer's High Priest. It answers the question, "Whatever happened to Jesus?"

C. The book of Hebrews has been called the fifth Gospel. The first four describe what Christ once did on earth; while Hebrews describes what he is now doing in heaven.

D. Hebrews 10:11 reveals that the book was written before the destruction of the temple by Titus in A.D. 70.

E. Hebrews may be compared to Romans.
   1. Romans reveals the *necessity* of the Christian faith.
   2. Hebrews reveals the *superiority* of the Christian faith.

F. There are six key words in this book. They are:
   1. Perfect (used 14 times)
   2. Eternal, forever (used 15 times)
   3. Better (used 13 times)
   4. Partakers (used nine times)
   5. Heaven (used 17 times)
   6. Priest, high priest (used 32 times)

G. There are at least 86 direct references to the Old Testament in Hebrews, taken from 100 passages.

H. Hebrews is the only one of the 27 New Testament books whose author is unknown. There are (at least) three suggested authors:
   1. Paul
      a. Because the early church believed he was the author
      b. Because of the characteristic closing of the epistle (13:25; cf. 2 Thess. 3:17-18)
      c. Because of the expression "the just shall live by faith"—This expression is an Old Testament quote (Hab. 2:4) which is used three times in the New Testament (Rom. 1:17; Gal. 3:11; Heb. 10:38). The argument here is that inasmuch as Paul used the expression the first two times, he probably also used it on the third occasion here in Hebrews.
      d. Because of Peter's statement in 2 Peter 3:15-16—Here Peter states that Paul had written to the same people he was addressing, the Jews of the dispersion (1 Pet. 1:1; 2 Pet. 3:1). Peter then refers to Paul's letter as Scripture. The book of Hebrews is the only New Testament book which fits this description.
      e. Because it was written from Italy (13:24) by a friend of Timothy (13:23) who was in prison at the time (10:34). This would tie in with Paul's imprisonment as recorded in Acts 28.
   2. Barnabas
      a. Because he was a Levite, and the book of Hebrews seems to have been written by a Levite
      b. Because of the comparison between Acts 4:36 and Hebrews 13:22
   3. Apollos
      a. Because of the eloquent Greek style of Hebrews
      b. Because the Old Testament quotes in Hebrews are taken from the Septuagint, while Paul usually quoted from the Hebrew Old Testament

I. The book provides the most extended biblical record of those conversations between the Father and the Son.
   1. First conversation: Concerning the superiority of Christ over angels (1:5-13).
   2. Second conversation: Concerning Christ's relationship to his people (2:12-13).
   3. Third conversation: Concerning the superior priesthood of Christ (7:17, 21).
   4. Fourth conversation: Concerning the obedience of Christ (10:5-9) Note: These are the first recorded words of Jesus in regard to his earthly mission, apparently uttered as he entered the womb of Mary.

J. It is the only New Testament book to explain the purpose of the Old Testament tabernacle (7–10).

K. It is the first of two New Testament books which refer to the heavenly tabernacle (6:10, 20; 8:1-5; 9:11-12, 23-24). (For the other book, see Rev. 11:19; 5:5.)

L. Hebrews 11 is the greatest chapter on faith in the Bible.

M. This book records the final (of three) New Testament references to that Old Testament quotation, "The just shall live by faith" (Hab. 2:4). (They are: Gal. 3:11; Rom. 1:17; Heb. 10:38.)

N. It lists the second (of three) statements concerning the shepherding ministry of Christ.
   1. Jesus said he was the Good Shepherd (John 10:11).
   2. Hebrews says he is the Great Shepherd (Heb. 13:20).
   3. Peter says Christ is the Chief Shepherd (1 Pet. 5:4).

O. Hebrews offers Scripture's greatest analogy between the Old Testament pilgrim and the New Testament pilgrim (3:7–4:16).
P. This epistle also has one of the most controversial passages in the entire Word of God. (See 6:4-6.)
Q. It includes the most extended passage on the subject of divine discipline. (See 12:1-15.)
R. Hebrews 4:12 is probably the Bible's most concise description of itself.
S. It records the third and final instance of the Savior's tears.
  1. John 11:35 (in Bethany)
  2. Luke 19:41 (near Jerusalem)
  3. Hebrews 5:7 (In Gethsemane)
T. It is the only New Testament book referring to Melchizedek (see chapter 7). (Compare with Gen. 14:18-20.)
U. It is the only New Testament book referring to the New Covenant 8:7-13; 10:16-17). (Compare with Jer. 31:31-32.)
V. It mentions by name more Old Testament people than any other New Testament book, a total of 21 individuals.
W. It includes at least eight warnings, writing against:
  1. Carelessness (3:1-3)
  2. Unbelief (3:12)
  3. Immaturity (5:11-14)
  4. Overt sin (6:4-6)
  5. Inconsistency (10:25)
  6. Fear (10:38)
  7. Discouragement (12:3-5)
  8. Bitterness (12:15)
X. Hebrews is the ninth longest New Testament book, and 31st longest biblical book, with 13 chapters, 303 verses, and 6,913 words. There are quotations or allusions from 21 Old Testament books in Hebrews.
Y. Great passages would include:
  1. 2:5-18
  2. 4:9-16
  3. 6:17-20
  4. 9:24-28
  5. 10:12-14
  6. 10:19-20
  7. 10:35-39
  8. 11:1-2
  9. 11:32-40
  10. 12:1-2
  11. 13:20-21

THE BOOK OF HEBREWS

I. Christ, the Superior Person (Heb. 1:1–5:10)
  A. He is better than the prophets (Heb. 1:1-3).

1. Because of the Father's declaration to him—"God, who at sundry times and in divers manners spake in time past unto the fathers by the prophets, hath in these last days spoken unto us by his Son" (Heb. 1:1-2).

---

†1:1 *The phrase "at sundry times and in divers manners," is literally, "by various means and in various ways." We know God spoke to human beings, but how did he speak? A careful examination of the Bible reveals at least nine different modes of communication. These are:*
A. Through angels (Dan. 9:21-27; Luke 1:11-20, 26-37)
B. Through a loud voice (Gen. 3:9-19; 6:13-21; 12:1-3)
C. Through a still, small voice (1 Kings 19:11-12)
D. Through nature (Psa. 19:1-3; Rom. 1:18-20)
E. Through an animal (Num. 22:28)
F. Through dreams (Gen. 28:12; Matt. 1:20; 2:13)
G. Through visions (Gen. 46:2; Isa. 6:1-8)
H. Through Christophanies—A Christophany is an Old Testament, pre-Bethlehem appearance of Christ (Gen. 32:24-30; Exod. 3:2; Judg. 6:11).
I. Through the earthly body of Christ (Heb. 1:1-2)

---

2. Because of the Father's description of him—"Whom he hath appointed heir of all things, by whom also he made the worlds; who being the brightness of his glory, and the express image of his person, and upholding all things by the word of his power, when he had by himself purged our sins, sat down on the right hand of the Majesty on high" (Heb. 1:2b-3).
   a. He is the creator of all things.
   b. He is the upholder of all things.
   c. He is the heir of all things.
   d. He is the redeemer of all things.

B. He is better than the angels (Heb. 1:4–2:18).
   1. Because of his reputation (Heb. 1:4)—"Having become as much better than the angels, as He has inherited a more excellent name than they" (Heb. 1:4, NASB).
   2. Because of his rank—"Thou hast loved righteousness, and hated iniquity; therefore God, even thy God, hath anointed thee with the oil of gladness above thy fellows. But to which of the angels said he at any time, Sit on my right hand, until I make thine enemies thy footstool?" (Heb. 1:9, 13).

---

†1:6 *John Bunyan once wrote: "If Jesus be not God, then heaven will be filled with idolaters."*

---

   3. Because of his relationship—"For unto which of the angels said he at any time, Thou art my Son, this day have I begotten thee? And again, I will be to him a Father, and he shall be to me a Son?" (Heb. 1:5).
   4. Because of his righteousness—"A sceptre of righteousness is the sceptre of thy kingdom" (Heb. 1:8b).
   5. Because of his reign—"But unto the Son he saith, Thy throne, O God, is for ever and ever" (Heb. 1:8a).

†1:8a *This verse, a quotation of Psalm 45:6, provides one of Scripture's strongest declarations of Christ's deity, for here we read of the Father calling the Son* God.

---

6. Because of his reliability—"And, Thou, Lord, in the beginning hast laid the foundation of the earth; and the heavens are the works of thine hands: they shall perish; but thou remainest; and they all shall wax old as doth a garment; and as a vesture shalt thou fold them up, and they shall be changed: but thou art the same, and thy years shall not fail" (Heb. 1:10-12).
7. Because of his redemptive ministry (Heb. 2:1-18)
   a. Redemption: The warning involved—"Therefore we ought to give the more earnest heed to the things which we have heard, lest at any time we should let them slip. For if the word spoken by angels was stedfast, and every transgression and disobedience received a just recompence of reward" (Heb. 2:1-2). "How shall we escape, if we neglect so great salvation?" (Heb. 2:3a).

---

†2:3a

A. There is no answer to this question, of course, because there is no escape.

B. Hebrews contains five key warnings. This is the first. Here is the argument. If Israel in Old Testament times was punished for disobeying the word of angels, how much greater would be punishment for disobeying God's Word as spoken by his own Son. (Gen. 19; Deut. 33:2; Psa. 68:17; Acts 7:53; Gal. 3:19; cf. Luke 4:18-21; 19:10; Matt. 16:21; 20:28.)

---

b. Redemption: The witness involved—"Which at the first began to be spoken by the Lord, and was confirmed unto us by them that heard him; God also bearing them witness, both with signs and wonders, and with divers miracles, and gifts of the Holy Ghost, according to his own will?" (Heb. 2:3b-4).

---

†2:3b-4 *God did indeed confirm his message through both Christ and his followers by signs and wonders.*

A. Christ (John 2:23; 3:2)

B. His followers

1. Peter and the apostles (Acts 2:43; 4:30; 5:12)
2. Stephen (Acts 6:8)
3. Philip (Acts 8:6, 13)
4. Paul (Acts 14:3; 15:12; Rom. 15:19; 2 Cor. 12:12)

---

c. Redemption: The works involved
   (1) Christ came to recapture our lost destiny (Heb. 2:5-9).
      (a) This destiny reviewed (Heb. 2:5-8)—"But one in a certain place testified, saying, What is man, that thou art mindful of him? or the son of man, that thou visitest him? Thou madest him a little lower than the angels; thou crownedst him with glory and honour, and didst set him over the works of thy hands" (Heb. 2:6-7). "Thou hast

put all things in subjection under his feet. For in that he put all in subjection under him, he left nothing that is not put under him" (Heb. 2:8a).

---

†2:8a

A. *God placed all things under man during the Creator's first recorded words to his creatures (Adam and Eve): "And God blessed them, and God said unto them, Be fruitful, and multiply, and replenish the earth, and subdue it: and have dominion over the fish of the sea, and over the fowl of the air, and over every living thing that moveth upon the earth" (Gen. 1:28).*

B. *Author Ray C. Stedman writes the following: "The writer insists that when David says 'all things,' he means all things, everything. For he adds,* Now in putting *everything in subjection to him, he left nothing outside his control. Here is man's intended destiny, his authorized dominion. Man was made to be king over all God's universe. Surely this passage includes far more than the earth. It envisions the created universe of God as far as man has ever been able to discover it, in all the illimitable reaches of space and whatever lies beyond that. All this is to be put under man's dominion. It is a vast and tremendous vision.*

"But man's authority was derived authority. Man himself was to be subject to the God who indwelt him. He was to be the means by which the invisible God became visible to His creatures. He was to be the manifestation of God's own life which dwelt in the royal residence of his human spirit. As long as man was subject to the dominion of God within him, he would be able to exercise dominion over all the universe around. Only when man accepted dominion could he exercise dominion.

"The writer further points out that man was made lower than the angels for a limited time to learn what the exercise of that dominion meant. He was given a limited domain: this earth, this tiny planet whirling its way through the great galaxy to which we belong, amid all the billions of galaxies of space! And he was also given a limited physical body so that within that limited area man should learn the principles by which his dominion could be exercised throughout the universe. This limitation is described as being lower than the angels" (What More Can God Say? *p. 20).*

(b) This destiny revoked—"But now we see not yet all things put under him" (Heb. 2:8c).

---

†2:8b *Man's lofty position was revoked as described by the saddest verse in Scripture: "And when the woman saw that the tree was good for food, and that it was pleasant to the eyes, and a tree to be desired to make one wise, she took of the fruit thereof, and did eat, and gave also unto her husband with her; and he did eat" (Gen. 3:6).*

Stedman continues: "But the passage goes on to describe man's present state of futility. As it is we do not yet see everything in subjection to him. *There is the whole story of human history in a nutshell. How visibly true this is: we do not yet see everything in subjection to him. Man attempts to exercise his dominion but he no longer can do so adequately. He has never forgotten the position God gave him, for throughout the history of the race there is a continual restatement of the dreams of man for dominion over the earth and the universe. This is why we cannot keep off the highest mountain. We have to get up there, though we have not lost a thing up there and we know when we get there we will only see what the bear saw: the other side of the mountain. But we have to be there. We have to explore the depths of the sea. We have to get out into space. Why? Because it is there.*

"Man consistently manifests a remarkable racial memory, a vestigial recollection of what God told him to do. The trouble is that when he tries to accomplish this now he creates a highly explosive and dangerous situation, for his ability to exercise dominion is no longer there. Things get out of balance. This is why we are confronted with an increasingly serious situation in our day when our attempt to control insects by pesticides and other poisons creates an imbalance that threatens serious results. The history of man is one of continually precipitating a crisis by attempting to exercise dominion.

"If we go back into recorded history to the earliest writings of men, the most ancient of history, we find that men were wrestling with the same moral problems then that we are wrestling with today. We have made wonderful advances in technology, but have made absolutely zero progress when it comes to moral relationships. Somewhere man has lost his relationship with God. The fall of man is the only adequate explanation of this. Since then the universe is stamped with futility. Everything man does is a dead-end to a successful conclusion. Even in the individual life this is true. How many have realized the dreams and ideals they began with? Who can say, 'I have done all that I wanted to do; I have been all that I wanted to be'? Paul in Romans puts it,'The creation was subjected to futility' *(Rom. 8:20)"* (What More Can God Say? *p. 21).*

(c) This destiny revived (Heb. 2:9)—"But we see Jesus, who was made a little lower than the angels for the suffering of death, crowned with glory and honour; that he by the grace of God should taste death for every man" (Heb. 2:9).

---

†2:9

A. But the writer of Hebrews says, "We see Jesus!" This is our one hope. With the eye of faith we see Jesus already crowned and reigning over the universe, the man Jesus fulfilling our own lost destiny.

B. By way of summary, consider these three tremendous truths described in Hebrews 2:5-9.

1. In regard to the past—The revealing. "But . . . [we see] thou hast put all things . . . under his feet." This may well have included everything from animals to angels, and from the grass of the fields, to the galaxies of the skies.

2. In regard to the present—The revoking. "But we see not . . . all things . . . under him." Apart from the new birth, human beings cannot subdue their own sinful nature, let alone their environment.

3. In regard to the future—The realizing. "But we see Jesus!" In a nutshell, one of the reasons Jesus left heaven's glory 20 centuries ago was to guarantee redeemed humanity of his original destiny, namely, to help rule the universe. This glorious truth is proclaimed no less than five times in the New Testament. (See 2 Tim. 2:12; Rev. 5:10; 20:4, 6; 22:5.)

---

(2) Christ came to restore our lost fellowship (Heb. 2: 10-18).

(a) His suffering ministry—"For it became him, for whom are all things, and by whom are all things, in bringing many sons unto glory, to make the captain of their salvation perfect through sufferings" (Heb. 2:10).

(b) His sanctifying ministry—"For both he that sanctifieth and they who are sanctified are all of one: for which cause he is not ashamed to call them brethren" (Heb. 2:11).

(c) His singing ministry—"Saying, I will declare thy name unto my brethren, in the midst of the church will I sing praise unto thee" (Heb. 2:12).

---

†**2:12** *This passage (Heb. 2:11-17) is the final of only two New Testament passages where believers are referred to as the brothers (and sisters) of Christ. (See also Rom. 8:29.) This precious relationship is predicted in Psalm 22:22 and Isaiah 8:18. Thus, as a child of God, Jesus is not only my Creator (John 1:3), my Redeemer (Rev. 5:9), and my Shepherd (John 10:11), but also my elder Brother.*

(d) His suppressing ministry—"Forasmuch then as the children are partakers of flesh and blood, he also himself likewise took part of the same; that through death he might destroy him that had the power of death, that is, the devil; and deliver them who through fear of death were all their lifetime subject to bondage" (Heb. 2:14-15).

(e) His sympathizing ministry

1) He understands our *nature*—"For verily he took not on him the nature of angels; but he took on him the seed of Abraham" (Heb. 2:16).

2) He understands our *need*—"Wherefore in all things it behoved him to be made like unto his brethren, that he might be a merciful and faithful high priest in things pertaining to God, to make reconciliation for the sins of the people. For in that he himself hath suffered being tempted, he is able to succour them that are tempted" (Heb. 2:17-18).

C. He is better than Moses (Heb. 3:1-4, 7, 9-16).

1. *Moses* was but a servant in the Father's house—"And Moses verily was faithful in all his house, as a servant, for a testimony of those things which were to be spoken after" (Heb. 3:5).

2. Moses was not able to provide a rest for his people.

a. Israel's sin—"Wherefore (as the Holy Ghost saith, To day if ye will hear his voice, Harden not your hearts, as in the provocation, in the day of temptation in the wilderness: When your fathers tempted me, proved me, and saw my works forty years. Wherefore I was grieved with that generation, and said, They do alway err in their heart; and they have not known my ways" (Heb. 3:7-10).

b. Israel's sentence—"So I sware in my wrath, They shall not enter into my rest.) For some, when they had heard, did provoke: howbeit not all that came out of Egypt by Moses. . . . But with whom was he grieved forty years? was it not with them that had sinned, whose carcases fell in the wilderness? And to whom sware he that they should not enter into his rest, but to them that believed not? So we see that they could not enter in because of unbelief" (Heb. 3:11, 16-19).

3. *Christ* is the unique Son in the Father's house—"For this man was counted

worthy of more glory than Moses, inasmuch as he who hath builded the house hath more honour than the house. . . . But Christ as a son over his own house; whose house are we, if we hold fast the confidence and the rejoicing of the hope firm unto the end" (Heb. 3:3, 6).

4. Only Christ is able to provide a rest for his people.
   a. An illustration of this rest—Creation. "And in this place again, If they shall enter into my rest. Seeing therefore it remaineth that some must enter therein, and they to whom it was first preached entered not in because of unbelief" (Heb. 4:5-6).
   b. The exhortation concerning this rest—"For the word of God is quick, and powerful, and sharper than any twoedged sword, piercing even to the dividing asunder of soul and spirit, and of the joints and marrow, and is a discerner of the thoughts and intents of the heart. Neither is there any creature that is not manifest in his sight: but all things are naked and opened unto the eyes of him with whom we have to do. Seeing then that we have a great high priest, that is passed into the heavens, Jesus the Son of God, let us hold fast our profession. For we have not an high priest which cannot be touched with the feeling of our infirmities; but was in all points tempted like as we are, yet without sin" (Heb. 4:12-15). "Let us therefore fear, lest, a promise being left us of entering into his rest, any of you should seem to come short of it. . . . There remaineth therefore a rest to the people of God. For he that is entered into his rest, he also hath ceased from his own works, as God did from his. Let us labour therefore to enter into that rest, lest any man fall after the same example of unbelief" (Heb. 4:1, 9-11).

---

†4:11

A. Concerning the phrase, "Let us"—This chapter (Heb. 4) records the first of 13 "Let us" admonitions to be found in Hebrews. Note:

1. *"Let us therefore fear" (4:1).*
2. *"Let us labour therefore to enter into that rest" (4:11).*
3. *"Let us hold fast our profession" (4:14).*
4. *"Let us therefore come boldly unto the throne of grace" (4:16).*
5. *"Let us go on unto perfection" (6:1).*
6. *"Let us draw near with a true heart in full assurance of faith" (10:22).*
7. *"Let us hold fast the profession of our faith without wavering" (10:23).*
8. *"Let us consider one another to provoke unto love and to good works" (10:24).*
9. *"Let us lay aside every weight" (12:1).*
10. *"Let us run with patience the race that is set before us" (12:1).*
11. *"Let us have grace" (12:28).*
12. *"Let us go forth therefore unto him without the camp" (13:13).*
13. *"Let us offer the sacrifice of praise to God continually" (13:15).*

B. Concerning the word "rest"

1. *The word "rest" as found in Hebrews 3 and 4 is a very important concept, being used no less than nine times (see 3:11, 18; 4:1, 3, 5, 8-11).*
2. *In essence, there are three facts concerning this rest:*
   a. The sin of unbelief once kept Israel from entering God's rest (3:11, 18; 4:11).
   b. The sin of unbelief will keep the believer from entering God's rest (4:1).

c. Faith will assure us of entering God's rest (4:9-10).

3. Here it should be stated that this is the rest of sanctification and not that of salvation. For example, Moses died a saved man (Heb. 11:24-29), but because of one tragic act of unbelief (Num. 20:7-12), he was prevented from entering the Promised Land.

4. Some have claimed, however, that the rest here is the rest of salvation, based on Hebrews 4:2: "For unto us was the gospel preached, as well as unto them: but the word preached did not profit them, not being mixed with faith in them that heard it."

To be sure, the word gospel *does mean "good news." Zane Hodges writes: "But this good news does not always refer to the plan of salvation from sin. In some circles the word 'gospel' has acquired a sense too technical and narrow to do justice to the writer's ideas here. What was preached to the Israelites of old was, quite clearly, God's offer of rest. This, of course, was 'good news' for them just as it is for people now, but it is not exactly what is meant today by 'gospel.' The Greek verb used,* euangelizomai, *was fully capable of having a nontechnical sense in the New Testament (cf. its use in Luke 1:19; 1 Thess. 3:6), but naturally the writer here did not sharply distinguish the 'good news' about rest, which his readers had heard, from the 'good news' to which the term 'gospel' is more usually applied (cf. 1 Cor. 15:1-4). But as the whole context shows, his concern was with the good news about a future rest for God's people (cf. Heb. 4:10), not with the fundamental facts Paul spoke of in 1 Corinthians 15"* (Bible Knowledge Commentary, *New Testament Volume, p. 788).*

5. We have now, listed for us, three great biblical rests:

a. The rest of creation (4:4)
b. The rest of salvation (4:10)
c. The rest of consecration (4:11)

---

c. The appropriation of this rest—How is it obtained? Answer: Through obedience to the Word of God—"For unto us was the gospel preached, as well as unto them: but the word preached did not profit them, not being mixed with faith in them that heard it. . . . For the word of God is quick, and powerful, and sharper than any twoedged sword, piercing even to the dividing asunder of soul and spirit, and of the joints and marrow, and is a discerner of the thoughts and intents of the heart. Neither is there any creature that is not manifest in his sight: but all things are naked and opened unto the eyes of him with whom we have to do" (Heb. 4:2, 12-13).

---

†**4:13** *These verses give us one of nine symbols for the Word of God as found in the Bible itself. These symbols are:*

A. A mirror (James 1:23-25)
B. A seed (James 1:18; 1 Pet. 1:23)
C. Water (Eph. 5:25-27)
D. A lamp (Psa. 119:105; Prov. 6:23; 2 Pet. 1:19)
E. Precious metals
1. Gold (Psa. 19:10; 119:127)
2. Silver (Psa. 12:6)
F. Nourishing food
1. Milk (1 Pet. 2:2)

2. Meat (Heb. 5:12-14)
3. Bread (John 6:51)
4. Honey (Psa. 19:10)
G. A hammer (Jer. 23:29)
H. A fire (Jer. 20:9)
I. A sword (Heb. 4:12; Eph. 6:17)

---

d. The location of this rest—Where can it be found? "Seeing then that we have a great high priest, that is passed into the heavens, Jesus the Son of God, let us hold fast our profession. For we have not an high priest which cannot be touched with the feeling of our infirmities; but was in all points tempted like as we are, yet without sin. Let us therefore come boldly unto the throne of grace, that we may obtain mercy, and find grace to help in time of need" (Heb. 4:14-16).

---

†**4:16** *Luther, Zwingli, and Calvin nailed to the masthead of their movement three great principles taken from Hebrews:*
A. No sacrifice but Calvary
B. No priest but Christ
C. No confessional but the throne of grace

D. He is better than Joshua (Heb. 4:8)—"For if Joshua had given them rest, He would not have spoken of another day after that" (Heb. 4:8, NASB).
E. He is better than Aaron (Heb. 5:1-10).
1. Christ possessed perfectly that which Aaron had in part.
a. Like Aaron, he was taken from among men—"For every high priest taken from among men is ordained for men in things pertaining to God" (Heb. 5:1).
b. Like Aaron, he offered up a sacrifice—"That he may offer both gifts and sacrifices for sins" (Heb. 5:1). He is obligated to offer sacrifices for sins, "as for the people" (Heb. 5:3, personal paraphrase).
c. Like Aaron, he possessed compassion—"Compassion on the ignorant, and on them that are out of the way" (Heb. 5:2).

---

†**5:2a** *While upon this earth, our Lord showed great compassion:*
A. Upon the sick multitudes (Matt. 14:14)
B. Upon the shepherdless multitudes (Matt. 9:36)
C. Upon the hungry multitudes (Matt. 15:32)
D. Upon a widow (Luke 7:13)
E. Upon a leper (Mark 1:41)
F. Upon a father (Mark 9:22-23)
G. Upon a demoniac (Mark 5:19)

---

d. Like Aaron, he experienced the infirmities of the flesh—"For that he himself also is compassed with infirmity" (Heb. 5:2).

---

†5:2b *Jesus took upon himself at Bethlehem all the sinless infirmities associated with humanity.*

A. He possessed flesh and blood (Heb. 2:14).
B. He grew (Luke 2:40).
C. He asked questions (Luke 2:46).
D. He was tempted (Matt. 4:1).
E. He hungered (Matt. 4:2).
F. He thirsted (John 4:7).
G. He became weary (John 4:6).
H. He slept (Matt. 8:24).
I. He wept (John 11:35).
J. He experienced joy (Heb. 12:2; Luke 10:21).
K. He was troubled (John 12:27).
L. He suffered (1 Pet. 4:1).
M. He bled (John 19:34).
N. He died (Matt. 27:50).

---

e. Like Aaron, he was chosen by God—"And no man taketh this honour unto himself, but he that is called of God, as was Aaron" (Heb. 5:4).
f. Like Aaron, he prayed—"Who in the days of his flesh, when he had offered up prayers and supplications with strong crying and tears unto him that was able to save him from death, and was heard in that he feared" (Heb. 5:7).
g. Like Aaron, he learned obedience—"Though he were a Son, yet learned he obedience" (Heb. 5:8).
h. Like Aaron, he suffered—"By the things which he suffered" (Heb. 5:8).

---

†5:8b *Zane Hodges observes: "In a real sense not fully comprehensible, the Incarnation gave the already infinitely wise and perfect Son of God the experiential acquisition of knowledge about the human condition. Suffering thus became a reality that He tasted and from it He can sympathize deeply with His followers. (The Greek has an interesting play on words in the verbs He learned* (emathen) *and He suffered* (epathen)" (Bible Knowledge Commentary, *p. 792).*

---

2. Christ possessed perfectly that which Aaron lacked completely.
   a. Unlike Aaron, he offered no sacrifice for his own self (Heb. 5:3).
   b. Unlike Aaron, he is God's Son—"Thou art my Son, today have I begotten thee" (Heb. 5:5).
   c. Unlike Aaron, he is God's eternal High Priest—"Thou art a priest forever" (Heb. 5:6).
   d. Unlike Aaron, he is a priest like Melchizedek—"Called of God an high priest after the order of Melchisedec" (Heb. 5:10).
   e. Unlike Aaron, he became the source of eternal salvation —"And being made perfect, he became the author of eternal salvation unto all them that obey him" (Heb. 5:9).

II. Maturity, the Superior Purpose (Heb. 5:11–6:20)—"Therefore leaving the elementary teaching about the Christ, let us press on to maturity" (Heb. 6:1, NASB).
   A. The appeal for spiritual maturity (Heb. 5:11–6:12)

1. Be faithful in dividing the Word of God—"Of whom we have many things to say, and hard to be uttered, seeing ye are dull of hearing. For when for the time ye ought to be teachers, ye have need that one teach you again which be the first principles of the oracles of God; and are become such as have need of milk, and not of strong meat. For every one that useth milk is unskilful in the word of righteousness: for he is a babe. But strong meat belongeth to them that are of full age, even those who by reason of use have their senses exercised to discern both good and evil" (Heb. 5:11-14).

---

†5:14 *Author Ray Stedman writes: "I read of a principal in a high school who had an administrative post to fill. He promoted one of his teachers with ten years of teaching experience to the job. When the announcement was made, another teacher in this school came to him terribly upset. She said, 'Why did you put that teacher in this position? He has only had ten years of experience and I've had twenty-five years, yet you passed me over in favor of him.' And the principal said, 'I'm sorry; you're wrong. You haven't had twenty-five years of experience. You have had one year's experience twenty-five times'"* (What More Can God Say?)

The reason for this uncertainty and immaturity is explained in 5:13-14; cf. 1 Corinthians 3:1-2; 1 Peter 2:1-2. See also Joshua 5:12, where we are told that the manna ceased after *Israel entered the Promised Land.*

---

2. Be faithful in doing the work of God.
   a. The futility of dead works—"Therefore let us leave the elementary teachings about Christ and go on to maturity, not laying again the foundation of repentance from acts that lead to death, and of faith in God, instruction about baptisms, the laying on of hands, the resurrection of the dead, and eternal judgment. . . . It is impossible for those who have once been enlightened, who have tasted the heavenly gift, who have shared in the Holy Spirit, who have tasted the goodness of the word of God and the powers of the coming age, if they fall away, to be brought back to repentance, because to their loss they are crucifying the Son of God all over again and subjecting him to public disgrace. Land that drinks in the rain often falling on it and that produces a crop useful to those by whom it is farmed receives the blessing of God. But land that produces thorns and thistles is worthless and is in danger of being cursed. In the end it will be burned" (Heb. 6:1-2, 4-8, NIV).

---

†6:8

A. Perhaps no other single biblical passage has been the subject of more speculation and interpretation than these words in Hebrews 6:4-6. Various theories hold that these verses describe one of the following kinds of people.

1. *Saved people who lose their salvation through some horrible sin—Of course, if this were true, then the same passage also teaches that they could never be saved again.*
2. *Professed believers who have only "tasted" the things of God and never really "swallowed" them—However, this is entirely unsupportable, for the same Greek word is used also in Hebrews 2:9 concerning Jesus who, "by the grace of God should taste death for every man."*

3. *Jewish professed believers living while the temple was still standing—The Scofield Bible presents this view: "Hebrews 6:4-8 presents the case of Jewish professed believers who halt short of faith in Christ after advancing to the very threshold of salvation, even 'going along with' the Holy Spirit in His work of enlightenment and conviction (John 16:8-10). It is not said that they had faith. This supposed person is like the spies at Kadesh-barnea (Deut. 1:19-26) who saw the land and had the very fruit of it in their hands, and yet turned back" (p. 1,295).*
4. *A hypothetical case of what could not happen—"If one could 'fall away' (v. 6), it would be impossible to renew him again to repentance; for, in such an instance, it would be necessary for Christ to be crucified a second time. Obviously, this will not occur (Heb. 10:12, 14); thus to fall away is impossible"* (The New Scofield Bible, *p. 1,315).*
5. *Backsliders who are in danger of committing the sin unto death (see 1 Cor. 11:30; Acts 5:1-11; 1 John 5:16-17)—None of these views is without its problems.*

B. *It should be noted (v. 8) that here it is* not *the field which is destroyed, but the fruit. (See also 1 Cor. 3:15; John 15:6; Heb. 10:30.)*

---

b. The fruits of dedicated works—"But, beloved, we are persuaded better things of you, and things that accompany salvation, though we thus speak. For God is not unrighteous to forget your work and labour of love, which ye have shewed toward his name, in that ye have ministered to the saints, and do minister. And we desire that every one of you do shew the same diligence to the full assurance of hope unto the end: that ye be not slothful, but followers of them who through faith and patience inherit the promises" (Heb. 6:9-12).

---

†6:12 *Thus, while good works will not save a sinner from hell, they will spare a saint from judgment. (See 1 Cor. 11:31.)*

B. The anchor for spiritual maturity (Heb. 6:13-20)

1. The promise of the Father—"When God made his promise to Abraham, since there was no one greater for him to swear by, he swore by himself, saying, 'I will surely bless you and give you many descendants.' And so, after waiting patiently, Abraham received what was promised. Men swear by someone greater than themselves, and the oath confirms what is said and puts an end to all argument. Because God wanted to make the unchanging nature of his purpose very clear to the heirs of what was promised, he confirmed it with an oath. God did this so that, by two unchangeable things in which it is impossible for God to lie, we who have fled to take hold of the hope offered to us may be greatly encouraged" (Heb. 6:13-18, NIV).
2. The priesthood of the Savior—"Which hope we have as an anchor of the soul, both sure and stedfast, and which entereth into that within the veil; whither the forerunner is for us entered, even Jesus, made an high priest for ever after the order of Melchisedec" (Heb. 6:19-20).

---

†6:20 *Jesus is described here as our forerunner. This word has been associated with a small boat called a forerunner. In the ancient world large ocean vessels often experienced difficulty when approaching* *the shallow Greek harbors. To counteract this, a small forerunner boat would often be sent out to help secure the vessel's anchor within the harbor itself. Dr. Kenneth Wuest writes: "The anchor of the believer is, therefore, fastened within the veil of the Holy of Holies of heaven. We have some rich figures here. This present life is the sea; the soul . . . of the believer, as a tempest-tossed ship, is held by the anchor within the veil, fastened by faith to the blessed reality within the veil"* (Hebrews in the Greek New Testament, *p. 125).*

III. Melchizedek, the Superior Priesthood (Heb. 7:1–10:39)
 A. It offers a better source—From Aaron to Melchizedek (Heb. 7).
  1. It is a royal priesthood (Heb. 7:1-2)—"For this Melchisedec, king of Salem, priest of the most high God, who met Abraham returning from the slaughter of the kings, and blessed him; to whom also Abraham gave a tenth part of all; first being by interpretation King of righteousness, and after that also King of Salem, which is, King of peace" (Heb. 7:1-2).

---

†**7:2** *Who was this mysterious Melchizedek who appeared in the time of Abraham (Gen. 14:18-20) and is later spoken of in the Psalms (Psa. 110)? The following theories have been advocated concerning his identity:*
 A. That he was Shem, one of Noah's three sons
 B. That he was a godly priest-king over the city of Salem (thought to be a reference to Jerusalem, and thus the first mention of the Holy City in the Bible)
 C. That he was Christ himself—This theory is based on Hebrews 7:3 which says of Melchizedek: "Without father, without mother, without descent, having neither beginning of days, nor end of life." This does not *necessarily mean that Melchizedek was actually Christ (although he may have been), but that inasmuch as we have no record of his birth or death he* does *become a type of Christ, not only in his* office, *but also in his origin.*
 D. That he was a heavenly creature—Zane Hodges suggests: "If this is correct, Melchizedek may have been an angelic being who reigned for a time at Salem (i.e., Jerusalem). If so, the statement that he was 'without beginning of days' would not mean that he was eternal, but simply that he had a pretemporal origin. Nor would this concept of Melchizedek as an angel elevate him to the same level as God's Son, since the author painstakingly asserted the Son's superiority to the angels (1:5-14). There is indeed evidence that, at Qumran, Melchizedek was regarded as an angelic personage" (Bible Knowledge Commentary, *p. 798).*

---

  2. It is a timeless priesthood (Heb. 7:3)—"Without father, without mother, without descent, having neither beginning of days, nor end of life; but made like unto the Son of God; abideth a priest continually" (Heb. 7:3).
  3. It is an authoritative priesthood (Heb. 7:4-10).
   a. Fact: Abraham tithed to Melchizedek.
   b. Fact: Abraham was the ancestor of Levi, founder of the Levitical priesthood.
   c. Conclusion: The yet unborn Levi tithed to Melchizedek while he was still in the loins of Abraham.
   d. Conclusion: The Melchizedek priesthood is therefore greater than the Levitical priesthood, for it received tithes from it. "And without all contradiction the less is blessed of the better" (Heb. 7:7).

4. It is an independent priesthood (Heb. 7:11-15).
   a. Independent of the Law (Heb. 7:11-12)—"If therefore perfection were by the Levitical priesthood, (for under it the people received the law,) what further need was there that another priest should rise after the order of Melchisedec, and not be called after the order of Aaron? For the priesthood being changed, there is made of necessity a change also of the law" (Heb. 7:11-12).
   b. Independent of the tribe of Levi (Heb. 7:13-15)—"For he of whom these things are spoken pertaineth to another tribe, of which no man gave attendance at the altar. For it is evident that our Lord sprang out of Juda; of which tribe Moses spake nothing concerning priesthood" (Heb. 7:13-14).

---

†**7:14** *Christ was given an independent priesthood. Melchizedek was ordained by an oath from God and not by the tribe of Levi. In the Old Testament no one could serve as a priest unless he was descended from Aaron (Ezra 2:61-62). However, neither Melchizedek nor Christ came from this tribe.*

---

5. It is an everlasting priesthood (Heb. 7:16-17)—"Who is made, not after the law of a carnal commandment, but after the power of an endless life. For he testifieth, Thou art a priest for ever after the order of Melchisedec" (Heb. 7:16-17).
6. It is a perfecting priesthood (Heb. 7:19, 25).
   a. The fact of this perfection—"For the law made nothing perfect, but the bringing in of a better hope did; by the which we draw nigh unto God" (Heb. 7:19).
   b. The extent of this perfection—"Wherefore he is able also to save them to the uttermost that come unto God by him, seeing he ever liveth to make intercession for them" (Heb. 7:25).

---

†**7:25** *This verse is usually applied to the salvation of the lost (from "the uttermost to the uttermost"), but in its context it refers to the preservation of the saved. Thus, Christ died down here on Calvary to bring us salvation, and now lives up there in glory to keep us saved. (See also Rom. 8:34; Rev. 1:18.)*

---

7. It is a guaranteed priesthood (Heb. 7:20-22)—"And inasmuch as not without an oath he was made priest: (For those priests were made without an oath; but this with an oath by him that said unto him, The Lord sware and will not repent, Thou art a priest for ever after the order of Melchisedec:) by so much was Jesus made a surety of a better testament" (Heb. 7:20-22).
8. It is a continuous priesthood (Heb. 7:23)—"And the former priests, on the one hand, existed in greater numbers, because they were prevented by death from continuing" (Heb. 7:23, NASB).
9. It is a permanent priesthood (Heb. 7:24)—""But He, on the other hand, because He abides forever, holds His priesthood permanently" (Heb. 7:24, NASB).

10. It is a holy priesthood (Heb. 7:26)—"For such an high priest became us, who is holy, harmless, undefiled, separate from sinners, and made higher than the heavens" (Heb. 7:26).

---

†**7:26** *This is in contrast to the Levitical priesthood, whose representatives often allowed corruption and idolatry to control their lives (see Exod. 32:1-6, 21-25; 1 Sam. 2:12-17; 8:1-3).*

---

11. It is an all-sufficient priesthood (Heb. 7:27)—"Who needeth not daily, as those high priests, to offer up sacrifice, first for his own sins, and then for the people's: for this he did once, when he offered up himself" (Heb. 7:27).

---

†**7:27** *Author Ray Stedman writes: "As a priest, Jesus Christ could find no unblemished sacrifice that He could offer except Himself, so He offered Himself as a sacrifice; there was found no other priest worthy of offering such a sacrifice, so Christ became both Priest and Victim"* (What More Can God Say? *p. 115).*

This dual arrangement can be seen by listening to his seven final sentences while on the cross. The first three demonstrate his priestly ministry while the final four speak of his sacrificial role.

A. His priestly ministry:

1. *"Father, forgive them; for they know not what they do" (Luke 23:34).*
2. *"Verily, I say unto thee, today shalt thou be with me in paradise" (Luke 23:43).*
3. *"Woman, behold thy son! . . . Behold thy mother!" (John 19:26-27).*

B. His sacrificial ministry

1. *"My God, my God, why hast thou forsaken me?" (Matt. 27:46).*
2. *"I thirst" (John 19:28).*
3. *"It is finished" (John 19:30).*
4. *"Father, into thy hands I commend my spirit" (Luke 23:46).*

---

12. It is a divine priesthood (Heb. 7:28)—"For the law maketh men high priests which have infirmity; but the word of the oath, which was since the law, maketh the Son, who is consecrated for evermore" (Heb. 7:28).

B. It offers a better script—From the Old Covenant to the New Covenant (Heb. 8).

---

†*The Old Testament Hebrew word for "covenant" was* berit, *meaning "to cut or divide." (See Gen. 15:10; Jer. 34:18-19.) This cutting was in reference to the cutting of sacrificial animals. Between these bloody pieces of flesh the two parties of the* berit *would walk. However, in the Genesis 15 account, God put Abraham to sleep and walked through alone, thus signifying that particular* berit *to be unconditional. This ceremony was also known as a blood covenant. This Old Testament concept is brought out in the New Testament by the Greek word* diatheke. *A* diatheke *is a treaty between two parties, but binding only on one, according to the terms fixed by the others. This important word appears no less than 22 times in the book of Hebrews. It is always translated by the English words "covenant" and/or "testament." (See also Luke 22:20; 1 Cor. 11:25; 2 Cor. 3:6.) Another Greek word,* suntheke, *although it is the regular term employed for a treaty, is used but four times and always in a bad light (see John 9:22; Luke 22:5; Acts 23:20; 24:9). Thus, a covenant* (berit *in the Old Testament Hebrew;* diatheke *in the New Testament Greek) is a promise or*

agreement between God and man. It may be a conditional or an unconditional agreement. In Hebrews 8, the author refers to both a conditional agreement (the Old Covenant), and an unconditional agreement (the New Covenant).

---

1. The Old Covenant
   a. Mediated by Moses—"Who serve unto the example and shadow of heavenly things, as Moses was admonished of God when he was about to make the tabernacle: for, See, saith he, that thou make all things according to the pattern shewed to thee in the mount" (Heb. 8:5).
   b. Conditional (Heb. 8:7-9)
      (1) The terms—Obedience by Israel
      (2) The tragedy—Disobedience by Israel—"Not according to the covenant that I made with their fathers in the day when I took them by the hand to lead them out of the land of Egypt; because they continued not in my covenant, and I regarded them not, saith the Lord" (Heb. 8:9).
   c. Condemning—"For finding fault with them" (Heb. 8:8)
   d. Written on dead stones (Exod. 32:15)

---

†**8:9** *Thus, to summarize the Old Covenant:*
A. It was mediated by Moses (Exod. 19; John 1:17; Gal. 3:19).
B. It was conditional (see Deut. 28).
C. It could not produce the necessary righteousness (8:8)
D. It was written on dead stones (Exod. 32:15).

---

2. The New Covenant
   a. Mediated by Christ (Heb. 8:1-4)—"Now of the things which we have spoken this is the sum: We have such an high priest, who is set on the right hand of the throne of the Majesty in the heavens; a minister of the sanctuary, and of the true tabernacle, which the Lord pitched, and not man" (Heb. 8:1-2).
   b. Unconditional—"But now hath he obtained a more excellent ministry, by how much also he is the mediator of a better covenant, which was established upon better promises" (Heb. 8:6).
   c. Justifying—"For I will be merciful to their unrighteousness, and their sins and their iniquities will I remember no more" (Heb. 8:12).
   d. Written on living hearts (Heb. 8:10-11)
      (1) Producing a special relationship with God—"For this is the covenant that I will make with the house of Israel after those days, saith the Lord; I will put my laws into their mind, and write them in their hearts: and I will be to them a God, and they shall be to me a people" (Heb. 8:10).
      (2) Producing a special revelation from God—"And they shall not teach every man his neighbour, and every man his brother, saying, Know the Lord: for all shall know me, from the least to the greatest" (Heb. 8:11).

---

†**8:11** *Thus, to summarize the New Covenant:*
A. The features involved

1. It is mediated by Christ (Heb. 9:15; John 1:17), but originally given by God to Jeremiah the prophet (see Jer. 31:31-34).
2. It is unconditional (8:9).
3. It can produce the necessary righteousness (8:11).
4. It is written on living hearts (8:10).

B. The theories involved—There are at least four theories concerning the recipients of this New Covenant. These are:
1. The church has replaced Israel as the participant in the New Covenant. This is totally refuted by Paul in Romans 9–11.
2. The New Covenant is with the nation Israel only. However, this seems to be out of context with Hebrews 8.
3. There are two new covenants in this chapter. One refers to Israel, and the other to the church.
4. There is but one New Covenant which will be fulfilled eschatologically with Israel, but participated in soteriologically by the church today. Of these four views it would seem that while the third is possible, the fourth is probable.

C. It offers a better sanctuary—From the earthly to the heavenly (Heb. 9).
1. The earthly tabernacle
a. It was of this world—"Then verily the first covenant had also ordinances of divine service, and a worldly sanctuary" (Heb. 9:1).
b. Its work was external in nature—"Which stood only in meats and drinks, and divers washings, and carnal ordinances, imposed on them until the time of reformation" (Heb. 9:10).
c. It was temporary—"The Holy Ghost this signifying, that the way into the holiest of all was not yet made manifest, while as the first tabernacle was yet standing" (Heb. 9:8).
d. It was a shadow of the real—"Which was a figure for the time then present, in which were offered both gifts and sacrifices, that could not make him that did the service perfect, as pertaining to the conscience" (Heb. 9:9).
e. It was inaccessible—"But into the second went the high priest alone once every year, not without blood, which he offered for himself, and for the errors of the people" (Heb. 9:7).
f. It was made by human hands—"For Christ is not entered into the holy places made with hands, which are the figures of the true; but into heaven itself, now to appear in the presence of God for us" (Heb. 9:24).
g. It featured animal blood—"For if the blood of bulls and of goats, and the ashes of an heifer sprinkling the unclean, sanctifieth to the purifying of the flesh" (Heb. 9:13).
h. It had daily sacrifice—"Now when these things were thus ordained, the priests went always into the first tabernacle, accomplishing the service of God. Nor yet that he should offer himself often, as the high priest entereth into the holy place every year with blood of others" (Heb. 9:6, 25).
i. It was serviced by sinful priests (Heb. 9:7).
j. It could not purge sin (Heb. 9:9).
k. It had no abiding hope (Heb. 9:10).
2. The heavenly tabernacle

a. It was of heaven—"It was therefore necessary that the patterns of things in the heavens should be purified with these; but the heavenly things themselves with better sacrifices than these" (Heb. 9:23).
b. Its work was internal in nature (Heb. 9:9).
c. It was permanent—"Neither by the blood of goats and calves, but by his own blood he entered in once into the holy place, having obtained eternal redemption for us" (Heb. 9:12).
d. It was the real thing (Heb. 9:24).
e. It was accessible to all—"Let us therefore come boldly unto the throne of grace, that we may obtain mercy, and find grace to help in time of need" (Heb. 4:16). "Having therefore, brethren, boldness to enter into the holiest by the blood of Jesus" (Heb. 10:19).
f. It was made by God himself (Heb. 9:24).
g. It featured the blood of Christ (Heb. 9:12).
h. It had but one sacrifice (Heb. 9:12).
i. It was serviced by the Holy Spirit—"How much more shall the blood of Christ, who through the eternal Spirit offered himself without spot to God, purge your conscience from dead works to serve the living God?" (Heb. 9:14).
j. It was able to purge sin (Heb. 9:12).
k. It has an abiding hope.
   (1) Because of Christ's past work—"So Christ was once offered to bear the sins of many" (Heb. 9:28a).
   (2) Because of Christ's present work—"For Christ is . . . entered . . . into heaven itself, now to appear in the presence of God for us" (Heb. 9:24).
   (3) Because of Christ's future work—"And unto them that look for him shall he appear the second time without sin unto salvation" (Heb. 9:28b).

---

†9:28b *At this point the author of Hebrews has described for us the full sevenfold ministry of our Lord.*

A. His incarnation (1:2; 2:16-17)
B. His ministration (5:7-9)
C. His crucifixion (6:6; 7:27; 2:9)
D. His resurrection (13:20)
E. His ascension (4:4; 6:20)
F. His intercession (7:25; 8:1; 9:12, 24)
G. His revelation (9:28)

D. It offers a better sacrifice—From animal lambs to God's Lamb (Heb. 10)
1. The Shepherd and his sacrifice (Heb. 10:1-18)—Here Jesus, the sovereign Shepherd, is pictured as the sacrificial Lamb.
   a. The need for his sacrifice—"For the law having a shadow of good things to come, and not the very image of the things, can never with those sacrifices which they offered year by year continually make the comers thereunto perfect. For it is not possible that the blood of bulls and of goats should take away sins" (Heb. 10:1, 4).

---

†10:4 *These sacrifices could (for awhile)* cover *sin; but these sacrifices could not* cleanse *it. (See also 10:6, 11; Isa. 1:11; Jer. 6:20; Hos. 6:6; Amos 5:21-22.)*

---

b. The obedience in his sacrifice (Heb. 10:5-9)—"Wherefore when he cometh into the world, he saith, Sacrifice and offering thou wouldest not, but a body hast thou prepared me: in burnt offerings and sacrifices for sin thou hast had no pleasure. Then said I, Lo, I come (in the volume of the book it is written of me,) to do thy will, O God" (Heb. 10:5-7).

---

†10:7 *These may be considered as our Lord's first recorded words in reference to his earthly ministry, uttered perhaps as he left the ivory palaces of glory to join himself to that tiny mass of human flesh within Mary's womb.*

---

c. The results from his sacrifice (Heb. 10:10-14)
 (1) His followers have been forever sanctified (Heb. 10:10, 14)—"For by one offering he hath perfected for ever them that are sanctified" (Heb. 10:14).
 (2) His Father has been forever satisfied (Heb. 10:11-13) —"And every priest standeth daily ministering and offering oftentimes the same sacrifices, which can never take away sins: but this man, after he had offered one sacrifice for sins for ever, sat down on the right hand of God; from henceforth expecting till his enemies be made his footstool" (Heb. 10:11-13).

d. The witness to his sacrifice (Heb. 10:15-18)—"Whereof the Holy Ghost also is a witness to us: for after that he had said before, This is the covenant that I will make with them after those days, saith the Lord, I will put my laws into their hearts, and in their minds will I write them; and their sins and iniquities will I remember no more" (Heb. 10:15-17).

2. The sheep and their Savior (Heb. 10:19-39)
 a. Concerning supplication—Be bold. "Having therefore, brethren, boldness to enter into the holiest by the blood of Jesus" (Heb. 10:19).
 b. Concerning past sins—Be assured. "Let us draw near with a true heart in full assurance of faith, having our hearts sprinkled from an evil conscience, and our bodies washed with pure water" (Heb. 10:22).
 c. Concerning service—Be steadfast. "From henceforth expecting till his enemies be made his footstool. . . . Not forsaking the assembling of ourselves together, as the manner of some is; but exhorting one another: and so much the more, as ye see the day approaching" (Heb. 10:13, 25).

---

†10:25 *The "day" here may be a reference to the predicted destruction of Jerusalem (Matt. 24:1-2), or the coming of the Lord. The context strongly suggests the second meaning (see Heb. 10:37).*

---

 d. Concerning other saints—Be helpful. "And let us consider one another to provoke unto love and to good works" (Heb. 10:24).
 e. Concerning sacrilege—Be careful. "For if we sin wilfully after that we have received the knowledge of the truth, there remaineth no more sacrifice for sins. . . . For we know him that hath said, Vengeance belongeth unto me, I

will recompense, saith the Lord. And again, The Lord shall judge his people. It is a fearful thing to fall into the hands of the living God" (Heb. 10:26, 30-31).

---

†**10:31** *Do these fearful verses refer to saved or unsaved people? While one cannot be absolutely dogmatic here, it would seem from the phrase in verse 30, "The Lord shall judge his people," that the author had believers in mind. If this is correct, then the sin unto death may be intended here. Thus (if that is true), this passage can be tied into Hebrews 6:4-6. (See also 1 Pet. 4:17.)*

---

f. Concerning suffering—Be mindful. "But call to remembrance the former days, in which, after ye were illuminated, ye endured a great fight of afflictions. . . . For ye had compassion of me in my bonds, and took joyfully the spoiling of your goods, knowing in yourselves that ye have in heaven a better and an enduring substance" (Heb. 10:32, 34).

g. Concerning the second coming—Be watchful. "Cast not away therefore your confidence, which hath great recompence of reward. For ye have need of patience, that, after ye have done the will of God, ye might receive the promise. For yet a little while, and he that shall come will come, and will not tarry" (Heb. 10:35-37).

h. Concerning spirituality—Be faithful. "Now the just shall live by faith: but if any man draw back, my soul shall have no pleasure in him. But we are not of them who draw back unto perdition; but of them that believe to the saving of the soul" (Heb. 10:38-39).

---

†**10:39** *This marks the third and final New Testament quotation of that phrase found in the Old Testament, "The just shall live by faith" (Hab. 2:4). The first two references are Romans 1:17; Galatians 3:11.*

IV. Faith, the Superior Principle (Heb. 11:1–13:25)

---

†*The author of Hebrews has just ended chapter 10 with a summary statement concerning the believer and his great High Priest. The statement is: "Now the just shall live by faith" (10:38).*

Having come this far in the epistle, some of the readers might be wondering: Exactly what is this faith like? Has anyone really lived like this before? The author now answers these questions. This chapter has been called the divine Hall of Fame and the Westminster Abbey of Scripture.

A. The people of faith (Heb. 11)—"Now faith is the substance of things hoped for, the evidence of things not seen. For by it the elders obtained a good report. Through faith we understand that the worlds were framed by the word of God, so that things which are seen were not made of things which do appear. . . . But without faith it is impossible to please him: for he that cometh to God must believe that he is, and that he is a rewarder of them that diligently seek him" (Heb. 11:1-3, 6).

†11:6 *Various attempts have been made to define the word "faith." Here are but a few:*
A. Faith is the confident assurance of things hoped for, the proof of things not seen (11:1, loosely paraphrased).
B. "Faith enables the believing soul to treat the future as present, and the invisible as seen" (J. Oswald Sanders). According to verse 3, faith is vital if we are to go beyond the very first verse in Genesis 1. (See also 11:6.)
C. Faith is trust in the unseen, but not the unknown. (See also 11:27.)
D. "Faith is the title-deed of things hoped for" (Moulton and Milligan).

---

1. Who they were
   a. Abel (Heb. 11:4)

---

†11:4 *Abel was the second baby to be born in history and the first martyr (Gen. 4:2, 8).*

---

b. Enoch (Heb. 11:5)

---

†11:5 *Enoch was the first of two human beings who left this earth without dying (Gen. 5:24). Elijah was the other person (2 Kings 2:11).*

---

c. Noah (Heb. 11:7)

---

†11:7
A. By faith Enoch was removed before the great flood and becomes a type of the Christian who will be taken out before the coming great tribulation.
B. By faith Noah was preserved during the great flood and becomes a type of Israel, who will be protected during the great tribulation.

---

d. Abraham (Heb. 11:8-10, 17-19)

---

†11:8 *It has been observed that by faith Abraham obeyed God when he did not know* where *(11:8-10); when he did not know* how *(11:11-12); when he did not know* when *(11:13-16); and when he did not know* why *(11:17-19).*

---

e. Sarah (Heb. 11:11-12)
f. Isaac (Heb. 11:20)

---

†11:21
A. Isaac predicted the future of Jacob (Gen. 27:26-40).
B. Jacob predicted the future for both his 12 sons and two grandsons of Joseph (Gen. 48–49).

---

g. Jacob (Heb. 11:21)

h. Joseph (Heb. 11:22)
i. Moses' parents (Heb. 11:23)
j. Moses (Heb. 11:24-29)
k. Joshua (Heb. 11:30)
l. Rahab (Heb. 11:31)
m. Gideon (Heb. 11:32)
n. Barak (Heb. 11:32)
o. Samson (Heb. 11:32)
p. Jephtah (Heb. 11:32)
q. David (Heb. 11:32)
r. Samuel (Heb. 11:32)

2. What they did
    a. Offered proper sacrifices—"By faith Abel offered unto God a more excellent sacrifice than Cain, by which he obtained witness that he was righteous, God testifying of his gifts: and by it he being dead yet speaketh" (Heb. 11:4).
    b. Left the earth without dying—"By faith Enoch was translated that he should not see death; and was not found, because God had translated him: for before his translation he had this testimony, that he pleased God" (Heb. 11:5).
    c. Survived the great flood—"By faith Noah, being warned of God of things not seen as yet, moved with fear, prepared an ark to the saving of his house; by the which he condemned the world, and became heir of the righteousness which is by faith" (Heb. 11:7).
    d. Inherited a land—"By faith Abraham, when he was called to go out into a place which he should after receive for an inheritance, obeyed; and he went out, not knowing whither he went" (Heb. 11:8).
    e. Bore children in their old age—"Through faith also Sara herself received strength to conceive seed, and was delivered of a child when she was past age, because she judged him faithful who had promised" (Heb. 11:11).
    f. Predicted the future (Heb. 11:20-21)
    g. Defied kings—"By faith Moses, when he was born, was hid three months of his parents, because they saw he was a proper child; and they were not afraid of the king's commandment" (Heb. 11:23).
    h. Forsook the pleasures of sin—"By faith Moses, when he was come to years, refused to be called the son of Pharaoh's daughter; choosing rather to suffer affliction with the people of God, than to enjoy the pleasures of sin for a season; esteeming the reproach of Christ greater riches than the treasures in Egypt: for he had respect unto the recompence of the reward" (Heb. 11:24-26).
    i. Left Egypt—"By faith he forsook Egypt, not fearing the wrath of the king: for he endured, as seeing him who is invisible" (Heb. 11:27).
    j. Kept the Passover—"Through faith he kept the passover, and the sprinkling of blood, lest he that destroyed the firstborn should touch them" (Heb 11:28).
    k. Crossed the Red Sea—"By faith they passed through the Red sea as by dry land: which the Egyptians assaying to do were drowned" (Heb. 11:29).
    l. Shouted down a city—"By faith the walls of Jericho fell down, after they were compassed about seven days" (Heb. 11:30).
    m. Subdued kingdoms (Heb. 11:33)
    n. Performed acts of righteousness (Heb. 11:33)

o. Obtained promises (Heb. 11:33)
p. Shut the mouths of lions (Heb. 11:33)

---

†*Faith accomplished this for at least three Old Testament individuals:*
A. Samson (Judg. 14:5-6)
B. David (1 Sam. 17:34-37)
C. Daniel (Dan. 6:22)

---

q. Quenched the power of fire (Heb. 11:34)
r. Escaped the edge of the sword (Heb. 11:34)
s. Saw their weakness turned into strength (Heb. 11:34)
t. Put foreign armies to flight (Heb. 11:34)

---

†*A number of Old Testament men won battles without using a single sword or arrow.*
A. Joshua (Josh. 6:20)
B. Gideon (Judg. 7:20-21)
C. Samuel (1 Sam. 7:9-12)
D. Elijah (2 Kings 1:1-12)
E. Elisha (2 Kings 6:15-18)
F. Asa (2 Chron. 14:9-13)
G. Jehoshaphat (2 Chron. 20:1-32)
H. Hezekiah (2 Kings 19:35)

---

u. Saw their dead raised (Heb. 11:35)

---

†*Two Old Testament mothers experienced this:*
A. The widow of Zarephath (1 Kings 17:17-24)
B. The woman at Shunem (2 Kings 4:30-37)

---

3. What they endured
   a. Terrible torture (Heb. 11:35)
   b. Ridicule (Heb. 11:36)
   c. Beatings (Heb. 11:36)
   d. Imprisonment (Heb. 11:36)
   e. Stoning (Heb. 11:37)
   f. Being cut in half (Heb. 11:37)

---

†*There is a tradition that wicked Judean king Manasseh ordered the prophet Isaiah to be sawn assunder.*

---

g. Severe temptation (Heb. 11:37)
h. Extreme poverty—"They were stoned, they were sawn asunder, were tempted, were slain with the sword: they wandered about in sheepskins

and goatskins; being destitute, afflicted, tormented; (of whom the world was not worthy:) they wandered in deserts, and in mountains, and in dens and caves of the earth" (Heb. 11:37-38).

4. Why they endured—"For he looked for a city which hath foundations, whose builder and maker is God. . . . These all died in faith, not having received the promises, but having seen them afar off, and were persuaded of them, and embraced them, and confessed that they were strangers and pilgrims on the earth. For they that say such things declare plainly that they seek a country. And truly, if they had been mindful of that country from whence they came out, they might have had opportunity to have returned. But now they desire a better country, that is, an heavenly: wherefore God is not ashamed to be called their God: for he hath prepared for them a city. . . . And these all, having obtained a good report through faith, received not the promise" (Heb. 11:10, 13-16, 39).

B. The pattern of faith (Heb. 12)
   1. Perform the work of God (Heb. 12:1-3).
      a. The patience involved—"Wherefore seeing we also are compassed about with so great a cloud of witnesses, let us lay aside every weight, and the sin which doth so easily beset us, and let us run with patience the race that is set before us" (Heb. 12:1).

---

†12:1 *Many believe Paul to be the author of Hebrews.*

A. This amazing apostle was many things. He was a missionary, a soul winner, a pastor, a great theologian, a tentmaker. But in his spare time he also seemed to be a sports lover. Often in his writings, Paul uses sports as an analogy to get his point across. For example:
   1. Wrestling—"For we wrestle not against flesh and blood, but against principalities, against powers, against the rulers of the darkness of this world, against spiritual wickedness in high places" (Eph. 6:12).
   2. Boxing—"I have fought a good fight" (2 Tim. 4:7). "So fight I, not as one that beateth the air" (1 Cor. 9:26).
   3. Racing—"Know ye not that they which run in a race run all, but one receiveth the prize? So run that ye may obtain . . . I therefore so run" (1 Cor. 9:24, 26). Here in Hebrews 12, Paul chooses the third analogy—that of a foot race.

B. At least four phrases in this verse merit special attention:
   1. "So great a cloud of witnesses"
      a. Great—*We often feel (wrongly so) that we are all alone, as Elijah once did (1 Kings 19:10, 14, 18).*
      b. Cloud—*This underlines the word "great." The Greek here is not* nephele, *which refers to a detached and sharply outlined cloud, but* nephos, *speaking of a huge mass of clouds, covering the entire visible space of the heavens.*
      c. Witnesses—*Who are these witnesses? They are not angels, for the Greek word is* marturos, *referring to one who has both seen, heard, and performed something, usually while suffering. It speaks of a well-qualified expert. The context strongly suggests that these witnesses are the faith heroes mentioned in chapter 11.*
   2. "Let us lay aside every weight"—Here the word is onkos *and refers to a bulk or mass. The concern of the Greek runner was not simply whether something was immoral or moral, but rather how it would affect his race. Thus, the enemy of the best is often not the worst, but the good.*

3. "And the sin which doth so easily beset us"—The word "beset" means "to surround, to cleverly encircle, to ambush." It speaks of a loosely fitting robe. Paul may have had in mind the sin of unbelief here, but it also refers to any sin the believer allows to upset him.
4. "Let us run with patience the race that is set before us"—Note the implications of this statement.
a. Every believer has been entered in this race by God himself. It is not just for pastors and missionaries. Note: The usual word for race (dromos) *is not used here, but rather the Greek word* agon, *from which we get our English word "agony." This is a serious race.*
b. The pace of each runner is set by God.
c. The object of the race is to please God and win rewards. Its goal is not *heaven.*
d. Every runner is expected to win.

---

b. The person involved—"Looking unto Jesus the author and finisher of our faith; who for the joy that was set before him endured the cross, despising the shame, and is set down at the right hand of the throne of God. For consider him that endured such contradiction of sinners against himself, lest ye be wearied and faint in your minds" (Heb. 12:2-3).

---

†12:3

A. "Looking unto Jesus" (12:2)—The phrase here speaks of a steadfast, intent, and continuous gaze. How easy it is to get our eyes off him and look to the left or right. Perhaps to our left we see another runner behind us. It may be that a runner is far ahead of us to the right. This then can produce pride (as we view the left runner) and envy (as we view the runner on the right). Both are sin and cause us to slow down. We are instead to keep looking at Jesus.
1. If you would be disappointed, look to others.
2. If you would be discouraged, look to yourself.
3. If you would be delighted, look at Jesus.
B. "The author and finisher of our faith" (12:2)—Christ is both Founder and Finisher of the Christian faith. Confucius, Buddha, and Mohammed founded three worldwide religious movements, but death finished Confucius, Buddha, and Mohammed.
C. "For the joy that was set before him endured the cross" (12:2)—The nature of this joy is explained in Jude 24: "Now unto him [Jesus] that is able to keep you from falling, and to present you faultless before the presence of his glory with exceeding joy" (see also John 17:6-12, 26).
D. "Despising the shame, and is set down at the right hand . . . of God" (12:2; see Phil. 2:5-11).
E. "For consider him" (12:3)—Time and again we are driven back to the Gospel accounts by the writers of the epistles.

---

2. Ponder the discipline of God (Heb. 12:4-11).

---

†*If rightly understood and accepted, the discipline of God upon his children can prove to be a very fruitful experience indeed.*

---

a. The reasons for discipline—"For whom the Lord loveth he chasteneth, and scourgeth every son whom he receiveth. If ye endure chastening, God dealeth with you as with sons; for what son is he whom the father chasteneth not? But if ye be without chastisement, whereof all are partakers, then are ye bastards, and not sons" (Heb. 12:6-8).

---

†12:8

A. The word "chasten" here refers to that instruction in right behavior. The word "scourge" speaks of that correction in wrong behavior.

B. Thus, divine chastisement upon a sinning Christian does not *imply* condemnation, *but rather* confirmation, *demonstrating that we belong to God.*

---

b. The reaction to discipline
   (1) We can despise it (underreact to it)—"My son, despise not thou the chastening of the Lord" (Heb. 12:5).
   (2) We can faint under it (overreact to it)—"Nor faint when thou art rebuked of him" (Heb. 12:5).
   (3) We can be exercised by it—"Furthermore we have had fathers of our flesh which corrected us, and we gave them reverence: shall we not much rather be in subjection unto the Father of spirits, and live? For they verily for a few days chastened us after their own pleasure; but he for our profit, that we might be partakers of his holiness" (Heb. 12:9-10).

---

†12:10 *The real question is not simply how many mistakes a Christian makes, but how much he learns through those mistakes. The Psalms speak concerning this: "Blessed is the man whom thou chastenest, O LORD, and teachest him out of thy law" (94:12). "Before I was afflicted I went astray: but now have I kept thy word" (119:67). "It is good for me that I have been afflicted: that I might learn thy statutes" (119:71). "I know, O LORD, that thy judgments are right and that thou in faithfulness hast afflicted me" (119:75).*

---

c. The results of discipline—"Now no chastening for the present seemeth to be joyous, but grievous: nevertheless afterward it yieldeth the peaceable fruit of righteousness unto them which are exercised thereby" (Heb. 12:11).

3. Prepare for the kingdom of God (Heb. 12:11).
   a. Straighten up (Heb. 12:12-14)—"Wherefore lift up the hands which hang down, and the feeble knees; and make straight paths for your feet, lest that which is lame be turned out of the way; but let it rather be healed. Follow peace with all men, and holiness, without which no man shall see the Lord" (Heb. 12:12-14).

---

†12:14 *Homer Kent writes: "If one's feet are lame, special care must be taken that the path on which they walk has no dangerous obstacles. Spiritually speaking, the one whose faith is weak must not venture into areas where his spiritual strength is insufficient. Otherwise the . . . lame believer may aggravate his lameness into a dislocation of the limbs"* (Epistle to the Hebrews, *p. 265).*

---

   b. Measure up (Heb. 12:15-17).
      (1) The attitude involved—"Looking diligently lest any man fail of the grace

of God; lest any root of bitterness springing up trouble you, and thereby many be defiled" (Heb. 12:15).

(2) The apostate involved—"Lest there be any fornicator, or profane person, as Esau, who for one morsel of meat sold his birthright. For ye know how that afterward, when he would have inherited the blessing, he was rejected: for he found no place of repentance, though he sought it carefully with tears" (Heb. 12:16-17).

---

†12:17

A. The birthright here had to do with the spiritual responsibility of the eldest son in continuing the family faith. Esau, being both irreverent and immoral, had no desire whatsoever in this matter (Gen. 25:27-34).

B. The blessing here had to do with receiving a double portion of the family wealth plus a prophetical prayer from the father asking God to protect and prosper the son. This, of course, Esau very much desired (Gen. 27).

---

c. Look up (Heb. 12:18-24).

(1) From—Mount Sinai, the old life under the Law (Heb 12:18-21). "For ye are not come unto the mount that might be touched, and that burned with fire, nor unto blackness, and darkness, and tempest. . . . (And so terrible was the sight, that Moses said, I exceedingly fear and quake)" (Heb. 12:18, 21).

(2) To—Mount Zion, the new life under grace (Heb. 12: 22-24). "But ye are come unto mount Sion, and unto the city of the living God, the heavenly Jerusalem, and to an innumerable company of angels, to the general assembly and church of the firstborn, which are written in heaven, and to God the Judge of all, and to the spirits of just men made perfect, and to Jesus, the mediator of the new covenant, and to the blood of sprinkling, that speaketh better things than that of Abel" (Heb. 12:22-24).

d. Become wise (Heb. 12:25-27)—"See that ye refuse not him that speaketh. For if they escaped not who refused him that spake on earth, much more shall not we escape, if we turn away from him that speaketh from heaven" (Heb. 12:25).

e. Cheer up (Heb. 12:28-29)—"Wherefore we receiving a kingdom which cannot be moved, let us have grace, whereby we may serve God acceptably with reverence and godly fear" (Heb. 12:28).

C. The performance of faith (Heb. 13)

1. What the Savior has done—"Jesus Christ the same yesterday, and to day, and for ever" (Heb. 13:8).

a. He died to save us—"Wherefore Jesus also, that he might sanctify the people with his own blood, suffered without the gate" (Heb. 13:12).

b. He lives to sanctify us—"Now the God of peace, that brought again from the dead our Lord Jesus, that great shepherd of the sheep, through the blood of the everlasting covenant, make you perfect in every good work to do his will, working in you that which is wellpleasing in his sight, through Jesus Christ; to whom be glory for ever and ever. Amen" (Heb. 13:20-21).

2. What the saints are to do
   a. We are to display charity—"Let brotherly love continue. Be not forgetful to entertain strangers: for thereby some have entertained angels unawares" (Heb. 13:1-2).

---

†13:2 *At least two Old Testament individuals come to mind here:*
A. Abraham (Gen. 18:1-8)
B. Lot (Gen. 19:1-3)

---

   b. We are to display compassion—"Remember them that are in bonds, as bound with them; and them which suffer adversity, as being yourselves also in the body" (Heb. 13:3).
   c. We are to display chastity—"Marriage is honourable in all, and the bed undefiled: but whoremongers and adulterers God will judge" (Heb. 13:4).
   d. We are to display contentment—"Let your conversation be without covetousness; and be content with such things as ye have: for he hath said, I will never leave thee, nor forsake thee" (Heb. 13:5).
   e. We are to display courage—"So that we may boldly say, The Lord is my helper, and I will not fear what man shall do unto me" (Heb. 13:6).
   f. We are to display consideration—This consideration and respect is to be directed toward our spiritual leaders.
      (1) Their divine appointment—"Remember them which have the rule over you, who have spoken unto you the word of God: whose faith follow, considering the end of their conversation" (Heb. 13:7).
      (2) Their divine accountability—"Obey them that have the rule over you, and submit yourselves: for they watch for your souls, as they that must give account, that they may do it with joy, and not with grief: for that is unprofitable for you" (Heb. 13:17).
   g. We are to display consistency—"Be not carried about with divers and strange doctrines. For it is a good thing that the heart be established with grace; not with meats, which have not profited them that have been occupied therein" (Heb. 13:9).
   h. We are to display commitment—"Let us go forth therefore unto him without the camp, bearing his reproach. For here have we no continuing city, but we seek one to come" (Heb. 13:13-14).
   i. We are to display consecration—"By him therefore let us offer the sacrifice of praise to God continually, that is, the fruit of our lips giving thanks to his name. But to do good and to communicate forget not: for with such sacrifices God is well pleased" (Heb. 13:15-16).

---

†13:16 *In addition to offering up a sacrifice of praise, the believer is commanded to offer up the sacrifice of his own body (Rom. 12:1), and that of good works (Heb. 13:16).*

JAMES

THIS NEW TESTAMENT BOOK
IS THE PROVERBS OF THE NEW TESTAMENT.

A. The book of James aptly fits this description.
B. His epistle is perhaps the earliest in the New Testament, dated around A.D. 45. The synagogue is mentioned as the place of meeting, rather than the church (see 2:2). It was thus written when the church was still in the circle of Judaism.
C. It is the most Jewish book in the New Testament. M. F. Unger writes: "If the several passages referring to Christ were eliminated, the whole epistle would be as proper in the canon of the Old Testament as it is in the New Testament. In fact, the epistle could be described as an interpretation of the Old Testament law and the Sermon on the Mount in the light of the Gospel of Christ" (*Unger's Bible Handbook,* p. 783).
D. It may be considered the Proverbs of the New Testament.
E. The Greek language of James is of the highest quality.
F. There are only four Old Testament direct quotes, but at least 53 Old Testament references in the epistle of James.
G. It is the only New Testament book specifically addressed to the 12 tribes (1:1).
H. James gives God's present-day plan for healing (5:13-18).
I. James was the oldest half brother of Jesus (Mark 6:3; Matt. 13:55). He was the full brother of Jude, who wrote the book of Jude.
J. James was an unbeliever prior to the resurrection (John 7:3-10).
K. James then appeared in the Upper Room awaiting Pentecost (Acts 1:13).
L. He became the first pastor of the Jerusalem church (Acts 12:17; 15:13; Gal. 2:1, 9-10, 12). "He was known as an unusually good man, and was surnamed 'the Just' by his countrymen. It is said that he spent so much time on his knees in prayer that they became hard and callused like a camel's knees. He is thought to have been married" (1 Cor. 9:5). (*Halley's Bible Handbook,* p. 657).
M. Like Jude, James does not "pull his rank" by pointing out the physical relationship between himself and Christ. He simply refers to himself as "a servant of God and of the Lord Jesus Christ" (1:1).
N. James, like Jesus, loved to use Old Testament characters and the realm of nature as illustrations. Note:
  1. Old Testament characters
    a. Abraham (2:21)
    b. Isaac (2:21)
    c. Rahab (2:25)
    d. Job (5:11)
    e. Elijah (5:17)
  2. Realm of nature
    a. Wind-tossed waves of the sea (1:6)
    b. Withering grass and fading flowers (1:10-11)

c. Fire (3:5)
d. Fountains of water (3:11)
e. Figs and olives (3:12)
f. Sowing and harvesting (3:18)
g. Early and latter rains (5:7)
h. Drought (5:17)

O. Some have imagined a contradiction between James and Paul. Martin Luther believed this, and referred to the book as "a right strawy epistle"! James wrote: "Ye see, then, that by works a man is justified, and not by faith only" (2:24). Paul wrote: "For by grace are ye saved through faith; and that not of yourselves; it is the gift of God: not of works, lest any man should boast" (Eph. 2:8-9). Luther and others were, of course, wrong on this conclusion. There is no contradiction here. Note:
1. Paul speaks of justification before God.
2. James describes justification before people.
3. We are justified by faith, says Paul.
4. We are justified for works, says James.
5. Paul is interested in the root of justification.
6. James is concerned about the fruit of justification.
7. It was John Calvin who said: "Faith alone saves, but the faith that saves is not alone."
8. Furthermore, on occasion Paul stresses works (1 Tim. 6:18; Titus 3:8; Eph. 2:10), while James emphasizes faith (James 2:5).

P. James met Paul during his (Paul's) first trip to Jerusalem after his Damascus Road conversion (Gal. 1:18-19).

Q. He also conferred with Paul during the apostle's last trip to Jerusalem (Acts 21:18-25).

R. Tradition says that shortly before Jerusalem was destroyed, when many Jews were accepting Christ, Annas the high priest assembled the Sanhedrin and commanded James publicly to renounce Christ as Israel's Messiah. Upon his refusal, he was thrown from the pinnacle of the temple and stoned to death as he lay dying from the fall.

S. The most extended discussion on the human tongue is found in James 3.

T. James is the 15th longest New Testament book, and 46th longest biblical book, with five chapters, 108 verses, and 2,309 words. There are quotations or allusions from 17 Old Testament books in James.

U. Great passages would include:
1. 1:2-8
2. 1:12-27
3. 4:6-10
4. 4:13-15
5. 5:8-11
6. 5:16-20

THE BOOK OF JAMES

"James, a servant of God and of the Lord Jesus Christ, to the twelve tribes which are scattered abroad, greeting. My brethren, count it all joy when ye fall into divers temptations; knowing this, that the trying of your faith worketh patience. But let patience have her perfect work, that ye may be perfect and entire, wanting nothing" (James 1:1-4). The word "perfect" (a reference to maturity) is found many times in James. Thus the term "maturity" will be used in outlining this book.

I. Suffering Makes a Mature Person (James 1:1-15).
  A. The background of sufferings—Both God and Satan are usually involved in the sufferings of a Christian.
    1. God's purpose is to purify and strengthen us. He wants to make us better. "My brethren, count it all joy when ye fall into divers temptations" (James 1:2). "Blessed is the man that endureth temptation" (James 1:12).

---

†1:1-5 *To summarize these verses:*
A. The facets of temptation—The word "temptation" carries with it a twofold meaning.
1. First meaning—To test in a good sense with the goal of confirming one in matters of righteousness. (See Gen. 22:1; Deut. 8:2-3; Exod. 20:20.)
2. Second meaning—To test in a bad sense with the goal of corrupting one in matters of righteousness. (See Gen. 3:1-6; Matt. 4:1.)
B. The facts about temptations (according to James 1:2)
1. They are often sudden—"When ye fall" (1:2).
2. They are certain—James says when *ye fall, not,* if *ye fall.*
3. They are sorted—"Into divers [various] temptations." These are financial, physical, spiritual, mental, and social trials.

---

    2. Satan's purpose is to pervert and weaken us—He wants to make us bitter. "Let no man say when he is tempted, I am tempted of God: for God cannot be tempted with evil, neither tempteth he any man: but every man is tempted, when he is drawn away of his own lust, and enticed. Then when lust hath conceived, it bringeth forth sin: and sin, when it is finished, bringeth forth death" (James 1:13-15).
  B. The purpose of suffering
    1. It produces endurance down here—"Knowing this, that the trying of your faith worketh patience. But let patience have her perfect work, that ye may be perfect and entire, wanting nothing" (James 1:3-4).
    2. It promises rewards up there—"Blessed is the man that endureth temptation: for when he is tried, he shall receive the crown of life, which the Lord hath promised to them that love him" (James 1:12).
  C. The response to suffering
    1. Positive
      a. We are to praise God for it (James 1:2).
      b. We are to pray while in it—"If any of you lack wisdom, let him ask of God, that giveth to all men liberally, and upbraideth not; and it shall be given him" (James 1:5).
    2. Negative
      a. We are not to become as tossed waves—"But let him ask in faith, nothing wavering. For he that wavereth is like a wave of the sea driven with the wind and tossed. For let not that man think that he shall receive any thing of the Lord. A double minded man is unstable in all his ways" (James 1:6-8).

b. We are not to become as wilted flowers—"Let the brother of low degree rejoice in that he is exalted: but the rich, in that he is made low: because as the flower of the grass he shall pass away. For the sun is no sooner risen with a burning heat, but it withereth the grass, and the flower thereof falleth, and the grace of the fashion of it perisheth: so also shall the rich man fade away in his ways" (James 1:9-11).

II. Scripture Study Makes a Mature Person (James 1:16-25).

A. Its author—"Every good gift and every perfect gift is from above, and cometh down from the Father of lights, with whom is no variableness, neither shadow of turning" (James 1:17).

B. Its accomplishments—"Of his own will begat he us with the word of truth, that we should be a kind of firstfruits of his creatures" (James 1:18).

C. Its admonitions (James 1:19-22)

1. Our talk is to be pure—"Wherefore, my beloved brethren, let every man be swift to hear, slow to speak, slow to wrath" (James 1:19).

2. Our walk is to be pure—"Wherefore lay apart all filthiness and superfluity of naughtiness, and receive with meekness the engrafted word, which is able to save your souls. But be ye doers of the word, and not hearers only, deceiving your own selves" (James 1:21-22). "Pure religion and undefiled before God and the Father is this, To visit the fatherless and widows in their affliction, and to keep himself unspotted from the world" (James 1:27).

D. Its analogy—"For if any be a hearer of the word, and not a doer, he is like unto a man beholding his natural face in a glass: For he beholdeth himself, and goeth his way, and straightway forgetteth what manner of man he was" (James 1:23-24).

E. Its assurance—"But whoso looketh into the perfect law of liberty, and continueth therein, he being not a forgetful hearer, but a doer of the work, this man shall be blessed in his deed" (James 1:25).

III. Sincerity Makes a Mature Person (James 2:1-13).

A. Commands against partiality (James 2:1-8)—"My brethren, have not the faith of our Lord Jesus Christ, the Lord of glory, with respect of persons. If ye fulfil the royal law according to the scripture, Thou shalt love thy neighbour as thyself, ye do well" (James 2:1, 8).

---

†2:8 *This "royal law" was given in Leviticus 19:18 and reaffirmed by Jesus in Matthew 22:36-40. It is considered royal or regal because it was decreed by the King of kings and functions as the Law of laws. Note its features: "Jesus said unto him, Thou shalt love the Lord thy God with all thy heart, and with all thy soul, and with all thy mind. This is the first and great commandment. And the second is like unto it, Thou shalt love thy neighbor as thyself. On these two commandments hang all the law and the prophets" (Matt. 22:37-40).*

A. The first part of the royal law (loving one's God) is vertical and fulfills laws 1-4 in the Ten Commandments (Exod. 20:3-11).

B. The second part of the royal law (loving one's neighbor) is horizontal and fulfills laws 5-10 in the Ten Commandments (Exod. 20:12-17).

---

1. An earthly example—"For if there come unto your assembly a man with a gold ring, in goodly apparel, and there come in also a poor man in vile raiment; and

ye have respect to him that weareth the gay clothing, and say unto him, Sit thou here in a good place; and say to the poor, Stand thou there, or sit here under my footstool: Are ye not then partial in yourselves, and are become judges of evil thoughts?" (James 2:2-4).

2. A heavenly example—"Hearken, my beloved brethren, Hath not God chosen the poor of this world rich in faith, and heirs of the kingdom which he hath promised to them that love him?" (James 2:5).

B. Consequences of partiality (James 2:9-13)

1. To be guilty of the Law—"But if ye have respect to persons, ye commit sin, and are convinced of the law as transgressors. For whosoever shall keep the whole law, and yet offend in one point, he is guilty of all. For he that said, Do not commit adultery, said also, Do not kill. Now if thou commit no adultery, yet if thou kill, thou art become a transgressor of the law" (James 2:9-11)
2. To be judged by the Law—"So speak ye, and so do, as they that shall be judged by the law of liberty. For he shall have judgment without mercy, that hath shewed no mercy; and mercy rejoiceth against judgment" (James 2:12-13).

IV. Christian Service Makes a Mature Person (James 2: 14-26).

A. The problem—Some have imagined a contradiction between James and Paul. Note:

1. Paul's words—"For by grace are ye saved through faith; and that not of yourselves: it is the gift of God: not of works, lest any man should boast" (Eph. 2:8-9).
2. James's words—"What doth it profit, my brethren, though a man say he hath faith, and have not works? can faith save him? . . . Ye see then how that by works a man is justified, and not by faith only" (James 2:14, 24).

B. The particulars

1. Paul speaks about vertical justification before God.
2. James speaks about horizontal justification before other people.

---

†*These verses are not meant to be* saving *texts, but* sign *texts. The proof of the pudding is still in the eating. The only test of a man's salvation is through his works. A silent believer may indeed be considered a saint before God, but he remains a sinner before man until he walks the walk and talks the talk of Christian service.*

C. The pattern

1. Two examples of head faith only
   a. Concerning the destitute—"If a brother or sister be naked, and destitute of daily food, and one of you say unto them, Depart in peace, be ye warmed and filled; notwithstanding ye give them not those things which are needful to the body; what doth it profit?" (James 2:15-16).
   b. Concerning the devil—"Thou believest that there is one God; thou doest well: the devils also believe, and tremble" (James 2:19).
2. Two examples of head and heart faith
   a. Abraham—"Was not Abraham our father justified by works, when he had offered Isaac his son upon the altar? Seest thou how faith wrought with his works, and by works was faith made perfect? And the scripture was fulfilled which saith, Abraham believed God, and it was imputed unto him for righteousness: and he was called the Friend of God" (James 2:21-23).

---

†**2:23** *The chronology of Abraham's life is important to note here. He was justified before God at the age of 85 (Gen. 15:6; 16:16). He was justified before humanity at the age of (approximately) 137 (Gen. 22:1-14; 23:1).*

---

b. Rahab—"Likewise also was not Rahab the harlot justified by works, when she had received the messengers, and had sent them out another way?" (James 2:25).

---

†**2:25** *Rahab's* salvation *is recorded in Joshua 2:1-14, and the* service *in 2:15-16. Dr. Charles Ryrie writes: "Unproductive faith cannot save, because it is not genuine faith. Faith and works are like a two-coupon ticket to heaven. The coupon of works is not good for passage, and the coupon of faith is not valid if detached from works"* (Ryrie Study Bible, *p. 421).*

D. The principle—"Even so faith, if it hath not works, is dead, being alone. Yea, a man may say, Thou hast faith, and I have works: shew me thy faith without thy works, and I will shew thee my faith by my works. . . . But wilt thou know, O vain man, that faith without works is dead? . . . For as the body without the spirit is dead, so faith without works is dead also" (James 2:17-18, 20, 26).

---

†**2:26** *In a nutshell:*

A. We are saved not by *good works, but rather* for *good works. (See Eph. 2:8-10.)*

B. Workless faith is worthless faith.

C. Faith is the basis of one's salvation, while works become the barometer of that salvation.

V. Sound Speech Makes a Mature Person (James 3:1-18; 1:26-27).

A. Importance of the tongue—"For in many things we offend all. If any man offend not in word, the same is a perfect man, and able also to bridle the whole body" (James 3:2).

---

†**3:2** *Taken in proper context, this is one of the most profound and far-reaching statements in the entire Bible. It has been suggested that the body is the congregation and the tongue is its teacher.*

B. Illustrations of the tongue

1. How it can control

a. It is as a bridle to a horse—"Behold, we put bits in the horses' mouths, that they may obey us; and we turn about their whole body" (James 3:3).

b. It is as a rudder to a ship—"Behold also the ships, which though they be so great, and are driven of fierce winds, yet are they turned about with a very small helm, whithersoever the governor listeth" (James 3:4).

2. How it can consume—"Even so the tongue is a little member, and boasteth great things. Behold, how great a matter a little fire kindleth!" (James 3:5).

C. Iniquity of the tongue (James 3:5-6: 1:26)

1. It can destroy our witness for God—"If any man among you seem to be religious, and bridleth not his tongue, but deceiveth his own heart, this man's religion is vain" (James 1:26).

2. It can defile our walk with God—"And the tongue is a fire, a world of iniquity: so is the tongue among our members, that it defileth the whole body, and setteth on fire the course of nature; and it is set on fire of hell" (James 3:6).

D. Incorrigibility of the tongue (James 3:7-8)—"For every kind of beasts, and of birds, and of serpents, and of things in the sea, is tamed, and hath been tamed of mankind: but the tongue can no man tame; it is an unruly evil, full of deadly poison" (James 3:7-8).

E. Inconsistency of the tongue (James 3:9-12)

1. The contradiction—"Therewith bless we God, even the Father; and therewith curse we men, which are made after the similitude of God. Out of the same mouth proceedeth blessing and cursing. My brethren, these things ought not so to be" (James 3:9-10).

---

†3:10 *An Egyptian king named Amasis once sent a sacrifice to his god and requested the priest to send back the best and worst part of the animal. The priest sent back the tongue, which organ, said he, represented both demands. It has been said that the Christian should so live that he would not hesitate to sell his talking parrot to the town gossip.*

---

2. The conclusion—"Doth a fountain send forth at the same place sweet water and bitter? Can the fig tree, my brethren, bear olive berries? either a vine, figs? so can no fountain both yield salt water and fresh" (James 3:11-12). "But above all things, my brethren, swear not, neither by heaven, neither by the earth, neither by any other oath: but let your yea be yea; and your nay, nay; lest ye fall into condemnation" (James 5:12).

F. Instructions for the tongue

1. Seek and speak the wisdom of God—"Who is a wise man and endued with knowledge among you? let him shew out of a good conversation his works with meekness of wisdom. But the wisdom that is from above is first pure, then peaceable, gentle, and easy to be intreated, full of mercy and good fruits, without partiality, and without hypocrisy. And the fruit of righteousness is sown in peace of them that make peace" (James 3:13, 17-18).
2. Refuse and renounce the slander of Satan—"But if ye have bitter envying and strife in your hearts, glory not, and lie not against the truth. This wisdom descendeth not from above, but is earthly, sensual, devilish. For where envying and strife is, there is confusion and every evil work" (James 3:14-16).

VI. Submission to God Makes a Mature Person (James 4:1-17).

A. What we escape when we do this

1. The flesh (James 4:1-3, 11-12, 16-17)—"From whence come wars and fighting among you? come they not hence, even of your lusts that war in your members? Ye lust, and have not: ye kill, and desire to have, and cannot obtain: ye fight and war, yet ye have not, because ye ask not. Ye ask, and receive not, because ye ask amiss, that ye may consume it upon your lusts" (James 4:1-3).

---

†4:3

A. Concerning spiritual things—They had not received because they had not asked (example, the gift of wisdom; see 1:5).

B. Concerning sinful things—They had not received even though they had asked.

---

2. The world—"Ye adulterers and adulteresses, know ye not that the friendship of the world is enmity with God? whosoever therefore will be a friend of the world is the enemy of God. Do ye think that the scripture saith in vain, The spirit that dwelleth in us lusteth to envy?" (James 4:4-5).
3. The devil—"Submit yourselves therefore to God. Resist the devil, and he will flee from you" (James 4:7).

B. What we enjoy when we do this
1. God's grace—"But he giveth more grace. Wherefore he saith, God resisteth the proud, but giveth grace unto the humble" (James 4:6).

---

†**4:6** *There are numerous biblical examples of God rejecting the haughty but receiving the humble.*
A. Cain and Abel (Gen. 4:1-7)
B. Jacob and Esau (Rom. 9:13)
C. Moses and Korah (Num. 12:3; 16:1-4)
D. Barak and Sisera (Judges 4–5)
E. David and Saul (1 Sam. 24:9-22; 26:17-25)
F. Nehemiah and Sanballat (Neh. 6:1-14)
G. Daniel and Nebuchadnezzar (Dan. 4)
H. Daniel and Belshazzar (Dan. 5)
I. Mordecai and Haman (book of Esther)
J. Amos and Amaziah (Amos 7)
K. The Pharisee and the publican (Luke 18:9-14)
L. Diotrephes and Demetrius (3 John 1:9-12)

---

2. God's guarantee
   a. Of his presence—"Draw nigh to God, and he will draw nigh to you. Cleanse your hands, ye sinners; and purify your hearts, ye double minded" (James 4:8).
   b. Of his promotion—"Humble yourselves in the sight of the Lord, and he shall lift you up" (James 4:10).

---

†**4:10** *The classic Old Testament example of this statement can be seen in the life of Joseph, whom God promoted from being a prisoner* in *Egypt, to being prime minister* over *Egypt. (See Gen. 39–41.)*

---

3. God's guidance—"Go to now, ye that say, To day or to morrow we will go into such a city, and continue there a year, and buy and sell, and get gain: Whereas ye know not what shall be on the morrow. For what is your life? It is even a vapour, that appeareth for a little time, and then vanisheth away. For that ye ought to say, If the Lord will, we shall live, and do this, or that" (James 4:13-15).

VII. Simplicity in Life Makes a Mature Person (James 5:1-6)—Here James contrasts this virtue by referring to the selfish rich.
   A. The consternation of the selfish rich—"Go to now, ye rich men, weep and howl for your miseries that shall come upon you" (James 5:1).

B. The corruption of the selfish rich—"Your riches are corrupted, and your garments are motheaten. Ye have lived in pleasure on the earth, and been wanton; ye have nourished your hearts, as in a day of slaughter" (James 5:2, 5).

C. The cruelty of the selfish rich—"Behold, the hire of the labourers who have reaped down your fields, which is of you kept back by fraud, crieth: and the cries of them which have reaped are entered into the ears of the Lord of Sabaoth. . . . Ye have condemned and killed the just; and he doth not resist you" (James 5:4, 6).

D. The condemnation of the selfish rich—"Your gold and silver is cankered; and the rust of them shall be a witness against you, and shall eat your flesh as it were fire. Ye have heaped treasure together for the last days" (James 5:3).

VIII. Steadfastness Makes a Mature Person (James 5:7-11).

A. A past example—Job and his trials (James 5:10-11)—"Take, my brethren, the prophets, who have spoken in the name of the Lord, for an example of suffering affliction, and of patience. Behold, we count them happy which endure. Ye have heard of the patience of Job, and have seen the end of the Lord; that the Lord is very pitiful, and of tender mercy" (James 5:10-11).

---

†5:11

A. The misery Job received from Satan is recorded in Job 1–2.

B. The mercy Job received from God is recorded in Job 42:7-17.

B. A present example—A farmer and his crops. "Be patient therefore, brethren, unto the coming of the Lord. Behold, the husbandman waiteth for the precious fruit of the earth, and hath long patience for it, until he receive the early and latter rain" (James 5:7).

C. A future example—The Savior and his return. "Be ye also patient; stablish your hearts: for the coming of the Lord draweth nigh. Grudge not one against another, brethren, lest ye be condemned: behold, the judge standeth before the door" (James 5:8-9).

IX. Supplication Makes a Mature Person (James 5:12-18).

A. The season of prayer—When should one pray?

1. In times of trouble—"Is any among you afflicted?" (James 5:13). "Is any sick among you?" (James 5:14).
2. In times of triumph—"Is any merry? let him sing psalms" (James 5:13).

B. The reasons for prayer—Why should one pray?

1. Prayer can alleviate the infirm—"Is any sick among you? let him call for the elders of the church; and let them pray over him, anointing him with oil in the name of the Lord: and the prayer of faith shall save the sick, and the Lord shall raise him up; and if he have committed sins, they shall be forgiven him. Confess your faults one to another, and pray one for another, that ye may be healed. The effectual fervent prayer of a righteous man availeth much" (James 5:14-16).

---

†5:16 *These verses have been the object of much speculation.*

A. What is meant by the anointing of a sick person with oil?

1. Negative

a. *This is not a reference to extreme unction, a Roman Catholic practice which prepares a dying person for death. The practice in these verses is to restore the sick, not to bury them.*
b. *This does not give sanction to faith healers. We note instead that several elders of the church are to be involved here.*

2. *Positive*
a. *The men involved—"The elders of the church" (5:14). As we have already stated, these were the spiritual leaders of the church.*
b. *The medicine involved—"Anointing him with oil" (5:14). The Greek word here is a reference to olive oil, used as a common medicinal remedy in the ancient East (see Isa. 1:6; Luke 10:34). In his book* The Game of Life, *author Roy Roberts gives the following helpful words as taken from professor James E. Rosscup:*

"In brief, oil did have therapeutic value in ancient times as well as today, but it is best to understand it here as a symbol of God's miraculous work in healing. That it had good medicinal effects is clear. It possessed soothing and curative value for animals, like sheep (Psa. 23:5), and men (Isa. 1:6). The good Samaritan in Christ's parable applied oil to the wounds of the man he helped (Luke 19:34). But, it is not the meaning of James for various reasons. Though it was therapeutic in some cases, it would not be a cure in all sicknesses in general. Further, James does not say in v. 15 that the oil will cure the sick or even that the oil plus the prayer will make him well. Specifically, he does say that 'the prayer of faith shall save the sick,' and makes no claim for the oil. It is not the oil, but the Lord who 'shall raise him up.' It is more adequate to say that the anointing is for the purpose of symbolizing tangibly the setting apart of the man to the miraculous healing work of God. It would be an aid to his faith by prompting a sense of expectancy. Christ Himself applied saliva to men at times evidently to symbolize, by physical contact, the healing that God would effect (Mark 7:33; 8:23). There is Old Testament support for the idea that the anointing could signify the setting apart of the man to God for His will and operation. There are numerous applications of oil, not to cure but to set disciples, they 'anointed with oil many that were sick, and healed them'" (Mark 6:13) (The Game of Life, *pp. 171-172).*

B. *Will all sick people be automatically healed by this action? To rephrase the question: Is it ever God's will for believers to experience prolonged illness? It is sometimes not God's will to heal sick Christians. Suffering, if rightly understood and endured by the believer, can bring about the glory of God. (See Exod. 4:11; 1 Tim. 5:23; 2 Tim. 4:20; 2 Cor. 12:1-10; John 9:1-3.) Sometimes, of course, sickness* is *penalty for sin (see John 5:14).*

C. *What is involved in the confession of 5:16? James says we are to confess our faults one to another. As we have already noted, there are times when unconfessed sin does bring suffering. James may have reference to this very thing here at this point. If a sick believer had wronged another Christian in the church, he was now encouraged to confess this, that God might be able to bless him both spiritually and physically. James then says: "The effectual fervent prayer of a righteous man availeth much" (5:16). The "righteous man" spoken of here may refer either to the elder who prays for the sick believer, or the believer himself who, having been restored to fellowship through confession, can now pray effectively. James mentions Elijah as an Old Testament example of effective prayer (5:17; cf. 1 Kings 17–18).*

---

2. Prayer can accomplish the impossible—"Elias was a man subject to like passions as we are, and he prayed earnestly that it might not rain: and it rained

not on the earth by the space of three years and six months. And he prayed again, and the heaven gave rain, and the earth brought forth her fruit" (James 5:17-18).

X. Soul Winning Makes a Mature Person (James 5:19-20)—"Brethren, if any of you do err from the truth, and one convert him; let him know, that he which converteth the sinner from the error of his way shall save a soul from death, and shall hide a multitude of sins" (James 5:19-20).

1 PETER

SOME SOUND ADVICE TO SOME SUFFERING SAINTS

This is what 1 Peter is all about.

A. Of the original 12 apostles, three were chosen to write inspired New Testament books or epistles. The three are Matthew, John, and Peter.

B. This epistle is the final fulfillment of a twofold commission given to Peter by Christ. Both were issued at the Sea of Galilee.
   1. The first part—"Catch fish" (Luke 5:10). This Peter did, through the spoken word at Pentecost (Acts 2:14).
   2. The second part—"Feed sheep" (John 21:15-17). This Peter does, through the written word at Babylon (1 Pet. 2:2; 5:13).

C. Peter's name appears 210 times in the New Testament. Paul's name is found 162 times. The names of the remaining 11 apostles combined appear 142 times.

D. Peter has been called "the apostle of hope" (see 1:3, 13, 21; 3:15). Paul could thus be classified as the apostle of faith, and John the apostle of love.

E. A key word in this epistle is "suffering." It, or its equivalent is used 16 times. Six times it speaks of Christ's suffering and ten times that of believers. Another important word is "grace," which appears eight times.

F. The letter was probably written at the end of his life. It is thought that after this epistle he was arrested and tried. Between his trial and execution he wrote 2 Peter (2 Pet. 1:13-21).

G. It must have been written around A.D. 64 on the eve of the outbreak of persecution by Nero. Nero died in A.D. 68.

H. In 5:13 he identifies the place of writing as Babylon. There are two main theories concerning the location of Babylon.
   1. It is literal Babylon on the Euphrates River—This would seem to be the natural interpretation of the passage. Furthermore, the list of countries in 1 Peter 1:1 is from East to West, which suggests that the writer was in the East at the time of writing. J. Vernon McGee writes: "There was at this time a large colony of Jews in ancient Babylon who had fled Rome due to severe persecution under Claudius and at the time of writing bloody Nero was on the throne" (*Through the Bible*, p. 256).

      In addition to this, the descendants of those Jews taken captive by Nebuchadnezzar were still living in and around Babylon.
   2. It is Rome—Charles Ryrie writes: "The place of the writing was Babylon (5:13), a symbolic name for Rome much used by writers who wished to avoid trouble with Roman authorities. . . . Peter was in Rome during the last decade of his life and wrote this epistle about A.D. 63, just before the outbreak of Nero's persecution in 64. Peter was martyred about 67" (*The Ryrie Study Bible*, p. 425). Furthermore, it is argued that Peter states Mark (5:13) was with him at the

time the epistle was written. However, just prior to this, Paul had written Timothy to bring Mark to Rome with him (2 Tim. 4:11).

I. The church apparently was affected by worldliness in the pews (2:11) and materialism in the pulpit (5:1-3).

J. Because of its many passages on suffering (1:6-7; 4:12-19; 5:10) this epistle can be looked upon as the Job of the New Testament.

K. Chapter 3 can be considered the marriage chapter (vv. 1-12) because of the advice Peter gives to both husbands and wives.

L. In a remarkable passage (3:18-22) Peter explains the activities of Christ during that time between his death and resurrection.

M. The book of 1 Peter provides the final of three descriptive phrases concerning the shepherding ministry of Christ.
   1. Jesus said he was the Good Shepherd (John 10:11).
   2. Hebrews said he is the Great Shepherd (Heb. 13:20).
   3. Peter says he is the Chief Shepherd (1 Pet. 5:4).

N. Satan is referred to as a roaring lion in this epistle (5:8).

O. Peter has much to say about the Word of God. He says it is incorruptible (1:23), eternal (1:25), and is, to the believer, as wholesome milk (2:2).

P. Peter develops the doctrine of Christ in a remarkable way in this short epistle. He discusses:
   1. The incarnation of Christ (1:20)
   2. The names for Christ
      a. A spotless Lamb (1:19)
      b. The chief Cornerstone—His relationship to the Scriptures (2:6)
      c. The precious Stone—His relationship to believers (2:7)
      d. The stumbling Stone—His relationship to unbelievers (2:8)
      e. The Bishop of our souls (2:25)
      f. The Chief Shepherd (5:4)
   3. His sinless life (1:19; 2:22)
   4. His suffering and death (1:11; 2:23-24; 3:18; 4:1, 13; 5:1)
   5. His resurrection (3:21-22)
   6. His ascension (3:22)
   7. His presence at God's right hand (3:22)
   8. His second coming (1:13, 17; 4:13; 5:1, 4)

Q. He also offers a number of titles which describe believers. Perhaps in no other New Testament book are so many given. We are referred to as:
   1. Obedient children (1:14)
   2. Newborn babes (2:2)
   3. Living stones (2:5)
   4. A holy priesthood (2:9)
   5. A royal priesthood (2:9)
   6. A holy nation (2:9)
   7. A peculiar people (2:9)
   8. Strangers and pilgrims (2:11)
   9. Christians (4:16)
   10. The righteous (4:18)
   11. The elect of God (1:2)
   12. The people of God (2:10)

13. The oracles of God (4:11)
14. The flock of God (5:2)

R. This epistle recounts the last of three instances where believers are called Christians.
1. Acts 11:26 (as used by the unbelievers at Antioch)
2. Acts 26:28 (as used by King Agrippa)
3. 1 Peter 4:16 (as used by Peter)

S. The book of 1 Peter can be compared to Colossians.
1. For its size, Colossians has more to say about the Person of Christ than any other New Testament book.
2. For its size, 1 Peter has more to say about the work of Christ than any other New Testament book.

T. This epistle contains the final of three New Testament passages commanding believers to be good citizens.
1. Romans 13:1-7
2. 1 Timothy 2:1-4
3. 1 Peter 2:13-17

U. Peter and John are the only two New Testament authors to refer to Christ as a Lamb (John 1:29, 36; Rev. 5:6; 1 Pet. 1:19).

V. A careful reading of 1 Peter and Ephesians shows more than 100 parallels in teaching and wording.

W. Peter was also familiar with the book of Romans, and perhaps other epistles from Paul (see 2 Pet. 3:15-16).

X. It is generally considered that the Gospel of Mark reflects the teaching of Peter. Young John Mark had, no doubt, often heard Peter speak and preach.

Y. The book of 1 Peter is the 14th longest New Testament book, and 45th longest biblical book, with five chapters, 105 verses, and 2,483 words. There are quotations or allusions from 15 Old Testament books in 1 Peter.

Z. Great passages would include:
1. 1:3-12
2. 1:18-25
3. 2:1-10
4. 2:21-25
5. 4:12-19
6. 5:1-11

THE BOOK OF 1 PETER

I. The Salvation of the Believer
A. The facts concerning our salvation
1. The source of our salvation—The entire Trinity
a. Elected by the Father—"Elect according to the foreknowledge of God the Father" (1 Pet. 1:2).

---

†**1:2a** *We are not told the basis of this election, it should be noted. However, God's selection is based squarely upon foreknowledge. Note: "For whom he did foreknow, he also did predestinate" (Rom.*

8:29). It should be quickly noted, though, that both man's responsibility (John 3:16; Rom. 10:13; Rev. 22:17) and God's sovereignty (Eph. 1:4-5) are clearly taught in the Bible.

In one single statement, our Lord combined both doctrines of election and free will. Note his words: "All that the Father giveth me shall come to me [this is election]; and him that cometh to me I will in no wise cast out [this is free will]" (John 6:37).

---

b. Redeemed by the Son—"And sprinkling of the blood of Jesus Christ" (1 Pet. 1:2).

---

†1:2c *Richard DeHaan writes: "The basis for this statement is found in the Old Testament ceremonial system. In certain of the rituals, the blood of the sacrificial animals was sprinkled in special areas. This sprinkling had three different meanings:*

A. First, it signified cleansing—The person who had been cured of leprosy, for example, went before the priest, and blood was sprinkled to indicate that he was now free from the disease and clean (Lev. 14:1-7).

B. Second, this act was used to symbolize the ratification of a covenant between God and man. Whenever Jehovah and His people entered into a covenant, it was sealed by the sprinkling of the blood of a sacrificial animal (see Exod. 24:3-8).

C. Third, the application of blood designated certain articles of the tabernacle or temple as set apart for worship. From that point on, the vessel was used exclusively for the service of the Lord (see Exod. 29:20-22)" (Good News for Bad Times, *p. 15).*

---

c. Sanctified by the Spirit—"Through sanctification of the Spirit" (1 Pet. 1:2).

2. The blessing of our salvation (1 Pet. 1:3-4)

a. A living hope—"Blessed be the God and Father of our Lord Jesus Christ, which according to his abundant mercy hath begotten us again unto a lively hope by the resurrection of Jesus Christ from the dead" (1 Pet. 1:3).

---

†1:3 *In light of all this, the triune God is to be blessed by the believer (v. 3). The Greek word for "blessed" is* eulogetos, *meaning "to speak well of." From this we get our word* eulogize. *Thus, the child of God is to speak well of the triune God. By doing this we "bless" God. Note his reaction to this. "Then they that feared the Lord spake often one to another; and the Lord hearkened, and heard it, and a book of remembrance was written before him for them that feared the Lord, and that thought upon his name" (Mal. 3:16).*

In this epistle Peter mentions three living things:

A. A living hope (1:3)

B. A living word (1:23)

C. A living stone (2:4)

---

b. A lasting hope—"To an inheritance incorruptible, and undefiled, and that fadeth not away, reserved in heaven for you" (1 Pet. 1:4).

---

†1:4

A. This inheritance is perfect (incorruptible).

B. This inheritance is pure (undefiled).
C. This inheritance is permanent (it "fadeth not away").

---

3. The guarantee of our salvation—"Who are kept by the power of God through faith unto salvation ready to be revealed in the last time" (1 Pet. 1:5).
4. The trials in our salvation (1 Pet. 1:6-9)
   a. The necessity of these trials—"Wherein ye greatly rejoice, though now for a season, if need be, ye are in heaviness through manifold temptations" (1 Pet. 1:6).
   b. The reasons for these trials
      (1) They strengthen our faith in Christ—"That the trial of your faith, being much more precious than of gold that perisheth, though it be tried with fire, might be found unto praise and honour and glory at the appearing of Jesus Christ" (1 Pet. 1:7).

---

†1:7 *Peter speaks of how precious is the trial of our faith. In this epistle he also refers to precious* blood *(1:19), a* cornerstone, *(2:4, 6-7), and a humble* spirit *(3:4). All these, says Peter, are precious. In his second epistle he adds two more: "precious faith" (1:1) and "precious promises" (1:4).*

Dr. Kenneth Wuest writes the following concerning verse 7: "Peter tells us that this approval of our faith is much more precious than the approval of gold, even though that gold be approved through firetesting. . . . The picture here is of an ancient goldsmith who puts his crude gold ore in a crucible, subjects it to intense heat, and thus liquifies the mass. The impurities rise to the surface and are skimmed off. When the metal-worker is able to see the reflection of his face clearly mirrored in the surface of the liquid, he takes it off the fire, for he knows that the contents are pure gold.

"So it is with God and His child. He puts us in the crucible of Christian suffering, in which process sin is gradually put out of our lives, our faith is purified from the slag of unbelief that somehow mingles with it so often, and the result is the reflection of the face of Jesus Christ in the character of the Christian. This, above all, God the Father desires to see. Christlikeness is God's ideal for His child. Christian suffering is one of the most potent means to that end" (First Peter in the Greek New Testament, *p. 27).*

---

      (2) They strengthen our love for Christ—"Whom having not seen, ye love; in whom, though now ye see him not, yet believing, ye rejoice with joy unspeakable and full of glory" (1 Pet. 1:8).
5. The Old Testament prophets and our salvation (1 Pet. 1:10-12)
   a. Their scrutiny—"Of which salvation the prophets have enquired and searched diligently, who prophesied of the grace that should come unto you" (1 Pet. 1:10).

---

†1:10

A. The Old Testament prophets (like Isaiah) did not always understand their inspired prophecies about the Messiah.
B. When they sought to know, they were told the predictions would be understood only at a later date (New Testament times). Our Lord once referred to this during his earthly ministry while

speaking to his disciples. "For verily I say unto you, that many prophets and righteous men have desired to see those things which ye see, and have not seen them; and to hear those things which ye hear, and have not heard them" (Matt. 13:17). (See also Dan. 12: 8-13.)

---

b. Their source—"The Spirit of Christ, which was in them . . . testified beforehand" (1 Pet. 1:11).

c. Their summary (1 Pet. 1:11-12)

(1) They predicted the nature of his first coming—"The sufferings of Christ" (1 Pet. 1:11). (See Isa. 53.)

(2) They predicted the nature of his second coming—"And the glory that should follow" (1 Pet. 1:11). (See Isa. 9, 11.)

---

†*All Bible prophecy concerning the Lord Jesus Christ is summarized in this little sentence: "The sufferings of Christ, and the glory that should follow." Here Peter connects Christ's first coming (the sufferings) with his second coming (the glory). This, in a nutshell, is a panorama of the purpose, plan, and program of Almighty God. Note this beautiful outline as we trace it through the Word of God:*

A. The sufferings—A Baby, wrapped in swaddling clothes (Luke 2:12). The glory—A King, clothed in majestic apparel (Psa. 93:1).

B. The sufferings—He was the wearied traveler (John. 4:6). The glory—He will be the untiring God (Isa. 40:28-29).

C. The sufferings—He had nowhere to lay his head (Luke 9:58). The glory—He will become heir to all things (Heb. 1:2).

D. The sufferings—He was rejected by Israel (John 1:11). The glory—He will be accepted by all the nations (Isa. 9:6).

E. The sufferings—Wicked people took up stones to throw at him (John 8:59). The glory—Wicked people will cry for stones to fall upon them to hide them from him (Rev. 6:16).

F. The sufferings—A lowly Savior, acquainted with grief (Isa. 53:3). The glory—The mighty God, anointed with the oil of gladness (Heb. 1:9).

G. The sufferings—He was clothed with a scarlet robe in mockery (Luke 23:11). The glory—He will be clothed with a vesture dipped in the blood of his enemies (Rev. 19:13).

H. The sufferings—He was smitten with a reed (Matt. 27:30). The glory—He will rule the nations with a rod of iron (Rev. 19:15).

I. The sufferings—Wicked soldiers bowed their knees and mocked (Mark 15:19). The glory—Every knee shall bow and acknowledge him (Phil. 2:10).

J. The sufferings—He wore the crown of thorns (John 19:5). The glory—He will wear the crown of gold (Rev. 14:14).

K. The sufferings—His hands were pierced with nails (John 20:25). The glory—His hands will carry a sharp sickle (Rev. 14:14).

L. The sufferings—His feet were pierced with nails (Psa. 22:16). The glory—His feet will stand on the Mount of Olives (Zech. 14:4).

M. The sufferings—He had no form or comeliness (Isa. 53:2). The glory—He will be beautiful (Psa. 27:4).

N. The sufferings—He delivered up his spirit (John 19:30). The glory—He is alive forevermore (Rev. 1:18).

O. The sufferings—He was laid in the tomb (Matt. 27:59-60). The glory—He will sit on his throne (Heb. 8:1). Note: Peter refers to the sufferings and glory theme again in 4:13 and 5:1. But on these occasions he includes the believer. In other words, to share in Christ's pain is to share in Christ's reign.

---

6. The holy angels and our salvation—"Which things the angels desire to look into" (1 Pet. 1:12).

---

†1:12 *One of the accomplishments of our salvation is to serve as an object lesson to heaven's elect angels. They do not experience our redemption but they are intensely interested in observing it. The following passages clearly bring this out: "Then I Daniel looked and behold, there stood other two [angels], the one on this side of the bank of the river, and the other on that side of the bank of the river. And one said . . . How long shall it be to the end of these wonders?" (Dan. 12:5-6). "For I think that God hath set forth us the apostles last, as it were appointed to death: for we are made a spectacle unto the world, and to angels, and to men" (1 Cor. 4:9). "To the intent that now unto the principalities and powers in the heavenly places might be known by the church the manifold wisdom of God" (Eph. 3:10).*

---

7. The desired response in light of our salvation (1 Pet. 1:13-17)
   a. God desires our determination—"Wherefore gird up the loins of your mind, be sober, and hope to the end for the grace that is to be brought unto you at the revelation of Jesus Christ" (1 Pet. 1:13).

---

†1:13 Gird up the loins of your mind. *Peter will repeat this in his second epistle: "This second epistle, beloved, I now write unto you: in both which I stir up your pure minds by way of remembrance" (2 Pet. 3:1). This girding calls to mind a patriarch of the Old Testament who wore a long flowing robe. Around that robe he had a big belt called a girdle. When the time came that he had to move swiftly, he pulled the robe up and lapped it over the belt. He girded up his loins and was ready for action.*

---

   b. God desires our repudiation—"As obedient children, not fashioning yourselves according to the former lusts in your ignorance" (1 Pet. 1:14).
   c. God desires our sanctification—"But as he which hath called you is holy, so be ye holy in all manner of conversation; because it is written, Be ye holy; for I am holy" (1 Pet. 1:15-16).
8. The awesome cost of our salvation (1 Pet. 1:18-22)
   a. The price involved—"Forasmuch as ye know that ye were not redeemed with corruptible things, as silver and gold, from your vain conversation received by tradition from your fathers; but with the precious blood of Christ, as of a lamb without blemish and without spot" (1 Pet. 1:18-19).
   b. The planning involved—"Who verily was foreordained before the foundation of the world, but was manifest in these last times for you" (1 Pet. 1:20).
9. The vehicle of our salvation (1 Pet. 1:23-25)—"Being born again, not of corruptible seed, but of incorruptible, by the word of God, which liveth and abideth for ever. For all flesh is as grass, and all the glory of man as the flower of grass. The grass withereth, and the flower thereof falleth away: but the word of the

Lord endureth for ever. And this is the word which by the gospel is preached unto you" (1 Pet. 1:23-25).

B. The fellowship involved concerning our salvation (1 Pet. 1:1-11)
   1. We are members of the same family.
      a. We have experienced the same birth (1 Pet. 1:23).
      b. We partake of the same food—"As newborn babes, desire the sincere milk of the word, that ye may grow thereby" (1 Pet. 2:2).

---

†2:2

A. The word "desire" speaks of an intense yearning. David has this desire for God's Word. "The judgments of the Lord are true and righteous altogether. More to be desired are they than gold, yea, than much fine gold, sweeter also than honey and the honeycomb" (Psa. 19:9-10).

The nation Israel had shown no desire for the Word of God in the Old Testament. Thus, when the Son of God appeared they viewed him in the same manner. "And when we shall see him, there is no beauty that we should desire him" (Isa. 53:2).

B. The word "sincere" is literally "unadulterated"—That is, nothing mixed with it. See Revelation 14:10 concerning a similar passage dealing with God's unadulterated wrath during the tribulation.

---

   2. We are stones in the same building—"You also, as lively stones, are built up a spiritual house" (1 Pet. 2:5a).
   3. We have been joined to the same cornerstone—"Wherefore also it is contained in the scripture, Behold, I lay in Sion a chief corner stone, elect, precious: and he that believeth on him shall not be confounded" (1 Pet. 2:6).
      a. To believers, this is a security stone.
      b. To unbelievers, this is a stumbling stone—"And a stone of stumbling, and a rock of offence, even to them which stumble at the word, being disobedient: whereunto also they were appointed" (1 Pet. 2:8).

---

†2:8 *The word "rock" or "stone" appears five times and the word "precious" is found three times in 1 Peter 2:3-8. Note the various usages of this Redeemer-like rock as described in the Bible.*

A. He is the smitten Rock to all who will drink (Exod. 17:6; 1 Cor. 10:4; John 4:13-14; 7:37-39).
B. He is the precious Stone to all who have drunk (1 Pet. 2:3, 7).
C. He is the chief Cornerstone to the church (Eph. 2:20).
D. He is the stumbling Stone to the Jews at his first coming (Rom. 9:32-33; 1 Cor. 1:23).
E. He is the Headstone of the corner to the Jews at his second coming (Zech. 4:7).
F. He is the smiting Stone cut without hands to Gentile world powers at his second coming (Dan. 2:34).
G. He is the crushing Stone of judgment to all unbelievers (Matt. 21:44). Peter says (2:4) this great Stone was "disallowed" by Israel. This word means "to put to a test and then repudiate." After examining Christ for 34 years, Israel rejected him. He simply was not what they were looking for in a Messiah.

Note, furthermore, the apostle's statement in 2:6: "Wherefore also it is contained in the scripture, Behold, I lay in Sion a chief cornerstone." Certainly here is the fulfillment of Christ's promise in Matthew 16:16, 18. Peter was not *that foundation; Christ was. Finally (see 2:5), all believers are "lively stones, built up [into] a spiritual house, an holy priesthood, to offer up spiritual sacrifices, acceptable to God by Jesus Christ." (See also Rev. 1:6.)*

---

4. We are ministers in the same priesthood—"An holy priesthood, to offer up spiritual sacrifices, acceptable to God by Jesus Christ" (1 Pet. 2:5b). "But ye are a chosen generation, a royal priesthood" (1 Pet. 2:9a).
5. We are citizens of the same nation—"An holy nation, a peculiar people" (1 Pet. 2:9b).

---

†2:9b

A. Old Testament Israel had a priesthood, but the church is a priesthood. The New Scofield Bible *(p. 1,334) offers the following summary of the priesthood.*

1. Until the Law was given, the head of each family was the family priest (Gen. 8:20; 26:25; 31:54).

2. When the Law was proposed, the promise to perfect obedience was that Israel should be unto God 'a kingdom of priests' (Exod. 19:6); but Israel violated the Law, and God shut up the priestly office to the Aaronic family, appointing the tribe of Levi to minister to Israel, thus constituting the typical priesthood. (Compare Exod. 13:2 and 19:6 with Num. 8:16. See also Exod. 28:1.)

3. In the church age, all Christians are unconditionally constituted 'a kingdom of priests' (v. 9; Rev. 1:6), the distinction which Israel failed to achieve by works.

4. The priesthood of the Christian is, therefore, a birthright, just as every descendant of Aaron was born to the priesthood (Heb. 5:1).

5. The chief privilege of a priest is access to God. Under the Law the high priest only could enter 'the holiest of all,' and that but once a year (Heb. 9:7). But when Christ died, the veil, a type of Christ's human body (Heb. 10:20), was rent, so that now believers—priests, equally with Christ the High Priest—have access to God in the holiest (Heb. 10:19-22).

6. The High Priest is corporeally there (Heb. 4:14-16; 9:24; 10:19-22)."

B. In the exercise of his office, the New Testament believer-priest is:

1. A sacrificer who offers a fourfold sacrifice:

a. His own living body (Rom. 12:1; Phil. 2:17; 2 Tim. 4:6; James 1:27; 1 John 3:16)

b. Praise to God, "the fruit of our lips giving thanks to his name," to be offered continually (Heb. 13:15; cf. Exod. 25:22: "I will commune with thee from above the mercy seat").

c. His substance (Rom. 12:13; Gal. 6:6, 10; Titus 3:14; Heb. 13:2, 16; 3 John 5–8)

d. His service, i.e., "to do good" (Heb. 13:16)

2. An Intercessor (Col. 4:12; 1 Tim. 2:1)

---

6. We are pilgrims on the same journey—"Dearly beloved, I beseech you as strangers and pilgrims, abstain from fleshly lusts, which war against the soul" (1 Pet. 2:11).

II. The Submission of the Believer (1 Pet. 2:12–3:12)

A. Peter's exhortation for submission

1. Our responsibilities to the unsaved (1 Pet. 2:12)—"Be careful how you behave among your unsaved neighbors; for then, even if they are suspicious of you and talk against you, they will end up praising God for your good works when Christ returns" (1 Pet. 2:12, TLB).

2. Our responsibilities to civil authorities (1 Pet. 2: 13-17)—"Submit yourselves to every ordinance of man for the Lord's sake: whether it be to the king, as supreme; or unto governors, as unto them that are sent by him for the

punishment of evildoers, and for the praise of them that do well. Honour all men. Love the brotherhood. Fear God. Honour the king" (1 Pet. 2:13-14, 17).

3. Our responsibilities to our employers (1 Pet. 2:18-20) —"Servants, be subject to your masters with all fear; not only to the good and gentle, but also to the froward" (1 Pet. 2:18).
4. Our responsibilities in the home (1 Pet. 3:1-12)
   a. The wife (1 Pet. 3:1-6)
      (1) Her attitude—"In the same way, you wives, be submissive to your own husbands so that even if any of them are disobedient to the word they may be won without a word by the behavior of their wives" (1 Pet. 3:1, NASB).
      (2) Her apparel (1 Pet. 3:3-4)—"Whose adorning let it not be that outward adorning of plaiting the hair, and of wearing of gold, or of putting on of apparel; but let it be the hidden man of the heart, in that which is not corruptible, even the ornament of a meek and quiet spirit, which is in the sight of God of great price" (1 Pet. 3:3-4).

---

†**3:4** *It should be quickly noted that this verse does not forbid a Christian woman to visit a beauty shop or a jewelry store. Those who would insist it does have a problem here, for Peter also refers to the wearing of clothes. What the passage does teach is that believing women are not to dress in a gaudy manner. History tells us the Roman women of that day went to ridiculous lengths in the adornment of the hair. The hair was arranged layer upon layer and interlaced with golden combs and nets. After the styling ordeal was completed many would stay up all night lest they spoil their coiffures for the next day's festivities. This godless external display had already been soundly condemned by the prophet Isaiah centuries ago (Isa. 3:16-26).*

---

      (3) Her example (1 Pet. 3:5-6)—"For after this manner in the old time the holy women also, who trusted in God, adorned themselves, being in subjection unto their own husbands: even as Sara obeyed Abraham, calling him lord: whose daughters ye are, as long as ye do well, and are not afraid with any amazement" (1 Pet. 3:5-6).
   b. The husband (1 Pet. 3:7)—"Likewise, ye husbands, dwell with them according to knowledge, giving honour unto the wife, as unto the weaker vessel, and as being heirs together of the grace of life; that your prayers be not hindered" (1 Pet. 3:7).

---

†**3:7** *Here the Christian husband is to do two things in regard to his wife:*

A. He is to "dwell with [her] according to knowledge." That is, he must have an intelligent recognition of the marriage relationship. He simply must understand that:

1. His wife is a weaker vessel. This weakness is limited to the physical realm, however. She is not weaker intellectually or spiritually.

2. His wife is his fellow-heir. She shares the same spiritual equality before God as he does. Thus, the arrogant husband who lightly dismisses his wife to "the kitchen and the bedroom," insults not only her, but God himself.

B. He is to give "honour unto the wife." That is, he is to assign her a special place in his heart. If these principles are not followed, then every prayer coming from that household will be hindered.

---

c. The entire family (1 Pet. 3:8-12)—"Finally, be ye all of one mind, having compassion one of another, love as brethren, be pitiful, be courteous" (1 Pet. 3:8).

B. Peter's example of submission (2:21-25)—"For even hereunto were ye called, because Christ also suffered for us, leaving us an example, that ye should follow his steps" (1 Pet. 2:21).

---

†*"The word 'leaving' is literally 'leaving behind.' When Peter used the Greek word here translated 'example,' he went back to his boyhood days for an illustration. The word means literally 'writing under.' It was used of words given children to copy, both as a writing exercise and as a means of impressing a moral. Sometimes it was used with reference to the act of tracing over written letters . . . just as a child slowly, with painstaking effort and close application, follows the shape of the letters of his teacher and thus learns to write, so saints should, with like painstaking effort and by close application, endeavor to be like the Lord Jesus in their own personal lives" (Kenneth Wuest,* First Peter in the Greek New Testament, *p. 67).*

---

1. The sinless Savior—"Who did no sin, neither was guile found in his mouth" (1 Pet. 2:22).
2. The silent Savior—"Who, when he was reviled, reviled not again; when he suffered, he threatened not, but committed himself to him that judgeth righteously" (1 Pet. 2:23).
3. The sacrificial Savior—"Who his own self bore our sins in his own body on the tree, that we, being dead to sins, should live unto righteousness; by whose stripes ye were healed" (1 Pet. 2:24).

---

†**2:24** *Note especially Peter's statement, "by whose stripes ye were healed" (2:24). Is there physical healing in the atonement? According to Matthew 8:16-17, this was indeed predicted by Isaiah (53:4) and was fulfilled during the earthly ministry of Christ. But in 1 Peter chapter 2 the apostle definitely links up Christ's stripes to the healing of our souls and* not *our bodies.*

†*Kenneth Wuest writes: "The word 'stripes' in the Greek presents a picture of our Lord's lacerated back after the scourging He endured at the hands of the Roman soldiers. The Romans used a scourge of cords or thongs to which latter were attached pieces of lead or brass, on small, sharp-pointed bones. Criminals condemned to crucifixion were ordinarily scourged before being executed. The victim was stripped to the waist and bound in a stooping position, with the hands behind the back, to a post or pillar. The suffering under the lash was intense. The body was frightfully lacerated. The Christian martyrs at Smyrna about A.D. 155 were so torn by the scourges that their veins were laid bare, and the inner muscles and sinews and even the intestines were exposed. . . . Peter remembered the body of our Lord after the scourging, the flesh so dreadfully mangled that the disfigured form appeared in his eyes as one single bruise"* (First Peter in the Greek New Testament, *p. 69).*

---

4. The shepherd Savior—"For ye were as sheep going astray, but are now returned unto the Shepherd and Bishop of your souls" (1 Pet. 2:25).

III. The Suffering of the Believer (1 Pet. 3:13–4:19)

A. Suffering justifies the sinner.

1. Christ's ministry on the cross (1 Pet. 3:18)—"For Christ also hath once suffered for sins, the just for the unjust, that he might bring us to God, being put to death in the flesh, but quickened by the Spirit" (1 Pet. 3:18).
2. Christ's ministry under the earth (1 Pet. 3:19-20)—"By which also he went and preached unto the spirits in prison; which sometime were disobedient, when once the longsuffering of God waited in the days of Noah, while the ark was a preparing, wherein few, that is, eight souls were saved by water" (1 Pet. 3:19-20).

---

†**3:20** *Richard DeHaan observes: "Just who were these spirits? Your answer determines your interpretation of this perplexing passage, and dictates the answer to a second question, 'What message was preached?' The word 'preached' means 'to herald' or 'to proclaim,' and can refer either to communicating the Gospel or giving an announcement. Four main views are held regarding the identification of these 'spirits in prison.'*

A. They were the souls of the people to whom Christ preached by the Holy Spirit through Noah during the 120 years the ark was being built. Many good scholars hold this view, but it is not without problems. The word of God seldom calls human beings 'spirits.' This term seems to be reserved for supernatural and nonhuman beings.

B. The 'spirits in prison' were the mongrel offspring of a union between fallen angels (the 'sons of God' of Genesis 6:1-2) and women. Those who take this position contend that when Jesus died, He descended immediately into hades and announced to these imprisoned spirits that He had paid the price for sin. Objections to this view are that the purpose for this declaration is not given, and that one must accept the theory that fallen angels were actually able to live in the marriage relationship with human women and produce offspring.

C. These spirits were wicked angels of Noah's day who engaged in some kind of monstrous evil, but who probably did not actually marry women. The people who hold this view consider the 'sons of God' of Genesis 6 to be fallen angels who entered into or possessed the bodies of violent men. These men in turn fathered children with even more lawless traits. The term nephilum, *translated 'giants' in Genesis 6:4, thus would denote men who 'fall upon' or attack others rather than 'fallen ones' or 'giants.' Scholars who give this explanation of the 'spirits in prison' see the sinning angels of Genesis as the same ones to whom Peter referred as 'delivered . . . into chains of darkness' (2 Pet. 2:4). They say the purpose of Christ's entrance into hades was to tell this special group of wicked angels that their doom was certain. He had paid the price for sin and would soon demonstrate that He was indeed their Master by rising from the dead. This interpretation is possible only for those who feel that the 'sons of God' of Genesis 6 were fallen angels, and that they possessed men's bodies and personalities for the purpose of leading the human race away from God.*

D. The 'spirits in prison' are wicked beings and Old Testament believers. Those who hold this view say that Christ descended into hades between His death and resurrection to make an announcement to all wicked spirits, and to release the Old Testament saints being kept there in a special compartment. Paul declares that Jesus 'descended first into the lower parts of the earth' and 'led captivity captive' (Eph. 4:8-10). Some Bible scholars see a dual purpose for our Lord's descent into hades. They say He first announced to fallen angels that He had conquered sin and paid its penalty. Then, contending that the believers of the ages before Calvary were not fully forgiven until Christ had presented His sacrifice, they maintain that He went to them immediately after His death to take them to heaven. This view can be held only if one is convicted that the 'compartment' theory of hades is biblical, and that Old Testament saints were not permitted to enter heaven until Jesus had died on the cross" (Good News for Bad Times, *pp. 103-104).*

---

3. Christ's ministry in the heavens (1 Pet. 3:22)—"Who is gone into heaven, and is on the right hand of God; angels and authorities and powers being made subject unto him" (1 Pet. 3:22).

B. Suffering purifies the saint.

1. Concerning the godly believer
   a. It gives him scriptural maturity—"Forasmuch then as Christ hath suffered for us in the flesh, arm yourselves likewise with the same mind: for he that hath suffered in the flesh hath ceased from sin; if ye be reproached for the name of Christ, happy are ye; for the spirit of glory and of God resteth upon you: on their part he is evil spoken of, but on your part he is glorified. Wherefore let them that suffer according to the will of God commit the keeping of their souls to him in well doing, as unto a faithful Creator" (1 Pet. 4:1, 14, 19).
   b. It gives him scriptural answers (1 Pet. 3:15-17)—"But sanctify the Lord God in your hearts: and be ready always to give an answer to every man that asketh you a reason of the hope that is in you with meekness and fear: having a good conscience; that, whereas they speak evil of you, as of evildoers, they may be ashamed that falsely accuse your good conversation in Christ. For it is better, if the will of God be so, that ye suffer for well doing, than for evil doing" (1 Pet. 3:15-17).
2. Concerning the carnal believer
   a. It is meant to bring about repentance for the sinfulness of the flesh—"But let none of you suffer as a murderer, or as a thief, or as an evildoer, or as a busybody in other men's matters" (1 Pet. 4:15).
   b. It is meant to bring about respect for the holiness of God—"For the time is come that judgment must begin at the house of God: and if it first begin at us, what shall the end be of them that obey not the gospel of God? And if the righteous scarcely be saved, where shall the ungodly and the sinner appear?" (1 Pet. 4:17-18).

---

†4:18 *Peter here refers to judgment beginning at the house of God. He may have been thinking of Ananias and Sapphira (see Acts 5:1-11).*

C. Suffering anticipates the second coming—"But the end of all things is at hand: be ye therefore sober, and watch unto prayer" (1 Pet. 4:7).

D. Suffering verifies the separated life—"For the time past of our life may suffice us to have wrought the will of the Gentiles, when we walked in lasciviousness, lusts, excess of wine, revellings, banquetings, and abominable idolatries: Wherein they think it strange that ye run not with them to the same excess of riot, speaking evil of you: who shall give account to him that is ready to judge the quick and the dead" (1 Pet. 4:3-5).

E. Suffering multiplies future rewards—"Beloved, think it not strange concerning the fiery trial which is to try you, as though some strange thing happened unto you:

but rejoice, inasmuch as ye are partakers of Christ's sufferings; that, when his glory shall be revealed, ye may be glad also with exceeding joy" (1 Pet. 4:12-13).

---

†4:13 *Note the phrase "the fiery trial" in 4:12. This is the second time Peter speaks of our faith being tried by fire (see 1:7). The intended meaning here can be metaphorical or historical, referring to the actual burning of believers by Nero in Rome.*

F. Suffering unifies the local church—"And above all things have fervent charity among yourselves: for charity shall cover the multitude of sins. Use hospitality one to another without grudging. As every man hath received the gift, even so minister the same one to another, as good stewards of the manifold grace of God" (1 Pet. 4:8-10).

G. Suffering glorifies the Lord—"If any man speak, let him speak as the oracles of God; if any man minister, let him do it as of the ability which God giveth: that God in all things may be glorified through Jesus Christ, to whom be praise and dominion for ever and ever. Amen. . . . Yet if any man suffer as a Christian, let him not be ashamed; but let him glorify God on this behalf" (1 Pet. 4:11, 16).

---

†4:16 *Note: Peter refers to a believer as a Christian. This title is used but two other times in the entire Bible (Acts 11:26 and 26:28). What Peter is saying in these verses is that suffering glorifies the Savior if one suffers as a Christian, that is, for his faith. But if he suffers as an evildoer, the Lord is not glorified. We are to suffer because of our position, and not our disposition.*

"For even hereunto were ye called" (2:21a).

---

†2:21a *This call to suffer here is the final of seven divine calls from God to the believer, proceeding from the very counsels of eternity past itself. Here are these "Seven Sovereign Summons":*

A. The call to salvation *(Rom. 8:30)*

B. The call to sanctification *(1 Thess. 5:23-24)*

C. The call to service *(1 Cor. 1:26-27)*

D. The call to separation *(2 Cor. 6:17-18)*

E. The call to sonship *(1 John 3:1)*

F. The call to subjection

1. *Children to their parents (Eph. 6:1)*
2. *Wives to their husbands (Eph. 5:22)*
3. *Employees to their employers (1 Pet. 2:18)*
4. *Citizens to their country (1 Pet. 2:13-14)*
5. *Believers to God (Rom. 12:1-2)*

G. The call to suffering *(Phil. 1:29; 1 Pet. 2:21)*

IV. The Service of the Believer (1 Pet. 5:1-14)

A. Serving as a shepherd (1 Pet. 5:1-4)

1. The responsibilities—"The elders which are among you I exhort, who am also an elder, and a witness of the sufferings of Christ, and also a partaker of the

glory that shall be revealed: Feed the flock of God which is among you, taking the oversight thereof, not by constraint, but willingly; not for filthy lucre, but of a ready mind; neither as being lords over God's heritage, but being ensamples to the flock" (1 Pet. 5:1-3).

2. The rewards—"And when the chief Shepherd shall appear, ye shall receive a crown of glory that fadeth not away" (1 Pet. 5:4).

---

†5:4 *This is one of at least five possible rewards a believer may earn. These are:*

A. *The incorruptible crown—Given to those who master the old nature (1 Cor. 9:25-27)*

B. *The crown of rejoicing—Given to soul winners (Prov. 11:30; 1 Thess. 2:19-20; Dan. 12:3)*

C. *The crown of life—Given to those who successfully endure temptation (James 1:12; Rev. 2:10)*

D. *The crown of righteousness—Given to those who especially love the doctrine of the Rapture (2 Tim. 4:8)*

E. *The crown of glory—Given to faithful preachers and teachers (1 Pet. 5:2-4; 2 Tim. 4:1-2; Acts 20:26-28) It has been suggested that these "crowns" will actually be talents and abilities with which to glorify Christ. Thus, the greater the reward, the greater the ability.*

B. Serving as a servant (1 Pet. 5:5-7)

1. Subject yourselves to the saints—"Likewise, ye younger, submit yourselves unto the elder. Yea, all of you be subject one to another, and be clothed with humility: for God resisteth the proud, and giveth grace to the humble" (1 Pet. 5:5).
2. Submit yourselves to the Savior—"Humble yourselves therefore under the mighty hand of God, that he may exalt you in due time: casting all your care upon him; for he careth for you" (1 Pet. 5:6-7).

---

†5:7 *"Humble yourselves . . . that he may exalt you." Our Lord both declared and demonstrated this principle.*

A. *The declaration—"For whosoever exalteth himself shall be abased; and he that humbleth himself shall be exalted" (Luke 14:11).*

B. *The demonstration—"Let this mind be in you, which was also in Christ Jesus: who, being in the form of God, thought it not robbery to be equal with God: but made himself of no reputation, and took upon him the form of a servant, and was made in the likeness of men: and being found in fashion as a man, he humbled himself, and became obedient unto death, even the death of the cross. Wherefore God also hath highly exalted him, and given him a name which is above every name: that at the name of Jesus every knee should bow, of things in heaven, and things in earth, and things under the earth; and that every tongue should confess that Jesus Christ is Lord, to the glory of God the Father" (Phil. 2:5-11).*

C. Serving as a soldier (1 Pet. 5:8-11)

1. The predator—"Be sober, be vigilant; because your adversary the devil, as a roaring lion, walketh about, seeking whom he may devour" (1 Pet. 5:8).
2. The plan—"Whom resist stedfast in the faith, knowing that the same afflictions are accomplished in your brethren that are in the world" (1 Pet. 5:9).
3. The purpose—"But the God of all grace, who hath called us unto his eternal

glory by Christ Jesus, after that ye have suffered a while, make you perfect, stablish, strengthen, settle you. To him be glory and dominion for ever and ever. Amen" (1 Pet. 5:10-11).

---

†**5:10** *Especially to be noted are the words "the God of all grace." This is the story of the Christian life. The believer is to go from grace to grace. (See John 1:16.) James says, "He giveth more grace" (James 4:6). The Scriptures speak of:*

A. Saving grace (Eph. 2:8-9)
B. Serving grace (1 Cor. 15:9-10)
C. Sanctifying grace (Rom. 5:17; 6:17)
D. Sacrificing grace (2 Cor. 8:1-9)
E. Singing grace (Col. 3:16)
F. Speaking grace (Col. 4:6)
G. Strengthening grace (2 Tim. 2:1)
H. Suffering grace (1 Pet. 5:10; 2 Cor. 12:9) In closing, Peter refers to Silvanus, "a faithful brother" (5:12). He was the messenger of this epistle and Peter's secretary. Silvanus is the lengthened form of Silas and doubtless this was the same individual who was Paul's traveling companion. (See Acts 15:40; 2 Cor. 1:19; 1 Thess. 1:1; 2 Thess. 1:1.)

2 PETER

THE FINAL WORDS OF A FORMER FISHERMAN

A. The book of 2 Peter contains Simon Peter's last words.
B. This epistle contains the only interconnective reference from one apostolic epistle to another. In other words, Peter refers to Paul's writing (3:15-16).
C. It is very similar to the book of Jude. Out of 25 verses in Jude, no less than 19 are reiterated in some fashion in 2 Peter.
D. The theme of 1 Peter is suffering, while that of 2 Peter is full knowledge. It appears some 16 times with cognate words.
E. The book of 2 Peter may be compared to 2 Timothy, in matters of both authorship and content. For example:
   1. One (Paul) was the official messenger to the Gentiles, while the other (Peter) was God's spokesman to the Jews (Gal. 2:7-8).
   2. Both played important roles in the Jerusalem Council (Acts 15).
   3. Both healed a lame man (Acts 3:1-8; 14:8-12).
   4. Both dealt with satanic pretenders.
      a. Peter confronted Simon the sorcerer at Samaria (Acts 8: 9-24).
      b. Paul confronted Bar-jesus the sorcerer at Salamis on the Isle of Cyprus (Acts 13:5-11).
   5. Both were released from prison miraculously.
      a. God sent an angel to free Peter (Acts 12:5-10).
      b. God sent an earthquake to free Paul (Acts 16:25-29).
   6. Both raised the dead.
      a. Peter raised Dorcas from the dead (Acts 9:40).
      b. Paul raised Eutychus from the dead (Acts 20:12).
   7. Both received heavenly visions to minister to the lost.
      a. Peter saw his vision at Joppa (Acts 10:9-23).
      b. Paul saw his vision at Troas (Acts 16:8-10).
   8. Both authored New Testament books.
      a. Peter wrote two epistles.
      b. Paul wrote 13 (and possibly 14) epistles
   9. Both wrote key passages on the subjects of biblical inspiration (2 Pet. 1:19-21; 2 Tim. 3:16-17)
   10. Both knew they would die as martyrs for Christ.
      a. Peter's testimony—"Yea, I think it meet, as long as I am in this tabernacle, to stir you up by putting you in remembrance; knowing that shortly I must put off this my tabernacle, even as our Lord Jesus Christ hath shewed me" (2 Pet. 1:13-14).
      b. Paul's testimony—"For I am now ready to be offered, and the time of my departure is at hand. I have fought a good fight, I have finished my course, I have kept the faith" (2 Tim. 4:6-7).

F. The book of 2 Peter is the only biblical book which discusses God's sovereign dealings with the former, present, and future worlds.
   1. The former world—Destroyed by the great flood (3:4-6)
   2. The present world—To be destroyed by a great fire (3:7-12)
   3. The future world—To be created in righteousness (3:13-14)

G. This epistle is the only New Testament book after the four Gospels to mention Christ's transfiguration (1:16-18).

H. The book of 2 Peter is the 21st longest New Testament book, and 55th longest biblical book, with three chapters, 61 verses, and 1559 words. There are quotations or allusions from six Old Testament books in 2 Peter.

I. Great passages would include:
   1. 1:4-8
   2. 3:1-2
   3. 3:13-14

THE BOOK OF 2 PETER

I. The Proclamation of the Power of God (2 Pet. 1:1-3)—"According as his divine power hath given unto us all things that pertain unto life and godliness, through the knowledge of him that hath called us to glory and virtue" (2 Pet. 1:3).

II. The Application of the Promises of God (2 Pet. 1:4-9)—"Whereby are given unto us exceeding great and precious promises: that by these ye might be partakers of the divine nature, having escaped the corruption that is in the world through lust" (2 Pet. 1:4).

---

†**1:4** *Henrietta Mears writes concerning 1:3-4: "Look at a criminal condemned to be hanged. Suppose a messenger comes to him and says: 'The governor has taken your case into consideration, and I have brought you a purse of a thousand dollars.' The criminal will say, 'What good will it do me? I am to be hanged tomorrow.' 'Well, I have another message. He has considered your case and sent you the deed to a million-dollar estate.' The condemned man despairingly shakes his head and says, 'What can I do with that? I must be hanged tomorrow.' But the messenger goes on. 'Stop! I have another offer to make. I have brought you the governor's own inauguration robe for you to wear with special favor.' The condemned man bursts into tears, as he says, 'Do you intend to mock me? How would I appear ascending the steps of the gallows, wearing the governor's own robe?' Then the messenger says, 'Wait, I have one more message. The governor has sent you a pardon. What do you say to that? The poor man looks at him and says he doesn't believe it. But the messenger hands the pardon, signed by the governor, with the official stamp upon it. Then the man leaps for joy, while tears of gratitude run down his face. Then the messenger says, 'I am not through yet. I have brought you the pardon, the purse of gold, the deed, and the royal robe which are yours in addition.' These are the 'all things' God has given us in Christ, His Son. With these, nothing can defeat the young Christian. The way I can escape the awful sins in this world every day and all the day is by partaking of His nature and letting Him live through me. Lay hold of the great and precious promises: that by these ye might be partakers of the divine nature"* (What the Bible Is All About, *pp. 622-633).*

A. The *what* of these promises (2 Pet. 1:5-7)—"And beside this, giving all diligence, add to your faith virtue; and to virtue knowledge; and to knowledge temperance; and to temperance patience; and to patience godliness; and to godliness brotherly kindness; and to brotherly kindness charity" (2 Pet. 1:5-7).

---

†1:7 *By encouraging his readers to supply themselves with these Christian virtues, Peter literally fulfilled Jesus' twofold command to him.*

A. The command before the resurrection—"And the Lord said, Simon, Simon, behold, Satan hath desired to have you, that he may sift you as wheat: but I have prayed for thee, that thy faith fail not: and when thou art converted, strengthen thy brethren" (Luke 22:31-32).

B. The command after the resurrection—"Feed my lambs. . . . Feed my sheep" (John 21:15-16).

B. The *why* of these promises (2 Pet. 1:8-9)

1. To apply them leads to fruitfulness—"For if these things be in you, and abound, they make you that ye shall neither be barren nor unfruitful in the knowledge of our Lord Jesus Christ" (2 Pet. 1:8).
2. To avoid them leads to blindness—"But he that lacketh these things is blind, and cannot see afar off, and hath forgotten that he was purged from his old sins" (2 Pet. 1:9).

III. The Examination of the Calling of God (2 Pet. 1:10-12)—"Wherefore the rather, brethren, give diligence to make your calling and election sure: for if ye do these things, ye shall never fall" (2 Pet. 1:10).

---

†1:10 *Peter is saying here that we are to possess that necessary confidence concerning both our* salvation *from God, and our* service *for God. No child of God is effective if he has doubts concerning either of these.*

IV. The Revelation to the Apostle of God (2 Pet. 1:13-15) —"Yea, I think it meet, as long as I am in this tabernacle, to stir you up by putting you in remembrance; knowing that shortly I must put off this my tabernacle, even as our Lord Jesus Christ hath shewed me" (2 Pet. 1:13-14).

---

†1:14 Peter *knew of his approaching death (John 21:18), as did* Moses *(Deut. 4:22; 31:14), and* Paul *(2 Tim. 4:6). He speaks of his death as "my decease" (1:15). The word here is actually "my exodus," and is also used to describe the death of Jesus (Luke 9:31).*

V. The Transfiguration of the Son of God (2 Pet. 1:16-18)

A. The glorious sight—"For we have not followed cunningly devised fables, when we made known unto you the power and coming of our Lord Jesus Christ, but were eyewitnesses of his majesty" (2 Pet. 1:16).

B. The glorious sound—"For he received from God the Father honour and glory, when there came such a voice to him from the excellent glory, This is my beloved Son, in whom I am well pleased. And this voice which came from heaven we heard, when we were with him in the holy mount" (2 Pet. 1:17-18).

VI. The Inspiration of the Word of God (2 Pet. 1:19-21)

A. Its importance—"We have also a more sure word of prophecy; whereunto ye do well that ye take heed, as unto a light that shineth in a dark place, until the day dawn, and the day star arise in your hearts" (2 Pet. 1:19).

---

†**1:19** *It should be noted that Peter had just described the mighty transfiguration, but now declares that the written Word (the Scriptures) become a surer confirmation for the believer than even Peter's eyewitness account on that mountain. This of course does not contradict Christian experience, but it does say that Christian experience should be confirmed by the Word of God. Note Peter's beautiful description of Christ here: "Until the day dawn, and the day star arise in your hearts." To the* church, *he is the day star (see Rev. 22:16), but to* Israel, *he becomes the Sun of righteousness (Mal. 4:2).*

B. Its interpretation—"Knowing this first, that no prophecy of the scripture is of any private interpretation" (2 Pet. 1:20).

---

†**1:20** *This teaches that no single verse in the Bible should be interpreted in and of itself, apart from the remaining 31,172 verses. For example:*

A. Proxy baptism is not taught in 1 Corinthians 15:29 (whatever else it may teach), for no other verse in the Bible confirms this.

B. Baptismal regeneration cannot be concluded from Acts 2:38, for many other verses clearly refute it. It is still true that a text taken out of context is a pretext.

C. Its impartation—"For the prophecy came not in old time by the will of man: but holy men of God spake as they were moved by the Holy Ghost" (2 Pet. 1:21).

---

†**1:21** *Here we are told that the authors of the Bible were carried along by the Spirit of God as (it may be said) a sailboat is carried along by the wind. They did* not *go into a coma or trance, but were fully aware of what was happening (see also 2 Tim. 3:16; Luke 1:70; Acts 3:18). One final thought here. The same Holy Spirit who originally gave the Word now desires to teach it both to and through God's people today. (See 1 Cor. 2:9-16; John 14:26; 16:13-14.)*

VII. The Deviation of the Enemies of God (2 Pet. 2:1–3:4)—"But there were false prophets also among the people, even as there shall be false teachers among you, who privily shall bring in damnable heresies, even denying the Lord that bought them, and bring upon themselves swift destruction" (2 Pet. 2:1).

---

†*Kenneth Gangel writes: "When the Edict of Milan was passed in* A.D. *313 the church was then free to move into the world, legally and openly propagating its doctrines. But at the same time, the world also began to move into the church, diluting its message for the next 1,200 years until the Reformation broke forth on the scene. But it is obvious from 2 Peter chapter 2 that the world was already in the church well before the time of Constantine. Believers in all ages must be constantly on guard against its attack"* (The Bible Knowledge Commentary, *p. 869).*

A. The identity of these enemies
  1. In former days
    a. Wicked angels (2 Pet. 2:4)—""For if God spared not the angels that sinned, but cast them down to hell, and delivered them into chains of darkness, to be reserved unto judgment" (2 Pet. 2:4).

---

†2:4 *All angels who sided in with Lucifer during his great revolt (Isa. 14:12-15; Ezek. 28:11-19; Rev. 12:3-4) will, of course, along with Satan, someday be judged by God. However, it is believed by many that in this passage Peter has in mind a special group of fallen angels who added to their original iniquity by the sin described in Genesis 6:1-5. As a result, these evil spirits are already "delivered . . . into chains [literally, pits] of darkness, to be reserved [kept, confined] unto judgment" (see also Jude 6).*

---

    b. Those living in Noah's day (2 Pet. 2:5)
      (1) The godless—"And spared not the old world . . . bringing in the flood upon the world of the ungodly" (2 Pet. 2:5).
      (2) The godly—"But saved Noah the eighth person, a preacher of righteousness" (2 Pet. 2:5).
    c. Those living in Lot's day (2 Pet. 2:6-9)
      (1) The godless—"And turning the cities of Sodom and Gomorrah into ashes condemned them with an overthrow, making them an ensample unto those that after should live ungodly" (2 Pet. 2:6).
      (2) The godly—"And delivered just Lot, vexed with the filthy conversation of the wicked: (for that righteous man dwelling among them, in seeing and hearing, vexed his righteous soul from day to day with their unlawful deeds;) the Lord knoweth how to deliver the godly out of temptations, and to reserve the unjust unto the day of judgment to be punished" (2 Pet. 2:7-9).

---

†2:9

A. In these verses we are given some additional facts about Lot not recorded in the Genesis 19 account:

  1. Facts about his salvation—*He is referred to as just and righteous. It would have been difficult to deduce this at times from the Old Testament account, "Nevertheless, the foundation of God standeth sure, having this seal, the Lord knoweth them that are his" (2 Tim. 2:19).*

  2. Facts about his soul—*We are told that he "vexed his righteous soul from day to day with their unlawful deeds" (2:8). Also note the phrase, "And delivered just Lot, vexed with the filthy conversation [conduct] of the wicked" (2:7). The verb "vexed" is found twice in these verses. Each comes from a different Greek word. In 2:7 the word is* kataphoneo, *which means "to wear down with toil, to exhaust with labor, to oppress." The second word is* basanizo, *meaning "to torture, to torment." Thus, through compromise, Lot subjected his righteous soul to exhausting labor and cruel torment.*

  3. Facts about his Savior—*"The Lord knoweth how to deliver the godly out of temptation" (2:9; see Gen. 19:15, 17, 22; Psa. 34:15, 17, 19; 1 Cor. 10:13). During his earthly ministry our Lord used the historical account of both Noah and Lot to illustrate those conditions which will prevail just prior to the final judgment. (See Luke 17:26-30.)*

B. In passing it may be said here that Lot is a type of the church, which will be taken out prior to judgment, while Noah is a foreshadow of Israel, which nation will be preserved during *judgment.*

---

d. False prophets (2 Pet. 2:1)—"But there were false prophets" (2 Pet. 2:1). "Which have forsaken the right way, and are gone astray, following the way of Balaam the son of Bosor, who loved the wages of unrighteousness; but was rebuked for his iniquity: the dumb ass speaking with man's voice forbad the madness of the prophet" (2 Pet. 2:15-16).

---

†2:16

A. This is the first of three New Testament passages which speak of the Old Testament false prophet Balaam. He is condemned in all three passages.

1. The way of Balaam (2 Pet. 2:15)

2. The error of Balaam (Jude 11)

3. The doctrine of Balaam (Rev. 2:14)

B. Balaam's ass is the second of two brute creatures recorded as speaking in the Old Testament.

1. A serpent, as used by the devil (Gen. 3:1-4)

2. An ass, as used by the Lord (Num. 22:28-30)

---

2. In the latter days
   a. False teachers (2 Pet. 2:1)
   b. Scoffers—"Knowing this first, that there shall come in the last days scoffers, walking after their own lusts" (2 Pet. 3:3).

B. The iniquity of these enemies
   1. Inventors of heresies (2 Pet. 2:1)

---

†*They bring in destructive heresies. These heresies are introduced along with and alongside the truth. A tiny portion of deadly poison placed in a gallon of wholesome milk is far more dangerous than a bottle of marked poison, for the fatal milk is often unrecognized until it is too late.*

---

2. Christ deniers (2 Pet. 2:1)
3. Sensuous flesh indulgers (2 Pet. 2:2, 10, 14)
4. Truth maligners (2 Pet. 2:2)

---

†*They speak evil of the way of truth. In doing this they gather to themselves many disciples. "And many shall follow their pernicious [lustful] ways." False followers will go after false teachers. The passage in 1 Corinthians 11:19 explains why God permits the cults of the day. "For there must also be factions among you, in order that those who are approved may have become evident among you" (1 Cor. 11:19, NASB).*

---

5. Greedy materialists (2 Pet. 2:3)
6. Exploiters (2 Pet. 2:3)

---

†*They will exploit (if possible) the very elect of God. "And through covetousness shall they with feigned words make merchandise of you" (2:3). The phrase translated "feigned works" is* plastos *in the Greek. We get our word "plastic" from this. Peter is saying that their work may be stretched or shortened to fit any and all theological systems. However, the heretics will be punished, for "their damnation slumbereth not" (see also Deut. 32:35).*

---

7. Despisers of all authority (2 Pet. 2:10)
8. Self-willed (2 Pet. 2:10)
9. Unreasoning brute animals (2 Pet. 2:12)
10. Ignorant revilers (2 Pet. 2:12)
11. Committed to the playboy philosophy (2 Pet. 2:13)
12. Cancers within the Christian community (2 Pet. 2:13)

---

†*They pretend to have roots in historic Christianity—"Sporting [revealing] themselves with their own deceivings while they feast with you." This is thought to have referred to that love feast held in the early church before the Lord's Supper (1 Cor. 11:17-34).*

---

13. Eaten with lust (2 Pet. 2:14)
14. Totally forsaking the right way (2 Pet. 2:15)
15. Empty clouds (2 Pet. 2:17)

---

†*They are empty "clouds that are carried with a tempest; to whom the mist of darkness is reserved for ever" (2:17). Dr. Kenneth Wuest writes: "Tempest is* lailaps *in the Greek, referring to a whirlwind, a tempestuous wind, a squall, violent wind. It is never a single gust, nor a steadily blowing wind, however violent, but a storm breaking from black thunder clouds in furious gusts . . . throwing everything topsy-turvy"* (In These Last Days, *p. 59).*

---

16. Waterless wells (2 Pet. 2:17)
17. Arrogant rabble rousers (2 Pet. 2:18)
18. Blind captives attempting to lead other blind captives (2 Pet. 2:19)

---

†*"While they promise them liberty, they themselves are the servants of corruption." On at least two occasions our Lord referred to this characteristic while he was on earth. "Let them alone; they be blind leaders of the blind. And if the blind lead the blind, both shall fall into the ditch" (Matt. 15:14). "Woe unto you, scribes and Pharisees, hypocrites! For ye compass sea and land to make one proselyte, and when he is made, ye make him twofold more the child of hell than yourselves" (Matt. 23:15).*

---

19. Cold-blooded apostates (2 Pet. 2:21)

†*Their "latter end is worse with them than the beginning" (2:20). One of our Lord's most frightening accounts on demonic activity vividly illustrates the 23rd characteristic of the enemies of the faith. He said: "When the unclean spirit is gone out of a man, he walketh through dry places, seeking rest, and findeth none. Then he saith, I will return into my house from whence I came out; and when he is come, he findeth it empty, swept, and garnished. Then goeth he, and taketh with himself seven other spirits more wicked than himself, and they enter in and dwell there: and the last state of that man is worse than the first. Even so shall it be also unto this wicked generation" (Matt. 12:43-45). Here is a case of reformation without regeneration. Peter then concludes: "For it had been better for them [false teachers] not to have known the way of righteousness, than, after they have known it, to turn from the holy commandment delivered unto them" (2:21). Again it should be observed that Christ had previously spoken concerning this subject. "And that servant, which knew his lord's will, and prepared not himself, neither did according to his will, shall be beaten with many stripes. But he that knew not, and did commit things worthy of stripes, shall be beaten with few stripes. For unto whomsoever much is given, of him shall be much required: and to whom men have committed much, of him they will ask the more" (Luke 12:47-48).*

---

20. Filthy hogs and dogs (2 Pet. 2:22)

---

†*"The dog is turned to his own vomit again; and, the sow that was washed [in the Greek tense it is literally the sow that washed itself] to her wallowing in the mire." Is Peter teaching here that a Christian can lose his salvation? He is not. See his statements on eternal security in 1 Peter 1:3-5. Nowhere in the Bible does God call a believer a hog or a dog. These are false teachers.*

---

21. Scoffers of the second coming (2 Pet. 3:3-4)
22. Closed-minded fools (2 Pet. 3:5)

---

†*They utterly and eternally close their minds to those truths revealed in both God's world and in his Word. "For this they willingly are ignorant of" (3:5). An agnostic is therefore not a person who says "I can't believe," but rather, "I won't believe." They are without excuse. (See Rom. 1:18-20.)*

VIII. The Condemnation of the Former World of God (2 Pet. 3:5-6)—"But they deliberately forget that long ago by God's word the heavens existed and the earth was formed out of water and by water. By these waters also the world of that time was deluged and destroyed" (2 Pet. 3:5-6, NIV).

---

†**3:6** *The phrase, "The earth was formed out of the water and by the water," may be a reference to the statement in Genesis 1:7: "And God made the firmament [space], and divided the waters which were under the firmament from the waters which were above the firmament." A number of Bible students have advocated a canopy theory which teaches that prior to the great flood much of the ocean's present water volume was suspended in the upper atmosphere in the form of invisible water vapor. Thus, as early as the second day of creation, God had already prepared for the watery judgment he would employ in Noah's day. These atmospheric oceans then came*

pouring down as recorded in Genesis 7:11. The word "overflowed" in the Greek is katakluzo, *from whence our English word "cataclysm" comes.*

IX. The Annihilation of the Present World of God (2 Pet. 3: 7-12)

A. The coming calamity (2 Pet. 3:7-10)

1. The certainty involved—"But the heavens and the earth, which are now, by the same word are kept in store, reserved unto fire against the day of judgment and perdition of ungodly men. But, beloved, be not ignorant of this one thing, that one day is with the Lord as a thousand years, and a thousand years as one day" (2 Pet. 3:7-8).

---

†3:8

A. Some have attempted to twist this passage to say:

1. That the "days" in Genesis 1 are not six literal 24-hour days, as indicated by the phrase, "one day is with the Lord as a thousand years."

2. That the "years" in Revelation 20 are not 1,000 literal years, as indicated by the phrase, "a thousand years [is] as one day."

B. Both assumptions are false, however. Peter is simply saying God is not conditioned by time. He both created it and controls it. We measure time against time. He measures time against eternity. In essence, a single day in his sight is no shorter than a thousand years, nor is a thousand years longer than a single day.

---

2. The compassion involved—"The Lord is not slack concerning his promise, as some men count slackness; but is longsuffering to us-ward, not willing that any should perish, but that all should come to repentance" (2 Pet. 3:9).

3. The chronology involved—"But the day of the Lord will come as a thief in the night; in the which the heavens shall pass away with a great noise, and the elements shall melt with fervent heat, the earth also and the works that are therein shall be burned up" (2 Pet. 3:10).

---

†3:10 *Dr. Henry Morris writes: "Question: 'Will the world eventually be destroyed in a nuclear holocaust?' Answer: The over-forty generation still remembers the awful destruction in Hiroshima, when the first atomic bomb was unveiled and the world entered the nuclear age. Bible-believing Christians recall how they thought immediately of the great prophecy in 2 Peter 3:10. Yes, the earth will eventually undergo a cataclysmic destruction, which may well consist of actual atomic disintegration. The Greek word translated 'elements' in the above passage actually means the basic subdivisions of matter, corresponding quite closely to the modern scientific concept of the chemical elements. The word translated 'melt' means 'break apart.' The phrase 'pass away' does not mean 'be annihilated' but, rather 'pass out of sight.' The 'heavens' are not the stars, but the 'sky' or 'air.' Finally, 'great noise' and 'fervent heat' are intrinsically associated with atomic explosions.*

"Peter's prophecy may well describe, therefore, a final cataclysm when the earth itself, with its atmosphere, will experience a vast nuclear chain reaction and perish in a tremendous atomic holocaust. Although it is conceivable that man's activities may lead to this final conflagration, it seems likely that God Himself will bring it about.

"The very existence of such a remarkable prophecy in the Bible is evidence of inspiration. The

scientific discovery that matter can be converted into energy is one of the greatest triumphs of twentieth-century science, and yet this plain forecast of atomic disintegration into 'fervent heat' has been in the Bible for 1900 years" (The Bible Has the Answer, *p. 344).*

B. The current challenge—"Seeing then that all these things shall be dissolved, what manner of persons ought ye to be in all holy conversation and godliness, looking for and hasting unto the coming of the day of God, wherein the heavens being on fire shall be dissolved, and the elements shall melt with fervent heat?" (2 Pet. 3:11-12).

X. The New Creation of the Future World of God (2 Pet. 3:13-18)

A. The anticipation of this new world—"Nevertheless we, according to his promise, look for new heavens and a new earth, wherein dwelleth righteousness. "Wherefore, beloved, seeing that ye look for such things, be diligent that ye may be found of him in peace, without spot, and blameless" (2 Pet. 3:13-14).

B. The preparation for this new world

1. Maintain a proper relationship to the Scriptures—"And account that the longsuffering of our Lord is salvation; even as our beloved brother Paul also according to the wisdom given unto him hath written unto you; as also in all his epistles, speaking in them of these things; in which are some things hard to be understood, which they that are unlearned and unstable wrest, as they do also the other scriptures, unto their own destruction. Ye therefore, beloved, seeing ye know these things before, beware lest ye also, being led away with the error of the wicked, fall from your own stedfastness" (2 Pet. 3:15-17).

---

†**3:17** *Peter's statement about Paul here brings out four facts:*

A. He and Paul apparently continued to be good friends, following their confrontation in Antioch (see Gal. 2:11-14). This is indicated by the phrase "our beloved brother Paul."

B. Peter attested to the divine inspiration of Paul's writings.

C. Peter stated some of Paul's writings were "hard to be understood."

D. Peter realized that (even back then) some of the cults and false religious systems of the day were twisting and perverting Paul's writings as they continue to do in modern times.

---

2. Maintain a proper relationship to the Savior—"But grow in grace, and in the knowledge of our Lord and Saviour Jesus Christ. To him be glory both now and forever" (2 Pet. 3:18).

1 JOHN

INTIMATE INSIGHTS ON THE FATHER, FELLOWSHIP, AND THE FAMILY OF GOD

A. John the apostle writes his first epistle to develop this wonderful theme.
B. It has more to say about the Father than does any other epistle. He is referred to 12 times.
C. The *New Scofield Bible* suggests: "It [1 John] is a family letter from the Father to His 'little children' who are in the world. With the possible exception of the Song of Solomon, it is the most intimate of the inspired writings. The sin of a Christian is treated as a child's offense against his Father, and is dealt with as a family matter (1:9; 2:1)" (p. 1,342).
D. The word *love* is found 37 times, more often in this epistle than in any other Old or New Testament book, with the single exception of the Psalms.
E. The Spirit of God directed John the apostle to pen five of the New Testament books. Apart from Paul, no other author would write as many books in the New Testament as he did. His five books are: The Gospel of John, the three epistles of John, and the Revelation. The following distinction between these books is offered:
   1. Gospel of John
      a. Speaks of salvation
      b. The past
      c. Christ the Prophet
      d. The cross
   2. Epistles of John
      a. Speak of sanctification
      b. The present
      c. Christ the Priest
      d. The *koinonia* (fellowship)
   3. Revelation of John
      a. Speaks of glorification
      b. The future
      c. Christ the King
      d. The crown
F. A comparison can be made between John's Gospel account and the epistle of 1 John.
   1. John begins his Gospel account by proving the *deity* of Christ (John 1:1).
   2. John begins his epistle by proving the *humanity* of Christ (1 John 1:1-3).
   3. John ends his Gospel account with the following words: "But these are written, that ye might believe that Jesus is the Christ, the Son of God; and that believing ye might have life through his name" (John 20:31).
   4. John ends his epistle with the following words: "These things have I written unto you that believe on the name of the Son of God; that ye may know that ye have eternal life, and that ye may believe on the name of the Son of God" (1 John 5:13).

G. In the Gospel, John describes believers as sheep in God's fold; in the epistle as members in his family; and in the Revelation as priests in his kingdom (John 10; 1 John 2; Rev. 1).
H. It is believed by some that John directed his epistles to the same readers who would later receive the book of Revelation—that is, the seven churches in Asia Minor.
I. This epistle describes several great contrasts. In it John speaks of light versus darkness, love versus hatred, Christ versus Antichrist, belief versus unbelief, and truth versus error.
J. It is the first of but two biblical books referring to the coming world dictator, the Antichrist (see 1 John 2:18, 22; 4:3; 2 John 7).
K. It is the only biblical book containing the phrase, "sin unto death" (5:16), describing what had already taken place in Acts 5:1-11 and 1 Corinthians 11:29-30.
L. It is the only biblical book classifying sin and temptation into three categories (2:15-17).
M. It has more to say about a Christian's sin and confession than any other biblical book for its size.
N. The book of 1 John is the 13th longest New Testament book, and 44th longest biblical book with five chapters, 105 verses, and 2,523 words. There are quotations or allusions from seven Old Testament books in the first epistle of John.
O. Great passages would include:
   1. 1:5-9
   2. 2:1-2
   3. 2:15-17
   4. 3:1-3
   5. 3:18-23
   6. 4:7-10
   7. 5:11-15

THE BOOK OF 1 JOHN

"That which we have seen and heard declare we unto you, that ye also may have fellowship with us: and truly our fellowship is with the Father, and with his Son Jesus Christ" (1 John 1:3).

This epistle is outlined with the word "fellowship" in mind.

I. The Source of This Fellowship
   A. The incarnation of Jesus Christ (1 John 1:1-2; 3:5, 8)
      1. The reality of his incarnation—"That which was from the beginning, which we have heard, which we have seen with our eyes, which we have looked upon, and our hands have handled, of the Word of life; (for the life was manifested, and we have seen it, and bear witness, and shew unto you that eternal life, which was with the Father, and was manifested unto us)" (1 John 1:1-2).

---

†**1:2** *The Apostle John was well qualified to give witness concerning the validity of the incarnation. For over three action-packed and life-changing years he listened to the Savior's sermons, learned*

from his parables, and marveled at his miracles. John, along with Peter and James, enjoyed a special relationship with Jesus.

A. They alone witnessed the transfiguration (Matt. 17:1-2).
B. They alone were present at the raising of Jairus's daughter (Luke 8:51-56).
C. They alone were taken to a special place in the Garden of Gethsemane (Matt. 26:36-38).
D. John leaned on the bosom of Christ during the Last Supper (John 13:23).
E. John witnessed the trial of Jesus before the Jewish high priest (John 18:15-16).
F. John was the only apostle present at the crucifixion (John 19:26-27).
G. John and Peter were the first two apostles at the empty tomb (John 20:1-8).

---

2. The reason for his incarnation—"And ye know that he was manifested to take away our sins; and in him is no sin. . . . He that committeth sin is of the devil; for the devil sinneth from the beginning. For this purpose the Son of God was manifested, that he might destroy the works of the devil" (1 John 3:5, 8).

---

†3:8 *It must be understood that Jesus did* not *come to preach the gospel. He came rather that there might be a gospel to be preached.*

B. The atonement of Jesus Christ (1 John 2:2; 3:16; 4: 9-10, 14)
   1. The divine extent—For whom did Christ die? "And he is the propitiation for our sins: and not for ours only, but also for the sins of the whole world" (1 John 2:2).

---

†2:2 *The word "propitiation" is from the Greek* hilasmos *and is found four times in the New Testament (Rom. 3:25; Heb. 9:5; 1 John 2:2; 4:10). Its literal meaning is "mercy seat" (as translated in Heb. 9:5). In the Old Testament, once yearly, the high priest made atonement for Israel by sprinkling the blood of a sacrificial animal upon the lid of the Ark of the Covenant, also known as the mercy seat (Lev. 16:13-19). Thus, the theological meaning of "propitiation" is to render favorable, to satisfy, to appease. In a nutshell, John is saying here in 2:2 that the sacrifice of Christ is looked upon as our mercy seat whereby God's holiness is satisfied by the blood of his Son. Note also this propitiation is sufficient not only for the nation Israel (as was the case in the Old Testament) but for the entire world.*

---

   2. The divine example—Why did Christ die? "Hereby perceive we the love of God, because he laid down his life for us: and we ought to lay down our lives for the brethren. . . . In this was manifested the love of God toward us, because that God sent his only begotten Son into the world, that we might live through him. Herein is love, not that we loved God, but that he loved us, and sent his Son to be the propitiation for our sins. And we have seen and do testify that the Father sent the Son to be the Saviour of the world" (1 John 3:16; 4:9-10, 14).

II. The Goal of This Fellowship
   A. That we might know more about the Father
      1. He is light—"This then is the message which we have heard of him, and declare unto you, that God is light, and in him is no darkness at all" (1 John 1:5).

2. He is love—"He that loveth not knoweth not God; for God is love. . . . And we have known and believed the love that God hath to us. God is love; and he that dwelleth in love dwelleth in God, and God in him" (1 John 4:8, 16). "Hereby perceive we the love of God, because he laid down his life for us: and we ought to lay down our lives for the brethren" (1 John 3:16).
3. He is life—"And this is the record, that God hath given to us eternal life, and this life is in his Son. He that hath the Son hath life; and he that hath not the Son of God hath not life" (1 John 5:11-12).
4. He is righteous—"Little children, let no man deceive you: he that doeth righteousness is righteous, even as he is righteous" (1 John 3:7).
5. He is all-knowing—"For if our heart condemn us, God is greater than our heart, and knoweth all things" (1 John 3:20).

---

†3:20 *There are two difficult phrases used by John, the first in this verse and the second in the next:*

A. "If our heart condemn us" (3:20).

B. "If our heart condemn us not" (3:21). The first phrase may result from an oversensitive conscience, revealing how frail we really are. If so, a classic illustration here can be seen in the answer given by a distraught father of a demon-possessed son when asked by Christ if he had faith for the healing of his son. "And straightway the father of the child cried out, and said with tears, Lord, I believe; help thou mine unbelief" (Mark 9:24).

The second phrase would thus become a reality when one realizes that God knows all about us and yet still loves us. "Like as a father pitieth his children, so the LORD pitieth them that fear him. For he knoweth our frame; he remembereth that we are dust" (Psa. 103:13-14). "Watch and pray, that ye enter not into temptation: the spirit indeed is willing, but the flesh is weak" (Matt. 26:41).

---

6. He is invisible—"No man hath seen God at any time" (1 John 4:12a).

B. That we might allow the Father's love to be perfected in us—"But whoso keepeth his word, in him verily is the love of God perfected: hereby know we that we are in him" (1 John 2:5).

C. That we might love the family of God—"If we love one another, God dwelleth in us, and his love is perfected in us" (1 John 4:12b).

D. That we might experience the fullness of joy—"And these things write we unto you, that your joy may be full" (1 John 1:4).

E. That we might receive assurance

1. Concerning our salvation—"These things have I written unto you that believe on the name of the Son of God; that ye may know that ye have eternal life, and that ye may believe on the name of the Son of God" (1 John 5:13).
2. Concerning our supplications—"And whatsoever we ask, we receive of him, because we keep his commandments, and do those things that are pleasing in his sight" (1 John 3:22). "And this is the confidence that we have in him, that, if we ask any thing according to his will, he heareth us: and if we know that he hear us, whatsoever we ask, we know that we have the petitions that we desired of him" (1 John 5:14-15).

III. The Requirements for This Fellowship

A. Help my brother—"But whoso hath this world's good, and seeth his brother have need, and shutteth up his bowels of compassion from him, how dwelleth the love of God in him?" (1 John 3:17).

B. Abide in Christ—"And now, little children, abide in him; that, when he shall appear, we may have confidence, and not be ashamed before him at his coming" (1 John 2:28).

C. Keep his commandments (1 John 2:3-8; 5:2-3)—"And hereby we do know that we know him, if we keep his commandments. He that saith, I know him, and keepeth not his commandments, is a liar, and the truth is not in him" (1 John 2:3-4). "For this is the love of God, that we keep his commandments: and his commandments are not grievous" (1 John 5:3).

1. The old commandment—"Brethren, I write no new commandment unto you, but an old commandment which ye had from the beginning. The old commandment is the word which ye have heard from the beginning" (1 John 2:7). The old commandment was to love others as you love yourself (Lev. 19:34; Deut. 10:19).
2. The new commandment—"Again, a new commandment I write unto you, which thing is true in him and in you: because the darkness is past, and the true light now shineth" (1 John 2:8).

D. Recognize my sin—"If we say that we have no sin, we deceive ourselves, and the truth is not in us" (1 John 1:8).

---

†1:8 *Those who hold to sinless perfection make claim to something that neither John nor Paul would make claim to (see Phil. 3:12-14).*

E. Confess my sin—"If we confess our sins, he is faithful and just to forgive us our sins, and to cleanse us from all unrighteousness" (1 John 1:9).

---

†1:9 *The word "confess" here is the Greek word* homologeo, *which means "to agree with." Thus, when the Holy Spirit points out a sin in our life we are immediately to agree with him. While the blood of Christ will cleanse us from every sin, it will not cleanse us of even one excuse.*

F. Walk in the light—"But if we walk in the light, as he is in the light, we have fellowship one with another, and the blood of Jesus Christ his Son cleanseth us from all sin" (1 John 1:7).

IV. The Tests of This Fellowship—A quick quiz to determine our fellowship

A. Do I conduct my life down here in view of the Rapture?—"And every man that hath this hope in him purifieth himself, even as he is pure" (1 John 3:3).

B. Do I continually dwell in sin?—"If ye know that he is righteous, ye know that every one that doeth righteousness is born of him" (1 John 2:29). "Whosoever abideth in him sinneth not: whosoever sinneth hath not seen him, neither known him. . . . Whosoever is born of God doth not commit sin; for his seed remaineth in him: and he cannot sin, because he is born of God. In this the children of God are manifest, and the children of the devil: whosoever doeth not righteousness is not of God, neither he that loveth not his brother" (1 John 3:6, 9-10). "For whatsoever is born of God overcometh the world: and this is the victory that overcometh the world, even our faith. Who is he that overcometh the world, but he that believeth that Jesus is the Son of God? . . . We know that whosoever is born of God sinneth not; but he that is begotten of God keepeth himself, and that wicked one toucheth him not" (1 John 5:4-5, 18).

---

†**5:18** *These verses, of course, do not teach sinless perfection. The Greek verbs are all in the present tense, referring to the* constant *practice of sin. Thus, while we may not be* sinless, *John nevertheless states that we should* sin less.

C. Do I hate my spiritual brother?—"If a man say, I love God, and hateth his brother, he is a liar: for he that loveth not his brother whom he hath seen, how can he love God whom he hath not seen?" (1 John 4:20).

D. Do I desire to help my brother?—"But whoso hath this world's good, and seeth his brother have need, and shutteth up his bowels of compassion from him, how dwelleth the love of God in him? My little children, let us not love in word, neither in tongue; but in deed and in truth" (1 John 3:17-18).

E. Do I really love my brother?—"He that loveth his brother abideth in the light, and there is none occasion of stumbling in him" (1 John 2:10). "Not as Cain, who was of that wicked one, and slew his brother. And wherefore slew he him? Because his own works were evil, and his brother's righteous. . . . We know that we have passed from death unto life, because we love the brethren. He that loveth not his brother abideth in death. Whosoever hateth his brother is a murderer: and ye know that no murderer hath eternal life abiding in him" (1 John 3:12, 14-15). "Beloved, let us love one another: for love is of God; and every one that loveth is born of God, and knoweth God. . . . And this commandment have we from him, That he who loveth God love his brother also" (1 John 4:7, 21).

---

†**4:21** *The word "love" is mentioned no less than eight times in these few verses. What is real Christian love? Consider these suggested definitions:*

A. Christian love is unselfish concern for the welfare of another.

B. Christian love is the act of one person seeking the highest good for another person. Thus, acting upon these definitions, we can love those individuals we may not even like.

F. Do I really love God?—"By this we know that we love the children of God, when we love God, and keep his commandments" (1 John 5:2).

G. Do I enjoy a rapport with other servants of God?—"We are of God: he that knoweth God heareth us; he that is not of God heareth not us. Hereby know we the spirit of truth, and the spirit of error" (1 John 4:6).

H. Am I plagued with constant fear?—"There is no fear in love; but perfect love casteth out fear: because fear hath torment. He that feareth is not made perfect in love" (1 John 4:18).

I. Can I recognize false doctrine when it comes my way? —"Beloved, believe not every spirit, but try the spirits whether they are of God: because many false prophets are gone out into the world. Hereby know ye the Spirit of God: Every spirit that confesseth that Jesus Christ is come in the flesh is of God: and every spirit that confesseth not that Jesus Christ is come in the flesh is not of God: and this is that spirit of antichrist, whereof ye have heard that it should come; and even now already is it in the world" (1 John 4:1-3).

---

†4:3 *The title "Antichrist" is found but four times in the Bible, all employed by John the apostle (1 John 2:18, 22; 4:3; 2 John 1:7). According to John:*
A. The Antichrist will appear during the last days (2:18; 4:3).
B. He has, however, many prototypes throughout history (2:18; 4:3).
C. The Antichrist denies the deity of Christ (2:22).
D. The Antichrist denies the humanity of Christ (4:3; 2 John 7).

J. Am I straight on the deity of Christ?—"Whosoever shall confess that Jesus is the Son of God, God dwelleth in him, and he in God" (1 John 4:15).
K. Am I straight on the work of Christ?—"And ye know that he was manifested to take away our sins; and in him is no sin. . . . He that committeth sin is of the devil; for the devil sinneth from the beginning. For this purpose the Son of God was manifested, that he might destroy the works of the devil" (1 John 3:5, 8). "Marvel not, my brethren, if the world hate you. . . . For if our heart condemn us, God is greater than our heart, and knoweth all things" (1 John 3:13, 20).
L. Do I have the witness of the Spirit?—"And he that keepeth his commandments dwelleth in him, and he in him. And hereby we know that he abideth in us, by the Spirit which he hath given us" (1 John 3:24). "Hereby know we that we dwell in him, and he in us, because he hath given us of his Spirit" (1 John 4:13). "If we receive the witness of men, the witness of God is greater: for this is the witness of God which he hath testified of his Son. He that believeth on the Son of God hath the witness in himself: he that believeth not God hath made him a liar; because he believeth not the record that God gave of his Son" (1 John 5:9-10).

V. The Maintenance of This Fellowship
A. Accomplished through the occupation of the Son of God
1. He serves as our advocate—"My little children, these things write I unto you, that ye sin not. And if any man sin, we have an advocate with the Father, Jesus Christ the righteous" (1 John 2:1).

---

†2:1 *The word "advocate" here is the Greek word* parakletos, *meaning "to call alongside of." The New Scofield Bible defines this office as follows: "Advocacy is that work of Jesus Christ for sinning believers which He carries on with the Father, whereby, because of the eternal efficacy of Christ's sacrifice, He restores them to fellowship"* (New Scofield Bible, *p. 1,343).*

---

2. He serves as our atoning sacrifice—"And he is the propitiation for our sins: and not for ours only, but also for the sins of the whole world" (1 John 2:2).

---

†2:2 *As brought out before in this study, the root Greek word here translated "propitiation" is rendered "mercy seat" in Hebrews 9:5. The mercy seat was a part of that sacred Ark of the Covenant which rested in the holy of holies. Upon this golden mercy seat, every day of atonement, was* *sprinkled the blood of an animal (Lev. 16:14). This meant that the righteous sentence of the Law had been executed, changing a judgment seat into a mercy seat (Heb. 9:11-15). It signified that humanity had thus been reconciled to God. The work of Christ thus served as a propitiation, whereby God's righteousness was forever satisfied. (See also 4:10.)*

B. Accomplished through the habitation of the Spirit of God—"But ye have an unction from the Holy One, and ye know all things. . . . But the anointing which ye have received of him abideth in you, and ye need not that any man teach you: but as the same anointing teacheth you of all things, and is truth, and is no lie, and even as it hath taught you, ye shall abide in him" (1 John 2:20, 27).

---

†2:27 *This verse does* not, *of course, deny the office of a human teacher (see Eph. 4:11-12). What it does say is that we are to test any system of teaching by the Word of God.*

C. Accomplished through the cooperation of the saint of God —"If we say that we have no sin, we deceive ourselves, and the truth is not in us. If we confess our sins, he is faithful and just to forgive us our sins, and to cleanse us from all unrighteousness" (1 John 1:8-9).

VI. The Family Members in This Fellowship—"Behold, what manner of love the Father hath bestowed upon us, that we should be called the sons of God: therefore the world knoweth us not, because it knew him not" (1 John 3:1).

A. Little children (new converts)—"I write unto you, little children, because your sins are forgiven you for his name's sake" (1 John 2:12). "I write unto you, little children, because ye have known the Father" (1 John 2:13b).

B. Young men (those saved for awhile)—"I write unto you, young men, because ye have overcome the wicked one" (1 John 2:13). "I have written unto you, fathers, because ye have known him that is from the beginning. I have written unto you, young men, because ye are strong, and the word of God abideth in you, and ye have overcome the wicked one" (1 John 2:14).

C. Fathers (those mature in the faith)—"I write unto you, fathers, because ye have known him that is from the beginning" (1 John 2:13).

VII. The Enemies of This Fellowship—"Love not the world, neither the things that are in the world. If any man love the world, the love of the Father is not in him" (1 John 2:15). "And we know that we are of God, and the whole world lieth in wickedness" (1 John 5:19).

---

†5:19 *A definition of this world—In the Bible there are several kinds of worlds.*

A. The physical world (Acts 17:24)

B. The human world (John 3:16)

C. The evil world (1 John 5:19; John 12:31; 15:18) Obviously John had this third "world" in mind here. A believer lives *on the first world, is a* member *of the second, but must* avoid *the third.*

A. The evil systems in this world

1. The divisions (1 John 2:16)

a. The lust of the flesh

b. The lust of the eyes
c. The pride of life

---

†*As John penned these words his thoughts may well have gone back to a beautiful garden and a terrible wilderness where two individuals were subjected to these satanic temptations by the devil himself.*
A. Eve and the beautiful garden (Gen. 3:6)
1. "The woman saw that the tree was good for food"—The lust of the flesh.
2. "And that it was pleasant to the eyes"—The lust of the eyes.
3. "And a tree . . . to make one wise"—The pride of life.
B. Christ and the terrible wilderness (Matt. 4:3, 8, 6)
1. "Command that these stones be made bread" (4:3)—The lust of the flesh.
2. "He [Satan] sheweth him [Jesus] all the kingdoms of the world" (4:8)—The lust of the eyes.
3. "Cast thyself down [from the pinnacle of the temple] . . . for he shall give his angels charge concerning thee" (4:6)—The pride of life.

---

2. The destruction (1 John 2:17)—"And the world passeth away, and the lust thereof: but he that doeth the will of God abideth for ever" (1 John 2:17).

B. The evil seducers in this world—"These things have I written unto you concerning them that seduce you" (1 John 2:26).
1. Their appearance—"Little children, it is the last time: and as ye have heard that antichrist shall come, even now are there many antichrists; whereby we know that it is the last time" (1 John 2:18).
2. Their apostasy—"They went out from us, but they were not of us; for if they had been of us, they would no doubt have continued with us: but they went out, that they might be made manifest that they were not all of us" (1 John 2:19).

---

†**2:19** *The actions of the following individuals serve to illustrate John's words here:*
A. Cain (Gen. 4:1-8; 1 John 3:10-12)
B. Korah (Num. 16:1-3)
C. Achan (Josh. 7:20)
D. Saul (1 Sam. 28:3-20)
E. Ahithophel (2 Sam. 15:31)
F. Judas (Matt. 26:14-16)
G. Demas (2 Tim. 4:10)

C. The evil spirits in this world
1. The fruit of these spirits—"Who is a liar but he that denieth that Jesus is the Christ? He is antichrist, that denieth the Father and the Son" (1 John 2:22). "Beloved, believe not every spirit, but try the spirits whether they are of God: because many false prophets are gone out into the world. Hereby know ye the Spirit of God: Every spirit that confesseth that Jesus Christ is come in the flesh is of God" (1 John 4:1-2).
2. The root of these spirits—"And every spirit that confesseth not that Jesus Christ is come in the flesh is not of God: and this is that spirit of antichrist, whereof ye

have heard that it should come; and even now already is it in the world" (1 John 4:3).

VIII. The Witnesses to This Fellowship (1 John 5:6-8)

A. The witnesses in heaven—"For there are three that bear record in heaven, the Father, the Word, and the Holy Ghost: and these three are one" (1 John 5:7).

B. The witnesses on earth—"And there are three that bear witness in earth, the spirit, and the water, and the blood: and these three agree in one" (1 John 5:8).

---

†**5:8** *These verses are not among the easiest to interpret. Let us begin by observing that the last part of verse 7 is not listed in most ancient manuscripts. Thus, the first part of the verse should read, "Because there* are *three that bear record." This apparently refers to the three witnesses already mentioned in verse 6 and amplified in verse 8. What are these witnesses?*

A. The identity of the witnesses:

1. The water

2. The blood

3. The Spirit

B. The interpretation of the witnesses—There are at least four theories here.

1. The baptism and death of Christ

2. The water and blood that flowed from his side

3. A symbolic reference to purification and redemption

4. A symbolic reference to the ordinances of baptism and the Lord's Supper—Most conservative theologians prefer the first of these, the baptism and death of Christ (Matt. 3:13-17; Heb. 9:12).

C. The implications of these witnesses—A twofold witness is all that is necessary (Deut. 19:15; Matt. 18:16; John 8:17), but God has given us three.

IX. The Separation from This Fellowship (1 John 5:16-17) —Sin causes a break in our fellowship with God. "If anyone sees his brother committing a sin not leading to death, he shall ask and God will for him give life to those who commit sin not leading to death. There is a sin leading to death; I do not say that he should make request for this. All unrighteousness is sin, and there is a sin not leading to death" (1 John 5:16-17, NASB).

---

†**5:17** *"There is a sin unto death" (5:16). The Bible teaches that my union with Christ is so strong that nothing can break it; but my communion with him is so fragile that the slightest sin shatters it. M. F. Unger writes: "Prayer and the Problem of Serious Sin, 16-17. It is possible for a true believer to fall into sin, 16a. If and when this happens, a fellow believer is to pray for him, 16b. As a result God will give the sinning Christian preservation of physical life (not eternal life, for this life is eternal and unforfeitable). However, this intercession is effective only in the case of sin not unto physical death, 16c. 'There is a sin unto death,' 16d. This is persistent, willful sinning in a believer in which 'the flesh is destroyed' (physical death) so 'that the spirit might be saved' (1 Cor. 5:1-5; Acts 5:1-11; 1 Cor. 11:30). Both Saul and Samson are types of this very severe chastening in the Old Testament. This sin is not to be prayed for because it involved the execution of an immutable law of God unaltered by prayer, 16e. Sin has different degrees of seriousness, 16. 'All unrighteousness is sin, but there is a sin which is not unto [physical] death' (involving lesser chastisements, cf. 1 Cor. 11:30)"* (Unger's Bible Handbook, *p. 829).*

X. The Encouragements for This Fellowship

A. The promise of eternal life—"And this is the promise that he hath promised us, even eternal life" (1 John 2:25).

B. The promise of a new body—"Beloved, now are we the sons of God, and it doth not yet appear what we shall be: but we know that, when he shall appear, we shall be like him; for we shall see him as he is" (1 John 3:2).

C. A life without fear—"And hereby we know that we are of the truth, and shall assure our hearts before him. . . . Beloved, if our heart condemn us not, then have we confidence toward God" (1 John 3:19, 21). "There is no fear in love; but perfect love casteth out fear: because fear hath torment. He that feareth is not made perfect in love" (1 John 4:18).

D. Confidence at the Rapture—"And now, little children, abide in him; that, when he shall appear, we may have confidence, and not be ashamed before him at his coming" (1 John 2:28).

E. Boldness at the judgment—"Herein is our love made perfect, that we may have boldness in the day of judgment: because as he is, so are we in this world" (1 John 4:17).

2 JOHN

THE EPISTLE FROM AN ELDER TO AN ELECT LADY

A. This is John's second epistle. It is the only book in the Bible addressed to a woman. It holds the same place in John's writing that Philemon holds in Paul's epistles.
B. John does not mention his own name or the name of this woman. This may have been to prevent persecution from the Roman authorities of the time, who viewed Christianity as an unlawful religion.
C. The book of 2 John is the 26th longest New Testament book and 65th longest biblical book, with one chapter, 13 verses, and 303 words. There are quotations or allusions to one Old Testament book in 2 John.
D. Its great passage is found in verses 7-8.

THE BOOK OF 2 JOHN

I. She Is Commended by the Apostle—"The elder unto the elect lady and her children, whom I love in the truth; and not I only, but also all they that have known the truth; for the truth's sake, which dwelleth in us, and shall be with us for ever. Grace be with you, mercy, and peace, from God the Father, and from the Lord Jesus Christ, the Son of the Father, in truth and love. I rejoiced greatly that I found of thy children walking in truth, as we have received a commandment from the Father" (2 John 1-4).

---

†**v. 4** *Here it perhaps should be noted that some Bible students believe the "elect lady" of this epistle was actually a local church. If this is the case, then the children here are church members. However, it is the view of this author that it is written to an actual woman and these are her children.*

II. She Is Commanded by the Apostle.
   A. That she walk in love—"And now I beseech thee, lady, not as though I wrote a new commandment unto thee, but that which we had from the beginning, that we love one another" (2 John 5).
   B. That she walk in truth—"And this is love, that we walk after his commandments. This is the commandment, That, as ye have heard from the beginning, ye should walk in it" (2 John 6).

---

†**v. 6** *In verses 5 and 6 John exhorts to walk in love and truth. How important it is not to separate these two. To practice truth without love leads to legalism. To employ love without truth leads to liberalism. Paul likewise combines these two: "But, speaking the truth in love, may grow up into him in all things, which is the head, even Christ" (Eph. 4:15).*

III. She Is Cautioned by the Apostle.
   A. Look out for Satan.
      1. The deception of his ministers—"For many deceivers are entered into the world, who confess not that Jesus Christ is come in the flesh. This is a deceiver and an antichrist" (2 John 7).
      2. The rejection of his ministers
         a. What the elect lady was to do—"If there come any unto you, and bring not this doctrine, receive him not into your house, neither bid him God speed" (2 John 10).

---

†**v. 10** *Perhaps this lady was extending hospitality to all those who claimed to be Christians, though some were heretics.*

---

         b. Why she was to do it—"For he that biddeth him God speed is partaker of his evil deeds" (2 John 11).

---

†**v. 11** *This may have been one of the reasons why Paul denounced a demon-possessed girl in Philippi in spite of the fact that she attempted to identify with his message. "The same followed Paul and us, and cried, saying, These men are the servants of the most high God, which shew unto us the way of salvation. And this did she many days. But Paul, being grieved, turned and said to the spirit, I command thee in the name of Jesus Christ to come out of her. And he came out the same hour" (Acts 16:17-18).*

   B. Look out for self—"Look to yourselves, that we lose not those things which we have wrought, but that we receive a full reward" (2 John 8).

---

†**v. 8** *John wanted this beloved lady to receive a full reward for faithful service at the judgment seat of Christ (see 1 Cor. 3:5-17).*

IV. She Is Comforted by the Apostle—"Having many things to write unto you, I would not write with paper and ink: but I trust to come unto you, and speak face to face, that our joy may be full" (2 John 12).

3 JOHN

AN EPISTLE FROM AN ELDER CONCERNING AN EXHORTER, AN EGOTIST, AND AN EXAMPLE

A. The epistle is 3 John. The elder is John. The exhorter is Gaius; the egotist, Diotrephes; and the example, Demetrius.
   J. Vernon McGee says: "This is a letter similar to John's second epistle, in that it is personal in character, and it carries the same theme of truth. However, this letter deals with principalities. In his second epistle, John says that truth is worth standing for; and in the third epistle that truth is worth working for!" (*Third John*, p. 291).
B. In his second epistle John dealt with the problem of welcoming deceivers (which should not have been done); in this epistle he discusses the error of not receiving believers (which should have been done).
C. This is the shortest book in the Bible.
D. Both 2 and 3 John end in similar fashion.
   1. In 2 John—"Having many things to write unto you, I would not write with paper and ink: but I trust to come unto you, and speak face to face, that our joy may be full" (2 John 12).
   2. In 3 John—"I had many things to write, but I will not with ink and pen write unto thee: but I trust I shall shortly see thee, and we shall speak face to face. Peace be to thee. Our friends salute thee. Greet the friends by name" (3 John 13-14).
E. This epistle gives an excellent (though brief) glimpse of church life at the close of the first century.
F. The book of 3 John is the smallest biblical book, with one chapter, 14 verses, and 299 words. There are quotations or allusions from one Old Testament book in 3 John.
G. Its great passage is verse 11.

THE BOOK OF 3 JOHN

I. The Prosperity of Gaius the Exhorter (3 John 1-8)
   A. John's prayer for him—"The elder unto the wellbeloved Gaius, whom I love in the truth. Beloved, I wish above all things that thou mayest prosper and be in health, even as thy soul prospereth. . . . I had many things to write, but I will not with ink and pen write unto thee: but I trust I shall shortly see thee, and we shall speak face to face. Peace be to thee. Our friends salute thee. Greet the friends by name" (3 John 1-2, 13-14).

---

†**v. 14** *Note the phrase in verse 2, "that thou mayest prosper and be in health." One of America's most famous faith healers during the latter part of the 20th century, by his own testimony, had*

based his entire healing ministry squarely upon this little verse, claiming he found in it God's will for every believer to enjoy continual health and considerable wealth. Even the most casual reading of John's letter here, however, would totally reject this bizarre interpretation. The Greek word here translated "prosper" is euodoumai, *meaning "to have a good journey."*

B. John's praise of him

1. His faithfulness to the message of God—"For I rejoiced greatly, when the brethren came and testified of the truth that is in thee, even as thou walkest in the truth. I have no greater joy than to hear that my children walk in truth" (3 John 3-4).
2. His helpfulness to the messengers of God—"Beloved, thou doest faithfully whatsoever thou doest to the brethren, and to strangers; which have borne witness of thy charity before the church: whom if thou bring forward on their journey after a godly sort, thou shalt do well: because that for his name's sake they went forth, taking nothing of the Gentiles. We therefore ought to receive such, that we might be fellowhelpers to the truth" (3 John 5-8).

---

†v. 8 *Note two phrases here in verse 6:*

A. "Which have borne witness of thy charity before the church." John seems to be saying here that his church had heard of Gaius's love for both the Savior and the saints. At this time John may have been pastor of the church at Ephesus. If so, the quality of Gaius's love was sadly absent among the apostle's congregation (see Rev. 2:4).

B. "Bring forward on their journey after a godly sort." John here instructs Gaius and his church to perform a twofold ministry for visiting Christian workers.

1. *Provide for them while they were there.*
2. *Anticipate their needs when they leave, that is, send them away with an offering.*

II. The Pride of Diotrephes the Egotist (3 John 9-11)

A. He attempted to occupy the leading place (3 John 9).
B. He refused to receive the Apostle John (3 John 9).
C. He had slandered the apostles (3 John 10).
D. He had refused to entertain missionaries (3 John 10).
E. He attempted to excommunicate believers (3 John 10).
F. He was not of God (3 John 11).

---

†v. 11 *J. Vernon McGee summarizes the actions of both Gaius and Diotrephes: "The missionaries of the early church were itinerants. They went from place to place. Since the local inn was a wretched and dirty place, and there were no Holiday Inns or Howard Johnson Motels, these missionaries were entertained in the homes of believers. Gaius opened his home, for which John congratulates him. Diotrephes opposed this practice, and John censors him for it. His 'hang-up' was that he loved to have recognition and attention, and be the center of attraction. He had to rule or ruin. There is generally one like him in every church who wants to control the church and the preacher. He tried to be the first pope. He was Diotrephes, the dictator"* (Through the Bible, *p. 292.)*

III. The Praise of Demetrius, the Example—"Demetrius hath good report of all men, and of the truth itself: yea, and we also bear record; and ye know that our record is true" (3 John 12).

---

†**v. 12** *After issuing a sixfold condemnation of Diotrephes, John now gives a threefold commendation of Demetrius.*

A. A public commendation—"A good report of all men"
B. A scriptural commendation—"Of the truth itself"
C. A personal commendation—"We also bear record."

JUDE

THE ARROGANT APOSTATE, DESCRIBED AND DENOUNCED

A. Such is the message of the book of Jude.
B. Jude was the brother of James (author of the book of James and first pastor of the Jerusalem church in Acts 15) and half brother of Jesus (see Mark 6:3).
C. Along with his brothers, Jude did not believe in the ministry of Jesus until after the resurrection (John 7:3-8). But sometime between the resurrection and ascension both men were gloriously saved. They were present (along with their mother Mary) in the Upper Room just prior to Pentecost (Acts 1:13).
D. Jude was apparently married and was accompanied by his wife as he performed missionary work (1 Cor. 9:5).
E. "The beginning of the age of the Church is described in the Acts of the Apostles. The end of the Church Age is set forth in the Epistle of Jude, which might well be called the Acts of the Apostates. Jude is the only book in all God's Word entirely devoted to the great apostasy which is to come upon Christendom before the Lord Jesus Christ returns. This brief message of 25 verses is the vestibule to the Revelation . . . without Jude, the prophetic picture which begins with the teachings of Christ in the Gospels and develops throughout the epistles would be incomplete. (See Luke 18:8; 2 Thess. 2:3; 1 Tim. 4:1–2 Tim. 4:3; 2 Pet. 2:1; 3:3.) Jude brings the teachings of the entire Bible about apostasy to a tremendous climax. He takes us back to the very dawn of human history. We are reminded of apostasy at the gate of Eden and within God's ancient people Israel. Our thoughts are turned to princes and prophets, to saints and sinners, to eternal fire and everlasting darkness, to the sea and to the stars, to past judgments and future glory" (Dr. S. Maxwell Coder, *Jude, the Acts of the Apostates*, pp. 3-4).
F. Jude can be compared to 2 Peter.
   1. Both epistles give the marks of false teachers.
      a. See 2 Peter 2:1-3, 10-22.
      b. See Jude 4, 10-19.
   2. Peter placed the ministry of false teachers in the future (2:1), whereas Jude saw them as already present (v. 4).
   3. Both epistles refer to fallen angels (2 Pet. 2:4; Jude 6).
   4. Both mention Sodom and Gomorrah (2 Pet. 2:6; Jude 7).
   5. Both use Balaam as an example of apostasy (2 Pet. 2:15-16; Jude 11).
   6. Both liken apostasy to waterless clouds (2 Pet. 2:17; Jude 12)
G. Jude has been called the Judges of the New Testament.
H. Jude refers to two noncanonical books. These are:
   1. The Assumption of Moses (Jude 9)
   2. The book of Enoch (Jude 14-15)—Paul had previously also done this. (See Acts 17:28; Titus 1:12.)

I. "Jude was intending to write an epistle regarding 'our common salvation' (v. 3), when the Spirit detoured him to write concerning the apostasy. It is a graphic and striking description of the apostasy. What was a little cloud the size of a man's hand in Jude's day is, in our day, a storm of hurricane proportions—because we are in the apostasy of which he foretold. It is a question now of how much worse it can become before genuine believers are taken out by the Rapture" J. Vernon McGee (*Through the Bible*, p. 293).

J. It is the first of two New Testament books referring to Michael the archangel. Both deal with his encounter with Satan (Jude 9; Rev. 12:7).

K. The book of Jude is the only New Testament book to provide for us a sample of the kind of preaching preflood sinners once heard. (See Jude 14-15.)

L. Jude concludes his epistle with one of the New Testament's greatest doxologies. (See Jude 24-25.)

M. The epistle of Jude is the 24th longest New Testament book, and 63rd longest biblical book, with one chapter, 25 verses, and 613 words. There are quotations or allusions from eight Old Testament books in Jude.

N. Great passages would include:
   1. Jude 3
   2. Jude 20-23

THE BOOK OF JUDE

I. The Problem of Apostasy (Jude 1-4)
   A. Jude's commendation—"Jude, the servant of Jesus Christ, and brother of James, to them that are sanctified by God the Father, and preserved in Jesus Christ, and called: Mercy unto you, and peace and love, be multiplied" (Jude 1-2).

---

†v. 2

A. We note that neither Jude nor James, half brothers of Jesus, ever attempted in their epistles to "pull rank" by reminding their readers of that fact (see Matt. 13:55). In fact, to the contrary, both brothers refer to themselves as servants of Jesus Christ. (See James 1:1; Jude 1.)

B. The phrase "preserved in Jesus Christ" should be translated "kept for *Jesus Christ." It is used of Peter's and Paul's imprisonments in Acts 12:5 and 25:4, 21. (See also 1 Pet. 1:4.) Even before Jude warns about the terrible apostasy which had already settled down upon the world of his day and would grow progressively worse, he reassures the believers that they are kept for Christ. Here he supplies us with the inspired answer to the prayer of Christ: "Holy Father, keep through thine own name those whom thou hast given me" (John 17:11). (See also 1 Thess. 5:23.)*

C. Jude continues with: "Mercy unto you, and peace, and love, be multiplied" (v. 2). S. Maxwell Coder writes: "There is an upward *look in the word* mercy, *an* inward *look in the word* peace, *and an* outward *look in the word* love. *These three related us properly to* God, *to our* own inner being, *and to our* brethren *around us. When they are multiplied, and only then, will we be able to cope with the great apostasy"* (Jude, the Acts of the Apostates, *p. 13).*

B. Jude's compulsion—"Beloved, when I gave all diligence to write unto you of the common salvation, it was needful for me to write unto you, and exhort you that ye should earnestly contend for the faith which was once delivered unto the saints" (Jude 3).

---

†**v. 3**

A. The meaning of the word needful *is "to bear down upon, to compress." God literally pressured Jude to write this (see also 1 Cor. 9:16).*

B. He said we are to contend, but not be contentious. For the latter, see Titus 3:9. To contend *involves both defense and offense. An excellent Old Testament example of this is found in Nehemiah 4:17-18. Note also what we are to contend for. It is the* faith, *that is, the entire Word of God. Furthermore, this faith (in the Greek language) was once for all delivered unto the saints. John would later warn all not to* add to *or* take from *this faith (see Rev. 22:18-19).*

C. Jude's concern—"For there are certain men crept in unawares" (Jude 4).

---

†**v. 4** *The word "unawares" is literally "having settled down alongside." (See also 2 Pet. 2:1.)*

II. The Description of Apostasy

---

†*In no less than 14 terse and terrible terms, Jude describes the filthy fruit of apostasy. Before listing these, let us define what an apostate really is. S. Maxwell Coder writes: "An apostate has received light, but not life. He may have received, in some degree, the written Word; but he has not received the living Word, the Son of God." (See also 2 Thess. 2:10; Acts 8:13-23.)* (Jude, the Acts of the Apostates, *p. 21.)*

A. Apostates are ungodly (Jude 4).
B. Twisters of God's grace (Jude 4)
C. Christ deniers (Jude 4)
D. Sensuous (Jude 8)
E. Flesh defilers (Jude 8)
F. Despisers of authority (Jude 8)
G. Ignorant critics (Jude 10)
H. Unreasoning animals (Jude 10)
I. Immoral fault-finders (Jude 16)
J. Arrogant to the core (Jude 16)
K. Lying flatterers for personal gain (Jude 16)
L. Divisive (Jude 19)
M. Worldly minded (Jude 19)
N. Devoid of the Spirit (Jude 19)

III. Historical Example and Causes of Apostasy. (See also Num. 14:22-23,; Psa. 106:6-33; Heb. 3:8-19.)

A. The nation Israel, caused by unbelief—"I will therefore put you in remembrance, though ye once knew this, how that the Lord, having saved the people out of the land of Egypt, afterward destroyed them that believed not" (Jude 5).

---

†v. 5

A. *Question: When and where did this take place? It began at Kadesh-barnea shortly after Israel had left Egypt for Palestine. Here at Kadesh they were influenced by the "mixed multitude" (an unsaved group of Egyptians and non-Hebrews) who had left Egypt with them, causing them to rebel against God's Word.*

B. *Question: Does this mean that all the children of Israel became apostates, and, upon dying, went into eternal hell? It does not, for God never sends his people to hell. (See Exod. 3:7; 5:1; Deut. 33:29.) What it does mean is that it is tragically possible for even believers to become ensnared into the trap of apostasy and suffer for it without actually becoming apostates themselves. (See also 1 Cor. 10:1-12; Heb. 3:12, 18-19; 4:1.) The word* apollumi, *translated "destroyed" in this verse, is used elsewhere as "physical death" (Luke 15:17).*

B. The fallen angels, caused by disloyalty. (See also Gen. 6:1-4; 1 Pet. 3:18-20; 2 Pet. 2:4; Rev. 12:3-4.)

C. The citizens of Sodom and Gomorrah, caused by sexual perversion. (See Gen. 13:13; 18:20-21; 19:4-13; 2 Pet. 2:6.) "Even as Sodom and Gomorrha, and the cities about them in like manner, giving themselves over to fornication, and going after strange flesh, are set forth for an example, suffering the vengeance of eternal fire" (Jude 7).

---

†v. 7 *Some of the most depraved sexual perverts of ancient times lived in Sodom. God destroyed this cesspool of sin in Genesis 19. Let us now go back to the wicked angels of verse 6, for a similarity may exist between their sin and that of Sodom. Here we must consider two things:*

A. *The fact of their sin—The Scriptures are explicit that there exist two kinds of fallen angels, the unchained and those chained. The unchained at present have access to high places and to the bodies of the unsaved (Eph. 6:12; Luke 8:27; Mark 1:23). These unchained angels will, of course, someday be judged by God. Their one main sin was that of following Satan in his foul rebellion against God (1 Cor. 6:3; Isa. 14:12-17; Ezek. 28:12-19). The chained are at present already incarcerated, as stated by both Peter (2 Pet. 2:4) and Jude. It was apparently to this place that certain unchained fallen angels on two separate occasions begged Christ not to send them "before their time" (Mark 1:24; Luke 8:31; Matt. 8:28).*

B. *The nature of their sin. It is believed that the sin which led to this premature punishment of a limited number of fallen angels can be directly linked to Genesis 6. It will be remembered that in this chapter we read of the "sons of God'" marrying the "daughters of men." Many believe this to be a reference to fallen angels (sons of God) actually mating with earthly women (daughters of men). Dr. Kenneth Wuest, Greek scholar, brings out the fact that the words in Jude "in like manner" are an adverbial accusative, referring back to the phrase "giving themselves over to fornication." In other words, the comparison is made between the sin of Sodom and the sin of the angels. What was the sin of Sodom? The answer, of course, was the sexual perversion. Wuest writes: "The word 'strange' is the translation of the Greek word* heteras *which means 'another of a different kind.' In committing this sin of fornication, the angels transgressed the limits of their own kind, and invaded the realm of another order of being. The sin of Sodom was the transgressing of the male beyond the limitations imposed by God"* (Word Studies in First Peter, *p. 103).*

C. *One final thought concerning this passage and this subject. Jude is admonishing his readers to remember three well-known Old Testament examples of apostasy. These were:*
   1. *The historical example of Israel's unbelief*
   2. *The historical example of those angels who kept not their first estate*
   3. *The historical example of Sodom's destruction*

D. *Concerning the first example, the minds of Jude's readers would immediately go back to Numbers 14, the account of Israel's great rebellion at Kadesh-barnea. As they read the third example, they would at once remember the frightful passage recorded in Genesis 19, the fiery destruction of Sodom on the plains. But what other chapter would come to mind concerning the second historical example if Genesis 6 is ruled out? Note: At this point we have described for us representatives of each of the three great classes of God's creatures mentioned in Scripture:*
   1. *Saved people*
   2. *Angels*
   3. *Unsaved people*

D. The devil, caused by pride and self-will. (See Isa. 14:12-15; Ezek. 28:11-19.) "Yet Michael the archangel, when contending with the devil he disputed about the body of Moses, durst not bring against him a railing accusation, but said, The Lord rebuke thee" (Jude 9).

---

†**v. 9** *In this passage Satan is indirectly brought in as an apostate.*

A. *The source of this statement—It appears to have been quoted from a first-century book entitled* The Assumption of Moses. *A copy of this was found in 1861. This, of course, does not mean that the entire book was inspired simply because Jude takes one little part from it. Paul quoted from Titus 1:12. He also mentions the name of two of the magicians in Egypt, although their names are not mentioned in the Old Testament (2 Tim. 3:8). James also tells us that Elijah's prayer caused a three-and-a-half-year drought, a fact not recorded in the Old Testament account (James 5:17 cf. 1 Kings 17:1; 18:1).*

B. *The theology of this statement—Why did Satan desire Moses' body?* The Assumption of Moses *gives two reasons why Moses should not have a decent burial.*
   1. *Because Moses had formerly murdered an Egyptian.*
   2. *Because he (Satan) was king of death and had a right to all dead bodies. Two other reasons have been offered by church theologians to explain this, both of which seem more reasonable than the above two.*
   3. *Because Satan wanted the body to be found by Israel and worshiped as a sacred relic—We do know that the nation would later worship the serpent of brass he had once made (2 Kings 18:4).*
   4. *Because Satan desired to keep Moses from appearing with Elijah on the Mount of Transfiguration (Matt. 17).*

C. *The hero of this statement—In Deuteronomy 34:5-6 we read, "So Moses, the servant of the Lord, died there in the land of Moab, according to the word of the Lord. And he buried him in a valley in the land of Moab . . . but no man knoweth of his sepulchre unto this day." Apparently the "he" in this verse is reference to the archangel Michael, the hero of this statement. He is mentioned three times in the Old Testament (Dan. 10:13, 21; 12:1), and again in the New Testament, in addition to the reference in Jude (Rev. 12:7-9).*

E. Cain, caused by religious perversion (see Gen. 4:1-8; 1 John 3:12)—"Woe unto them! for they have gone in the way of Cain" (Jude 11).

†**v. 11a** *The way (apostasy) of Cain is described in Genesis 4:1-7. He brought a bloodless sacrifice to God. That is the way of the apostate liberals of our day. They look to culture instead of Calvary. (See 1 John 3:11-12.)*

F. Balaam, caused by greed for money (see Num. 22:15-17)—"And ran greedily after the error of Balaam for reward" (Jude 11).

†**v. 11b** *Balaam was a money-grabbing false prophet mentioned in Numbers 22–25. Thus the error of Balaam was making merchandise of the gospel ministry. Many modern apostates do this.*

G. Korah, caused by rejection of divine authority (see Num. 16:1-3)—"And perished in the gainsaying of Core" (Jude 1:11).

†**v. 11c** *In Numbers 16, Korah (Core) led a rebellion against Moses, the official spokesman for God. For this great sin he was sent down into the pit, the earth opening up its bowels and swallowing him. Present-day apostates speak evil against pastors, missionaries, Bible teachers, and other God-appointed men. In summarizing this section, note the words of S. Maxwell Coder: "Cain was a tiller of the soil; Balaam was a prophet; Korah was a prince in Israel. One reason for this selection of three men may be to demonstrate that apostasy is not confined to one class of person. This evil is not peculiar to religious leaders. It touches prophets, princes, and people alike. There are apostates in pulpit, palace, and poorhouse"* (Jude, the Acts of the Apostates, *p. 66).*

IV. The Metaphors of Apostasy (Jude 12-13)

†*"The more minutely we examine this great epistle, the most impressive becomes its delineation of the doctrine of apostasy. Jude has now covered the whole creation, from angels to men and brute beasts. There yet remains the realm of nature, and in five flashing inspired word-pictures he brings before us the earth, the air, the trees, the sea, and the starry heavens, to complete the panorama needed to provide the church with a magnificent final summary of conditions as they are to be in Christendom just before the scenes of Revelation are unveiled"* (Jude, the Acts of the Apostates, *p. 75).*

A. Hidden rocks—"These men are those who are hidden reefs in your love-feasts when they feast with you without fear, caring for themselves" (Jude 12, NASB). This describes the unseen dangers of apostasy.

†**v. 12a** *We note that these rocks are hidden in the Christian love-feasts, a reference to the Lord's table in the early days of the church. How are we to understand this? Paul explains it in 1 Corinthians 11:17-30. The first-century church had a full meal in connection with the Holy Communion. But some of these apostates (or perhaps believers influenced by apostasy) had joined themselves to these*

gatherings. As a result, some practiced gluttony and drunkenness, while others were actually going hungry. Divine judgment had taken many in death due to this.

B. Waterless clouds—"Clouds they are without water, carried about of winds" (Jude 12). This describes the false claims of apostasy.

---

†v. 12b *See also Proverbs 25:14. These clouds are said to be carried along by the winds. Doubtless the "winds" here are demonic activity. Apostates are the captives of Satan. For a refreshing contrast, see 2 Peter 1:21.*

C. Dead autumn trees—"Autumn trees without fruit, doubly dead, uprooted" (Jude 12, NASB). This describes the wasted efforts of apostasy.

---

†v. 12c *The Greek phrase here is literally "late autumn trees," suggesting the fact that the great apostasy is to come as the autumn of the Church Age is waning and the winter of judgment is nigh. (See also Matt. 13:30; 15:30; Prov. 2:22.)*

D. Wandering stars—"Wandering stars, to whom is reserved the blackness of darkness forever" (Jude 13). This describes the aimless purpose of apostasy.

---

†v. 13a *This is perhaps both the most descriptive and horrifying characteristic of apostasy. A quote from S. Maxwell Coder is appropriate here: "By way of contrast, true believers enjoy a lifelong love-feast. They are borne along by the Holy Spirit, unmoved by winds of false doctrine. After a life of fruitfulness, they go home to be with Christ, in glory and honor. Forever afterward they dwell in light unutterable. Instead of being lifeless, dangerous rocks, they are living stones (1 Pet. 2:5). Rather than waterless clouds they are sources of living water (John 7:38). Far from being dead trees, they are called 'trees of righteousness, the planting of the LORD' (Isa. 61:3). In contrast with raging waves, their peace is like a river and their righteousness as the waves of the sea (Isa. 48:18). Whereas wandering stars have reserved for them the blackness of darkness forever, true believers shall shine as the stars forever and ever" (Dan. 12:3)* (Jude, the Acts of the Apostates, *pp. 82-83).*

V. The Judgment upon Apostasy (Jude 14-15)
   A. The messenger—"And Enoch also, the seventh from Adam, prophesied of these, saying" (Jude 14).
   B. The message—"Behold, the Lord cometh with ten thousands of his saints, to execute judgment upon all, and to convince all that are ungodly among them of all their ungodly deeds which they have ungodly committed, and all of their hard speeches which ungodly sinners have spoken against him" (Jude 14-15).

---

†v. 15

A. The source of this statement—Around 100 B.C., a noncanonical book entitled The Book of Enoch was written. It contained 108 chapters. In 1773 a copy of this work was discovered. The Apostle Jude was inspired by God to take the words which are found here in verses 14-15 from this book.

B. The speaker of this statement—The book, of course, was not written by Enoch, but the statement here was apparently taken from his text. Both Enoch and Noah were fearless preachers of prophecy and righteousness. (See also 2 Pet. 2:5.) The amazing faith of this preflood prophet may be seen in that he predicted the second coming of Christ centuries before our Lord came the first time. Enoch thus predicts his coming in Genesis, while John proclaims it in Revelation (see Rev. 19:11-14). Both men refer to the same event.
1. He comes with his saints (Col. 3:4; 1 Thess. 3:13).
2. He comes to judge (Heb. 9:26-28; 2 Pet. 3:7).

VI. The Safeguards against Apostasy (Jude 20-25)
A. The believer and himself
1. He is to build on the Word of God—"But ye, beloved, building up yourselves on your most holy faith" (Jude 20).
2. He is to pray with the Spirit of God—"Praying in the Holy Ghost" (Jude 20).
3. He is to keep in the love of God—"Keep yourselves in the love of God" (Jude 21).

---

†v. 21a *In verse 1 Jude tells us we are kept for Jesus, but here he says we are to keep in God's love. How is this done? While the believer cannot escape the boundary of God's love (Psa. 139:7-12), he can withdraw himself from the full blessings of this love (John 15:9).*

---

4. He is to look for the return of God—"Looking for the mercy of our Lord Jesus Christ unto eternal life" (Jude 21).
5. He is to testify to the glory of God—"To the only wise God our Saviour, be glory and majesty, dominion and power, both now and ever. Amen" (Jude 25).

B. The believer and the lost
1. Concerning those in great doubt—"And have mercy on some, who are doubting" (Jude 22, NASB).
2. Concerning those who are in great danger—"Save others, snatching them out of the fire" (Jude 23, NASB).
3. Concerning those who are in great depravity—"And on some have mercy with fear, hating even the garment polluted by the flesh" (Jude 23, NASB).

---

†v. 23 *S. Maxwell Coder writes: "In a brief manual for personal work, three groups of people are set before us:*
A. Those who need compassionate tenderness, because sincere doubts trouble them.
B. Those requiring urgent boldness if they are to be snatched from an eternity of fiery judgment.
C. Those who must be dealt with in cautious compassion lest the soul winner himself be contaminated by their sins" (Jude, the Acts of the Apostates, *p. 113.)*

C. The believer and the Lord
1. What he does for us now—"Now unto him that is able to keep you from falling" (Jude 24).
2. What he will do for us later—"And to present you faultless before the presence of his glory with exceeding joy" (Jude 24).

REVELATION

THE STORY HAS A HAPPY ENDING—THE BRIDEGROOM AND THE BRIDE ARE MARRIED AND LIVE HAPPILY IN A BEAUTIFUL CITY FOREVER.

A. Revelation is the only prophetical book in the New Testament (in contrast to 17 books in the Old Testament).

B. Revelation is the only book in all the Bible that begins by promising a special blessing on those who study it, and ends by promising a special curse on those who add to or take away from it.

C. It was written by the Apostle John, who had already written four other New Testament books. They are: the Gospel of John, 1 John, 2 John, 3 John. The author had previously reached farther back into eternity than any other Bible writer (see John 1:1-3). In Revelation he reaches farther on into eternity than any other writer (see Rev. 21–22).

D. Revelation may be compared to the book of *Daniel.*

1. Concerning the indestructible Jewish nation (Dan. 3, 6; cf. Rev. 12).
2. Concerning the ministry of the Antichrist (Dan. 3:1-7; 7:7-8, 24-25; 8:9-12, 23-25; 9:27; 11:36-45; cf. Rev. 13).
3. Concerning the length of the tribulation (Dan. 9:24-27; cf. Rev. 11:2; 12:6, 14; 13:5). Note, however, that Daniel was a sealed book (Dan. 12:9), whereas Revelation is not (Rev. 22:10).

E. Revelation may be compared to the book of *Genesis*.

1. In Genesis we read: "In the beginning God created the heaven and the earth" (1:1). In Revelation we read: "I saw a new heaven and a new earth" (21:1).
2. In Genesis we see described the *first Adam* with his wife Eve in the Garden of Eden, reigning over the earth (1:27-28). In Revelation we see described the *last Adam* with his wife, the church, in the City of God, reigning over all the universe (21:9).
3. In Genesis we are told: "And the gathering together of the waters called he Seas" (1:10). In Revelation we are told: "and there was no more sea" (21:1).
4. In Genesis God created the sun and moon, the day and the night (1:5-16). In Revelation "There shall be no night there" (22:5). "And the city had no need of the sun, neither of the moon, to shine in it: for the glory of God did lighten it, and the Lamb is the light thereof" (21:23).
5. In Genesis the Tree of Life is denied to sinful humans (3:22). In Revelation the Tree of Life "yielded her fruit every month: and the leaves of the tree were for the healing of the nations" (22:2).
6. In Genesis people hear God say: "Cursed is the ground for thy sake" (3:17). In Revelation people will hear God say: "And there shall be no more curse" (22:3).
7. In Genesis Satan appears to torment human beings (3:1). In Revelation Satan disappears, himself to be tormented forever (20:10).
8. In Genesis the old earth was punished through a flood (7:12). In Revelation the new earth shall be purified through a fire (2 Pet. 3:6-12; Rev. 21:1).

9. In Genesis man's early home was beside a river (2:10). In Revelation our eternal home will be beside a river—"And he shewed me a pure river of water of life, clear as crystal, proceeding out of the throne of God and of the Lamb" (22:1).
10. In Genesis the patriarch Abraham weeps for Sarah (23:2). In Revelation the children of Abraham will have God himself wipe away all tears from their eyes (21:4).
11. In Genesis God destroys an earthly city, wicked Sodom, from the sands (chapter 19). In Revelation, God presents a heavenly city, New Jerusalem, from the skies (21:1).
12. Genesis ends with a believer in Egypt, lying in a coffin (50:1-3). Revelation ends with all believers in eternity, reigning forever (22:5).

F. J. Vernon McGee writes: "This book is like a great union station where the great trunk lines of prophecy come in from other portions of Scripture. Revelation does not originate, but consummates. It is imperative to a right understanding of the book to be able to trace each great subject of prophecy from the first reference to the terminal" (*Reveling Through Revelation*, p. 4).

G. Some of the great subjects of prophecy that find their consummation here are:
1. The Lord Jesus Christ (Gen. 3:15; cf. Rev. 1:13; 12:5)
2. The church (Matt. 16:18; cf. Rev. 19:7-9)
3. The resurrection of saints (Dan. 12:2-3; 1 Thess. 4:13-18; 1 Cor. 15:51-52; Rev. 20:4-6)
4. The great tribulation (Deut. 4:30-31; Isa. 24; cf. Rev. 6–18)
5. Satan (Isa. 14:12-15; Ezek. 28:11-19; cf. Rev. 20:1-10)
6. The man of sin (2 Thess. 2:1-12; cf. Rev. 19:19-21)
7. False religion (Gen. 11:1-9; Matt. 13; cf. Rev. 17)
8. The times of the Gentiles (Dan. 2:37; Luke 21:23; cf. Rev. 18)
9. The second coming of Christ (Jude 14-15; cf. Rev. 19:11-16)

H. There are at least four main interpretations to this last book in the Bible:
1. It is pure fiction—This is the view of the agnostics.
2. It is allegorical—This says no part of the book may be taken literally. It is simply a symbolic account of the agelong struggle between good and evil. This is the view of most liberals.
3. It is historical—Here two kinds of history are in mind.
   a. Past history—This is often called the preterist theory. "Preterist" is from a Latin word that means "past." Dr. Charles Ryrie writes: "Thus, the preterist interpreters are those who see Revelation as having already been fulfilled in the early history of the church. Chapters 5–11 are said to record the church's victory over Judaism; chapters 12–19 her victory over pagan Rome; and 20–22 her glory because of these victories. The persecutions described are those of Nero and Domitian, and the entire book was fulfilled by the time of Constantine (A.D. 312)" (*Revelation*, p. 8).
   b. Continuous history—Again to quote Ryrie: "This interpretative viewpoint states that in Revelation there is a panorama of the history of the church from the days of John to the end of the age. It holds that the book has been in the process of being fulfilled throughout the whole Christian era. Those who hold this view see in the symbols the rise of papacy, the corruption of the church and the various wars throughout church history. Most of the reformers interpreted the book in this manner" (*Revelation*, pp. 8-9).

4. It is prophetical—This view sees those events from chapter 4 onward as yet to be fulfilled. This view alone does justice to the book. Revelation, like all other books in the Bible, is to be taken in the plain, normal sense of the words. To do otherwise is to dishonor Christ, the divine Author. Dr. David L. Cooper once suggested: "When the plain sense of Scripture makes common sense, seek no other sense."

I. This book lists more titles for the Savior than does any other book in the Bible. Note but some of them:
1. Jesus Christ (1:1)
2. The faithful witness (1:5)
3. The first begotten of the dead (1:5)
4. The Prince of kings of the earth (1:5)
5. The Alpha and Omega (1:8)
6. The first and the last (1:8)
7. The Son of man (1:13)
8. The Son of God (2:18)
9. The keeper of David's keys (3:7)
10. The keeper of the keys of hell and death (1:18)
11. The Lion of the tribe of Judah (5:5)
12. The Root of David (5:5)
13. The slain Lamb (5:6)
14. The angry Lamb (6:16-17)
15. The tender Lamb (7:17)
16. Our Lord (11:8)
17. The man child (12:5)
18. The King of saints (15:3)
19. The faithful and true (19:11)
20. The Word of God (19:13)
21. The King of kings (19:16)
22. The Lord of lords (19:16)
23. The beginning and the end (22:13)
24. The bright and morning Star (22:16)

J. The numbers seven and 12 are predominant in the book of Revelation.
1. The number seven
   a. Seven spirits (1:4)
   b. Seven stars (1:16)
   c. Seven lamps (4:5)
   d. Seven seals (5:1)
   e. Seven horns (5:6)
   f. Seven eyes (5:6)
   g. Seven angels (8:2)
   h. Seven trumpets (8:2)
   i. Seven thunders (10:3)
   j. Seven heads (12:3)
   k. Seven crowns (12:3)
   l. Seven plagues (15:1)
   m. Seven vials (17:1)
   n. Seven mountains (17:9)

o. Seven kings (17:10)

2. The number 12
   a. 12,000 from each of the 12 tribes (7:4-8)
   b. A crown of 12 stars (12:1)
   c. 12 gates (21:12)
   d. 12 angels (21:12)
   e. 12 foundations (21:14)
   f. 12,000 furlongs (21:16)

K. In essence, the book of Revelation contains:

1. The last of three New Testament passages describing Balaam, the false prophet of the Old Testament (see Num. 22–25)—*Peter* speaks of the way of Balaam (2 Pet. 2:15). *Jude* speaks of the error of Balaam (Jude 11); *Revelation* speaks of the doctrine of Balaam (Rev. 2:14).
2. The most detailed description of the ascended Christ in the Bible (1:9-20)
3. The last words of Christ to his churches (Rev. 2–3)
4. The most vivid description of heaven in all Scripture (Rev. 4–5; 21–22)
5. The only description of four specialized angelic creatures (4:6-8)
6. The most detailed account of heaven's activities (Rev. 4–5; 8:1-5; 11:19; 15:1-8; 19:1-10)
7. The greatest prayer meeting of the unsaved in history (6:15-17)
8. History's most severe judgments (chapters 6, 8, 10, 16)
9. The only New Testament listing of Israel's 12 tribes (7:4-8)
10. The world's greatest revival (7:9-17)
11. The only description of demons in the Bible (chapter 9)
12. The most descriptive account of the age-old battle between Satan and Israel (chapter 12)
13. The only biblical book to describe both the Antichrist and his false prophet (chapter 13)
14. The only biblical book to record the preaching of angels (14:6-7)
15. Scripture's most frightening descriptions of hell (14:10-11)
16. The most vivid account of Armageddon and the second coming (14:14-20; 16:16-21; 19:11-21)
17. The world's greatest earthquake and hailstorm (16:18-21)
18. The only biblical book to distinguish between the two Babylons:
    a. Religious Babylon is described in chapter 17.
    b. Political Babylon is described in chapter 18.
19. The only biblical book that gives the actual duration of the millennium (20:5)
20. The most detailed description of the great white throne judgment (20:11-15)
21. The most Old Testament quotations and allusions of any New Testament book
22. The last of three attempts by Satan to consolidate his religious system around a project:
    a. First attempt—A tower in Shinar (Gen. 11)
    b. Second attempt—A statue in Babylon (Dan. 3)
    c. Final attempt—A statue in the temple (Rev. 13)
23. It is the second of two biblical books offering a description of the Father (Dan. 7:9-10; Rev. 4:2-3).
24. It is the only biblical book to use that greatest of all praise words, Alleluia. (See 19:1, 3-4, 6.)

25. It is the only biblical book given almost in its entirety by vision form.
26. It is the only biblical book written from a small island (1:9).

L. The book of Revelation is the sixth longest New Testament book, and 24th longest biblical book, with 22 chapters, 404 verses, and 12,000 words. There are quotations or allusions from 32 Old Testament books in Revelation.

M. Great passages would include:
1. 1:5-8
2. 2:2-5
3. 3:2-3
4. 3:8-12
5. 3:20-21
6. 4:8-11
7. 5:9-13
8. 7:13-17
9. 11:15-18
10. 12:10-11
11. 15:3-4
12. 19:6-9
13. 19:11-16
14. 20:11-15
15. 21:1-4
16. 21:23-27
17. 22:1-4
18. 22:12-14
19. 22:16-17

THE BOOK OF REVELATION

PART ONE: The Witnesses of the Lamb Instructed (Rev. 1–3)

I. The Servant of God (Rev. 1:1-10)—A heavenly message was revealed to a man on a lonely island some 20 centuries ago.
  A. The source of the message—"The Revelation of Jesus Christ, which God gave unto him . . . and he sent and signified it by his angel" (Rev. 1:1).
  B. The recorder of the message—"Unto his servant John: who bare record of the word of God, and of the testimony of Jesus Christ, and of all things that he saw" (Rev. 1:1b-2).
  C. The nature of the message—"To shew unto his servants things which must shortly come to pass" (Rev. 1:1).
  D. The promise of the message—"Blessed is he that readeth, and they that hear the words of this prophecy, and keep those things which are written therein: for the time is at hand" (Rev. 1:3).

---

†1:3

A. This is the first of seven beatitudes in Revelation. See also:
  1. Revelation 14:13—"Blessed are the dead which die in the Lord."

2. Revelation 16:15—"Blessed is he that watcheth."
3. Revelation 19:9—"Blessed are they which are called unto the marriage supper of the Lamb."
4. Revelation 20:6—"Blessed . . . is he that hath part in the first resurrection."
5. Revelation 22:7—"Blessed is he that keepeth the sayings . . . of this book."
6. Revelation 22:14—"Blessed are they that do his commandments."

B. Note the phrase, "for the time is at hand." Here the word is not chronos *(regular word for clock-time) but* kairos, *referring to a fixed season. This "fixed season" is that described by Daniel in 9:24-27. Someday a group of Jews will be able to rightly conclude by comparing both Daniel and Revelation, that this "fixed, determined season" is indeed at their very doorsteps.*

C. In addition to this, God is desirous to "shew unto his servants things which must shortly be done" (22:6b)—as God records time. See 2 Peter 3:9; Romans 16:20 (1:1). The word "shortly" can also mean rapidly. Note the following verses which reveal God's desire to lift back the curtain of the future for his saints.

1. "Surely the Lord GOD will do nothing but he revealeth his secret unto his servants" (Amos 3:7).
2. "But there is a God in heaven that revealeth secrets" (Dan. 2:28).
3. "I thank thee, O Father, Lord of heaven and earth, because thou hast hid these things from the wise and prudent, and hast revealed them unto babes" (Matt. 11:25).
4. "Unto you it is given to know the mysteries of the kingdom of God" (Luke 8:10).

E. The recipients of the message—"To the seven churches which are in Asia" (Rev. 1:4)

F. The greetings in the message
1. From the Father—"Grace be unto you, and peace, from him which is, and which was, and which is to come" (Rev. 1:4).
2. From the seven Spirits (or, sevenfold spirit, a possible reference to the Holy Spirit and his perfection) (Rev. 1:4).
3. From the Son—"And from Jesus Christ" (Rev. 1:5)

G. The theme of the message—Jesus Christ.
1. Who he is—"Who is the faithful witness, and the first begotten of the dead, and the prince of the kings of the earth" (Rev. 1:5a).
2. What he has done—"Unto him that loved us, and washed us from our sins in his own blood, and hath made us kings and priests unto God and his Father; to him be glory and dominion for ever and ever. Amen" (Rev. 1:5b-6).
3. What he shall do—"Behold, he cometh with clouds; and every eye shall see him, and they also which pierced him: and all kindreds of the earth shall wail because of him. Even so, Amen" (Rev. 1:7).

H. The authority behind the message—"I am Alpha and Omega, the beginning and the ending, saith the Lord, which is, and which was, and which is to come, the Almighty" (Rev. 1:8).

I. The place of the message—"I John, who also am your brother, and companion in tribulation, and in the kingdom and patience of Jesus Christ, was in the isle that is called Patmos, for the word of God, and for the testimony of Jesus Christ" (Rev. 1:9).

---

†1:9

A. John now explains why he was on this isle. He was exiled there from about A.D. *86 to 96. Patmos was a rugged, volcanic island off the coast of Asia Minor. It was about ten miles long and six miles wide. He was probably put there by the Roman Emperor Domitian. Domitian was the brother of Titus (who destroyed the city of Jerusalem). Thus, God allowed one pagan to destroy his earthly city, but would use his brother to allow the heavenly new Jerusalem to first be described to humans. Marvelous and mysterious indeed are the workings of grace.*

B. John speaks of being in tribulation. There were at least four reasons why Rome persecuted Christians:

1. For political purposes—The Christian took no part in the pantheon (worship of many gods). In fact, Christians were regarded as atheists, for they worshiped no visible God.

2. For economic purposes—No money or sacrifices were forthcoming from believers to Roman idols.

3. For "moral" purposes—Christians were often looked upon as cannibals, for did they not secretly "eat the flesh and drink the blood" of their religious founder?

4. For scapegoat purposes—Nero attempted to blame various state problems upon the Christians living in Rome.

J. The day of the message—"I was in the Spirit on the Lord's day, and heard behind me a great voice, as of a trumpet," (Rev. 1:10).

---

†1:10

A. The time involved—"The Lord's day." This was probably on a Sunday (see Matt. 28:1; Acts 20:7; 1 Cor. 16:1-2).

B. The trumpet involved—The trumpet call is heard many more times in this book (see 4:1; 8:2, 7-8, 10, 12; 9:1, 13; 11:15).

II. The Son of God (Rev. 1:11-20)

A. The designation—"Saying, I am Alpha and Omega, the first and the last: and, What thou seest, write in a book, and send it unto the seven churches which are in Asia; unto Ephesus, and unto Smyrna, and unto Pergamos, and unto Thyatira, and unto Sardis, and unto Philadelphia, and unto Laodicea" (Rev. 1:11).

B. The description—"And I turned to see the voice that spake with me. And being turned, I saw seven golden candlesticks; and in the midst of the seven candlesticks one like unto the Son of man, clothed with a garment down to the foot, and girt about the paps with a golden girdle. His head and his hairs were white like wool, as white as snow; and his eyes were as a flame of fire; and his feet like unto fine brass, as if they burned in a furnace; and his voice as the sound of many waters. And he had in his right hand seven stars: and out of his mouth went a sharp twoedged sword: and his countenance was as the sun shineth in his strength" (Rev. 1:12-16).

---

†1:16 *This is the only detailed description of the ascended Christ in the entire New Testament.*

C. The devastation—"And when I saw him, I fell at his feet as dead. And he laid his right hand upon me, saying unto me, Fear not; I am the first and the last" (Rev. 1:17).

†1:17 *The effect of this dazzling sight upon John was nothing less than paralyzing. John had once walked with Christ for three years. He had witnessed his miracles and heard his sermons. He had leaned upon his breast in the Upper Room and watched him die on the cross. Finally he had rejoiced in his resurrection and viewed his ascension. But that had all happened some 60 years before. Now, he sees the resplendent Redeemer in all his blinding brightness and drops at his feet as though dead. John became struck as by the sun. But John's loving Lord quickly performed that tender task the apostle had so often seen him do. He reached out and touched the one in need. Compare Revelation 1:17 with the following Gospel accounts:*

A. Matthew 8:14-5—"And when Jesus was come into Peter's house, he saw his wife's mother laid, and sick of a fever. And he touched her hand, and the fever left her."

B. Matthew 9:27-30a—"Two blind men followed him saying and crying, Thou Son of David, have mercy on us . . . then touched he their eyes . . . and their eyes were opened."

C. Matthew 17:7—"And Jesus came and touched them [Peter, James, and John, who became terrified after watching his transfiguration on a mountain] and said, Arise, and be not afraid."

D. John 9:6—"He spat on the ground and he anointed the eyes of the blind man."

E. Luke 5:12-13—"And it came to pass when he was in a certain city, behold a man full of leprosy: who seeing Jesus fell on his face and besought him saying, Lord, if thou wilt, thou canst make me clean. And he put forth his hand and touched him."

F. Luke 7:14—"And he came and touched the bier [of the widow's dead son in Nain] . . . and said, Young man, I say unto thee, arise."

G. Luke 22:51—"And he touched his ear [of one of his enemies whom Peter had wounded in the garden] and healed him."

D. The declaration—"I am he that liveth, and was dead; and, behold, I am alive for evermore, Amen; and have the keys of hell and of death" (Rev. 1:18).

---

†1:18

A. Jesus assures John that "I am alive!" The real symbol of Christianity is not the cross, but the empty tomb. History relates the account of Julian the apostate, a nephew of the Roman Caesar Constantine. Julian was reared in a Christian home. But in his youth he renounced his faith and embraced paganism. When he became Emperor in A.D. 361, he sought to blot out Christianity. In the days of his cruel reign, one of his cronies said to a humble Christian, "And your Jesus—what is your carpenter of Nazareth doing now?" The Spirit-filled believer quietly replied, "He is building a coffin for your emperor!" In 363, after he had reigned but two years, Julian died on the battlefield, facing a Persian army. One of the most famous incidents of history then followed. As they carried the Emperor off the field and as he lay dying, he lifted up his dimming eyes to heaven, and with a gasp, cried out, "O Galilean, thou hast conquered at last!"

B. Jesus furthermore assures John that, "I have the keys of hell and of death." There are five keys mentioned in the New Testament and our Lord carries them all. The other four are:

1. The keys of the kingdom (Matt. 16:19)

2. The key of knowledge (Luke 11:52)

3. The key of the throne of David (Rev. 3:7)

4. The key to the bottomless pit (Rev. 9:1; 20:1)

E. The dictation—"Write the things which thou hast seen, and the things which are, and the things which shall be hereafter" (Rev. 1:19).

†1:19

A. This is the first of at least 11 instances where John is commanded to write down something.
- *1. He was to write concerning the seven churches in Asia Minor (2:1, 8, 12, 18; 3:1, 7, 14).*
- *2. He was to write concerning the martyred dead (14:13).*
- *3. He was to write concerning the marriage supper of the Lamb (19:9).*
- *4. He was to write concerning the New Jerusalem (21:5).*

B. On one occasion, however, he was commanded not to write down what he had seen and heard (see 10:4).

F. The delineation—"The mystery of the seven stars which thou sawest in my right hand, and the seven golden candlesticks. The seven stars are the angels of the seven churches: and the seven candlesticks which thou sawest are the seven churches" (Rev. 1:20)

---

†1:20

A. The seven stars were the angels of the seven churches. J. Vernon McGee writes: "Angels can be either human or divine—the word here is messenger. *It could refer to a member of the angelic host of heaven; it could refer to a ruler or teacher of the congregation. Personally, I think that it refers to the local pastors. It is good to hear a pastor being called an angel—sometimes we are called other things!"* (Reveling Through Revelation, *p. 1.).*

B. The seven lampstands were seven specific churches. Upon hearing this, John could understand why he saw Christ dressed the way he was. He is now appearing as our great High Priest. The golden lampstands speak of his present work in heaven in maintaining the lights. Aaron lighted the lamps in the tabernacle, put them out with snuffers, filled them with oil, and trimmed the wicks. Christ now does this with his present lights, which are the local churches.

III. The Churches of God (Rev. 2–3)

---

†*At the time Revelation was written (around* A.D. *95–100) there may have existed well over 100 separate and independent local churches in the world. Paul had, of course, personally planted dozens of churches by himself. Other apostles would doubtless have done the same thing. But out of the many, Christ chose seven representative churches and addressed himself to these. It has been suggested that the listing of these seven appears in the sacred record to accomplish at least the following purposes:*

A. The contemporary purpose—That Christ had a direct message to seven literal churches existing at that time.

B. The composite purpose—That these messages are meant to be applied by all churches existing in all ages.

C. The chronological purpose—That the characteristics of these churches serve as a prophetical preview of the seven great periods in Christendom from Pentecost to the Rapture. A suggested outline of this predictive panorama may be seen as follows:
- *1. Ephesus (*A.D. *30–300)—Name means "desirable": The Apostolic church*
- *2. Smyrna (100–313)—Name means "myrrh": The martyr church*
- *3. Pergamos (314–590)—Name means "marriage": The compromising church*
- *4. Thyatira (590–1517)—Name means "continual sacrifice": The Roman Catholic church*

5. Sardis (1517–1700)—Name means "remnant": The Reformation church
6. Philadelphia (1700–1900)—Name means "brotherly love": The revival church
7. Laodicea (1900–Rapture)—Name means "people's rights": The worldly church

In Revelation 2–3, the Savior speaks his mind to his churches. It is therefore in these chapters (and not in Matt. 28 or Acts 1) that the final words of Christ to the church are recorded.

A. The church at Ephesus (Rev. 2:1-7)

---

†*J. Vernon McGee describes Ephesus for us: "Ephesus was the chief city of the province of Asia. It was called 'the Vanity Fair of Asia.' It was both the religious and commercial center of that entire area which influenced both east and west—Europe and Asia. The temple of Diana was there, which was one of the seven wonders of the ancient world, being the largest Greek temple ever constructed (418 feet by 240 feet). There were over 100 external columns about 56 feet in height, of which 36 were hand-carved. It was built over a marsh on an artificial foundation of skins and charcoal so that it was not affected by earthquakes. The doors were of cypress wood; columns and walls were of Parian marble; the staircase was carved out of one vine from Cyprus. The temple served as the bank of Asia and was the depository of vast sums of money. It was an art gallery displaying the masterpieces. . . . Behind a purple curtain was the lewd and crude image of Diana, the goddess of fertility. She was many-breasted, carried a club in one hand and a trident in the other"* (Reveling Through Revelation, *p. 19). Ephesus was a large city with a population of 225,000 and possessed a huge harbor.*

---

1. The counselor (what Jesus says about himself)—"Unto the angel of the church of Ephesus write; these things saith he that holdeth the seven stars in his right hand, who walketh in the midst of the seven golden candlesticks" (Rev. 2:1).
2. The commendation (the good things he says about the church)—"I know thy works, and thy labour, and thy patience, and how thou canst not bear them which are evil: and thou hast tried them which say they are apostles, and are not, and hast found them liars: and hast borne, and hast patience, and for my name's sake hast laboured, and hast not fainted. . . . But this thou hast, that thou hatest the deeds of the Nicolaitanes, which I also hate" (Rev. 2:2-3, 6).

---

†2:6

A. Our Lord begins by making a statement that will be repeated to every one of the seven churches. The statement is, "I know thy works" (2:2, 9, 13, 19; 3:1, 8, 15).

B. According to the Savior:

1. Ephesus was an evangelistic church.
2. It was a patient church (unlike the Christians Peter wrote to; see 2 Pet. 1:6).
3. It was a separated church (unlike the Corinthian church; cf. 1 Cor. 5).
4. It was an orthodox church.
5. It was a persecuted but persistent church (unlike the Christians in the book of Hebrews; see Heb. 12:1-15).
6. It was a democratic church—"Thou hatest the deeds of the Nicolaitanes, which I also hate" (2:6). The word "Nicolaitanes" comes from two Greek words, nikao, *meaning "to conquer,"*

and laos, *meaning "people." Many believe John was speaking here to the growing distinction between clergy and laity. Thus: This church was zealous, long-suffering, orthodox, separated, and reliable.*

---

3. The condemnation (the bad things he says about the church)—"Nevertheless I have somewhat against thee, because thou hast left thy first love" (Rev. 2:4).

---

†2:4

A. *It is tragically possible to be so busy* working *for Christ that one neglects Christ. God did not create Adam to evangelize the world with the gospel, or to build the largest Sunday school in Eden (as important as these may be), but to* fellowship *with his Creator.*

B. *The spiritual temperature of the church had apparently cooled drastically since Paul had written his epistle to them, observing their "faith in the Lord Jesus, and love unto all the saints" (Eph. 1:15). (See also Eph. 3:14-19.)*

---

4. The counsel (his advice to the church)—"Remember therefore from whence thou art fallen, and repent, and do the first works; or else I will come unto thee quickly, and will remove thy candlestick out of his place, except thou repent" (Rev. 2:5).

---

†2:5

A. *In essence, the church was to do three things:*
   1. *Remember—Their heads were to be given over to Christ.*
   2. *Repent—Their hearts were to be given over to Christ.*
   3. *Repeat—Their hands were to be given over to Christ. Unless this was done, fearful results would transpire. "I will come unto thee quickly, and will remove thy candlestick out of his place" (2:5).*

B. *The child of God need never pray the words of Psalm 51:11, "Cast me not away from thy presence, and take not thy holy spirit from me." However, every Bible-believing local church should often repeat these words. There is absolutely no eternal security for any local church presented in the Bible. A believer can never fall from grace, but his church can. History records the sad fact that Christ did indeed later remove the lampstand of the church in Ephesus. It has been gone for centuries, smothered by the Muslims. There is today no local church within miles of Ephesus.*

---

5. The challenge (his encouragement to the church) (Rev. 2:7)

---

†2:7 *This tree, once given to Adam, disappears after his sin (Gen. 3:24). Here (Rev. 2:7) it is mentioned again for the first time. (See also Rev. 22:2, 14.) The definition and method of overcoming is given in 1 John 5:4-5.*

B. The church at Smyrna (Rev. 2:8-11)

†*Facts about the city of Smyrna:*
- A. *It was some 40 miles north of Ephesus.*
- B. *It was a splendid city of rare beauty on a fine bay.*
- C. *It was on a direct trade route from India and Persia to Rome.*
- D. *It was celebrated for its schools of science and medicine, for its handsome buildings and wide paved streets.*
- E. *The temple of Bacchus, god of wine, was there.*
- F. *Many apostate Jews lived here.*
- G. *It was the traditional birthplace of Homer.*

---

1. The counselor—"And unto the angel of the church in Smyrna write; These things saith the first and the last, which was dead, and is alive" (Rev. 2:8).
2. The commendation—"I know thy works, and tribulation, and poverty, (but thou art rich) and I know the blasphemy of them which say they are Jews, and are not, but are the synagogue of Satan" (Rev. 2:9).

---

†2:9
- A. *They had suffered poverty for Christ (but God saw them as rich). Many believers doubtless belonged to the various city labor guilds of that day prior to their conversion. But because of their newfound faith they apparently had lost the right to guilds. Many may have gone bankrupt. (See also Matt. 6:20; 2 Cor. 6:10.)*
- B. *They had suffered persecution for Christ (but God promised them a reward). Dr. Charles Ryrie writes: "The instigators of the persecution were apostate Jews who were in reality instruments of Satan. At the martyrdom of Polycarp (disciple of John the Apostle) in 158, these Jews eagerly assisted by gathering* on the Sabbath *wood and faggots for the fire in which he was burned." (See also Rom. 2:28-29; John 8:44; Rev. 3:9.)* (Revelation, *p. 23).*

---

3. The condemnation (none given)
4. The counsel—"Fear none of those things which thou shalt suffer: behold, the devil shall cast some of you into prison, that ye may be tried; and ye shall have tribulation ten days: be thou faithful unto death, and I will give thee a crown of life" (Rev. 2:10).

---

†2:10
- A. *Jesus warns his church that they would have "tribulation ten days" (2:10). He may have referred to an actual ten-day period of fearful bloodletting. Or he might have meant the ten intensive periods of persecution by ten Roman Emperors. It has been estimated that at least five million saints were martyred during this period. This would be over 100 million, in proportion to today's world population.*
- B. *These ten Roman persecution periods are:*
  1. *Nero (64–68)—Killed Peter and Paul.*
  2. *Domitian (81–96)—Thought Christianity was atheistic. Killed thousands of believers. Banished John to Patmos.*
  3. *Trajan (98–117)—Was the first to pass laws against Christianity. Burned Ignatius at the stake.*

4. Pius (137–161)—Killed Polycarp, disciple of John.
5. Marcus Aurelius (161–180)—Thought Christianity an absurd superstition. Beheaded the great writer and defender of the faith, Justin Martyr.
6. Severus (193–211)—Killed Origen's father.
7. Thracian (235–238)—Brutal barbarian; commanded all Christian leaders to die.
8. Decius (249–251)—Determined to exterminate Christianity.
9. Valerian (253–260)—Killed Cyprian, Bishop of Carthage.
10. Diocletian (284–305)—Last and most severe persecution. For ten years believers were hunted in caves and forests. They were burned, thrown to wild beasts, and put to death by every torture cruelty could devise. But Diocletian's own wife and daughter accepted Christ.

---

5. The challenge—"He that hath an ear, let him hear what the Spirit saith unto the churches; He that overcometh shall not be hurt of the second death" (Rev. 2:11).

C. The church at Pergamos (Rev. 2:12-17)

---

†*Facts about the city of Pergamos:*
A. It was the political capital city of Asia, some 75 miles north of Ephesus.
B. It boasted one of the finest libraries of antiquity which contained some 200,000 volumes. This library was later given by Mark Antony to Cleopatra.
C. It was in this city that parchment was first used.

---

1. The counselor—"And to the angel of the church in Pergamos write; These things saith he which hath the sharp sword with two edges" (Rev. 2:12).
2. The commendation—"I know thy works, and where thou dwellest, even where Satan's seat is: and thou holdest fast my name, and hast not denied my faith, even in those days wherein Antipas was my faithful martyr, who was slain among you, where Satan dwelleth" (Rev. 2:13).

---

†2:13
A. They had kept the faith, even though living in the very city Satan had chosen as his temporary headquarters. For centuries the devil had carried on his empire from Babylon. (See Gen. 11:1-9; Dan. 5.) But when that nation fell he apparently transferred it (at least for awhile) to Pergamos. The city worshiped, among other objects, a living serpent. Satan will later move his capital back to Babylon (Rev. 17–18).
B. Many in Pergamos had been martyred for their faith. One is mentioned here, Antipas by name. His name never appears in any other historical record. But God knew all about this anonymous humble believer who lived and died for Christ some 20 centuries ago. (See John 10:3; 2 Tim. 2:19.)

---

3. The condemnation
   a. The church was tolerating the doctrine of Balaam—"But I have a few things against thee, because thou hast there them that hold the doctrine of Balaam, who taught Balac to cast a stumblingblock before the children of Israel, to eat things sacrificed unto idols, and to commit fornication" (Rev. 2:14).

†**2:14** *Some were practicing the doctrine of Balaam. Balaam was a false Old Testament prophet who attempted to put a curse on the nation Israel (Num. 22:1–25:9). The New Testament refers to his doctrine, his error and his way.*

A. His way (2 Pet. 2:15)—His way was his covetousness. Balaam's services could be readily bought.
B. His error (Jude 11)—He wrongly supposed a holy God would be forced to curse sinful Israel.
C. His doctrine (Rev. 2:14)—He concluded that if you can't curse them, then you can corrupt them through immorality and idolatry. Some were practicing the doctrine of the Nicolaitanes (2:15). This philosophy had already been condemned by Christ in the church at Ephesus (2:6). However, we see that what was once deeds *in the first church had now become hardened into* doctrine.

---

b. The church was tolerating the doctrine of the Nicolaitanes—"So hast thou also them that hold the doctrine of the Nicolaitanes, which thing I hate" (Rev. 2:15).

4. The counsel—"Repent; or else I will come unto thee quickly, and will fight against them with the sword of my mouth" (Rev. 2:16).
5. The challenge—"He that hath an ear, let him hear what the Spirit saith unto the churches; to him that overcometh will I give to eat of the hidden manna, and will give him a white stone, and in the stone a new name written, which no man knoweth saving he that receiveth it" (Rev. 2:17).

---

†**2:17** *Charles Ryrie writes: "The meaning of the white stone with the new name written is derived from either one or both of two customs of the day. The first was that of judges who determined a verdict by placing in an urn a white and black pebble. If the white one came out it meant acquittal; thus the white stone would mean the assurance that there is no condemnation to those who are in Christ Jesus. The other custom was the wearing of amulets, a good luck charm worn around the neck. If this is the reference, then the stone is the Lord's way of reminding the people that they had Him and needed no other thing"* (Revelation, *p. 25).*

D. The church at Thyatira (Rev. 2:18-29)

---

†*Facts about the city of Thyatira:*

A. It was 35 miles southeast of Pergamos.
B. The city may have been founded by Alexander the Great around 300 B.C.
C. It was a union city, and headquarters for the trade guilds, such as tanners, potters, weavers, dyers, and robemakers.
D. Lydia, the first convert of Paul in Europe (Acts 16:14), was a native of this city. Today it has a population of 25,000.

---

1. The counselor—"And unto the angel of the church in Thyatira write; These things saith the Son of God, who hath his eyes like unto a flame of fire, and his feet are like fine brass" (Rev. 2:18).
2. The commendation—"I know thy works, and charity, and service, and faith, and thy patience, and thy works; and the last to be more than the first" (Rev. 2:19).
3. The condemnation—"Notwithstanding I have a few things against thee,

because thou sufferest that woman Jezebel, which calleth herself a prophetess, to teach and to seduce my servants to commit fornication, and to eat things sacrificed unto idols" (Rev. 2:20).

---

†**2:20** *God's main objection to this church centered on the fact that they were allowing the ministry of a false prophetess aptly named Jezebel.*

A. Her Old Testament counterpart—This Jezebel was the pagan murderous wife of King Ahab (1 Kings 16:28–19:21; 21:1-29; 2 Kings 9:22-37).

B. Her sin in the church

1. She was teaching men, which was forbidden (see 1 Tim. 2:12-14).

2. She was teaching immorality and idolatry.

---

4. The counsel—"But unto you I say, and unto the rest in Thyatira, as many as have not this doctrine, and which have not known the depths of Satan, as they speak; I will put upon you none other burden. But that which ye have already hold fast till I come" (Rev. 2:24-25).
5. The challenge—"And he that overcometh, and keepeth my works unto the end, to him will I give power over the nations: and he shall rule them with a rod of iron; as the vessels of a potter shall they be broken to shivers: even as I received of my Father. And I will give him the morning star" (Rev. 2:26-28).

E. The church at Sardis (Rev. 3:1-6)

---

†*Facts about the city of Sardis:*

A. It was 30 miles south of Thyatira and the capital of Lydia.

B. The city was thought to be impregnable, but Cyrus the Great captured it by following a secret path up the cliff.

C. Coins were first minted here.

D. It was noted for its great wealth, the chief of which was its flourishing carpet industry.

---

1. The counselor—"These things saith he that hath the seven Spirits of God, and the seven stars" (Rev. 3:1).
2. The commendation—"Thou hast a few names even in Sardis which have not defiled their garments; and they shall walk with me in white: for they are worthy" (Rev. 3:4).

---

† **3:4** *God always has his remnant in every church and church age (see 1 Kings 19:10, 18; Rom. 11:5).*

---

3. The condemnation—"I know thy works, that thou hast a name that thou livest, and art dead" (Rev. 3:1).

---

†**3:1** *J. Vernon McGee observes: "This is a picture of Protestantism. The great truths which were recovered in the Reformation have been surrendered by a compromising church. Although the great*

denominations and churches still repeat by rote the creeds of the church; in mind, heart and life they have repudiated them. Imposing programs, elaborate rituals, and multiplication of organizations have been substituted for the Word of God and real spiritual life. There is activity, but no actions, motion without movement, promotion without progress, and program without power. Although the outward form remains, the living creature has vacated the shell" (Reveling Through Revelation, *p. 28). The word to Sardis proves that the Reformation was not a restoration to the New Testament ideal church.*

---

4. The counsel—"Remember therefore how thou hast received and heard, and hold fast, and repent. If therefore thou shalt not watch, I will come on thee as a thief, and thou shalt not know what hour I will come upon thee" (Rev. 3:3).
5. The challenge—"He that overcometh, the same shall be clothed in white raiment; and I will not blot out his name out of the book of life, but I will confess his name before my Father, and before his angels" (Rev. 3:5).

---

†**3:5** *Here the challenge is twofold to the overcomers:*

A. His name would remain in the Book of Life. Often this book is referred to in both Old and New Testament (Exod. 32:32; Dan. 12:1; Psa. 69:28; Luke 10:20; Phil. 4:3; Heb. 12:23; Rev. 3:5; 13:8; 17:8; 20:12, 15; 21:27; 22:19). Whatever else may be involved here, these verses do not teach that a saved person can ever be lost. In fact, quite the opposite, for many prove one cannot be lost because each saved person's name is written in this book. (See especially Dan. 12:1; Luke 10:20; Rev. 13:8; 17:8; 21:27.)

B. His name would be confessed by Jesus before the Father (Luke 12:8-9).

F. The church at Philadelphia (Rev. 3:7-13)

---

†*Facts about the city of Philadelphia:*

A. It was built as a center of Greek culture around 200 B.C.

B. It is located some 30 miles southeast of Sardis.

C. Philadelphia was celebrated for its excellent wine.

D. The city had a large Jewish population.

E. It was destroyed by an earthquake in A.D. 17, but soon rebuilt by Tiberius Caesar.

---

1. The counselor—"And to the angel of the church in Philadelphia write; these things saith he that is holy, he that is true, he that hath the key of David, he that openeth, and no man shutteth; and shutteth, and no man openeth" (Rev. 3:7).

---

†**3:7** *J. Vernon McGee writes the following concerning Christ's description here: "Christ reminds them that He is holy—holy at His birth (Luke 1:35), holy at His death (Acts 2:27), and holy in His present priestly office (Heb. 7:26). He is likewise true (John 1:9; 14:6; 15:1). 'True' means genuine with an added note of perfection and completeness. Moses did not give the true bread. See John 6:32-35. He also has the Key of David (see Isa. 22:22). This is different from the keys of hades and*

death (1:18). This speaks of His regal claims as the Ruler of this universe (Luke 1:32). He will sit on the throne of David in the Millennium, but today He is sovereign" (Reveling Through Revelation, *p. 31).*

---

2. The commendation—"I know thy works: behold, I have set before thee an open door, and no man can shut it: for thou hast a little strength, and hast kept my word, and hast not denied my name" (Rev. 3:8).

---

†3:8 *This is the first of four special doors in Revelation. These are:*
A. The door of service (3:8). (See also Acts 14:27; 1 Cor. 16:9; 2 Cor. 2:12; Col. 4:3.)
B. The door of the human heart (Rev. 3:20)
C. The door of Rapture (4:1)
D. The door of the second coming (19:11)

---

3. The condemnation—None given
4. The counsel—"Behold, I come quickly: hold that fast which thou hast, that no man take thy crown" (Rev. 3:11).
5. The challenge
   a. To be given power—"Behold, I will make them of the synagogue of Satan, which say they are Jews, and are not, but do lie; behold, I will make them to come and worship before thy feet, and to know that I have loved thee" (Rev. 3:9).

---

†3:9 *"The synagogue of Satan"—Both Jesus and Paul had previously spoken out concerning this group. (See John 8:44; Matt. 23:1-35; 1 Thess. 2:14-16.)*

---

   b. To be given protection—"Because thou hast kept the word of my patience, I also will keep thee from the hour of temptation, which shall come upon all the world, to try them that dwell upon the earth" (Rev. 3:10).
   c. To be given privilege—"Him that overcometh will I make a pillar in the temple of my God, and he shall go no more out: and I will write upon him the name of my God, and the name of the city of my God, which is new Jerusalem, which cometh down out of heaven from my God: and I will write upon him my new name" (Rev. 3:12).

---

†3:12 *This is the first mention in the Scriptures of that shining city in the stars, our ultimate and eternal home, the New Jerusalem. (See also 21:2.)*

G. The church at Laodicea (Rev. 3:14-22)

---

†*Facts about the city of Laodicea: "These seven churches lie within a great arc beginning with Ephesus, swinging upward and eastward through Smyrna and Pergamum and back down to Laodicea. Thus, this last city is about ninety miles due east of Ephesus and about forty-five miles*

southeast of Philadelphia. The name of the town means 'judgment of the people' (Reveling Through Revelation, *p. 31).*

A. *This city was founded by Antiochus II and named after his wife. It was a very common name for women.*

B. *It was a banking center and possessed immense wealth.*

C. *It was graced with resplendent temples and theaters.*

D. *An excellent and well-known medical school was built there.*

E. *The city was famous for its eye salve called cellyrium.*

F. *It was noted for the manufacture of rich garments of black glossy wool. Several mineral streams were located nearby.*

---

1. The counselor—"And unto the angel of the church of the Laodiceans write; these things saith the Amen, the faithful and true witness, the beginning of the creation of God" (Rev. 3:14).

---

†**3:14** *We now move from the best of the seven churches, Philadelphia, to the worst, Laodicea. While nothing bad was said about the former, nothing good is said about this one. John Phillips writes: "He introduces Himself to Laodicea as 'the beginning of the creation of God,' or as the margin of the American Standard version puts it, 'the origin of the creation of God.' He it was who flung the stars into space, plowed out the basins of the sea, reared against the skyline of the world the mighty Himalayan range. Not a blade of grass grows without His permission nor a speck of dust moves. He is the origin of the creation of God, the all-controlling one of the dynamic Christ"* (Exploring Revelation, *p. 89).*

---

2. The commendation (none given)
3. The condemnation
   a. The indictment of the Lord—"I know thy works, that thou art neither cold nor hot: I would thou wert cold or hot. So then because thou art lukewarm, and neither cold nor hot, I will spue thee out of my mouth" (Rev. 3:15-16).

---

† **3:16** *The word "spue" or "spew" is the Greek* emeo, *meaning "to vomit." Charles Ryrie writes: "Near Laodicea were hot mineral springs whose water could be drunk only if very hot. When lukewarm it became nauseating"* (Exploring Revelation, *31). According to Christ's words here, he apparently has more respect for fiery hot fanaticism or icy cold formalism than for lifeless and lame lukewarmness.*

---

   b. The ignorance of the Laodiceans—"Because thou sayest, I am rich, and increased with goods, and have need of nothing; and knowest not that thou art wretched, and miserable, and poor, and blind, and naked" (Rev. 3:17).

4. The counsel—"I counsel thee to buy of me gold tried in the fire, that thou mayest be rich; and white raiment, that thou mayest be clothed, and that the shame of thy nakedness do not appear; and anoint thine eyes with eyesalve, that thou mayest see. As many as I love, I rebuke and chasten: be zealous therefore, and repent" (Rev. 3:18-19).

5. The challenge—"Behold, I stand at the door, and knock: if any man hear my voice, and open the door, I will come in to him, and will sup with him, and he with me. To him that overcometh will I grant to sit with me in my throne, even as I also overcame, and am set down with my Father in his throne" (Rev. 3:20-21).

---

†3:21 *J. Vernon McGee writes: "His invitation is to the evening meal, the last call for dinner. It is an invitation to come to Him before the night of the Great Tribulation"* (Reveling Through Revelation, *p. 36). Millions of Christians have doubtless viewed Holman Hunt's famous picture of Christ as the Light of the World. Here the artist has depicted Jesus wearing a crown of thorns and standing outside a door which represents the human heart. This painting now hangs in Saint Paul's Cathedral in London. Phillips writes: "When it was first displayed, critics came to comment on the work. One of them turned to the painter and said, 'Mr. Hunt, you have painted a masterpiece, but you have made one very serious mistake. You have painted a door without a handle.' 'That is no mistake,' replied the artist. 'The handle is on the inside'"* (Exploring Revelation, *p. 93).*

Dr. John Walvoord aptly summarizes the Savior's words to his people here in Revelation 2–3. "The letters to the seven churches are a remarkably complete treatment of problems that face the church today. The recurring dangers of losing their first love (2:4), of being afraid of suffering (2:10), doctrinal defection (2:14-15), moral departure (2:20), spiritual deadness (3:1-2), not holding fast (v. 11), and lukewarmness (vv. 15-16) are just as prevalent today as they were in first century churches. Because these letters come from Christ personally, they take on significance as God's final word of exhortation to the church down through the centuries. The final appeal is to all individuals who will hear. People in churches today would do well to listen" (Bible Knowledge Commentary, *New Testament Volume, p. 942).*

PART TWO: The Worship of the Lamb Invited (Rev. 4–5)

This section is in reality the story of two songs of praise.

I. The Creation Hymn of Worship (Rev. 4)

A. The place—"After this I looked, and, behold, a door was opened in heaven: and the first voice which I heard was as it were of a trumpet talking with me; which said, Come up hither, and I will shew thee things which must be hereafter" (Rev. 4:1).

---

†4:1 *John begins this new section with the words "after this" (4:1). The Greek phrase is* meta tauta, *"after these things." What things? The context would suggest that he refers to the Rapture which occurs between chapters 3 and 4. The* meta tauta *phrase both opens and closes this verse in the original language. The church has been referred to some 19 times in the first three chapters. It now completely drops from the pages of the book until the end of the tribulation in Revelation 19. The only godly group Satan can find to torment during the tribulation is the nation Israel. Only two conclusions may be reached from these facts.*

A. The church has been wiped out, through persecution by Satan. This concept is, of course, totally unscriptural (see Matt. 16:18).

B. The church has been taken out, through the Rapture, by Christ. Various New Testament passages would strongly support this (see 1 Cor. 15:51; 1 Thess. 4:16). Now John:

1. Sees a door (John 10:9)

2. Hears a trumpet (1 Thess. 4:16)

B. The persons

1. The Father—"And immediately I was in the spirit: and, behold, a throne was set in heaven, and one sat on the throne. And he that sat was to look upon like a jasper and a sardine stone: and there was a rainbow round about the throne, in sight like unto an emerald" (Rev. 4:2-3).

---

†**4:3** *John now becomes the second of two recorded human beings who are allowed a glimpse of that dazzling kingdom in the sky called heaven. (For the other, see 2 Cor. 12:2-4.) He sees the glory of the Father upon the throne (4:2-3). Revelation is a* throne *book, the word being used 45 times, as compared with only 15 other occurrences of the word in the entire New Testament. John could distinguish no form or give no description of the awesome One upon this throne, save to say, "He that sat was to look upon like a jasper and a sardine stone" (4:3). Here the jasper, a white stone, and the sardine, a fiery red stone, may refer to God's two basic characteristics, his glory and his grace. These were also the first and last stones among the 12 that the Old Testament high priest bore upon his breastplate. These stones represented the 12 tribes of Israel, arranged according to the births of the 12 sons of Jacob (Exod. 28). Reuben was the first tribe, which name meant "Behold a son"; and Benjamin was the last, meaning "Son of my right hand." This may be God's way of reminding all creatures throughout all eternity of:*

A. The incarnation of Christ (his humanity) via the jasper stone, Reuben ("Behold a son").

B. The exaltation of Christ (his deity) via the sardine stone, Benjamin ("Son of my right hand").

---

2. The 24 elders—"And round about the throne were four and twenty seats: and upon the seats I saw four and twenty elders sitting, clothed in white raiment; and they had on their heads crowns of gold" (Rev. 4:4).

---

†**4:4**

A. He sees 24 elders with golden crowns (4:4). These 24 may consist of a special representative body of both Old Testament and New Testament saints (1 Chron. 24:3-5, 18; Luke 1:5-9; Rev. 21:12-14). The Greek tells us they are all wearing stephanos *crowns (martyr crowns) rather than* diadems *(monarch crowns). Thus they must be human beings rather than angels. John saw these thrones being set up—not "cast down," as Daniel saw them (see Dan. 7:9). They were empty in Daniel's day. John sees them occupied now.*

B. He hears lightnings and thunderings, which means that the awful storm of the great tribulation is about to unleash its fury (4:5). In the Old Testament at Mount Sinai, God thundered when he gave his Law. Now he does the same when he prepares to judge people for breaking that Law.

---

3. The seven spirits of God—"And out of the throne proceeded lightnings and thunderings and voices: and there were seven lamps of fire burning before the throne, which are the seven Spirits of God" (Rev. 4:5).

---

†**4:5** *He sees "seven lamps of fire burning before the throne, which are the seven spirits of God" (4:5). Several suggestions have been offered to explain this verse:*

A. It refers to the earthly ministry of Christ as prophesied in Isaiah 11:1-3.

B. It refers to the sevenfold ministry of the Holy Spirit (restraining, convicting, regenerating, sealing, baptizing, indwelling, filling).
C. It refers to the seven angels of judgment later spoken of in Revelation 8:1-6.

---

4. The four living creatures
   a. The description of these creatures—"And before the throne there was a sea of glass like unto crystal: and in the midst of the throne, and round about the throne, were four beasts full of eyes before and behind. And the first beast was like a lion, and the second beast like a calf, and the third beast had a face as a man, and the fourth beast was like a flying eagle" (Rev. 4:6-7).

---

†4:7

A. He sees a crystal sea of glass (Rev. 4:6). Dr. Donald Barnhouse has written concerning this sea: "Before the throne there was a glassy sea, like crystal. The concordance immediately takes us to the temple built by Solomon after the model of the tabernacle. 'And he made a molten sea, ten cubits from one brim to the other; it was round all about and his height was five cubits' (1 Kings 7:23). This great basin, fifteen feet in diameter, was supported on the backs of twelve oxen of brass, facing outward. Here the priests came for their cleansing. Each time before they entered the holy place they stopped for the cleansing ceremony. But thank God the laver will be turned to crystal. The day will come when none of the saints will ever need confession. One of the greatest joys in the anticipation of Heaven is that the laver is of crystal. I shall never have to go to the Heavenly Father again to tell Him I have sinned. I shall never have to meet that gaze of Christ that caused Peter to go out and weep bitterly. The laver is of crystal only because I and all the saints of the ages will have been made like unto the Lord Jesus Christ" (Revelation, an Expository Commentary, *p. 94).*

B. He sees and hears the testimony of four special angelic creatures (4:6-8). The Greek for "wild beast" is therion. *But here the word used is* zoa *(root word for zoology), meaning "living creatures." Who are these four living creatures? J. Vernon McGee writes: "These creatures, of the highest intelligence, are in God's presence. They resemble the Cherubim of Ezekiel 1:5-10; 10:20 and the seraphim of Isaiah 6:2-3. Are they a new order of creatures in heaven that have not been revealed before in Scripture?"* (Reveling Through Revelation, *p. 43). What is their purpose? Perhaps to remind all creatures throughout all eternity of the blessed earthly and heavenly ministry of Christ. This is suggested by their appearance:*

1. *The first was like a lion. He communicates the office of Christ as King as seen in the Gospel of Matthew.*
2. *The second was like a calf. He communicates the office of Christ as a servant as seen in the Gospel of Mark.*
3. *The third was like a man. He communicates the humanity of Christ as seen in the Gospel of Luke.*
4. *The fourth was like an eagle. He communicates the deity of Christ as seen in the Gospel of John.*

---

   b. The duties of these creatures—"And the four beasts had each of them six wings about him; and they were full of eyes within: and they rest not day and night, saying, Holy, holy, holy, Lord God Almighty, which was, and is, and is to come" (Rev. 4:8).

C. The praise
   1. The singers—"And when those beasts give glory and honour and thanks to him that sat on the throne, who liveth for ever and ever, the four and twenty elders fall down before him that sat on the throne, and worship him that liveth for ever and ever, and cast their crowns before the throne" (Rev. 4:9-10).
   2. The song—"Saying, Thou art worthy, O Lord, to receive glory and honour and power: for thou hast created all things, and for thy pleasure they are and were created" (Rev. 4:11).

---

†4:11 *It may be said that everything God has ever done, is doing, or will do, can be placed in one of two basic categories, his work in* creation *(Gen. 1–2), and his work in* redemption *(Gen. 3—Rev. 22). Throughout eternity these two works will be celebrated in song by the redeemed. Here is the first glorious hymn, thanking God for his work in creation. For the second song, see Revelation 5:9.*

II. The Redemption Hymn of Worship (Rev. 5)
   A. The proclamation—"And I saw in the right hand of him that sat on the throne a book written within and on the backside, sealed with seven seals. And I saw a strong angel proclaiming with a loud voice, Who is worthy to open the book, and to loose the seals thereof?" (Rev. 5:1-2).

---

†5:2 *What is this book (actually a rolled-up scroll), sealed so securely with seven seals? Whatever it contained, the scroll was extremely important, for history informs us that under Roman law all legal documents pertaining to life and death were to be sealed seven times. A number of theologians believe that this is actually the legal title deed to the earth. Thus the angel's proclamation was, in effect, "Who is worthy to reclaim the earth's title deed? Who is able to pour out the seven-sealed judgment to purify this planet, and to usher in the long-awaited golden-age millennium?" Who indeed was worthy? (See also Jer. 32:6-16.)*

   B. The investigation—"And no man in heaven, nor in earth, neither under the earth, was able to open the book, neither to look thereon" (Rev. 5:3).

---

†5:3 *Let us follow the angel as he begins his threefold search.*

A. The search in heaven—Was there any among the redeemed worthy to claim the earth's title deed? There was not.
   1. Adam originally possessed this title deed (Gen. 1:28-29), but was cheated out of it by the devil (Gen. 3:1-19).
   2. Noah, the hero of the flood, subsequently became the drunkard of the vineyard, thus disqualifying himself (Gen. 6–9).
   3. Abraham, the father of Israel, backslid and went to Egypt temporarily (Gen. 12). David, the man after God's own heart (1 Sam. 16:7), later broke God's heart through lust and murder (2 Sam. 11).
   4. John the Baptist, the forerunner of Christ, in a moment of weakness doubted that same Messiah (Matt. 11:3).
   5. Peter, the "rock," denied his Lord in the hour of need (Matt. 26:70).

6. Paul, perhaps the greatest Christian who ever lived, compromised his testimony (Acts 21).
B. The search on earth—Who could accomplish in the sinful environment of earth what no man could achieve even in the sinless environment of heaven? Preachers and priests might minister on the earth, and kings rule over sections of it, but claim it they could not.
C. The search under the earth (in Hades). If no saint or angel could *purify this earth, then certainly no sinner or demon* would, *even if this were possible.*

C. The lamentation—"And I wept much, because no man was found worthy to open and to read the book, neither to look thereon" (Rev. 5:4).

---

†5:4 *Why did John weep? Perhaps because (among other reasons) he realized that the ultimate resurrection and glorification of his own body was directly connected with the removal of the curse placed upon this earth. (See Rom. 8:17-23.) This passage marks the final instance of a believer weeping. Sorrow, sufferings, and death have combined to carve out an ocean of human tears since Adam's tragic rebellion against God.*

D. The manifestation
1. The Lion of Judah—"And one of the elders saith unto me, Weep not: behold, the Lion of the tribe of Juda, the Root of David, hath prevailed to open the book, and to loose the seven seals thereof" (Rev. 5:5).
2. The Lamb of Jehovah
   a. His appearance—"And I beheld, and, lo, in the midst of the throne and of the four beasts, and in the midst of the elders, stood a Lamb as it had been slain, having seven horns and seven eyes, which are the seven Spirits of God sent forth into all the earth" (Rev. 5:6).

---

†5:6 *"John turned to behold a Lion. But instead of a shaggy mane and gaping jaws and dreadful teeth, he saw—a Lamb! Was there ever a more dramatic moment in the history of the universe? The Lion was none other than the Lamb!"* (Exploring Revelation, *p. 106). Who is this heavenly Hero who so boldly removes the scroll from the Father's right hand? We need not speculate for one second about his identity, for he is the Lord Jesus Christ himself. The proof is overwhelming.*
A. He has the characteristics of a lamb. Our Lord is referred to as a lamb 29 times in the New Testament. In all but one instance (1 Pet. 1:19) it is the Apostle John who employs this title. Furthermore,
1. It is a pet lamb. There are two words for "lamb" in the Greek New Testament. One is amnos *(a lamb in general) and the other is* arnion *(a special household pet lamb). Here in Revelation 5:6 the second Greek word is used. (For a related Old Testament passage, see 2 Sam. 12:1-4.)*
2. It is a slain lamb. Here the Greek word for slain is sphatto, *and refers to a violent death of some sort. The same word is found in the following passage: "We should love one another. Not as Cain, who was of that wicked one, and slew his brother" (1 John 3:11-12). The word* sphatto *is found only seven times in the New Testament, and four of these usages refer to the death of Christ (Rev. 5:6, 9, 12; 13:8).*
3. It is an all-powerful lamb. The lamb is pictured as possessing seven horns, which in biblical symbolic language refers to power and authority.

4. It is an all-knowing lamb. The lamb is pictured as possessing seven eyes, referring to perfect knowledge and wisdom.

B. He has the characteristics of a lion. John calls him "The Lion of the tribe of Judah, the Root of David"; and so he is. Three key Bible chapters explain this title.

1. In Genesis 49, the dying Jacob predicted that Judah, his fourth son, would be like a lion, and that the later kings of Israel, including Christ himself, would come from his tribe (Gen. 49:8-10).

2. In 2 Samuel 7, God told David (who was of the tribe of Judah) that his kingdom would be eternal and that his household would rule forever (2 Sam. 7:8-17).

3. In Luke 1, the angel Gabriel explained to Mary (who was of the house of David) that her virgin-born son would inherit all the Old Testament promises as found in Genesis 49 and 2 Samuel 7 (Luke 1:30-33). Thus John sees Christ as a Lamb, since he once came to redeem his people. This was his past *work. John also sees him as a lion, for he shall come again to reign over his people. This will be his* future *work. The source of his claim to the earth's scepter is therefore related to his slain Lamb characteristics while the strength of his claim is due to his mighty Lion characteristics.*

---

b. His action—"And he came and took the book out of the right hand of him that sat upon the throne" (Rev. 5:7).

E. The adoration

1. The song—"And they sung a new song, saying, Thou art worthy to take the book, and to open the seals thereof: for thou wast slain, and hast redeemed us to God by thy blood out of every kindred, and tongue, and people, and nation; and hast made us unto our God kings and priests: and we shall reign on the earth. . . . Saying with a loud voice, Worthy is the Lamb that was slain to receive power, and riches, and wisdom, and strength, and honour, and glory, and blessing" (Rev. 5:9-10, 12).

---

†5:12

A. "And they sung a new song." This is the second hymn of praise, thanking God for his work in redemption.

B. "Worthy is the Lamb." The Bible can be aptly summarized by three lamb-centered statements:

1. The statement of Isaac—"Where *is the lamb?" (Gen. 22:7).*

2. The statement of John—"Behold, *the lamb!" (John 1:29).*

3. The statement of the redeemed—"Worthy *is the lamb!" (Rev. 5:12).*

---

2. The singers—"And I beheld, and I heard the voice of many angels round about the throne and the beasts and the elders: and the number of them was ten thousand times ten thousand, and thousands of thousands. . . . And every creature which is in heaven, and on the earth, and under the earth, and such as are in the sea, and all that are in them, heard I saying, Blessing, and honour, and glory, and power, be unto him that sitteth upon the throne, and unto the Lamb for ever and ever. And the four beasts said, Amen. And the four and twenty elders fell down and worshipped him that liveth for ever and ever" (Rev. 5:11, 13-14).

†**5:14** *Two aspects of this celestial choir can be noted:*

A. *Its diversity—Both angels and humans will participate. Inasmuch as angels had previously been allowed to be present at the creation of the world (Job 38:1, 4, 7) and its redemption (Luke 2:8-14), it is only appropriate that they be permitted to join in this celebration.*

B. *Its universality—We note every creature, saved and unsaved alike, will give honor to the Lamb. This of course in no way suggests that all will be saved. A similar passage is found in Philippians 2:5-11: "Let this mind be in you, which was also in Christ Jesus: who, being in the form of God, thought it not robbery to be equal with God: but made himself of no reputation, and took upon him the form of a servant, and was made in the likeness of men: and being found in fashion as a man, he humbled himself, and became obedient unto death, even the death of the cross. Wherefore God also hath highly exalted him, and given him a name which is above every name: that at the name of Jesus every knee should bow, of things in heaven, and things in earth, and things under the earth; and that every tongue should confess that Jesus Christ is Lord, to the glory of God the Father." What these verses are saying is that no creature has a choice concerning whether he or she will acknowledge the glory of Christ, but only how that acknowledgment will be made. He will either be recognized as one's Savior and Lord of all on earth, or as one's Judge and Lord of all throughout eternity.*

PART THREE: The Wrath of the Lamb Invoked (Rev. 6–19)

I. He Pours Out the Seven Seal Judgments (Rev. 6–11).

---

†*"For two breathtaking, soul-inspiring chapters, we have been in heaven. The scroll has changed hands, and the right to judge and rule the world has been placed upon Jesus. Now we must come down from the mount and out of the ivory palaces. Down here, on the rebel planet of earth, the tempo is increasing, passions are rising. Evil men and seducers are waxing worse and worse. Disobedience to parents has grown up into brawling maturity, defying all authority. Men have become inventors of evil things, and their fearful inventions have become Frankenstein monsters, threatening to destroy the globe. The time has come for God to intervene in human affairs, so judgment is given to the Son"* (Exploring Revelation, *p. 110). At the beginning of chapter 4, John took us up from earth to heaven by means of the rapture of Christ. Here in chapter 6 we abruptly return to earth to view the wrath of Christ. The wrath of Jesus is invoked along the following six avenues (in these chapters):*

A. *He pours out the seven seal judgments (6–11).*
B. *He allows the devil and the Antichrist to reign on earth (12–13).*
C. *He pours out the seven vial (bowl) judgments (14–16).*
D. *He destroys the world's religious systems (17).*
E. *He destroys the world's political and economic systems (18).*
F. *He defeats his enemies at Armageddon (19).*

A. First seal (Rev. 6:1-2)—"And I saw, and behold a white horse: and he that sat on him had a bow; and a crown was given unto him: and he went forth conquering, and to conquer" (Rev. 6:2).

---

†**6:2** *This is doubtless a symbolic picture of the Antichrist as he subdues to himself the ten nations of*

the revived Roman Empire. This may be thought of as the "cold war" period. We note that he carries no arrow, which may indicate conquest by diplomacy rather than a shooting war.

B. Second seal (Rev. 6:3-4)—"And there went out another horse that was red: and power was given to him that sat thereon to take peace from the earth, and that they should kill one another: and there was given unto him a great sword" (Rev. 6:4).

---

†6:4 *The uneasy peace which the rider on the white horse brings to earth is temporary and counterfeit. The Antichrist promises peace, but only God can actually produce it. As Isaiah would write, "But the wicked are like the troubled sea, when it cannot rest, whose waters cast up mire and dirt. There is no peace, saith my God, to the wicked" (Isa. 57:20-21). Now open and bloody hostility breaks out among some of the nations.*

C. Third seal (Rev. 6:5-6)—"And when he had opened the third seal, I heard the third beast say, Come and see. And I beheld, and lo a black horse; and he that sat on him had a pair of balances in his hand. And I heard a voice in the midst of the four beasts say, A measure of wheat for a penny, and three measures of barley for a penny; and see thou hurt not the oil and the wine" (Rev. 6:5-6).

---

†6:6 *Dr. Charles Ryrie observes: "The third judgment brings famine to the world. The black horse forebodes death, and the pair of balances bespeaks a careful rationing of food. Normally, a 'penny' (a Roman denarius, a day's wages in Palestine in Jesus' day, Matt. 20:2) would buy eight measures of wheat or twenty-four of barley. Under these famine conditions the same wage will buy only one measure of wheat or three of barley. In other words, there will be one-eighth of the normal supply of food. The phrase 'see thou hurt not the oil and the wine' is an ironic twist in this terrible situation. Apparently luxury food items will not be in short supply, but of course most people will not be able to afford them. This situation will only serve to taunt the populace in their impoverished state"* (Revelation, *pp. 45-46).*

D. Fourth seal (Rev. 6:7-8)—"And I looked, and behold a pale horse: and his name that sat on him was Death, and Hell followed with him. And power was given unto them over the fourth part of the earth, to kill with sword, and with hunger, and with death, and with the beasts of the earth" (Rev. 6:8).

---

†6:8

A. The identity of these riders—John calls them "Death" and "Hell," apparently referring to physical and spiritual death. Thus the devil will destroy the bodies and damn the souls of multitudes of unbelievers during this third-seal plague.

B. The damage done by these riders—One fourth of all humanity perishes during this plague. It is estimated that during the Second World War one out of 40 persons lost their lives, but this seal judgment alone will claim one out of four persons—nearly one billion human beings. We note the phrase, "with the beasts of the earth." Here John Phillips has written: "The beasts are closely linked with the pestilence, and this might be a clue. The most destructive creature on earth as far as mankind is concerned, is not the lion or the bear, but the rat. The rat is clever, adaptable, and destructive. If ninety-five percent of the rat population is exterminated in a given area, the rat population will replace itself within a year. It has killed more people than all the wars in history, and makes its home wherever man is found. Rats carry as many as thirty-five diseases. Their fleas carry bubonic plague, which killed a third of the population of Europe in the fourteenth century. Their fleas also carry typhus, which in four centuries has killed an estimated two hundred million people. Beasts, in this passage, are linked not only with pestilence, but with famine. Rats menace human food supplies, which they both devour and contaminate, especially in the more underdeveloped countries which can least afford to suffer loss" (Exploring Revelation, *p. 116).*

E. Fifth seal (Rev. 6:9-11)

1. The altar for the saints—"And when he had opened the fifth seal, I saw under the altar the souls of them that were slain for the word of God, and for the testimony which they held" (Rev. 6:9).
2. The anger of the saints—"And they cried with a loud voice, saying, How long, O Lord, holy and true, dost thou not judge and avenge our blood on them that dwell on the earth?" (Rev. 6:10).
3. The answer to the saints—"And white robes were given unto every one of them; and it was said unto them, that they should rest yet for a little season, until their fellowservants also and their brethren, that should be killed as they were, should be fulfilled" (Rev. 6:11).

---

†**6:11** *Here is religious persecution as never before. These three verses are loaded with theological implications.*

A. They refute the false doctrine of soul sleep.

B. They correct the error of one general resurrection. It is evident that these martyred souls did not receive their glorified bodies at the Rapture, as did the church-age saints. Therefore it can be concluded that these are Old Testament saints who will experience the glorious bodily resurrection after the tribulation (see Rev. 20:4-6).

C. They suggest the possibilities of an intermediate body. (See also 2 Cor. 5:1-3.) Dr. John Walvoord writes: "These martyred dead here pictured have not been raised from the dead and have not received their resurrection bodies. Yet it is declared that they are given robes. The fact that they are given robes would almost demand that they have a body of some sort. A robe could not hang upon an immaterial soul or spirit. It is not the kind of body that Christians now have, that is, the body of earth; nor is it the resurrection body of flesh and bones of which Christ spoke after His own resurrection. It is a temporary body suited for their presence in heaven but replaced in turn by their everlasting resurrection body given at the time of Christ's return" (The Revelation of Jesus Christ, *p. 134).*

F. Sixth seal (Rev. 6:12-17)

1. The destruction of earth's surface—"There was a great earthquake" (Rev. 6:12). "And every mountain and island were moved out of their places" (Rev. 6:14).
2. The darkening of earth's skies—"And I beheld when he had opened the sixth seal, and, lo, there was a great earthquake; and the sun became black as sack-cloth of hair, and the moon became as blood; and the stars of heaven fell unto

the earth, even as a fig tree casteth her untimely figs, when she is shaken of a mighty wind. And the heaven departed as a scroll when it is rolled together; and every mountain and island were moved out of their places" (Rev. 6:12-14).

---

†6:14 *As it can be seen, this fearful judgment ushers in:*

A. The greatest earthquake in history—There have, of course, been hundreds of severe earthquakes in human history.

1. The earliest recorded was in July of 365 in the Middle East.

2. The most destructive was in January of 1556 in China. Nearly one million lost their lives. Note: At the end of the tribulation there will be an earthquake even worse than the one occurring here at the time of the sixth seal. (See Rev. 16:18.)

B. The greatest cosmic disturbances in history—These may be a result of nuclear war. Hal Lindsey writes: "Do you know what happens in a nuclear explosion? The atmosphere rolls back on itself! It's this tremendous rush of air back into the vacuum that causes much of the destruction of a nuclear explosion. John's words in this verse are a perfect picture of an all-out nuclear exchange. When this happens, John continues, every mountain and island will be jarred from its present position. The whole world will be literally shaken apart!" (There's a New World Coming, *p. 110).*

C. The greatest prayer meeting in history—But they prayed for the wrong thing. The only object to protect the sinner from the wrath *of the Lamb is the* righteousness *of the Lamb.*

---

3. The despair of earth's sinners
   a. The classification of these sinners—"And the kings of the earth, and the great men, and the rich men, and the chief captains, and the mighty men, and every bondman, and every free man, hid themselves in the dens and in the rocks of the mountains" (Rev. 6:15).
   b. The consternation of these sinners—"And said to the mountains and rocks, Fall on us, and hide us from the face of him that sitteth on the throne, and from the wrath of the Lamb: for the great day of his wrath is come; and who shall be able to stand?" (Rev. 6:16-17).

G. Interlude (Rev. 7:1-17)

1. On earth—The sealing of the servants of God (Rev. 7:1-8)—"And after these things I saw four angels standing on the four corners of the earth, holding the four winds of the earth, that the wind should not blow on the earth, nor on the sea, nor on any tree" (Rev. 7:1).
   a. The sealers—"And I saw another angel ascending from the east, having the seal of the living God: and he cried with a loud voice to the four angels, to whom it was given to hurt the earth and the sea, Saying, Hurt not the earth, neither the sea, nor the trees, till we have sealed the servants of our God in their foreheads" (Rev. 7:2-3).
   b. The sealed—"And I heard the number of them which were sealed: and there were sealed an hundred and forty and four thousand of all the tribes of the children of Israel" (Rev. 7:4).

---

†7:4 *This passage does not mean that God will save only Jews during the tribulation, for in Revelation 7:9-17, the Bible declares that a great multitude from every nation will be saved. What this chapter does teach, however, is that God will send out 144,000 "Hebrew Billy Sundays" to* *evangelize the world. This will be a massive number indeed, especially when we consider that there are less than 35,000 missionaries of all persuasions in the world today. Our Lord doubtless had the ministry of the 144,000 in mind when He said, "And this gospel of the kingdom shall be preached unto all nations; and then shall the end come" (Matt. 24:14). Judah heads up this list, and not Reuben, the firstborn. Both Dan and Ephraim are missing. Both tribes were guilty of going into idolatry (Judg. 18; 1 Kings 11:26; Hosea 4). The tribes of Levi and Manasseh here take their place. However, both are listed in Ezekiel's millennial temple (Ezek. 48), so they simply forfeit their chance to preach during the tribulation. Some have concluded on the basis of Genesis 49:17 and Jeremiah 8:16 that the Antichrist will come from the tribe of Dan.*

---

2. In heaven—The singing of the servants of God (Rev. 7:9-17)—"After this I beheld, and, lo, a great multitude, which no man could number, of all nations, and kindreds, and people, and tongues, stood before the throne, and before the Lamb, clothed with white robes, and palms in their hands. . . . And one of the elders answered, saying unto me, What are these which are arrayed in white robes? and whence came they? And I said unto him, Sir, thou knowest. And he said to me, These are they which came out of great tribulation, and have washed their robes, and made them white in the blood of the Lamb" (Rev. 7:9, 13-14).
   a. Their song—"And cried with a loud voice, saying, Salvation to our God which sitteth upon the throne, and unto the Lamb" (Rev. 7:10).
   b. Their support—"And all the angels stood round about the throne, and about the elders and the four beasts, and fell before the throne on their faces, and worshipped God, Saying, Amen: Blessing, and glory, and wisdom, and thanksgiving, and honour, and power, and might, be unto our God for ever and ever. Amen" (Rev. 7:11-12).
   c. Their service—"Therefore are they before the throne of God, and serve him day and night in his temple: and he that sitteth on the throne shall dwell among them" (Rev. 7:15).
   d. Their Savior—"For the Lamb which is in the midst of the throne shall feed them, and shall lead them unto living fountains of waters: and God shall wipe away all tears from their eyes" (Rev. 7:17).

H. Seventh seal (Rev. 8–11)—The seventh seal actually consists of seven trumpets.
1. The silence before the trumpets (Rev. 8:1-5)—"And when he had opened the seventh seal, there was silence in heaven about the space of half an hour. And I saw the seven angels which stood before God; and to them were given seven trumpets. And another angel came and stood at the altar, having a golden censer; and there was given unto him much incense, that he should offer it with the prayers of all saints upon the golden altar which was before the throne. And the smoke of the incense, which came with the prayers of the saints, ascended up before God out of the angel's hand. And the angel took the censer, and filled it with fire of the altar, and cast it into the earth: and there were voices, and thunderings, and lightnings, and an earthquake" (Rev. 8:1-5).

---

†8:5 *This marks the only occasion in recorded history that heaven is silent. There is not the slightest sound or movement.*

A. The purpose of the silence—During the sixth seal, mankind seemed to weaken for the first time during the tribulation. A merciful and patient God now awaits further repentance, but all to no avail. God takes no pleasure in the death of the wicked (Ezek. 33:11).

B. The duration of the silence—It lasted for 30 minutes. The number 30 in the Bible is often associated with mourning. Israel mourned for 30 days over the death of both Aaron (Numb. 20:29) and Moses (Deut. 34:8).

---

2. The sounding of the trumpets (Rev. 8:6)—"And the seven angels which had the seven trumpets prepared themselves to sound" (Rev. 8:6).
   a. First trumpet (Rev. 8:7)—"The first angel sounded, and there followed hail and fire mingled with blood, and they were cast upon the earth: and the third part of trees was burnt up, and all green grass was burnt up" (Rev. 8:7).

---

†8:7 *It has been observed that plant life was the first to be created, and it is the first to be destroyed (Gen. 1:11-12).*

---

   b. Second trumpet (Rev. 8:8-9)—"And the second angel sounded, and as it were a great mountain burning with fire was cast into the sea: and the third part of the sea became blood; and the third part of the creatures which were in the sea, and had life, died; and the third part of the ships were destroyed" (Rev. 8:8-9).

---

†8:9 *Dr. Herman A. Hoyt writes: "Here we read of a great mountain burning with fire. This may refer to a meteoric mass from the sky falling headlong into the sea, perhaps the Mediterranean Sea. The result is to turn a third part of the sea a blood-red color and bring about the death of a third part of the life in the sea. Death may be caused by the chemical reaction in the water, such as radioactivity following atomic explosion. The third part of ships may be destroyed by the violence of the waters produced by the falling of the mass"* (Revelation, *p. 49).*

---

   c. Third trumpet (Rev. 8:10-11)—"And the third angel sounded, and there fell a great star from heaven, burning as it were a lamp, and it fell upon the third part of the rivers, and upon the fountains of waters; and the name of the star is called Wormwood: and the third part of the waters became wormwood; and many men died of the waters, because they were made bitter" (Rev. 8:10-11).

---

†8:11 *This star could refer to a meteor containing stifling and bitter gases, which fall on the Alps or some other freshwater source. During the second trumpet a third of the salt water was contaminated. Now a third of earth's fresh water suffers a similar fate. Many species of wormwood grow in Palestine. All species have a strong, bitter taste.*

---

   d. Fourth trumpet (Rev. 8:12-13)
      (1) The fearful darkening—"And the fourth angel sounded, and the third part of the sun was smitten, and the third part of the moon, and the third

part of the stars; so as the third part of them was darkened, and the day shone not for a third part of it, and the night likewise" (Rev. 8:12).

---

†8:12

A. Our Lord may have had this trumpet judgment in mind when he spoke the following words: "And except those days should be shortened, there should no flesh be saved; but for the elect's sake those days shall be shortened" (Matt. 24:22). "And there shall be signs in the sun, and in the moon, and in the stars" (Luke 21:25).

B. The Old Testament prophecy of Amos is also significant here: "And it shall come to pass in that day, saith the Lord God, that I will cause the sun to go down at noon, and I will darken the earth in the clear day" (Amos 8:9).

C. It was on the fourth day that God created the sun, moon, and stars (Gen. 1:14-16). They were to be for "signs, and for seasons, and for days, and years." After the flood, God promised not to alter this divine arrangement (Gen. 8:22). But in the tribulation, during the fourth trumpet, earth's very light will be limited by judgment.

---

(2) The future destruction—"And I beheld, and heard an angel flying through the midst of heaven, saying with a loud voice, Woe, woe, woe, to the inhabiters of the earth by reason of the other voices of the trumpet of the three angels, which are yet to sound!" (Rev. 8:13).

---

†8:13 *The word "angel" here should be translated "eagle." An eagle is sometimes pictured as God's method of judgment (Deut. 28:49; Hosea 8:1). Thus, even the brute creation will be used by God during the tribulation. This marks the last of three occasions on which a creature speaks in the Bible. (For the other two, see Gen. 3:1-5—a serpent; and Num. 22:28-30—an ass.)*

---

e. Fifth trumpet (Rev. 9:1-12)—This trumpet unleashes the first hellish invasion of demons upon the earth.

---

†*The ninth chapter of Revelation, which contains both fifth and sixth trumpet judgments, may be the most revealing section in all the Bible concerning the subject of demonology. Prior to this, God has already made it known that there are two kinds of unfallen angels. These are the Cherubim (Gen. 3:24; Exod. 25:18-22; Ezek. 10:1-20), and the Seraphim (Isa. 6:1-8). Here he may be describing for us the two kinds of fallen angels.*

---

(1) Their location—"And the fifth angel sounded, and I saw a star fall from heaven unto the earth: and to him was given the key of the bottomless pit. And he opened the bottomless pit; and there arose a smoke out of the pit, as the smoke of a great furnace; and the sun and the air were darkened by reason of the smoke of the pit" (Rev. 9:1-2).

---

†9:2

A. Literally, the phrase "bottomless pit" is "shaft of the abyss." The word "shaft" here indicates that there is an entrance from the surface of the earth to the heart of our planet. In this chapter we learn for the first time of a place called the bottomless pit. God mentions it no less than seven times in the book of Revelation (9;1-2, 11; 11:7; 17:8; 20:1-3).

B. *Some have identified these with the sons of God in Genesis 6:1-2. Here the theory is that these demons attempted sexual relations with women, resulting in immediate confinement in the bottomless pit. We do know that some demons are already chained and others at present have access to the bodies of people.*
   1. *Unchained demons (Luke 4:34; Matt. 8:29; Luke 8:27-31).*
   2. *Chained demons (Jude 6-7; 2 Pet. 2:4; 1 Pet. 3:18-20). Thus another name for this bottomless pit may be the* tartarus *mentioned in the Greek text of 2 Peter 2:4. Here Satan will be confined during the millennium (Rev. 20:3).*

---

(2) Their leader—"And they had a king over them, which is the angel of the bottomless pit, whose name in the Hebrew tongue is Abaddon, but in the Greek tongue hath his name Apollyon" (Rev. 9:11).

---

†9:11 *This "fallen star" mentioned in 9:1 seems to be Satan himself. (See also Isa. 14:12; Luke 10:18; 2 Cor. 11:14.) Prior to this time, Christ has held the key to the pit (Rev. 1:18), but now he allows the devil to use it for a specific purpose.*

---

(3) Their torment—"And there came out of the smoke locusts upon the earth: and unto them was given power, as the scorpions of the earth have power. And it was commanded them that they should not hurt the grass of the earth, neither any green thing, neither any tree; but only those men which have not the seal of God in their foreheads" (Rev. 9:3-4). "And their torment was as the torment of a scorpion when he striketh a man" (Rev. 9:5b).

---

†9:5 *The pain from the sting of a scorpion, though not generally fatal, is perhaps the most intense that any animal can inflict upon the human body. The insect itself is the most malignant that lives, and its poison is in kind.*

---

(4) Their duration—"And to them it was given that they should not kill them, but that they should be tormented five months" (Rev. 9:5). "And in those days shall men seek death, and shall not find it; and shall desire to die, and death shall flee from them" (Rev. 9:6).

---

†9:6 *Charles Ryrie writes: "Horrible as the torment will be, God will place certain limitations on the activity of these demons. They will be limited as to what they may strike and as to how far they may go and as to how long they may do what they will do. They will not attack the vegetation of the earth (as common locusts do); they may only attack certain men, that is, those who have not the seal of God in their foreheads (the 144,000; cf. 7:3). The wicked will persecute God's servants, the 144,000; but in turn they will be tormented by this plague which God allows. The demon-locusts will also be limited in that they may not kill men, just torment them. Further, the duration of this* *plague will be five months. The effect of this torment is to drive men to suicide, but they will not be able to die. Although men will prefer death to the agony of living, death will not be possible. Bodies will not sink and drown; poisons and pills will have no effect; and somehow even bullets and knives will not do their intended job"* (Revelation, *p. 62).*

---

(5) Their description—"And the shapes of the locusts were like unto horses prepared unto battle; and on their heads were as it were crowns like gold, and their faces were as the faces of men. And they had hair as the hair of women, and their teeth were as the teeth of lions. And they had breastplates, as it were breastplates of iron; and the sound of their wings was as the sound of chariots of many horses running to battle. And they had tails like unto scorpions, and there were stings in their tails: and their power was to hurt men five months" (Rev. 9:7-10).

f. Sixth trumpet (Rev. 9:13-21)—This trumpet unleashed the second hellish invasion of demons upon the earth.

(1) Their four leaders—"And the sixth angel sounded, and I heard a voice from the four horns of the golden altar which is before God, saying to the sixth angel which had the trumpet, Loose the four angels which are bound in the great river Euphrates" (Rev. 9:13-14).

---

†9:14

A. *"Loose the four angels"—These may function to Satan as the four living creatures do to God (see Rev. 4:6-8).*

B. *"The great river Euphrates"—This is where evil began on earth (Zech. 5:8-11; Gen. 3), where false religion began (Gen. 4:3; 10:9-10; 11:4), and where it will come to its end (Rev. 17–18).*

---

(2) Their mission—"And the four angels were loosed, which were prepared for an hour, and a day, and a month, and a year, for to slay the third part of men" (Rev. 9:15).

---

†9:15 *One third of humanity is killed through fire, smoke, and brimstone. One fourth had already been slain by the fourth seal (6:8). This would be approximately one billion. Now one third is killed, meaning another billion die. This invasion is therefore the opposite of the fifth trumpet judgment during which no man was able to die.*

---

(3) Their number—"And the number of the army of the horsemen were two hundred thousand thousand: and I heard the number of them" (Rev. 9:16).

---

†9:16 *By normal standards, this mighty army would occupy a territory one mile wide and 87 miles long.*

---

(4) Their description—"And thus I saw the horses in the vision, and them that sat on them, having breastplates of fire, and of jacinth, and brimstone:

and the heads of the horses were as the heads of lions; and out of their mouths issued fire and smoke and brimstone" (Rev. 9:17).

(5) Their torment—"For their power is in their mouth, and in their tails: for their tails were like unto serpents, and had heads, and with them they do hurt" (Rev. 9:19).

(6) Their effect—"And the rest of the men which were not killed by these plagues yet repented not of the works of their hands, that they should not worship devils, and idols of gold, and silver, and brass, and stone, and of wood: which neither can see, nor hear, nor walk: neither repented they of their murders, nor of their sorceries, nor of their fornication, nor of their thefts" (Rev. 9:20-21).

---

†9:21 *At this point over one half of the world's population has been wiped out. And what is the response of the survivors? Total unrepentance and intensified rebellion. That very year the F.B.I. reports will probably show a thousand percent increase in murder, drug-related crimes (the word "sorceries" is the Greek* pharmakeion, *from which we get our "pharmacy." It is the Greek word for drugs), sex, felonies, and robbery.*

---

g. Interlude (Rev. 10:1–11:14)—Seven events occur between the sixth and seventh trumpets.

(1) The message of the angel of God (Rev. 10:1-7)

(a) The vision—"And I saw another mighty angel come down from heaven, clothed with a cloud: and a rainbow was upon his head, and his face was as it were the sun, and his feet as pillars of fire: and he had in his hand a little book open: and he set his right foot upon the sea, and his left foot on the earth" (Rev. 10:1-2).

---

†10:2

A. "Another mighty angel"—This angel may well be Michael the Archangel (see Dan. 12:1). He is probably the same angel referred to in 5:2; 7:2; 8:3; and 18:2.

B. "A little book"—This is probably the seven-sealed book mentioned in Revelation 5:1.

(b) The voice—"And cried with a loud voice, as when a lion roareth: and when he had cried, seven thunders uttered their voices" (Rev. 10:3).

(c) The veto—"And when the seven thunders had uttered their voices, I was about to write: and I heard a voice from heaven saying unto me, Seal up those things which the seven thunders uttered, and write them not" (Rev. 10:4).

---

†10:4 *This passage contains the only sealed part of the book of Revelation.*

(d) The vow—"And the angel which I saw stand upon the sea and upon the earth lifted up his hand to heaven, and sware by him that liveth for ever and ever, who created heaven, and the things that therein are, and the earth, and the things that therein are, and the sea, and the things which are therein, that there should be time no longer" (Rev. 10:5-6).

(e) The victory—"But in the days of the voice of the seventh angel, when he shall begin to sound, the mystery of God should be finished, as he hath declared to his servants the prophets" (Rev. 10:7).

(2) The mission of the apostle of God (Rev. 10:8-11)—"And the voice which I heard from heaven spake unto me again, and said, Go and take the little book which is open in the hand of the angel which standeth upon the sea and upon the earth. And I went unto the angel, and said unto him, Give me the little book. And he said unto me, Take it, and eat it up; and it shall make thy belly bitter, but it shall be in thy mouth sweet as honey. And I took the little book out of the angel's hand, and ate it up; and it was in my mouth sweet as honey: and as soon as I had eaten it, my belly was bitter. And he said unto me, Thou must prophesy again before many peoples, and nations, and tongues, and kings" (Rev. 10:8-11).

(3) The measuring of the temple of God (Rev. 11:1-2)

---

†11:2 *Here John is put to work with a nine-foot ruler (see Ezek. 40:5), measuring the tribulation temple. He is also to record the identity of its worshipers. God is always interested in those who worship him. However, the outer court was to be left out, "for it is given unto the Gentiles: and the holy city shall they tread under foot forty and two months" (11:2).*

---

(4) The ministry of the witnesses of God (Rev. 11:3-6)

(a) The duration involved in their ministry—"And I will give power unto my two witnesses, and they shall prophesy a thousand two hundred and threescore days, clothed in sackcloth. These are the two olive trees, and the two candlesticks standing before the God of the earth" (Rev. 11:3-4).

(b) The devastation caused by their ministry—"And if any man will hurt them, fire proceedeth out of their mouth, and devoureth their enemies: and if any man will hurt them, he must in this manner be killed. These have power to shut heaven, that it rain not in the days of their prophecy: and have power over waters to turn them to blood, and to smite the earth with all plagues, as often as they will" (Rev. 11:5-6).

---

†11:6 *Who are these witnesses?*

A. Some hold that they are Elijah and Enoch—Hebrews 9:27 states that all men are appointed to die, and since these two men did not experience physical death, they will be sent back to witness and eventually to die a martyr's death.

B. Some hold that they are Elijah and Moses.

1. Elijah—Because of Malachi 4:5-6, which predicts that God will send Elijah during that great and dreadful day of the Lord. (See also Matt. 17:11.) Because Elijah appeared with Moses on the Mount of Transfiguration to talk with Jesus (Matt. 17:3). Because Elijah's Old Testament ministry of preventing rain for some three years will be repeated by one of the witnesses during the tribulation (1 Kings 17:1; cf. Rev. 11:6).

2. *Moses—Because of Jude 9, where we are informed that after the death of Moses, Satan attempted to acquire his dead body, so that God would not be able to use him against the Antichrist during the tribulation. Because Moses' Old Testament ministry of turning water into blood will be repeated by one of the witnesses during the tribulation (Exod. 7:19; cf. Rev. 11:6). Because Moses appeared with Elijah on the Mount of Transfiguration (Matt. 17:3).*

---

(5) The martyrdom of the witnesses of God (Rev. 11:7-10)

(a) The person involved—"And when they shall have finished their testimony, the beast that ascendeth out of the bottomless pit shall make war against them, and shall overcome them, and kill them" (Rev. 11:7).

---

†**11:7** *The Antichrist is finally allowed to kill them. The word "beast" is first mentioned here in 11:7. There are 35 other references to him in Revelation. It should also be noted that he could not kill the witnesses until "they shall have finished their testimony." Satan cannot touch one hair on the head of the most humble saint until God gives him specific permission (see Job. 1:12; 2:6). These two, like Paul, finished their testimonies (2 Tim. 4:7). Contrast this with Belshazzar's sad death (Dan. 5:26-30).*

(b) The place involved—"And their dead bodies shall lie in the street of the great city, which spiritually is called Sodom and Egypt, where also our Lord was crucified" (Rev. 11:8).

---

†**11:8** *Their bodies will be on display in Jerusalem (11:8). It is called Sodom because of its immorality, and Egypt because of its worldliness.*

(c) The perversion involved—"And they of the people and kindreds and tongues and nations shall see their dead bodies three days and an half, and shall not suffer their dead bodies to be put in graves. And they that dwell upon the earth shall rejoice over them, and make merry, and shall send gifts one to another; because these two prophets tormented them that dwelt on the earth" (Rev. 11:9-10).

(6) The metamorphosis of the witnesses of God (Rev. 11:11-12)

(a) From death to life—"And after three days and an half the Spirit of life from God entered into them, and they stood upon their feet; and great fear fell upon them which saw them" (Rev. 11:11).

(b) From earth to heaven—"And they heard a great voice from heaven saying unto them, Come up hither. And they ascended up to heaven in a cloud; and their enemies beheld them" (Rev. 11:12).

(7) The manifestation of the judgment of God (Rev. 11:13) —"And the same hour was there a great earthquake, and the tenth part of the city fell, and in the earthquake were slain of men seven thousand: and the remnant were affrighted, and gave glory to the God of heaven" (Rev. 11:13).

h. Seventh trumpet (Rev. 11:15-19)
   (1) The proclamation—"And the seventh angel sounded; and there were great voices in heaven, saying, The kingdoms of this world are become the kingdoms of our Lord, and of his Christ; and he shall reign for ever and ever" (Rev. 11:15).
   (2) The adoration—"And the four and twenty elders, which sat before God on their seats, fell upon their faces, and worshipped God, saying, We give thee thanks, O Lord God Almighty, which art, and wast, and art to come; because thou hast taken to thee thy great power, and hast reigned" (Rev. 11:16-17).
   (3) The vindication—"And the nations were angry, and thy wrath is come, and the time of the dead, that they should be judged, and that thou shouldest give reward unto thy servants the prophets, and to the saints, and them that fear thy name, small and great; and shouldest destroy them which destroy the earth. And the temple of God was opened in heaven, and there was seen in his temple the ark of his testament: and there were lightnings, and voices, and thunderings, and an earthquake, and great hail" (Rev. 11:18-19).

---

†11:19 *Note the phrase, "And the temple of God was opened in heaven." It would appear that an actual tabernacle exists in heaven from this and other verses. (See Isa. 6:1-8; Exod. 25:9, 20; Heb. 8:2, 5; 9:24; Rev. 14:15, 17; 15:5-6, 8; 16:1, 17.)*

II. He Allows the Devil to Reign on Earth (Rev. 12–13).
   A. The devil and Israel (Rev. 12)
      1. Satan's former hatred for the Jews (Rev. 12:1-5)
         a. His sin in the beginning when he attempted to steal God's throne—"And there appeared another wonder in heaven; and behold a great red dragon, having seven heads and ten horns, and seven crowns upon his heads" (Rev. 12:3). "And his tail [influence] swept away a third of the stars [angels] of heaven, and threw them to the earth" (Rev. 12:4, NASB).

---

†12:4a *There is no question concerning the identity of this vicious creature. He is given at least five titles and subtitles in Revelation 12 alone.*

A. *The great red dragon (12:3)*—Great, *because of his vast power (see Matt. 4:8-9);* red, *because he was the first murderer (see John 8:44);* dragon, *because of his viciousness (see 2 Cor. 6:15).*
B. *The old serpent (12:9)*—Old, *which takes us back to the Garden of Eden (Gen. 3);* serpent, *which reminds us of the first body he used (Gen. 3).*
C. *The devil (12:9)—One who slanders (see 12:10; also Job 1–2; Zech. 3:1-7; Luke 22:31)*
D. *Satan (12:9)—The adversary (see 1 Pet. 5:8).*
E. *The deceiver of the world (12:9)—Note: He not only deceives men, but angels as well. In 12:4 we are told that his tail "drew [literally, 'pulled down,' or 'to drag'; see Acts 14:19 where the same word is used] the third part of the stars of heaven." This is apparently a reference to the number of angels Satan persuaded to join him in his original revolt against God (Isa. 14:12-15; Ezek. 28:11-19).*

---

b. Satan's sin at Bethlehem, when he attempted to slaughter God's Son—"And his tail drew the third part of the stars of heaven, and did cast them to the earth: and the dragon stood before the woman which was ready to be delivered, for to devour her child as soon as it was born" (Rev. 12:4).

c. Israel's rise—Israel began with Jacob's 12 sons. "And there appeared a great wonder in heaven; a woman clothed with the sun, and the moon under her feet, and upon her head a crown of twelve stars" (Rev. 12:1).

---

†12:1 *Here is the first of four symbolic women in Revelation:*

A. A suffering woman—Israel (Rev. 12)
B. A bloody harlot—The world's religious system (Rev. 17)
C. An arrogant queen—The world's economic system (Rev. 18)
D. A pure bride—The true church (Rev. 19)

---

d. Israel's prize—Israel gave birth to her Messiah. "And she being with child cried, travailing in birth, and pained to be delivered" (Rev. 12:2).

---

†12:2 *We note that she cries aloud in her agony. Dr. Herman A. Hoyt writes: "The activity of the woman from the time of Abraham to the birth of Christ is described in verse 2. The present tense of the verses provides a dramatic setting. The woman is continuously with child. She is continually crying . . . in the pain of travail. She is continuously experiencing labor to be delivered. . . . Herein, then, are pictured the experiences of Israel as a nation from the moment she was brought into existence with the call of Abraham until the day Christ was born in Bethlehem. The entire message of the Old Testament from Genesis to Malachi describes what is here set forth in one verse"* (Revelation, *p. 61).*

---

2. His future hatred for the Jews (Rev. 12:6-17)

a. His defeat in heaven—Satan is cast out of the very heavenlies during the tribulation. "And there was war in heaven: Michael and his angels fought against the dragon; and the dragon fought and his angels, and prevailed not; neither was their place found any more in heaven. And the great dragon was cast out, that old serpent, called the Devil, and Satan, which deceiveth the whole world: he was cast out into the earth, and his angels were cast out with him" (Rev. 12:7-9).

(1) Heaven's reaction to his defeat—"And I heard a loud voice saying in heaven, Now is come salvation, and strength, and the kingdom of our God, and the power of his Christ: for the accuser of our brethren is cast down, which accused them before our God day and night. And they overcame him by the blood of the Lamb, and by the word of their testimony; and they loved not their lives unto the death" (Rev. 12:10-11).

(2) Satan's reaction to his defeat—"Therefore rejoice, ye heavens, and ye that dwell in them. Woe to the inhabiters of the earth and of the sea! for the devil is come down unto you, having great wrath, because he knoweth that he hath but a short time" (Rev. 12:12).

b. His depravity on earth—Satan now instigates an all-out attempt to destroy Israel.

(1) The devil's persecution—"And when the dragon saw that he was cast unto the earth, he persecuted the woman which brought forth the man child. And the serpent cast out of his mouth water as a flood after the woman, that he might cause her to be carried away of the flood. And the dragon was wroth with the woman, and went to make war with the remnant of her seed, which keep the commandments of God, and have the testimony of Jesus Christ" (Rev. 12:13, 15, 17).

---

†12:17 *This marks the last and most severe anti-Semitic movement in history. A. W. Kac writes: "Next to the survival of the Jews, the most baffling historical phenomenon is the hatred which he has repeatedly encountered among the nations of the earth. This hostility to the Jews, which goes under the name of antisemitism, is as old as Jewish existence. It is endemic; i.e., like many contagious diseases it is always with us to some degree. But under certain circumstances it assumes epidemic proportions and characteristics. It is prevalent wherever Jews reside in sufficiently large numbers to make their neighbors aware of their presence. 'The growth of antisemitism,' Chaim Weizman declares, 'is proportionate to the number of Jews per square kilometre. We carry the germs of antisemitism in our knapsack on our backs'"* (Rebirth of the State of Israel, *p. 306).*

Throughout their long history, Satan has made every attempt to exterminate Israel. This he has done by resorting to:

A. Enslaving (Exod. 2)
B. Drowning (Exod. 14)
C. Starving (Exod. 16)
D. Tempting (Exod. 32: Num. 14)
E. Cursing (Num. 23)
F. Capturing (2 Kings 17–24)
G. Swallowing (Jonah 2)
H. Burning (Dan. 3)
I. Devouring (Dan. 6)
J. Hanging (Esther 3)

Of course, to all this could be added the gas ovens of Adolph Hitler. But the most vicious attack is yet to come.

---

(2) The Lord's protection—"And the woman fled into the wilderness, where she hath a place prepared of God, that they should feed her there a thousand two hundred and threescore days. . . . And to the woman were given two wings of a great eagle, that she might fly into the wilderness, into her place, where she is nourished for a time, and times, and half a time, from the face of the serpent. . . . And the earth helped the woman, and the earth opened her mouth, and swallowed up the flood which the dragon cast out of his mouth" (Rev. 12:6, 14, 16).

---

†12:16 *According to Zechariah 13:9 it would seem that at least one third of Israel will remain true to God and be allowed by him to escape into a special hiding place for the duration of the tribulation. We shall now consider the location of this hiding place. While it is not actually specified in*

Scripture, many Bible students believe that this place will be Petra. This is based on the following three passages:

A. Zechariah 14:5: "And ye shall flee to the valley of the mountains, for the valley of the mountains shall reach unto Azal; yea, ye shall flee . . . and the Lord my God shall come, and all the saints with thee." (The "Azal" mentioned here is thought to be connected with Petra.)

B. Isaiah 63:1: "Who is this that cometh from Edom, with dyed garments from Bozrah?" The first few verses of Isaiah 63 deal with the second coming of Christ. He comes to Edom (of which Petra is the capital) and Bozrah (a city in Edom) for some reason, many believe to receive his Hebrew remnant who are hiding there.

C. Daniel 11:41: "He shall enter also into the glorious land, and many countries shall be overthrown; but these shall escape out of his hand, even Edom." Thus for some reason the land of Edom will not be allowed to fall into the hands of the Antichrist. It is assumed by some that the reason is to protect the remnant. Many years ago the noted Bible scholar W. E. Blackstone, on the basis of these verses, hid thousands of copies of the New Testament in and around the caves and rocks of Petra. He felt that someday the terrified survivors of the Antichrist's bloodbath will welcome the opportunity to read God's Word, preferring it even over the Dow-Jones stock average and the Wall Street Journal. *Petra has been called "the rainbow city," and once had 267,000 inhabitants. It was a large market center at the junction of a great caravan route. The city is inaccessible except through the gorge or canyon in the mountains, which is wide enough for only two horses abreast. The perpendicular walls of the gorge are from 400 to 700 feet high and are brilliant in splendor, displaying every color of the rainbow. The old buildings, cut from the solid rock of the mountain, still stand. A clear spring bubbles over rose-red rocks. Wild figs grow on the banks. Everything awaits Israel.*

B. The devil and the world (Rev. 13)
   1. His false son, the Antichrist (Rev. 13:1-10)
      a. The description of the Antichrist—"And I stood upon the sand of the sea, and saw a beast rise up out of the sea, having seven heads and ten horns, and upon his horns ten crowns, and upon his heads the name of blasphemy" (Rev. 13:1). "And the beast which I saw was like unto a leopard, and his feet were as the feet of a bear, and his mouth as the mouth of a lion" (Rev. 13:2).

---

†13:2a

A. The frightful and vicious individual described by John here is given various names and titles in the Scriptures. He is called:

1. *The Antichrist*
2. *The man of sin (2 Thess. 2:8)*
3. *The son of perdition (2 Thess. 2:8)*
4. *The wicked one (2 Thess. 2:8)*
5. *The willful king (Dan. 11:36)*
6. *The beast—This title is found 36 times in the book of Revelation.*
7. *The little horn (Dan. 7:8)*
8. *The seven heads and ten horns may be a political reference to the Antichrist's rise to power. Many believe he will proceed from a ten-dictatorship confederation which will come into existence during the tribulation. These dictators are referred to as "ten horns" in Daniel 7:7;*

Revelation 12:3; 13:1; 17:7, 12. In his rise to power he will defeat three of these dictators (Dan. 7:8, 24). This ten-horned confederation is the revived Roman Empire. This is derived from the fact that the most important prophetic details concerning the old Roman Empire in Daniel 2:40-44 are still unfulfilled.

B. Both Daniel and John write concerning the Antichrist's personal characteristics:

1. He will be an intellectual genius (Dan. 8:23).
2. He will be an oratorical genius (Dan. 11:36).
3. He will be a political genius (Rev. 17:11-12).
4. He will be a commercial genius (Rev. 13:16-17; Dan. 11:43).
5. He will be a military genius (Rev. 6:2; 13:2).
6. He will be a religious genius (Rev. 13:8; 2 Thess. 2:4).

---

b. The authority of the Antichrist—"And the dragon gave him his power, and his seat, and great authority" (Rev. 13:2).

---

†13:2b

A. He begins by controlling the Western power bloc (Rev. 17:12).
B. He makes a seven-year covenant with Israel but breaks it after three and a half years (Dan. 9:27). There is ample scriptural evidence to show that the Antichrist will allow (and perhaps even encourage) the building of the temple and the rendering of its sacrifices during the tribulation. (See Dan. 9:27; Matt. 24:15; 2 Thess. 2:4; Rev. 13:14-15; 11:2.)
C. He gains absolute control over the Middle East after the Russian invasion (Ezek. 38–39).
D. He attempts to destroy all of Israel (Rev. 12).
E. He destroys the false religious system, so that he may rule unhindered (Rev. 17:16-17).
F. He thereupon sets himself up as God (Dan. 11:36; 2 Thess. 2:4-11; Rev. 13:5).
G. He briefly rules over all nations (Psa. 2; Dan. 11:36; Rev. 13:16).
H. He is utterly crushed by the Lord Jesus Christ at the battle of Armageddon (Rev. 19).
I. He is the first creature to be thrown into the lake of fire (Rev. 19:20).

---

c. The possible resurrection of the Antichrist—"And I saw one of his heads as it were wounded to death; and his deadly wound was healed: and all the world wondered after the beast" (Rev. 13:3).

d. The worship of the Antichrist—"And they worshipped the dragon which gave power unto the beast: and they worshipped the beast, saying, Who is like unto the beast? who is able to make war with him? . . . And all that dwell upon the earth shall worship him, whose names are not written in the book of life of the Lamb slain from the foundation of the world" (Rev. 13:4, 8).

e. The power of the Antichrist

(1) Its scope—"And it was given unto him to make war with the saints, and to overcome them: and power was given him over all kindreds, and tongues, and nations" (Rev. 13:7).

(2) Its duration—"And power was given unto him to continue forty and two months" (Rev. 13:5b).

f. The blasphemy of the Antichrist—"And there was given unto him a mouth speaking great things and blasphemies" (Rev. 13:5a). "And he opened his mouth in blasphemy against God, to blaspheme his name, and his tabernacle, and them that dwell in heaven" (Rev. 13:6).

2. His unholy spirit, the false prophet (Rev. 13:11-18)
   a. His militancy—"And I beheld another beast coming up out of the earth; and he had two horns like a lamb, and he spake as a dragon" (Rev. 13:11). "And he exerciseth all the power of the first beast" (Rev. 13:12).

---

†13:12 *Who is this second beast of Revelation 13 who is also called on three later occasions "the false prophet" (Rev. 16:13; 19:20; 20:10)? Some believe he will be a Jew (while the Antichrist will be a Gentile), and that he will head up the apostate church.*

---

   b. His mission—"And causeth the earth and them which dwell therein to worship the first beast, whose deadly wound was healed" (Rev. 13:12).
   c. His miracles
      (1) The deception—"And he doeth great wonders, so that he maketh fire come down from heaven on the earth in the sight of men" (Rev. 13:13).
      (2) The deceived—"And deceiveth them that dwell on the earth by the means of those miracles which he had power to do in the sight of the beast; saying to them that dwell on the earth, that they should make an image to the beast, which had the wound by a sword, and did live" (Rev. 13:14).
   d. His mark
      (1) The nature of this mark—"And he had power to give life unto the image of the beast, that the image of the beast should both speak, and cause that as many as would not worship the image of the beast should be killed. And he causeth all, both small and great, rich and poor, free and bond, to receive a mark in their right hand, or in their foreheads: and that no man might buy or sell, save he that had the mark, or the name of the beast, or the number of his name" (Rev. 13:15-17).
      (2) The number of this mark—"Here is wisdom. Let him that hath understanding count the number of the beast: for it is the number of a man; and his number is Six hundred threescore and six" (Rev. 13:18).

---

†13:18 *To understand this passage requires some basic information concerning the world 2,000 years ago. When the Apostle John wrote these words an identification system known as Gematria was widely practiced. Under this arrangement, the Greek, Latin, and Hebrew alphabetical letters also represented a specific number. We do not have this system in the English alphabet, but if we did, the letter A might stand for the number six, B for 12, C for 18, etc. Of course, all those speaking the language where this practice is observed would have to agree upon the numerical equivalent of each letter. With this in mind, what John is saying here is that the total number of the name used by the Antichrist during the tribulation will equal 666. The figure will then become all important in matters of buying, selling, etc. What does this mean? It seems to suggest that at the beginning of the tribulation the world will adopt some sort of letter-numbering system.*

III. He Pours Out the Seven Vial Judgments (Rev. 14–16).

A. Those events preceding the vial judgments (Rev. 14–15)

1. The song of the witnesses of God (Rev. 14:1-5)—"And I looked, and, lo, a Lamb stood on the mount Sion, and with him an hundred forty and four thousand, having his Father's name written in their foreheads. . . . And they sung as it were a new song before the throne, and before the four beasts, and the elders: and no man could learn that song but the hundred and forty and four thousand, which were redeemed from the earth" (Rev. 14:1, 3).

---

†**14:3** *This group is the same as mentioned in chapter 7. There they are redeemed. Here they are raptured. And note—not one is missing. J. Vernon McGee writes: "It is clear from Chapter 13 that this is the darkest day and the most horrible hour in history. It is truly hell's holiday. Every thoughtful mind must inevitably ask the question—How did God's people fare during this period? Could they make it through to the end with overwhelming odds against them? The Shepherd who began with 144,000 sheep is now identified with them as a Lamb with 144,000. He did not lose one"* (Reveling Through Revelation, *p. 21).*

---

2. The messages of the angels of God (Rev. 14:6-12)

a. First message—"Saying with a loud voice, Fear God, and give glory to him; for the hour of his judgment is come: and worship him that made heaven, and earth, and the sea, and the fountains of waters" (Rev. 14:7).

b. Second message—"And there followed another angel, saying, Babylon is fallen, is fallen, that great city, because she made all nations drink of the wine of the wrath of her fornication" (Rev. 14:8).

c. Third message

(1) Concerning the people who were worshiping the beast —"And the third angel followed them, saying with a loud voice, If any man worship the beast and his image, and receive his mark in his forehead, or in his hand" (Rev. 14:9).

(2) Concerning the punishment for worshipping the beast—"The same shall drink of the wine of the wrath of God, which is poured out without mixture into the cup of his indignation; and he shall be tormented with fire and brimstone in the presence of the holy angels, and in the presence of the Lamb: and the smoke of their torment ascendeth up for ever and ever: and they have no rest day nor night, who worship the beast and his image, and whosoever receiveth the mark of his name" (Rev. 14:10-11).

---

†**14:11** *Here is the last hellfire-and-brimstone message that will ever be preached to the unsaved, and it is delivered not by a Jonathan Edwards or a Billy Sunday, but by an angel. Apparently no one responds to the invitation. Here God will pour out his undiluted wrath, something he has done once before upon Christ at Calvary. How tragic that Christ once drank this same cup for the very unrepentant sinners who are now forced to drink it again.*

---

3. The assurance of the Spirit of God—"And I heard a voice from heaven saying unto me, Write, Blessed are the dead which die in the Lord from henceforth:

Yea, saith the Spirit, that they may rest from their labours; and their works do follow them" (Rev. 14:13).

---

†14:13 *It has been rightly observed that this world is the only* heaven *the unsaved will ever know, and the only* hell *the saved will ever experience.*

---

4. The reaping of the harvest of God (Rev. 14:14-20)
   a. The Judge (the Lord Jesus Christ, assisted by the angels)—"And I looked, and behold a white cloud, and upon the cloud one sat like unto the Son of man, having on his head a golden crown, and in his hand a sharp sickle" (Rev. 14:14).
   b. The judged—"And he that sat on the cloud thrust in his sickle on the earth; and the earth was reaped. . . . And the angel thrust in his sickle into the earth, and gathered the vine of the earth, and cast it into the great winepress of the wrath of God. And the winepress was trodden without the city, and blood came out of the winepress, even unto the horse bridles, by the space of a thousand and six hundred furlongs" (Rev. 14:16, 19-20).

---

†14:20 *This is the first of three references in Revelation to the Battle of Armageddon. It is mentioned again in 16:13-16 and 19:17-19. An overview of this battle is given under the final reference.*

---

5. The praise of the victors of God (Rev. 15:1-4)—"And I saw as it were a sea of glass mingled with fire: and them that had gotten the victory over the beast, and over his image, and over his mark, and over the number of his name, stand on the sea of glass, having the harps of God. And they sing the song of Moses the servant of God, and the song of the Lamb, saying, Great and marvellous are thy works, Lord God Almighty; just and true are thy ways, thou King of saints. Who shall not fear thee, O Lord, and glorify thy name? for thou only art holy: for all nations shall come and worship before thee; for thy judgments are made manifest" (Rev. 15:2-4).

---

†15:4 *There are two songs mentioned here, the song of Moses and the song of the Lamb. Note the contrast between the two: The song of Moses was sung beside the Red Sea (Exod. 15); the song of the Lamb will be sung beside the crystal sea. The song of Moses was sung over Egypt; the song of the Lamb will be sung over Babylon. The song of Moses described how God brought his people out; the song of the Lamb will describe how God brings his people in. The song of Moses was Scripture's first song; the song of the Lamb will be Scripture's last song.*

---

6. The events in the temple of God (Rev. 15:5-8)
   a. The guardians of the temple—"And after that I looked, and, behold, the temple of the tabernacle of the testimony in heaven was opened: and the seven angels came out of the temple, having the seven plagues, clothed in pure and white linen, and having their breasts girded with golden girdles. And one of the four beasts gave unto the seven angels seven golden vials

full of the wrath of God, who liveth for ever and ever" (Rev. 15:5-7).

b. The glory in the temple—"And the temple was filled with smoke from the glory of God, and from his power; and no man was able to enter into the temple, till the seven plagues of the seven angels were fulfilled" (Rev. 15:8).

---

†15:8 *John Phillips writes: "Since Calvary, the way into the holiest in heaven has been opened to all, because the blood of Christ has blazed a highway to the heart of God. But now, for a brief spell, that royal road is barred. God's wrath, once poured out upon His Son on man's behalf, is to be out-poured again. The world which crucified the Lamb and which now has crowned its rebellions with the worship of the beast, is to be judged to the full. So bright glory burns within the temple, filling it with smoke and standing guard at the door. The way into the holiest is barred again for a while"* (Exploring Revelation, *p. 198).*

B. Those events accompanying the vial judgments (Rev. 16)—"And I saw another sign in heaven, great and marvellous, seven angels having the seven last plagues; for in them is filled up the wrath of God. . . . And I heard a great voice out of the temple saying to the seven angels, Go your ways, and pour out the vials of the wrath of God upon the earth" (Rev. 15:1; 16:1).

1. First vial judgment (Rev. 16:2)—"And the first went, and poured out his vial upon the earth; and there fell a noisome and grievous sore upon the men which had the mark of the beast, and upon them which worshipped his image" (Rev. 16:2).

---

†16:2 *J. Vernon McGee writes: "God is engaged in germ warfare upon the followers of anti-christ. . . . These putrefying sores are worse than leprosy or cancer. This compares to the sixth plague in Egypt, and is the same type of sore or boil (Exod. 9:8-12)."* (Reveling Through Revelation, *p. 36).*

---

2. Second vial judgment (Rev. 16:3)—"And the second angel poured out his vial upon the sea; and it became as the blood of a dead man: and every living soul died in the sea" (Rev. 16:3).

---

†16:3 *Charles Ryrie states: "The second bowl is poured on the sea, with the result that the waters became blood and every living thing in the sea dies. The 'as' is misplaced in the Authorized Version, the correct reading being 'became blood as of a dead man.' The vivid image is of a dead person wallowing in his own blood. The seas will wallow in blood. Under the second trumpet, one third of the sea creatures died (8:9); now the destruction is complete. The stench and disease that this will cause along the shores of the seas of the earth are unimaginable"* (Revelation, *p. 97).*

---

3. Third vial judgment (Rev. 16:4-7)

a. The action—"And the third angel poured out his vial upon the rivers and fountains of waters; and they became blood" (Rev. 16:4).

b. The reaction—"And I heard the angel of the waters say, Thou art righteous, O Lord, which art, and wast, and shalt be, because thou hast judged thus.

For they have shed the blood of saints and prophets, and thou hast given them blood to drink; for they are worthy" (Rev. 16:5-6).

---

†16:6 *Two significant things may be noted in these verses:*

A. This third vial judgment is, among other things, an answer to the cry of the martyrs under the altar at the beginning of the tribulation. Their prayer at that time was, "How long, O Lord, holy and true, dost thou not judge and avenge our blood on them that dwell on the earth?" (Rev. 6:10).

B. These verses indicate that God has assigned a special angel as superintendent on earth's waterworks. When we compare this with Revelation 7:1, where we are told that four other angels control the world's winds, we realize that even during the hellishness of the tribulation, this world is still controlled by God.

---

4. Fourth vial judgment (Rev. 16:8-9)
   a. The action—"And the fourth angel poured out his vial upon the sun; and power was given unto him to scorch men with fire" (Rev. 16:8).
   b. The reaction—"And men were scorched with great heat, and blasphemed the name of God, which hath power over these plagues: and they repented not to give him glory" (Rev. 16:9).

---

†16:9 *Perhaps the two most illuminating passages in Scripture about man's total depravity can be found in Revelation 9:20-21 and 16:9. Both sections deal with the world's attitude toward God during the tribulation. What do these verses prove? They prove that in spite of horrible wars, of terrible famines, of darkened skies, of raging fires, of bloody seas, of stinging locusts, of demonic persecutions, of mighty earthquakes, of falling stars, and of cancerous sores, sinful mankind still will not repent.*

---

5. Fifth vial judgment (Rev. 16:10-11)
   a. The action—"And the fifth angel poured out his vial upon the seat of the beast; and his kingdom was full of darkness; and they gnawed their tongues for pain" (Rev. 16:10).
   b. The reaction—"And blasphemed the God of heaven because of their pains and their sores, and repented not of their deeds" (Rev. 16:11).

---

†16:11 *This plague, poured out upon "the seat of the beast" (literally, his "throne"), will apparently concentrate itself upon the ten nations of the revived Roman Empire. Again we read those tragic words "and repented not of their deeds."*

---

6. Sixth vial judgment (Rev. 16:12-16)
   a. The what of this judgment—"And the sixth angel poured out his vial upon the great river Euphrates; and the water thereof was dried up, that the way of the kings of the east might be prepared" (Rev. 16:12).

---

†16:12 *Here the God of heaven employs psychological warfare upon his enemies, conditioning them to gather themselves together in the near future at Armageddon. The Euphrates River is 1,800 miles* *long and in some places 3,600 feet wide. It is 30 feet deep. This river has been the dividing line between western and eastern civilization since the dawn of history. It served as the eastern border of the Old Roman Empire. Thus, the Euphrates becomes both the cradle and grave of man's civilization. Here the first godless city (Enoch, built by Cain; see Gen. 4:16-17) went up, and here the last rebellious city will be constructed (Babylon, built by the Antichrist; see Rev. 18).*

---

b. The who of this judgment—"And I saw three unclean spirits like frogs come out of the mouth of the dragon, and out of the mouth of the beast, and out of the mouth of the false prophet" (Rev. 16:13).

c. The why of this judgment—"For they are the spirits of devils, working miracles, which go forth unto the kings of the earth and of the whole world, to gather them to the battle of that great day of God Almighty. . . . And he gathered them together into a place called in the Hebrew tongue Armageddon" (Rev. 16:14, 16).

d. The warning of this judgment—"Behold, I come as a thief. Blessed is he that watcheth, and keepeth his garments, lest he walk naked, and they see his shame" (Rev. 16:15).

7. Seventh vial judgment (Rev. 16:17-21)—"And the seventh angel poured out his vial into the air; and there came a great voice out of the temple of heaven, from the throne, saying, It is done" (Rev. 16:17).

a. History's greatest earthquake—"And there were voices, and thunders, and lightnings; and there was a great earthquake, such as was not since men were upon the earth, so mighty an earthquake, and so great. And the great city was divided into three parts, and the cities of the nations fell: and great Babylon came in remembrance before God, to give unto her the cup of the wine of the fierceness of his wrath. And every island fled away, and the mountains were not found" (Rev. 16:18-20).

b. History's greatest hailstorm—"And there fell upon men a great hail out of heaven, every stone about the weight of a talent: and men blasphemed God because of the plague of the hail; for the plague thereof was exceeding great" (Rev. 16:21).

---

†**16:21** *The seventh and final vial judgment brings about two frightening events:*

A. The world's greatest earthquake takes place. The intensity of an earthquake is measured on an instrument called a Richter scale. The greatest magnitude ever recorded so far has been 8.9. The greatest loss of life due to an earthquake occurred on January 23, 1556, in Shensi Province, China, and killed some 830,000 people. However, that earthquake will be but a mild tremor compared to the tribulation earthquake, which, we are told, will level all the great cities of the world.

B. The world's greatest shower of hailstones comes crashing down on mankind. These gigantic icy chunks will weigh up to 125 pounds apiece.

IV. He Destroys the World's Religious Systems (Rev. 17).

---

†*This brutal, bloody, and blasphemous harlot is none other than the universal false church, the wicked wife of Satan. God had no sooner begun his blessed work in preparing for himself a people*

than the devil did likewise. In fact, the first baby to be born on this earth later became Satan's original convert. (See Gen. 4:8; 1 John 3:12.) We shall now consider the historical and future activities of this perverted prostitute.

A. The history of this harlot (Rev. 17:1-6)—"And there came one of the seven angels which had the seven vials, and talked with me, saying unto me, Come hither; I will shew unto thee the judgment of the great whore that sitteth upon many waters. . . . So he carried me away in the spirit into the wilderness: and I saw a woman sit upon a scarlet coloured beast, full of names of blasphemy, having seven heads and ten horns" (Rev. 17:1, 3).
   1. Depraved with the filth of hell—"With whom the kings of the earth have committed fornication, and the inhabitants of the earth have been made drunk with the wine of her fornication. . . . And upon her forehead was a name written, MYSTERY, BABYLON THE GREAT, THE MOTHER OF HARLOTS AND ABOMINATIONS OF THE EARTH" (Rev. 17:2, 5).
   2. Decked with the wealth of the world—"And the woman was arrayed in purple and scarlet colour, and decked with gold and precious stones and pearls, having a golden cup in her hand full of abominations and filthiness of her fornication" (Rev. 17:4).
   3. Drunken with the blood of saints—"And I saw the woman drunken with the blood of the saints, and with the blood of the martyrs of Jesus: and when I saw her, I wondered with great admiration" (Rev. 17:6).

---

†17:6

A. Satan's church began officially at the Tower of Babel in Genesis 11:1-9, nearly 24 centuries B.C. *Here, in the fertile plain of Shinar, probably very close to the original Garden of Eden, the first spade of dirt was turned for the purpose of devil-worship.*

B. The first full-time minister of Satan was Nimrod, Noah's wicked and apostate grandson (Gen. 10:8-10).

C. Secular history and tradition tell us that Nimrod married a woman who was as evil and demonic as himself. Her name was Semerimus. Knowing God's promise of a future Savior (Gen. 3:15), Semerimus brazenly claimed that Tammuz, her first son, fulfilled this prophecy.

D. Semerimus thereupon instituted a religious system which made both her and her son the objects of divine worship. She herself became the first high priestess. Thus began the mother-child cult which later spread all over the world. The city of Babylon was the seat of Satan worship until it fell, in 539 B.C.*, to the Persians.*

1. *From Babylon it spread to Phoenicia under the name of Ashteroth and Tammuz.*
2. *From Phoenicia it traveled to Pergamos in Asia Minor. This is the reason for John's admonition to the church at Pergamos in the book of Revelation: "I know thy works, and where thou dwellest, even where Satan's seat is" (Rev. 2:13).*
3. *In Egypt the mother-child cult was known as Isia and Horus.*
4. *In Greece it became Aphrodite and Eros.*
5. *In Rome this pair was worshiped as Venus and Cupid.*
6. *In China it became known as Mother Shing Moo and her child. Dr. J. Dwight Pentecost writes: "Several years ago I visited an archaeological museum in Mexico City. A recent find had just been put on display which Mexican archaeologists had authenticated as belonging*

to the period about 200 years before Christ. The object was the center of religious worship among some of the early Indians in Mexico. To my amazement, it was an image of a mother with a child in her arms. This Babylonian religion spread abroad to become the religion of the world" (Prophecy for Today, *p. 133).*

E. What was the teaching of Semerimus' satanic church?

1. That Semerimus herself was the way to God—She actually adopted the title "Queen of Heaven."

2. That she alone could administer salvation to the sinner through various sacraments, such as the sprinkling of holy water.

3. That her son Tammuz was tragically slain by a wild boar during a hunting trip.

4. That he was, however, resurrected from the dead 40 days later. Thus, each year afterward, the temple virgins of this cult would enter a 40-day fast as a memorial to Tammuz's death and resurrection.

5. After the 40-day fast, a joyful feast called Ishtar took place. At this feast colored eggs were exchanged and eaten as a symbol of the resurrection. An evergreen tree was displayed and a yule log was burned. Finally, hot cakes marked with the letter "T" (to remind everybody of Tammuz) were baked and eaten.

F. About 2000 B.C., *God called Abraham away from all this (see Josh. 24:2-3) and led him into the Promised Land. But by the ninth century* B.C., *Israel had returned to this devil-worship under the influence of wicked Jezebel (1 Kings 16:30-33). At this time the cult was worshiped under the name of Baal.*

G. Both Ezekiel and Jeremiah warned against this hellish thing. "Then he brought me to the door of the gate of the Lord's house which was toward the north; and behold, there sat women weeping for Tammuz" (Ezek. 8:14). "The children gather wood, and the fathers kindle the fire, and the women knead their dough, to make cakes to the queen of heaven . . . to burn incense to the queen of heaven, and to pour out drink offerings unto her" (Jer. 7:18; 44:25).

H. By the time of Christ, this cult had so influenced Roman life that the Caesars were not only crowned as emperors of Rome, but also bore the title Pontifex Maximus, *meaning "high priest." They were high priests of the Babylonian satanic church.*

B. The future of this harlot (Rev. 17:7-18)

1. To be teamed up (at first) with the Antichrist (Rev. 17:7-9)—"And the angel said unto me, Wherefore didst thou marvel? I will tell thee the mystery of the woman, and of the beast that carrieth her, which hath the seven heads and ten horns" (Rev. 17:7). It is thought that both the religious system (the mystery Babylon, v. 5), and the political system (the 10 kings of v. 12) join up with the Antichrist (the beast of vv. 7-8, 11-13) at the beginning of the tribulation. "These have one mind, and shall give their power and strength unto the beast" (Rev. 17:13).
2. To be torn up (at last) by the Antichrist (Rev. 17:15-17)—"And the ten horns which thou sawest upon the beast, these shall hate the whore, and shall make her desolate and naked, and shall eat her flesh, and burn her with fire. For God hath put in their hearts to fulfil his will, and to agree, and give their kingdom unto the beast, until the words of God shall be fulfilled" (Rev. 17:16-17).

---

†17:17 *In essence, the false church lends all her evil strength to elevate the Antichrist during the first part of the tribulation. For awhile she flourishes, luxuriating in surpassing wealth and opulence.*

But suddenly things change drastically. The Antichrist suddenly turns on her. The probable reason for all this is that after she has put the Antichrist into power, the harlot then attempts to control him. History gives us many examples of various religious systems attempting to control kings and rulers. But the Antichrist won't bow. He will turn on her, destroy her buildings, burn her "holy" books, and murder her priests. One of the most ironical turn of events in all history will be the destruction of the false church. For this evil organization will meet its doom not at the hands of Gabriel, or the Father, or the Son, or the Spirit, but the Antichrist.

V. He Destroys the World's Political and Economic Systems (Rev. 18).

---

†*Dr. J. Vernon McGee writes: "In chapters 17 and 18 two Babylons are brought before us. The Babylon of chapter 17 is ecclesiastical. The Babylon of chapter 18 is economic. The first is religious—the apostate church. The second is political and commercial. The apostate church is hated by the kings of the earth (Rev. 17:16); the commercial center is loved by the kings of the earth (Rev. 18:9). The apostate church is destoyed by the kings of the earth; political Babylon is destroyed by the judgment of God (verses 5, 8). Obviously, mystery Babylon is destroyed first—in the midst of the Great Tribulation; while commercial Babylon is destroyed at the Second Coming of Christ. These two Babylons are not one and the same city"* (Reveling Through Revelation, *p. 58).*

It is possible that a literal city will become the headquarters for both of these systems, probably built by the Antichrist himself. "What city is like unto this great city!" (Rev. 18:18).

---

†**18:18** *Charles Ryrie writes: "Whether the city will be rebuilt once again on the Euphrates is a matter of debate. Nevertheless, the name is used for more than a city in these chapters (17–18); it also stands for a system. This is much the same as the way Americans speak of Wall Street or Madison Avenue. They are actual streets, but they also stand for the financial or advertising enterprises"* (Revelation, *p. 100).*

A. The designation of the city—"That great city Babylon, that mighty city" (Rev. 18:10). A literal interpretation of this chapter would say ancient Babylon will be rebuilt by the Antichrist during the tribulation and become his headquarters.
B. The denunciation of the city—"And after these things I saw another angel come down from heaven, having great power; and the earth was lightened with his glory" (Rev. 18:1). "And he cried mightily with a strong voice, saying, Babylon the great is fallen, is fallen" (Rev. 18:2). "For her sins have reached unto heaven, and God hath remembered her iniquities. . . . And a mighty angel took up a stone like a great millstone, and cast it into the sea, saying, Thus with violence shall that great city Babylon be thrown down, and shall be found no more at all" (Rev. 18:5, 21).
C. The degeneration of this city
   1. Godless materialism—"Cargoes of gold and silver and precious stones and pearls and fine linen and purple and silk and scarlet, and every kind of citron wood and every article of ivory and every article made from very costly wood and bronze and iron and marble, and cinnamon and spice and incense and perfume and frankincense and wine and olive oil and fine flour and wheat and

cattle and sheep, and cargoes of horses and chariots" (Rev. 18:12-13, NASB).

2. Arrogance and pride—"How much she hath glorified herself, and lived deliciously, so much torment and sorrow give her: for she saith in her heart, I sit a queen, and am no widow, and shall see no sorrow" (Rev. 18:7).
3. Immorality—"For all nations have drunk of the wine of the wrath of her fornication, and the kings of the earth have committed fornication with her, and the merchants of the earth are waxed rich through the abundance of her delicacies" (Rev. 18:3).
4. Demonism and false religions—"And he cried mightily with a strong voice, saying, Babylon the great is fallen, is fallen, and is become the habitation of devils, and the hold of every foul spirit, and a cage of every unclean and hateful bird" (Rev. 18:2).
5. Drug peddling—"For by thy sorceries were all nations deceived" (Rev. 18:23b).
6. Slavery—"And slaves, and souls of men" (Rev. 18:13b).
7. Blood shedding—"And in her was found the blood of prophets, and of saints, and of all that were slain upon the earth" (Rev. 18:24).

D. The devastation of the city

1. The source of its destruction—God himself. "For strong is the Lord God who judgeth her" (Rev. 18:8b). "For God hath avenged . . . her" (Rev. 18:20b).
2. The means of its destruction—Possibly by nuclear energy. This is suggested because of the quickness and nature of the destruction. "Therefore shall her plagues come in one day, death, and mourning, and famine; and she shall be utterly burned with fire" (Rev. 18:8). "The kings of the earth . . . when they shall see the smoke of her burning, standing afar off for the fear of her torment, saying, Alas, alas . . . for in one hour is thy judgment come" (Rev. 18:9-10). "For in one hour so great riches is come to nought" (Rev. 18:17). "For in one hour she is made desolate" (Rev. 18:19).
3. The reaction to its destruction
    a. Despair on earth—"And the merchants of the earth shall weep and mourn over her; for no man buyeth their merchandise any more: and they cast dust on their heads, and cried, weeping and wailing, saying, Alas, alas, that great city, wherein were made rich all that had ships in the sea by reason of her costliness! for in one hour is she made desolate" (Rev. 18:11, 19).
    b. Delight in heaven—"Rejoice over her, thou heaven, and ye holy apostles and prophets; for God hath avenged you on her" (Rev. 18:20).

VI. He Defeats His Enemies at Armageddon (Rev. 19).

A. The celebration in heaven (Rev. 19:1-10)

1. Praising God for his wrath upon a cruel whore (Rev. 19:1-5)—"And after these things I heard a great voice of much people in heaven, saying, Alleluia; Salvation, and glory, and honour, and power, unto the Lord our God: for true and righteous are his judgments: for he hath judged the great whore, which did corrupt the earth with her fornication, and hath avenged the blood of his servants at her hand" (Rev. 19:1-2).
2. Praising God for his wedding to a chaste wife (Rev. 19:6-10)—"Let us be glad and rejoice, and give honour to him: for the marriage of the Lamb is come, and his wife hath made herself ready. And to her was granted that she should be arrayed in fine linen, clean and white: for the fine linen is the righteousness of saints. And he saith unto me, Write, Blessed are they which are called unto the

marriage supper of the Lamb. And he saith unto me, These are the true sayings of God" (Rev. 19:7-9).

---

†19:9 *There are three events in the tribulation which cause all of heaven to rejoice.*

A. When Satan is cast out (Rev. 12:12)

B. When Babylon is destroyed (Rev. 18:20)

C. When the Lamb is married to the church (Rev. 19:7) This glorious event is celebrated by the usage of heaven's greatest praise word. That word is Alleluia *(Halleluja)! Nowhere else in the New Testament can it be found. The Holy Spirit has reserved it for this occasion. (In the Old Testament it appears some 24 times in the Psalms.) Heaven now celebrates the Lamb's victory over the harlot, and his marriage to the bride. We are told that "to her was granted that she should be arrayed in fine linen, clean and white: for the fine linen is the righteousness of saints" (19:8). Dr. Charles Ryrie writes: "The bride's array, fine linen, which is explained as 'the righteousness,' requires the translation 'righteous deeds.' In other words, the wedding garment of the bride will be made up of the righteous deeds done in life. The bride is the bride because of the righteousness of Christ; the bride is clothed for the wedding because of her acts"* (Revelation, *p. 111). Dr. Lehman Strauss writes: "Has it ever occurred to you . . . that at the marriage of the Bride to the Lamb, each of us will be wearing the wedding garment of our own making?"*

B. The confrontation on earth (Rev. 19:11-21)

1. The appearance of heaven's King—"And I saw heaven opened, and behold a white horse; and he that sat upon him was called Faithful and True, and in righteousness he doth judge and make war" (Rev. 19:11).
2. The attire of heaven's King—"His eyes were as a flame of fire, and on his head were many crowns; and he had a name written, that no man knew, but he himself. And he was clothed with a vesture dipped in blood: and his name is called The Word of God. . . . And he hath on his vesture and on his thigh a name written, KING OF KINGS, AND LORD OF LORDS" (Rev. 19:12-13, 16).
3. The armies of heaven's King—"And the armies which were in heaven followed him upon white horses, clothed in fine linen, white and clean" (Rev. 19:14).
4. The action of heaven's King
   a. Armageddon—The victory over Satan's horseman. "And out of his mouth goeth a sharp sword, that with it he should smite the nations: and he shall rule them with a rod of iron: and he treadeth the winepress of the fierceness and wrath of Almighty God. . . . And I saw an angel standing in the sun; and he cried with a loud voice, saying to all the fowls that fly in the midst of heaven, Come and gather yourselves together unto the supper of the great God; that ye may eat the flesh of kings, and the flesh of captains, and the flesh of mighty men, and the flesh of horses, and of them that sit on them, and the flesh of all men, both free and bond, both small and great. . . . And the remnant were slain with the sword of him that sat upon the horse, which sword proceeded out of his mouth: and all the fowls were filled with their flesh" (Rev. 19:15, 17-18, 21).

---

†19:21 *Dr. Herman A. Hoyt aptly describes Armageddon: "The staggering dimensions of this conflict can scarcely be conceived by man. The battlefield will stretch from Megiddo on the north*

(Zech. 12:11; Rev. 16:16) to Edom on the south (Isa. 34:5-6; 63:1), a distance of sixteen hundred furlongs—approximately two hundred miles. It will reach from the Mediterranean Sea on the west to the hills of Moab on the east, a distance of almost one hundred miles. It will include the Valley of Jehoshaphat (Joel 3:2, 12) and the Plains of Esdraelon. At the center of the entire area will be the city of Jerusalem (Zech. 14:1-2). Into this area the multiplied millions of men, doubtless approaching 400 million, will be crowded for the final holocaust of humanity. The kings with their armies will come from the north and the south, from the east and from the west. . . . In the most dramatic sense this will be the 'Valley of decision' for humanity (Joel 3:14) and the great winepress into which will be poured the fierceness of the wrath of Almighty God (Rev. 19:15)" (The End of Times, *p. 163).*

---

b. Gehenna—The victory over Satan's henchman. "And I saw the beast, and the kings of the earth, and their armies, gathered together to make war against him that sat on the horse, and against his army. And the beast was taken, and with him the false prophet that wrought miracles before him, with which he deceived them that had received the mark of the beast, and them that worshipped his image. These both were cast alive into a lake of fire burning with brimstone" (Rev. 19:19-20).

PART FOUR: The Reign of the Lamb Instituted (Rev. 20)

I. The Great Chain (Rev. 20:1-3)
- A. The prisoner—"And I saw an angel come down from heaven, having the key of the bottomless pit and a great chain in his hand. And he laid hold on the dragon, that old serpent, which is the Devil, and Satan, and bound him a thousand years" (Rev. 20:1-2).
- B. The prison—"And cast him into the bottomless pit, and shut him up, and set a seal upon him, that he should deceive the nations no more, till the thousand years should be fulfilled: and after that he must be loosed a little season" (Rev. 20:3).

II. The Great Reign
- A. The resurrection of the just—"But the rest of the dead lived not again until the thousand years were finished. This is the first resurrection. Blessed and holy is he that hath part in the first resurrection: on such the second death hath no power, but they shall be priests of God and of Christ, and shall reign with him a thousand years" (Rev. 20:5-6).
- B. The rule of the just—"And I saw thrones, and they sat upon them, and judgment was given unto them: and I saw the souls of them that were beheaded for the witness of Jesus, and for the word of God, and which had not worshipped the beast, neither his image, neither had received his mark upon their foreheads, or in their hands; and they lived and reigned with Christ a thousand years" (Rev. 20:4).

III. The Great Revolt
- A. The adversary—"And when the thousand years are expired, Satan shall be loosed out of his prison" (Rev. 20:7).
- B. The arrogance—"And shall go out to deceive the nations which are in the four quarters of the earth, Gog and Magog, to gather them together to battle: the number of whom is as the sand of the sea" (Rev. 20:8).

†20:8 *Dr. J. Dwight Pentecost quotes F. C. Jennings, who writes: "Has human nature changed, at least apart from sovereign grace? Is the carnal mind at last at friendship with God? Have a thousand years of absolute power and absolute benevolence, both in unchecked activity, done away with all war forever and forever? These questions must be marked by a practical test. Let Satan be loosed once more from his prison. Let him range once more earth's smiling fields that he knew of old. He saw them last soaked with blood and flooded with tears, the evidence and accompaniments of his own reign; he sees them now 'laughing with abundance'. . . But as he pursues his way further from Jerusalem, the center of this blessedness, these tokens become fainter, until, in the far off 'corner of the earth,' they cease altogether, for he finds myriads who have instinctively shrunk from close contact with that holy center, and are not unprepared once more to be deceived"* (Things to Come, *p. 549).*

C. The attack—"And they went up on the breadth of the earth, and compassed the camp of the saints about, and the beloved city: and fire came down from God out of heaven, and devoured them" (Rev. 20:9).

D. The abyss—"And the devil that deceived them was cast into the lake of fire and brimstone, where the beast and the false prophet are, and shall be tormented day and night for ever and ever" (Rev. 20:10).

IV. The Great Throne (Rev. 20:11-15)

A. The Judge—"And I saw a great white throne, and him that sat on it, from whose face the earth and the heaven fled away; and there was found no place for them" (Rev. 20:11).

B. The judged—"And I saw the dead, small and great, stand before God; and the books were opened: and another book was opened, which is the book of life: and the dead were judged out of those things which were written in the books, according to their works. And the sea gave up the dead which were in it; and death and hell delivered up the dead which were in them: and they were judged every man according to their works" (Rev. 20:12-13).

C. The judgment—"And death and hell were cast into the lake of fire. This is the second death. And whosoever was not found written in the book of life was cast into the lake of fire" (Rev. 20:14-15).

PART FIVE: The Wife of the Lamb Introduced (Rev. 21–22)

"And there came unto me one of the seven angels which had the seven vials full of the seven last plagues, and talked with me, saying, Come hither, I will shew thee the bride, the Lamb's wife" (Rev. 21:9).

I. Her Habitation—The Fabulous City (Rev. 21:1–22:5). "And I saw a new heaven and a new earth: for the first heaven and the first earth were passed away; and there was no more sea. And I John saw the holy city, new Jerusalem, coming down from God out of heaven, prepared as a bride adorned for her husband. And I heard a great voice out of heaven saying, Behold, the tabernacle of God is with men, and he will dwell with them, and they shall be his people, and God himself shall be with them, and be their God. And God shall wipe away all tears from their eyes; and there shall be no more death, neither sorrow, nor crying, neither shall there be any more pain: for the former things are passed away. . . . And he carried me away in the spirit to a great and high mountain, and shewed me that great city, the holy Jerusalem, descending out of heaven from God, having the glory of God: and her light was like unto a stone most precious, even like a jasper stone, clear as crystal" (Rev. 21:1-4, 10-11). "And the city was pure gold, like unto clear glass" (Rev. 21:18).

A. Its purity—"But the fearful, and unbelieving, and the abominable, and murderers, and whoremongers, and sorcerers, and idolaters, and all liars, shall have their part in the lake which burneth with fire and brimstone: which is the second death. . . . And there shall in no wise enter into it any thing that defileth, neither whatsoever worketh abomination, or maketh a lie: but they which are written in the Lamb's book of life" (Rev. 21:8, 27).

B. Its wall—"And had a wall great and high" (Rev. 21:12). "And the wall of the city had twelve foundations, and in them the names of the twelve apostles of the Lamb. And he measured the wall thereof, an hundred and forty and four cubits, according to the measure of a man, that is, of the angel" (Rev. 21:14, 17). "And the building of the wall . . . was of jasper" (Rev. 21:18).

C. Its gates—"And had twelve gates, and at the gates twelve angels, and names written thereon, which are the names of the twelve tribes of the children of Israel" (Rev. 21:12). "On the east three gates; on the north three gates; on the south three gates; and on the west three gates" (Rev. 21:13). "And the twelve gates were twelve pearls; every several gate was of one pearl" (Rev. 21:21). And the gates of it shall not be shut at all by day: for there shall be no night there" (Rev. 21:25).

D. Its size and shape—"And he that talked with me had a golden reed to measure the city, and the gates thereof, and the wall thereof. And the city lieth foursquare, and the length is as large as the breadth: and he measured the city with the reed, twelve thousand furlongs. The length and the breadth and the height of it are equal" (Rev. 21:15-16).

---

†21:16 *According to our present-day measurements, this city would be roughly 1,500 miles long, wide, and high. If placed in America, it would reach from New York City to Denver, Colorado, and from Canada to Florida.*

E. Its foundation—Twelve foundations. "And the foundations of the wall of the city were garnished with all manner of precious stones" (Rev. 21:19).

F. Its street—"And the street of the city was pure gold, as it were transparent glass" (Rev. 21:21).

G. Its light source—"And the city had no need of the sun, neither of the moon, to shine in it: for the glory of God did lighten it, and the Lamb is the light thereof" (Rev. 21:23). "And there shall be no night there; and they need no candle, neither light of the sun" (Rev. 22:5).

H. Its river—"And he shewed me a pure river of water of life, clear as crystal, proceeding out of the throne of God and of the Lamb" (Rev. 22:1).

I. Its Tree of Life—"In the midst of the street of it, and on either side of the river, was there the tree of life, which bare twelve manner of fruits, and yielded her fruit every month: and the leaves of the tree were for the healing of the nations" (Rev. 22:2).

J. Its relationship to the earth—"And the nations of them which are saved shall walk in the light of it: and the kings of the earth do bring their glory and honour into it. . . .

And they shall bring the glory and honour of the nations into it" (Rev. 21:24, 26).

K. Its worship center—"And I saw no temple therein: for the Lord God Almighty and the Lamb are the temple of it" (Rev. 21:22).

L. Its activities—What will we do in heaven?

1. Learning about Christ—"And they shall see his face; and his name shall be in their foreheads" (Rev. 22:4).
2. Working for Christ—"And his servants shall serve him" (Rev. 22:3).
3. Reigning with Christ—"And they shall reign for ever and ever" (Rev. 22:5).

II. Her Husband, the Faithful Spouse (Rev. 22:6-21)

A. The blessings of the wife

1. The comfort from Christ

a. He promises to return—"And, behold, I come quickly; and my reward is with me, to give every man according as his work shall be" (Rev. 22:12).

b. He promises to reward—"And, behold, I come quickly; and my reward is with me, to give every man according as his work shall be. . . . Blessed are they that do his commandments, that they may have right to the tree of life, and may enter in through the gates into the city" (Rev. 22:12, 14).

2. The character of Christ—"I am Alpha and Omega, the beginning and the end, the first and the last. . . . I Jesus have sent mine angel to testify unto you these things in the churches. I am the root and the offspring of David, and the bright and morning star" (Rev. 22:13, 16).

3. The counsel of Christ—"And he saith unto me, Seal not the sayings of the prophecy of this book: for the time is at hand" (Rev. 22:10).

4. The concern of Christ

a. His concern about the water of life—"And the Spirit and the bride say, Come. And let him that heareth say, Come. And let him that is athirst come. And whosoever will, let him take the water of life freely" (Rev. 22:17).

b. His concern about the Word of Life

(1) That we not add to it—"For I testify unto every man that heareth the words of the prophecy of this book, If any man shall add unto these things, God shall add unto him the plagues that are written in this book" (Rev. 22:18).

(2) That we not take from it—"And if any man shall take away from the words of the book of this prophecy, God shall take away his part out of the book of life, and out of the holy city, and from the things which are written in this book" (Rev. 22:19).

B. The blunders of the writer—John the apostle is so enthralled by these glorious sights and sounds he has been writing about that on two occasions he attempts to worship the attending angel. Each time he is rebuked.

1. First occasion—"And I fell at his feet to worship him. And he said unto me, See thou do it not: I am thy fellowservant, and of thy brethren that have the testimony of Jesus: worship God: for the testimony of Jesus is the spirit of prophecy" (Rev. 19:10).

2. Second occasion—"And I John saw these things, and heard them. And when I had heard and seen, I fell down to worship before the feet of the angel which shewed me these things. Then saith he unto me, See thou do it not: for I am thy fellowservant, and of thy brethren the prophets, and of them which keep the sayings of this book: worship God" (Rev. 22:8-9).

BIBLIOGRAPHY

BOOKS

Donald Barnhouse, *Revelation, an Expository Commentary*, Zondervan, 1971.

J. Sidlow Baxter, *Explore the Book*, Vol. 6, Zondervan.

Herman A. Hoyt, *The End of Times*, BMH Books, 1983.

———, *Studies in Revelation*, BMH Books.

Dr. Allen Johnson, *Romans: the Freedom Letter*, Everyman's Bible Commentary Series, Moody Press, 1974.

A. W. Kac, *Rebirth of the State of Israel*.

Homer Kent, *Jerusalem to Rome*, Baker Books, 1973.

———, *Ephesians, the Glory of the Church*, Everyman's Bible Commentary Series, Moody Press, 1981.

———, *Epistle to the Hebrews*, BMH Books, 1972.

Hal Lindsey, *There's a New World Coming*, Bantam, 1975.

William MacDonald, *Letters to the Thessalonians*, Walterick Publications, 1952.

Henrietta Mears, *What the Bible Is All About*, Regal, 1982.

J. Vernon McGee, *Through the Bible*, Nelson, 1981.

———, *Exploring Through Ephesians*, Nelson, 1983.

———, *Second Timothy*, Nelson, 1983.

———, *Reveling Through Revelation*, Nelson, 1983.

J. Dwight Pentecost, *The Joy of Living*, Zondervan, 1973.

———, *Prophecy for Today*, Zondervan, 1984.

———, *Things to Come*, Zondervan, 1958.

John Phillips, *Exploring Romans*, Moody Press, 1971.

———, *Exploring Revelation*, Moody Press, 1987.

Roy Roberts, *The Game of Life*, BMH Books.

Charles Ryrie, *The Acts of the Apostles*, Everyman's Bible Commentary Series, Moody Press, 1967.

———, *Dispensationalism Today*, Moody Press, 1973.

———, *Balancing the Christian Life*, Moody Press, 1969.

———, *First and Second Thessalonians*, Everyman's Bible Commentary Series, Moody Press, 1968.

———, *Ryrie Study Bible*, 1976.

———, *Revelation*, Everyman's Bible Commentary Series, Moody Press, 1968.

Erich Sauer, *Dawn of World Redemption*, Eerdmans, 1951.

Ray C. Stedman, *What More Can God Say?* Regal, 1977.

Dr. Lehman Strauss, *God's Plan for the Future*, Zondervan, 1965.

Merrill Tenney, *New Testament Survey*, Eerdmans, 1985.

Stanley Toussaint, *Bible Knowledge Commentary*, New Testament edition, Victor Books, 1983.

Merrill F. Unger, *Unger's Bible Handbook*, Moody Press, 1966.

John Walvoord, *Philippians, Triumph in Christ*, Everyman's Bible Commentary Series, Moody Press, 1980.

———, *The Thessalonian Epistle*, Zondervan, 1958.

———, *The Revelation of Jesus Christ*, Moody Press, 1966.

Warren Wiersbe, *Be Free*, Victor Books, 1975.

———, *Be Joyful*, Victor Books, 1974.
Kenneth Wuest, *Word Studies in the Greek New Testament: Ephesians and Colossians*, Eerdmans.
———, *Word Studies in Philippians*, Eerdmans.
———, *By Paths in the Greek New Testament*, Eerdmans.
———, *Hebrews in the Greek New Testament*, Eerdmans.

COMMENTARIES
Bible Knowledge Commentary, John Walvoord and Roy Zuck, eds., Victor Books, 1983.